CRIMINAL JUSTICE RESEARCH METHODS

QUALITATIVE AND QUANTITATIVE APPROACHES

W. LAWRENCE NEUMAN

University of Wisconsin at Whitewater

BRUCE WIEGAND

University of Wisconsin at Whitewater

Allyn and Bacon

Boston   London   Toronto   Sydney   Tokyo   Singapore

For students of justice everywhere

Editor in Chief, Social Sciences: Karen Hanson
Editorial Assistant: Karen Corday
Marketing Manager: Brooke Stoner
Editorial-Production Administrator:
  Annette Joseph
Editorial-Production Coordinator: Susan Freese

Editorial-Production Service: TKM Productions
Electronic Composition: Modern Graphics
Composition Buyer: Linda Cox
Manufacturing Buyer: Megan Cochran
Cover Administrator: Jenny Hart

Library of Congress Cataloging-in-Publication Data
Neuman, W. Lawrence.
    Criminal justice research methods: qualitative and quantitative
approaches / W. Lawrence Neuman, Bruce Wiegand.
        p.   cm.
    Includes bibliographical references and index.
    ISBN 0-205-28710-7
    1. Criminology—Research.   2. Criminology—Methodology.
3. Criminal justice, Administration of—Research.   I. Wiegand,
Bruce.   II. Title.
HV6024.5.N48   1999
364'.07'2—dc21   98-43813
                                                            CIP

Printed in the United States of America

10   9   8   7   6   5   4   3   2   1   04   03   02   01   00   99

Contents

PART II
RESEARCH USING QUANTITATIVE DATA

PART III
RESEARCH USING QUALITATIVE DATA

CHAPTER 16
ANALYZING QUALITATIVE
DATA   391

PART IV
FINAL CONSIDERATIONS

CHAPTER 17
ETHICAL AND POLITICAL ISSUES IN
CRIMINOLOGICAL RESEARCH   412

APPENDIXES

The purpose of this book is to explore how research is done in the related fields of criminology and criminal justice. If criminology is the science of justice, then how scientists go about gathering and analyzing information is of considerable measure. Think of it this way: A textbook on research methods in criminology offers a practical guide as to how people might construct a more just society. It represents a unique combination of the ideal and the practical. This, of course, has been the history and objective of the science of justice. Over 200 years ago, Cesare Beccaria pressed for reforms in existing systems of criminal justice by calling for the discovery of "useful truths." In this textbook, we try to answer his call.

Not every student who reads this book will become a researcher. That should not be the most important point, however. We believe the more one knows about the process of conducting criminological research, the more fairly one can approach the issues of crime and justice. Our faith rests in the scientific method. Our idealism is grounded in empirical science.

Several features distinguish *Criminal Justice Research Methods*. Generally speaking, our approach is fairly broad. We make a concerted effort to go beyond narrow conceptions of criminal justice. We advocate a comparative perspective to counter ethnocentric tendencies that might be at play in the discipline. We also adopt a critical perspective by acknowledging the connection between criminal justice and social justice. This critical/comparative perspective is communicated in our selection of research examples. Many of the examples in this book pertain to criminal justice in the United States, but many others draw on criminological research from other countries. We have also selected examples of research that touch on topics not typically found in such research methods textbooks. Among these topics are white-collar crime, tax evasion, organized crime, war crime, and issues of human rights.

It is our dedicated belief that the shared disciplines of criminology and criminal justice studies should be moving in the critical/comparative direction we advocate here. This textbook in research methods is our conscientious effort to hasten that movement.

ACKNOWLEDGMENTS

We would be remiss if we were to let this opportunity go by without posting a full acknowledgment for the support we have received. Both of us wish to salute our colleagues in Wisconsin. Over the decades, our inspiring ringleader and chair of the Sociology Department, Professor Lanny Neider, has acted on our behalf with the university.

The University of Wisconsin System has provided us both with years of scholarship, upon which has been built a more solid critical/comparative point of view. The East-West Center of the University of Hawaii and the Fulbright program have both been instrumental in our efforts to apprehend the "big picture."

The editorial team at Allyn and Bacon, particularly Karen Hanson, Editor in Chief, has been more than helpful throughout. We also appreciate Lynda Griffiths of TKM Productions, with her keen eye for detail. The text reads smoother owing to her efforts.

In the final analysis, be sure that our families are found in these lines of typed print. With due respect and admiration to all, we offer a grand thank you.

SCIENCE AND RESEARCH

> *In a society more and more dominated by experts and computer printouts, the technology of decision-making excludes, by its very nature, a stratum of people who lack education.*
> —Michael Harrington, *The New American Poverty,* p. 247

INTRODUCTION

Read almost any daily newspaper, and in it you will find many different stories having to do with basic issues of crime and justice. For example, the authors recently read that the U.S. Federal Bureau of Investigation (FBI) is increasing its enforcement staff and budget at the very time most other federal agencies are being downsized; research in Germany indicates that recidivism rates for youthful offenders sent to prison are higher than rates for those given alternative sanctions; roughly every 20 minutes, an exploding antipersonnel land mine kills or maims, and more than 110 million active mines are scattered in some 64 countries. These news items come from the results of research. Indeed, to really understand the important issues of crime and justice, you should be familiar with basic research methods.

This book is about criminological research. In simple terms, research is a way of going about finding answers to questions. Research conducted by criminologists, sociologists, and other social scientists is a method to seek answers to questions about the social world. You probably already have some notion of what research entails. First, let us end possible misconceptions. When the authors ask students what they think research entails, the following answers are usually given:

- Based on facts alone, without theory or judgment
- Read or used only by experts or college professors
- Done only in universities by people with Ph.D. degrees
- Going to the library and finding articles on a topic
- Hanging around some exotic place and observing
- Conducting an experiment in which people are tricked into doing something
- Drawing a sample of people and giving them questionnaires
- Looking up lots of tables from government reports or books
- Using computers, statistics, charts, and graphs

The first three of these answers are wrong, and the others describe only part of what constitutes research. It is unwise to confuse one part with the whole. Just as you would never mistake wearing shoes for being fully dressed, you should not mistake any one of these items for scientific research.

Research involves many things. It is how a person finds out something new and original about the social world. To do this, a researcher needs to think logically, follow rules, and repeat steps over and over. A researcher combines theories or ideas with facts in a systematic way and uses his or her imagination and creativity. He or she quickly learns to organize and plan carefully and to select the appropriate technique to address a question. A researcher also must be sensitive to treating the people who are being studied in ethical and moral ways. In addition, a researcher must communicate to others clearly.

Social research is a collection of methods people use systematically to produce knowledge. It is an exciting process of discovery, but it requires persistence, personal integrity, tolerance for ambiguity, interaction with others, and pride in doing quality work. You will learn more about the diversity of social research in Chapter 2.

Do not expect this book to transform you into an expert researcher. It can teach you to be a bet-ter consumer of research results, give you an understanding of how the research enterprise works, and prepare you to conduct small research projects yourself. After reading this textbook, you will understand research, its meaning, what it can and cannot do, and its role in the larger society.

ALTERNATIVES TO CRIMINOLOGICAL RESEARCH

A great deal of what you know about crime and criminal behavior is based on what your parents and others have told you. You also have knowledge that you have learned from personal experience. The books and magazines you have read and the movies and television you have watched also have given you information. You may also use common sense to learn about crime.

In addition to being a collection of methods, social research is a process for producing knowledge about the social world. It is a more structured, organized, and systematic process than the alternatives. Knowledge from the alternatives is often correct, but knowledge based on research is more likely to be true and has fewer potential errors. It is important to recognize that research does not always produce perfect knowledge. Nonetheless, compared to the alternatives, it is less likely to be flawed. Let us review the alternatives before examining criminological research.

Authority

You gain knowledge from parents, teachers, and experts as well as from books and television and other media. When you accept something as being true just because someone in a position of authority says it is true or because it is in an authoritative publication, you are using authority as a basis of knowledge. Relying on the wisdom of authorities has advantages—it is a quick, simple, and cheap way to learn something. Authorities often spend time and effort to learn something, and you can benefit from their experience and work.

Relying on authorities also has limitations. It is easy to overestimate the expertise of other people. You may assume that they are right when they are not. Authorities may speak on fields they know little about; they can be plain wrong. An expert in one area may try to use his or her authority in an unrelated area. Have you ever seen television commercials where an expert in football uses that expertise to try to convince you to buy a car? In addition, there are the questions: Who is or is not an authority? Whom do you believe when different authorities disagree? For example, one criminologist might argue that reductions in violent crime are due to the increased likelihood of going to prison, whereas another might find little correlation between rates of crime and the number of people in prison.

The history of criminology is full of past experts who are now regarded as misinformed. For example, nineteenth-century, Italian criminologist Cesare Lombroso presented his research to support the idea that some criminals are atavistic (or biologically inferior). Lombroso's theory is now discounted, but can you be certain that today's experts will not become tomorrow's fools? Also, too much reliance on authorities can be dangerous to a democratic society. An overdependence on experts lets them keep others in the dark, and they may promote ideas that strengthen their power and position. When we have no idea of how the experts arrived at their knowledge, we lose some of our ability to make judgments for ourselves.

Tradition

People sometimes rely on tradition for knowledge. Tradition is a special case of authority—the authority of the past. Tradition means you accept something as being true because "it's the way things have always been." Consider, for example, the traditional approach of seeking to control prostitution by use of criminal law enforcement. Most people realize by now that this crime-control approach has not achieved the elimination or even a significant reduction in prostitution. Indeed, as some research suggests, the criminalization of prostitution just makes matters worse. Yet, many people continue to favor the approach because it is the way things have always been done.

Some traditional criminological knowledge begins as simple prejudice. A belief such as "people from that side of the tracks will never amount to anything" or "you never can trust anyone of that race" comes down from the past. Even if traditional knowledge was once true, it can become distorted as it is passed on, and soon it is no longer true. People may cling to traditional knowledge without real understanding; they assume that because something may have worked or been true in the past, it must always be true.

Common Sense

You know a lot about crime and criminal behavior from your ordinary reasoning or common sense. You rely on what everyone knows and what "just makes sense." For example, it "just makes sense" that murder rates are higher in nations that do not have a death penalty, because people are less likely to kill if they face execution for doing so. This and other widely held commonsense beliefs, such as that poor youth are more likely to commit deviant acts than those from the middle class or that the income gap in the United States is getting smaller are false.

Common sense is valuable in daily living, but it can allow logical fallacies to slip into your thinking.[1] For example, the "gambler's fallacy" says: "If I have a long string of losses playing a lottery, the next time I play, my chances of winning will be better." In terms of probability and the facts, this is false. Also, common sense contains contradictory ideas that go unnoticed because people use the ideas at different times—for example, "opposites attract" and "birds of a feather flock together." Common sense can originate in tradition. It is useful and sometimes correct, but it also contains errors, misinformation, contradiction, and prejudice.

Media Myths

Television shows, movies, and newspaper and magazine articles are important sources of information about social life. For example, most people who have no contact with criminals learn about crime by watching television shows and movies and by reading newspapers. However, the portrayals of crime and of many other things on television do not accurately reflect social reality. Instead, the writers who invent or "adapt" real life for television shows and movie scripts distort reality either out of ignorance or because they rely on authority, tradition, and common sense. Their primary goal is to entertain, not to present reality accurately. Although journalists who write for newspapers and newsmagazines try to present a realistic picture of the world, they must write stories in short time periods with limited information and within editorial guidelines.

Unfortunately, the media tend to perpetuate the myths of a culture. For example, television promotes a distorted image of crime and criminal justice in the United States. It portrays most criminals as violent, and implies that policing is very effective. But these media portrayals reflect and perpetuate cultural stereotypes more than they mirror reality. Also, a selective emphasis on an issue by the media can change public thinking about it (see Box 1.1). For example, television repeatedly shows low-income, inner-city, African American youth using illegal drugs.

Eventually, most people "know" that urban African Americans use illegal drugs at a much higher rate than other groups in the United States, even though this notion is false.

Personal Experience

If something happens to you, if you personally see it or experience it, you accept it as true. Personal experience, or "seeing is believing," has a strong impact and is a forceful source of knowledge. Unfortunately, personal experience can lead you astray. Something similar to an optical illusion or mirage can occur. What appears true may actually be due to a slight error or distortion in judgment. The power of immediacy and direct personal contact is very strong. Even knowing that, people sometimes make mistakes or fall for illusions. Sometimes people believe what they see or experience rather than what is revealed by careful research designed to avoid such errors.

The four errors of personal experience reinforce each other and can occur in other areas, as well. They are a basis for misleading people through propaganda, cons or fraud, magic, stereo-

---

Box 1.1 _____

Cyberporn Myths versus Research

In the competition for sales and advertising revenue, the media sometimes sensationalize an idea or finding based on scanty evidence. Yet widespread publicity may cause many people to accept the finding as true or to falsely believe that it is backed by a solid scientific study. In the summer of 1995, _Time_ magazine, the leading U.S. news weekly, ran a front-page story on cyberporn. The term refers to electronically sending and receiving pornography by way of computers on the Internet. The magazine's attention-grabbing cover showed a bewildered-looking child in front of a computer. The frightening story, citing a Carnegie Mellon University study, suggested that computer networks were being flooded with lurid pornography that any child with a computer could access. Major television news programs quickly amplified the alarm, and soon thereafter

politicians in Washington demanded tough new laws.

Upon closer inspection, it was learned that the hysteria was based on a single unpublished study conducted by an undergraduate and riddled with serious methodological flaws. In the rush to get the story out, the magazine failed to have proper research professionals evaluate it. Besides circumventing the scientific community's review process and depending on a single, shoddy study by someone who was unqualified, the article had a misleading tone. It failed to emphasize that less than one-half of 1 percent of Internet messages at that time involved pornography. Whatever the moral offense of cyberporn, the media's message lacked solid evidence and careful research.

typing, and some advertising. The first problem, which is the most frequent, is *overgeneralization.* It occurs when you have some evidence that you believe and then assume that it applies to many other situations, too. Limited generalization may be appropriate; under certain conditions, a small amount of evidence can explain a larger situation. The problem is that people often generalize well beyond limited evidence. There are many individuals, areas, and situations about which people know little or nothing, so generalizing from the little they do know might seem reasonable. For example, suppose you read in the newspaper about a serious crime committed by a person on parole. Would this affect your attitude to parole, in general? Would you be apt to dismiss research showing that parolees actually have lower rates of recidivism than prisoners who serve their full term?

A second common error is *selective observation.* It occurs when you take special notice of some people or events and generalize from them. People often focus on or observe particular cases or situations, especially when they fit preconceived ideas. We often seek out evidence that confirms what we already know or believe and ignore the range of cases and contradictory information. We are sensitive to features that confirm our ideas—features that might otherwise go unnoticed. For example, research on the policing of minorities has shown that the police often "overinterpret" the behavior of minority suspects. Without realizing it, some police officers apply preconceived notions they hold as to the "violent tendencies" and "disrespect for authority" allegedly characteristic of minorities. These preconceptions can result in the selective way in which these officers view minority behavior, and ultimately in their selective treatment of minority suspects.

A third error is *premature closure.* It often operates with and reinforces the first two errors. Premature closure occurs when you feel you have all the answers and do not need to listen, seek information, or raise questions any longer. Unfortunately, most of us are a little lazy or get a little sloppy in everyday experiences. We take a few pieces of evidence or look at events for a short while and then think we have it figured out. We look for evidence to confirm or reject an idea and stop when a small amount of evidence is present. In a word, we jump to conclusions, such as: I know three people who smoked six packs of cigarettes a day and lived to be 80 years old; therefore, people who smoke lots of cigarettes will live to age 80.

The last error is the *halo effect.* It comes in various forms, but basically, it says we overgeneralize from what we interpret to be highly positive or prestigious. We give things or people we respect a halo, or a strong reputation. We let the prestige "rub off" on other things or people about which we know little. Thus, we pick up an annual report published by the White House, replete with a glowing introduction by the president, who says the United States is finally winning the War on Drugs. We assume, perhaps unquestioningly, that the president's diagnosis is correct, and accept his premise that "more drug arrests" is an indication of the victory at hand.

HOW SCIENCE WORKS

The critical factor that separates criminological research from other ways of knowing about crime and criminal behavior is that it uses a scientific approach. *Criminological research* is more than a collection of methods and a process for creating knowledge; it is a process for producing new knowledge about the social world that uses a *scientific* approach. Let us take a brief look at "science," a subject to which we will return in Chapter 4.

Science

When most people hear the word *science*, the first image that comes to mind is one of test tubes, computers, rocket ships, and people in white lab coats. These outward trappings are a part of science. Some sciences, such as the natural sciences—biology, chemistry, physics, and zoology—deal with the physical and material world (e.g., rocks, plants, chemicals, stars, blood, electricity, etc.). The natural sciences are the basis of new technology and receive a lot of publicity. Most people first think of them when they hear the word *science.*

The social sciences, such as anthropology, criminology, political science, and sociology, involve the study of people—their beliefs, behavior, interaction, institutions, and so forth. Fewer people associate these disciplines with the word *science.* They are sometimes called *soft sciences.* This is not because their work is sloppy or lacks rigor but because their subject matter, human social life, is fluid, formidable to observe, and hard to measure precisely with laboratory instruments. The subject matter of a science (e.g., criminal behavior, the weather, or galaxies) determines the techniques and instruments (e.g., surveys, microscopes, or telescopes) used by it.

Science is a social institution and a way to produce knowledge. It has not always been around; it is a human invention. What people now call science grew from a major shift in thinking that began with the Age of Reason or Enlightenment period in western European history, which occurred between the 1600s and the early 1800s. The Enlightenment ushered in a wave of new thinking. It included a faith in logical reasoning, an emphasis on experiences in the material world, a belief in human progress, and a questioning of traditional religious authority. It began with the study of the natural world and spread to the study of social life. The importance of science in modern society and as a basis for seeking knowledge is associated with the societal transformation called the Industrial Revolution. The advancement of science or of fields within science, such as criminology, does not just happen. It is punctuated by the triumphs and struggles of individual researchers. It is also influenced by significant social events such as war, depression, government policy, or shifts in public support.[2]

At one time, all people created new knowledge using prescientific or nonscientific methods. These included the alternatives discussed previously and other methods that are less widely accepted in modern society (e.g., oracles, mysticism, magic, astrology, or spirits). Before science became fully entrenched, such prescientific systems were generally accepted. They were an unquestioned way to produce knowledge that people took to be true. Such prescientific methods still exist but are secondary to science. Some people use nonscientific methods to study topics beyond the scope of science (e.g., religion, art, or philosophy). People in advanced modern society believe that most aspects of the social and natural world are within the scope of science. Today, few people seriously question science as a legitimate way to produce knowledge about modern society.

Science refers to both a system for producing knowledge and the knowledge produced from that system. The system evolved over many years and is slowly but constantly changing. It combines assumptions about the nature of the world and knowledge; an orientation toward knowledge; and sets of procedures, techniques, and instruments for gaining knowledge. It is visible in a social institution called the scientific community.

The knowledge of science is organized in terms of theories. For now, *criminological theory* can be defined as a system of interconnected abstractions or ideas that condense and organize knowledge about criminal behavior and the criminal justice system. Several types of criminological theory are discussed in Chapter 3. Theory is like a map; it helps people visualize the complexity in the world and explains why things happen.

Scientists gather data using specialized techniques and use the data to support or reject theories. *Data* are the empirical evidence or information that one gathers carefully according to rules or procedures. The data can be *quantitative* (i.e., expressed as numbers) or *qualitative* (i.e., expressed as words, pictures, or objects). *Empirical* evidence refers to observations that people experience through the senses—touch, sight, hearing, smell, and taste. This confuses people, because researchers cannot use their senses to directly observe many aspects of the social world about which they seek answers (e.g., intelligence, attitudes, opinions, feelings, emotions, power, authority, etc.). Researchers have many specialized techniques to observe and indirectly measure such aspects of the social world.

The Scientific Community

Science is given life through the operation of the scientific community, which sustains the assumptions, attitudes, and techniques of science. The *scientific community* is a collection of people and a set of norms, behaviors, and attitudes that bind them together to sustain the scientific ethos. It is a community because it is a group of interacting people who share ethical principles, beliefs and values, techniques and training, and career paths. It is not a geographic community. Rather, it is a professional community whose members share an outlook on and a commitment to scientific research. For the most part, the scientific community includes both the natural and social sciences.[3]

Many people outside the core scientific community use scientific research techniques. A range of practitioners and technicians apply research techniques that have been developed and refined by the scientific community. They apply the knowledge and procedures originated within the scientific community. For example, many people use a research technique created by the scientific community (e.g., a survey) without possessing a deep knowledge of research, without inventing new methods of research, and without advancing science itself. Yet, those who use the techniques or results of science will be able to do so better if they also understand the principles and processes of the scientific community.

The boundaries of this community and its membership are defined loosely. There is no membership card or master roster. Many people treat a Ph.D. degree in a scientific field as an informal "entry ticket" to membership in the scientific community. The Ph.D., which stands for doctorate of philosophy, is an advanced graduate degree beyond the master's that prepares one to conduct independent research. Some researchers do not have Ph.D.s and not all those who receive Ph.D.s enter occupations in which they conduct research. They enter many occupations and may have other responsibilities (e.g., teaching, administration, consulting, clinical practice, advising, etc.). In fact, about one-half of the people who receive scientific Ph.D.s do not follow careers as active researchers.

At the core of the scientific community are researchers who conduct studies on a full-time or half-time basis, usually with the help of assistants. Many research assistants are graduate students, and some are undergraduates. Working as a research assistant is the way that most scientists gain a real grasp on the details of doing research.

Colleges and universities employ most members of the scientific community's core. Some scientists work for the government or private industry in organizations such as Bell Labs, the National Opinion Research Center, or the Rand Corporation. Most are found at the approximately 200 research universities and institutes located in half a dozen advanced industrialized countries. Thus, the scientific community may be scattered geographically, but its members tend to work together in small clusters.

How big is the scientific community? This is not an easy question to answer. Using the broadest definition (including all scientists and those in science-related professions, such as engineers), about 15 percent of the labor force in advanced industrialized countries are members of the scientific community. A better way to look at the scientific community is to look at the basic unit of the larger community: the discipline (e.g., criminology and criminal justice). Scientists are most familiar with a particular discipline because knowledge is specialized. In just the United States, for example, there are thousands of academic criminologists who keep abreast of the latest research findings on crime and justice. They usually belong to professional organizations, such as the American Society of Criminology, and often attend and participate in research conferences.

Not all criminologists teach and conduct research at universities, however. A growing number work in applied settings, such as in the criminal justice system, or with nongovernmental organizations (NGOs), such as Amnesty International. Rather than conduct research for a living, their job is to use the latest research findings in order to promote social justice. Indeed, the scientific community of criminologists is reaching well beyond traditional boundaries. It is rapidly becoming international in perspective and expanding its range of research interests, including everything from foreign policy implications of the War on Drugs, to international war crimes and human rights abuses, to economic crimes such as money laundering. It is a very exciting time to be involved in criminological research.

The Norms of the Scientific Community

Behavior in any human community is regulated by social norms. The scientific community is governed by a set of professional norms and values that researchers learn and internalize during many years of schooling. The norms are mutually reinforcing and contribute to the unique role of the scientist.[4] The settings in which active researchers work and the very operation of the system of science reinforces the norms.[5] Like other social norms, professional norms are ideals of proper conduct. Because researchers are real people, their prejudices, egos, ambitions, personal lives, and the like may affect their professional behavior. The norms of science do not always work perfectly in practice and are occasionally violated.[6] Likewise, it is important to remember that the operation of science does not occur in a vacuum isolated from the real world. Diverse social, political, and economic forces affect its development and influence how it operates.

The five basic norms of science are listed in Box 1.2. They differ from those in other social institutions (e.g., business or government) and set scientists apart. Scientists largely check on each other to see that the norms are followed. For example, consistent with the norm of *universalism*, scientists will admire a brilliant, creative researcher even if he or she has strange personal habits or a disheveled appearance. Scientists may argue intensely with one another and "tear apart" a research report as part of the norm of *organized skepticism*. They usually listen to new ideas, no matter how strange. Following *disinterestedness*, scientists take results as being tentative, to be

Box 1.2 _____

Norms of the Scientific Community

1. *Universalism.* Irrespective of who conducts research (e.g., old or young, male or female) and regardless of where it was conducted (e.g., United States or France, Harvard or Unknown University), the research is to be judged only on the basis of scientific merit.
2. *Organized skepticism.* Scientists should not accept new ideas or evidence in a carefree, uncritical manner. Instead, all evidence should be challenged and questioned. Each research study is subjected to intense criticism and scrutiny. The purpose of the criticism is not to attack the individual; rather, it is to ensure that the research can stand up to close examination.
3. *Disinterestedness.* Scientists must be neutral, impartial, receptive, and open to unexpected observations or new ideas. They should not be rigidly wedded to a particular idea or point of view. They should accept, even look for, evidence that runs against their positions and should honestly accept all findings based on high-quality research.
4. *Communalism.* Scientific knowledge must be shared with others; it belongs to everyone. Creating scientific knowledge is a public act, and the findings are public property, available for all to use. The way in which the research is conducted must be described in detail. New knowledge is not formally accepted until other researchers have reviewed it and it has been made publicly available in a special form and style.
5. *Honesty.* This is a general cultural norm, but it is especially strong in scientific research. Scientists demand honesty in all research; dishonesty or cheating in scientific research is a major taboo.

accepted only until something better comes along. They love to have other scientists read and react to their research, and some have led fights against censorship. This is consistent with the norm of *communalism*. Scientists expect *honesty* in the conduct and reporting of research and are aghast when anyone cheats at research.

The Scientific Method and Attitude

You have probably heard of the scientific method, and you may be wondering how it fits into all this. The *scientific method* is not one single thing. It refers to the ideas, rules, techniques, and approaches that the scientific community uses. The method arises from a loose consensus within the community of scientists. It is better to focus on the *scientific attitude,* or a way of looking at the world. It is an attitude that values craftsmanship, with pride in creativity, high-quality standards, and hard work. As Grinnell (1987:125) stated:

> Most people learn about the "scientific method" rather than about the scientific attitude. While the "scientific method" is an ideal construct, the scientific attitude is the way people have of looking at the world. Doing science includes many methods; what makes them scientific is their acceptance by the scientific collective.

Journal Articles in Science

You may be familiar with certain criminolgy scholarly journals or specialized magazines. When the scientific community creates new knowledge, it appears in academic books or scholarly journal articles. A more detailed discussion of scholarly journals is in Chapter 5. The primary forms in which research findings or new scientific knowledge appear are *scholarly journal articles.* They are how scientists formally communicate with one another and disseminate the results of scientific research. They are also part of the much discussed explosion of knowledge. Each discipline or field has over 100 journals, each of which publishes many articles every year. For example, one of the leading criminology journals in the world is called *Justice Quarterly,* an official publication of the Academy of Criminal Justice Sciences (ACJS). The journal contains research reports, book reviews, and theoretical essays. To be sure, journals such as this publish scholarly articles that play a critical part of the research process and the scientific community, but they are not always well understood.[7]

Consider what happens once a researcher completes a study. First, he or she writes a description of the study and the results as a research report or a paper in a special format. Often, he or she gives an oral presentation of the paper at a meeting of a professional association, such as the American Society of Criminology, and sends a copy of it to a few scientists for their comments and suggestions. Next, the researcher sends copies to the editor of a scholarly journal such as the *Justice Quarterly* or *Criminology.* Each editor, a respected researcher who has been chosen by other scientists to oversee the journal, removes the title page, which is the only place the author's name appears, and sends the paper to several referees for a *blind review.* The referees are scientists who have conducted research in the same specialty area or topic. The review is "blind" because the referees do not know who conducted the research and the author does not know the referees. This reinforces the norm of universalism, because referees judge the paper on its merits alone. They evaluate the research on the basis of its clarity, originality, standards of good research, and contribution to knowledge. Journals want to publish research that is well done and that significantly advances knowledge. The referees return their evaluations to the editor, who decides to reject the paper, ask the author for revisions, or accept it for publication.

Some scholarly journals are widely read and highly respected. They receive many more papers than they can publish. This means that most of the papers are rejected, and only a very select few are accepted. For example, a few leading journals reject over 90 percent of the papers sent to them. Even less highly esteemed journals may reject half of the research papers submitted for consideration. Thus, before an article is published in a scholarly journal, it has been screened. In this way, its publication represents tentative acceptance by the scientific community. Once published, the article becomes a piece of knowledge added to that which is already considered science.

Unlike the authors of articles for the popular magazines found at newsstands, who are paid for writing, scientists are not paid for publishing in scholarly journals. In fact, they may have to pay a small fee to help defray costs just to have their papers considered. Researchers are happy to make their research available to their peers (i.e., other scientists and researchers) through scholarly journals. Likewise, the referees are not paid for reviewing papers. They consider it an honor to be asked to conduct the reviews and a responsibility of membership in the scientific community. The scientific community imparts great respect to researchers who publish many articles in the foremost scholarly journals because the articles confirm that these researchers are leaders in advancing the primary goal of the scientific community—to contribute to the accumulation of scientific knowledge.

A researcher gains prestige and honor within the scientific community, respect from peers, and a reputation as an accomplished researcher through such publications. Researchers want to earn the respect of their peers—other highly trained scientists who are most knowledgeable about the research issues. In addition, an impressive record of respected publications helps a researcher obtain grants, fellowships, job offers, a following of students, improved working conditions, and increases in salary.[8]

You may never publish an article in a scholarly journal, but you will likely read such articles. They are a vital component of the system of scientific research. The results of most research (i.e., most new scientific knowledge) first appear in scholarly journals. Researchers read the journals to learn about the research others conducted, the methods they used, and the results they obtained. You can participate in the process by which new knowledge is communicated.

Science as a Transformative Process

You can think of research as the use of scientific methods to transform ideas, hunches, and questions, sometimes called *hypotheses,* into scientific knowledge. This book reveals the transformative process of social science research. *Transformation* means altering something, converting it from one thing into another. In the research process, a researcher starts with guesses or questions and applies specialized methods and techniques to this raw material. At the end of the process, a finished product of value appears: scientific knowledge. A highly productive researcher is one who creates a great deal of new knowledge that greatly improves people's understanding of the world.

You may be starting to feel that the research process is beyond you. After all, it involves complex technical skills and the high-powered scientific community. Yet, the fundamentals of conducting research are accessible to most people. With education and practice, you can learn to do scientific research. In addition to assimilating the scientific attitude or culture, you will need to master how and when to apply research techniques. After reading this book, you should grasp them. Soon you will be able to conduct small-scale research projects yourself.

STEPS OF THE RESEARCH PROCESS

The Steps

The research process requires a sequence of steps. Various approaches suggest somewhat different steps, but most seem to follow the seven discussed here. (Different types of research are covered in Chapters 2 and 4.)

The process begins with a researcher selecting a *topic*—a general area of study or issue such as violent behavior or tax crime. A topic is too broad for conducting research. This is why the next step is crucial. The researcher narrows down, or *focuses,* the topic into a specific research question that he or she can address in the study (e.g., "Are authoritarian governments more corrupt than democratic ones?"). When learning about a topic and narrowing the focus, the researcher usually reviews past research, or the *literature*, on a topic or question. (Chapter 5 discusses how to do a literature review.) The researcher also develops a possible answer, or hypothesis. As Chapter 3 will show, theory can be important at this stage.

After specifying a research question, the researcher plans how he or she will carry out the specific study or research project. The third step involves making decisions about the many practical details of doing the research (e.g., whether to use a survey or observe in the field, how many subjects to use, which questions to ask, etc.). Now the researcher is ready to *gather the data* or evidence (e.g., ask people the questions, record answers, etc.).

Once the researcher has collected the data, his or her next step is to manipulate or *analyze the data* to see any patterns that emerge. The patterns or evidence help the researcher give meaning to or *interpret the data* (e.g., "Governments that are selling off or privatizing public property and assets are more corrupt than those that are not"). Finally, the researcher *informs others* by writing a report that describes the background to the study, how he or she conducted it, and what he or she discovered.

The neat seven-step process shown in Figure 1.1 is oversimplified. In practice, researchers rarely complete step 1, then leave it to move to step 2, and so on. Research is more of an interactive process in which steps blend into each other. A later step may stimulate reconsideration of a previous one. The process is not strictly linear; it may flow in several directions before reaching an end. Research does not abruptly end at step 7. It is an ongoing process, and the end of one study often stimulates new thinking and fresh research questions.

The seven steps are followed for one research project. A researcher applies one cycle of the steps in a single research project or a research study on a specific topic. Each project builds on prior research and contributes to a larger body of knowledge. The larger process of scientific discovery and accumulating new knowledge requires the involvement of many researchers in numerous research projects all at the same time. A single researcher may be working on multiple research projects at once, or several researchers may collaborate on one project. Likewise, one project may result in one scholarly article or several, and sometimes several smaller projects are reported in a single article. It may help to look at Figure 1.1 for a summary of the steps after reading the following examples.

Examples

The parts of the research process can be seen in two published studies on very different topics. The parts in each will be identified. In the first example, author Lonnie Athens conducted a series of in-depth interviews with a number of dangerous, violent criminals in order to explore what social experiences they had in common. The second example is a national survey of taxpayers to determine the extent of tax noncompliance.

Example 1.   In 1992, Lonnie Athens published a book summarizing his 20 years of research on violence, called *The Creation of Dangerous Violent Criminals.*

Choose a Topic.   The study looks at the social experiences that lead a person to become a dangerous violent criminal. Athens was interested in discovering how relatively benign individuals undergo lengthy, at times brutal, development that transforms them into vicious criminals.

Focus the Project.   Athens was a student of the well-known sociologist, Herbert Blumer. His early thinking about the topic was largely shaped by Blumer's theory of symbolic interaction. This

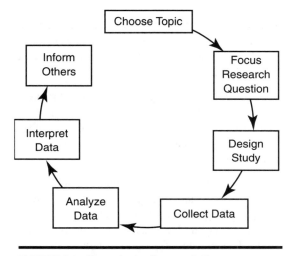

FIGURE 1.1 Steps in the Research Process

theory suggests that criminals must be studied from their own perspective to learn how they define their situation. Athens stated, "In reading this book one should find that one is undergoing similar thoughts and feelings as the subjects." Athens was concerned with only a particularly impulsive type of violent behavior, which he called dangerous violent behavior. This is an extremely violent behavior toward another that occurs with little or no provocation.

Design the Study.   Rather than going into the study with clear-cut hypotheses to test, Athens decided to design a study that would be open to the perspectives of his subjects. He also decided that, for his purposes, it was better to study 50 people in depth than to study, say, 5,000 people superficially. The research method Athens decided on was in-depth personal interviews. His strategy was to get the dangerous violent criminals talking about the formative experiences they, not the researcher, felt were significant for their lives.

Gather the Data.   In applying his research strategy, Athens spent hundreds of hours interviewing a group of 8 male adult offenders imprisoned for committing serious violent crimes and who had been previously convicted of at least two prior serious violent crimes. He also conducted in-depth interviews with a group of 30 young adult violent offenders, including males and females. Their ages ranged from early to late teens, and all were serving time in a correctional institution for serious violent crimes. All the subjects candidly admitted (to Athens) committing previous violent criminal acts for which they were never arrested or convicted.

Analyze the Data.   Athens's main strategy for analyzing the data was to look for patterns in the developmental experiences of his violent subjects. Were there certain social experiences, he wondered, that were shared and unique to these subjects that might in turn provide the basis for their impulsive violence? (Athens also interviewed a control group of nonviolent individuals to see if, indeed, the experiences were unique to his subjects.)

Interpret the Findings.   As it turned out, Athens discovered four significant experiences that were commonly endured by his sample of dangerous violent criminals. All four experiences, by the way, were suffered at an early stage in each subject's life, usually in early adolescence. The first experience is brutalization, which involves the subject's physical abuse by someone in his or her primary group. It also involves the horrifying experience of witnessing the physical abuse of someone emotionally close to the subject, such as his or her mother. The second experience is belligerency, which involves the subject's introspection and resolution to respond in kind to violence—that is, the subject's internalizing of an "eye for an eye" philosophy of violence. The third experience is violent performance, which involves the subject's involvement in a fight and, in it, harming someone quite seriously. The fourth experience is virulency, which involves a "violent label" being put on the subject by his or her peers, and the subject's (perverse) satisfaction at the social trepidation others now feel toward him or her. It is the sum total of these four experiences, Athens claims, that transforms a nonviolent person into a dangerous violent criminal.

Inform Others.   The study was published as a book.

Example 2.   In 1988, the research division of the Internal Revenue Service (IRS) published a benchmark study of income tax compliance in the United States.

Choose a Topic.   The IRS mission statement calls for taxes to be collected fairly, and in a way that ensures tax compliance. Thus, the topic of tax noncompliance is at the very center of the IRS's research agenda.

Focus the Project.   Before being able to estimate the size and dimensions of the tax noncompliance problems, it was necessary for the IRS to define the basic terms or concepts of the study. The concept of *tax gap* is perhaps the most basic of them. It refers to the gross amount of income tax owed but not voluntarily paid by the taxpayer. In this case, the IRS included both individual and corporate taxpayers in its study. Thus, the tax gap consisted of unpaid individual and business taxes on legally earned income. (The IRS made no attempt at measuring the taxes due on illegal income, even though such income is taxable.) The tax gap exists because taxpayers underestimate income, overstate deductions, or fail to file tax returns altogether. It includes taxpayers who willfully evade, as well as those who mistakenly or inadvertently fail to comply with, the law. (The IRS study dealt with many more technical concepts, but these are the main ones used to focus the research.)

Design the Study. The IRS designed a Taxpayer Compliance Measurement Program (TCMP) to carry out this study. TCMP is used to estimate the noncompliance of filers (i.e., taxpayers who file a tax return). It is a survey of approximately 50,000 randomly selected taxpayers. The taxpayers are thoroughly audited to measure their degree of compliance. (To study nonfilers, the IRS matched data from a national household survey with Social Security and IRS data, which gave an estimate of numbers and incomes of nonfilers.)

Gather the Data. TCMP data from tax years 1973, 1976, 1979, and 1982 were used to measure the tax gap. (TCMP surveys take about three years to complete.) These data were then projected to 1992, taking into account the impact of subsequent tax law changes.

Analyze the Data. The data analysis uncovered truly shocking results. The 1992 tax gap was estimated to be over $113 billion! Moreover, trends showed the tax gap was growing. The single biggest source of tax noncompliance is underreported income, comprising nearly 60 percent of the tax gap. Compliance was highest for wage earners whose taxes are withheld by their employers, and worst for those with no tax withholding (e.g., business income).

Interpret the Findings. The tax gap estimates have been interpreted by researchers in various ways. However, the IRS has maintained that income tax compliance is fostered by the tax withholding system. The IRS has also used the findings to argue for increasing its tax enforcement resources.

Inform Others. Besides encouraging social scientists to study the TCMP data, the IRS has convened several research conferences and published various reports. The U.S. Congressional General Accounting Office (GAO) sponsored a symposium in 1995 to discuss the tax gap problem.

QUALITATIVE AND QUANTITATIVE RESEARCH

You will learn about both qualitative and quantitative styles of doing social research in this book. After the first several chapters, the two styles will be used to help organize most remaining chapters. Chapters 6 through 12 focus on quantitative research, and Chapters 13 through 16 focus on qualitative research. Each category uses several specific research techniques (e.g., survey, interview, and historical analysis), yet there is much overlap between the type of data and the style of research. Most qualitative-style researchers examine qualitative-type data, and vice versa. However, sometimes qualitative researchers examine quantitative data, and vice versa. Both styles are widely used in social research, but each is rooted on a distinct logic or approach to social science (discussed in Chapter 4).

Unfortunately, there is a lot of ill will between the followers of each style of research, as some find it difficult to understand or appreciate the other style. Thus, Levine (1993:xii) wrote, "Quantitative social science," which he called "real social science," faced opposition but it "won the battle." Denzin and Lincoln (1994) argued that qualitative research has expanded greatly in the recent decades and is rapidly displacing outdated quantitative-style research.

Although both styles of research share basic principles of science, the two approaches differ in significant ways (see Table 1.1). Each has its strengths and limitations, topics or issues where it glitters, and classic studies that provide remark-

TABLE 1.1   Quantitative Style versus Qualitative Style

QUANTITATIVE STYLE	QUALITATIVE STYLE
Measure objective facts	Construct social reality, cultural meaning
Focus on variables	Focus on interactive processes, events
Reliability is key	Authenticity is key
Value free	Values are present and explicit
Independent of context	Situationally con-strained
Many cases, subjects	Few cases, subjects
Statistical analysis	Thematic analysis
Researcher is detached	Researcher is involved

Sources: Cresswell (1994), Denzin and Lincoln (1994), Guba and Lincoln (1994), and Mostyn (1985).

able insights into social life. The authors agree with King, Keohane, and Verba (1994:5), who stated that the best research "often combines the features of each."

No matter what style they adopt, researchers try to avoid the errors discussed earlier in this chapter, to be systematic in gathering data, and to use the idea of comparison extensively. By understanding both styles, you will know about a broader range of research and can use both in complementary ways. Ragin (1994:92) has explained one way the styles complement each other:

> The key features common to all qualitative methods can be seen when they are contrasted with quantitative methods. Most quantitative data techniques are data condensers. They condense data in order to see the big picture. . . . Qualitative methods, by contrast, are best understood as data enhancers. When data are enhanced, it is possible to see key aspects of cases more clearly.

WHY CONDUCT RESEARCH?

Where can you find people conducting research? Students, professors, professional researchers, and scientists in universities, research centers, and the government, with an army of assistants and technicians, conduct much research. This research is not visible to the average person. Although the results may appear only in specialized publications or textbooks, the basic knowledge and research methods that professional researchers develop become the basis for all other research.

In addition to those in universities, people who work for newspapers, television networks, market research firms, schools, hospitals, social service agencies, political parties, consulting firms, government agencies, personnel departments, public interest organizations, insurance companies, or law firms may conduct research as part of their jobs. Numerous people make use of social research techniques. The findings from this social research usually yield better informed, less biased decisions than the guessing, hunches, intuition, and personal experience that were previously used (see Box 1.3). Unfortunately, those being studied may feel overstudied or overloaded by the research. For example, the many exit poll studies by the mass media during elections have prompted a backlash of people refusing to vote and debates over legal restrictions on such polling.

Also, some people misuse or abuse social research—use sloppy research techniques, misinterpret findings, rig studies to find previously decided results, and so on. But the hostile reactions to such misuse may be directed at research in general instead of at the people who misuse it.

Criminologists and other social scientists conduct research for many reasons. Some seek to answer practical questions (e.g., "What is the size of the tax gap? Is it growing larger or getting smaller?"). Others want to expand basic theoretical understanding of issues of crime and justice (e.g., "What transforms a nonviolent person into a dangerous violent criminal? What causes violent behavior to become intergenerational?"). Regardless of why the social research is conducted, all researchers in one way or another subscribe to the goal of changing society for the better.

Box 1.3 _____

The Practitioner and Social Science

Science does not, and cannot, provide people with fixed, absolute Truth. This is because science is a slow, incomplete process of reducing untruth. It is a quest for the best possible answers carried out by a collection of devoted people who labor strenuously in a careful, systematic, and open-minded manner. Many people are uneasy with the painstaking pace, hesitating progress, and incertitude of science. They demand immediate, absolute answers. Many turn to religious fanatics or political demagogues who offer final, conclusive truths in abundance.

What does this mean for diligent practitioners (e.g., criminal justice professionals, social activists, policy analysts, and the like) who have to make prompt decisions in their daily work? Must they abandon scientific thinking and rely only on common sense, personal conviction, or political doctrine? No. They, too, can use social scientific thinking. Their task is difficult but possible. They must conscientiously try to locate the best knowledge currently available; use careful, independent reasoning; avoid known errors or fallacies; and be wary of any doctrine offering complete, final answers. Practitioners must always be open to new ideas, use multiple information sources, and constantly question the evidence offered to support a course of action.

CONCLUSION

In this chapter, you learned what research is, how the research process operates, and who conducts research. You also learned about alternatives to research—ways to get fast, easy, and practical knowledge that, nonetheless, often contains error, misinformation, and false reasoning. You saw how the scientific community works, how research fits into the scientific enterprise, and how the norms of science and journal articles are crucial to the scientific community. You also learned the steps of research.

Criminological research is for, about, and conducted by *people*. Despite the attention to the principles, rules, or procedures, remember that it is a human activity. Researchers are people, not unlike yourself, who became absorbed in a desire to create and discover knowledge. Many find research to be fun and exciting. They conduct it to discover new knowledge and to gain a richer understanding of crime, criminal behavior, and the criminal justice system. Whether you become a professional researcher, someone who applies a few research techniques as part of a job, or just someone who uses the results of research, you will benefit from learning about the research process. You will be enriched if you can begin to create a personal link between yourself and the research process.

Mills offered the following valuable advice in his *Sociological Imagination* (1959:196):

> *You must learn to use your life experiences in your intellectual work: continually to examine and interpret it. In this sense craftsmanship is the center of yourself and you are personally involved in every intellectual product upon which you may work.*

KEY TERMS _____

blind review	overgeneralization	scientific method
communalism	premature closure	selective observation
data	qualitative data	social research
disinterestedness	quantitative data	social theory
empirical	scholarly journal article	universalism
halo effect	scientific attitude	
organized skepticism	scientific community	

REVIEW QUESTIONS

1. What sources of knowledge are alternatives to social research?
2. Why is social research usually better than the alternatives?
3. Is social research always right? Can it answer any question? Explain.
4. What is the scientific community? What is its role?
5. What are the norms of the scientific community? What are their effects?
6. How does a study get published in a scholarly social science journal?
7. What steps are involved in conducting a research project?
8. What does it mean to say that research steps are not rigidly fixed?
9. What types of people do social research? For what reasons?

NOTES

1. For more on fallacies, see Babbie (1995:23–25), Kaplan (1964), and Wallace (1971).
2. The rise of science is discussed in Camic (1980), Lemert (1979), Merton (1970), Wuthnow (1979), and Ziman (1976). For more on the historical development of the social sciences, see Eastrope (1974), Laslett (1992), Ross (1991), and Turner and Turner (1991).
3. For more on the scientific community, see Cole (1983), Cole, Cole, and Simon (1981), Collins (1983), Collins and Restivo (1983), Hagstrom (1965), Merton (1973), Stoner (1966), and Ziman (1968).
4. For more on the social role of the scientist, see Ben-David (1971), Camic (1980), and Tuma and Grimes (1981).

5. Norms are discussed in Hagstrom (1965), Merton (1973), and Stoner (1966).
6. Violations of norms are discussed in Blume (1974) and Mitroff (1974).
7. The communication and publication system is described in Bakanic and colleagues (1987), Blau (1978), Cole (1983), Crane (1967), Gusfield (1976), Hargens (1988), Mullins (1973), Singer (1989), and Ziman (1968).
8. For more on the system of reward and stratification in science, see Cole and Cole (1973), Cole (1978), Fuchs and Turner (1986), Gaston (1978), Gustin (1973), Long (1978), Meadows (1974), and Reskin (1977).

RECOMMENDED READINGS

Agnew, Neil McK., and Sandra W. Pyke. (1991). *The science game: An introduction to research in the social sciences*, 5th ed. Englewood Cliffs, NJ: Prentice Hall. This short book provides an overview of social research with whimsical examples and creative diagrams. The authors discuss the general system of science and experimental research.

Beirne, Piers. (1987). Adolphe Quetelet and the origins of positivist criminology. *American Journal of Sociology* 92(5):1140–1169.

———. (1993). *Inventing criminology: Essays on the rise of "Homo Criminalis."* Albany, NY: State University of New York Press. These two references provide a good starting place for young criminologists wishing to learn more about the

origins of the discipline and criminological research.

Frost, Peter, and Ralph Stablein, eds. (1992). *Doing exemplary research.* Newbury Park, CA: Sage. This is a look at the human side of research. It scrutinizes seven articles in organizational analysis, detailing each author's personal autobiographic adventure to create and publish the article. It provides commentary on the nuts and bolts of research and lots of practical tips.

Hunt, Morton. (1985). *Profiles of social research: The scientific study of human interactions.* New York: Russell Sage Foundation. Hunt provides an overview of different methods of doing social research and stories of how five research studies were conducted. He reveals the drama and excitement of discovery in social research in descriptions of the social lives of researchers and the evolution of ideas during the research process.

Mills, C. Wright. (1959). *The sociological imagination.* New York: Oxford University Press. In this classic on sociological thinking and research, Mills comments on developing an overall orientation to social science and discusses several important issues of social research. His appendix on intellectual craftsmanship gives valuable practical advice to the beginning social researcher.

Ziman, John. (1976). *The force of knowledge: The scientific dimension of society.* New York: Cambridge University Press. Ziman provides a broad outline of the growth of science and technology over the past 200 years. He argues that science is fundamentally a social activity in which the public communication of how research was done and of its findings is central.

CHAPTER 2

DIMENSIONS OF RESEARCH

> *The point is rather that a more accurate perception of crime patterns might help societies fix more rationally the level of resources that they allocate for combatting crime, and to concentrate those resources more efficiently.*
> —The Economist, p. 23

INTRODUCTION

A friend of the authors is an anthropologist doing research in Africa. Specifically, she is working on an applied project to explore ways of reducing interethnic violence in southern Sudan. Her longitudinal study spans a two-year period and relies primarily on field research.

To the new researcher, the above description is probably a little confusing. It uses unfamiliar terminology, such as *applied* project and *longitudinal* study, to explain specific details of a person's research. These terms, however, are important to grasp because they convey the dimensions of the study. They explain precisely what the researcher is doing. Every research project, irrespective of scientific discipline, can be described in terms of four research dimensions: (1) the purpose of doing it, (2) its intended use, (3) how it treats time, and (4) the research techniques used in it. The four dimensions reinforce one

another; that is, a purpose tends to go with certain techniques and particular uses. Few studies are pure types, but the dimensions simplify the complexity of conducting research.

Before conducting a research project, a researcher makes several decisions. By understanding the dimensions of research, you will be better prepared to make such decisions. In addition, an awareness of the types of research and how they fit into the research process will make it easier for you to read and understand published studies.

DIMENSIONS OF RESEARCH

The Purpose of a Study

If you ask someone why he or she is conducting a study, you might get a range of responses: "My boss told me to"; "It was a class assignment"; "I was curious"; "My roommate thought it would be a good idea." There are almost as many reasons to do research as there are researchers. Yet, the purposes of social research may be organized into three groups based on what the researcher is trying to accomplish—explore a new topic, describe a social phenomenon, or explain why something occurs.[1] Studies may have multiple purposes (e.g., both to explore and to describe), but one purpose is usually dominant.

Exploration.   Perhaps you have explored a new topic or issue in order to learn about it. If the issue was new or researchers had written little on it, you began at the beginning. This is called *exploratory research.* The researcher's goal is to formulate more precise questions that future research can answer. Exploratory research may be the first stage in a sequence of studies. A researcher may need to conduct an exploratory study in order to know enough to design and execute a second, more systematic and extensive study.

The purpose of the authors' friend's research is "to explore ways of reducing interethnic violence in southern Sudan." It is exploratory because she is studying a topic about which very few social scientists know anything. The civil war in Sudan has been raging for decades, but the war's effect on levels of violent crime, especially on interethnic violence, is only poorly understood. Yet, hopes of finding a lasting peace in this region of Africa depend on the ability of social scientists to study and understand the problem of interethnic violence.

Social scientists are continually watching for new areas of society that deserve their research attention. When they find an area that interests them, they begin to investigate it by designing an exploratory study. This is exactly what is occurring, for example, in the former Soviet Union, as criminologists and other social scientists explore the many new manifestations of social conflict and crime.

Gudkov (1997), who is exploring the issue of ethnic phobias, is one such social scientist. Based on a 1996 public opinion survey, Gudkov argued that the mass ethnic phobias and trauma

Russians felt in the loss of their great-power staus has peaked. He has based his argument on the fact that a smaller percentage of Russians (40 percent) agree that "non-Russians have too much influence in Russia" than was the case in 1993 (54 percent).

Exploratory research rarely yields definitive answers. It addresses the "what" question: "What is this social activity really about?" It is difficult to conduct because there are few guidelines to follow. Everything about a topic is potentially important. The steps are not well defined and the direction of inquiry changes frequently. This can be frustrating for researchers, who may feel adrift or that they are "spinning their wheels."

Exploratory researchers are creative, open minded, and flexible; adopt an investigative stance; and explore all sources of information. Researchers ask creative questions and take advantage of *serendipity,* those unexpected or chance factors that have larger implications. For example, Dekeseredy and colleagues (1997) were surprised to discover in their study of dating violence among Canadian university students that women tended not to use violence in self-defense. These "findings throw doubt on the argument that dating violence is fully symmetrical, or mutual combat" (p. 201).

Exploratory researchers frequently use qualitative data. The techniques for gathering qualitative data are less wedded to a specific theory or research question. Qualitative research tends to be more open to using a range of evidence and discovering new issues (see Box 2.1).

Description.   You may have a more highly developed idea about a social phenomenon and want to describe it. *Descriptive research* presents a picture of the specific details of a situation, social setting, or relationship. Much of the social research found in scholarly journals or used for making policy decisions is descriptive.

Descriptive and exploratory research have many similarities. They blur together in practice. In descriptive research, the researcher begins with a well-defined subject and conducts research to describe it accurately. The outcome

Goals of Exploratory Research

- Become familiar with the basic facts, people, and concerns involved.
- Develop a well-grounded mental picture of what is occurring.
- Generate many ideas and develop tentative theories and conjectures.
- Determine the feasibility of doing additional research.
- Formulate questions and refine issues for more systematic inquiry.
- Develop techniques and a sense of direction for future research.

of a descriptive study is a detailed picture of the subject. For example, crime statistics published annually by the U.S. Federal Bureau of Investigation (FBI) give researchers a wealth of details about such things as arrests and types of crime.

Reviewing the FBI crime statistics on, say, homicide, reveals some interesting changes over the past 60 years or so that these figures have been available. The peak year for homicide was 1980. Homicide rates were over 10 per 100,000 people—practically as high as in the early 1930s. They then began to decline, and stayed relatively low throughout the decades of the 1940s and 1950s, when homicide rates were around 4 to 6 per 100,000 people. In the 1980s, homicide rates fluctuated a bit but remained relatively high. In the 1990s, rates went down somewhat, to around 7 to 8 per 100,000 people. This recent drop in the rate of homicide has touched off a debate among criminologists in the United States to explain the trend.

Descriptive research presents an accurate account of what is occurring. In some sense, it addresses the "how" and "who" questions: "How did it happen?" "Who is involved?" But descriptive research does not explore new issues or explain why something happens. Thus, the FBI

data on homicide does not really explain the reasons for this current decline in homicide. To answer, criminologists must draw on other kinds of research.

A great deal of social research is descriptive. Descriptive researchers use most data-gathering techniques—surveys, field research, content analysis, and historical-comparative research. Only experimental research is less ineffective (see Box 2.2).

Explanation. When you encounter an issue that is already known and have a description of it, you might begin to wonder *why* things are the way they are. The desire to know "why," to explain, is the purpose of *explanatory research*. It builds on exploratory and descriptive research and goes on to identify the reason something occurs. Going beyond focusing on a topic or providing a picture of it, explanatory research looks for causes and reasons. For example, a descriptive study of homicide might reveal that rates are dropping. But an explanatory study is more interested in learning *why* this is happening.

Part of the explanation, some criminologists have argued, has to do with levels of use of crack cocaine. They pointed to the strong correlation that exists between changes in crack use and homicide rates. During the late 1980s and early 1990s, they argued, homicide rates in a number of

Goals of Descriptive Research

- Provide an accurate profile of a group.
- Describe a process, mechanism, or relationship.
- Give a verbal or numerical picture (e.g., percentages).
- Find information to stimulate new explanations.
- Present basic background information or a context.
- Create a set of categories or classify types.
- Clarify a sequence, set of stages, or steps.
- Document information that contradicts prior beliefs about a subject.

U.S. cities closely paralleled levels of cocaine use among adult male arrestees. Thus, when the use of crack became more popular in the mid- and late-1980s, homicide rates likewise began to go up. Now that crack cocaine levels are decreasing, homicide rates are, as well.

Even this explanation does not settle the debate, however. Criminologists and others are currently trying to explain the specific relationship between crack and homicide. Some say it has to do with the pharmaceutical effects of crack cocaine (i.e., "the drug-crazed killer"), whereas others point to the growing racial segregation and income inequality in cities and to changes in illicit drug markets. In any event, one can see how explanatory research tries to uncover why something is occurring (see Box 2.3).

The Use of Research

Criminology really has two wings. Researchers in one adopt a more detached, scientific, and academic orientation; those in the other are more activist, pragmatic, and reform oriented. This is not a rigid separation. Researchers in the two wings cooperate and maintain friendly relations. Some move from one wing to another at different stages in their careers. The difference in orienta-

tion revolves around how to use criminological research. In simple terms, some focus on using research to advance general knowledge, whereas others use it to solve specific problems. Those who seek an understanding of the fundamental nature of social reality are engaged in *basic research* (also called *academic research* or *pure research*). Applied researchers, by contrast, primarily want to apply and tailor knowledge to address a specific practical issue. They want to answer a policy question or solve a pressing social problem.

Basic Research. Basic research advances fundamental knowledge about the social world. It focuses on refuting or supporting theories that explain how the social world operates, what makes things happen, why social relations are a certain way, and why society changes. Basic research is the source of most new scientific ideas and ways of thinking about the world. It can be exploratory, descriptive, or explanatory; however, explanatory research is the most common.

Many nonscientists criticize basic research and ask, "What good is it?" They consider basic research to be a waste of time and money because it does not have a direct use or help resolve an immediate problem. It is true that knowledge produced by basic research often lacks practical applications in the short term. Yet, basic research provides a foundation for knowledge and understanding that are generalizable to many policy areas, problems, or areas of study. Basic research is the source of most of the tools—methods, theories, and ideas—that applied researchers use. Really big breakthroughs in understanding and significant advances in knowledge usually come from basic research. In contrast to applied researchers, who want quick answers to questions for use within the next month or year, basic researchers painstakingly seek answers to questions that could have an impact on thinking for over a century.

The questions asked by basic researchers might often seem impractical. For instance, the authors have a friend who is a sociologist at a

---

Box 2.3 _____

Goals of Explanatory Research

- Determine the accuracy of a principle or theory.
- Find out which competing explanation is better.
- Advance knowledge about an underlying process.
- Link different issues or topics under a common general statement.
- Build and elaborate a theory so it becomes more complete.
- Extend a theory or principle into new areas or issues.
- Provide evidence to support or refute an explanation or prediction.

major urban university in the United States. Being interested in deviant behavior, she began to do field research on urban male prostitutes years ago. Sometimes she would even invite her subjects to speak in class to her students. All through the 1960s and 1970s, many may have wondered why she was doing this research and how anything of practical use could come from it. However, the AIDS epidemic soon erased any questions they may have had. In fact, this friend received a prestigious grant to study the spread of AIDS among male prostitutes. Ironically, even she did not know how important her basic research would someday become.

Police officers, officials trying to prevent delinquency, or counselors of youthful offenders may see little direct relevance to basic research on the question, "Why does deviant behavior occur?" Basic research rarely helps practitioners directly with their everyday concerns. Nevertheless, it stimulates new ways of thinking about deviance that have the potential to revolutionize and dramatically improve how practitioners deal with the problem. Although policymakers and service providers often feel that basic research is of little relevance, public policies and social services will be ineffective and misguided unless they are based on an understanding of actual causes.

A new idea or fundamental knowledge is not generated only by basic research. Applied research, too, can build new knowledge. Nonetheless, basic research is essential for nourishing the expansion of knowledge. Researchers at the center of the scientific community conduct most of the basic research.

Applied Research.   Applied researchers try to solve specific policy problems or help practitioners accomplish tasks.[2] Theory is less central to them than seeking a solution to a specific problem for a limited setting (e.g., "Does a negative public opinion toward the Internal Revenue Service encourage higher levels of tax crime?"). People employed by universities, human rights organizations, government agencies, and businesses conduct applied research. It often affects our daily

lives. For instance, decisions to choose one public policy over another, or to allocate resources in a particular way, should be based on sound applied research.

Applied research is frequently descriptive research, and its main strength is its immediate practical use. The scientific community is the primary consumer of basic research. The consumers of applied research findings are practitioners such as teachers, counselors, and caseworkers, or decision makers such as managers, committees, and officials. Often, someone other than the researcher who conducted the study uses the results of applied research. The use of the results may be beyond the researcher's control. This means that applied researchers have an obligation to translate findings from scientific technical language into the language of decision makers or practitioners.

The results of applied research are less likely to enter the public domain in publications. Results may be available only to a small number of decision makers or practitioners, who decide whether or how to put the research results into practice and who may or may not use the results wisely. For example, Neuberg (1988) found that the results of the famous Seattle–Denver "negative income tax" experiment of the 1960s and 1970s was seriously misinterpreted and distorted in newspaper accounts. Despite serious problems with the study and cautions from researchers, politicians used its results to justify cuts in government programs they disliked.

Because applied research has immediate implications or involves controversial issues, it often generates conflict. This is not new. For example, in 1903, Ellwood conducted an applied study of the jails and poorhouses in Missouri and documented serious deficiencies. His research report generated great public indignation, and he was accused of slandering the state that gave him employment (Turner and Turner, 1991:181).

Gagne's (1996) study of battered women also addresses a controversial issue. Gagne spent many hours interviewing a dozen different women who, as a result of their being physically abused either by a parent or husband, assaulted or killed their abuser. These women were incarcerated for their violent crimes. However, the point of Gagne's research was to underscore the horrifying victimization they had suffered. Her research and that done by others are proving useful in the legal defense and clemency appeals of battered women.

Applied and basic researchers adopt different orientations toward research methodology (see Table 2.1). Basic researchers emphasize high scientific standards and try to conduct near-perfect research. Applied researchers make more trade-offs. They may compromise scientific rigor to get quick, usable results. Compromise is no excuse for sloppy research, however. Applied researchers squeeze research into the constraints of an applied setting and balance rigor against practical needs. Such balancing requires an in-depth knowledge of research and an awareness of the consequences of compromising standards.

Types of Applied Research.   Practitioners use several types of applied research. Some of the major ones are discussed here.

Action research is applied research that treats knowledge as a form of power and abolishes the line between research and social action. There are several types of action research, but most share common characteristics: Those who are being studied participate in the research process; research incorporates ordinary or popular knowledge; research focuses on power with a goal of empowerment; research seeks to raise consciousness or increase awareness; and research is tied directly to political action.

Action researchers try to equalize power relations between themselves and research subjects, and they oppose having more control, status, and authority than those they study. These researchers try to advance a cause or improve conditions by expanding public awareness. They are explicitly political, not value neutral. Because the goal is to improve the conditions and lives of research participants, formal reports, articles, or books become secondary. Action researchers assume that knowledge develops from experience, particularly the experience of social-political action. They also assume that ordinary people can become aware of con-

---

TABLE 2.1   Basic and Applied Social Research Compared

BASIC	APPLIED
1. Research is intrinsically satisfying and judgments are by other criminologists.	1. Research is part of a job and is judged by sponsors who are outside the discipline of criminology.
2. Research problems and subjects are selected with a great deal of freedom.	2. Research problems are "narrowly constrained" to the demands of employers or sponsors.
3. Research is judged by absolute norms of scientific rigor, and the highest standards of scholarship are sought.	3. The rigor and standards of scholarship depend on the uses of results. Research can be "quick and dirty" or may match high scientific standards.
4. The primary concern is with the internal logic and rigor of research design.	4. The primary concern is with the ability to generalize findings to areas of interest to sponsors.
5. The driving goal is to contribute to basic, theoretical knowledge.	5. The driving goal is to have practical payoffs or uses for results.
6. Success comes when results appear in a scholarly journal and have an impact on others in the scientific community.	6. Success comes when results are used by sponsors in decision making.

Source: Adapted from Freeman and Rossi (1984:572–573).

ditions and learn to take actions that can bring about improvement.

Action research is typically associated with the critical social science approach discussed in Chapter 4. It attracts criminologists who hold specific perspectives (e.g., progressive, environmental, Native American, feminist, etc.). For example, Kraska and Kappeler (1997) conducted research on the "militarization of policing" in the United States. They were extremely critical of what they called "a dark side of contemporary policing" (p. 13). They were referring to the growing, heavily armed, paramilitary police units in minority neighborhoods. The researchers strongly criticized the police for this practice, and urged them not to adopt a military model of social control.

In one situation, action research involved working to preserve a town that was to be destroyed by a dam project. An action researcher worked together with union officials and management to redesign work to prevent layoffs. In developing nations, action researchers work among illiterate, impoverished peasants to teach literacy, study local conditions, and spread an awareness of conditions, and to attempt to improve them.[3] Gamson (1992:xviii) described a seminar on action research at Boston College that drew students from the Social Economy and Social Justice graduate program:

> The participants in this seminar . . . are activist-scholars oriented to the concrete problems involved in mobilizing people for collective action. Participants are or have been involved in the Central American solidarity movement, the nuclear freeze movement, the movements for more equitable health care and decent housing, the labor movement. . . . Members of the seminar write papers, run workshops, and consult on media strategy for various movement organizations, as well as conduct research.

A second type of applied research is *social impact assessment*.[4] It may be part of a larger environmental impact statement required by government agencies. Its purpose is to estimate the likely consequences of a planned change. Such an assessment can be used for planning and making choices among alternative policies. For example, racial impact statements have been suggested in a recent study (Donziger, 1996). Such statements would specifically anticipate how major changes in crime policy might affect minority communities. Proposed criminal justice legislation, as well as law enforcement initiatives, need to be assessed to ensure that arrests, pretrial detentions, plea negotiations, and sentencing are free of racial bias. In this way, an honest effort is being made to respond to complaints by minorities of bias in the system. The impact of a proposed community policing initiative, for example, can be assessed in various ways (see Box 2.4).

Evaluation research is a widely used type of applied research[5] that addresses the question, "Did it work?" Smith and Glass (1987:31) defined *evaluation* as "the process of establishing value judgments based on evidence." Evaluation research measures the effectiveness of a program, policy, or way of doing something. It is frequently descriptive but can be exploratory or explanatory. Evaluation researchers use several different research techniques (e.g., survey and field). If it can be used, the experimental technique is usually most effective.

Practitioners involved with a policy or program may conduct evaluation research for their own information or at the request of outside deci-

---

Box 2.4 _____

Areas Assessed in Community Policing Impact Studies

- Community relations (e.g., Does the policing initiative improve community-police relations?)
- Demographic consequences (e.g., Are patterns of arrest reflective of the ethnic composition of the community?)
- Psychological well-being (e.g., Are police officers adjusting well to the new forms of community policing?)
- Criminal behavior (e.g., Does community policing lower measured levels of criminal behavior?)

sion makers. For example, the U.S. General Accounting Office (GAO; Wray, 1993) was asked by Congress to evaluate the government's efforts to combat *money laundering,* which is the "disguising or concealing of illicit income to make it appear legitimate" (p. 1). Federal law enforcement officers estimate that somewhere between $100 billion and $300 billion in U.S. currency is laundered every year! The GAO conducted the evaluation by focusing on the legal requirement forcing banks to report large cash transactions to the federal government. The GAO found that the number of transaction reports has grown steadily, and that these reports are very helpful in detecting money laundering.

Ethical and political conflicts often arise in evaluation research because people have opposing interests in the findings about a program. Research results can affect getting a job, building political popularity, or promoting an alternative program. People who are personally displeased with the finding often try to attack the researcher or his or her methods as being sloppy, biased, or inadequate. In addition to creating controversy and being attacked, evaluation researchers are sometimes subjected to pressures to rig a study before they begin. Imagine the researchers' dilemma, for example, if their evaluation showed that past crime policies had indeed been biased against minorities. Furthermore, suppose their research findings were to be announced to the public just before an election. The political pressure on the researchers to "reinterpret" their findings would be tremendous. This raises all manner of ethical issues having to do with the politics of evaluation research. (You can read more about ethical issues in Chapter 17.)

Something similar to this scenario actually happened in 1994 (Donziger, 1996). A government study indicated that federal prisons incarcerate a substantial portion of nonviolent offenders for long terms. This information was not in keeping with conventional wisdom and could have been used to weaken political interests wishing to "get tough" on drugs and crime. However, the release of the report was postponed for several weeks, precisely at a time when such issues were being fiercely debated in Congress.

Two types of evaluation research are formative and summative. *Formative evaluation* is built-in monitoring or continuous feedback on a program used for program management. *Summative evaluation* looks at final program outcomes. Both are usually necessary. In the earlier example of money laundering, summative evaluation was used. The GAO conducted the research one time after the bank reporting requirements had been put into law. A formative evaluation could be added, as well. This would involve an ongoing evaluation on the part of the federal government to ensure banks are filing the required transaction reports and that they are accurate.

Applied researchers use two tools, needs assessment and cost-benefit analysis, in social impact assessment and evaluation research. In a *needs assessment,* a researcher collects data to determine major needs and their severity. Suppose you are conducting a needs assessment of refugees living in a camp run by a human rights organization. As a researcher, you are immediately faced with questions such as, "Whose needs should be assessed?" "Should the health needs of women be given more or less attention than the nutritional needs of children or the overall safety of the camp?" Quite obviously, the full complexity of needs inside the refugee camp cannot be satisfied equally, so they must be prioritized in terms of their severity.

A second, related issue is that needs are often not articulated in a way that links them directly to policies or long-term solutions. After studying the refugee camp, you might determine that the incidences of violence and theft in the camp have to do with the presence of competing political factions. Thus, the actual need goes beyond that of simply policing the facility to maintain order and civility in the camp. It really has to do with the long-term objective of striking some sort of political compromise between the competing factions.

This brings us to a third issue often accompanying needs assessment research. The issue involves a situation in which suggested solutions go beyond local control. The example of researching the needs of refugees illustrates this point. By definition, refugees are physically displaced from their homes because of tragic circumstances beyond their control. Thus, for instance, refugees might be caught up in a civil war not at all of their making. It is not clear what a needs assessment of the refugee camp can do about settling the civil war. Nevertheless, as the researcher, you might be able to suggest specific needs, such as hunger and malnutrion, that both warring sides can agree to address. This could in turn suggest other mutual needs that the sides might be willing to address, such as the need to limit the civilian proliferation of small arms and ammunition. The point is, the needs assessment should produce solutions that consider the short- and long-term needs of the subjects. However, powerful groups may attempt to put a stop to the needs assessment or try to censor its results. If locally felt needs are caused by major international relations, decisions made in distant corporate headquarters, or changes in the global economy, a needs assessment may be only a timid "Band-Aid solution."

Social impact studies often include a *cost-benefit analysis*. Economists developed cost-benefit analysis, in which the researcher estimates the future costs and benefits of one or several proposed actions and gives them monetary values. In brief, it works like this: A researcher identifies all the consequences of a proposed action. Next, he or she assigns each consequence a monetary value. The consequences may include intangibles such as less fear of crime, more attachment to one's community, lower crime rates, and even human life itself. Often, the researcher assigns a probability or likelihood to the occurrence of various consequences. Next, policymakers or others identify negative consequences (costs) and positive ones (benefits). Finally, costs are compared to benefits, and policymakers decide whether they balance.

Cost-benefit analysis appears to be a neutral, rational, and technical decision-making strategy, but it can be controversial. People do not necessarily agree on what are positive and negative consequences. For instance, one might apply a cost-benefit logic to crime and sentencing alternatives. The costs associated with crime are somewhat difficult to frame. However, health care costs associated with injuries caused by crime are estimated at $4 billion annually (Donziger, 1996). Another $65 billion is spent each year on private security systems. To be sure, for some (i.e., the prison-industrial complex) these might not be costs at all but rather benefits.

There are two ways to assign monetary values to costs and benefits. *Contingency evaluation* asks people how much something is worth to them. For example, the per capita expenditure for Wisconsin's correctional system was over $70 in 1997. A contingency evaluation might involve a survey of Wisconsin residents, asking them if they thought spending this much on jails and prisons was worth it. Results from this survey could then be compared with the results of surveys from the other states. This would tell us which state's residents are most (and least) satisfied with levels of criminal justice spending.

On the other hand, a reseacher might use *actual cost evaluation* to calculate costs and benefits. A criminal justice administrator, for example, would be very interested in having the relative cost of sentencing alternatives. His or her decision to emphasize a particular alternative over another depends, to some degree, on their relative costs. The cost of keeping a person in a U.S. prison for one year is over $22,000. The annual cost of, say, intensive probation supervision is about $6,500. All things being equal, intensive probation supervision is a better bargain than imprisonment. Thus, to balance the costs with benefits, the administrator must estimate (in terms of dollars) the advantages of prison over intensive probation. If he or she cannot balance the equation, then there is no cost-benefit rationale for preferring the more costly strategy of imprisonment.

A significant issue for cost-benefit analysis is the assumption that everything has a price (learning, health, love, happiness, human dignity, chastity, etc.) and that people assign similar valuations. It also raises serious moral and political concerns. Cost-benefit calculations usually favor upper-income people over low-income or poor people. This occurs because the relative value of a cost or benefit depends on one's wealth and income. A wealthy person, for instance, is better able to afford the annual cost of keeping an offender in prison, as opposed to the less costly alternatives such as intensive probation. He or she probably feels safer knowing that "a criminal is behind bars." Proponents of alternatives to imprisonment, on the other hand, need to point out that not only are relatively higher costs involved but also the perceived benefits of imprisonment (i.e., reducing one's chances of being a crime victim) are overstated. This will give the wealthy person a reason to take pause and reconsider his or her position vis-à-vis sentencing alternatives.

Cost-benefit analysis tends to conceal the moral-political aspect of questions. For instance, crime policies favoring imprisonment over probation for nonviolent offenders have a moral dimension that is often overlooked by cost-benefit economics. This concern for morality, it seems, becomes overpowering as one becomes intimately and emotionally tied to the specific individuals feeling the pains of punishment and victimization. The moral aspect can get lost in a decision that involves people who are not easily identified as individuals among a large group and for whom decision makers lack direct, personal contact. A moral aspect remains, even if the focus is on the economic costs and benefits.

The Time Dimension in Research

Another dimension of criminological research is the treatment of time. An awareness of the time dimension will help you read or conduct research because different research questions or issues incorporate time in different ways.

Some studies give you a snapshot of what is going on at a single, fixed time point and allow you to analyze it in detail. Other studies provide a moving picture that lets you follow events, people, or social relations over periods of time.

Quantitative research is divided into two groups: a single point in time (cross-sectional research) versus multiple time points (longitudinal research). Quantitative research looks at a large group of cases, people, or units and measures a limited number of features. A case study is more distinct. It usually involves qualitative methods and focuses on one or a few cases during a limited time period.

Cross-Sectional Research. Most criminological research takes a snapshot approach to the social world. In *cross-sectional research*, researchers observe at one point in time. Cross-sectional research is usually simpler and less costly than longitudinal research. Its disadvantage is that it cannot capture social processes or change. Cross-sectional research can be exploratory, descriptive, or explanatory but it is most consistent with a descriptive approach to research. The survey on dating violence among Canadian university students, mentioned earlier in the chapter, is a good example of cross-sectional research. The researchers actually collected the survey data at one point in time—over a several-month period in 1992.

Longitudinal Research. Researchers using *longitudinal research* examine features of people or other units at more than one time. It is usually more complex and costly than cross-sectional research but it is also more powerful, especially when researchers seek answers to questions about social change. Descriptive and explanatory researchers use longitudinal approaches. We will now consider three types of longitudinal research: time series, panel, and cohort.

Time-series research is a longitudinal study in which the same type of information is collected on a group of people or other units across multiple time periods. Researchers can observe stability or change in the features of the units or can track conditions over time. The earlier-mentioned study of ethnic phobias in Russia is a time-series design. Three times since 1990 the Russian Center for Public Opinion Research has asked random samples of the public about their concern over "non-

Russian nationalities" and the influence they might have in the country.

Marvell and Moody (1995) also used time series in their study on the impact of enhanced prison terms for felonies committed with guns. Their study is also a type of evaluation research, although few legislators base their actions on research, so the findings may not affect future laws or policy. The researchers examined the impact on firearm sentence-enhancement laws in the United States. The laws impose extra prison time or a minimum prison term for felonies committed with a gun. Such laws have been enacted in 49 states in the past 25 years. For 44 states that had strong sentence-enhancement laws, Marvell and Moody examined data on various features (e.g., prison population, crime rates, prison admissions, whether guns were used in specific crimes, etc.) for the years 1971 to 1993. They concluded, "We found little evidence to support the intended purposes of firearm sentencing enhancement, reducing crime rates and gun use" (1995:269).

The *panel study* is a powerful type of longitudinal research. It is more difficult to conduct than time-series research. In a panel study, the researcher observes exactly the same people, group, or organization across time periods. Panel research is formidable to conduct and very costly. Tracking people over time is often difficult because some people die or cannot be located. Nevertheless, the results of a well-designed panel study are very valuable. Even short-term panel studies can clearly show the impact of a particular life event. The most important criminological panel study in the United States is the National Crime Victimization Survey (NCVS). The survey collects data from approximately 58,000 housing units or households every six months for a three-year period, and then resamples another panel for the next three years.

Another panel study (Nagin et al., 1995) looked at the impact of deviance in youth on long-term criminal activity and problems in adulthood. The researchers examined data on 411 males from a working-class section of London who were first studied when they were about 8 years old, in 1961–62. The same men were followed until they were 32 years old, except for 8 who died. The men were interviewed at two-year intervals. Data were collected throughout the years on many personality, background, and deviant behavior measures. The men's families, teachers, and friends were also interviewed. The researchers classified the men into four groups based on self-reported delinquency, ranging from nondelinquent to high-level chronic. The main finding was that those who were deviant only in adolescence appeared to be very similar to nonoffenders by the age of 32, except they were more likely to drink alcohol to excess and use illegal drugs.

A *cohort analysis* is similar to the panel study, but rather than observing the exact same people, a category of people who share a similar life experience in a specified time period is studied. Cohort analysis is "explicitly macroanalytic," which means researchers examine the category as a whole for important features (Ryder, 1992:230). The focus is on the cohort, or category, not on specific individuals.

Wolfgang (1995) recently reported the results of a birth-cohort analysis of over 5,000 Chinese individuals all born in 1973 in the major port city of Wuhan, China. Less than 2 percent of the birth cohort had a record of delinquency by the age of 17. In contrast to cohort levels found in other studies—including those in Philadelphia, Racine (Wisconsin), Stockholm, and London, which typically show delinquency rates about 30 percent—the Chinese birth cohort had low rates, indeed. As with the other cohorts, however, the delinquents in the Wuhan cohort tended to possess lower levels of formal education, employment, and quarreling families than were the nondelinquents.

Case Studies. In cross-sectional and longitudinal research, a researcher examines features on many people or units, either at one time period or across time periods. In both, a researcher precisely measures a common set of features on many cases, usually expressed in numbers. In *case-study research*, he or she examines, in depth, many features of a few cases over a duration of time. Cases can be individuals, groups, organizations, movements, events, or geographic units. The data are usually more detailed, varied, and extensive. Most involve qualitative data about a few cases. Qualitative and case-study research are not identical, but "almost all qualitative research seeks to construct representations based on in-depth, detailed knowledge of cases" (Ragin, 1994:92).[6]

In a case study, a researcher may intensively investigate one or two cases or compare a limited set of cases, focusing on several factors. Case study uses the logic of analytic instead of enumerative induction. In it, the researcher carefully selects one or a few key cases to illustrate an issue and analytically study it (or them) in detail. He or she considers the specific context of the case and examines how its parts are configured. This contrasts with longitudinal studies in which the researcher collects data on many units or cases, then looks for patterns in the mass of numbers. The researcher looks more for averages or patterns across many units or cases.[7]

Case studies help researchers connect the micro level, or the actions of individual people, to the macro level, or large-scale social structures and processes (Vaughan, 1992). "The logic of the case study is to demonstrate a causal argument about how general social forces shape and produce results in particular settings" (Walton, 1992:122). Case-study research raises questions about the boundaries and defining characteristics of a case. Such questions help in the generation of new thinking and theory. "Case studies are likely to produce the best theory" (Walton, 1992:129).

Puri and colleagues (1997) conducted a case study of terrorism in two village areas in India. These two areas in the Punjab are "where large scale recruitment to terrorist groups and relatively extensive scale of terrorist activities and killings were noticed" (p. 39). Open-ended interviews with terrorists, their families, sympathizers, extorted shopkeepers, police officers, and others revealed intriguing results and demonstrated the "micro-macro" connection just mentioned. At the micro level of analysis, the case study developed profiles of individual terrorists. The terrorists were overwhelmingly young (less than 25 years of age) when recruited into terrorist activity.

There was a predominance of one case (Jat Sikh), and most were bound by kinship to other terrorists. However, contrary to popular notions, the terrorists were not particularly political or fundamentalist in orientation. Their socioeconomic backgrounds were quite similar—hailing mostly from poor farming or landless families.

At the macro level, Puri and associates (1997) found the effects of structural changes in the agrarian economy to be significant in the creation of terrorism in the region. The terrorists and their families had been displaced, and otherwise hurt economically and socially, by the changing economy. But it would be an unfair characterization to presume that these terrorists were, in some sense, driven by a coherent sociopolitical ideology. If in the beginning "they seemed to be working for a cause and attacked definite targets" (p. 55), as time went on, most of the terrorists were hardly more than "petty theives and bad characters."

DATA COLLECTION TECHNIQUES USED

Every researcher collects data using one or more techniques. This section is a brief overview of the main techniques. In later chapters, you will read about these techniques in detail and learn how to use them. The techniques may be grouped into two categories: *quantitative,* collecting data in the form of numbers, and *qualitative,* collecting data in the form of words or pictures. Some techniques are more effective when addressing specific kinds of questions or topics. It takes skill, practice, and creativity to match a research question to an appropriate data collection technique.

Quantitative Data

Experiments. Experimental research uses the logic and principles found in natural science research. Experiments can be conducted in laboratories or in real life. They usually involve a relatively small number of people and address a well-focused question. Experiments are most effective for explanatory research. They are often limited to topics for which a researcher can manipulate the situation in which people find themselves.

In most experiments, the researcher divides the people being studied into two or more groups. He or she then treats both groups identically, except that one group but not the other is given a condition he or she is interested in: the "treatment." The researcher measures the reactions of both groups precisely. By controlling the setting for both groups and giving only one the treatment, the researcher can conclude that any differences in the reactions of the groups are due to the treatment alone.

Rhodes and Gross (1997) conducted an experiment to find more effective ways to prevent the spread of HIV among the heavy drug-using and needle-using population. The subjects of the experiement were some 1,400 arrestees in Washington, DC, and in Portland, Oregon. Before being released, the arrestees were randomly assigned to one of three groups. The first group of arrestees were given a referral guide to community services (e.g., HIV counseling and testing centers, drug-treatment programs, and job training) and shown a related videotape. The second group not only saw the videotape and received the referral guide but also had one counseling session. The third group viewed the videotape, received the referral guide, and were given six months of intensive case management, meaning regular contacts with counselors and community service providers.

The subjects were then interviewed individually three times over the next six months. At each interview they were asked about their crime behavior, sexual behavior, and substance abuse. When the experiment was over, the researchers found that all three groups had improved their "HIV prevention" behavior. Among other things, the arrestees reported less needle sharing, and the case management group in particular showed far less "heavy drug use" during the course of the experiment. This led the researchers to conclude that case management could be used to reduce the spread of HIV among at-risk populations.

Surveys. Survey techniques are often used in descriptive or explanatory research. A survey researcher asks people questions in a written questionnaire (mailed or handed to people) or during an interview, then records answers. He or she manipulates no situation or condition; people simply answer questions. In *survey research,* the researcher asks many people numerous questions in a short time period. He or she typically summarizes answers to questions in percentages, tables, or graphs. Surveys give the researcher a picture of what many people think or report doing. A survey researcher often uses a sample or a smaller group of selected people, but generalizes results to a larger group from which the smaller group was chosen.

Shoemaker (1992) modified survey methods used in the United States for his study of delinquency in the Philippines. His study involved drawing a sample of 567 high school students from Oro City and asking them to reveal (or self-report) their delinquent behavior. Unfortunately, Shoemaker did not use random sampling, so his findings cannot be generalized to all high school students in the Philippines. Nevertheless, his study represents a good starting point.

Compared to high school students in the United States and other western countries, the Philippine teens in this sample had relatively low levels of delinquency. Shoemaker found, for example, that on a delinquency scale, ranging from 0.0 (no self-reported delinquency) to 48.0 (frequent acts of delinquency), the Philippine students had an average score of 3.1. He also used advanced statistical techniques (e.g., multiple regression analysis, which will be discussed in Chapter 12) to show a strong relationship between delinquency and one's attachment, involvement, and commitment to parents and peers. Shoemaker interpreted this specific finding as evidence for the social bond theory of crime. Finally, the researcher discovered that middle-class students had higher delinquency scores than students with more modest social class backgrounds.

Content Analysis. *Content analysis* is a technique for examining information, or content, in written or symbolic material (e.g., pictures, movies, song lyrics, etc.). In content analysis, a researcher first identifies a body of material to analyze (e.g., books, newspapers, films, etc.) and then creates a system for recording specific aspects of it. The system might include counting how often certain words or themes occur. Finally, the researcher records what was found in the material. He or she often measures information in the content as numbers and presents it as tables or graphs. This technique lets a researcher discover features in the content of large amounts of material that might otherwise go unnoticed. Content analysis is used for exploratory and explanatory research but is most often used in descriptive research.

Livingston and Eachus (1996) published a very interesting content analysis focusing on the media's willingness to report the U.S. government's involvement with Latin American paramilitary "death squads." Their basic argument, what they called "the indexing hypothesis," is that "journalism in the post–Cold War environment has greater latitude in including dissident voices and ideas" (p. 423).

To test the hypothesis, the researchers traced how major newspapers (e.g., *New York Times*) had covered stories of death squads in El Salvador and Guatemala. What they found was the initial media coverage emphasized the "moderating influence" played by the United States (Livingston and Eachus, 1996:426). There was no indication in these reports of any U.S. involvement or knowledge of the death squads' atrocities. However, by the mid-1990s, the newspapers had changed their position and were now reporting on the deep institutional links tying the U.S. government, military, and CIA (Central Intelligence Agency) to Latin America's "dirty war."

Their explanation for this change is thoughtful. Livingston and Eachus (1996) cited the post–Cold War period as one which "lacks a clear conceptual consensus regarding U.S. foreign policy" (p. 425). That is to say, ideological alignments have been reordered and are subject to further realignment.

Existing Statistics. In *existing statistics research,* a researcher locates a source of previously collected information, often in the form of government reports or previously conducted surveys. He or she then reorganizes or combines the information in new ways to address a research question. Locating sources can be time consuming, so the researcher needs to consider carefully the meaning of what he or she finds. Frequently, a researcher does not know whether the information of interest is available when he or she begins a study. Sometimes, the existing quantitative information consists of stored survey or other data that a researcher reexamines using various statistical procedures. This is called *secondary analysis research.* Existing statistics research can be used for exploratory, descriptive, or explanatory purposes but is most frequently used for descriptive research.

Koetting and Schiraldi (1997) brought together a wide variety of existing crime statistics in their comparative analysis of incarceration. They were interested in identifying, among other things, the world's highest incarceration rates. To do this, they had to compile data from sources such as Interpol (International Criminal Police Organization), the Council of Europe, Human Rights Watch's Prison Project, the Australian Institute of Criminology, the World Almanac, and the U.S. Department of Justice. The researchers found that California has the dubious distinction of having the world's highest rate of incarceration. The only territories with rates nearly as high are the occupied regions of Israel (i.e., the West Bank and the Gaza Strip).

Qualitative Data

Field Research. Most field researchers conduct case studies on a small group of people for some length of time. *Field research* begins with a loosely formulated idea or topic. Next, researchers select a social group or site for study. Once they gain access to the group or site, they adopt a social role in the setting and begin observing. The researchers observe and interact in the field setting for a period from a few months to several years. They get to know personally the people being studied and may conduct informal interviews. They take detailed notes on a daily basis. During the observation, they consider what they observe and refine or focus ideas about its significance. Finally, they leave the field site. They then reread their notes and prepare written reports. Field research is usually used for exploratory and descriptive studies; it is rarely used for explanatory research.

Wright and Decker (1997) recently published a book that provides a "street-level" view of armed robbery. Unlike most previous research on this topic, which tends to focus on armed robbers after they have been arrested and incarcerated, these two authors actually spent time in the social environment of active armed robbers in St. Louis, Missouri. Although this brand of field research has its dangers, it also offers fresh insights into the process of committing armed robbery. Field research put these criminologists in a position to get forthright, candid responses from armed robbers as to their motives and methods. Much of their book contains verbatim quotes from conversations with armed robbers on such topics as how and why certain victims are selected by the criminals. Field research also gave the researchers an ecological sense of the crime scene. That is, they were able to see how situational and spatial features of the crime scene contributed to the criminal's decision to rob. The authors drew on their unique perspective to suggest ways of bringing crime prevention policy into line with such scientific research on armed robbery.

Historical-Comparative Research. *Historical-comparative research* examines aspects of social life in a past historical era or across different cultures. Researchers who use this technique may focus on one historical period or several, compare one or more cultures, or mix historical periods and cultures. This kind of research combines theory with data collection. As with field research, a researcher begins with a loosely formulated question, refining and elaborating on it during the research process. Researchers often use a mix of evidence, including existing statistics, interviews, oral histories, footage from media archives, and

documents (e.g., newspapers, photographs, diaries, journals, maps, etc.). Historical-comparative research can be exploratory, descriptive, or explanatory and can blend types, but it is usually descriptive.

Farnsworth (1997) reported on some interesting criminological research from Australia. The country's origin as a penal colony laid the groundwork for its emerging policy of restorative justice. Between 1788 and 1868, some 160,000 British convicts were exiled to Australia. Upon their arrival, however, they soon discovered, to their good fortune, that Australia, being a settler society, afforded them a second chance to make an honest life for themselves. So celebrated are its "rehabilitated criminals" that even the $20 note has on it a horse-thief-made-good, Mary Reibey, Australia's first successful businesswoman.

Restorative justice is the practice of bringing victim and offender together to decide among themselves how to repair the crime's damage. Researchers point out that not only does this notion of criminal justice derive from Australia's history as a penal colony but it can also be credited to the Maori of New Zealand. The Maori have cultural traditions very similar to those evolving in nearby Australia, such as restorative justice.

CONCLUSION

This chapter gave you an overview of the dimensions of social research. You saw that research can be classified in a number of different ways (e.g., by its purpose, by its research technique, etc.) and that the dimensions of research loosely overlap with each other (see Table 2.2). The dimensions of research provide a "road map" through the terrain that is criminological research.

In the next chapter, we turn to criminological theory. You read about theory in Chapter 1 and it was mentioned again in this chapter. In Chapter 3, you will learn how theory and research methods work together and about several types of theory.

TABLE 2.2 Dimensions of Social Research

PURPOSE FOR STUDY	USE OF STUDY	TIME IN STUDY	DATA COLLECTION TECHNIQUE
Exploratory Descriptive Explanatory	Basic Applied: ■ Action ■ Impact ■ Evaluation	Cross-sectional Longitudinal: ■ Panel ■ Time series ■ Cohort analysis Case study	Quantitative data: ■ Experiment ■ Survey ■ Content analysis ■ Existing statistics Qualitative data: ■ Field research ■ Historical-comparative

KEY TERMS

action-oriented research
applied research
basic research
case-study research
cohort analysis
content analysis
cost-benefit analysis
cross-sectional research
descriptive research

evaluation research
existing statistics research
experimental research
explanatory research
exploratory research
field research
formative evaluation research
historical-comparative research
longitudinal research

needs assessment
panel study
secondary analysis research
serendipity
social impact assessment
summative evaluation research
survey research
time-series research

REVIEW QUESTIONS

1. When is exploratory research used, and what can it accomplish?
2. What types of results are produced by a descriptive research study?
3. What is explanatory research? What is its primary purpose?
4. What are the major differences between basic and applied research?
5. Who is likely to conduct basic research, and where are results likely to appear?
6. Explain the differences among the three types of applied research.
7. How do time-series, panel, and cohort studies differ?
8. What are some potential problems with cost-benefit analysis?
9. What is a needs assessment? What complications can occur when conducting one?
10. Explain the difference between qualitative and quantitative research.

NOTES

1. Explanatory, exploratory, and descriptive research are also discussed in Babbie (1995:84–86), Bailey (1987:38–39), and Churchill (1983:56–77).
2. Finsterbusch and Motz (1980), Freeman (1983), Lazarsfeld and Reitz (1975), Olsen and Micklin (1981), and Rubin (1983) discuss applied research. Also see Whyte's (1986) critique of social research that is not applied and instances in which social research affects

public issues. McGrath, Martin, and Kulka (1982) discuss judgment calls that are relevant in applied research.
3. See Cancian and Armstead (1992), Reason (1994), and Whyte (1989).
4. Social impact research is discussed in Chadwick, Bahr, and Albrecht (1984:313–342), Finsterbusch and Motz (1980:75–118), and Finsterbush and Wolf (1981). Also see Rossi, Wright, and Weber-Burdin (1982) and Wright and Rossi (1981) on "natural hazards" and social science.
5. For a brief introduction to evaluation research, see Adams and Schvaneveldt (1985:315–328), Finster-busch and Motz (1980:119–158), and Smith and Glass (1987). A more complete discussion can be found in Burnstein, Freeman, and Rossi (1985), Freeman (1992), Rossi (1982), Rossi and Freeman (1985), Saxe and Fine (1981), and Weiss (1972).
6. For discussions of case-study research, see Miller (1992), Mitchell (1984), Ragin (1992a, 1992b), Stake (1994), Vaughan (1992), Walton (1992), and Yin (1988).
7. See Mitchell (1984) and Stake (1994).

RECOMMENDED READINGS

Burnstein, Leigh, Howard E. Freeman, and Peter H. Rossi, eds. (1985). *Collecting evaluation data: Problems and solutions.* Beverly Hills, CA: Sage. This collection of 13 essays covers program evaluation in the areas of health, crime, education, and employment and training. The essays underscore the types of conditions and constraints faced by evaluation researchers. Difficulties in conducting experiments in field settings, in training nonresearchers, and in using administrative records are discussed. In addition to identifying data collection problems, the authors suggest possible solutions.

Finsterbusch, Kurt, and Annabelle Bender Motz. (1980). *Social research for policy decisions.* Belmont, CA: Wadsworth. Finsterbusch and Motz introduce applied social research. They discuss the role of applied research for policymaking within a societal context and provide separate chapters on social impact assessment and evaluation research.

Hakim, Catherine. (1987). *Research design: Strategies and choices in the design of social research.* Boston: Allen and Unwin. Hakim provides an overview of various research techniques. She discusses strategies and trade-offs to consider in selecting one technique over the other, as well as applied and basic research.

House, Ernest R. (1980). *Evaluating with validity.* Beverly Hills, CA: Sage. House gives an overview of the different types of evaluation research and discusses some strengths and weaknesses of each. He also describes principles to use in judging the quality of evaluation research. There is a discussion of moral principles involved in conducting evaluation research and a critique of some types of evaluation studies.

Yin, Robert K. (1988). *Case study research,* rev. ed. Beverly Hills, CA: Sage. This is a useful introduction to the case-study method. Yin describes the strengths of the method and important strategies for using it.

CHAPTER 3

THEORY AND RESEARCH

> *If everyone undertook to form all his own opinions and to seek for truth by isolated paths struck out by himself alone, it would follow that no considerable number would ever unite in any common belief.*
>
>   *But obviously without such common belief no society can prosper; say rather, no society can exist; for without ideas held in common there is no common action.*
>
> —Alexis de Tocqueville, *Democracy in America,* p. 298

INTRODUCTION

In a sense, theory is like the "common belief" to which de Tocqueville refers. Theory is the abstract way in which we make sense of our world. Without theory, there is no rational basis for predicting outcomes to our actions. Without theory, one set of crime policies is as good the next. In short, without theory, there can be no sustained progress in our eternal march toward a more just society.

   Theory must be held in common or shared. This does not imply that all criminologists subscribe to the same theory. In fact, they do not, as you shall see in Chapter 4. Rather, it suggests that

all criminologists (and all other scientists, for that matter) share a belief that theoretical knowledge is necessary to their discipline. By the same token, criminological theory is changing all the time. The dynamic force driving theoretical change is the constant interplay between theory and research. Thus, our theoretical understanding of why crimes occur, or how best to reduce them, rests on the quality of our criminological research.

   Of course, what we choose to do with our theoretical knowledge is another matter entirely. In the best of all possible worlds, our decisions

35

about crime policies would be predicated on the best criminological theory and research at hand.

Often, we fall short of this ideal, however. Consider, for example, the "three strikes and you're out" law that exists in one form or another in 24 states and in the federal government (Clark, Austin, and Henry, 1997). The general idea behind the law is simply to increase the prison sentence for a second offense and require life without parole for a third offense (Donziger, 1996). Unfortunately, there was no solid criminological theory or research to suggest that such a law would indeed lower recidivism (i.e., repeat criminal offenses). Still, the public, frustrated with violent crime, and the politicians, quick to cash in on the vote, strongly supported the new law.

States such as California are just now recognizing the unanticipated consequences of its "three strikes" law. First, implementing the law will cost 5 times more than originally estimated. Second, the law is bringing about a decline in plea bargaining, causing massive backlogs in the judicial system. Finally, there is evidence the law entails racial disparities. In Los Angeles County, for instance, minorities are being charged with the "three strikes" law at 17 times the rate of Whites (Donziger, 1996).

Clearly, the importance of theory and research in criminology, both for scientific understanding and as a tool in developing crime policy, is indisputable. It is necessary, therefore, that we examine more carefully the interconnection between theory and research.

WHAT IS THEORY?

In Chapter 1, *social theory* was defined as a system of interconnected abstractions or ideas that condenses and organizes knowledge about the social world. It is a compact way to think of the social world. People are always creating new theories about how the world works. Theory encounters data in research.

Criminological theory is a specific type of social theory. Social theory is much broader and touches on social phenomena besides crime and

justice. Yet, the debt criminological theory owes to social theory is great. For this reason, the authors refer to social theory in general throughout the book, unless addressing a specific criminological theory.

The history of criminological theory dates back to the eighteenth century. Of course, there have been spiritual and natural explanations of crime since time immemorial. But the first set of important concepts, such as proportionate punishment and crime prevention, appeared during this so-called classical period. Classical criminology is generally associated with the Italian scholar, Cesare Beccaria (1738–1794).

Whereas Beccaria's theory sought to humanize criminal justice policies and practices, the positivist criminology of the nineteenth century attempted to make a science out of criminology. For example, Andre-Michel Guerry (1802–1866) and Adolphe Quetelet (1796–1874) analyzed existing statistics in France to explore crime in relation to poverty, wealth, and other social factors. Cesare Lombroso (1835–1909), mentioned in Chapter 1, also employed a scientific approach in his study of the atavistic (or biologically inferior) characteristics of criminals. Although his theory is no longer considered valid, Lombroso's use of research techniques to test theory is an important contribution to the discipline.

Drawing from the sociological theories of Durkheim, Marx, and others, criminologists in the twentieth century have produced many different theories. Thus, the question facing researchers today is less *whether* one should use theory than *how* one should use it.

Being explicit about the theory makes it easier to read someone else's research or to conduct your own. An awareness of how theory fits into the research process helps to clarify murky issues. It also helps that theory has *parsimony*. A parsimonious theory has minimal complexity, with no excess or redundant elements. Using good theory helps the researcher conduct a better study. Indeed, most researchers disparage atheoretical or "crude empiricist" research.

Theories come in many shapes and sizes. In this chapter, the authors provide an elementary introduction to social theory. You will encounter theory in later chapters, as well.

SOCIAL THEORY VERSUS IDEOLOGY

Many people find the relationship between a social scientific theory and a sociopolitical ideology controversial and confusing. Few people outside the scientific community examine social scientific theories, but most people encounter diverse ideologies in the mass media or from the champions of particular points of view. Controversy arises because the scientific community recognizes theory as essential for clarifying and building scientific knowledge, while it condemns ideology as illegitimate obfuscation that is antithetical to science. Confusion also arises because each has multiple definitions, both explain similar events in the world, and they can overlap in places.

There are similarities between theory and ideology (see Box 3.1). Both theory and ideology explain many events in the world: why arrest rates are lower for the upper-income classes, why poor countries—such as Nigeria—have so much political corruption, and so on. Social scientific theory and an ideology both contain assumptions about the nature of the social world. They both focus on what is or is not important in it, contain a system of ideas or concepts, and specify relations among the concepts. Both provide explanations of why things are the way they are and what needs to be changed to alter conditions.

An *ideology* is a type of theory or explanation of events in the social world. It is a quasi-theory that lacks critical features required of a scientific theory. Many ideologies look a lot like legitimate scientific theories. One feature of ideologies is that they have fixed, strong, and unquestioned assumptions. They are full of unquestioned absolutes and normative categories (what is right/wrong, moral/immoral, good/bad, etc.). The assumptions may be founded on faith or rooted in particular social circumstances. Many ideologies advance or protect the interests of a particular group or sector of society.

Box 3.1 _____

Social Theory and Ideology

SIMILARITIES
- Contains a set of assumptions or a starting point
- Explains what the social world is like, how/why it changes
- Offers a system of concepts/ideas
- Specifies relationships among concepts, tells what causes what
- Provides an interconnected system of ideas

DIFFERENCES

Ideology
- Offers absolute certainty
- Has all the answers
- Fixed, closed, finished
- Avoids tests, discrepant findings
- Blind to opposing evidence
- Locked into specific moral beliefs
- Highly partial
- Has contradictions, inconsistencies
- Rooted in specific position

Social Theory
- Conditional, negotiated understandings
- Incomplete, recognizes uncertainty
- Growing, open, unfolding, expanding
- Welcomes tests, positive and negative evidence
- Changes based on evidence
- Detached, disconnected, strong moral stand
- Neutral, considers all sides
- Strongly seeks logical consistency, congruity
- Transcends/crosses social positions

Ideologies are closed belief and value systems that change very little. They are closed to contradictory evidence and use circular reasoning. Ideologies are logically "slippery" and prevent falsification. This makes them immune to significant change. Their capacity to develop or change is extremely limited, because they already have all the answers. In ideology, lines between assertions about what *is* the case (ideals or values) and beliefs about what *should be* the case blur together.

Ideologies selectively present and interpret empirical evidence. They often use techniques of personal experience or conviction (e.g., overgeneralization, selective observation, and premature closure) that fall short of a scientific approach. It is difficult to test ideological principles or confront them with opposing evidence. In a way, ideology is "blind"; it cannot acknowledge contradictory evidence. Even if overwhelming evidence is amassed, the ideology will not bend or change. A true, hard-core believer in an ideology will reject or refuse to recognize evidence. He or she will refuse to abandon core value premises and rigidly adhere to principles. It is a "don't confuse me with facts, I know I'm right" attitude. Supporters often react with fear and hostility to those who disagree or present carefully gathered contradictory information.

The distinction between ideology and theory has implications for how a person conducts research. A researcher can never test and show an ideology to be true or false. By contrast, a researcher can test a scientific theory or parts of it and show them to be false. Social scientific theories alone are empirically testable, and they are constantly evolving. Researchers try to directly confront a theory with evidence. They look at all relevant evidence, both that supporting and that opposing a theory, in a disinterested way. They do not know for sure whether the evidence will support a theory. If the evidence repeatedly fails to support a theory, it is changed or replaced.

Theories are logically consistent. If a contradiction occurs, researchers try to resolve it. Theories are also open ended, always growing or developing to higher levels. If theories fail to develop, they often get replaced by competing theories. Rarely do theories claim to have all the answers. Instead, they often contain areas of uncertainty or incomplete knowledge and only offer partial or tentative answers. Researchers constantly test theories and are skeptical toward them. The theory itself is often disinterested or detached from the position of any specific social group or sector of society. Most theories stand apart from specific social relationships. This makes them perplexing to people who are only self-interested or who operate from a particular social position.

THE PARTS OF THEORY

Concepts

Concepts are the building blocks of theory.[1] A *concept* is an idea expressed as a symbol or in words. Natural science concepts are often expressed in symbolic forms, such as Greek letters (e.g., π) or formulas (e.g., $s = d/t$; s = speed, d = distance, t = time). Most social science concepts are expressed as words. The exotic symbols of natural science theory make many people nervous, but the use of everyday words in specialized ways in social science theory can also create confusion.

One might think of concepts and social theories as making up a sort of specialized language that researchers use to communicate with one another. For example, criminologists have recently created the concept of *hate crime* to refer to a particular kind of criminal behavior. It is conceptually distinct from ordinary criminal behavior in that hate crimes are aimed at entire groups or categories of people rather than isolated individuals. Thus, teenagers drawing graffiti on a public building would be committing a property crime, as they are defacing public property. But if the graffiti they are drawing is a swastika, then the meaning of their behavior is something quite different. The swastika is a symbol of racial supremacy and expresses hatred toward a whole group of people in general (i.e., those who are Jewish). By using the new concept, criminologists are able to communicate the distinctiveness of such criminal behavior.

In a sense, a language is merely an agreement to represent ideas by sounds or written characters that people learned at some point in their lives. Learning concepts and theory is like learning a language.[2]

Concepts are everywhere, and you use them all the time. Height is a simple concept from everyday experience. What does it mean? It is easy to use the concept of *height,* but describing the concept itself is difficult. It represents an abstract idea about physical relations. How would you describe it to a very young child or a creature from a distant planet who was totally unfamiliar with it? A new concept from a social theory may seem just as alien to you when you encounter it for the first time. Height is a characteristic of a physical object, the distance from top to bottom. All people, buildings, trees, mountains, books, and so forth have a height. We can measure height or compare it. A height of zero is possible, and height can increase or decrease over time. As with many words, we use the word in several ways. You may have heard such expressions as *the height of the battle, the height of the summer,* and *the height of fashion.*

The word *height* refers to an abstract idea. We associate its sound and its written form with that idea. There is nothing inherent in the sounds that make up the word and the idea it represents. The connection is arbitrary, but it is still useful. People can express the abstract idea to one another using the symbol alone.

Concepts have two parts: a *symbol* (word or term) and a *definition.* The words *hate crime,* for instance, are symbols that stand for a definition (i.e., criminal behavior motivated by hatred toward a group or category of people). As a person is trained in criminology, he or she learns many different kinds of concepts and also learns to put them together into theories that are used to understand why crime occurs and what to do to prevent it. Criminologists must share basic symbols and definitions for concepts if they wish to communicate their research to the scientific community.

Everyday culture is filled with borrowed concepts from criminology. These concepts, such as

crime victimization and political corruption, to name just two, have diffused into the larger culture and become less precise. Far less attention is given to conceptual definitions; consequently, the popularization of criminological concepts often entails fundamental misconceptions and ideological biases.

Take, for example, the concept of *white-collar crime.* This term has become popular and widely used by the public. Much of the technical meaning of the concept gets lost in the popular translation, however. Criminologists use it to refer to the criminal behavior of one who is of high social standing and respectability. It involves either behavior that advances that individual's own economic interests (i.e., *occupational crime*) or behavior that advances the economic interests of the organization for which he or she works (i.e., *organizational crime*).

The specialized language that criminologists use is called *jargon.* Most fields have their own jargon. Physicians, lawyers, engineers, plumbers, and auto mechanics all have specialized languages. These languages are made up of related concepts. Terms such as *organizational crime, hate crime,* and *classical criminology* are examples of criminological jargon. For insiders, jargon is a speedy, effective, and efficient way to communicate. But jargon also has negative connotations. Some people may misuse it to confuse, exclude, or denigrate others. Using jargon among nonspecialists fails to communicate; it is like speaking English to people who know only Korean.

Concepts vary in their *level of abstraction.* They are on a continuum from most concrete to most abstract. Concrete ones refer to straightforward physical objects or familiar experiences, whereas abstract concepts refer to more difficult, diffuse, and indirect ideas and experiences.

In the study of income tax evasion, for example, criminologists must distinguish between concrete and abstract concepts. *Family income* is a fairly straightforward idea, referring to the total income earned from all sources by members of a family. (Note, however, that the idea of "family" is not as concrete as one might think.) On the other hand, *taxable income* is much more abstract, for it takes into account tax deductions and credits, nontaxable income, and the like. Yet, criminologists interested in this field must have a clear understanding of taxable income before they can do research on the *evasion of taxable income.*

Researchers define scientific concepts more precisely than those we use in daily discourse. Social theory requires well-defined concepts. The definition of a concept helps to link theory with research. A valuable goal of exploratory research, and of most good research, is to clarify and refine concepts. Weak, contradictory, or unclear definitions of concepts restrict the advance of knowledge. After noting that there are many definitions of a *gang* with little consensus, Ball and Curry (1995:239) argued,

> *Few if any gang researchers and theorists have been sufficiently conscious of their own definition strategies, with the result that their definitions carry too many latent connotations, treated correlations or consequences as properties or causes, or contributed to similar errors of logic.*

Concept Clusters. Concepts are rarely used in isolation. Rather, they form interconnected groups, or *concept clusters.* This is true for concepts in everyday language as well as for those in social theory. Theories contain collections of associated concepts that are consistent and mutually reinforcing. Together, they form a web of meaning. For example, if we want to discuss the concept of *hate crime,* we will need a set of associated concepts, such as *ethnicity, interethnic relations, majority/minority relations, social mobility,* and *relative deprivation.*

Some concepts take on a range of values, quantities, or amounts. Examples of this kind of concept are *size of the tax gap, homicide rate, per capita spending on criminal justice system,* and *length of prison sentence.* These are called *variables,* and you will read about them in Chapter 6. Other concepts express types of nonvariable phe-

nomena (e.g., *human rights, occupational crime,* and *dangerous violent behavior*).

Assumptions. Concepts contain built-in *assumptions,* statements about the nature of things that are not observable or testable. We accept them as a necessary starting point. Concepts and theories build on assumptions about the nature of human beings, social reality, or a particular phenomenon. Assumptions often remain hidden or unstated. One way for a researcher to deepen his or her understanding of a concept is to identify the assumptions on which it is based.

Consider again the concept of *hate crime.* Embedded in it is the assumption of a diverse, multiethnic community. There is also an assumption about the problematical condition of majority/minority relations in the community. Finally, the concept contains the assumption that ordinary crime victimizes individuals, whereas hate crime is also intended to terrorize an entire group or category of individuals in the community. If any or all of these assumptions were not accepted, then the concept itself would cease to be useful for criminological research. Almost all concepts used in criminological research contain assumptions about social relations or how people behave.

Classifications. Some concepts are simple; they have only one dimension and vary along a single continuum. Others are complex; they have multiple dimensions or many subparts. You can break complex concepts into a set of simple, or single-dimension, concepts. For example, the concept of *drug-related homicide* has three dimensions (Goldstein et al., 1997). It may mean (1) homicide caused by the psychopharmacological effects of a drug (i.e., "drug-crazed murderer"); (2) homicide related to an addict's need to obtain money to purchase more drugs (i.e., economic compulsion); or (3) homicide related to competition or territorial disputes among sellers in the illicit drug market (i.e., systemic dimension).

Classifications are important in many theories. They are partway between a single, simple concept and a theory.[3] They help to organize abstract, complex concepts. To create a new classification, a researcher logically specifies and combines the characteristics of simpler concepts. You can best grasp this idea by looking at some examples.

The *ideal type* is a well-known classification. Ideal types are pure, abstract models that define the essence of the phenomenon in question. They are mental pictures that define the central aspects of a concept. Ideal types are not explanations because they do not tell why or how something occurs. They are smaller than theories, and researchers use them to build a theory. They are broader, more abstract concepts that bring together several narrower, more concrete concepts. Qualitative researchers often use ideal types to see how well observable phenomena match up to the ideal model. For example, Max Weber developed an ideal type of the concept *bureaucracy.*

Many criminologists have used Weber's bureaucratic ideal type in their research. Clinard and Yeager (1980), for example, made the point that a corporation's ability to socialize employees into its corporate culture is a main characteristic of bureaucratic organizations. What this accomplishes is an organization constructed not of persons per se but of roles, positions, and expectations over which it has control. Clinard and Yeager found that this bureaucratic characteristic is also an important ingredient of organizational crime:

> *Pressures often exist at all levels of the corporation to promote attitudes and behaviors conducive to corporate goals regardless of means. . . . Many involved in illegal corporate activities regard their acquiescence and active participation as necessary to keep their jobs, although they have no illusions about the illegal and immoral nature of their behavior. (pp. 64, 66)*

Another type of classification is the *typology,* or taxonomy,[4] in which a researcher combines two or more unidimensional, simple concepts, such that the intersection of simple concepts forms new concepts. The new concepts or types express the complex interrelation between the simple concepts:

> *One of the chief merits of a typology is parsimony. . . . A well constructed typology can work miracles in bringing order out of chaos. It can transform the overwhelming complexity of an apparent eclectic congeries of numerous apparently diverse cases into a well-ordered set of a few rather homogenous types. (Bailey, 1992:2193)*

In a famous qualitative study, Humphreys (1970), a sociologist interested in deviance, set out to research homosexuality in the United States. In particular, Humphreys was interested in the rarely studied phenomenon of impersonal sex among men. He wondered why some men sought such impersonal sexual outlets, whereas others were more comfortable being identified with the "gay" or homosexual subculture.

Conducting field research in so-called tearooms (the subcultural term for public restrooms), Humphreys collected scientific data on the participants of this activity. He then gathered background information on the men by conducting a survey, which, by the way, brought him under intense criticism regarding research ethics. (The issue of research ethics is taken up in detail in Chapter 17.)

To explain differential involvement in tearoom sex (i.e., covert sexual activity), Humphreys developed a typology using two simple concepts: marital status (i.e., single or married) and type of employment (i.e., independent or dependent) (see Figure 3.1). Those least likely to be found in the tearooms were called "gay guys." These were unmarried men who had independent types of employment (e.g., self-employed businessmen). Humphreys reasoned that being single and financially independent, these men had relatively little to lose by openly identifying with the gay subculture. On the other hand, there were men Humphreys referred to as "trade." These individuals were married with dependent employment situations (e.g., wage-earning employees such as clerical workers). Having a great deal to lose if openly identified with the gay subculture, these men preferred the anonymity and social isolation

FIGURE 3.1 Tearoom Trade Typology

		MARITAL STATUS	
		Single	*Married*
EMPLOYMENT	*Independent*	"Gay Guys"	"Ambisexual"
	Dependent	"Closet Queen"	"Trade"

provided them in the tearoom encounters. Humphreys's typology thus suggested the types of men most likely to be involved in tearoom sex.

A second typology comes from the study of environmental crime by Williams (1996). One of the fundamental problems in attempting to prosecute individuals and corporations who destroy the environment is the way in which the law regards causation. Environmental law typically applies the notion of proximate causation in determining guilt. *Proximate causation* embodies the principle that the outcome of an act must have been reasonably foreseeable for it to constitute an offense. However, with respect to environmental crime, victimization is due to what might be thought of as "slow emergencies." Consequently, there is often a lapse of time from when an environmental crime occurs and when its victims realize the fact.

Williams introduced a typology to help clarify thinking on this point (see Figure 3.2). It suggests that criminal responsibility can be assigned in terms of human acts (i.e., acts of commission and acts of omission) and the presence or absence of an environmental agent. Cell A of the typology cross-classifies acts of commission and the pres-

ence of an environmental agent. An illustration of this is the methoisocyanate poisoning that occurred at the Union Carbide plant in Bhopal, India. Cell B represents acts of omission and the presence of an environmental agent. One example of this is the presence of harmful chemical agents (such as lead) in the drinking water due to a failure to test water safety. Cell C is characterized by acts of commission and the absence of an environmental agent. This occurs, for instance, whenever land-use policies are adopted that result in the runoff of fertile top soil. Cell D is characterized by acts of omission and the absence of an environmental agent. An example of this is the failing to add necessary chemicals (e.g., chlorine) to the public water supply.

This typology lays out the logical possibilities for identifying environmental crime. It thus systematizes our ability to assign criminal guilt to violators of environmental law.

Relationships

Theories contain many concepts, their definitions, and assumptions. More significantly,

FIGURE 3.2 A Typology of Environmental Victimization

		HUMAN ACTS	
		Commission	*Omission*
ENVIRONMENTAL AGENT	*Presence*	Cell A	Cell B
	Absence	Cell C	Cell D

theories specify how concepts relate to one another. Theories tell us whether concepts are related and, if they are, how they relate to each other. In addition, theories state why the relationship does or does not exist.

Beck and Tolnay (1990) presented a theory about lynching, the killing of African Americans by hanging carried out by mobs of White people in the southern United States from the late 1800s to the 1930s. They said that lynching was related to economic distress (i.e., lower prices received by Whites for the cotton grown in the area) but not to Blacks committing crimes (i.e., an increasing incidence of crimes committed by African Americans). Their theory stated connections among the three concepts—lynching, economic distress, and Black victimization.

Many theories make a causal statement, or a *proposition,* about the relation among variables. "A proposition is a theoretical statement that specifies the connection between two or more variables, informing us how variation in one concept is accounted for by variation in another" (Turner, 1985:25). It is a relationship expressed in a theory, such as: Economic distress among the White population caused an increase in mob violence against African Americans. When a researcher empirically tests or evaluates a relationship, it is called a *hypothesis.* You will learn more about hypotheses in Chapter 6. After many careful tests of a hypothesis confirm the proposition, the scientific community begins to develop confidence that the proposition is true.

A social theory contains concepts, a relationship among concepts, and a causal mechanism, or reason, for the relationship. A *causal mechanism* is a statement of how things work, such as: When people fear a loss, they strike out at those they believe to be their direct competitors and who have less social or political power. Reasons for a relationship are other logically connected assumptions and propositions. It could be an assumption, such as: After the Civil War, Whites in southern United States held a deep resentment over the loss of their racially based social status. This might be combined with a proposition: The absence of strong, legitimate,

and formal social control over perceived deviants or outgroup members, combined with a high level of frustration about deviant or outgroup actions, causes an ingroup to adopt nonlegal but traditional means of asserting social control. Propositions do not exist in isolation; they are part of a web of interconnected concepts, relations, and assumptions.

Scope

Some concepts are highly abstract, some are at a middle level of abstraction, and some are at a concrete level. Theories with many abstract concepts apply to a wider range of social phenomena than those with concrete concepts. An example of an abstract theoretical relationship is Sutherland's (1940) classic essay on white-collar crime that took issue with one of the widely accepted understandings of his day. The understanding in question had to do with social class and the propensity to commit crime.

Most criminologists accepted that poverty caused crime. Thus, the discipline's focus was on the criminal behavior of the lower class. Sutherland, however, stressed that this theoretical understanding was deeply flawed. As he put it, "The theory that criminal behavior in general is due either to poverty or to the psychopathic and sociopathic conditions associated with poverty can now be shown to be invalid. . . . The generalization is based on a biased sample which omits almost entirely the behavior of white-collar criminals" (p. 9). In arguing against this theoretical relationship, Sutherland was putting forth the idea that, from the perspective of causation, the behaviors of lower-class criminals and that of white-collar criminals are essentially no different. Both are normal learned behavior.

By contrast, the least abstract, simplest, or lowest level relationship is an *empirical generalization.* It is a simple relationship that is concrete and uncomplicated. A researcher creates one when he or she generalizes about a regularity he or she observes. A theory on a topic often implies many generalizations, which can be elementary hypotheses. Citing various newspaper accounts, such as the following that appeared in the *Wall Street Journal* on November 28, 1978, Clinard and Yeager (1980) made an empirical generalization about bribery. The *Journal* reported: "During that period Textron's Bell Helicopter division and at least six other U.S. suppliers funneled fees to Air Taxi Company, the Teheran sales agency that was owned in part by the late General Khatemi, Commander of the Iranian Air Force." Clinard and Yeager stated: "The most common method of channeling foreign payoffs is through a sales agent. . . . These sales agents are able to facilitate marketing arrangements, which are maintained by special favors" (pp. 172–173). To become a full theory, empirical generalizations need further elaboration on the conditions and greater breadth to explain why this occurs.

When building or extending a theory and specifying its relationships, a researcher needs to think clearly about the types of units, cases, or situations to which the theory applies:

> *Most theoretical ideas are formulated in general terms and thus applicable to some universe of cases. Sometimes these general claims are explicit (e.g., a theory of ethnic relations applies to all ethnic relations), and sometimes the claims are taken to be general because a theory's scope conditions have been left unspecified.* (Ragin, 1992b:219)

Thinking explicitly about a theory's scope will make it stronger and allow the researcher to communicate it more clearly to others.

Referring again to Clinard and Yeager's study (1980), we can see how an empirical generalization about bribery fits into their wider theory of corporate crime. Bribery is but a specific type of financial violation; others include violations of foreign currency laws, illegal political contributions, tax crime, and accounting violations. Financial violations are but a specific type of corporate crime; others are administrative violations, environmental violations, labor violations, managing violations, and unfair trade practices.

Discovering that U.S. corporations routinely break these laws (e.g., 42 percent of their sample of 477 corporations had multiple viola-

tions over a two-year period), the researchers developed a theory that is wide in scope. It explains, among other things, the role corporate culture plays in rationalizing corporate crime. The theory also explains how "the size and complex interrelationships of large corporations" make them exceedingly difficult to police (p. 313). Thus, the larger theory unites the myriad of empirical generalizations into a single, cogent explanation. The end result is a much clearer understanding of why corporate crime occurs.

FACT VERSUS THEORY

A long-standing issue in discussions of testing scientific theory is the line between fact and theory. There are two extreme positions. At one extreme is the unrefined *empiricist* position. It says that facts and theories are totally different. Theories belong to the world of soft, indistinct mental images, values, and ideas. Facts are part of the empirical world of hard, settled, observable things that are uncontaminated by theories or ideas. Ideas or theories belong to the world of thought that also contains illusions, dreams, imagination, speculation, and misconceptions. Theories can slide into speculation, illusion, or fiction. To avoid this, theory must be tested against the hard, empirical facts of "real" material reality. The extreme empiricist says that what we see is what there is. This position urges the researcher to improve measures until he or she approaches the position of a person with crystal clear, perfect vision and who is not fooled by optical illusions or visual tricks.

The opposite is the extreme *relativist* position. It says that reality is what we think it is. More precisely, what we take to be reality is very strongly shaped by our cultural beliefs, thoughts, or mental images of it. We can never fully escape the powerful influence of our thoughts. We cannot test theories against hard, objective facts, because all facts are shaped by formal or informal theories. An extreme relativist says that our desires, ideas, and beliefs so strongly distort our vision that the social world we see contains mirages that our minds create. We are unable to see things that our ideas and beliefs do not allow us to see.

Some researchers adopt one or the other extreme, but most fall somewhere in the middle. Those in the middle say that theories and our categories of thought influence what we take to be facts or observations of the world. Nevertheless, there is a separate reality "out there," independent of our ideas. The difficulty is that we can never get a pure, simple, direct, and unmodified measure of that reality. Our attempts to get at facts are forever clouded or tainted by our cultural beliefs, theories, and ideas. We only see a distorted image of what is really there. Our vision of reality is blurred, as if we are looking through a warped or cloudy glass. Facts we observe are always an imperfect, indirect, and distorted representation of what actually exists.

Deeper philosophical issues in the debate are further explored in Chapter 4. This debate affects how we do social research in two ways. First, it means we make allowances for the distortion. Everyone, except the most extreme empiricist, warns that our views of data might involve some distortion due to our ideas and beliefs. The issue becomes how to control for such distortion and the degree to which such control is possible or desirable. Second, the process of research by many different people over time is likely to reduce or control distortion. Except for some postmodernists (see Chapter 4), most scholars believe that many well-conducted studies by diverse, independent, open-minded, and freely communicating researchers will get closer to the reality "out there" in the long run.

THEORIES

Theory can be baffling to students and professionals because it comes in so many forms. We can categorize a theory by (1) the direction of reasoning, (2) the level of social reality that it explains, (3) whether it is formal or substantive (4) the forms of explanation it employs, and (5) the overall framework of assumptions and concepts in

which it is embedded. Fortunately, all logically possible combinations of direction, level, explanation, and framework are not equally viable. There are only about half a dozen serious contenders.

Direction

Researchers approach the building and testing of theory from two directions. Some begin with abstract thinking. They logically connect the ideas in theory to concrete evidence, then test the ideas against the evidence. Others begin with specific observations of empirical evidence. On the basis of the evidence, they generalize and build toward increasingly abstract ideas. In practice, most researchers are flexible and use both approaches at various points in a study.

Deductive.   In a *deductive approach,* you begin with an abstract, logical relationship among concepts, then move toward concrete empirical evidence. You may have ideas about how the world operates and want to test these ideas against "hard data." Beck and Tolnay's (1990) study on lynching, referred to earlier, used deductive logic. They began with a theory about lynching and economic distress. The theory suggested the evidence they should gather. After they had gathered and analyzed the data, they learned that the findings supported their theory.

Inductive.   If you use an *inductive approach,* you begin with detailed observations of the world and move toward more abstract generalizations and ideas. When you begin, you may have only a topic and a few vague concepts. As you observe, you refine the concepts, develop empirical generalizations, and identify preliminary relationships.

In Chapter 1, Athens's study of dangerous violent criminals was discussed. It is a good example of research using inductive reasoning. Athens began his qualitative interviews not knowing what social experiences dangerous violent criminals held in common. Only after much time in the field was the researcher able to refine concepts and begin to see empirical generalizations. Eventually, Athens developed a theory to explain how a nonviolent person becomes dangerous and violent.

Another example is Weatherford's (1986) qualitative study of the impact of the global market for cocaine on the culture and social structure of rural Bolivians. Using the inductive approach, Weatherford spent time in several small villages to observe the villagers' way of life. He was interested in describing changes in traditional culture that might be occurring with the arrival of the cocaine economy.

What he found, for instance, was an exodus of young men away from the village. The young men migrated to the cocaine-producing regions of Bolivia with hopes of finding employment. The migration created a demographic imbalance in the villages, which produced grave consequences on the village's ability to raise food. Hence, Weatherford's theory to explain the spread of rural poverty, malnutrition, and disease in terms of the cocaine economy is one that is "grounded" in reality. Theoretical generaliza-

tion generated by an inductive approach is called *grounded theory* (see Figure 3.3).

Level of Theory

Social theories can be divided into three broad groupings by the level of social reality with which they deal. Most of us devote the majority of our time to thinking about the micro level of reality, the individuals we see and interact with on a day-by-day basis. *Micro-level theory* deals with small slices of time, space, or numbers of people. The concepts are usually not very abstract. Routine activity theory has become fairly popular among criminologists in the last decade or so (Cohen and Felson, 1979). This micro-level theory tries to explain why certain street crimes (such as robbery or assault) occur by looking at the routine activities of those involved. For instance, the daily work routines of a taxi driver involves the handling of cash and often being alone. These routines are correlated with relatively high levels of criminal victimization. In contrast, family activities (such as the evening meal together) entail

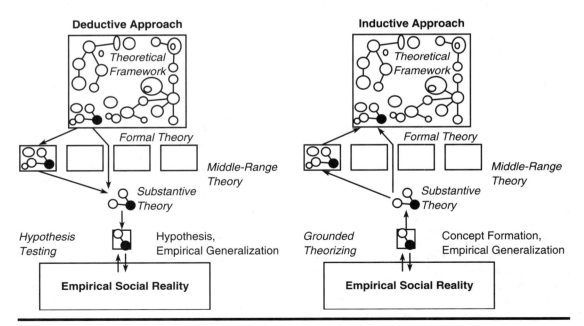

FIGURE 3.3 Deductive and Inductive Theorizing

lower risks of victimization. What makes this theory micro level is that it focuses on the daily routines and interactions of individuals (e.g., victims) that might bring them into direct contact with motivated predators.

Macro-level theory concerns the operation of larger aggregates such as social institutions, entire cultural systems, and whole societies. It uses more concepts that are abstract. Carlson and Michalowski (1997) have provided an interesting macro-level explanation of the unemployment/crime relationship. Past studies have been somewhat inconclusive, the authors argue, because they fail to take into account the different types of unemployment that correspond to historical periods of economic growth and stagnation (i.e., the capitalist accumulation process). Analyzing 60 years of U.S. data for unemployment and crime, Carlson and Michalowski discovered empirical evidence to support their theory. They found that the relationship is fairly weak when the economy is expanding and unemployment is frictional (i.e., the result of voluntary job-hopping). However, when the economy is in recession and unemployment is structural (i.e., the result of involuntary layoff), the relationship is significantly stronger. Thus, macro processes at the societal level alter the strength of the relationship between unemployment and crime.

Meso-level theory is relatively rare. It attempts to link macro and micro levels or to operate at an intermediate level. Theories of organizations, social movements, or communities are often at this level. Perry's (1997) study of a Senegalese immigrant community in New York City operates at the meso level. Her theoretical interest focused on the immigrant community's use of "rural ideologies" as a means of adapting to their new urban environment. Nostalgic memories of Senegal are continually invoked and become increasingly salient, the author reports, as the immigrants try to overcome the shock of displacement and relocation. To contend with exclusion, scorn, and the label of being a "Senegalese Mafia," the immigrant community idealizes Senegal as a sort of "imagined community." The incongruence of a rural ideology existing in an urban setting is explained in terms of a cultural adaptation to the condition of powerlessness.

Formal and Substantive Theories

We can distinguish substantive from formal theory (Layder, 1993:42–43). *Substantive theory* is developed for a specific area of social concern, such as bribery, drug-related homicide, or toxic-waste dumping. *Formal theory* is developed for a broad conceptual area in general theory, such as corruption, violent crime, or environmental crime. If you want to test, generate, or extend a substantive theory, then you should think of cases within the same substantive area. For example, you might compare bribery in several different cultural systems, but you would not have to theorize about all other forms of corruption. If you want to test, generate, or extend formal theory, then you should compare cases within the same formal area. For example, you might examine various forms of violent crime (e.g., dangerous violent behavior, gang-related violence, and homicide). You can do this without reference to the details of the substantive areas (e.g., the shared social experiences of dangerous violent criminals).

Eventually, substative and formal theory can be connected. There is no need to force all thinking into a single theory; in fact, "the cumulative progress of theory is enhanced by the encouragement of multiple substantive and formal theories" (Layder, 1993:44).

Forms of Explanation

Prediction and Explanation. A theory's primary purpose is to explain. Many people confuse prediction with explanation. Some researchers even argue that the prediction is a major goal of research, but most acknowledge that explanation is essential. There are two meanings or uses of the term *explanation*. Researchers focus on *theoretical explanation,* a logical argument that tells why something occurs. It refers to a general rule or principle. These are a researcher's theoretical argument or connections among concepts. The second type of explanation, *ordinary explanation,* makes something clear or describes something in a way that illustrates it and makes it intelligible. For example, a good teacher "explains" in the ordinary sense. The two types of explanation can blend together. This occurs when a researcher explains (i.e., makes intelligible) his or her explanation (i.e., a logical argument involving theory).

Prediction is a statement that something will occur. It is easier to predict than to explain, and an explanation has more logical power than prediction because good explanations also predict. An explanation rarely predicts more than one outcome, but the same outcome may be predicted by opposing explanations. Although it is less powerful than explanation, many people are entranced by the dramatic visibility of a prediction.

To illustrate a fundamental difference between prediction and explanation, let us return to the Lombroso's atavistic theory of crime. This theory explained criminal behavior in terms of the inferior biological characteristics of the offender. Such things as a large jaw, full lips, and excessive body hair were taken to be physical indications of "the ferocious instincts of primitive humanity and the inferior animal" (Lombroso, 1876, as quoted in Vold, Bernard, and Snipes, 1998:43). Lombroso's theory could have been used to predict that individuals with such characteristics will have higher rates of criminal behavior. But the explanation, we now know, is ludicrous. Individuals so described probably came from southern Italy, including Sicily. Any unusually high crime rates attributed to them would have been better explained in terms of their relatively low socioeconomic status in Italian society. As you can see, a weak explanation can produce an accurate prediction. A good explanation depends on a well-developed theory and is confirmed in research by empirical observations.

Now that you have an idea of what *explanation* means, we can turn to the three ways researchers explain: causal, structural, and interpretive. The forms of explanation refer to the way in which a researcher tells others why social events occur or why social relations assume a particular pattern.

Causal Explanation.   *Causal explanation,* the most common type, is used when the relationship is one of cause and effect. We use it all the time in everyday language, but everyday language tends to be sloppy and ambiguous. What do we mean when we say *cause?* For example, you may say that poverty causes crime or that looseness in morals causes an increase in divorce. This does not tell how or why the causal process works. Researchers try to be more precise and exact when discussing causal relations.

Philosophers have long debated the idea of cause. It has been a controversial idea since the writings of the eighteenth-century Scottish philosopher David Hume (1711–1776). Some people argue that causality occurs in the empirical world, but it cannot be proved. Causality is "out there" in objective reality, and researchers can only try to find evidence for it. Others argue that causality is only an idea that exists in the human mind, a mental construction, not something "real" in the world. This second position holds that causality is only a convenient way of thinking about the world. Without entering into the philosophical debate, many researchers pursue causal relationships.

You need three things to establish causality: temporal order, association, and the elimination of plausible alternatives. An implicit fourth condition is an assumption that a causal relationship makes sense or fits with broader assumptions or a theoretical framework. Let us examine the three basic conditions.

The *temporal order* condition means that a cause must come before an effect. This common-sense assumption establishes the direction of causality: from the cause toward the effect. You may ask: How can the cause come after what it is to affect? It cannot, but temporal order is only one of the conditions needed for causality. Temporal order is necessary but not sufficient to infer causality. Sometimes people make the mistake of talking about "cause" on the basis of temporal order alone.

For example, there is the notion that illicit drug use "causes" one's involvement in property crime. The implication is that one first uses such drugs, and, as a direct consequence of drug use, begins to commit property crimes. In terms of temporal order, drug use precedes and initiates criminal involvement. The research of Anglin and Speckart (1988) suggests otherwise, however. They found that the majority of their sample of patients at a methadone maintenance program had been arrested *before* the onset of drug addiction. Only 10 percent of the sample were arrested for the first time after becoming addicted. Indeed, in some cases, criminal involvement in certain forms of property crime (e.g., theft) was higher prior to addiction. Yet, despite this research, there is still the confusion of the temporal ordering of drug use and criminal behavior. The temporal order condition simply eliminates from consideration potential causes that occurred later in time.

It is not always easy to establish temporal order. With cross-sectional research, temporal order is tricky. For example, cross-sectional surveys on self-reported tax evasion reveal that taxpayers who believe the tax system is unfair are more likely to report cheating on their income taxes. This is indeed an interesting insight into the causes of tax evasion. Yet, simply based on such surveys, the researcher has no way of knowing if attitudes toward tax fairness were formed prior to one's decision to evade his or her taxes. Just as conceivable is the possibility that tax fairness attitudes are constructed after the fact as a way of rationalizing one's tax crime. It is a chicken-and-egg problem. To resolve it, a researcher needs to bring in other information or design research that specifically tests for the temporal order.

Simple causal relations are unidirectional, operating in a single direction from the cause to the effect. Most studies examine unidirectional relations. More complex theories specify reciprocal-effect causal relations—that is, a mutual causal relationship or simultaneous causality. For example, believing that the tax system is unfair contributes to one's decision to evade. But the reverse of that may also be true: Evading taxes contributes to one's belief that the tax system is unfair. Theories often have reciprocal or feedback relationships, but these are difficult to test. Some researchers call unidirectional relations nonrecursive and reciprocal-effect relations recursive.

A researcher also needs an *association* for causality. Two phenomena are associated if they occur together in a patterned way or appear to act together. People sometimes confuse correlation with association. Correlation has a specific technical meaning, whereas association is a more general idea. A correlation coefficient is a statistical measure that indicates the amount of association, but there are many ways to measure association. Sometimes, researchers call association *concomitant variation* because two variables vary together.

More people mistake association for causality than confuse it with temporal order. A good example of this is the relationship between rates of crime and the number of people in prison. Criminological research shows little or no correlation between the two. However, because increasing rates of incarceration will sometimes occur at the same time crime rates are going down, those who choose to use the data selectively can make it seem that the former "causes" the latter. This claim is frequently heard in the United States, particularly since crime rates have dropped over the past seven years. A broader historical perspective, on the other hand, reveals that putting more people in prison is not a primary determinant of crime.

A researcher needs to show association to demonstrate causality. If he or she cannot find an association, a causal relationship is unlikely. This is why researchers attempt to find correlations and other measures of association. Yet, a researcher can find an association without causality. The association eliminates potential causes that are not associated. It cannot definitely identify a cause. It is a necessary but not a sufficient condition. In other words, you need it for causality, but it is not enough alone. Finally, an association does not have to be perfect (i.e., every time one variable is present, the other is also present in proportion) to show causality.

Eliminating alternatives means that a researcher interested in causality needs to show that the effect is due to the causal variable and not to something else. It is also called *no spuriousness* because an apparent causal relationship that is actually due to an alternative but unrecognized cause is called a spurious relationship. You will read about spurious relationships in Chapter 6.

Researchers can observe temporal order and associations. They cannot observe the elimination of alternatives. They can only demonstrate it indirectly. Eliminating alternatives is an ideal because eliminating all possible alternatives is impossible. A researcher tries to eliminate major alternative explanations in two ways: through built-in design controls and by measuring potential hidden causes. Experimental researchers build controls into the study design itself to eliminate alternative causes. They isolate an experimental situation from the influence of all variables except the main causal variable.

Researchers also try to eliminate alternatives by measuring possible alternative causes. This is common in survey research and is called *controlling for* another variable. Researchers use statistical techniques to learn whether the causal variable or something else operates on the effect variable.

Causal explanations are usually in a linear form or state cause and effect in a straight line: *A* causes *B, B* causes *C, C* causes *D.* Consider Carlson and Michalowski's (1997) study of unemployment and crime mentioned earlier in the chapter. The basic research question was this: Does unemployment cause crime? In other words, the researchers were asking if changes in the level of unemployment cause changes in the level of crime. We can also restate the research question as a linear causal proposition, such as: The higher the unemployment rate, the higher the level of crime.

Good causal explanations not only identify a causal relationship (e.g., unemployment causes crime) but they also specify the causal mechanism. In other words, a complete explanation tells us what causes crime and explains the specific mechanism or process by which the causal effect is felt. For example, Carlson and Michalowski (1997) explain changes in the crime rate in relation to the type of unemployment. Thus, in their theory, not only does the rate of unemployment influence the rate of crime but the type of unemployment (i.e., frictional or structural) does, as well. Simply put, having high rates of frictional unemployment, in and of itself, would have no causal impact on the crime rate. On the other hand, high rates of structural unemployment would exercise a causal effect over the crime rate.

The unemployment/crime example illustrates both a causal relationship and a causal mechanism. A typical research strategy is to divide a larger theory into parts and test various relationships against the data.

Diagrams of Causal Relations among Variables. Researchers express theories in words as well as in symbols. They often draw diagrams of the causal relations to present a simplified picture of a relationship and see it at a glance. Such symbolic representations supplement verbal descriptions of causal relations and convey complex information. They are a shorthand way to show theoretical relations.

The simplest diagram is a two-variable model, as in Figure 3.4(a). Researchers represent variables using letters, circles, or boxes. The convention is to represent a cause by an X and the effect by a Y. The arrow shows the direction of causality (e.g., from independent to dependent variable). Sometimes, researchers use subscripts when there is more than one cause (e.g., X_1, X_2), as in Figure 3.4(b). Relationships among variables are symbolized by lines with arrows. Causal relations are represented by straight lines. Associations that do not imply a causal relationship are represented by curved lines with arrows on each end. A single arrow on a line represents a unidirectional relationship. Arrows on both ends of a straight line represent reciprocal relationships.

Relationships between variables can be positive or negative. Researchers imply a positive relationship if they say nothing. A *positive rela-*

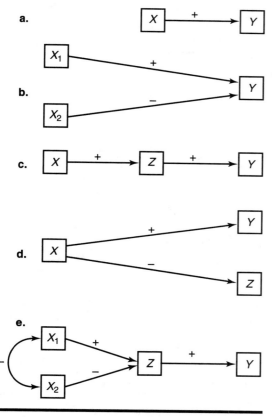

FIGURE 3.4 Causal Diagrams of Theories Explaining Hate Crimes

tionship means that a higher value on the causal variable goes with a higher value on the effect variable. For example, the more education a person has, the longer his or her life expectancy is. A *negative relationship* means that a higher value on the causal variable goes with a lower value on the effect variable. For example, as the number of taxpayers perceiving the tax system as being unfair increases, the level of voluntary tax compliance decreases.

Figure 3.4 illustrates some of the causal diagrams in Albrecht's (1997) sociological theory of "hate violence." This is a theory to explain violence toward ethnic and foreign minorities. His theory is written with Germany in mind, but it can also be applied more generally to other countries, as well. In all of the diagrams, what is

being explained—that is, the dependent variable—is the level of hate violence. It is symbolized by (Y).

Diagram (a) is the least complex. It is a two-variable, linear, positive relationship. Variable (X) is the level of frustration-aggression in the German population. Thus, as the frustration-aggression increases, so too does the level of hate violence. Diagram (b) is a slightly more complex relationship. It involves two causal (or independent) variables. Variable (X_1) is the level of fear of violent crime among the public, and it has a positive relationship to the level of hate violence. Variable (X_2) is the level of employment, and it has a negative relationship to the dependent variable. (Thus, as level of employment rise, levels of hate violence decrease.)

Diagram (c) shows a simple linear causal chain. It says X affects Z, which in turn affects Y. Both relationships are positive. Variable (X) is the level of nationalist ideologies held by the public. It affects variable (Z), which is level of fear of immigrants. Fear of immigrants, in turn, affects the level of hate violence in society. Diagram (d) states that X affects Y and Z, but that Y and Z are distinct. Variable (X) is the level of nationalist ideologies. It has a positive affect on variable (Y), which is the level of hate violence. The level of nationalist ideologies also has an effect (negative) on variable (Z), which is the level of residential integration.

Diagram (e) is the most complex of the five diagrams. It illustrates a theoretical model that has two causal (or independent) variables: (X_1) and (X_2). They are associated in a negative way, but neither is the cause of the other. Variable (X_1) is the level of nationalist ideologies and variable (X_2) is the level of employment in society. (Thus, increasing levels of nationalist ideology is associated with decreasing levels of employment.) Variable (X_1) has a positive effect on variable (Z), which is the level of fear of ethnic and foreign minorities. Variable (X_2) has a negative effect on variable (Z). (Thus, as levels of employment go up, levels of fear of ethnic and foreign minorities goes down.) Variable (Z), level of fear of ethnic and foreign minorities, has a positive effect on variable (Y), which is the level of hate violence.

As you can see, causal diagrams are a shorthand, useful way of characterizing complex theoretical relationships. We will return to the topic of causal diagrams in Chapter 6.

Structural Explanation.   A *structural explanation* is used with functional and pattern theories. Unlike a causal effect chain, which is similar to a string of balls lined up that hit one another in sequence, it is more similar to a wheel with spokes from a central idea or a spider web in which each strand forms part of the whole. A researcher making a structural explanation uses a set of interconnected assumptions, concepts, and relationships. Instead of causal statements, he or she uses metaphors or analogies so that relationships "make sense." The concepts and relations within a theory form a mutually reinforcing system. In structural explanations, a researcher specifies a sequence of phases or identifies essential parts that form an interlocked whole.

There are several types of structural explanation. One type is *network theory*.[5] A network theorist says that a behavior or social relationship occurs when certain patterns of interaction take place, when aspects of social relations overlap in time or space, or when relationships follow a developmental sequence.

A network theorist explains something by referring to a broader pattern, a set of syntax rules, or structures. His or her explanation shows how a specific event is just one part of a larger pattern, is one building block in a bigger structure, or is a one link within a much larger system of linkages. It is a form of reasoning like that used to explain why people use language in specific ways; that is, there are syntax rules that state that X goes with Y or that sentences need a noun and a verb. The researcher explains an event by identifying the syntax rule that covers the event.

Gould's (1991) theory of the social mobilization in the Paris Commune of 1871 is an example of a structural explanation. The Paris Commune was a famous rebellion and takeover of the city of Paris—and very nearly of the government of France—by masses of poor and working people who were led by socialists, Marxists, and radicals. It was a two-month experiment in democratic socialism with free education, worker cooperatives, and radical social reforms. The Commune ended with a brutal battle in which 25,000 Parisians died, most of them shot after surrendering to the national army.

Gould said that people came from different social networks, which shaped their involvement in collective action. Thus, prior to their recruitment into the Paris Commune rebellion, people had social ties to one another. By knowing these ties, Gould predicted who was likely to join. His theory said that isolated people are unlikely to join. People join when those with whom they have intimate social relations join. In addition, a person's location within a web of social ties is important. People at the center of a dense web of ties (i.e., those who have multiple strong ties) are pulled more strongly than those on the periphery (i.e., those with only one or a few weak ties). Gould found that people from the same Paris neighborhood were recruited into a single battalion in the revolutionary defense guard. The new organization, the guard, was built on previous informal ties from the neighborhood—ties of family, neighbor, co-worker, or friend. This created intense intrabattalion loyalty. At the same time, a few people from the neighborhood, some whom were central in it, went to other battalions. This created loyalty across guard battalions.

Gould predicted the pattern of battalion behavior from the positions people held in the overlapping social networks of the neighborhood and the guard battalion. He explained the actions of battalions and their responses to events by referring to a broader pattern of social ties among people.

Structural explanation is also used in *functional theory*.[6] Functional theorists explain an event by locating it within a larger, ongoing, balanced social system. They often use biological metaphors. These researchers explain something by identifying its function within a larger system or the need it fulfills for the system. Functional explanations are in this form: "*L* occurs because it serves needs in the system *M*." Theorists assume that a system will operate to stay in equilibrium and to continue over time.

Emile Durkheim's theorizing about the concept of social control is a classic example of functional explanation. He explored notions of conformity and deviance in the philosophical context of morality. Morality is understood to be a system of rules of conduct. These rules bind one with a sense of obligation to conform. However, one's moral conscience is an individualized expression of a much larger collective morality.

The collective morality gets internalized into one's individual morality to the extent that the collective set of rules appear desirable from the individual perspective. The mechanism that allows this to happen—that is, which connects acts to consequences—is called *sanctions*. Thus, for example, homicide on the part of soldiers at war carries no consequence of punishment or negative sanction, as is the case of homicide in times of peace. In other words, punishment does not arise automatically with every instance of homicide, but rather is defined within the context of the collective morality of society. There is nothing intrinsic to the act of homicide, Durkheim theorized, which makes it immoral.

As the individual learns and internalizes (i.e., accepts as desirable) the conduct rules associated with the collective morality, then he or she contributes to the social order of society. In this way, the sanctions function to discourage deviance and crime. They contribute to the overall equilibrium of society.

Interpretive Explanation. The purpose of *interpretive explanation* is to foster understanding. The interpretive theorist attempts to discover the meaning of an event or practice by placing it within a specific social context. He or she tries to comprehend or mentally grasp the operation of the social world, as well as get a feel for something or to see the world as another person does. Because each person's subjective world view shapes how he or she acts, the researcher attempts to discern others' reasoning and view of things.

The process is similar to decoding a text or work of literature. Meaning comes from the context of a cultural symbol system.

Lachmann (1988) used an interpretive explanation in his study of the illegal art form of graffiti in New York City. He noted that the career of a deviant is shaped by how nondeviants label and respond to deviants. He explored how graffiti mentors recruit new artists and teach the young artists that there is an audience for graffiti. Lachmann described the career of graffiti artists by placing it in the social context of low-income, inner-city neighborhoods. For example, escaping from police is part of the excitement of the career, and many artists are arrested for other crimes. Skilled artists create murals covering 60-foot subway cars and develop an independent style. Lachmann explained the search for fame and advancement in a career by referring to the culture, constraints, and values of ghetto neighborhoods. Nondeviant artists who appreciate the talent displayed by graffiti artists also shape their career paths.

Theoretical Frameworks

So far, you have learned about theory and empirical generalization. Many researchers use middle-range theory. Middle-range theories are slightly more abstract than empirical generalizations or specific hypotheses. As Merton (1967:39) stated, "Middle-range theory is principally used in sociology to guide empirical inquiry."

Middle-range theories can be formal or substantive. We can organize the terms about theory by the degree of abstraction suggested. From the most concrete to the most abstract are empirical generalizations, middle-range theories, and frameworks. A *theoretical framework* (also called a paradigm or theoretical system) is more abstract than a formal or substantive theory. Figure 3.3 (page 46) shows the levels and how they are used in inductive and deductive approaches to theorizing.

Researchers do not make precise distinctions among the degrees of abstraction. When they conduct a study, they primarily use middle-range theory and empirical generalization. They rarely use a theoretical framework directly in empirical research. A researcher may test parts of a theory on a topic and occasionally contrast parts of the theories from different frameworks. Box 3.2 illustrates the various degrees of abstraction with Albrecht's (1997) review of sociological theories of hate violence in Germany.

Criminology has several major theoretical frameworks.[7] The frameworks are orientations or sweeping ways of looking at the social world. They provide collections of assumptions, concepts, and forms of explanation. Frameworks include various formal or substantive theories (e.g., theories of hate violence, theories of corporate crime, etc.). Thus, there are conflict, structural-functional, and symbolic interactionist theories of crime, to name three of the primary ones.

Theories within the same framework share assumptions and major concepts. Some frameworks are oriented more to the micro level, others focus on more macro-level phenomena. As you will see in Chapter 4, each is associated with an approach to research methodology. Box 3.3 shows three major frameworks in criminology and briefly describes the key concepts and assumptions of each.

THEORY AND RESEARCH:
THE DYNAMIC DUO

You have seen that theory and research are interrelated. Only the naive, new researcher mistakenly believes that theory is irrelevant to research or that a researcher just collects the data. Researchers who attempt to proceed without theory or fail to make it explicit may waste time collecting useless data. They easily fall into the trap of hazy and vague thinking, faulty logic, and imprecise concepts. They may find it difficult to converge onto a crisp research issue or to generate a lucid account of their study's purpose. Researchers of this type often find themselves adrift as they attempt to design or conduct empirical research.

Box 3.2 _____

Albrect's (1997) Levels of Sociological Theory to Explain Hate Violence

THEORETICAL FRAMEWORK

The theory of culture conflict can be used to understand the likelihood a country will experience hate violence. Hate violence erupts as social stability and integration deteriorate. In industrialized societies, there is no single set of shared social values or cultural consensus. Rather, there are competing and conflicting interpretations of society. Under conditions of material prosperity, relative social solidarity and integration arise to quiet the potential for culture conflict. However, in times of economic insecurity, the material basis for social solidarity and integration in industrialized societies weakens. This often produces manifestations of culture conflict.

FORMAL THEORY

Social disintegration and anomie accompany rapid sociopolitical change, such as the reintegration of postwar Germany. During these periods in society, minority/majority relations are strained, and various forms of social segregation appear. In this context, downward social mobility and economic insecurity amplify ethnic and cultural differences. Collective reaction to these perceived differences are reflected in xenophobic behavior.

MIDDLE-RANGE SUBSTANTIVE THEORY

A theory of hate violence underscores the relationship between nationalist ideologies and the scapegoating of immigrant and minority populations. These populations are perceived as being responsible for economic and social problems, such as crime. There occurs the "ghettoization" of these populations who are targeted by elements of the majority population bearing the brunt of sociopolitical change and economic insecurity.

EMPIRICAL GENERALIZATION

Germans who are young, male, poorly educated, and denied access to the benefits of material culture in the reintegrated Germany are more likely to adopt nationalist ideologies and engage in hate violence than other segments of majority population.

The reason is simple. Theory frames how we look at and think about a topic. It gives us concepts, provides basic assumptions, directs us to the important questions, and suggests ways for us to make sense of data. Theory enables us to connect a single study to the immense base of knowledge to which other researchers contribute. To use an analogy, theory helps a researcher see the forest instead of just a single tree. Theory increases a researcher's awareness of interconnections and of the broader significance of data.

Theory has a place in virtually all research, but its prominence varies. It is generally less central in applied-descriptive research than in basic-explanatory research. Its role in applied and descriptive research may be indirect. The concepts are often more concrete, and the goal is not to create general knowledge. Nevertheless, researchers use theory in descriptive research to refine concepts, evaluate assumptions of a theory, and indirectly test hypotheses.

Theory does not remain fixed over time; it is provisional and open to revision. Theories grow into more accurate and comprehensive explanations about the make-up and operation of the social world in two ways. They advance as theorists toil to think clearly and logically, but this effort has limits. The way a theory makes significant progress is by interacting with research findings.

The scientific community expands and alters theories based on empirical results. Researchers who adopt a more deductive approach use theory to guide the design of a study and the interpretation of results. They refute, extend, or modify the theory on the basis of results. As researchers continue to conduct empirical research testing a theory, they develop confidence that some parts of it are true. Researchers may modify some propositions of a theory or reject them if several well-conducted studies have negative findings. A theory's core propositions and central tenets are more difficult to test and are refuted less often. In a slow process, researchers may decide to abandon or change a theory as the evidence against it mounts over time and cannot be logically reconciled (see Table 3.1).

Box 3.3

Three Major Theoretical Frameworks in Criminology

STRUCTURE FUNCTIONALISM

Major Concepts: Social system, collective conscience, anomie, dysfunction, equilibrium, division of labor

Key Assumptions: A certain amount of crime is ubiquitous and normal in society. It functions as a means of maintaining social solidarity. An underlying consensus on values exerts pressure for conformity against deviance. However, the traditional basis of social solidarity takes on a new form as society differentiates and modernizes.

SYMBOLIC INTERACTIONISM

Major Concepts: Self, perception, social construction, social reaction, differential association

Key Assumptions: Criminal behavior is learned in the process of communication and interaction. People learn motives, rationalizations, attitudes, and techniques; or, to put it simply, definitions favorable to law violation. Emphasis is given to the meaning of behavior to the actor, as well as the social reaction to that behavior. The construction of notions of crime and justice emerge out of micro-level, social interaction.

CONFLICT CRIMINOLOGY

Major Concepts: Inequality of power, social class, alienation, struggle

Key Assumptions: All societies are composed of conflicting values and economic interests. In industrialized societies, conflict is manifested in terms of competing social classes. There is an inverse or negative relationship between power and official crime rates. Thus, those individuals and groups with more power tend to have lower official crime rates. Solutions to the crime problem entail the redistribution of power in society.

Researchers adopting an inductive approach follow a slightly different process. Inductive theorizing begins with a few assumptions and broad

TABLE 3.1   Aspects of Social Theory

DIRECTION OF APPROACH	LEVEL OF REALITY	FORMAL OR SUBSTANTIVE	FORM OF EXPLANATION	DEGREE OF ABSTRACT	THEORETICAL FRAMEWORK
Inductive	Micro	Substantive	Interpretative	Empirical generalization	Symbolic interaction
			Causal	Middle range	
Deductive	Macro	Formal			
					Structural functional
			Structural	Framework	
					Conflict

orienting concepts. Theory develops from the ground up as the researchers gather and analyze the data. Theory emerges slowly, concept by concept and proposition by proposition in a specific area. The process is similar to a long pregnancy. Over time, the concepts and empirical generalizations emerge and mature. Soon, relationships become visible, and researchers weave together knowledge from different studies into more abstract theory.

CONCLUSION

In this chapter, you learned about social theory—its parts, purposes, and types. The dichotomy between theory and research is an artificial one. The value of theory and its necessity for conducting good research should be clear. Researchers who proceed without theory rarely conduct top-quality research and frequently find themselves in a quandary. Likewise, theorists who proceed without linking theory to research or anchoring it to empirical reality are in jeopardy of floating off into incomprehensible speculation and conjecture. You are now familiar with the scientific community, the dimensions of research, and social theory. In the next chapter, you will examine the competing approaches researchers adopt when they do criminological science.

KEY TERMS

association
assumption
causal explanation
classification
concept cluster
deductive approach
empirical generalization
functional theory

grounded theory
ideal type
inductive approach
jargon
level of abstraction
macro-level theory
meso-level theory
micro-level theory

negative relationship
network theory
parsimony
positive relationship
prediction
proposition
temporal order
typology

REVIEW QUESTIONS

1. How do concrete and abstract concepts differ? Give examples.
2. How do researchers use ideal types and classifications to elaborate concepts?

3. How do concepts contain built-in assumptions? Give examples.

4. What is the difference between inductive and deductive approaches to theorizing?

5. Describe how the micro, meso, and macro levels of social reality differ.

6. Discuss the differences between prediction and theoretical explanation.

7. What are the three conditions for causality? Which one is never completely demonstrated? Why?

8. Why do researchers use diagrams to show causal relationships?

9. How do structural and interpretive explanations differ from one another?

10. What is the role of the major theoretical frameworks in research?

NOTES

1. For more detailed discussions of concepts, see Chafetz (1978:45–61), Hage (1972:9–85), Kaplan (1964:34–80), Mullins (1971:7–18), Reynolds (1971), and Stinchcombe (1973a).

2. Turner (1980) has provided an interesting discussion of how sociological explanation and theorizing can be conceptualized as translation.

3. Classifications are discussed in Chafetz (1978: 63–73) and Hage (1972).

4. For more on typologies and taxonomies, see Blalock (1969:30–35), Chafetz (1978:63–73), Rey-nolds (1971: 4–5), and Stinchcombe (1968:41–47).

5. Network theory is discussed in Collins (1988: 412–428) and Galaskiewicz and Wasserman (1993).

6. An introduction to functional explanation can be found in Chafetz (1978:22–25).

7. Introductions to alternative theoretical frameworks and social theories are provided in Phillips (1985:44–59) and Skidmore (1979). An elementary introduction is given in Chapter 1 of Bart and Frankel (1986).

RECOMMENDED READINGS

Giddens, Anthony. (1971). *Capitalism and modern social theory: An analysis of the writings of Marx, Durkheim and Max Weber.* New York: Cambridge University Press. This is a respected summary and discussion of the three major classical theories—those of Marx, Weber, and Durkheim.

Little, Daniel. (1991). *Varieties of social explanation: An introduction to the philosophy of social science.* Boulder, CO: Westview. Little emphasizes the major forms of explanation used in social science. He provides examples from specific studies and evaluates recent developments in social theory. He discusses causal, interpretive, and functional theories.

Vold, George, Thomas J. Bernard, and Jeffrey B. Snipes. (1998). *Theoretical criminology.* Oxford: Oxford University Press. This book, now in its fourth edition, is perhaps the standard bearer for criminological theory. It does a very good job of placing theories in their historical context. It covers the full range of theories and concisely summarizes their underlying assumptions about human nature, society and crime.

CHAPTER 4

QUESTIONS OF METHODOLOGY

*Being first virtues of human activities, truth and justice are
uncompromising.*
   —John Rawls, *A Theory of Justice*, p. 4

INTRODUCTION

The notion of justice exists in every culture.
People believe in it; institutions are erected
to uphold it; and whole industries make a
practice of finding profit in it. But what, exactly,
is justice? How do humans come to learn its
hard lessons? Can there be a science of justice? Would this science mimic the natural sciences? Or would it require different approaches?
What distinguishes the science of justice from
ideology?

This chapter examines these questions. We
begin with the premise that criminology is a science—more specifically, a social science. Other
social sciences include sociology, anthropology,
and psychology. Much of our discussion focuses
on what makes criminology, as well as the other
social sciences, scientific. In short, we are interested in research methodology.

Research methodology refers to the ways in
which scientists seek knowledge. It is emphatically not subject matter that distinguishes science
from ideology. Rather, it is that science demands
clearly articulated methodologies, whereas ideology does not. Thus, a science of justice is possible, provided its scientists (i.e., criminologists)
adhere to certain systematic ways of knowing.

It would be a mistake to think that there is
only one right research methodology all criminologists must adopt. On the other hand, it would be
foolish to think that anything goes in doing criminological science. The fact is, there are a number
of *alternative methodologies* (or ways of knowing) in criminology. Each methodology has its
own history, philosophical assumptions, and
logic. Each methodology requires that scientific
research be conducted in concert with these

assumptions and logic. Rarely, however, do criminologists explicitly articulate the methodology underlying their research. Yet, research methodology plays a central role in the development of criminology and the other social sciences and their related fields.[1]

Collins (1989:134) argued that the debate over whether the social sciences are scientific comes from an overly rigid definition of *science*. He remarked, "Modern philosophy of science does not destroy sociological science; it does not say that science is impossible, but gives us a more flexible picture of what science is." The approaches in this chapter help link abstract issues in philosophy to concrete research techniques. They proscribe what good social research involves, justify why one should do research, relate values to research, and guide ethical behavior. They are broad frameworks within which researchers conduct studies. Couch (1987:106) summarized it as follows:

> *The ontological and epistemological positions of these . . . research traditions provide the foundation of one of the more bitter quarrels in contemporary sociology. . . . Each side claims that the frame of thought they promote provides a means for acquiring knowledge about social phenomena, and each regards the efforts of the other as at best misguided. . . . They differ on what phenomena should be attended to, how one is to approach phenomena, and how the phenomena are to be analyzed.*

By the end of this chapter, you should have three answers to the question: What is scientific about social scientific research? One answer will be for each of the three approaches to be discussed. You may find the pluralism of approaches confusing at first, but once you learn them, you will find that other aspects of research and theory become clearer. Specific research techniques are based on the general approaches discussed in this chapter. The techniques (e.g., experiments and participant observation) will make more sense to you and will be learned faster if you are aware of the logic and assumptions on which they are based. In addition, the approaches presented here will help you understand the diverse perspectives you may encounter as you read criminological studies. Also, the three approaches give you an opportunity to make an informed choice among alternatives for the type of research you may want to pursue.

THE THREE APPROACHES

We need to begin by recognizing that the meaning of science was not written in stone or handed down as a sacred text; it has been an evolving human creation. Prior to the early 1800s, there was really no scientific explanations of criminal behavior. Instead, people tended to rely on spiritual or other worldly explanations. Vold, Bernard, and Snipes (1998:5) underlined the weakness: "Spiritual explanations provide a way of understanding crime that is satisfactory to some people. The problem is that, because spiritual explanations cannot be observed, these theories cannot be falsified."

The classical theorists, most notably Cesare Beccaria (1738–1794), ushered in a new perspective on crime that emphasized human rationality and free will. Thus, crime was to be explained not in spiritual terms, but in terms of free choice based on the individual's rational assessments of the potential costs and benefits of committing a crime. Indeed, the modern theory of crime deterrence traces back to this school of thought, as do such human rights reforms as the ban against torture. Shortly after the classical period of criminology, a more scientific approach was adopted. Like social scientists in other fields, the criminologists of the early 1800s began to argue that the social world could be studied using science. They contended that rigorous, systematic observation of the social world, combined with careful, logical thinking, could provide a new and valuable type of knowledge about criminal behavior. In modern times, science has become the accepted way to gain knowledge. So when people accepted the claim that society could be studied by using science, it was a revolutionary idea with important ramifications.

Once the idea of a science of the social world gained acceptance, the issue became: What does such a science look like, and how is it conducted? Some people went to the already accepted natural sciences (e.g., physics and biology) and copied their methods. Their argument was simple: The legitimacy of the natural sciences rests on the scientific method, so social scientists should adopt this same approach.

Many researchers accepted this answer, but it poses certain difficulties. First, there is a debate over what *science* means, even in the natural sciences. The scientific method is only a loose set of abstract, vague principles that provide little guidance. Scholars who specialize in the history and philosophy of science have explored multiple ways to do scientific research and have found that scientists use several methods. Second, some scholars say that human beings are qualitatively different from the objects of study in the natural sciences (stars, rocks, plants, chemical compounds, etc.). Humans think and learn, have an awareness of themselves and their past, and possess motives and reasons. These unique human characteristics mean that a special science is needed to study the social life of people.

Social researchers did not stop while the philosophers debated. Practicing researchers developed ways to do research based on their informal notions of science. This added to the confusion. Leading researchers used techniques to conduct social research that sometimes deviated from the philosopher's ideal model of good science.

The three approaches in this chapter are based on a major reevaluation of social science that began in the 1960s.[2] The three alternatives to social science are the core ideas distilled from many specific arguments. They are ideal types or idealized, simplified models of more complex arguments. In practice, few social researchers agree with all parts of an approach. Often, they mix elements from each. Yet, these approaches represent fundamental differences in outlook and alternative assumptions about social science research.[3] The approaches are different ways of looking at the world—ways to observe, measure, and understand social reality. They begin from very different positions, even when all end up looking at the same thing or saying the same thing.

To simplify the discussion, we have organized the assumptions and ideas of the approaches into answers to the following eight questions:

1. Why should one conduct criminological research?
2. What is the fundamental nature of social reality? (the ontological question)
3. What is the basic nature of human beings?
4. What is the relationship between science and common sense?
5. What constitutes an explanation or theory of social reality?
6. How does one determine whether an explanation is true or false?
7. What does good evidence or factual information look like?
8. Where do sociopolitical values enter into science?

The three approaches are *positivist criminology, interpretive criminology*, and *critical criminology*. Most ongoing social research is based on the first two. Positivism, as it is generally known, is the oldest and the most widely used approach. Miller (1987:4), a philosopher of science, observed, "Positivism is the most common philosophical outlook on science. Yet there are current alternatives to it with extremely broad appeal." Interpretive criminology has held a strong minority position in debates for nearly a century. Critical criminology is perhaps the least commonly seen in scholarly journals. Yet, it is included here to give you the full range of debate over the meaning of social science and because it criticizes the other approaches and tries to move beyond them.

Each approach is associated with different traditions in criminological theory and diverse research techniques. The linkage of the broad approaches to science to criminological theories and research techniques is not strict. The approaches are similar to a research program, research tradition, or scientific paradigm. A *paradigm*, an idea made famous by Kuhn (1970), another philosopher of science, means a basic orientation to theory and research. There are many definitions of *paradigm*. In general, a scientific paradigm is a whole system of thinking. It includes basic assumptions, the important questions to be answered or puzzles to be solved, the research techniques to be used, and examples of what good scientific research looks like. For example, criminology is a multiparadigm science. No single paradigm has complete dominance, although positivism does tend to be favored (DiCristina, 1997).[4]

POSITIVIST CRIMINOLOGY

Positivist criminology is used so widely that most people never think of alternative approaches. They assume that the positivist approach *is* science. There are many versions of positivism, and it has a long history within the philosophy of science and among researchers.[5] Yet, for many researchers, it has come to be a pejorative label to be avoided. Turner (1992:1511) observed, "*Positivism* no longer has a clear referent, but it is evident that, for many, being a positivist is not a good thing." The answers to the eight questions give you a picture of what a positivist approach sees as constituting criminology.

Positivist criminology owes a great debt to the country of France (Beirne, 1993). The first annual national crime statistics were published there in 1827. From those statistics, it became clear that certain crime patterns such as homicide rates were relatively constant from one year to the next. This empirical regularity implied that the classical explanation of crime was deficient. Vold, Bernard, and Snipes (1998:27) commented on this:

> [The] free will theory of crime expected random changes in the number of crimes, especially in the number of unpremeditated crimes such as passion murders. The regularity of crime statistics suggested that Beccaria had been right in his argument that, rather than being entirely the product

of free will, crime must be influenced by factors in larger society. . . .

> But the new crime statistics also made it clear that crime rates were going up, not down. . . . People who had received the prompt, proportionate punishments provided by the new French code [of law] were committing more new offenses rather than fewer. . . .

> The new crime statistics clearly revealed the failure of classical punishment policies [i.e., the deterrence doctrine], while at the same time suggesting that other social factors might influence the level of crime in society. This gave rise to a new brand of criminology, which eventually became known as positivism.

Positivism is associated with many specific criminological theories. Positivist researchers prefer precise quantitative data and often use experiments, surveys, and statistics. They seek rigorous, exact measures and "objective" research, and they test hypotheses by carefully analyzing statistics. Many applied researchers (e.g., police scientists, crime policy analysts, and crime prevention program evaluators) embrace positivism. Critics charge that positivism reduces people to numbers and that its concerns with abstract laws or formulas are not relevant to the actual lives of real people.

Positivism says that "there is only *one* logic of science, to which any intellectual activity aspiring to the title of 'science' must conform" (Keat and Urry, 1975:25, emphasis in original). Thus, the social sciences and the natural sciences must use the same method. In this view, differences between the natural and social sciences are due to the immaturity or youth of the social sciences and their subject matter. Eventually, all science, including the social sciences, will be like the most advanced science, physics. Differences among the sciences may exist as to their subject matter (e.g., geology requires techniques different from astrophysics or microbiology because of the objects being studied), but all sciences share a common set of principles and logic.

Positivism sees social science as an *organized method for combining deductive logic with precise empirical observations of individual behavior in order to discover and confirm a set of probabilistic causal laws that can be used to predict general patterns of human activity.*

The Questions

1. Why should one conduct criminological research?

The ultimate purpose of research is scientific explanation—to discover and document universal laws of human behavior. Another important reason is to learn about how the world works so that people can control or predict events. This latter idea is sometimes called an *instrumental orientation*. It is a technical interest that assumes knowledge can be used as a tool or instrument to satisfy human wants and to control the physical and social environment. Once people discover the laws that govern human life, we can use them to alter social relations, to improve how things are done, and to predict what will happen.

For example, a criminologist might be interested in identifying the key factors of military organizations (e.g., informal norms, leadership styles, etc.) that predict increased rates of war crimes. The researcher carefully specifies the factors in his or her theory, and then devises a strategy for measuring them to test the "war crimes" theory. The results of the study are then communicated to, say, the United Nations, which in turn uses them to assist in its efforts to reorganize military institutions in different countries. This positivist view is summarized generally by Turner (1985:39), who stated that the "social universe is amenable to the development of abstract laws that can be tested through the careful collection of data" and that researchers need to "develop abstract principles and models about invariant and timeless properties of the social universe."

Positivists say that scientists are engaged in a never-ending quest for knowledge. As more is learned, new complexities are discovered and there is still more to learn. Early versions of positivism maintained that humans can never know everything because only God possesses such knowledge; however, as creatures placed on this planet with great capacity for knowledge, humans have a duty to discover as much as they can.

2. What is the fundamental nature of social reality?

Positivist criminologists hold that social reality exists "out there"—that is, it is external to the researcher and not determined by his or her personal biases and interests. Social reality, in other words, is waiting to be discovered. This idea notes that human perception and intellect may be flawed, and reality may be difficult to pin down, but it does exist. Moreover, social reality is not random; it is patterned and has order. Without this assumption (i.e., if the world were chaotic and without regularity), logic and prediction would be impossible. Science lets humans discover this order and the laws of nature. "The basic, observational laws of science are considered to be true, primary and certain, because they are built into the fabric of the natural world. Discovering a law is like discovering America, in the sense that both are already waiting to be revealed" (Mulkay, 1979:21).

Two other assumptions are that basic patterns of social reality are stable and knowledge of them is additive. The regularity in social reality does not change over time, and laws discovered today will hold in the future. We can study many parts of reality one at a time, then add the fragments together to get a picture of the whole. Some early versions of this assumption said that the order in nature was created by and is evidence of the existence of God or a supreme being.

3. What is the basic nature of human beings?

In positivism, humans are assumed to be self-interested, pleasure-seeking, rational individuals. People operate on the basis of external causes, with the same cause having the same effect on everyone. We can learn about people by observing their behavior, what we see in external reality.

This is more important than what happens in internal, subjective reality. Sometimes, this is called a *mechanical model of man* or a behaviorist approach. It means people respond to external forces that are as real as physical forces on objects. Durkheim (1938:27) stated, "Social phenomena are things and ought to be studied as things." External reality suggests that researchers may not have to examine unseen, internal motivations of an individual's behavior.

Positivists say that human behavior or social institutions do not just happen because of what a person wants. Human events can be explained with reference to *causal laws*, which describe causes and effects. They identify forces that operate in a manner similar to natural laws in the physical sciences. This suggests that the idea of free will is largely fiction and describes only aspects of human behavior that science has not yet conquered.

Few positivists believe in absolute determinism, wherein people are mere robots or puppets who must always respond exactly the same. Rather, the causal laws are probabilistic. Laws hold for large groups of people or occur in many situations. Researchers can estimate the odds of a predicted behavior. In other words, the laws permit us to make accurate predictions of how often criminal behavior will occur within a large group. The causal laws cannot predict the specific behavior of a specific person in each situation. However, they can say that under conditions *X, Y,* and *Z,* there is a 95 percent probability that one-half of the people will engage in a specified behavior.

For example, criminologists cannot predict which individual soldier will commit a war crime such as torture or rape. However, scientific research could uncover the factors that structure military organizations in ways that increase the likelihood that a significant proportion of soldiers will violate statutes of international law governing armed conflicts. Thus, the researcher can speak with authority that one army is 95 percent more likely to commit double the number of war crimes as another army.

4. What is the relationship between science and common sense?

Positivists see a clear separation between science and nonscience. Of the many ways to seek truth, science is special—the "best" way. Scientific knowledge is better than and will eventually replace the inferior ways of gaining knowledge (e.g., magic, religion, astrology, personal experience, and tradition). Science borrows some ideas from common sense, but it replaces the parts of common sense that are sloppy, logically inconsistent, unsystematic, and full of bias. The scientific community—with its special norms, scientific attitudes, and techniques—can regularly produce "Truth," whereas common sense does so only rarely and inconsistently.

A researcher working in a positivist tradition often creates a whole new vocabulary—a set of scientific ideas and associated terms. He or she wants to use ideas that are more logically consistent and carefully thought out and refined than the ideas found in everyday common sense. The positivist researcher "should formulate new concepts at the outset and not rely on lay notions. . . . There is a preference for the precision which is believed possible in a discipline-based language rather than the vague and imprecise language of everyday life" (Blaikie, 1993:206). In his *Rules of the Sociological Method,* Durkheim warned the researcher to "resolutely deny himself the use of those concepts formed outside of science" and to "free himself from those fallacious notions which hold sway over the mind of the ordinary person" (quoted in Gilbert, 1992:4).

5. What constitutes an explanation or theory of social reality?

Positivist scientific explanation is *nomothetic* (*nomos* means law in Greek); it is based on a system of general laws. Science explains why social life is the way it is by discovering causal laws. Explanation takes the form; *Y* is caused by *X* because *Y* and *X* are specific instances of a causal law. In other words, a positivist explanation states the general causal law that applies to or covers specific observations about social life. This is why positivism is said to use a *covering law model* of explanation.

Positivism assumes that the laws operate according to strict, logical reasoning. Researchers connect causal laws and the specific facts observed about social life with deductive logic. Positivists believe that eventually laws and theories of criminology will be expressed in formal symbolic systems, with axioms, corollaries, postulates, and theorems. Someday, criminological theories will look similar to those in mathematics and the natural sciences.

The laws of human behavior should be universally valid, holding in all historical eras and in all cultures. As noted before, the laws are stated in a probabilistic form for aggregates of people. For example, a positivist explanation of a rise in the crime rate in Toronto in the 1990s refers to factors (e.g., rising divorce rate, declining commitment to traditional moral values, etc.) that could be found any where at any time: in Bombay in the 1890s, Chicago in the 1940s, or Singapore in the 2010s. The factors, as it were, logically obey a general law (e.g., the breakdown of a traditional moral order causes an increase in the rate of criminal behavior).

6. *How does one determine whether an explanation is true or false?*

Positivism developed during the Enlightenment (post–Middle Ages) period of Western thinking (see Bernard, 1988:12–21). It includes an important Enlightenment idea: People can recognize truth and distinguish it from falsehood by applying reason, and, in the long run, over centuries, the human condition can improve through the use of reason and the pursuit of truth. As knowledge grows and ignorance declines, conditions will improve. This optimistic belief that knowledge accumulates over time plays a role in how positivists sort out true from false explanations.

In positivism, to be seriously considered, explanations must meet two conditions: they must (1) have no logical contradictions and (2) be con-

sistent with observed facts. Yet, this is not sufficient. *Replication* is also needed (see Hegtvedt, 1992). Any researcher can replicate or reproduce the results of others. This puts a check on the whole system for creating knowledge. It ensures honesty because it repeatedly tests explanations against hard, objective facts. An open competition exists among opposing explanations, impartial rules are used, neutral facts are accurately observed, and logic is rigorously followed. Over time, scientific knowledge accumulates as different researchers conduct independent tests of a theory and add up the findings.

Consider the example of war crimes. A *war crime,* as defined by the United Nations' Security Council Resolution 827, "is usually a crime committed by a person demonstrably linked to one side of an armed conflict against persons or property on the other side" (Reisman and Antoniou, 1994:387). A "war crimes" theory that predicts levels of criminal behavior based on the organizational structure of armies and military institutions would not be proven with just one study. Confirming a causal relationship depends on replication of the original study by other researchers working in other countries, studying other armies, and even at different periods in history. Determining the truthfulness of a causal explanation involves a long, careful process of doing research.

7. *What does good evidence or factual information look like?*

Positivism is dualist; it assumes that the cold, observable facts are fundamentally distinct from ideas, values, or theories. Empirical facts exist apart from personal ideas or thoughts. We can observe them by using our sense organs (eyesight, smell, hearing, and touch) or special research techniques that extend the senses (e.g., victimization surveys, experiments, and content analysis). Some researchers express this idea as a language of empirical fact and a language of abstract theory. If people disagree over facts, it must be due to the improper use of measurement instruments or to sloppy or inadequate observation. "Scientific explanation involves the accurate and precise measurement of phenomena" (Derksen and Gartrell, 1992:1714). Knowledge of observable reality obtained using our senses is superior to other knowledge (e.g., intuition, emotional feelings, etc.); it allows us to separate true from false ideas about social life.

Positivists combine this idea of the privileged status of empirical observation with the assumption that subjective understanding of the empirical world is shared. Factual knowledge is not based on just one person's observations and reasoning. It must be capable of being communicated and shared by others. Rational people who independently observe facts will agree on them. This is called *intersubjectivity*, or the shared subjective acknowledgment of the facts. Many positivists accept a version of falsification doctrine outlined by the Anglo-Austrian philosopher Sir Karl Popper (1902–1991) in the *Logic of Scientific Discovery* (1959). Popper argued that claims to knowledge "can never be proven or fully justified, they can only be refused" (Phillips, 1987:3). Good evidence for a causal law involves more than piling up supporting facts; it involves looking for evidence that contradicts the causal law. Even if, for example, we studied 10 different armies and found the predicted relationship between military organization and levels of war crimes, that does not prove our theory. Indeed, finding only one army in which the relationship did not hold would be enough for us to refute our causal explanation and seek to refine it. Negative or disconfirming evidence is very powerful, indeed.

8. *Where do sociopolitical values enter into science?*

Positivists argue for a *value-free science* that is objective. There are two meanings of the term *objective*: that observers agree on what they see and that science is not based on values, opinions, attitudes, or beliefs (Derksen and Gartrell, 1992:1715). Positivists see science as a special, distinctive part of society that is free of personal, political, or religious values. It operates independently of the social and cultural forces affecting other human activity. It

involves applying strict rational thinking and systematic observation in a manner that transcends personal prejudices, biases, and values. The norms and operation of the scientific community keep science objective. Scientists are socialized to unique professional norms and values. Researchers accept and internalize the norms as part of their membership in the scientific community. The scientific community has created an elaborate system of checks and balances to guard against value bias. A researcher's proper role is to be a "disinterested scientist."[6] The positivist view on values has had an immense impact on how people see ethical issues and knowledge:

> To the degree that a positivist theory of scientific knowledge has become the criterion for all knowledge, moral insights and political commitments have been delegitimized as irrational or reduced to mere subjective inclination. Ethical judgments are now thought of as personal opinion. (Brown, 1989:37)

Summary

You probably find many positivist assumptions familiar because the positivist approach is widely taught as being the same as science. Few people are aware of the origins of positivist assumptions. An early religious aspect exists in some assumptions because the scholars who developed them in western Europe during the eighteenth and nineteenth centuries had religious training and lived in a cultural-historical setting that assumed specific religious beliefs. Many positivist assumptions will reappear when you read about quantitative research techniques and measurement in later chapters. A positivist approach implies that a researcher begins with a general cause-effect relationship that he or she logically derives from a possible causal law in general theory. He or she logically links the abstract ideas of the relationship to precise measurements of the social world. The researcher remains detached, neutral, and objective as he or she measures aspects of social life, examines evidence, and replicates the research of others. These processes lead to an empirical test of and confirmation for the laws of social life as outlined in a theory.

There is little doubt that positivist criminology is the dominant methodology in the discipline. As DiCristina (1997:191) has stated, "Because of the existing cultural and structural conditions, quantitative information [i.e., positivism] is more likely to receive serious and favorable reviews from the conforming intellectuals; consequently it is more likely to sell." The interesting question, however, is: What, exactly, is it that makes positivism so much more marketable?

DiCristina (1997) has suggested two possible reasons. One of them has to do with the discipline's preoccupation with appearing "scientific." Criminology, like the other social sciences, suffers a crisis of status. And since most people equate positivism with science, criminology stands to gain legitimacy to the degree it embraces a positivist methodology. Another reason is that positivism produces and manipulates numbers, which allows for precise bureaucratic accounting. This tends to the practical concern of the criminal justice bureaucracy, such as the U.S. Department of Justice. But, perhaps more fundamentally, positivist methodology is "congruent with the technical control interests of modern capitalism" (p. 191). Positivism thus opens a political space for criminological research within the broader political-economic framework of the United States as well as other countries.

INTERPRETIVE CRIMINOLOGY

Interpretive criminology can be traced to German sociologist Max Weber (1864–1920). Weber formulated the notion of *verstehen,* which entails a full measure of empathetic understanding between researcher and subject. To quote Weber (1978:5) directly: "Empathetic or appreciative accuracy is attained when, through sympathetic participation, we can adequately grasp the emotional context in which the act took place." Weber (1981:159) later stated:

We shall speak of "social action" wherever human action is subjectively related in meaning to the behavior of others. An unintended collision of two cyclists, for example, shall not be called social action. But we will define as such their possible prior attempts to dodge one another. . . . Social action is not the only kind of action significant for sociological causal explanation, but it is the primary object of an "interpretive sociology."

Weber's notion of an interpretive methodology has intrigued criminologists in the United States for decades. The so-called Chicago School in sociology of the 1920s and 1930s used this approach to study a colorful assortment of urban deviants, delinquents, "jackrollers" and bums. Since then, criminological field research or participant observation has evolved into an accepted, if underutilized, alternative to positivist methodology. Indeed, criminology, perhaps more than any other social science, has added to the scientific respectability of interpretive methodology.

Ferrell (1997:10) addressed criminology's seeming affinity for this methodology:

The concept of verstehen *can be defined somewhat more narrowly and more modestly as a situated strategy in the always partial and imperfect process of research into criminality. . . . [A] researcher, through attentiveness and participation, at least can begin to apprehend and appreciate the specific roles and experiences of criminals, crime victims, crime control agents, and others caught up in the day-to-day reality of crime.*

A positivist researcher will precisely measure selected quantitative details about thousands of people and use statistics, whereas an interpretive researcher may live a year with a dozen people and use careful methods to gather large quantities of detailed qualitative data to acquire an in-depth understanding of how they create meaning in everyday life.

In contrast to positivism's instrumental orientation, the interpretive approach adopts a *practical orientation.* It is concerned with how ordinary people manage their practical affairs in everyday life, or how they get things done.

Interpretive criminology (IC) is concerned with how people interact and get along with each other. In general, the interpretive approach is *the systematic analysis of socially meaningful action through the direct detailed observation of people in natural settings in order to arrive at understandings and interpretations of how people create and maintain their social worlds.*

The Questions

1. Why should one conduct criminological research?

For interpretive researchers, the goal of research is to develop an understanding of social life and discover how people construct meaning in natural settings. An interpretive researcher wants to learn what is meaningful or relevant to the people being studied, or how individuals experience daily life. The researcher does this by getting to know a particular social setting and seeing it from the point of view of those in it. The researcher shares the feelings and interpretations of the people he or she studies and sees things through their eyes.

Interpretive researchers study *meaningful social action*, not just the external or observable behavior of people. Social action is the action to which people attach subjective meaning—it is activity with a purpose or intent. Nonhuman species lack culture and the reasoning to plan out things and attach purpose to their behavior; therefore, social scientists should study what is unique to human social behavior. The researcher must take into account the social actor's reasons and the social context of action. Consider, for example, how recent changes in U.S. immigration law and policies might suggest research questions for interpretive criminologists. Clearly, these changes, which call for harsher criminal enforcement and control of illegal immigration and employment, have altered the social context of meaning for entire immigrant communities in the United States. Yet, the emerging perspective of the undocumented workers who are being marginal-

ized and criminalized by the new immigration policies is virtually unmapped (e.g., How are notions of justice and criminality being redefined? What consequences could this have on future criminality?). Unfortunately, we have at this point little scientific research on this subject of growing concern.

The interpretive approach notes that human action has little inherent meaning. It acquires meaning among people who share a meaning system that permits them to interpret the action as a socially relevant sign or action. Thus, it may well be that criminalizing undocumented workers conveys a meaning to the immigrant community distinctly different, perhaps even antithetical, to that which is intended by immigration officials.

2. What is the fundamental nature of social reality?

The interpretive approach sees human social life as an accomplishment. It is intentionally created out of the purposeful actions of interacting social beings. In contrast to the realist idea (shared by positivist and critical social science) that social life is "out there," independent of human consciousness, interpretive criminology says social reality is not waiting to be discovered. Instead, the social world is largely what people perceive it to be. Social life exists as people experience it and give it meaning. It is fluid and fragile. People maintain it by interacting with others in ongoing processes of communication and negotiation. They operate on the basis of untested assumptions and taken-for-granted knowledge about people and events around them.

The interpretive approach holds that social life is based on social interactions and socially constructed meaning systems. People possess an internally experienced sense of reality. This subjective sense of reality is crucial to grasp human social life. External human behavior is an indirect and often obscure indicator of true social meaning. This approach says that "access to other human beings is possible, however, only by indirect means: what we experience initially are gestures, sound, and actions and only in the process of understanding do we take the step from external signs to the underlying inner life" (Bleicher, 1980:9).

For interpretive criminologists, the "reality" of crime evaporates into subjective definitions of crime. Even legalistic definitions of crime are viewed as resulting from a social construction of reality that processes and appoints one preferred set of definitions of crime over others. Quinney's theory of the social reality of crime emerges out of an interpretive paradigm, as the following quote reveals:

> The term crime *can be taken to refer to concrete happenings that individuals personally experience, or it can refer to conceptions of reality that are created and communicated to individuals through various forms of social interaction, including the media. Different conceptions of crime can be created and communicated as part of the political process of promoting a particular set of values and interests. (Vold, Bernard, and Snipes, 1998:239)*

Positivists assume that everyone shares the same meaning system and that we all experience the world in the same way. The interpretive approach says that people may or may not experience social or physical reality in the same way. Key questions for an interpretive researcher are: How do people experience the world? Do they create and share meaning? Interpretive criminology points to numerous examples in which several people have seen, heard, or even touched the same physical object, yet come away with different meanings or interpretations of it. The interpretive researcher argues that positivists avoid important questions and impose one way of experiencing the world on others. By contrast, IC assumes that multiple interpretations of human experience, or realities, are possible. In sum, the IC approach sees social reality as consisting of people who construct meaning and create interpretations through their daily social interaction.

3. *What is the basic nature of human beings?*
Ordinary people are engaged in a process of

creating flexible systems of meaning through social interaction. They then use such meanings to interpret their social world and make sense of their lives. Human behavior may be patterned and regular, but this is not due to preexisting laws waiting to be discovered. The patterns are created out of evolving meaning systems or social conventions that people generate as they socially interact. Important questions for the interpretive researcher are: What do people believe to be true? What do they hold to be relevant? How do they define what they are doing?

Interpretive researchers want to discover what actions mean to the people who engage in them. It makes little sense to try to deduce social life from abstract, logical theories that may not relate to the feelings and experiences of ordinary people. People have their own reasons for their actions, and researchers need to learn the reasons people use. Individual motives are crucial to consider even if they are irrational, carry deep emotions, and contain false facts and prejudices.

Criminological *verstehen* communicates not only a sense of human nature but it also supports a particular etiology of crime. From this perspective, the symbolic experience of crime is of utmost importance. Ferrell (1997:11) summarizes this etiology: "An understanding of crime and criminality as constructed from the immediate interactions of criminals, control agents, victims, and others, and therefore as emerging from a tangled experiential web of situated dangers and situated pleasures, certainly refocuses theories of criminal causality on the criminal moment."

4. *What is the relationship between science and common sense?*
Positivists see common sense as inferior to science. By contrast, interpretive researchers argue that ordinary people use common sense to guide them in daily living; therefore, one must first grasp common sense. People use common sense all the time. It is a stockpile of everyday theories people use to organize and explain events in the world. It is critical to understand common

sense because it contains the meanings that people use when they engage in routine social interactions.

An interpretive approach says that common sense and the positivist's laws are alternative ways to interpret the world; that is, they are distinct meaning systems. Neither common sense nor scientific law has all the answers. Neither is inferior or superior to the other. Instead, interpretive researchers see each as important in its own domain; each is created in a different way for a different purpose.

The interpretive approach says that common sense is a vital source of information for understanding people. A person's common sense and sense of reality emerge from a pragmatic orientation and set of assumptions about the world. People do not know that common sense is true with absolute certainty, but they must assume that it is true in order to get anything accomplished. The interpretive philosopher, Alfred Schutz (1899–1959), called this the *natural attitude*. It is the assumption that the world existed before you arrived and it will continue to exist after you depart. People develop ways to maintain or reproduce a sense of reality based on systems of meaning that they create in the course of social interactions with others.

5. *What constitutes an explanation or theory of social reality?*

Positivists believe that social theory should be similar to natural science theory with deductive axioms, theorems, and interconnected causal laws. Instead of a maze of interconnected laws and propositions, theory for IC tells a story. Interpretive criminology theory describes and interprets how people conduct their daily lives. It contains concepts and limited generalizations, but it does not dramatically depart from the experience and inner reality of the people being studied.

The interpretive approach is ideographic and inductive. *Ideographic* means the approach provides a symbolic representation or "thick" description of something else. An interpretive research report may read more like a novel or a biography than like a mathematical proof. It is rich in detailed description and limited in abstraction. An interpretive analysis of a social setting, like the interpretation of a literary work, has internal coherence and is rooted in the text, which here refers to the meaningful everyday experiences of the people being studied.

Interpretive theory gives the reader a feel for another's social reality. The theory does this by revealing the meanings, values, interpretive schemes, and rules of living used by people in their daily lives. For example, it may describe major typifications people use in a setting to recognize and interpret their experiences. A *typification* is an informal model, scheme, or set of beliefs that people use to categorize and organize the flow of the daily events they experience.

Thus, interpretive theory resembles a map that outlines a social world or a tourist guidebook that describes local customs and informal norms. For example, interpretive research on war crimes might reveal the socialization experiences of soldiers so as to understand the making of a war criminal. The researcher studies how soldiers are taught to view their enemy, as well as the rationalizations they use to overcome reluctance to commit heinous acts. The study should produce a grounded explanation of behavior based on a detailed description of the military socialization. The grounded theory and evidence are interwoven to create a unified whole; the concepts and generalizations are wedded to their context.

6. *How does one determine whether an explanation is true or false?*

Positivists evaluate a theory by using set procedures to test hypotheses. They logically deduce from theory, collect data, and analyze facts in ways that other scientists can replicate. An explanation is considered to be true when it stands up to replication. For interpretive criminology, a theory is true if it makes sense to those being studied and if it allows others to understand more deeply the constructed reality of those being studied. The theory or description is accurate if the researcher conveys a deep understanding of the way others reason, feel, and see things. Prediction may be possible, but it is a type of prediction that occurs when two people are very close, as when they have been married for a long time. An interpretive explanation documents the actor's point of view and translates it into a form that is intelligible to readers. Smart (1976:100) calls this the *postulate of adequacy:*

> *The postulate of adequacy asserts that if a scientific account of human action were to be presented to an individual actor as a script it must be understandable to that actor, translatable into action by the actor and furthermore comprehensible to his fellow actors in terms of a common sense interpretation of everyday life.*

An interpretive researcher's description of another person's meaning system is a *secondary account.* Like a traveler telling about a foreign land, the researcher is not a native. Such an outside view never equals a primary account given by those being studied, but the closer it is to the native's primary account, the better. Or, to use Ferrell's (1997:11) words: "Criminologists must situate themselves as close to the (inter)action as possible—perhaps even inside the interaction— if they are to catch the constructed reality of crime."

7. *What does good evidence or factual information look like?*

Good evidence in positivism is observable, precise, and independent of theory and values. By contrast, interpretive criminology sees the unique features of specific contexts and meanings as essential to understand social meaning. Evidence about social action cannot be isolated from the context in which it occurs or the meanings assigned to it by the social actors involved.

Interpretive criminologists see facts as fluid and embedded within a meaning system in the interpretive approach; they are not impartial, objective, and neutral. Facts are context-specific actions that depend on the interpretations

of particular people in a social setting. What the positivist assumes—that neutral outsiders observe behavior and see unambiguous, objective facts—an IC researcher takes as a question to be addressed: How do people observe ambiguities in social life and assign meaning? Interpretive researchers say that social situations contain a great deal of ambiguity. This makes it almost impossible to discover straightforward, objective facts. Most behaviors or statements can have several meanings and can be interpreted in multiple ways. In the flow of ambiguous social life, people are constantly "making sense" by reassessing clues in the situation and assigning meanings until they "know what's going on."

For example, to grasp the meaning of war crimes in the conflicts of former Yugoslavia, one must place them in the context of ethnic cleansing. *Ethnic cleansing* means "rendering an area ethnically homogeneous by using force or intimidation to remove persons of given groups from the area" (Reisman and Antoniou, 1994:389). Thus, from the soldier's point of view, acts such as mass rape, extrajudicial executions, and so on, are more expressions of military loyalty and nationalism than they are criminal behavior.

Interpretive researchers rarely ask objective survey questions, aggregate the answers of many people, and claim to have something meaningful. Each person's interpretation of the survey question must be placed in a context (e.g., the individual's previous experiences or the survey interview situation), and the true meaning of a person's answer will vary according to the interview or questioning context. Moreover, because each person assigns a somewhat different meaning to the question and answer, combining answers only produces nonsense.

8. *When do sociopolitical values enter into science?*

The positivist researcher calls for eliminating values and operating within an apolitical environment. The interpretive researcher, by contrast, argues that researchers should reflect on, reexamine, and analyze personal points of view and feelings as a part of the process of studying others. The interpretive researcher needs, at least temporarily, to empathize with and share in the social and political commitments or values of those he or she studies. In this way, Ferrell (1997:11) reveals his own social and political values in the following passage on criminological *verstehen*:

> *The spreading disintegration of the work process, the growing confinement of youths and adults in relatively meaningless work situations (when they can find work at all), surely will continue to heighten the seduction of edgework and adrenaline rush experiences as moments of cleansing terror and desperate rehumanization.*

Interpretive research does not try to be value free. Indeed, it questions the possibility of achieving it. This is because interpretive research sees values and meaning infused everywhere in everything. What the positivist calls value freedom is just another meaning system and value—the value of positivist science. The interpretive researcher urges making values explicit and does not assume that any one set of values is to be a "passionate participant" (Guba and Lincoln, 1994:115), involved with those being studied.

Summary

The interpretive approach existed for many years as the loyal opposition to positivism. Although some positivist criminologists accept the interpretive approach as useful in exploratory research (see Chapter 2), few positivists consider it to be scientific. You will read again about the interpretive outlook when you examine field research and, to a lesser degree, historical-comparative research in later chapters. The interpretive approach is the foundation of criminological techniques that are sensitive to context, that use various methods to get inside the ways others see the world, and that are more concerned with achieving an empathic understand-

ing of feelings and world views than with testing laws of human behavior.

CRITICAL CRIMINOLOGY

Critical criminology offers a third alternative to the meaning of methodology. Sometimes called the "new criminology," critical criminology (CC) mixes nomothetic and ideographic approaches. It agrees with many of the criticisms the interpretive approach directs at positivism, but it adds some of its own and disagrees with the interpretive paradigm on some points.

Critical criminology is "characterized particularly by an argument that it is impossible to separate values from the research agenda, and by a need to advance a progressive agenda favoring disprivileged peoples" (Schwartz and Friedrichs, 1994, as quoted in Vold, Bernard, and Snipes, 1998:260). This approach is traced back to Karl Marx (1818–1883) and his theory of class conflict. Writing in the soot of the Industrial Revolution, Marx argued that capitalism tends to polarize the classes. Marx termed those at the very bottom the *lumpenproletariat*. Largely unemployed, powerless, and alienated, this declassed element of society was susceptible to the temptations of crime.

Of course, Marx's sociology has had a profound impact on social science methodology. It is tied, for example, to critical social theory first developed by the Frankfurt School in Germany in the 1930s.[7] Out of this has come a strong tradition of scholarship criticizing positivism as being narrow, antidemocratic, and nonhumanist in its use of reason. This was outlined in Adorno's essays, "Sociology and Empirical Research" (1976a) and "The Logic of the Social Sciences" (1976b). The well-known living representative of the school, Jurgen Habermas (1929–   ), advanced critical social science in his *Knowledge and Human Interests* (1971). In the field of education, Freire's *Pedagogy of the Oppressed* (1970) also falls within the critical approach.

More recently, critical criminology has been influenced by a "left realism" approach (Vold, Bernard, and Snipes, 1998).[8] This approach offers a more moderate solution to crime in capitalist society, one involving cooperation with the criminal justice system as opposed to bringing down the entire capitalist political economy, as Marxists might have it.

Interpretive criminology criticizes positivism for failing to deal with the meanings of real people and their capacity to feel and think. It also believes positivism ignores the social context and is antihumanist. Critical criminology agrees with these criticisms of positivism. It also believes that positivism defends the status quo because it assumes an unchanging social order instead of seeing current society as a particular stage in an ongoing process.

Critical researchers criticize the interpretive approach for being too subjective and relativist. The critical researcher says that interpretive criminology sees all points of view as equal. The interpretive approach treats people's ideas as more important than actual conditions and focuses on localized, micro-level, short-term settings while ignoring the broader and long-term context. Interpretive criminology is overly concerned with subjective reality. To critical researchers, interpretive criminology is amoral and passive. It does not take a strong value position or actively help people to see false illusions around them so that they can improve their lives. In general, critical criminology can be thought of as a *critical process of inquiry that goes beyond surface illusions to uncover the real structures in the material world in order to help people change conditions and build a better world for themselves.*

The Questions

1. Why should one conduct criminological research?

Critical researchers conduct research to critique and transform social relations. They do this by revealing the underlying sources of social relations and empowering people, especially less powerful people. The purpose of critical research is to change the world. More specifically, social research should uncover myths, reveal hidden truths, and help people to change the world for themselves.

The critical criminologist is action oriented. He or she is dissatisfied with the way things are and seeks dramatic improvements. A positivist researcher usually tries to solve problems as they are defined by government or corporate elites, without "rocking the boat." By contrast, the critical researcher may create problems by "intentionally raising and identifying more problems than the ruling elites in politics and administration are able to accommodate, much less to 'solve'" (Offe, 1981:34–35). The critical researcher asks embarrassing questions, exposes hypocrisy, and investigates conditions in order to encourage dramatic grass-roots action. "The point of all science, indeed all learning, is to change and develop out of our understandings and reduce illusion.... Learning is the reducing of illusion and ignorance; it can help free us from domination by hitherto unacknowledged constraints, dogmas and falsehoods" (Sayer, 1992:252).

For example, Lopez (1996) investigated the U.S. government's ties to human rights violators in Colombia, South America. In particular, he pointed out that almost half (105 out of 246) of the military and police officials cited in a 1992 Inter-American Commission report as being responsible for human rights abuses had been trained at the U.S. Army School of the Americas (SOA) at Fort Benning, Georgia. He also pointed out that "over 6,894 Colombians trained at the SOA during the height of the Colombian 'dirty war,' 1984–1992, the main period when torture, assassination, and state terrorism manuals were in use.... Between 1988 and 1995, the U.S. spent over US$13 million on Colombian soldiers in the program" (p. 38). The goal of Lopez's research and all critical research is to empower. Kincheloe and McLaren (1994:140) stated:

Critical research can be best understood in the context of the empowerment of individuals.

Inquiry that aspires to the name critical must be connected to an attempt to confront the injustice of a particular society or sphere within the society. Research thus becomes a transformative endeavor unembarrassed by the label "political" and unafraid to consummate a relationship with an emancipatory consciousness.

2. What is the fundamental nature of social reality?

Like positivism, critical criminology adopts a realist position (i.e., social reality is "out there" to be discovered). It differs from positivism in that it is historical realism in which reality is seen as constantly shaped by social, political, cultural, and similar factors. Social reality evolves over time. It may be misleading on the surface and have unobservable enduring real structures of power underneath. Critical criminology assumes that social reality always changes and the change is rooted in the tensions, conflicts, or contradictions of social relations. It focuses on change and conflict, especially paradoxes or conflicts that are inherent in the very way social relations are organized. Such paradoxes or inner conflicts reveal much about the true nature of social reality.

This idea of a paradoxical inner conflict or contradiction that brings about social change is called the *dialectic.* It traces back to Marx's notion of class conflict. A dialectical perspective is quite useful for understanding the situation Lopez (1996) described in Colombia.

At the heart of the problem, according to Lopez, is a society at war with itself. The Trujillo massacre serves as a bloody example. "Beginning in April 1989, over 250 people were tortured and murdered by police, army, and hired killers *(sicarios)* working for locally based drug traffickers" (Lopez, 1996:42). The victims were trade union leaders, landless farmers *(campesinos),* and human rights workers who publicly spoke out against official corruption and the government's connection to the cocaine cartels. According to an eyewitness, an army officer trained at the SOA

sprayed them [the victims] in the face with pressurized water from a hose. He pried off their fingernails with a pocket knife, cut off pieces of the bottoms of their feet with a nail clipper, he poured salt in their cuts, then with a blow torch he burned them on different parts of their bodies and their flesh cracked and the skin peeled off, he pointed the blow torch at the genital area, cut off their penises and testicles and put them in their mouths, and finally quartered them with a chain saw. . . . To this day none of the officers responsible for the Trujillo massacre has been tried or convicted. (Lopez, 1996:42)

Such heinous crimes as this, according to the dialectical perspective, will generate oppositional forces which, in turn, give rise to societal change.

Critical criminology generally promotes a social change that goes well beyond the criminal justice system. Indeed, some have called for "social justice," implying the need to redress basic social problems such as economic inequality and powerlessness. The critical criminologist thus analyzes crime from the broader perspective of social justice.

Change can be uneven—extremely slow for long periods of time, then suddenly speed up. The critical researcher studies the past or different societies in order to better see change or to discover alternative ways to organize social life.

A critical approach notes that social change and conflict are not always apparent or observable. The social world is full of illusion, myth, and distortion. Initial observations of the world are only partial and often misleading because the human senses are limited and so is our knowledge. Illusion and myth are how social reality operates. The appearances in surface reality do not have to be based on conscious deception. The immediately perceived characteristics of objects, events, or social relations rarely reveal everything. These illusions allow some groups in society to hold power and exploit others. Karl Marx, German sociologist and political thinker, stated this forcefully (Marx and Engels, 1947:39): "The ideas of the ruling class are in every epoch the ruling ideas; . . . The class which

has the means of material production at its disposal, has control at the same time over the
means of mental production, so that . . . the
ideas of those who lack the means of mental production are subject to it."

The critical science approach argues that
social reality has multiple layers. Behind the
immediately observable surface reality lie deep
structures or unobservable mechanisms. The
events and relations of superficial social reality
are based on deep structures beneath the surface
of casual observation. We can uncover or
expose such structures with effort. Intense and
directed questioning, a good theory about where
to look, a clear value position, and a historical
orientation help the critical researcher probe
below the surface reality and discover the deep
structures.

Interpretive criminology and critical criminology both see social reality as changing and
subject to socially created meanings. The critical
science approach disagrees with the IC emphasis
on micro-level interpersonal interactions and its
acceptance of any meaning system. Critical criminology says that although subjective meaning is
important, there are real, objective conditions that
shape social relations. The critical researcher
questions social situations and places them in a
larger, macro-level historical context. Vold,
Bernard, and Snipes (1998:265) make this point
quite clear:

> This new and more rigorous Marxist criminology
> [which began to take shape in the mid-1970s]
> attempts to relate criminal behavior and crime
> policies to the political economy of the particular
> societies in which they occur, and relies primarily
> on historical and cross-cultural studies for sup-
> port, since only in such studies can societies with
> different political economies be compared.

3. What is the basic nature of human beings?

Positivism views social forces almost as if
they had a life of their own and operated regardless of people's personal wishes. Such social
forces have power over and operate on people.
The critical science approach rejects this idea as
reification. *Reification* is giving the creations of

your own activity a separate, alien existence. It
is separating or removing yourself from what
you have created, until you no longer recognize
it as part of you or as something you helped to
bring about. Once you no longer see your contributions and treat what you have helped to create
as an outside force, you lose control over your
destiny.

The critical researcher says that people have
a great deal of unrealized potential. People are
creative, changeable, and adaptive. Despite their
creativity and potential for change, however, people can also be misled, mistreated, and exploited
by others. They become trapped in a web of social
meanings, obligations, and relationships. They
fail to see how change is possible and thus lose
their independence, freedom, and control over
their lives. This happens when people allow
themselves to become isolated and detached from
others in similar situations. The potential of people can be realized if they dispel their illusions
and join collectively to change society. People
can change the social world, but delusion, isolation, and oppressive conditions in everyday life
often prevent them from realizing their dreams.
Lopez (1996: 44), for example, encourages others
to muster an activism to close down the U.S.
School of the Americas. He ends his article with
the words of Bishop Romero of El Salvador, who
himself was shot dead by an alumnus of the SOA:
"We who have a voice, we have to speak for the
voiceless."

*4. What is the relationship between science and
common sense?*

The critical criminology position on common sense is based on the idea of *false consciousness*—that people are mistaken and act
against their own true best interests as defined
in objective reality. Objective reality lies behind
myth and illusion. False consciousness is meaningless for interpretive criminology because it
implies that a social actor uses a meaning system that is false or out of touch with objective
reality. The interpretive approach says that people create and use such systems and that researchers can only describe such systems, not

judge their value. The critical science approach says that social researchers should study subjective ideas and common sense because these shape human behavior. Yet, they are full of myth and illusion. Critical criminology assumes that there is an objective world in which there is unequal control over resources and power on which common sense is based.

The structures that critical researchers talk about are not easy to see. In order to see structures, researchers must first demystify them and pull back the veil of their surface appearances. Careful observation is not enough. It does not tell what to observe, and observing an illusion does not dispel it. A researcher must use theory to dig beneath surface relations, to observe periods of crisis and intense conflict, to probe interconnections, to look at the past, and to consider future possibilities. Uncovering the deeper level of reality is difficult, but it is essential because surface reality is full of ideology, myth, distortion, and false appearances. "Common sense tends to naturalize social phenomena and to assume that what is, must be. A social science which builds uncritically on common sense . . . reproduces these errors" (Sayer, 1992:43).

5. *What constitutes an explanation or theory of social reality?*

Positivism is based on the idea of *determinism:* Human behavior is determined by causal laws over which humans have little control. Interpretive criminology assumes *voluntarism:* People have a large amount of free will to create social meanings. The critical science approach falls between the other two. It is partially deterministic and partially voluntaristic. Critical criminology says that people are constrained by the material conditions, cultural context, and historical conditions in which they find themselves. The world people live in limits their options and shapes their beliefs and behavior. Yet, people are not locked into an inevitable set of social structures, relationships, or laws. People can develop new understandings or ways of seeing that enable them to change these structures, relationships, and laws. They need first to develop a vision of the future and work together for change, then they can overcome those who oppose them. In a nutshell, people do shape their destiny, but not under conditions of their own choosing.

A complete critical science explanation does several things: It demystifies illusion, describes the underlying structure of conditions, explains how change can be achieved, and provides a vision of a possible future. Critical theory does more than describe the unseen mechanisms that account for observable reality; it also critiques conditions and implies a plan of change.

The critical science approach focuses less on fixed laws of human behavior because the laws are seen as changing. Human behavior is only partially governed by laws or constraints imposed by underlying social structures. People can change most of the apparent laws of society, although this is difficult and involves a long struggle. By identifying the causal mechanisms, the trigger or the levers of social relations, CC explains how and why certain actions will bring about change.

6. *How does one determine whether an explanation is true or false?*

Positivists test theories by deducing hypotheses, testing hypotheses with replicated observations, and then combining results to support laws. Interpretive researchers collect support for theories by seeing whether the meaning system and rules of behavior make sense to those being studied. Critical theory seeks to provide people with a resource that will help them understand and change their world. A researcher tests critical theory by accurately describing conditions generated by underlying structures then by applying that knowledge to change social relations. A good critical theory teaches people about their own experiences, helps them understand their historical role, and can be used by ordinary people to improve conditions.

Critical theory informs practical action or suggests what to do, but theory is also modified on the basis of its use. A critical theory grows and interacts with the world it seeks to explain. Because a critical approach tries to explain and change the world by penetrating hidden structures that are in constant change, the test of an explanation is not static. Testing theory is a dynamic, ongoing process of applying theory and modifying it. Knowledge grows by an ongoing process of eroding ignorance and enlarging insights through action.

The critical approach uses *praxis* to separate good from bad theory. It puts the theory into practice and uses the outcome of practical applications to reformulate theory. *Praxis* means that explanations are valued when they help people really understand the world and to take action that changes it. As Sayer (1992:13) argued, "Knowledge is primarily gained through activity both in attempting to change our environment (through labor or work) and through interaction with other people."

Critical research tries to eliminate the division between the researcher and those being researched, the distinction between science and everyday life. It is thus common to find critical criminological studies published in scientific journals, as well as rewritten (in a jargon-free style) and published in magazines dedicated to activism and social justice. Lopez's (1996) article on the U.S. School of the Americas, for example, is immediately followed by "urgent action requests." These requests implore readers to send "telegrams/telexes/faxes/express/airmail letters" to the President of Colombia, his Attorney General and other ministers, urging "the government to immediately fulfill its commitment to disband paramilitary forces presently operating as auxiliaries of the armed forces or with armed forces' complicity, and to bring to justice members of such forces responsible for human rights violations" (p. 46).

7. What does good evidence or factual information look like?

Positivism assumes that there are incontestable neutral facts on which all rational people agree. Its dualist doctrine says that social facts are like objects. They exist separate from values or theories. The interpretive approach sees the social world as made up of created meaning, with people creating and negotiating meanings.

It rejects positivism's dualism, but it substitutes an emphasis on the subject. Evidence is whatever resides in the subjective understandings of those involved. The critical approach tries to bridge the object-subject gap. It says that the facts of material conditions exist independent of subjective perceptions, but that facts are not theory neutral. Instead, facts require an interpretation from within a framework of values, theory, and meaning. DiCristina (1997:192) underscores this inextricable connection between empirical fact and political value that lies at the heart of critical criminology:

> *Numerical data can be found, constructed or interpreted to support (or challenge) a wide variety of competing perspectives on a broad range of criminal justice issues. If it is true that few criminal justice policies can be consistent with all data sets and all interpretations, a large proportion of criminal justice data is bound to be discounted during the policy making process.*

Theory helps a critical researcher find new facts and separate the important from the trivial ones. Theory is a type of map telling researchers where to look for facts and how to interpret them once they are uncovered. For example, in *Inequality in Africa*, Nafziger (1988) used a critical perspective. He criticized "facts" on income inequality because they measured only money income in societies where money is not widely used. He also criticized interpretations of "facts" on issues such as land distribution and infant mortality rates. Such facts ignored the number of people living on a farm and ignored those outside one group in a nation (South African Whites) that has drastically lower infant mortality rates than others in the same nation. Instead, Nafziger used theory to identify a wide variety of facts (e.g., birth rates, urban-rural gaps, ethnic divisions, international trade, political power) and went beyond the surface to connect them to one another. He asked: Why is Africa the only region in the world to become more impoverished since World War II? His theory helped him identify a number of major social groups (e.g., government leaders) and classes (e.g., peasants). Nafziger also asked whether various trends or policies served the interests of each group.

All theories are not equally useful for finding and understanding key facts. Theories are based on beliefs and assumptions about what the world is like and on a set of moral-political values. Critical criminology says that some values are better than others.[9] Thus, in order to interpret facts, one must understand history, adopt a set of values, and know where to look for underlying structures. Different versions of critical science offer different value positions (e.g., Marxism versus feminism).

8. *When do sociopolitical values enter into science?*

The critical approach has an activist orientation. Social research is a moral-political activity that requires the researcher to commit to a value position. Critical criminology rejects positivist value freedom as a myth. It also attacks the interpretive approach for its *relativism* (the idea that everything is relative and nothing is absolute). In the interpretive approach, the reality of the genius and the reality of the idiot are equally valid and important. There is little, if any, basis for judging between alternative realities or conflicting viewpoints. For example, the interpretive researcher does not call a racist viewpoint wrong, because any viewpoint is true for those who believe in it. The critical approach says that there is only one, or a very few, correct points of view. Other viewpoints are plain wrong or misleading. All social research *necessarily* begins with a value or a moral point of view. For CC, being objective is not being value free. Objectivity means a nondistorted, true picture of reality; "it challenges the belief that science must be protected from politics. It argues that some politics—the politics for emancipatory social change—can increase the objectivity of science" (Harding, 1986:162).

Critical criminology says that to deny that a researcher has a point of view is itself a point of view. It is a technician's point of view: Conduct research and ignore the moral questions; satisfy a sponsor and follow orders. Such a view says that science is a tool or instrument anyone can use. This view was strongly criticized when Nazi scientists committed inhumane experiments and then claimed that they were blameless because they "just followed orders" and were "just scientists." Positivism adopts such an approach and produces technocratic knowledge—a form of knowledge best suited for use by the people in power to dominate or control other people.[10] For critical criminology, "the political use of behavioral science has made positivism into a legitimating ideology of dominant groups . . . value-freedom itself has come to provide an ethic for calculated bureaucratic control" (Brown, 1989:39).

The critical approach rejects positivism and interpretive criminology as being detached and concerned with studying the world instead of acting on it. Critical criminology holds that knowledge is a type of power. Knowledge can be used to control people, it can be hidden in ivory towers for intellectuals to play games with, or it can be given to people to help them take charge of and improve their lives. What a researcher studies, how he or she studies it, and what happens to the results involve values and morality, because knowledge can have tangible effects on people's lives. The researcher who studies trivial behavior, who fails to probe beneath the surface, or who buries the results in a university library is making a moral choice. The choice is to take information from the people being studied without involving them or liberating them. Critical science questions the morality of such a choice, even if it is not a conscious one. The researcher's proper role is to be the "transformative intellectual" (Guba and Lincoln, 1994:115).

Summary

Much of what we have said here about the three criminological methodologies parallels similar divides and approaches in the other social sciences (e.g., sociology, anthropology, and women's studies), as well. Referring generally to these social science methodologies, Habermas

(1971, as quoted in DiCristina, 1997:190–191) summarized their differences in this way:

> Empirical-analytic science [i.e., positivism] emphasizes hypothetico-deductive reasoning and controlled observation, and incorporates a "cognitive interest in technical control over objectified processes." Historical-hermeneutical science stresses interpretation (not observation), and incorporates a "practical cognitive interest" that is associated with mutual understanding. Critical social science focuses on "self-reflection" that is associated with the "critique of ideology" and is "determined by an emancipatory cognitive interest."

EXPANDING CRITICAL/COMPARATIVE CRIMINOLOGY: FEMINIST AND POSTMODERN APPROACHES

There are two other perspectives on the horizon, which, along with Marxism, constitute what is now considered to be critical criminology (Vold, Bernard, and Snipes, 1998; Schwartz and Friedrichs, 1994): feminist and postmodern perspectives. Not fully seasoned but already containing the fire and urgency of Marxist theory and praxis, feminism and postmodern criminology are jettisoning the value-free notion harnessing positivism. In the spirit of activism and social movement, feminism far outreaches postmodernist practitioners. This is doubtless due to the inherent diffuse qualities of what is loosely termed "postmodern criminology." We will come back to this point.

Feminist research is conducted by people, almost all of them women, who hold a feminist self-identity and consciously use a feminist perspective. They use multiple research techniques. Feminist methodology attempts to give a voice to women and to correct the male-oriented perspective that has predominated in the development of criminology.

The feminists register their critique of criminal justice. They fault the justice system and the discipline for ignoring domestic abuse for so long, and for ignoring differences pertaining to crime etiology and relationship to the underlying power structure upon which, and for which, the system stands (Donzinger, 1996; Simpson, 1989; Daly and Chesney-Lind, 1988; Naffine, 1987; Klein, 1973). Theirs is an intricate and necessary critique of the presently existing science of criminal justice.

Feminist research is based on a heightened awareness that the subjective experience of women differs from an ordinary interpretative perspective (Olsen, 1994). Feminist criminologists launch a full attack on the discipline. Criminological theory and research has not, to their liking, addressed the differences in the ways men and women experience crime and justice. They believe the discipline accepts untested beliefs that men and women experience crime similarly, justice similarly, and are similarly motivated to commit crime. To correct this, there needs to be a distinct methodology in criminology to account for the position of women in society. It is even felt in some corners that positivism itself aggrandizes the male point of view; it is objective, logical, task oriented, and instrumental. It reflects a male emphasis on individual competition, on dominating and controlling the environment, and on the hard facts and forces that act on the world. In contrast, women emphasize accommodation and gradually developing human bonds. They see the social world as a web of interconnected human relations, full of people linked together by feelings of trust and mutual obligation. Women tend to emphasize the subjective, empathetic, process-oriented, and inclusive sides of social life. Feminist research is also action oriented and seeks to advance feminist values (see Box 4.1).

Feminist researchers argue that much nonfeminist research is sexist, largely as a result of broader cultural beliefs and a preponderance of male researchers. The research overgeneralizes from the experience of men to all people, ignores gender as a fundamental social division, focuses on men's problems, uses male as points of reference, and assumes traditional gender roles.

Box 4.1 _____

Characteristics of Feminist Criminology

- Advocacy of a feminist value position and perspective
- Rejection of sexism in assumptions, concepts, and research questions
- Creation of empathic connections between the researcher and those he or she studies
- Sensitivity to how relations of gender and power permeate all spheres of social life
- Incorporation of the researcher's personal feelings and experiences into the research process
- Flexibility in choosing research techniques and crossing boundaries between academic fields
- Recognition of the emotional and mutual-dependence dimensions in human experience
- Action-oriented research that seeks to facilitate personal and societal change

The feminist approach sees researchers as fundamentally gendered beings. Researchers necessarily have a gender that will shape how they experience reality, and therefore it affects their research (Cook and Fonow, 1990). In addition to gender's impact on individual researchers, basic theoretical assumptions and the scientific community appear as gendered cultural contexts. Gender has a pervasive influence in culture and shapes basic beliefs and values that cannot be simply isolated and insulated in the social processes of scientific inquiry (Longino, 1990).

Feminist researchers are not objective or detached; they interact and collaborate with the people they study. They fuse their personal and professional lives. For example, feminist researchers will attempt to comprehend an interviewee's experiences while sharing their own feelings and experiences. This process may give birth to a personal relationship between researcher and interviewee that might mature over time. Reinharz (1992:263) argued, "This blur-

ring of the disconnection between formal and personal relations, just as the removal of the distinction . . . between the research project and the researcher's life, is a characteristic of much, if not all, feminist research."

A science of justice must include a vibrant and active feminist criminology. Signs of such a perspective are already appearing in critical criminology. They can be found, for example, in new works attacking "get tough" crime policies and in others that question the very premise of a capitalist justice system (e.g., see Miller, 1998; Chesney-Lind, 1997; or any number of others). Signs of progress can also be seen in the emerging research agenda of criminal justice institutions in the United States. For example, the U.S. National Institute of Justice committed $1.3 million in 1997 to assess the impact of the Violence Against Women Act of the Violent Crime Control and Law Enforcement Act of 1994. Clearly, it is in the interest of feminist criminologists to see such support continue.

Postmodern criminology is part of the larger postmodern movement or evolving understanding of the contemporary world that includes art, music, literature, and cultural criticism. It began in the humanities and has roots in the philosophies of existentialism, nihilism, and anarchism and in the ideas of Heidegger, Nietzsche, Sartre, and Wittgenstein. Postmodernism is a rejection of modernism. _Modernism_ refers to basic assumptions, beliefs, and values that arose in the Enlightenment era. Modernism relies on logical reasoning; it is optimistic about the future and believes in progress, it has confidence in technology and science, and it embraces humanist values (i.e., judging ideas based on their effect on human welfare). Modernism holds that there are standards of beauty, truth, and morality about which most people can agree (Brannigan, 1992).

There is debate over the shift from modernism to postmodernism (Gartman, 1998). Marxists theory attributes it to the change in industrial capitalism—a change, that is, from standardized mass production (i.e., "Fordism") to diverse forms of flexible production, employment, and subcontracting (i.e., "post-Fordism"). The accompanying cultural shift is toward one of "difference, superficiality, and ahistoricality" (Gartman, 1998:119).

Be that as it may, postmodern research sees no separation between the arts or humanities and social sciences. It shares the critical social science goal of demystifying the social world. It seeks to deconstruct or tear apart surface appearances to reveal the internal hidden structure. Like extreme forms of interpretive criminology, postmodernism distrusts abstract explanation and holds that research can never do more than describe, with all descriptions equally valid. A researcher's description is neither superior nor inferior to anyone else's and only describes the researcher's personal experiences. As Vold, Bernard, and Snipes (1998:270) phrased it, "Postmodernists, in contrast, do not give scientific thinking a special position, and describe it instead as being no more nor less valid than other types of thinking."

A main premise of postmodern theory is the belief that scientific reasoning (e.g., linear causality and objectivity) has contributed to the oppression of individuals rather than to their liberation. The postmodern charge, therefore, is to replace the notion of a nomothetic science with variegated perspectives that free up human potential. Postmodernists distrust all systematic empirical observation and doubt that knowledge is generalizable or accumulates over time. They see knowledge as taking numerous forms and as unique to particular people or specific locales. Rosenau (1992:77) argued, "Almost all postmodernists reject truth as even a goal or ideal because it is the very epitome of modernity. . . . Truth makes reference to order, rules, and values; depends on logic, rationality and reason, all of which the postmodernists question."

Postmodernists object to presenting research results in a detached and neutral way. The researcher or author of a report should never be hidden when someone reads it; his or her presence needs to be unambiguously evident in the report. Thus, a postmodern research report is similar to a work of art. Its purpose is to stimulate others, to give pleasure, to evoke a response, or to arouse curiosity. Postmodern reports often have a theatrical, expressive, or dramatic style of presentation. They may be in the form of a work of fiction, a movie, or a play. The postmodernist argues that the knowledge about social life created by a researcher may be better communicated through a skit or musical piece than by a scholarly journal article. Its value lies in telling a story that may stimulate experiences within the people who read or encounter it. Postmodernism is antielitist and rejects the use of science to predict and to make policy decisions. Postmodernists oppose those who use positivist science to reinforce power relations and bureaucratic forms of control over people (see Box 4.2).

Postmodern criminology has only begun to bear fruit in the discipline. Its most notable contri-

---

Box 4.2 _____

Characteristics of Postmodern Social Research

- Rejection of all ideologies and organized belief systems, including all social theory
- Strong reliance on intuition, imagination, personal experience, and emotion
- Sense of meaninglessness and pessimism, belief that the world will never improve
- Extreme subjectivity in which there is no distinction between the mental and the external world
- Ardent relativism in which there are infinite interpretations, none superior to another
- Espousal of diversity, chaos, and complexity that is constantly changing
- Rejection of studying the past or different places since only the here and now is relevant
- Belief that causality cannot be studied because life is too complex and rapidly changing
- Assertion that research can never truly represent what occurs in the social world

bution thus far is its critique of the discourse of criminal justice. The discourse of criminal justice practitioners and academicians, according to the postmodernist, is a language of domination and control by the powerful.

Schissel (1997:169) "tears a text apart," as he has termed it, so as "to deconstruct" official discourse in Canada that marginalizes young people. As he sees it, official discourse serves up a "moral panic against youth in Canada [and] is an issue of power and social control" (p. 169). The postmodern attack on such "framed discourse" is illustrated in Schissel's quote:

> Constructing images of crime and criminalization is a social control strategy that creates the illusion that the "dangerous class" is located at the bottom of the social hierarchy. This illusion melds poverty and criminality and proposes them as the effects of moral inferiority. As a consequence, the "dangerous class" deserves both poverty and punishment. [The] ideology of child-hating is subtle. (p. 169)

Although postmodern criminology is less articulated than either Marxist or feminist criminology, there are signs of it being used to deconstruct the central metaphor of criminal justice. The metaphor of a "war on crime" clearly drives much of the professional and popular thinking about crime and justice. Therefore, a number of criminologists are attempting to frame an alternative discourse, that of "criminology as peacemaking" (Fuller, 1998; Pepinsky and Quinney, 1991). The peacemaking perspective, according to Fuller (1998:41), "emphasizes social justice, conflict resolution, rehabilitation, and a belief that people need to cooperate in democratic institutions in order to develop meaningful communities."

CONCLUSION

This chapter began by asking whether a science of justice is possible, and, if so, what methodologies it would employ. This opened our discussion of the competing approaches to criminological research. These approaches contain different philosophical assumptions about the purpose of science and the nature of social reality. We then described in detail three ideal approaches to criminological research (see Table 4.1).

The positivist deduces hypotheses from a general theory and then tests these hypotheses empirically. The researcher uses statistics in this process. The interpretive criminologist takes an entirely different tack. He or she personally interacts with his or her research subject, using a field research technique called ethnography. Underlying the research is the logic of *verstehen.* That is, the criminologist attempts to understand the meaning of social action from the perspective of those directly involved. In this case, an inductive logic is used to generate grounded theory. The critical criminologist focuses on the larger social and historical context. He or she emphasizes the moral/critical purpose of research and uses both quantitative and qualitative research techniques.

That criminology has these three fundamental approaches to research methodology should suggest to you that there is no single, absolutely correct approach to doing scientific research. This does not mean than anything goes, of course, nor that there is no ground for tentative agreement (see Box 4.3). Rather, it means that the basis for doing criminological research is not settled in favor of one approach or another, and perhaps never will be. Nevertheless, being aware of these different approaches will help you when you read research reports or their findings reported in the mass media.

The various techniques used in criminological research (e.g., survey, random sampling, and ethnography) are ultimately based on the assumptions of the three approaches to a science of justice. Often, you will see reference made to one of these techniques without the methodological reasoning on which it is based. By knowing about the approaches, you can better understand the principles on which the specific research techniques are based. You will also be in a much stronger position to criticize and improve on

TABLE 4.1 A Summary of Differences among the Three Approaches to Criminology

	POSITIVIST CRIMINOLOGY	INTERPRETIVE CRIMINOLOGY	CRITICAL CRIMINOLOGY
1. Reason for research	To discover natural laws so people can predict and control events	To understand and describe meaningful social action	To smash myths and empower people to change society radically
2. Nature of social reality	Stable preexisting patterns or order that can be discovered	Fluid definitions of a situation created by human interaction	Conflict filled and governed by hidden underlying structures
3. Nature of human beings	Self-interested and rational individuals who are shaped by external forces	Social beings who create meaning and who constantly make sense of their worlds	Creative, adaptive people with unrealized potential, trapped by illusion and exploitation
4. Role of common sense	Clearly distinct from and less valid than science	Powerful everyday theories used by ordinary people	False beliefs that hide power and objective conditions
5. Theory looks like	A logical, deductive system of interconnected definitions, axioms, and laws	A description of how a group's meaning system is generated and sustained	A critique that reveals true conditions and helps people see the way to a better world
6. An explanation that is true	Is logically connected to laws and based on facts	Resonates or feels right to those who are being studied	Supplies people with tools needed to change the world
7. Good evidence	Is based on precise observations that others can repeat	Is embedded in the context of fluid social interactions	Is informed by a theory that unveils illusions
8. Place for values	Science is value free, and values have no place except when choosing a topic	Values are an integral part of social life: no group's values are wrong, only different	All science must begin with a value position; some positions are right, some are wrong

Box 4.3 _____

Common Features of the Three Approaches to Criminology

1. *All are empirical.* Each is rooted in the observable reality of the sights, sounds, behaviors, situations, discussions, and actions of people. Research is never based on fabrication and imagination alone.

2. *All are systematic.* Each emphasizes meticulous and careful work. All reject haphazard, shoddy, or sloppy thinking and observation.

3. *All are theoretical.* The nature of theory varies, but all emphasize using ideas and seeing patterns. None holds that social life is chaos and disorder; all hold that explanation or understanding is possible.

4. *All are public.* All say a researcher's work must be candidly expressed to other researchers; it should be made explicit and shared. All oppose keeping the research processes hidden, private, or secret.

5. *All are self-reflective.* Each approach says researchers need to think about what they do and

be self-conscious. Research is never done in a blind or unthinking manner. It involves serious contemplation and requires self-awareness.

6. *All are open-end processes.* All see research as constantly moving, evolving, changing, asking new questions, and pursuing leads. None see it as static, fixed, or closed. Current knowledge or research procedures are not "set in stone" and settled. They involve continuous change and an openness to new ways of thinking and doing things.

Thus, despite their differences, all the approaches say that criminology strives to create systematically gathered, empirically based theoretical knowledge through public processes that are self-reflective and open ended.

---

existing criminological research. This is exactly what is needed to advance criminology as the science of justice.

Speaking to the American Society of Criminologists in his presidential address in 1996, Charles F. Wellford (1997:7) had this to say: "Fewer than five percent of the articles [in

Criminology, perhaps the discipline's most prestigious scientific journal] have any connection to testing or achieving justice. . . . We may have lost our historical focus." Thus, as you can see, there is considerable room in the discipline for methodologically sound research that seeks to advance justice in society.

KEY TERMS _____

causal laws	intersubjectivity	postulate of adequacy
critical social science	meaningful social action	practical orientation
dialectic	mechanical model of man	praxis
feminist research	nomothetic	relativism
ideographic	paradigm	value-free science
instrumental orientation	positivist social science	*verstehen*
interpretive social science	postmodern research	

REVIEW QUESTIONS _____

1. What is the purpose of criminological research according to each approach?

2. How does each approach define social reality?

3. What is the nature of human beings according to each approach?

4. How are science and common sense different in each approach?

5. What is criminological theory according to each approach?

6. How does each approach test a criminological theory?

7. What does each approach say about facts and how to collect them?

8. How is value-free science possible in each approach? Explain.

9. How are the criticisms of positivism by the interpretive and critical criminologists similar?

10. How does the model of science and the scientific community presented in Chapter 1 relate to each of the three approaches?

NOTES

1. For educational research, see Bredo and Feinberg (1982) and Guba and Lincoln (1994); for psychology, see Harre and Secord (1979) and Rosnow (1981); for political science, see Sabia and Wallulis (1983); and for economics, see Hollis (1977) and Ward (1972). A general discussion of alternatives can be found in Nowotny and Rose (1979).

2. See especially Friedrichs (1970), Giddens (1976), Gouldner (1970), and Phillips (1971). General introductions are provided by Harre (1972), Suppe (1977), and Toulmin (1953).

3. Divisions of the philosophies of social science similar to the approaches discussed in this chapter can be found in Benton (1977), Blaikie (1993), Bredo and Feinberg (1982), Fay (1975), Fletcher (1974), Guba and Lincoln (1994), Keat and Urry (1975), Lloyd (1986), Mulkay (1979), Sabia and Wallulis (1983), Smart (1976), and Wilson (1970).

4. For discussions of paradigms, see Eckberg and Hill (1979), Kuhn (1970, 1979), Masterman (1970), Ritzer (1975), and Rosnow (1981).

5. In addition to the works listed in note 3, Halfpenny (1982) and Turner (1984) have provided overviews of positivism in sociology. Also see Giddens (1978). Lenzer (1975) is an excellent introduction to Auguste Comte.

6. See Couch (1987). Also see Longino (1990:62–82) for an excellent analysis of objectivity in positivism and more broadly.

7. For a discussion of the Frankfurt School, see Bottomore (1984), Held (1980), Martin (1973), and Slater (1977). For more on the works of Habermas, see Holub (1991), McCarthy (1978), Pusey (1987), and Roderick (1986).

8. For discussions of realism, see Bhaskar (1975), Miller (1987), and Sayer (1992).

9. See Sprague and Zimmerman (1989) on feminists' privileged perspectives of women and see Rule (1978a, 1978b) on constituencies that researchers favor.

10. See Habermas (1971, 1973, 1979) for a critical science critique of positivism as being technocratic and used for domination. He has suggested an emancipatory alternative. Also see note 7.

RECOMMENDED READINGS

Berger, Peter, and Thomas Luckman. (1967). *The social construction of reality: A treatise in the sociology of knowledge.* Garden City, NY: Anchor. This is a classic work within the interpretive approach to social science. It gives a forceful statement of how what people consider to be real is based on social meanings that are constructed and reconstructed by people during social interactions with each other.

Blaikie, Norman. (1993). *Approaches to social inquiry.* Cambridge, MA: Polity Press. Blaikie offers a clear overview of a wide variety of approaches and issues in how social science is to be conducted. He gives special attention to the contrast between a critical-realist and an interpretive or constructivist approach.

DiCristina, Bruce. (1995). *Method in criminology: A philosophical primer.* Albany, NY: Harrow and

Heston. This book explores the epistemological underpinnings of criminology. It is useful for understanding the philosophical issues that make a science of justice possible.

Fay, Brian. (1987). *Critical social science: Liberation and its limits*. Ithaca, NY: Cornell University Press. This is Fay's second book on the different approaches to social science. Here, he presents a clear statement of what a critical social science should involve, its major parts, and its weaknesses.

Fuller, John R. (1998). *Criminal justice: A peacemaking perspective*. Boston: Allyn and Bacon. This is a short, readable introduction into peacemaking criminology. This perspective draws from various sources, including Marxist, feminist, and postmodern criminology.

Guba, Egon G., and Yvonna S. Lincoln. (1994). Competing paradigms in qualitative research. In *Handbook of qualitative research*, edited by Norman K. Denzin and Yvonna S. Lincoln, pp. 105–117. Thousand Oaks, CA: Sage. This is an overview of the three major approaches written from an interpretive point of view.

Reinharz, Shulamit. (1992). *Feminist methods in social research*. New York: Oxford University Press. Reinharz discusses how a feminist approach to research differs from other approaches and identifies its common features. In addition, she explains how feminist researchers use many specific research techniques, case studies, content analysis, oral history, cross-cultural research, experimental, survey, field research, and survey research. She cites hundreds of example studies taken from social science fields.

Rosenau, Pauline Marie. (1992). *Post-modernism and the social sciences*. Princeton, NJ: Princeton University Press. This is a relatively accessible and even-handed introduction to postmodernism in the social sciences. Rosenau traces its origins and outlines its implications for methodology. She also identifies two major tendencies in contemporary postmodern thinking and evaluates its potential.

READING OTHER PEOPLE'S RESEARCH

justice - *n.* **1.** *moral rightness; equity.* **2.** *Honor; fairness.* **3.** *Good reason.* **4.** *Fair handling; due reward or treatment.* **5.** *The administration and procedure of law.* **6.** *Abbr.* **J.** *A judge.* **7.** *A justice of the peace.* *[Middle English, from Old French, from Latin* justus, *JUST]*
—*The American Heritage Dictionary of the English Language*

INTRODUCTION

People go to the dictionary to find out what a word means and how it is used in a sentence. For example, the word *justice* means moral rightness or equity, such as in the sentence: *Democratic societies are erected on the principle of justice for all.* For researchers, the process is similar. But instead of consulting a dictionary, researchers find out what a concept means and how it has been used by other researchers by reviewing the scientific literature on a topic. In this chapter, you will explore how and why criminologists begin their own research by first reading what other criminologists have done.

Reviewing the accumulated knowledge about a question is an essential early step in the research process, no matter which approach to criminology you adopt. As in other areas of life, it is best to find out what is already known about a question before trying to answer it yourself. The cliché about wasting time reinventing the wheel is a reminder to do your homework before beginning an endeavor that requires an investment of time and effort. This is true for the consumer of research and for the professional researcher beginning a study.

This chapter examines the literature review as part of the research process. After reading it, you should understand the role of the literature review and its purpose in a specific study. You should know how to conduct a review. You will have another reason for learning about your college library, although this chapter cannot substitute for a visit to the library and assistance from a professional librarian. Finally, you will learn about six types of reviews, and you will see differences between good and bad reviews. The skills you use to conduct a high-quality literature review will improve your understanding of the research process.

We begin by looking at the various purposes the review can serve. We will also discuss what the *literature* is, where to find it, and what it contains. Then, we will explore techniques for systematically conducting a review. Finally, we will look at how to write a review and its place in a research report.

REASONS TO CONDUCT A LITERATURE REVIEW

A literature review is based on the assumption that knowledge accumulates and that we learn from and build on what others have done. Scientific research is not an activity of isolated hermits who ignore others' findings. Rather, it is a collective effort of many researchers who share their results with one another and who pursue knowledge as a community. Although some studies may be especially important and individual researchers may become famous, a specific research project is just a tiny part of the overall process of creating knowledge. Today's studies build on those of yesterday. Researchers read studies to compare, replicate, or criticize them for weaknesses.

Reviews vary in scope and depth. Different kinds of reviews are stronger at fulfilling one or another of four goals (see Box 5.1). It may take a researcher over a year to complete an extensive professional summary review of all the literature on a broad question. The same researcher might complete a highly focused review in a very specialized area in a few weeks. When beginning a review, a researcher decides on a topic or field of knowledge to examine, how much depth to go into, and the kind of review to conduct. The six kinds listed in Box 5.2 are ideal

Box 5.1 _____

Goals of a Literature Review

1. *To demonstrate a familiarity with a body of knowledge and establish credibility.* A review tells a reader that the researcher knows the research in an area and knows the major issues. A good review increases a reader's confidence in the researcher's professional competence, ability, and background.

2. *To show the path of prior research and how a current project is linked to it.* A review outlines the direction of research on a question and shows the development of knowledge. A good review places a research project in a context and demonstrates its relevance by making connections to a body of knowledge.

3. *To integrate and summarize what is known in an area.* A review pulls together and synthesizes different results. A good review points out areas where prior studies agree, where they disagree, and where major questions remain. It collects what is known up to a point in time and indicates the direction for future research.

4. *To learn from others and stimulate new ideas.* A review tells what others have found so that a researcher can benefit from the efforts of others. A good review identifies blind alleys and suggests hypotheses for replication. It divulges procedures, techniques, and research designs worth copying so that a researcher can better focus hypotheses and gain new insights.

types. A specific review often combines features of several kinds.

All reviews follow the first goal—to show familiarity and establish credibility—to some degree. It is one reason teachers ask students to write library research term papers. A review that only demonstrates familiarity with an area is rarely published, but it often is part of an educational program. When this goal is combined with the fourth goal, it is a *self-study review*. In addition to giving others confidence in a reviewer's command of a field, it has the side benefit of building the reviewer's self-confidence.

Box 5.2 _____

Six Types of Reviews

1. Self-study reviews increase the reader's confidence.
2. Context reviews place a specific project in the big picture.
3. Historical reviews trace the development of an issue over time.
4. Theoretical reviews compare how different theories address an issue.
5. Integrative reviews summarize what is known at a point in time.
6. Methodological reviews point out how methodology varies by study.

The most common reason for writing a literature review is the second goal: creating links to a developing body of knowledge. This is a background or *context review*. It usually appears at the beginning of a report or article. It introduces the rest of a research report and establishes the significance and relevance of a research question. It tells the reader how a project fits into the big picture and its implications for a field of knowledge. The review can emphasize how the current research continues a developing line of thought, or it can point to a question or unresolved conflict in prior research to be addressed.

Another kind of review combines the second and third goals. The *historical review* traces the development of an idea or shows how a particular issue or theory has evolved over time. Researchers conduct historical reviews only on the most important ideas in a field. These reviews are also used in studies of the history of thought. Sometimes they are helpful, when students are introduced to an area, to show how we got to where we are today. They may show how, during the advance of knowledge, a single past idea split into different parts or separate ideas combined into broad thought.

The *theoretical review* primarily follows the third goal. It presents different theories that purport to explain the same thing, then evalu-ates how well each accounts for findings. In addition to examining the consistency of predictions with findings, a theoretical review may compare theories for the soundness of their assumptions, logical consistency, and scope of explanation. Researchers also use it to integrate two theories or extend a theory to new issues. It sometimes forms a hybrid—the historical-theoretical review.

The *integrative review* presents the current state of knowledge and pulls together disparate research reports in a fast-growing area of knowledge. Researchers may publish such valuable reviews as an article to provide a service to other researchers. For example, a researcher may discover that criminological studies which have used existing U.S. Department of Justice statistics tend to ignore economic inequality as a causal variable.

The *methodological review* is a specialized type of the integrative review. In it, a researcher evaluates the methodological strength of past studies. It describes conflicting results and shows how different research designs, samples, measures, and so on account for different results. For example, a researcher may discover that all experiments that studied only males yielded different results than those that studied both sexes.

A *meta-analysis* is a special technique researchers use in an integrative review, or more often, in a methodological review.[1] The researcher gathers the details about a large number of research projects (e.g., sample size, when published, size of the effects of variables) and then statistically analyzes this information.

Cox and Davidson (1995) used meta-analysis to examine findings on whether alternative education programs help juvenile delinquents. These nontraditional programs are designed specifically for troubled youth, using low student/teacher ratios, an unstructured environment, and individualized learning. The authors first conducted a computerized search of three sources: ERIC (Educational Resources Information Circuit), PSYCHLIT, and NCJRS (National Criminal Justice Reference Service) for the years 1966 to 1993. They looked for all citations that mentioned alternative education programs for youth and found 241 citations. They next read each to see whether the article met three criteria: (1) mentioned a separate curriculum, (2) was held in a separate location or building, (3) included quantitative measures of program outcomes. Of the 241 studies, only 87 met all three criteria. The researchers then checked whether the studies used specific statistical measures or tests; they found that 57 studies had the statistics. After statistically analyzing the results of the 57 studies, the authors learned that such programs slightly improve school performance and self-esteem but do not directly reduce delinquent behavior.

WHERE TO FIND RESEARCH LITERATURE

Researchers present reports of their research projects in several written forms. For the most part, you can find them only in a college or university library. Researchers publish studies as books, scholarly journal articles, dissertations, government documents, or policy reports. They also present them as papers at the meetings of professional societies. This section briefly discusses each type and gives you a simple road map on how to access them.

You can find the results of research in textbooks, newspapers, popular magazines (e.g., *Economist, The Nation,* and *In These Times*), and radio or television news, but these are not true reports of scientific research. Rather, they are condensed summaries of true reports. Authors or journalists selected them for their popular appeal or teaching usefulness and rewrote them for a general audience. Such popularizations lack essential details that the scientific community requires for a serious evaluation of the research and for use in building the knowledge base.

Scholarly Journals

A researcher who conducts a complete literature review will examine all research outlets. Different types of reports require different search strategies. Let us begin with scholarly journals because they are the place in which most reports appear and are the most crucial outlet. As you saw in Chapter 1, they are central to the communication system of science.

A growing number of scientific journals, such as *Criminology* and *Justice Quarterly,* publish criminologists' research results. There are quite a few others, many of which have a broader emphasis than simply criminal justice in the United States. Some of these emphasize an international perspective, such as *International Journal of Comparative and Applied Criminal Justice, Crime, Law, and Social Change; The Australian and New Zealand Journal of Criminology*; and *The British Journal of Criminology*. Others emphasize a broader conception of justice (i.e., social justice), such as *Social Justice, Crime and Social Justice,* and *Social Problems*. Still others emphasize human rights issues, such as *Human Rights Watch* and *Humanity and Society*. These scientific journals and others are of considerable interest to criminologists.

Your college library has a section for scholarly journals and magazines, or, in some cases, they may be mixed with books. Look at a map of library facilities or ask a librarian to find this section. The most recent issues, which look like thin paperbacks or thick magazines, are often physically separate in a "current periodicals" section. This is done to store them temporarily and make them available until the library receives all the issues of a volume. Most often, libraries bind all issues of a volume together as a book before adding it to their permanent collection.

Scholarly journals from many different fields are placed together with popular magazines. All are periodicals, or *serials* in the jargon of librarians. Thus, you will find popular magazines (e.g., *Time, Road and Track, Cosmopolitan,* and *Atlantic Monthly*) next to journals for philosophy, criminology, literature, sociology, chemistry, corrections, human rights, and so on. Some areas of study have more scholarly journals than others. For instance, the "pure" academic fields, such as criminology, usually have more than the "applied" or practical fields, such as criminal justice or police studies. The journals are listed by title in a card catalog or in a computerized catalog system. Libraries can provide you with a list of periodicals to which they subscribe.

Many libraries do not retain physical, paper copies of older journals. To save space and costs, they retain only microfilm versions. There are hundreds of scholarly journals in most academic fields, with each costing $50 to $1,500 per year. Only the large research libraries subscribe to all of them. You may have to borrow a journal or photocopy of an article from a distant library through an *interlibrary loan service*, a system by which libraries lend books or materials to other libraries. Few libraries allow people to check out recent issues of scholarly journals. You should plan to use these in the library. A few experimental scholarly journals are available in an electronic form, to be read using computers via the Internet.

Once you find the periodicals section, wander down the aisles and skim what is on the shelves. You will see volumes containing many research reports. Each title of a scholarly journal has a call number like that of a regular library book. Libraries often arrange them alphabetically by title. Because journals change titles, it may create confusion if the journal is shelved under its original title.

Scholarly journals differ by field and by type. Most contain articles that report on research in an academic field. Some cover an entire academic field or discipline (e.g., criminology, sociology, etc.) and contain reports from the entire field. Topics may thus range from the etiology of crime to terrorism. Others specialize in a subfield of criminology, such as corrections, policing, corporate crime, criminal law, to mention a few. There are scholarly journals that try to bridge the gap between academic disciplines, such as criminology and psychology or criminology and public policy, and others that try to popularize academic research in order to reach a wider audience. One journal even focuses on the teaching of criminology (i.e., *Journal of Criminal Justice Education*).

Scholarly journals are published as rarely as once a year or as frequently as weekly. Most appear four to six times a year. For example, *Justice Quarterly* appears four times a year. To assist in locating articles, librarians and scholars have developed a system for tracking scholarly journals and the articles in them. Each issue is assigned a date, volume number, and issue number. This information makes it easier to locate an article. Such information—along with details such as author, title, and page number—is called an article's *citation* and is used in bibliographies. When a journal is first published, it begins with volume 1, number 1, and continues increasing the numbers thereafter. Although most journals follow a similar system, there are enough exceptions that you have to pay close attention to citation information. For most journals, each volume is one year. If you see a journal issue with volume 52, it probably means that the journal has been in existence for 52 years. Most, but not all, journals begin their publishing cycle in January.

Most journals number pages by volume, not by issue. The first issue of a volume usually begins with page 1, and page numbering continues throughout the entire volume. For example, the first page of volume 52, issue 4, may be page 547. Most journals have an index for each volume and a table of contents for each issue that lists the title, the author's or authors' names, and the page on which the article begins. Issues contain as few as 1 or 2 articles or as many as 50. Most have 8 to 18 articles, which may be 5 to 50 pages long. The articles often have *abstracts*, short summaries on the first page of the article or grouped together at the beginning of the issue.

An article's citation is the key to locating it. Suppose, for example, you wish to read more about the theory of restorative justice. One of the citations you would find in the card catalog is:

Sarre, Rick. (1997). Justice as restoration. *Peace Review* 9(4):541–547.

This tells you that the article was written by Rick Sarre and that is was published in 1997 in volume 9, issue 4 of *Peace Review*. The article is seven pages long, from page 541 to page 547.

There are many ways to cite the literature. Formats for citing literature in the text itself vary, with the internal citation format of using an author's last name and date of publication in parentheses being very popular. The full citation appears in a separate bibliography or reference section. There are many styles for full citations of journal articles, with books and other types of works each having a separate style. When citing articles, it is best to check with an instructor, journal, or other outlet for the desired format. Almost all include the names of authors, article title, journal name, and volume and page numbers. Beyond these basic elements, there is great variety. Some include the authors' first names, others use initials only. Some include all authors, others give only the first one. Some include information on the issue or month of publication, others do not (see Figure 5.1).

Citation formats can get complex. Two major reference tools on the topic in social science are the *Chicago Manual of Style*, which has nearly 80 pages on bibliographies and reference formats, and the *American Psychological Association Publication Manual*, which devotes about 60 pages to the topic. Criminology journals generally use the American Sociological Association reference style.

Books

Books communicate many types of information, provoke thought, and entertain. There are many types of books: picture books, textbooks, short story books, novels, popular fiction or nonfiction, religious books, children's books, and others. Our concern here is with those books containing reports of original research or collections of research articles. Libraries shelve these books and assign call numbers to them, as they do with other types of books. You can find citation information on them (e.g., title, author, publisher) in the library's catalog system.

It is not easy to distinguish a book that reports on a piece of research from other books. You are more likely to find such books in a college or university library. Some publishers, such as university presses, specialize in publishing

---

FIGURE 5.1   Different Reference Citations for a Journal Article

A recent article by Kraska and Cubellis on paramilitary policing in the United States appeared in *Justice Quarterly*. Below are various ways to cite the article. (*Justice Quarterly* uses the ASA style.)

ASA STYLE

Kraska, Peter B., and Luis J. Cubellis. 1997. "Militarizing Mayberry and beyond: Making sense of American paramilitary policing." *Justice Quarterly* 14:607–29.

APA STYLE

Kraska, P., & Cubellis, L. (1997). Militarizing Mayberry: Making sense of American paramilitary policing. *Justice Quarterly, 14*(4), 607–629.

OTHER STYLES

Kraska Peter B., and Louis J. Cubellis, 1997. "Militarizing Mayberry and beyond: Making sense of American paramilitary policing." *Justice Q.*14(4): 607–629.

Kraska, P. & L. Cubellis. (1997). Militarizing Mayberry and beyond: Making sense of American paramilitary policing. *Justice Quarterly* 14, 607–629.

them. Nevertheless, there is no guaranteed method for identifying one without reading it.

Certain types of criminological research are more likely to appear in book form than others. For example, ethnographic studies and comparative-historical studies are more likely to be published as a book, whereas quantitative survey research is often published as an article. Of course, there are exceptions to this. Indeed, quite often a criminologist will publish two or three articles on a specific topic and then publish a book on that same topic. Books are invariably more nuanced than articles, often giving a more thorough treatment to the criminological issues addressed in the original articles.

Locating original research articles in books can be difficult because there is no single source listing them. Three types of books contain collections of articles or research reports. The first is designed for teaching purposes. Such books, called *readers*, may include original research reports. Usually, articles on a topic from scholarly journals are gathered and edited to be easier for nonspecialists to read and understand.

The second type of collection is designed for scholars and may gather journal articles or may contain original research or theoretical essays on a specific topic. Some collections contain articles from journals that are difficult to locate. They may include original research reports organized around a specialized topic. The table of contents lists the titles and authors. Libraries shelve these collections with other books, and some library catalog systems include them.

Finally, there are annual research books that contain reports on studies that are not found elsewhere. These are hybrids between scholarly journals and collections of articles. They appear year after year, with volume numbers for each year, but they are not journals. Some annual books specialize in literature reviews, touching on issues of deviance, crime, and social control (e.g., *Annual Review of Sociology* and *Annual Review of Anthropology*). There is no comprehensive list of these books as there is for scholarly journals. The only way someone new to an area can find out about them is by spending a lot of time in the library or asking a researcher who is already familiar with a topic area.

Citations or references to books are easier than article citations. They include the author's name, book title, year and place of publication, and publisher's name.

Dissertations

All graduate students who receive the Ph.D. degree are required to complete a work of original research, which they write up as a dissertation thesis. The dissertation is bound and shelved in the library of the university that granted the Ph.D. About half of all dissertations are eventually published as books or articles. Because dissertations report on original research, they can be valuable sources of information. Some students who receive the master's degree conduct original research and write a master's thesis, but fewer master's theses involve serious research, and they are much more difficult to locate than unpublished dissertations.

Specialized indexes list dissertations completed by students at accredited universities. For example, *Dissertation Abstracts International* lists dissertations with their authors, titles, and universities. This index is organized by topic and contains an abstract of each dissertation. You can borrow most dissertations via interlibrary loan from the degree-granting university if the university permits this. An alternative is to purchase a copy from a national dissertation microfilm/photocopy center like the one at the University of Michigan, Ann Arbor, for U.S. universities. Some large research libraries contain copies of dissertations from other libraries if others have previously requested them.

Government Documents

The federal government of the United States, the governments of other nations, state or provincial-level governments, the United Nations, and other international agencies such as the World Bank, all sponsor studies and publish reports of the research. Many college and university libraries have these documents in their holdings, usually in a special "government documents" section. These reports are rarely found in the catalog system. You must use specialized lists of publications and indexes, usually with the help of a librarian, to locate these reports. Most college and university libraries hold only the most frequently requested documents and reports.

Policy Reports and Presented Papers

A researcher conducting a thorough review of the literature will examine these two sources, which are difficult for all but the trained specialist to obtain. Research institutes and policy centers (e.g., Brookings Institute, Institute for Research on Poverty, Rand Corporation, etc.) publish papers and reports. Some major research libraries purchase these and shelve them with books. The only way to be sure of what has been published is to write directly to the institute or center and request a list of reports.

Each year, the professional associations in academic fields (e.g., sociology, criminology, criminal justice, etc.) hold annual meetings. Hundreds of researchers assemble to give, listen to, or discuss oral reports of recent research. Most of these oral reports are available as written papers to those attending the meeting. People who do not attend the meetings but who are members of the association receive a program of the meeting, listing each paper to be presented with its title, author, and author's place of employment. They can write directly to the author and request a copy of the paper. Many, but not all, of the papers are later published as articles. The papers may be listed in indexes or abstract services (to be discussed).

HOW TO CONDUCT A SYSTEMATIC REVIEW

Define and Refine a Topic

Just as a researcher must plan and clearly define a topic and research question when beginning a research project, you need to begin a literature review with a clearly defined, well-focused research question and a plan. A good review topic should be as focused as a research question. (You can read more about focusing research questions in the next chapter.) For example, "crime" is much too broad. A more appropriate review topic might be "economic inequality and crime rates across nations." If you conduct a context review for a research project, it should be slightly broader than the specific research question being tested. Often, a researcher will not finalize a specific research question for a study until he or she has reviewed the literature. The review helps bring greater focus to the research question.

Design a Search

After choosing a focused research question for the review, the next step is to plan a search strategy. The reviewer needs to decide on the type of review, its extensiveness, and the types of materials to include. The key is to be careful, systematic, and organized. Set parameters on your search: how much time you will devote to it, how far back in time you will look, the minimum number of research reports you will examine, how many libraries you will visit, and so forth.

Also, decide how to record the bibliographic citation for each reference you find and how to take notes (e.g., in a notebook, on 3 × 5 cards, in a computer file). Develop a schedule, because several visits are usually necessary. You should begin a file folder or computer file in which you can place possible sources and ideas for new sources. As the review proceeds, it should become more focused.

Locate Research Reports

Locating research reports depends on the type of report or "outlet" of research being searched. As a general rule, use multiple search strategies in order to counteract the limitations of a single search method.

Articles in Scholarly Journals.   As discussed earlier, most criminological research is likely published in scholarly journals. These journals are the vehicles of communication in science. Before beginning a search, pick up a journal in an area with which you are somewhat familiar and skim its contents. There are dozens of journals, many going back decades, each containing many articles. The task of searching for articles can be formidable. Luckily, specialized publications make the task easier.

You may have used an index for general publications such as the *Reader's Guide to Periodical Literature*. Many academic fields have "abstracts" or "indexes" for the scholarly literature. For education-related topics, the Educational Resources Information Center (ERIC) system is especially valuable. There are over 100 such publications. You can usually find them in the reference section of a library. Many abstracts or index services as well as ERIC are available via computer access, which speeds the search process (see Appendix C).

Abstracts or indexes are published on a regular basis (monthly, six times a year, etc.) and allow a reader to look up articles by author name or subject. The journals covered by the abstract or index are listed in it, often in the front. An index, such as the *Social Sciences Index*, lists only the citation, whereas an abstract such as *Criminologcial Abstracts* lists the citation and has a copy of the article's abstract. Abstracts do not give you all the findings and details of a research project. Researchers use abstracts to screen articles for relevance, then locate the more relevant articles. Abstracts may also include papers presented at professional meetings.

It may sound as if all you have to do is to go find the index in the reference section of the library and look up a topic. Unfortunately, things are more complicated than that. In order to cover the studies across many years, you may have to look through many issues of the abstracts or indexes. Also, the subjects or topics listed in the abstracts or indexes are broad. The specific research question that interests you may fit into several subject areas. You should check each one. For example, for the topic of illegal drugs in high schools, you might look up these subjects: drug addiction, drug abuse, substance abuse, drug laws, illegal drugs, high schools, and secondary schools. Many of the articles under a subject area will not be relevant for your literature review. Also, there is a 3- to 12-month time lag between the publication of an article and its appearance in the abstracts or indexes. Unless you are at a major research library, the most useful article may not be available in your library. You can obtain it only by using an interlibrary loan service, or it may be in a foreign language that you do not read.

Most research-oriented libraries subscribe to the *Social Science Citation Index (SSCI)* of the Institute for Scientific Information. This is a valuable resource with information on over 1,400 journals. It is similar to other indexes and abstracts, but it takes time to learn how to use it. The SSCI comes in four books. One is a source index, which provides complete citation information on journal articles. The other three books refer to articles in the source book. They are organized by subject, by the university or research center for which the researcher works, or by authors who are cited in the reference sections of other articles.

You can begin a SSCI search in one of three ways: (1) with a subject (e.g., alcohol use among children), (2) with a known research center (e.g., the Austrian Institute of Criminology), or (3) with an earlier article (e.g., Russell's "Reintegrative Shaming and the 'Frozen Antithesis': Braithwaite and Elias" in the November 1998 issue of the *Journal of Sociology*). The first search directs you to the authors of current research reports. The second search identifies all authors from the same research center who published articles. The third search directs you to all citations included in earlier article's reference section. This last type of search is important when a researcher wants to trace research that influenced other research. For example, suppose you wanted to trace the evolution of the notion of "reintegrative shaming" in criminological research. You could do this by looking at the SSCI to identify the key references used in articles published on the topic. Even if your library does not have the *Social Science Citation Index*, a good search principle is to examine the bibliography of articles to find additional articles or books on a topic.

Another resource for locating articles is the computerized literature search, which works on the same principle as an abstract or an index. Researchers organize computerized searches in several ways—by author, by article title, by subject, or by keyword. A *keyword* is an important term for a topic that is likely to be found in a title. You will want to use six to eight keywords in most computer-based searches and consider several synonyms. The computer's searching method can vary and most only look for a keyword in a title or abstract. If you choose too few words or very narrow terms, you will miss a lot of relevant articles. If you choose too many words or very broad terms, you will get a huge number of irrelevant articles. The best way to learn the appropriate breadth and number of keywords is by trial and error.

There are numerous computer-assisted search databases or systems. Some may be on line at your library, some are on CD-ROM, and others are available through the Internet or another long-distance connection. (The Internet is explained more in Appendix C.) For now, it is sufficient to say that the Internet connects millions of computers around the world to each other. A person with a computer and an Internet hook-up can search some article index collections, the catalogs of libraries, and other information sources around the globe if they are available on the Internet.

All computerized searching methods share a similar logic, but each has its own method of operation to learn. Often, the same articles will appear in multiple scholarly literature databases, but each database may identify a few new articles not found in the others. This points to a critical lesson: "Do not rely exclusively on com-

puterized literature searches, on abstracting services, [or] on the literature in a single discipline, or on an arbitrarily defined time period" (Bausell, 1994:24).

Scholarly Books. Finding scholarly books on a subject can be difficult. The subject topics of library catalog systems are usually incomplete and too broad to be useful. Moreover, they list only books that are in a particular library system, although you may be able to search other libraries for interlibrary loan books. Libraries organize books by call numbers based on subject matter. Again, the subject matter classifications may not reflect the subjects of interest to you or all the subjects discussed in a book. Once you learn the system for your library, you will find that most books on a topic will share the main parts of the call number. In addition, librarians can help you locate books that may be in other libraries. For example, the *Library of Congress National Union Catalog* lists all books in the U.S. Library of Congress. Librarians have access to sources that list books at other libraries, or you can use Internet. There is no sure-fire way to locate relevant books. Use multiple search methods, including a look at journals that have book reviews and the bibliographies of articles.

Of course, there is still no substitute for the tried-and-true strategy of going to the library and spending time just browsing scholarly books of interest. Naturally, this strategy is most useful when used in conjunction with more systematic reviews of the literature, including computerized book searches.

Dissertations. A publication called *Dissertation Abstracts International* lists most dissertations. Like the indexes and abstracts for journal articles, it organizes dissertations by broad subject category, author, and date. Researchers look up all titles in the subject areas that include a topic. Unfortunately, after you have located the dissertation title and abstract, you may find that obtaining a copy of it takes time and involves added costs.

Government Documents. The "government documents" sections of libraries contain specialized lists of government documents. A useful index for documents issued by the U.S. federal government is the *Monthly Catalog of Government Documents,* which is often available on computer. It has been issued since 1885, but other supplemental sources should be used for research into documents more than a decade old. The catalog has an annual index, and monthly issues have subject, title, and author indexes. *Indexes to Congressional Hearings,* another useful source, lists committees and subjects going back to the late 1930s. *The Congressional Record* contains debate of the U.S. Congress with synopses of bills, voting records, and changes in bills. *United States Statutes* lists each individual U.S. federal law by year and subject. *The Federal Register,* a daily publication of the U.S. government, contains all rules, regulations, and announcements of federal agencies. It has both monthly and annual indexes. There are other indexes that cover treaties, technical announcements, and so forth.

Of particular interest to criminologists in the United States is the U.S. Bureau of Justice Statistics (BJS) publications. These publications cover a wide range of criminal justice topics—including criminal victimization, drug crimes, and female victims of violent crime—and are available through the National Criminal Justice Reference Service. Materials are kept up to date and are available on CD-ROM. Of course, other governments also publish similar indexes.

Do not overlook the documents published by international and nongovernmental organizations. Those relevant to criminologists include the United Nations Interregional Crime and Justice Research Institute, the United Nations Crime and Justice Information Network, and the United Nations Center for Human Rights. It is usually best to rely on the expertise of librarians for assistance in using these specialized indexes. The topics used by index makers may not be the best ones for your specific research question.

Policy Reports and Presented Papers. The most difficult sources to locate are policy reports and presented papers. They are listed in some bibliographies of published studies; some are listed in the abstracts or indexes. To locate these studies, try several methods: Write to research centers and ask for lists of publications, obtain lists of papers presented at professional meetings, and so forth. Once you locate a research report, try writing to the relevant author or institute.

What to Record

After you locate a source, you should write down all details of the reference (full names of authors, titles, volume, issue, pages, etc.). It is usually best to record more than the minimum needed to form a citation. Most researchers create one set of cards or a computer file with the full references and another with notes on the research report. Create a code or indicator to link unambiguously the reference or source of the notes to each note card or file. For example, put the last name of the first author and the year of the book or article on each note card or record. You can quickly look up the complete reference in a set of reference cards or file organized by author's last name and date. You will find it much easier to take all notes on the same type and size of paper or card, rather than having some notes on sheets of papers, others on cards, and so on. Researchers have to decide what to record about an article, book, or other source. It is better to err in the direction of recording too much rather than too little. In general, record the hypotheses tested, how major concepts were measured, the main findings, the basic design of the research, the group or sample used, and ideas for future study (see Box 5.3). It is wise to examine the report's bibliography and note sources that you can add to your search.

Photocopying all relevant articles or reports will save you time recording notes and will ensure that you will have an entire report. You can make notes on the photocopy. There are several warnings about this practice. First, photocopying can be expensive for a large literature search. Second, be aware of and obey copyright laws. U.S. copyright laws permit photocopying for personal research use. Third, remember to record or photocopy the entire article, including all citation information. Fourth, organizing entire articles can be cumbersome, especially if several different parts of a single article are being used. Finally, unless you highlight carefully or take good notes, you may have to reread the entire article later.

Organize Notes

After gathering a large number of references and notes, you need an organizing scheme. One approach is to group studies or specific findings by skimming notes and creating a mental map of how they fit together. Try several organizing schemes before settling on a final one. Organizing is a skill that improves with practice. For example, place notes into piles representing common themes, or draw charts comparing what different reports state about the same question, noting agreements and disagreements.

In the process of organizing notes, you will find that some references and notes do not fit and should be discarded as irrelevant. Also, you may discover gaps or areas and topics that are relevant but that you did not examine. This necessitates return visits to the library.

There are many organizing schemes. The best one depends on the purpose of the review. A context review implies organizing recent reports around a specific research question. A historical review implies organizing studies by major theme and by the date of publication. An integrative review implies organizing studies around core common findings of a field and the main hypotheses tested. A methodological review implies organizing studies by the topic and, within topic, by

---

Box 5.3 _____

How to Read Journal Articles

1. Read with a clear purpose or goal in mind. Are you reading for basic knowledge or to apply it to a specific question?
2. Skim the article before reading it all. What can you learn from the title, abstract, summary and conclusions, and headings? What are the topic, major findings, method, and main conclusion?
3. Consider your own orientation. What is your bias toward the topic, the method, the publication source, and so on, that may color your reading?
4. Marshal external knowledge. What do you already know about the topic and the methods used? How credible is the publication source?
5. Evaluate as you read the article. What errors are present? Do findings follow the data? Is the article consistent with assumptions of the approach it takes?
6. Summarize information as an abstract with the topic, the methods used, and the findings. Assess the factual accuracy of findings and cite questions about the article.

Source: Adapted from Katzer, Cook, and Crouch (1991: 199–207).

---

the design or method used. A theoretical review implies organizing studies by the theories and major thinkers being examined.

Write the Review

A literature review requires planning and good, clear writing, which requires a lot of rewriting. This step is often merged with organizing notes. All the rules of good writing (e.g., clear organizational structure, an introduction and conclusion, transitions between sections, etc.) apply to writing a literature review. Keep your purposes in mind when you write, and communicate clearly and effectively.

To prepare a good review, read articles and other literature critically. Recall that skepticism is a norm of science. It means that you should not accept what is written simply on the basis of the authority of its having been published. Question what you read, and evaluate it. The first hurdle to overcome is thinking something must be perfect just because it has been published.

Critically reading research reports requires skills that take time and practice to develop. Despite a peer review procedure and high rejection rates, errors and sloppy logic slip in. When reading an article, read carefully to see whether the introduction and title really fit with the rest of the article. Sometimes, titles, abstracts, or the introduction are misleading. They may not fully explain the research project's method and results. An article should be logically tight, and all the parts should fit together. Strong logical links should exist between parts of the argument. Weak articles make leaps in logic or omit transitional steps. Likewise, articles do not always make their theory or approach to research explicit. Be prepared to read the article more than once to determine its underlying theory or approach. (See Box 5.4 on taking notes on an article.)

The most critical areas of an article to read are the methods and results sections. Few studies are perfect. Researchers do not always describe the methods they used as fully as they should. Sometimes, the results presented in tables or charts do not match what the researcher says. For example, an author might overlook an important result in a table, while giving minor results too much attention. The careful reader evaluates how the research project was done and reads the data that are presented. Too frequently, authors give one interpretation and ignore equally possible interpretations. Also be careful when reading conclusions. Do not assume that they are entirely consistent with all the data; check the data for yourself.

WHAT A GOOD REVIEW LOOKS LIKE ONCE IT IS WRITTEN

An author should communicate a review's purpose to the reader by its organization. The *wrong* way to write a review is to list a series of research reports with a summary of the findings of each. This fails to communicate a sense of purpose. It reads as a set of notes strung together. Perhaps the reviewer got sloppy and skipped over the important organizing step in writing the review. The *right* way to write a review is to organize common findings or arguments together. A well-accepted approach is to address the most important ideas first, to logically link statements or findings, and to note discrepancies or weaknesses in the research (see Box 5.5, p. 100, for an example). You should paraphrase a few critical quotes and summarize the key findings (also see Appendix B).

CONCLUSION

Literature reviews allow consumers of criminology access to the information in research reports. They show the reviewer's familiarity with a body of knowledge; they show the path prior research has taken and how a current project is linked to it; they can integrate and summarize the current knowledge in a topic area; they are a way for researchers to learn from others; and they often stimulate new ideas and insights.

In this chapter, you learned about six types of literature reviews. You also learned the many outlets for research studies. Most are found only in college or university libraries. The most important outlets are scholarly journals and books. Other outlets include Ph.D. dissertations, government documents and policy reports, and papers presented at professional meetings.

A literature review requires a plan and a clear idea of the topic. When conducting a literature search, researchers use multiple search strategies because each single way of conducting a search has weaknesses. It is often necessary to consult with a reference librarian and use specialized publications called abstracts or indexes. Computerized searches can also be helpful, although they have limitations. Once you have located studies, take good notes and record and file details about the citation. A good review communicates with the reader and is organized around themes.

Box 5.4 _____

Example of Notes on an Article

FULL CITATION ON BIBLIOGRAPHY CARD

Kraska, Peter B., and Louis J. Cubellis. (1997). Militarizing Mayberry: Making sense of American paramilitary policing. *Justice Quarterly* 14:607–29.

NOTE CARD

Kraska and Cubellis, 1997

Topics: paramilitary policing, Swat teams, state violence

Research Question   The research question is: To what extent has the use of paramilitary police units (e.g., SWAT teams) become a normal practice in small-town police departments? There is relatively little empirical research on this topic.

Method   A sampling frame of all police departments (excluding federal) serving communities with between 25,000 and 50,000 inhabitants was constructed. There were 770 different police departments on the sampling frame. In March 1996, a 40-item questionnaire was mailed out. The response rate was 72% ($n = 552$). However, 79 departments were excluded, as they had more than 100 sworn officers (i.e., they were too large to be included in the sample). In addition, 40 departments were chosen for follow-up telephone interviews. The interviews lasted about 30 minutes and tended to be qualitative.

Findings   Over 65% of the U.S. small-town police departments have a paramilitary unit. Another 28% plan to develop one within the next few years. Most are equipped with the latest "tactical gear" such as semiautomatic shotguns, night vision equipment, sniper rifles, flash-bang grenades, battle dress uniforms, and dynamic entry tools.

A dramatic increase is seen in the number of units and in "call-outs" since 1980. Around two-thirds of the call-outs are for executing search and arrest warrants.

Around 17% of the departments use the units as proactive patrol forces in high-crime areas; they conduct "terry stops" (i.e., interrogate suspicious persons).

Most SWAT teams receive military training, usually by for-profit, tactical training schools.

There are about 18 police paramilitary officers for every 100 regular patrol officers in small-town police departments.

Box 5.5 _____

Examples of Good and Bad Reviews

EXAMPLE OF GOOD REVIEW

There is a long-running critique of prevailing conceptions of justice, particularly conceptions of criminal justice narrowly focused on the punishment of the individual offender. Mead (1918), in his essay on the psychology of punitive justice, noted how, on the one hand, "the attitude of hostility toward the lawbreaker has the unique advantage of uniting all members of the community in the emotional solidarity of aggression." But, as Mead also noted, "Hostility toward the lawbreaker inevitably brings with it the attitudes of retribution, repression, and exclusion. These provide no principles for the eradication of crime" (p. 465, as quoted in Coser and Rosenberg, 1976). More recently, Fuller (1998), Quinney (1993), and Pepinsky and Quinney (1991) have rejected punitive notions of violence embedded in the criminal justice system. They offer, in their place, a "peacemaking" perspective.

Other scholars have attempted to broaden the prevailing conception of criminal justice into one of social justice. A social justice conception, according to Rawls (1971:7), calls into question "the way in which the major social institutions distribute fundamental rights and duties and determine the division of advantages from social cooperation." Reiman (1998), Phillips (1986), and others find moral legitimacy only in legal systems that foster and regulate the just distribution of wealth and opportunity. Institutions of justice (e.g., law enforcement, judiciary, etc.) claim legitimacy to the extent they uphold a legal and social order that fosters social justice.

An emerging conception is that of "justice as restoration." In essence, this conception supports the reliance on informal community mechanisms for problem solving and victim-offender restoration (Sarre, 1997). For example, offenders can be brought back in line through processes of reintegrative shaming and family conferencing.

Finally, Wellford (1997:9) encourages criminologists to "make a more significant contribution to achieving a condition of justice that approximates the ideals of democratic societies."

EXAMPLE OF BAD REVIEW

There are different conceptions of justice. Sarre (1997) took the point of view that justice involves the repair of social injury. He suggests ways of doing that. Another approach has been to evaluate social institutions as to their degree of justice. Quite a number of philosophers and social scientists have taken this tack (e.g., Rawls, 1971; Phillips, 1986; Reiman, 1998). Even long ago, scholars have noted different conceptions of justice. Mead (1918) wrote at length about the psychology of punitive justice. Wellford (1997) stressed the need for criminologists to spend more time exploring the development of justice theory and research. It is likely that different conceptions of justice will continue to develop.

KEY TERMS _____

abstract	integrative review	methodological review
citation	interlibrary loan service	self-study review
context review	keyword	theoretical review
historical review	meta-analysis	

REVIEW QUESTIONS _____

1. What are the four major goals of a review of the literature?
2. What type of review is likely to organize studies in chronological order?
3. What is the major purpose of a theoretical review?
4. Which outlet of reports on research studies is easiest to locate?

5. How would you go about locating a dissertation?

6. What is the page-numbering system used in most scholarly journals?

7. What are the three types of books that contain collections of research articles, and which of the three contains all original research studies?

8. List the first several steps in conducting a systematic review.

9. How does one go about doing a computerized literature search? What are its advantages and disadvantages?

10. What distinguishes a strong from a weak literature review?

NOTE

1. See Hunter, Schmidt, and Jackson (1982).

RECOMMENDED READINGS

Bart, Pauline, and Linda Frankel. (1986). *The student sociologist's handbook*, 4th ed. New York: Random House. This is an introduction to using the research literature for the sociology student. It has excellent discussion of the mechanics of library research, and it describes a variety of sociology journals and indexes. There is even an overview of government documents.

Beasley, David. (1988). *How to use a research library.* New York: Oxford University Press. As the title suggests, this book describes how to use a major research library. Many of the procedures described in the book apply to any research library. The examples in the book are taken from the New York Public Library, which is one of the few city public research libraries. Most research libraries are located at major universities. There are also specialized research libraries (e.g., the Newberry Library in Chicago) and the major U.S. government research library, the Library of Congress.

Captor, Renee S. (1998). *Library research for the analysis of public policy.* New York: Council on International Public Affairs. This short but helpful book serves as a general introduction to library research as well as a specific guide to public policy research. Exercises include the use of reference books, periodicals, newspapers, and so on.

Light, Richard J., and David B. Pillemer. (1984). *Summing up: The science of reviewing research.* Cambridge, MA: Harvard University Press. The authors provide an innovative approach to conducting a comprehensive review of research literature and synthesizing it. The book is organized around four themes: A review needs a precise research question to guide it; disagreements among findings are valuable; quantitative and qualitative studies both have important roles to play; and, despite their usefulness, statistical techniques are not a substitute for conceptual clarity in determining what a body of literature says.

Rose, Gerry. (1982). *Deciphering sociological research.* Beverly Hills, CA: Sage. This book is divided into two parts. Part I explains how to read and figure out what is said in a research report; Part II presents 12 articles published between 1953 and 1976. The author emphasizes the importance of identifying the type of study and its link to theory (as Chapter 2 in this book discussed) and the approach to research used (as discussed in Chapter 3) in order to decipher an article.

QUANTITATIVE RESEARCH DESIGNS

The control of statistics is one of the critical functions of power in a democratic society. The numbers define the limits of the possible; they confer the awesome mathematical legitimacy of "fact" upon some parts of reality and deny it to others. . . . [I]t must always be kept in mind that the statistical columns are the surrogates for human misery.

—Michael Harrington, *The New American Poverty*, p. 71

INTRODUCTION

Numbers seem to have an almost hypnotic effect on people. Once cited, statistical facts drive the machinery of political persuasion. They circulate in conversation, spreading out from person to person, back and forth in debate among scholars and scientists, and into the media. The mass media can be counted on to give statistical data a blunt treatment. The media tend to simplify statistics into sound bites and entirely ignore methodological caveats that might undermine the intended effect of media coverage. Yet, this is how most people become acquainted with statistical data, and too often how legislative issues are orchestrated. At each turn, the facts gain in the

power to define what is real and what can be done to change it. In short, people tend to reify numbers.

There is an old saying, "The devil is in the details." How true. Indeed, "the devil" lays hidden in the methodological details of any crime or justice statistic. It is encoded in the research question being asked, in the operational definitions being applied, in the level of measurement, in the choice of sample and technique, and so on. Before any statistic can or should be applied, one must first lay bare the methodological details that went in to constructing the "fact." This is the only way to deal with "the devil," and, as Harrington (1984) argued, the only way to interpret statistical data democratically.

In this chapter, you will begin to learn the language of quantitative criminology—a language of variables, units of analysis, and causal relationships. As you become conversant in the language, you will also learn how to refine a diffuse topic into a well-focused research question. Additionally, you will have an opportunity to think critically about research design. These skills will not only improve your ability to do criminological research but it will also enable you to better evaluate the barrage of statistical claims that bombard each of us in modern society.

LEARNING THE LANGUAGE OF VARIABLES AND HYPOTHESES

What Is a Variable?

Variation and Variables. The *variable* is a central idea in quantitative research. Simply defined, a variable is a concept that varies. The language of quantitative research is a language of variables and relationships among variables. In Chapter 3, you learned about two types of concepts: those that refer to a fixed phenomenon (e.g., organized crime) and those that vary in quantity, intensity, or amount (e.g., dollar amount of money laundered).

The second type of concept and measures of the concepts are variables. Variables take on two or more values. Once you begin to look for them, you will see variables everywhere. For example, "nationality of organized crime groups" is a variable. We have the Russian *Mafiya,* the Sicilian *La Cosa Nostra,* the Colombian drug cartels, the Chinese Triads, the Japanese *Yakuza,* and the Jamaican posses, to cite a number of them. Another variable is "the number of murders committed by organized crime groups." In New York, for example, there were 200 Jamaican posse-related killings in 1988 alone (Sullivan, 1997). Yet another variable is the "number of illegal immigrants entering the United States."

The values or the categories of a variable are its *attributes.* It is easy to confuse variables with attributes. Variables and attributes are related, but they have distinct purposes. The confusion arises because the attribute of one variable can itself become a separate variable with a slight change in definition. The distinction is between concepts themselves that vary and conditions within concepts that vary. For example, the Japanese *Yakuza* is not a variable. Rather, it is one of the categories of the variable "nationality of organized crime groups." However, by slightly redefining it, it can be transformed into a distinct variable, such as "the number of *Yakuza* members." Knowing the number of members would be an important variable for criminologists studying the changing leadership and organizational structure of the *Yakuza.* (By the way, Scaramella [1997] estimated the *Yakuza* to have over 20,000 members.) Thus, we see that all variables take on a range of values or categories. To put it simply, variables vary.

You need to redefine concepts of interest in a quantitative research project into the language of variables. As the examples of variables and attributes illustrate, slight changes in definition change a nonvariable into a variable concept. As you saw in Chapter 3, concepts are the building blocks of theory; they organize thinking about the social world. Clear concepts with careful definitions are essential in theory.

Types of Variables. Researchers who focus on causal relations usually begin with an effect, then search for its causes. Variables are classified into three basic types, depending on their location in a causal relationship. The cause variable, or the one that identifies forces or conditions that act on something else, is the *independent variable.* The variable that is the effect or is the result or outcome of another variable is the *dependent variable.* The independent variable is "independent of" prior causes that act on it, whereas the dependent variable "depends on" the cause.

It is not always easy to determine whether a variable is independent or dependent. Two questions help you identify the independent variable. First, does it come before other variables in time? Independent variables come before any other type. Second, if the variables occur at the same time, does the author suggest that one variable has an impact on another variable? Independent variables affect or have an impact on other variables. Research topics are often phrased in terms of the dependent variables because the dependent variable is the phenomenon to be explained. For example, if a criminologist wanted to know why certain organized crime groups are able to distribute narcotics on an international scale while others are not, then the dependent variable is "the group's ability to distribute narcotics."

A basic causal relationship requires only an independent and a dependent variable. A third type of variable, the *intervening variable,* appears in more complex causal relations. It comes between the independent and dependent variables and shows the link or mechanism between them. Advances in knowledge depend not only on documenting cause-and-effect relationships but also on specifying the mechanisms that account for the causal relation. In a sense, the intervening variable acts as a dependent variable with respect to the independent variable and acts as an independent variable toward the dependent variable.[1]

Consider the example having to do with an organized crime groups's ability to market narcotics. What factors are involved in determining the scope or extent of a group's drug market (i.e., local, regional, national, international)? Perhaps one key independent variable is the number of members. Groups with a large number of members have at least the potential of maintaining a wider distribution network than crime groups with fewer members. But there is an intervening variable that seems to be just as important. The intervening variable is group cohesion. Those crime groups whose members are tightly bound to the culture of the group are better able to avoid police detection. Indeed, one of the most difficult challenges for law enforcement is trying to penetrate these secret crime organizations. Combining the three variables into a causal chain, we have theoretical relationships to explain differences in the scope of narcotics distribution networks. The independent variable

(i.e., the organized crime group's number of members) works through the intervening variable (i.e., the degree of group cohesion), which in turn determines the value of the dependent variable (i.e., the scope of the crime group's narcotics distribution network).

Social reality is complex, however. In order to formulate more comprehensive explanations, criminologists must construct complex theories. These theories may contain many different independent and intervening variables. Thus, to explain in precise terms why crime organizations have such different capacities for distributing narcotics, it is necessary to include more variables in the theoretical model. Besides number of members and group cohesion, a string of other variables are linked together in the causal chain. Among them are "the degree of cooperation among law enforcement agencies"; "the extent of international money laundering, drug trafficking, and conspiracy legislation"; "the financial assets of the organized crime group"; and "the degree of public support for drug enforcement." These six independent and intervening variables would be combined into a theory to explain the dependent variable (i.e., "the scope of the organized crime group's narcotics distribution network").

It is likely that there are other criminological theories trying to explain the same phenomenon. These theories may well use some of the same independent and intervening variables. They might also include different variables in their causal explanation. For example, a theory of drug trafficking networks may emphasize "the cultural differences of the crime groups" as one of its key independent variables. Or it might emphasize "the extent of political corruption" as an important independent variable. The point is, any particular theory and related research examines only a small segment of the overall causal chain. To put it differently, no single criminological theory has been able to include every single variable that goes into the full explanation of why something occurs. However unique, each theory gives only a partial explanation or understanding.

Causal Relationships and Hypotheses

The Hypothesis and Causality. A *hypothesis* is a proposition to be tested or a tentative statement of a relationship between two variables. Hypotheses are guesses about how the social world works; they are stated in a value-neutral form. Kerlinger (1979:35) noted that

> *hypotheses are much more important in scientific research than they would appear to be just by knowing what they are and how they are constructed. They have a deep and highly significant purpose of taking man out of himself, so to speak. . . . Hypotheses are powerful tools for the advancement of knowledge, because, although formulated by man, they can be tested and shown to be correct or incorrect apart from man's values and beliefs.*

A causal hypothesis has five characteristics (see Box 6.1). The first two characteristics define the minimum elements of a hypothesis. The third restates the hypothesis. For example, the hypothesis that stronger group cohesion increases a crime group's drug distribution network can be restated as a prediction: Crime groups that have stronger cohesion among its members have more expansive drug distribution networks than do crime groups with weaker cohesion. The prediction can be tested against empirical evidence. The fourth characteristic states that the hypothesis

should not be viewed in isolation. It should be logically tied to a research question and to a theory. Researchers test hypotheses to answer the research question or to find empirical support for a theory. The last characteristic requires that a researcher use empirical data to test the hypothesis. Statements that are necessarily true as a result of logic, or questions that are impossible to answer through scientific observation (e.g., Is taking illicit drugs a sin?) cannot be scientific hypotheses.

Causal hypotheses can be stated in several ways. Sometimes the word *cause* is used, but this is not necessary (see Box 6.2). For example, the hypothesis contained in our "narcotics distribution" theory can be stated in a variety of ways.

Researchers avoid using the term *proved* when testing hypotheses. You might hear the word *proof* used in journalism, courts of law, or advertisements, but you will rarely hear research scientists use it. A jury, for instance, says that the evidence "proves" a defendant is guilty or, conversely, that the evidence was not compelling enough "to prove" the defendant is guilty. This is

---

Box 6.1 _____

Five Characteristics of Causal Hypotheses

1. It has at least two variables.
2. It expresses a causal or cause-effect relationship between the variables.
3. It can be expressed as a prediction or an expected future outcome.
4. It is logically linked to a research question and a theory.
5. It is falsifiable; that is, it is capable of being tested against empirical evidence and shown to be true or false.

Box 6.2 _____

Ways to State Causal Relations

- Having more members causes a crime group's drug distribution network to expand.
- Increased group cohesion increases the likelihood a crime group's drug distribution network will expand.
- The degree of cooperation between law enforcement agencies is related to the scope of a crime group's drug distribution network.
- The number of international drug trafficking laws and treaties influences the scope of a crime group's drug distribution network.
- The *more* financial assets a crime group has, the *wider* the scope of its drug distribution network.
- The *greater* the public's support for drug enforcement, the *smaller* the crime group's drug distribution network.

not the language of scientific research. In the language of science, knowledge is tentative, and creating knowledge is an ongoing process that avoids premature closure.

Scientists do not say they have proved a hypothesis or the causal relationship it represents. Proof implies finality, absolute certainty, or something that does not need further investigation. *Proof* is too strong a term for the cautious world of science. Evidence supports or confirms, but does not prove, the hypothesis. Even after hundreds of studies show the same results, as with the link between cigarette smoking and lung cancer, scientists do not say that they have absolute proof.

The best science can say is that overwhelming evidence, or all studies to date, support or are consistent with the hypothesis. Scientists do not want to close off the possibility of discovering new evidence that might contradict past findings. They do not want to cut off future inquiry or stop exploring intervening mechanisms. History contains many examples of relationships that were once thought to be proved but were later found to be in error. *Proof* is used when referring to logical or mathematical relations, as in a mathematical proof, but not in discussing empirical research.

Testing and Refining Hypothesis.   Knowledge rarely advances on the basis of one test of a single hypothesis, although a researcher may test one hypothesis in a research project. In fact, it is easy to get a distorted picture of the research process by focusing on a single research project that tests one hypothesis. Knowledge develops over time as researchers throughout the scientific community test many hypotheses. It grows from shifting and winnowing through many hypotheses. Each hypothesis represents an explanation of a dependent variable. If the evidence fails to support some hypotheses, they are gradually eliminated from consideration. Those that receive support remain in contention. Theorists and researchers are constantly creating new hypotheses to challenge those that have received support.

Figure 6.1 represents an example of the process of shifting through hypotheses over time. At a given starting point (1960), there are eight contending hypotheses. Over the years, different researchers test the hypotheses until, by 2000, two hypotheses remain as possibilities. Neither had been developed in the beginning; the others were created as researchers sorted out existing evidence and developed new theories. The process continues into the future as the hypotheses are tested against empirical evidence.

Scientists are a skeptical group. Support for a hypothesis in one research project is not sufficient for them to accept it. The principle of replication says that a hypothesis needs several tests with consistent and repeated support to gain broad acceptance. Another way to strengthen confidence in a hypothesis is to test related causal linkages in the theory from which it comes.

The strongest contender or the hypothesis with the greatest empirical support is accepted as the best explanation at the time. The logic suggests that the more alternatives we test a hypothesis against, the greater our confidence in it. Some tests of hypotheses are called *crucial experiments* or crucial studies. This is a type of study where

> two or more alternative explanations for some phenomenon are available, each being compatible with the empirically given data; the crucial experiment is designed to yield results that can be accounted for by only one of the alternatives, which is thereby shown to be "the correct explanation." (Kaplan, 1964:151–152)

Thus, the infrequent crucial experiment or research project is an important test of theory. Hypotheses from two different theories confront each other in crucial experiments, and one is knocked out of the competition. It is rare, but significant, when it occurs.

Types of Hypotheses.   Hypotheses are links in a theoretical causal chain and can take several forms. Researchers use them to test the direction and strength of a relationship between variables. When a hypothesis defeats its competitors, or

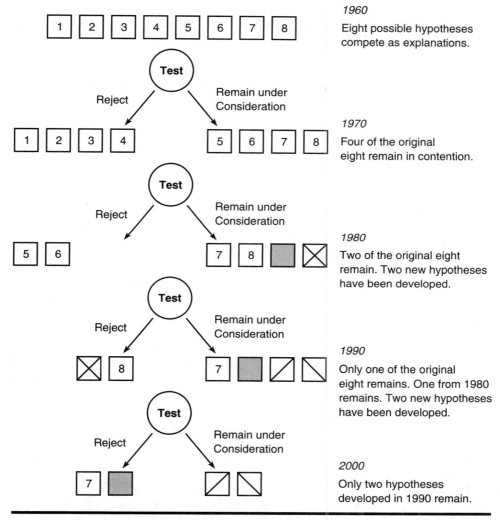

FIGURE 6.1 How the Process of Hypotheses Testing Operates over Time to Create New Knowledge and Contending Hypotheses

offers alternative explanations for a causal relation, it indirectly lends support to the researcher's explanation. A curious aspect of hypothesis testing is that researchers treat evidence that supports a hypothesis differently from evidence that opposes it. They give negative evidence more importance. The idea that negative evidence is critical when evaluating a hypothesis comes from

the *logic of disconfirming hypotheses.*[2] It is associated with Karl Popper's idea of falsification (see Chapter 4) and with the use of null hypotheses (see later in this section).

Recall the preceding discussion of proof. A hypothesis is never completely proved, but it can be disproved. A researcher with supporting evidence can say only that the hypothesis remains a possibility or that it is still in the running. Negative evidence is more significant because the hypothesis becomes "tarnished" or "soiled" if the evidence fails to support it. This is because a hypothesis makes predictions. Negative and disconfirming evidence shows that the predictions are wrong. Positive or confirming evidence for a hypothesis is less critical because alternative hypotheses may make the same prediction. A researcher who finds confirming evidence for a prediction may not elevate one explanation over its alternatives.

For example, a man stands on a street corner with an umbrella and claims that his umbrella protects him from falling elephants. His hypothesis that the umbrella provides protection has supporting evidence. He has not had a single elephant fall on him in all the time he has had his umbrella open. Yet, such supportive evidence is weak; it also is consistent with an alternative hypothesis—that elephants do not fall from the sky. Both predict that the man will be safe from falling elephants. Negative evidence for the hypothesis—the one elephant that falls on him and his umbrella, crushing both—would destroy the hypothesis for good.

Researchers test hypotheses in two ways: a straightforward way and a null hypothesis way. Many quantitative researchers, especially experimenters, frame hypotheses in terms of a *null hypothesis* based on the logic of the disconfirming hypotheses. They test hypotheses by looking for evidence that will allow them to accept or reject the null hypothesis. Most people talk about a hypothesis as a way to predict a relationship. The null hypothesis does the opposite. It predicts no relationship.

For example, if a criminologist has a hunch that public support for drug enforcement is related to the scope of a crime group's distribution network, then he or she might want to test the null hypothesis that there is no relationship between the two variables. The null hypothesis is then used with a corresponding *alternative hypothesis* or experimental hypothesis. The alternative hypothesis says that a relationship exists— that is, public support for drug enforcement serves to limit the scope of drug markets.

For most people, the null hypothesis approach is a backward way of hypothesis testing. Null hypothesis thinking rests on the assumption that researchers try to discover a relationship, so hypothesis testing should be designed to make finding a relationship more demanding. A researcher who uses the null hypothesis approach only directly tests the null hypothesis. If evidence supports or leads the researcher to accept the null hypothesis, he or she concludes that the tested relationship does not exist. This implies that the alternative hypothesis is false. On the other hand, if the researcher can find evidence to reject the null hypothesis, then the alternative hypotheses remain a possibility. The researcher cannot prove the alternative; rather, by testing the null hypothesis, he or she keeps the alternative hypotheses in contention. When null hypothesis testing is added to confirming evidence, the argument for an alterative hypothesis can grow stronger over time.

Many people find the null hypothesis to be confusing. Another way to think of it is that the scientific community is extremely cautious. It prefers to consider a causal relationship to be false until mountains of evidence show it to be true. This is similar to the Anglo-American legal idea of innocent until proved guilty. A researcher assumes, or acts as if, the null hypothesis is correct until *reasonable doubt* suggests otherwise. Researchers who use null hypotheses generally use it with specific statistical tests (e.g., *t*-test or *F*-test). Thus, a researcher may claim there is reasonable doubt in a null hypothesis if a statistical test suggests that the odds of it being false are 99 in 100. This is what a researcher means when he or she says that statistical tests allow him or her to "reject the null hypothesis at the .01 level of significance." (Inferential statistics are briefly discussed in Chapters 9 and 12.)

Another type of hypothesis is the *double-barreled hypothesis*.[3] Researchers should avoid using it; it shows unclear thinking and creates confusion. A double-barreled hypothesis puts two distinct relationships in one hypothesis. For instance, "public support for drug enforcement and international money laundering legislation cause the scope of drug markets to decrease." This hypothesis is double-barreled. It could mean either of two things: that public support *or* international money laundering legislation causes drug distribution networks to shrink in scope, or that *only* the combination of the two independent variables (i.e., public support and legislation) cause the distribution networks to shrink. If the "either one" hypothesis is intended, and only one independent has an effect, the results of the hypothesis testing are unclear. For example, if the evidence shows that public support affects the scope of the distribution network but the international legislation does not, is the hypothesis supported? If the combination hypothesis is intended, then a researcher really means that the joint occurrence of public support *and* international legislation only, and neither alone, causes a shrinking in drug-trafficking networks. If a researcher intends the combination meaning, it is not double-barreled. Researchers should be clear and state the combination hypothesis so that the particular form in which the variables go together or are combined is made explicit. This is often called an *interaction effect* (interaction effects are discussed later).

Other Aspects of Explanation

Clarity about Units and Levels of Analysis. It is easy to become confused at first about the ideas of units and levels of analysis. Nevertheless, they are important ideas for clearly thinking through and planning a research project. All studies have both units and levels of analysis, but few researchers explicitly identify them as such. The levels and units of analysis are restricted by the topic and the research question. In other words, there is a rough match between the topic or research question and the units or levels of analysis that one can use.

A *level of analysis* is the level of social reality to which theoretical explanations refer. The level of social reality varies on a continuum from micro level (e.g., small groups or individual

processes) to macro level (e.g., civilizations or structural aspects of society). The level includes a mix of the number of people, the amount of space, the scope of the activity, and the length of time. For example, very micro-level analysis can involve a few seconds of interaction between two people in the same small room. Very macro-level analysis can involve billions of people on several continents across centuries. Most social research uses a level of analysis that lies between these extremes.

The level of analysis delimits the kinds of assumptions, concepts, and theories that a researcher uses. For example, many criminologists are interested in knowing why delinquency and crime rates tend to be lower in Asian societies than in the United States and other Western societies. Some researchers suggest that the difference may have to do with different societal values. Asian societies tend to espouse communalism, whereas Western societies tend to espouse individualism. This plausible explanation lends itself to both micro and macro levels of analysis.

At the micro level, criminologists might wish to test the hypothesis that kinship solidarity (or communalism) is stronger in Asian families than in Western families. To do this, he or she might compare the norms, social relations, and parental expectations of Asian and Western families. Asian families, one might hypothesize, tend to display a greater degree of communalism, which serves as a means of informal social control over individualized forms of deviance and crime. What makes this a micro-level analysis is the study's attention to norms and social interaction within a relatively small group (i.e., the family). Indeed, the criminologist could collect comparative data from specific families to see if those with greater degrees of communalism have also less criminality and delinquency.

A macro level of analysis would be more apt to emphasize cultural and social structural differences between Asian and Western societies. Asian cultures place emphasis on conformity to group norms (i.e., "relational self"), whereas Western cultures place emphasis on self-expression and freedom (i.e., individualism). Likewise, patterns of social and geographic mobility in Western societies have led to the breakup of extended kinship networks more so than is seen in Asian societies. At the macro level, then, the criminologist would compare societal patterns, such as social mobility, to test the hypothesis. Be that as it may, the topic suggests theory and research at both micro and macro levels of analysis.

The *unit of analysis* refers to the type of unit a researcher uses when measuring variables. Common units in criminology are the individual, the group (e.g., youth gang), the organization (e.g., corporation), the social category (e.g., social class, gender, or race), the social institution (e.g., the criminal justice system), and the society (e.g., a nation or a tribe). Although the individual is the most commonly used unit of analysis, it is by no means the only one. Different theories emphasize one or another unit of analysis, and different research techniques are associated with specific units of analysis. For example, the individual is usually the unit of analysis in survey and experimental research. Criminologists often use crime statistics to compare individuals, households, towns or cities, states, regions of the country, or even countries. All of these are a different unit of analysis.

Sometimes criminologists are interested in studying criminal law. They might wish to compare countries in terms of their specific laws, such as laws regarding bank secrecy and money laundering. In this case, criminal law is the unit of analysis. Or perhaps criminologists wish to compare criminal court decisions over a period of time or from one jurisdiction to another. Here, the unit of analysis is the court decision.

The units of analysis determine how a researcher measures variables. They also correspond loosely to the level of analysis in an explanation. Thus, social-psychological or micro levels of analysis fit with the individual as a unit of analysis, whereas macro levels of analysis fit with the social category or institution as a unit. Theories and explanations at the micro level generally refer to features of individuals or interactions among individuals. Those at the macro level refer to social forces operating across a society or relations among major parts of a society as a whole.

Researchers use levels and units of analysis to design research projects, and being aware of them helps researchers avoid logical errors in causality (see the next section). For example, the National Narcotics Intelligence Consumers Committee (NNICC) publishes a report every year that examines the role other countries play in supplying illicit drugs to the United States. The unit of analysis in the report is the specific country (e.g., Colombia), and it is chosen because of the research question being asked (i.e., What role do other countries play?). The NNICC, which is comprised of various U.S. governmental agencies, no doubt uses "country" as the unit of analysis for political reasons. Having data on specific countries helps the U.S. government decide certain foreign policy questions, such as whether a country should be certified as significantly helping U.S. efforts in the War on Drugs.

However, researchers studying the same research topic might decide to select different levels or units of analysis. For instance, criminologists interested in studying trends in the effectiveness of drug enforcement might select "illicit drug seizures" as the pertinent unit of analysis. Another commonly used unit of analysis in this area is "emergency room drug abuse episode." The Drug Abuse Warning System (DAWN) tallies the number of nationwide emergency room drug abuse episodes in the United States as a way of anticipating particularly dangerous illicit drugs that are being sold to drug users. Still another commonly used unit of analysis is "illicit drug prices." The U.S. Drug Enforcement Administration (DEA), for example, keeps track of the retail and wholesale prices of cocaine in all major U.S. metropolitan areas as an indicator of drug supply.

The point is, there are any number of units of analysis to be used by criminologists. The choice must always depend on the theoretical questions being asked by the researcher.

Potential Errors in Causal Explanation.   Developing good explanations requires that researchers watch for statements that appear to be causal hypotheses on the surface but are not. Five fallacies or misleading statements are discussed next.

Ecological Fallacy. The *ecological fallacy* arises from a mismatch of units of analysis. It refers to a poor fit between the units for which a researcher has empirical evidence and the units for which he or she wants to make statements. It is due to imprecise reasoning and generalizing beyond what the evidence warrants. Ecological fallacy occurs when a researcher gathers data at a *higher* or an *aggregated* unit of analysis but wants to make a statement about a *lower* or *disaggregated* unit. It is a fallacy because what happens in one unit of analysis does not always hold for a different unit of analysis.[4] Thus, if a researcher gathers data for large aggregates (e.g., organizations, entire countries, etc.) and then draws conclusions about the behavior of individuals from those data, he or she is committing the ecological fallacy. You can avoid this error by ensuring that the unit of analysis you use in an explanation is the same as or very close to the unit on which you collect data (see Box 6.3).

Example. Consider again the example of crime rates in Asia. Japan has considerably lower rates of homicide and other forms of violent crime than does the United States. One important reason for this is the community-based, mutual-help organizations to which over 90 percent of Japanese households belong (Rifkin, 1995). These organizations *(jichikai)* are basically neighbors looking after neighbors. They provide individuals in the community with all manner of resources, such as loans, employment, medical support, housing, and community supervision. Underlying the *jichikai* is the Confucian tradition of cooperation and harmonious relations. And, as we are just now discovering in the United States, community policing of this sort is indeed a powerful hedge against crime and delinquency.

The problem of ecological fallacy enters in to the extent that criminologists attribute individual-based characteristics as accounting for the lower criminality of the Japanese. This in effect places the explanation not at the proper unit of analysis (i.e., the community), but at a lower or disaggregated unit (i.e., the individual). The ecological fallacy in this case is attributing to the individual what should properly be associated with the community.

Reductionism. Another problem involving mismatched units of analysis and imprecise reasoning about evidence is *reductionism,* also called the *fallacy of nonequivalence* (see Box 6.4). This error occurs when a researcher explains macro-level events but has evidence only about specific individuals. It occurs when a researcher observes a *lower* or *disaggregated* unit of analysis but makes statements about the operations of *higher* or *aggregated* units. It is a mirror image of the mismatch error in the ecological fallacy. A researcher who has data on how individuals behave but makes statements about the dynamics of macro-level units is committing the error of reductionism. It occurs because it is often easier to get data on concrete individuals. Also, the operation of macro-level units is more abstract and nebulous. Lieberson has argued that this error, which he says is common in criminological research, leads to inconsistencies, contradictions, and confusion. He (1985:108, 113–114) forcefully stated:

> *Associations on the lower level are irrelevant for determining the validity of a proposition about processes operating on the higher level. As a matter of fact, no useful understanding of the higher-level structure can be obtained from lower-level analysis. . . . If we are interested in the higher-level processes and events, it is because we operate with the understanding that they have distinct qualities that are not simply derived by summing up the subunits.*

As with the ecological fallacy, you can avoid this error by ensuring that the unit of analysis in your explanation is very close to the one for which you have evidence.

Researchers who fail to think precisely about the units of analysis and those who do not couple data with the theory are likely to commit the ecological fallacy or reductionism. They make a mis-

Box 6.3

Example of Ecological Fallacy

Hightop University has five sections of a course entitled Western History, each with 50 students. Last year, the dean discovered cheating in the sections and looked at the following data that included the gender composition of each section. The dean calculated a very high correlation between cheating and gender. It is plotted in Graph A.

Section	a	b	c	d	e
# Cheaters	2	4	6	8	10
% Women	80	60	40	30	20

Unfamiliar with the *ecological fallacy*, the dean concluded that men tend to be cheaters and instituted a policy to monitor male students.

You studied the *ecological fallacy* and recognize that the dean's data on characteristics on entire sections of students do not provide evidence on individual cheating behavior. You asked for data on the gender breakdown of the individual cheating students, which is shown in the following:

Section	a	b	c	d	e
Male Cheaters	1	2	3	4	5
Female Cheaters	1	2	3	4	5
Total Cheaters	2	5	6	8	10

You immediately notice that half of the cheaters are female in all sections, and there is no association between the percent of women in a section and the percent of male cheaters. Your plot of the data looks like Graph B. You then explain to the dean that men and women are equally likely to cheat and there is no gender difference in cheating.

The dean's chart is correct, in that it shows the data. The problem is that it is *not* evidence for a statement about gender differences in individual student behavior. Perhaps another unmeasured factor accounts for the pattern (i.e., it is a *spurious relationship*), or maybe a section with fewer women creates a social atmosphere in the classroom that supports a norm to cheat among both men and women equally. These are issues for additional study.

Despite a clear pattern of observations in Graph A, it is not the type of evidence to support a conclusion that men are more likely to cheat than women. One must have the right type of evidence (on individuals) to draw conclusions about individual cheating behavior.

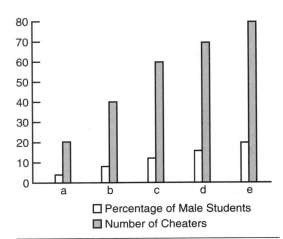

GRAPH A   Percentage of Men by Number of Cheaters in Five Sections of Western History

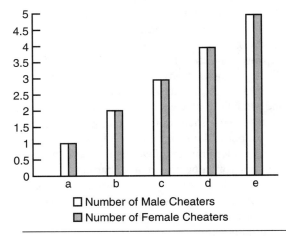

GRAPH B   Number of Cheaters by Gender in Five Sections of Western History

Box 6.4 _____

Error of Reductionism

To further explore the error of reductionism, we will examine a national survey of tax practitioners conducted by the U.S. Internal Revenue Service (1987). Tax practitioners are white-collar professionals—such as certified public accountants, commercial tax preparers, and lawyers—who prepare other people's federal income tax returns. The Internal Revenue Service (IRS) was interested in a number of research questions, including the extent to which tax practitioners have a hand in a client's tax evasion. (You might be interested in knowing that Professor Wiegand was project director of this survey.)

One set of survey questions concerned the practitioner's role in cautioning a client about "criminal violations when you suspect significant income is intentionally not fully reported." Three percent of the national sample of tax practitioners said that they did not caution their client, despite suspicions of the client being involved in a tax crime. This perhaps suggests that only a small proportion of tax professionals engage in this highly unethical conspiracy of silence (or, more precisely, that only a small proportion admit to

it). In other words, of the many tax practitioners in the United States, only a relatively few would not caution against a client committing a tax crime.

However, a related question seemed to reveal a much more troubling situation. This question focused on a more aggregated unit of analysis. Thus, instead of asking about the individual tax preparer's own behavior, the survey question asks if "other preparers do this action." Over half of the other preparers are perceived as "frequently" or "occasionally" failing to caution their clients against committing a tax crime. From this perspective, one might argue for the existence of a professional culture that tacitly approves of (or at least chooses to remain silent about) a client's criminal behavior.

This study revealed two distinct units of analysis: the individual tax practitioner and the tax practitioner culture. It would be reductionistic to interpret a cultural fact (regarding norms about cautioning clients) in terms of the self-reported behavior of individuals. Sociologically speaking, culture cannot be reduced to any specific individual.

---

take about the data appropriate for a research question, or they may seriously overgeneralize from the data.

You can make assumptions about units of analysis other than the ones you study empirically. Thus, research on individuals rests on assumptions that individuals act within a set of social institutions. Research on social institutions is based on assumptions about individual behavior. We know that many micro-level units form macro-level units. The danger is that it is easy to slide into using the causes or behavior of micro units, such as individuals, to explain the actions of macro units, such as social institutions. What happens among units at one level does not necessarily hold for different units of analysis.

Criminology, as mentioned earlier, has very close ties to other social sciences, particularly sociology. One distinct influence of sociology is the fundamental belief in criminology that social reality exists at levels beyond the individual. Or,

to paraphrase Emile Durkheim, one of the founding fathers of sociology, social facts are real. Thus, theoretical explanations of social phenomena cannot simply marshal individual-level data. The causes, forces, structures, and processes that exist among macro-level units cannot be reduced to individual behavior.

Example.   Consider the example of white-collar crime. Many people are willing to explain it in individual terms: "The bank executive was corrupt"; "The firm's accountant was dishonest"; "The corporate CEO was unethical." These are reductionistic explanations, for they ignore the social reality of the organization into which bank executives, accountants, CEOs, and others were socialized. Criminological research at the organizational level might reveal that, indeed, cultural norms and values, as well as structural incentives of the organization were such that individuals were being tacitly encouraged to break the law.

Moreover, organizational structure and culture cannot simply be reduced to the "criminal tendencies" of individuals. For this reason, criminologists since Clinard and Quinney (1973) have made the distinction between "occupational crime" (i.e., criminal behavior committed by individuals in the course of their white-collar occupation) and "corporate crime" (i.e., criminal behavior committed by corporate officials on behalf of their corporation). Explaining the latter in terms of the former is a classic example of reductionism.

Tautology. The *tautology* is circular reasoning—when something is "true by definition." A tautology looks like a causal relationship but is not one. It occurs through a slip in language, a confusion between a definition and a causal relationship. A scientific hypothesis must be capable of being shown to be false with empirical evidence. Tautologies cannot be empirically tested or shown to be false because they state a logical or semantic relationship, not an empirical, causal one. You can avoid this error by considering whether a hypothesis can be restated as a definition. If you can substitute an equal sign for the causal arrow between the independent and dependent variables, you probably have a tautology.

Example. Consider, for example, the War on Drugs. As it is currently being waged, "the enemy" (i.e., those who are arrested for drug offenses) are disproportionately minority, especially African American. Yet, if the War on Drugs was instead aimed at, say, university students (many of whom are consumers of illicit drugs), then they would be disproportionately represented and arrested, and they would be "the enemy." Thus, there is this circular logic: The War on Drugs is aimed at "the enemy." The enemy, by definition, are those who are arrested for drug offenses.

Teleology. This is another case in which something looks like a causal relationship but is not

one because it cannot be tested empirically. It is due to a slip in language. A *teleology* arises when a vague future condition or an abstract, diffuse idea about the "nature of the world" is used to explain something specific. It is untestable and violates temporal order in causal explanations. For example, human nature causes crime. You can avoid this error by carefully examining the independent variable or cause in an explanation.

Spuriousness. To call a relationship between variables spurious means that it is false, a mirage. Researchers get excited if they think they have found a spurious relationship because they can show the world to be more complex than it appears on the surface. Because any association between two variables might be spurious, researchers are cautious when they discover that two variables are associated; upon further investigation, it may not be the basis for a causal relationship. It may be an illusion, just like the mirage that resembles a pool of water on a road during a hot day.

Spuriousness occurs when two variables are associated but are not causally related because there is actually an unseen third factor that is the real cause (see Box 6.5). The third variable causes both the apparent independent and the dependent variable. It accounts for the observed association. In terms of conditions for causality, the unseen third factor represents a more powerful alternative explanation.

You now understand that you should be wary of correlations or associations, but how can you tell whether a relationship is spurious, and how do you find out what the mysterious third factor is? You will need to use statistical techniques (discussed later in this book) to test whether an association is spurious. To use them, you need a theory or at least a guess about possible third factors, based on how you think the world operates. Actually, spuriousness is based on some commonsense logic that you already use.

Consider, for example, one of the heated debates raging in criminology. The debate is over the relationship between incarceration and crime.

Box 6.5

Spuriousness Example

Mugford (1997) has raised an interesting research question: Why does the United States have a problem with crack cocaine use but Australia does not? The answer, according to Mugford, has partly to do with the spurious assumption often made in the United States about why people use crack.

The assumption is that people will use crack if it is available to them. Thus, law enforcement must interdict and interrupt the supply of crack cocaine in order to diminish consumption levels (see, for example, the annual NNICC report on the supply of illicit drugs to the United States). To put it differently, the causal relationship underlying U.S. drug enforcement policy is that the availability of crack cocaine determines the level of consumption. That is to say,

the availability (or supply) of crack cocaine creates its own demand.

To Mugford's mind, this relationship is somewhat spurious. As he stated, "In the case of Australia, supply is restricted, partly by geographical contingency but more importantly by the absence of a class of people for whom illicit crack sales is perhaps the only available means of material success" (p. 204).

From Mugford's point of view, it is the relative absence of an urban underclass in Australia that explains why crack cocaine consumption is less of a problem there than in the United States: "We have neither widespread, violent, illicit drug markets in our cities nor substantial numbers of heavy crack users who both suffer and *seem to 'cause'* (emphasis added) serious social problems" (p. 206).

Evidence over the last five years or so seems to suggest that increasing incarceration rates are causing crime rates to drop. However, there are quite a number of criminologists who feel the relationship is more spurious than real. By taking a wider historical perspective, they contend that the close correlation of the two variables (i.e., incarceration rates and crime rates) vanishes. In California, for instance, the prison population expanded 19 of the past 21 years. However, in 15 of those 19 years, violent crime actually rose (Donziger, 1996).

Various alternative hypotheses are presently being examined by criminological researchers to account for these recent drops in crime. They are looking at patterns of community policing, changes in illicit drug markets, and demographic factors as possible causal factors. As you can see, identifying spurious relationships depends in large measure on criminological theory. For it is theory that suggests other possible explanations for a spurious relationship.

Figure 6.2 shows in graphic form the five errors that have been discussed in this section.

SELECTING AND REFINING RESEARCH TOPICS

Selecting a Topic

Your first step when beginning a research project is to select your topic.[5] There is no cut-and-dry formula for this task. Whether you are an experienced researcher or just beginning, the best guide is to conduct research on something that interests you. There are many sources of research topics; Box 6.6 suggests various ways to make your selection. The techniques for choosing topics are not limited to quantitative research but apply to all types of research.

From a Topic to a Specific Research Question

Social researchers do not conduct research on a topic, although a topic is an essential starting point. A topic is just that—a starting point. Researchers refine and narrow down a topic into a problem or question. A common mistake of new researchers is to fail to narrow a topic sufficiently, or to try to jump from a

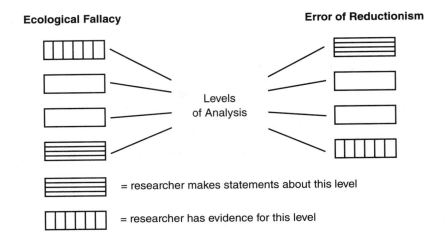

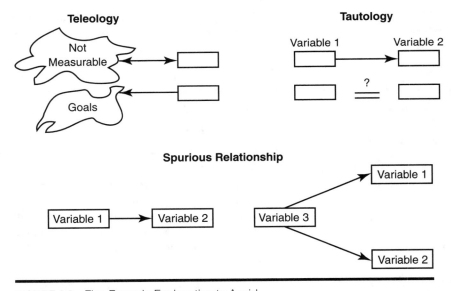

FIGURE 6.2 Five Errors in Explanation to Avoid

broad topic directly into a research project without first creating a research question. In quantitative research, you need a narrowly focused research question before you design a research project.

Research projects are designed around research problems or questions. Before designing a project, focus on a specific research problem within a broad topic. More times than not, the process of focusing on a research problem begins with a personal experience (see Box 6.6). Suppose, for example, you read in the newspaper that the Ku Klux Klan is sponsoring a rally in a nearby town. That makes you stop and think about why the rally is taking place, who will attend it, if there will be an anti-Klan rally, and so on. As your

Box 6.6 _____

Ways to Select Topics

1. *Personal experience*. Choose a research topic based on what is happening around you. Trust your instincts. If you find a topic personally interesting, then chances are you will be able to come up with a worthwhile research question. An example is: Why are we suddenly seeing a revival in White supremacy organizations like the Ku Klux Klan in the United States?

2. *Curiosity based on something in the media*. The idea of doing research on the White supremacy movement stems from a small announcement in the local newspaper. The announcement just seems to jump off the page at you, and you are open to finding research topics so long as they are personally interesting.

3. *The state of knowledge in the field*. Having had basic criminology and sociology courses, you are probably familiar with the dynamics of racial and ethnic conflict. So, you begin reviewing some recent journal articles on the topic to find out yourself what the state of knowledge is regarding topics such as the Ku Klux Klan, racism, hate crimes, and so on.

4. *Solving a problem*. Another way to approach the research topic is to think in terms of applied research. What type of organizations, government agencies, or business establishments might be willing to sponsor research on this topic? Once you have narrowed down an identified group of interested parties, you can contact them to discuss ways that your research might help solve a problem they are facing.

5. *Social premiums*. This is a term suggested by Singleton and colleagues (1988:68). It means that some topics are "hot" or offer an opportunity. For example, you may receive a request for proposals from the National Institute of Justice, which lists the research topics it is willing to fund. On its list you see the topic "hate crimes and the White supremacy movement," so you decide to submit a research proposal.

6. *Personal values*. Some people are highly committed to a set of religious, political, or social values. Perhaps, for instance, your parents have taught you that racial segregation is wrong. Your strong conviction in turn leads you to select research topics that address one of your fundamental values (e.g., the value of racial harmony).

---

curiosity is piqued, you decide to observe the rally and antirally with the idea in the back of your mind of maybe trying to do research on the topic.

When starting research on a topic, ask yourself: What is it about the topic that is of greatest interest? For a topic about which you know little, first get background knowledge by reading about it. Research questions refer to the relationships among a small number of variables. Identify a limited number of variables and specify the relationships among them.

A research question has one or a small number of causal relationships. Box 6.7 lists some ways to focus a topic into a research question. For example, the research question, What causes the revival of interest in White su-premacy organizations? can be sharpened a bit. A better research question is: To what extent is capital disinvestment associated with a revival in the White supremacy movement in a community?

Another technique for focusing a research question is to specify the *universe* to which the answer to the question can be generalized. All research questions, hypotheses, and studies apply to some group or category of people, organizations, or other units. The universe is the set of units that the researcher wishes to explain. For instance, your research question is about not just the Ku Klux Klan but also about the entire universe of White supremacy organizations. We will come back to a discussion of universe in Chapter 9.

Box 6.7 _____

Techniques for Narrowing a Topic into a Research Question

1. *Examine the literature.* Published articles are an excellent source of ideas for research questions. They are usually at an appropriate level of specificity and suggest research questions that focus on the following:
   a. Replicate a previous research project exactly or with slight variations.
   b. Explore unexpected findings discovered in previous research.
   c. Follow suggestions an author gives for future research at the end of an article.
   d. Extend an existing explanation or theory to a new topic or setting.
   e. Challenge findings or attempt to refute a relationship.
   f. Specify the intervening process and consider linking relations.
2. *Talk over ideas with others.*
   a. Ask people who are knowledgeable about the topic for questions about it that they have thought of.
   b. Seek out those who hold opinions that differ from yours on the topic and discuss possible research questions with them.
3. *Apply to a specific context.*
   a. Focus the topic onto a specific historical period or time period.
   b. Narrow the topic to a specific society or geographic unit.
   c. Consider which subgroups or categories of people/units are involved and whether there are differences among them.
4. *Define the aim or desired outcome of the study.*
   a. Will the research question be for an exploratory, explanatory, or descriptive study?
   b. Will the study involve applied or basic research?

_____

When refining a topic into a research question, when designing a research project, and when formulating hypotheses, you also need to consider practical limitations. Designing a perfect research project is an interesting academic exercise, but if you expect to carry out a research project, practical limitations will have an impact on its design.

Major limitations include time, costs, access to resources, approval by authorities, ethical concerns, and expertise. If you have 10 hours a week for five weeks to conduct a research project, but the answer to a research question will take five years to uncover, reformulate the research question more narrowly. Estimating the amount of time required to answer a research question is difficult. The hypotheses specified, the research technique used, and the type of data collected all play significant roles. Experienced researchers are the best source of good estimates.

Cost is another limitation. As with time, there are inventive ways to answer a question within limitations, but it may be impossible to answer some questions because of the expense involved. To study the whole universe of White supremacy organizations is obviously an enormous task. A more manageable task might be to compare two similar towns—one that had recently had a Ku Klux Klan rally, and one that had not. The towns' inhabitants could be studied to determine if one or the other had been more affected by capital disinvestment.

Access to resources is a common limitation. Resources can include the expertise of others, special equipment, or information. For example, a research question about burglary rates and family income in many different nations is almost impossible to answer because information on burglary and income is not collected or available for most countries. Some questions require the approval of authorities (e.g., to see medical records) or involve violating basic ethical principles (e.g., causing serious physical harm to a person to see the person's reaction). The expertise or background of the researcher is also a limitation. Answering some research questions involves the use of data collection techniques, statistical methods, knowledge of a foreign language, or skills that the researcher may not have. Unless the researcher can acquire the necessary training or can pay for another person's services, the research question may not be practical.

From the Research Question to Hypotheses

It is difficult to move smoothly from a broad topic to hypotheses, but the leap from a well-formulated research question to hypotheses is a short one. Hints about hypotheses are embedded within a good research question. In addition, hypotheses are tentative answers to research questions (see Box 6.8).

Consider again this research question: To what extent is capital disinvestment associated with a revival of the White supremacy movement? The question contains two variables: capital disinvestment and the revival of the White supremacy movement. To develop a hypothesis, a researcher asks: Which is the dependent variable? In this example, the dependent variable is "the revival of the White supremacy movement." It is the variable that is affected by the independent variable ("capital disinvestment"). The researcher also asks: What is the direction of the relationship? The hypothesis could be: The more affected a local community is by capital disinvestment, the more likely it is to experience a revival in White supremacy organizations.

Of course, several hypotheses can be developed from the same research question. Another related hypothesis is: Those individuals who have personally experienced a layoff (i.e., loss of job) are more likely to accept negative stereotyping of minorities. Perhaps the hypothesis could be: Those who accept negative stereotyping of minorities are more likely to agree with notions of White supremacy than those not accepting negative stereotypes.

Hypotheses can specify that a relationship holds under some conditions but not others. As Lieberson (1985:198) remarked, "In order to evaluate the utility of a given causal proposition, it is important that there be a clear-cut statement of the conditions under which it will operate. A

Box 6.8

Examples of Good and Bad Research Questions

BAD

Not Empirically Testable, Nonscientific Questions
- Is the Ku Klux Klan wrong?
- Should the Ku Klux Klan be illegal?

General Topics, Not Research Questions
- Hate violence
- White Supremacy movement

Set of Variables, Not Questions
- Capital disinvestment and White supremacy
- Racism and hate crime

Too Vague, Ambiguous
- Does capital disinvestment affect racism?
- What can be done to stop the Ku Klux Klan?

Need to Be Still More Specific
- Is White supremacy on the rise?
- How does being laid off affect attitudes toward minorities?

GOOD

Exploratory Questions
- Has the number of White supremacy groups increased in Wisconsin in the past 10 years?

Descriptive Questions
- Are White supremacy groups more active in communities that have suffered capital disinvestment or those that have not?

Explanatory Questions
- Does the emotional insecurity created by job lay-off increase the likelihood of accepting negative stereotyping of ethnic minorities?

hypothesis of this sort is: White middle-class and working-class individuals who have been laid off because of plant closings tend to accept negative stereotyping of minorities, unless they have close friends who are minorities.

Formulating a research question and developing a hypothesis do not have to proceed in fixed stages. A researcher can formulate a tentative research question, then develop possible hypotheses. The process of developing hypotheses helps a researcher state the research question more precisely. The process is interactive and involves creativity.

Where Is the Theory?

You may be wondering: Where does theory fit into the process of moving from a topic to a hypothesis I can test? Recall from Chapter 3 that theory takes many forms. Researchers use general theoretical issues and puzzles as a source of topics. Theories and theoretical frameworks provide researchers with concepts and ideas that they turn into variables. Theory provides the reasoning or mechanism that helps researchers connect variables into a research question. A hypothesis can be both an answer to a research question and an untested proposition from a theory. Researchers can express a hypothesis at an abstract, conceptual level. They can also restate it in a more concrete, measurable form, as you will see in the next chapter.

You first saw the steps of a research project in Chapter 1. Figure 6.3 gives a slightly different picture of the steps. It shows intermediate steps and the processes used to narrow a topic into a hypothesis. It also shows how the abstract theoretical level blends into the concrete empirical level as a researcher moves toward the data collection stage.

EXAMPLE STUDIES

Before looking at how to conduct a study, you should see how the ideas in this chapter—topic, research question, hypotheses, independent and dependent variables, universe, and unit of analysis—are used in real studies.

Experiment

The *topic* of Schwartz and Orleans's (1967) field experiment is taxpayer compliance. The authors are interested in knowing if social commitment and deterrence have an appreciable impact on voluntary compliance with tax laws. The *research question* is: Does social commitment or deterrence have the stronger effect in raising taxpayer compliance? The *independent variable* in this experiment is "motives for paying one's taxes" and the *dependent variable* is "level of taxpayer compliance."

Schwartz and Orleans (1967) used two questionnaires, one emphasizing social commitment (e.g., patriotism, guilt, etc.) as the main motive for paying one's income taxes, and the second emphasizing deterrence (e.g., likelihood of being audited, punishment, etc.). The experiment randomly assigned respondents to three groups. The first group received a social commitment questionnaire, the second group received a deterrence questionnaire, and the third group (the control group) received a questionnaire with neither social commitment nor deterrence questions on it.

After each respondent filled out his or her questionnaire, the authors examined IRS tax data for that year and the preceding year. They found a significant difference between the three groups. In particular, they discovered that only the "social commitment groups of taxpayers" reported a statistically significant (at the .05 level of confidence) increase in the amount of income reported and the amount of tax due in the second year. The authors concluded that normative appeals appear to have a stronger impact on increasing levels of tax compliance, whereas deterrence threats have little or no effect on compliance levels.

The Schwartz and Orleans (1967) study is perhaps the first that uses a randomized experiment to test compliance theories on actual tax-reporting behavior. The *universe* to which this study applies is all taxpayers. The *unit of analysis* is the individual taxpayer, because the variables measure characteristics of individuals

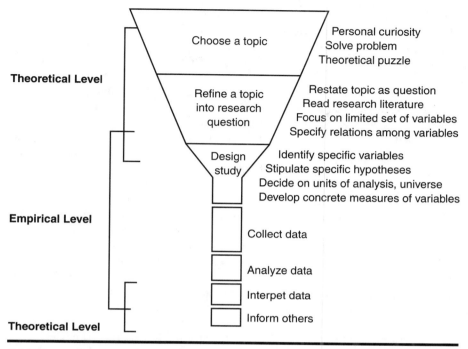

FIGURE 6.3 Steps in Research Revisited

(e.g., amount of income reported in a given year). This study is an explanation that attempts to advance basic knowledge but also has important implications for tax administration.

Survey Research

The *topic* of Bankston and Thompson's (1989) article, "Carrying Firearms for Protection," is evident in the title. The researchers discussed the research on firearms in the United States, which has largely examined the ownership of guns. They developed a focused *research question:* To what degree do people who carry firearms when away from home do so out of a fear of crime?

The authors mailed questionnaires to over 4,000 people in Louisiana, asking about their attitudes and background characteristics in addition to whether they carried a firearm.

Eventually, the authors limited the study to Whites and had full data on a little over 1,000 people. The main *hypothesis* they tested was whether people who fear crime the most and who believe that a gun will protect them are most likely to carry a firearm. The authors' main *independent variable* was fear of crime, and they specified an *intervening variable:* a belief that guns provide effective protection. The *dependent variable* was how often a person carried a gun when away from home. The authors found that about one-third of the respondents carried a firearm on at least some occasions.

In the Results section, the authors examined the effects of variables on how often a person carried a firearm. They found that a fear of crime did not directly affect how often a person carried a weapon, but a belief in the effectiveness of having a gun for protection had a large effect. People who thought that carrying a gun offered personal protection tended to be younger, less well educated rural males who thought crime was a serious problem and who feared crime.

The authors noted that Louisiana is a southern state with some of the least restrictive laws on purchasing or carrying firearms. The *universe* for the results may be limited to Whites in other areas of the southern United States. The *unit of analysis* of the study was the individual.

Content Analysis

The article by Barlow, Barlow, and Chiricos (1995), "Economic Conditions and Ideologies of Crime in the Media," used content analysis. The *topic* of the study was how the media portrays crime and criminals. The *hypothesis* was that the media give a distorted picture of crime, and the distortion is linked to changes in economic conditions. In particular, the authors predicted that more negative images of crime and criminals occur when unemployment is high or the economy is in a recession. Thus, the *independent variable* was the unemployment rate and the *dependent variable* was how negative the offender was presented. The authors also looked at overall distortion in terms of a mismatch between crime statistics and crime that gets media attention. The *research question* was: Does the news media give a distorted picture of crime, with the distortion based on a value and belief system that condemns offenders most harshly when economic conditions are bad?

The data for the study came from *Time* magazine. The authors sampled various years (1953, 1958, 1975, 1982) that had different economic conditions and looked at all articles during the year that dealt with crime, criminal justice, or criminals. They found 175 articles. The *unit of analysis* was the article. The *universe* for the study was all crime-related articles that appeared in major U.S. mass circulation newsmagazines from the 1950s to the 1980s.

The authors also looked at the crime rate, change in the crime rate, characteristics of offenders, and types of crime as violent or nonviolent during the selected years. They rated the image of the offender in each article as to how positive or negative it appeared. A negative image showed the offender as being without remorse, as lacking a reason for the crime, as unprincipled or lying, or as unlikely to be rehabilitated. A more positive image showed the offender as confused and willing to make changes, as trying to make the best of a bad situation, as forced into crime as a result of circumstances, or as caught up in the criminal justice system.

The authors found that negative images were more common in high unemployment periods. Specifically, 62 percent of the images in high unemployment periods were negative versus 32 percent in low unemployment periods. Other patterns of distortion were also found. For example, the authors discovered that 73 percent of the articles focused on violent crime, which made up about 10 percent of crimes known to police in the selected years. Some 74 percent of the articles that included a reference to the offender's race stated that the offender was non-White, whereas the percent of arrests involving non-Whites, in the selected years was 28 percent. Finally, despite the strong connection between employment conditions and crime, only 3 percent of the articles included information on whether the offender had a job or was unemployed.

Existing Statistics

Reuter's (1996) "The Mismeasurement of Illegal Drug Markets" gives us a good illustration of the existing statistics method. As the title implies, the *topic* involved the measurement of illegal drug markets. Indeed, the researcher pointed out weaknesses in the methodologies used to measure the size of these illegal markets. Reuter was particularly critical of estimates of drug prices and production levels; as he phrased it:

> *In recent years, the [U.S.] federal government has developed systematic estimates of domestic expenditures that do indeed provide a reasonable basis for scaling the size of these markets.*

However, these coexist with an essentially mad-cap series of federal figures on international production and prices that make a mockery of the whole enterprise. (p. 63)

The *research question* Reuter (1996) asked is: Does this measurement matter? In his opinion, the mismeasurement would be very serious if drug policies were rational or based on scientific research. His argument, however, was that "the numbers are in fact just decorations on the policy process, rhetorical conveniences for official statements. . . . a condemnation of drug policy decision making" (p. 64).

The *unit of analysis* in Reuter's (1996) research was the illegal drug market. For example, international price data pertains to "the price of the illegal drug." In theory, drug prices should be a fairly accurate indicator of supply, but obvious inconsistencies turn up in the U.S. government's "Illicit Drug Wholesale/Retail Price Report," which contains price data for foreign production covering both intermediate and final product. For instance, "the price of morphine, an intermediate product in refining illicit heroin, is sometimes recorded as higher than the final product" (p. 70). The price data, by the way, come from a data set called STRIDE (System to Retrieve Information from Drug Evidence), which is maintained by the U.S. Drug Enforcement Administration.

There are two different *universes* to which Reuter's (1996) findings can be generalized. His research can be generalized to illegal drug markets, both in the United States and abroad. But his research also generalizes to *official data sets* used by various countries to measure the size of illegal drug markets.

CONCLUSION

In this chapter, you learned about the components of quantitative research that are based on a posi-tivist approach to research. Quantitative research techniques share a language and logic from positivism that separates them from research techniques based on other approaches.

You learned that the language of quantitative research is one of variables, causal relations, and hypotheses. Quantitative research design uses a deductive logic. When using it, you begin with a general topic, narrow it down to research questions and hypotheses, and, finally, test hypotheses against empirical evidence.

You saw that theoretical explanations and concepts are a critical part of research design. Explanations and concepts are the basis of variables and their interrelationships.

You also learned about dangers in constructing causal explanations. Several types of logical errors (ecological fallacy, reductionism, tautology, teleology, and spuriousness) can plague causal explanations. As we saw in Chapter 4, positivist science emphasizes the importance of logical rigor, consistency, and an absence of contradiction in theoretical explanation. Efforts to avoid the logical errors in causal explanation are consistent with this emphasis.

Once you have narrowed topics, explanations, and research into hypotheses and variables, the next step is to measure the variables to test hypotheses with empirical evidence. Positivist approaches give special importance to precise measurement. They demand careful, objective measurement of the empirical world.

Precise quantitative measures of variables should be used whenever possible. In the next two chapters, we will examine measurement in quantitative research. They extend the discussion of variables and use a similar logic. It is important to address general issues of measurement before we examine how the four quantitative research techniques measure variables and collect data so you can test hypotheses.

KEY TERMS

alternative hypothesis	crucial experiment	double-barreled
attributes	dependent variable	hypothesis

ecological fallacy	logic of disconfirming	tautology
hypothesis	hypotheses	teleology
independent variable	null hypothesis	unit of analysis
intervening variable	reductionism	universe
level of analysis	spuriousness	variable

REVIEW QUESTIONS

1. Describe the differences between independent, dependent, and intervening variables.

2. Why don't we *prove* results in criminological research?

3. How are units of analysis and levels of analysis related to each other?

4. What two hypotheses are used if a researcher uses the logic of disconfirming hypotheses? Why is negative evidence stronger?

5. Restate the following in terms of a hypothesis with independent and dependent variables: "The amount of capital disinvestment in a year affects the level of hate crime, and there is a positive unidirectional relationship between the variables."

6. What is the unit of analysis for the hypothesis in question 5?

7. What would a diagram of the variables for a spurious relationship look like?

8. How can you determine whether an explanation is a tautology?

9. In what ways do ecological fallacy and reductionism involve problems with the units of analysis?

10. What is the relationship between a topic, a research question, and a hypothesis?

NOTES

1. See Lieberson (1985:185–187) for a discussion of basic and superficial variables in a set of causal linkages. Davis (1985) and Stinchcombe (1968) provide good general introductions to making linkages among variables in social theory.

2. The logic of disconfirming hypothesis is discussed in Singleton and associates (1988:56–60).

3. See Bailey (1987:43) for a discussion of this term.

4. The general problem of aggregating observation and making causal inferences is discussed in somewhat technical terms in Blalock (1982:-237–264) and in Hannan (1985). O'Brien (1992) argues that the ecological fallacy is one of a whole group of logical fallacies in which levels and units of analysis are confused and overgeneralized.

5. Problem choice and topic selection are discussed in Campbell and associates (1982) and in Zuckerman (1978).

RECOMMENDED READINGS

Blalock, Hubert M., Jr. (1969). *Theory construction: From verbal to mathematical formulations.* Englewood Cliffs, NJ: Prentice-Hall. As the subtitle suggests, this book explains how to take verbal sociological theories and convert them into a mathematical form. The mathematics required is fairly low level (an appendix reviews elementary calculus). The book is very helpful for seeing how complex explanations of social relations can be turned into precise, logical, quantifiable statements.

Campbell, John P., Richard L. Daft, and Charles L. Hulin. (1982). *What to study: Generating and developing research questions.* Beverly Hills, CA: Sage. This unusual book is primarily about how to look for and ask research questions. The main topic area with which the authors are concerned is organizations, but their suggestions have applicability to most topic areas.

Davis, James A. (1985). *The logic of causal order.* Beverly Hills, CA: Sage. This very short (66 pages) book elaborates on the system for diagramming causal relationships among variables. In addition to providing many examples and rules for the logic of causal diagrams, the author gives an introduction to using various statistics to examine the meaning of different patterns of causal relationships.

QUANTITATIVE CRIMINOLOGICAL MEASUREMENT

Whereas one can be reasonably assured of estimates of automobile production in the United States in a given year, we are less confident of the estimates offered for tax compliance, domestic marijuana production, the volume of illegal gambling, or the extensiveness of barter trade. Hence we dig deeper and ask, how were these numbers made?

—Susan Pozo, *Exploring the Underground Economy*, p. 1

INTRODUCTION

A science of justice must embrace measurement with open arms. It must welcome the challenge of trying to measure crime and quantify justice. But this deep-seated respect for precision in observation can never entirely overcome the inherent ingredient in crime; it thwarts detection. Here, the litany is practically endless; the police see only the tip of the iceberg—in the United States, only half or less of serious street crimes are reported. Even community policing cannot scale the walls of homes behind which hide domestic brutalities and cruel attacks.

As Pozo (1996) and other criminologists who study the crime economy know, the measurement of economic crime is notorious. Some of the most quantitative methodologies conclude in boggling, almost bizarre claims. Take Feige's (1996) research as a case in point. Using an economist's rigor, Feige has followed the trail of U.S. currency being held abroad. The many charts, mathematical formulas, and statistical tables point to this conclusion: "The world economy appears to subsume a U.S.-sized unrecorded economy that employs U.S. currency as its medium of exchange" (p. 57). Are we seeing the financial outlines of a global underground economy? Could it be that the economics of crime is operating at such a scale? Are the "missing" dollars being taxed? These are still open questions.

It is amazing. We have evidence of huge stores of U.S. dollars in the world economy—Feige (1996) has estimated around 40 percent—but we do not know where the money came from or who has it. Criminologists have hardly begun thinking about, let alone measuring, the implications of a "U.S.-sized unrecorded economy" for corporate crime. The point is, measurement of white-collar crime is the next great frontier to be explored and charted. These measurements will invariably take criminologists across national borders.

This chapter extends the discussion on research design in two ways. First, research design and measurement share common positivist assumptions and principles. Second, the process of designing, arranging, and planning a research project prior to collecting data extends into the measurement process. Clear thinking about the variables is needed before a researcher can use measures to collect data.

In quantitative research, the process of measurement begins after a researcher has formulated a research question and determined the variables and units of analysis that he or she will use in a research project. When developing measures, the researcher is not primarily concerned with whether a variable is the independent or dependent in a hypothesis; rather, the main concern is to develop clear definitions and to create measures that will yield precise, accurate findings.

Quantitative measurement is a deductive process. It involves taking a concept, *construct*,[1] or idea, then developing a measure (a device, procedure, or instrument) to observe it empirically. The process begins with concepts and ends with specific, concrete indicators. A researcher then uses the measures to produce data in the form of numbers. Actually, the process is interactive, because concepts become clearer and better defined as a researcher develops measures for them.

WHY MEASURE?

The need to measure is by no means unique to criminologists. We all strive to measure the world around us; whether with scientific precision or everyday intuition, we all benefit from putting our observations into more exact terms. This is the essence of measurement.

In addition to adding precision and objectivity, scientific measurement helps people observe what is otherwise invisible. Measurement extends human senses. It lets us observe things that were once unseen and unknown but were predicted by theory.

Before you can measure, you need a clear idea about what you are interested in. For example, you cannot directly observe the unrecorded U.S. currency in the world economy; for that matter, nor can the U.S. government or any other single government. You can only observe its effects indirectly, and make sense out of them in the context of a theory about the unrecorded currency. Like the natural scientist who invents measures of the "invisible" objects and forces of the physical world (e.g., magnetism, planets, molecules, etc.), the criminological researcher devises measures for difficult-to-observe aspects of crime and justice. Therefore, as criminologists raise new research questions and build new theories, they must also invent new ways of measuring their new concepts and testing their new hypotheses.[2]

Parts of the Measurement Process

Before you can measure, you need to begin with a concept. You also need to distinguish what you are interested in from other things. The idea that you first need a construct or concept of what is to be measured simply makes sense. How can you observe or measure something unless you know what you are looking for? For example, a biologist cannot observe a cell unless he or she first knows what a cell is, has a microscope, and has learned to distinguish it from noncell "stuff" or "junk" under the microscope.

The process of measurement involves more than just having a measurement instrument (e.g., a microscope). In order to measure, the researcher needs three things: a construct, a measurement instrument, and an ability to recognize what he or she is looking for.[3] Say, for instance, a criminologist is interested in the crime of smuggling. He or she must first define *smuggling*. What does the concept mean? To make it into a variable, the criminologist thinks of the different values that smuggling can take on (e.g., high versus low). Then, the researcher decides on a strategy for measuring the concept. This, in a nutshell, is the measurement process. Only after measurement issues have been ironed out are observations (or data) collected.

MEASUREMENT AND RESEARCH DESIGN

A researcher needs measures to test hypotheses and gather data. He or she chooses a general topic and refines it into a focused research problem or question. The researcher further refines it into testable hypotheses or statements about causal relationships with at least two variables. After the variables are identified in hypotheses, he or she is ready to begin the task of measurement, and measurement begins with conceptualization.

Conceptualization

At the beginning of the measurement process, a researcher conceptualizes and operationalizes each variable in a hypothesis. *Conceptualization* is the process of taking a construct or concept and refining it by giving it a conceptual or theoretical definition. A *conceptual definition* is a definition in abstract, theoretical terms. It is the researcher's way of communicating what he or she is studying. There is no magical way of turning a concept into a precise conceptual definition. It involves a process of combing over the scholarly literature, consulting with experts, and trying out possible candidates for an appropriate conceptual definition. It refers to other ideas or constructs. There is also no magical way to turn a construct into a precise conceptual definition. It involves thinking carefully, observing directly, consulting with others, reading what others have said, and trying possible definitions.

A good definition has one clear, explicit, and specific meaning. There is no ambiguity or vagueness. Some scholarly articles have been devoted to conceptualizing key concepts.

Gibbs (1989) delved into the conceptual meaning of *terrorism*. Ball and Curry (1995) discussed ways to conceptualize a *street gang*. Witte (1996) struggled to find a clear definition of the *underground economy*. These are just several of countless examples in which criminologists presented a conceptual definition.

A single construct can have several definitions, and people may disagree over definitions. Conceptual definitions are linked to theoretical frameworks and to value positions. For example, a conflict theorist may define *social class* as the power and property a group of people in society has or lacks. A structural functionalist defines it in terms of individuals who share a social status, life-style, or subjective identification. Although people disagree over definitions, it is always important to state explicitly which definition is being used.

Some constructs are more abstract than others. For example, some constructs (e.g., alienation) are highly abstract and complex. They contain lower-level concepts within them (e.g., powerlessness), which can be made even more specific (e.g., a feeling of little power over where one can live). Other constructs are concrete and simple (e.g., age). When developing definitions, you need to be aware of how complex and abstract a construct is. For example, a concrete construct such as *age* is easier to define (e.g., the number of years that have passed since birth) than is a complex, abstract concept such as *environmental crime.*

How might a criminologist develop a conceptual definition of *smuggling?* An obvious place to begin is with the dictionary definition of the word. *Smuggling* means to bring in or take out illegally, according to the *American Heritage Dictionary.* But conceptual definitions go far beyond ordinary dictionary meaning. They build on how other researchers have defined terms. The most important conceptual definitions, the ones vital to maintenance of the paradigm, are generally agreed upon by researchers in the field. Conceptual definitions will not enjoy such agreement indefinitely, however. Conceptual definitions are fluid; they represent research traditions yet spawn theoretical breakthroughs.

Let us continue with our example. One way to conceptualize smuggling is to look at the dollar value of the contraband being smuggled (Wiegand, 1993). This relationship suggests a dichotomy between petty and commercial amounts. To recall an earlier argument (Wiegand, 1994), petty smuggling does not supply stock to markets. Its small scale-of-operation prohibits that. The flat social structure of petty smuggling networks are often ethnic based. This socioethnic structure makes petty smuggling relationships very difficult to penetrate from the

outside and very difficult to detect and control. Commercial smuggling, on the other hand, brings into play elaborate systems capable of seizing and selling commercial quantities of contraband in a very short time. Surprisingly, research has shown that these complex social systems are also usually embedded in primary ethnic ties (Wiegand, 1994).

We have just constructed a simple example of a conceptual definition. We did this by conceptualizing *smuggling* based on the value of the contraband being smuggled. In our conceptual definition of *smuggling,* we have two dimensions or subparts: petty smuggling and commercial smuggling. Are there others? Of course. There is no one right answer to this question. But the researcher must give serious thought to selecting that conceptual definition which best addresses the main research question.

Invariably, the researcher will need to distinguish the main concept from related ones. This need is more easily met with a clear and appropriate conceptual definition. Thus, our conceptual definition must be able to distinguish smuggling from other related crimes such as tax evasion, corruption, or money laundering. By insisting on theoretically important distinctions, the concept has been made more precise and, subdivided into dimensions, is easier to measure. Measurement depends on having well-crafted conceptual definitions.

The best conceptual definitions are grounded in empirical reality. Familiarity with a topic is indispensable. Let us use another example with which you probably have personal experience: family unity. We define *family unity* as the feeling of closeness and sharing many daily living and leisure time activities within a family. It combines three ideas: shared feelings, shared activities, and family. One critical part of our definition is the family. What is a family? A *family* is traditionally defined as two adults who are legally married to each other and who have natural or adopted children. This seems simple, but this definition creates problems. For example, perhaps you know two people who are legally married, but who have not lived together for many years and will probably never get a legal divorce. Are they a family? What about the following relationships, none of which fits a standard definition of a family:

— A married couple who are raising children who are not biologically their own and whom they have not legally adopted
— A married couple who do not have any children
— A divorced woman who lives with her two young children
— A couple who have lived together for six years without getting legally married and who have three children
— A stable homosexual couple who have lived together as marital partners for 10 years
— Two elderly neighbors who have moved in together to look after and care for each other, and who share their pension money and all living arrangements

Most official or legal definitions of a family for purposes of insurance, inheritance, and the like define the foregoing relationships as nonfamilies, although some are now being contested. Yet, if you talked to the people in these relationships, saw how they lived, and probed into their feelings about each other, you would find few differences from the social relations in a traditional family.

The point is that conceptual definitions need to be consistent with your meaning of the construct. Our construct of *family* includes all the relationships listed here, many of which others do not call a family. Thus, our definition includes the relationships from our construct. If it did not, we would not be measuring the construct in which we are really interested.

Operationalization

After you have a working definition ("working" because it can be modified), you are ready for *operationalization*—the process of developing an operational definition for the construct. An *operational definition* is a definition in terms of specific operations, measurement instruments, or procedures. It is sometimes referred to as the *indicator* or measure of a construct.

There are usually multiple ways to measure a construct. Some are better or worse and more or less practical than others. The key is to fit your measure to your specific conceptual definition, to the practical constraints within which you must operate (e.g., time, money, available subjects, etc.) and to the research techniques you know or can learn. You can develop a new measure from scratch, or it can be a measure that is already being used by other researchers (see Box 7.1).

Operationalization links the language of theory with the language of empirical measures. Theory is full of abstract concepts, assumptions, relationships, definitions, and causality. Empirical measures describe how people concretely measure specific variables. They refer to specific operations or things people use to indi-

---

Box 7.1 _____

Five Suggestions for Coming Up with a Measure

1. *Remember the conceptual definition.* The underlying principle for any measure is to match it to the specific conceptual definition of the construct that will be used in the study.
2. *Keep an open mind.* Do not get locked into a single measure or type of measure. Be creative and constantly look for better measures. Avoid what Kaplan (1964:28) called the "law of the instrument," which means being locked into using one measurement instrument for all problems.
3. *Borrow from others.* Do not be afraid to borrow from other researchers, as long as credit is given. Good ideas for measures can be found in other studies or modified from other measures.
4. *Anticipate difficulties.* Logical and practical problems often arise when trying to measure variables of interest. Sometimes a problem can be anticipated and avoided with careful forethought and planning.
5. *Do not forget your units of analysis.* Your measure should fit with the units of analysis of the study and permit you to generalize to the universe of interest.

---

cate the presence of a construct that exists in observable reality.

The link between indicators and constructs is a central issue for quantitative measurement. During operationalization, a researcher links the world of ideas to observable reality. *Rules of correspondence* or auxiliary theory link the conceptual definitions of constructs to concrete measures or operations for measuring constructs.[4] They are logical statements of how an indicator corresponds to an abstract construct. For example, a rule of correspondence might state that a shipment of contraband exceeding a certain dollar amount is evidence of commercial smuggling. Likewise, an *auxiliary theory* explains how and why indicators and constructs connect. Such theories play a crucial role in research. Carmines and Zeller (1979:11) noted, "The auxiliary theory specifying the relationship between concepts and indicators is equally important to social research as the substantive theory linking concepts to one another." For example, an auxiliary theory would explain why the cut-off value denoting petty or commercial smuggling is set at one particular dollar amount rather than another.

Figure 7.1 illustrates the measurement process for two variables that are linked together in a theory and a hypothesis. There are three levels to consider: conceptual, operational, and empirical.[5] At the most abstract level, the researcher is interested in the causal relationship between two constructs, or a *conceptual hypothesis*. At the level of operational definitions, the researcher is interested in testing an *empirical hypothesis* to determine the degree of association between indicators. This is the level at which correlations, statistics, questionnaires, and the like are used. The third level is the concrete empirical world. If the operational indicators of variables (e.g., questionnaires) are logically linked to a construct (e.g., racial discrimination), they will capture what actually happens in the empirical social world and relate it to the conceptual level.

The measurement process links together the three levels, moving deductively from the abstract to the concrete. A researcher first conceptualizes a variable, giving it a clear conceptual definition. Next, he or she operationalizes it by developing an operational definition or set of indicators for it. Last, he or she uses the indicators by applying them in the empirical world. The links from abstract constructs to empirical reality allows the researcher to test empirical hypotheses. Those

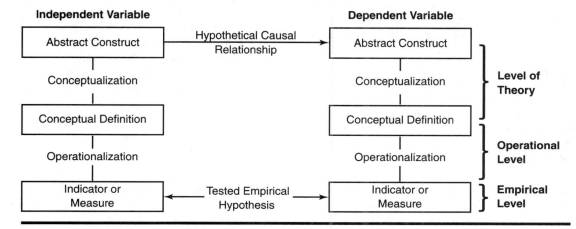

Abstract Construct to Concrete Measure

FIGURE 7.1 Conceptualization and Operationalization

empirical tests are logically linked back to a conceptual hypothesis and causal relations in the world of theory.

A hypothesis has at least two variables, and the processes of conceptualization and operationalization are necessary for each variable. To go back to our example, smuggling is a concept transformed into a variable with two attributes: petty and commercial smuggling. Depending on one's theoretical framework, it could be used as an independent or dependent variable.

Here is another example of measuring criminological concepts. Donziger (1996) developed a conceptual definition of *public safety*. He and his colleagues identified five dimensions or subparts of the construct: (1) the level of violence, (2) the rational use of prison space, (3) the level of poverty, (4) violence prevention initiatives, and (5) hope for the future. They then operationalized each dimension by selecting a variety of existing statistical data. Homicide rates, for instance, were used as a measure of "level of violence." In this way, the researchers created a concrete quantitative indicator of public safety.

RELIABILITY AND VALIDITY

Reliability and validity are central issues in all scientific measurement. Both concern how concrete measures, or indicators, are developed for constructs. Reliability and validity are salient in criminological research because constructs in criminological theory are often ambiguous, diffuse, and not directly observable. Perfect reliability and validity are virtually impossible to achieve. Rather, they are ideals researchers strive for. Researchers want to maximize the reliability and validity of indicators. *Reliability* tells us about an indicator's dependability and consistency. *Validity* tells us whether an indicator actually captures the meaning of the construct in which we are interested. If indicators have a low degree of reliability or validity, then the final results will be questionable.

Reliability

Definition.   Reliability deals with an indicator's dependability. If you have a reliable indicator or measure, it gives you the same result each time the same thing is measured (as long as what you are measuring is not changing). *Reliability* means that the information provided by indicators (e.g., a questionnaire) does not vary as a result of characteristics of the indicator, instrument, or measurement device itself.

For example, the issue of reliability came into play in Donziger's decision to use the homicide rate as an indication of level of violence. Donzinger (1996:Appendix A) wrote, "Homicide is the only crime it [the FBI Uniform Crime Report] measures accurately enough to make cross-jurisdictional comparisons." In other words, the very act of counting how many homicides have occurred is more reliable than that of other crimes. Of course, the difficulty of disposing of the victim's body contributes to the reliability of homicide rates.

Three Types of Reliability.   The three types of reliability are stability reliability, representative reliability, and equivalence reliability.[6]

Stability Reliability.   *Stability reliability* is reliability across time. It addresses the question: Does the measure or indicator deliver the same answer when applied in different time periods? You can examine an indicator's degree of stability reliability by using the *test-retest method,* with which you retest or readminister the indicator to the same group of people. If what you are measuring is stable and the indicator has stability reliability, then you will get the same results each time. Thus, homicide rates have stability reliability if the rates for a specific location are the same, irrespective of who calculated them or when (assuming the time between test and retest is relatively short).

Representative Reliability.   *Representative reliability* is reliability across subpopulations or groups of people. It addresses the question: Does the indicator deliver the same answer when applied to different groups? An indicator has high representative reliability if it yields the same result for a construct when applied to different subpopulations (e.g., different classes, races, sexes, age groups, etc.). For example, you ask a question about a person's age. If people in their twenties answered your question by overstating their true age, whereas people in their fifties understated their true age, then the indicator has a low degree of representative reliability. To have representative reliability, the measure needs to give accurate information for every age group.

A *subpopulation analysis* determines whether an indicator has this type of reliability. The analysis involves comparing the indicator across different subpopulations or subgroups and uses independent knowledge about subpopulations. For instance, suppose a researcher wants to test the representative reliability of a victimization questionnaire that asks about reporting the crime to the police. He or she could conduct a subpopulation analysis to see whether the questionnaire works equally well for men and women. By asking both men and women the questions, and then checking their responses with independent information, such as official police reports, the researcher is able to determine if there are differences between them in terms of crime reporting. The questionnaire has representative reliability if there are no significant differences.

Equivalence Reliability. *Equivalence reliability* applies when researchers use *multiple indicators*— that is, when multiple specific measures are used in the operationalization of a construct (e.g., several items in a questionnaire all measure the same construct). It addresses the question: Does the measure yield consistent results across different indicators? If several different indicators measure the same construct, then a reliable measure gives the same result with all indicators.

Researchers examine equivalence reliability on examinations and long questionnaires with the *split-half method*. This involves dividing the indicators of the same construct into two groups, usually by a random process, and determining whether both halves give the same results. For example, the National Crime Victimization Survey

(NCVS) in the United States was recently redesigned so as "to encourage more complete recall and recounting of crime events" (Kinderman et al., 1997). To test the equivalence reliability of the new design, the researchers used the split-half method, as described here:

> From 1992 through June 1993, the full NCS-NCVS sample was divided into two parts. Half of the sample was administered the NCVS method [i.e., a new set of questions to measure victimization], and the other half, the NCS method [i.e., the old set of questions]. The overlap procedure was designed to permit continuous publication of estimates of the year-to-year change in crime rates with comparable data while the new design was introduced. The procedure was also intended to provide measurable differences between the halves. (p. 2)

In general, the new NCVS questions prompted higher estimates of crime rates than had the previous questions.

A special type of equivalence reliability is *interrater* or *intercoder reliability*. It arises when there are several observers, raters, or coders of information. In a sense, each person who is observing is an indicator. A measure is reliable if the observers, raters, or coders agree with each other. It is a common type of reliability reported in content analysis studies, but it can be used whenever multiple raters or coders are involved. If, for example, a researcher wanted to study the editorial slant of television evening news coverage of the new crime legislation, the researcher may have multiple coders. Until the researcher measures intercoder reliability, he or she will never know whether the actual analysis is biased or not, because viewers tend to code the same television content differently. If intercoder reliability is poor, then the study lacks equivalence reliability.

How to Improve Reliability. It is rare to have perfect reliability. There are four principles to follow to increase the reliability of measures: (1) clearly conceptualize constructs, (2) use a precise level of measurement, (3) use multiple indicators, and (4) use pilot tests.

Clearly Conceptualize All Constructs.   Reliability increases when a single construct or subdimension of a construct is measured. This means developing unambiguous, clear theoretical definitions. Constructs should be specified to eliminate "noise" (i.e., distracting or interfering information) from other constructs. Each measure should indicate one and only one concept. Otherwise, it is impossible to determine which concept is being "indicated." As you might expect, this applies directly to questionnaire construction, which we take up in Chapter 10. There, the terminology speaks of double-barreled questions in which the referent remains lost in illogic. One is never clear if the measure is of this concept or that. The correct way to improve reliability is to unload double-barreled questions by separating the constituent parts.

In some cases, an indicator may provide an indirect measure of related concepts. In using the homicide rate to indicate level of violence, researchers in the "public safety" study (Donziger, 1996) assumed that "homicide is an 'indicator' crime." Their assumption was unfounded to the extent that they had no direct measures of the homicide-related crimes (e.g., "assaults, robberies, and other types of violent crime").

Increase the Level of Measurement.   Levels of measurement are discussed in greater detail later. Indicators at higher or more precise levels of measurement are more likely to be reliable than less precise measures because the latter pick up less detailed information. If more specific information is measured, then it is less likely that anything other than the construct will be captured. The general principle is: Try to measure constructs at the most precise level possible. However, it is more difficult to measure at higher levels of measurement. For example, given the choice of measuring homicide in terms of rates or "low" or "high" categories, it is advisable to use the more precise measure (i.e., rates).

Use Multiple Indicators of a Variable.   A third way to increase reliability is to use *multiple indicators,* because two (or more) indicators of the same construct are better than one.[7] Figure 7.2 illustrates the use of multiple indicators in hypothesis testing. Three indicators of the one independent variable construct are combined into an overall measure, *A,* and two indicators of a dependent variable are combined into a single measure, *B.*

Getting back to the public safety example, we find three indicators of the "rational use" variable. *Rational use* is defined as "how rationally a state employs its prison resources" (Donziger, 1996). The three indicators are (1) "the ratio of violent to nonviolent new commitments to state prison," (2) "the change in the rate of incarceration over the previous ten years," and (3) "the rate of incarceration of each (U.S.) State."

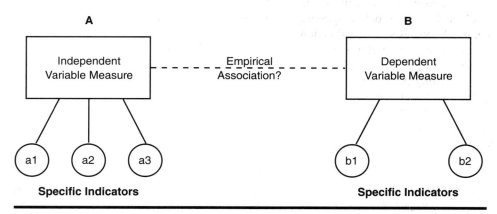

FIGURE 7.2   Measurement Using Multiple Indicators

TABLE 7.1 Summary of Measurement Reliability and Validity Types

RELIABILITY (Dependable Measure)	VALIDITY (True Measure)
Stability—over time	Face—in the judgment of others
Representative—across subgroups	Content—captures the entire meaning
Equivalence—across indicators	Criterion—agrees with an external source
	▬ Concurrent—agrees with a preexisting measure
	▬ Predictive—agrees with future behavior
	Construct—multiple indicators are consistent
	▬ Convergent—alike ones are similar
	▬ Discriminant—different ones differ

Multiple indicators do two things. First, they let a researcher take measurements from a wider range of the content of a conceptual definition. Some writers call this *sampling from the conceptual domain*. Different aspects of the construct can be measured, each with its own indicator. Second, one indicator (e.g., one question on a questionnaire) may be imperfect, but several measures are less likely to have the same (systematic) error. Multiple indicator measures tend to be more stable than measures with one item.

Use Pretests, Pilot Studies, and Replication. A fourth principle for improving reliability is to use a pretest or pilot version of a measure first. Develop one or more draft or preliminary versions of a measure and try them before applying the final version in a hypothesis-testing situation. This takes more time and effort, but it is likely to produce reliable measures.

The principle of using pilot tests extends to replicating the measures other researchers have used. It is wise to learn from past research. If good measures of a concept can be found already in the literature, then why not cite the source and reuse it in your own study? Replicating measures has the added advantage of giving the researcher the opportunity to compare replicated and new measures. In this way, the quality of the measure can improve over time, as long as the same definition

is used. (See Table 7.1 for a summary of reliability types.)

Validity

Definition. A measurement has no meaning without validity. *Measurement validity* refers to measurement being appropriate (or valid) for the research at hand. When a researcher says that an indicator is valid, he or she means it to be appropriate for one research project but not necessarily for another having a different research question, variables, and the like.[8] The first concern in measurement is that the measure be valid.

At its core, measurement validity is the degree of fit between a construct and indicators of it. It refers to how well the conceptual and operational definitions mesh with each other. The better the fit, the greater the measurement validity. Validity is more difficult to achieve than reliability. We cannot have absolute confidence about validity, but some measures are *more valid* than others. The reason we can never achieve absolute validity is that constructs are abstract ideas, whereas indicators refer to concrete observation. This is the gap between our mental pictures about the world and the specific things we do at particular times and places. Bohrnstedt (1992b) has argued that validity is a matter of degree; it cannot be determined directly. Validity is part of a dynamic process that grows by accumulating evidence over time, and without it, all measurement becomes meaningless.

Another way of talking about measurement validity is the *epistemic correlation*. This refers to a make-believe or hypothetical correlation between a specific indicator and the essence of the construct that the indicator measures. We cannot measure such correlations directly because correlations between a measure and an abstraction are impossible, but they can be estimated with advanced statistical techniques.[9]

Four Types of Measurement Validity.   The four types of measurement validity are face validity, content validity, criterion validity, and construct validity.

Face Validity.   The easiest type of validity to achieve and the most basic kind of validity is *face validity*. It is a judgment by the scientific community that the indicator really measures the construct. In other words, it addresses the question: On the face of it, do people believe that the definition and method of measurement fit? It is a consensus method of measurement validity.

For example, few experts would quibble with the face validity of measuring the rational use of prison resources in terms of the ratio of violent to nonviolent prisoners, as Donziger (1996) did. The tacit point of agreement is that it is rational to have proportionately more violent prisoners than nonviolent prisoners. Recall that the principle of organized skepticism in the scientific community means that aspects of the research are scrutinized by others. This serves to enforce the significance of face validity.[10] (See Table 7.1 for a summary of types of measurement validity. Figure 7.3 presents them in pictorial form.)

Content Validity.   *Content validity* is actually a special type of face validity. It addresses the question: Is the full content of a definition represented in a measure? A conceptual definition holds ideas; it is a "space" containing ideas and concepts. Measures should sample or represent all ideas or areas in the conceptual space. Content

validity involves three steps. First, specify the content in a construct's definition. Next, sample from all areas of the definition. Finally, develop an indicator that taps all of the various parts of the definition.

The public safety study cited earlier in the chapter serves as a good illustration of content validity. "Public safety," you might recall, contained five dimensions: level of violence, rational use of prison resources, poverty, violence prevention initiatives, and hope for the future. Establishing good content validity requires that each of the five dimensions has its own set of measures. The study met this requirement. To measure level of violence, the researchers used one indicator (i.e., the homicide rate), rational use had three indicators, poverty had two indicators, violence prevention initiatives had one indicator, and hope for the future had two indicators. For a content-valid measure, each dimension needs one or more indictor or measure of it.

Criterion Validity.   *Criterion validity* uses some standard or criterion that is known to indicate a construct accurately. In other words, the validity of an indicator is verified by comparing it with another measure of the same construct in which a researcher has confidence. There are two subtypes of this kind of validity.[11]

Concurrent.   To have *concurrent validity*, an indicator must be associated with a preexisting indicator that is judged to be valid (i.e., it has face validity). For example, if the homicide rate is an indicator of level of violence, then one would expect it to be associated with other existing measures of violent crime, such as assault rates, robbery rates, and so on. The two measures (e.g., homicide and assault rates) may not be perfectly associated, but if they measure the same or a similar construct (i.e., level of violence), it is logical for them to yield similar results.

Predictive.   Criterion validity whereby an indicator predicts future events that are logically related to a construct is called *predictive validity*. It cannot be used for all measures. The measure and the action predicted must be distinct from but

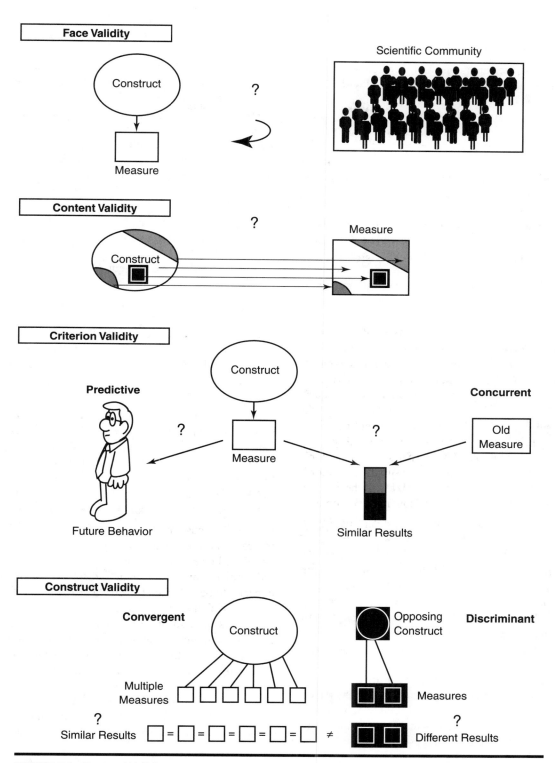

FIGURE 7.3 Types of Validity

indicate the same construct. Predictive measurement validity should not be confused with prediction in hypothesis testing, where one variable predicts a different variable in the future. For instance, one of the ways the public safety study (Donziger, 1996) measures poverty is as the percentage of children living below the official poverty line. If this measure has predictive validity, then it will be associated with some other future measure logically related to the poverty construct, such as the high school dropout rate.

Another way to test predictive validity is to select a group of people who have specific characteristics and predict how they will score (very high or very low) vis-à-vis the construct. If a researcher developed a "fear of crime" measure, for example, he or she could try it out on different groups to see if the measure operates in the predicted direction. Thus, elderly women will score higher on it than young women, elderly men higher than young men, and so on.

Construct Validity.   *Construct validity* is for measures with multiple indicators. It addresses the question: If the measure is valid, do the various indicators operate in a consistent manner? It requires a definition with clearly specified conceptual boundaries. The two types are convergent validity and discriminant validity.

Convergent validity.   This kind of validity applies when multiple indicators converge or are associated with one another. *Convergent validity* means that multiple measures of the same construct hang together or operate in similar ways. Consider, for example, the way researchers in the public safety study measured "hope for the future" in two ways: (1) percentage of teens who dropped out of high school and (2) the salary ratio between public school teachers and prison guards. Having convergent validity, these two measures behave in a similar fashion. Thus, a low dropout rate would be associated with a high salary ratio (i.e., teachers make more money than prison guards). Both suggest hope.

Discriminant validity.   Also called divergent validity, *discriminant validity* is the opposite

of convergent validity. It means that the indicators of one construct hang together or converge, but also diverge or are negatively associated with opposing constructs. It says that if two constructs *A* and *B* are very different, then measures of *A* and *B* should not be associated. The public safety study, for example, has discriminate validity built into it. Measures of poverty (i.e., percentage of children in poverty) would be negatively associated with measures of hope for the future (e.g., salary ratio of teachers to prison guards). In other words, the two opposing constructs (i.e., poverty and hope for the future) have measures that are likewise opposing or divergent.

Other Uses of the Terms *Reliable* and *Valid*

Many words have multiple definitions, including *reliability* and *validity*. This creates confusion unless we distinguish among alternative uses of the same word.

Reliability.   We use *reliability* in everyday language. A reliable person is one who is dependable, stable, and responsible; a reliable car is dependable and trustworthy. This means the person responds in similar, predictable ways in different times and conditions; the same can be said for the car. In addition to measurement reliability, researchers sometimes say a study or its results are reliable (e.g., Yin, 1988). By this, they mean that the method of conducting a study or the results from it can be reproduced or replicated by other researchers.

Internal Validity.   *Internal validity* means there are no errors internal to the design of the research project.[12] It is used primarily in experimental research to talk about possible errors or alternative explanations of results that arise despite attempts to institute controls. High internal validity means there are few such errors. Low internal validity means that such errors are likely.

External Validity.   *External validity* is used primarily in experimental research. It is the ability to generalize findings from a specific setting and small group to a broad range of settings and people. It addresses the question: If something happens in a laboratory or among a particular group of subjects (e.g., college students), can the findings be generalized to the "real" (nonlaboratory) world or to the general public (nonstudents)? High external validity means that the results can be generalized to many situations and many groups of people. Low external validity means that the results apply only to a very specific setting.

Statistical Validity.   *Statistical validity* means that the correct statistical procedure is chosen and its assumptions are fully met. Different statistical tests or procedures are appropriate for different conditions, which are discussed in textbooks that describe the statistical procedures.

All statistics are based on assumptions about the mathematical properties of the numbers being used. A statistic will be invalid and its results nonsense if the major assumptions are violated. For example, to compute an average (actually the mean, which is discussed in a later chapter), one cannot use information at the nominal level of measurement (to be discussed). For example, suppose we measure the race of a class of students. We give each race a number: White = 1, African American = 2, Asian = 3, others = 4. It makes no sense to say that the "mean" race of a class of students is 1.9 (almost African American?). This is a misuse of the statistical procedure, and the results are invalid even if the computation is correct. The degree to which statistical assumptions can be violated or bent (the technical term is *robustness*) is a topic in which professional statisticians take great interest.

RELATIONSHIP BETWEEN RELIABILITY AND VALIDITY

Reliability is necessary for validity and is easier to achieve than validity. Although reliability is necessary in order to have a valid measure of a concept, it does not guarantee that a measure will be valid. It is not a sufficient condition for validity. A measure can produce the same result over and over (i.e., it

has reliability), but what it measures may not match the definition of the construct (i.e., validity).

A measure can be reliable but invalid. For example, the FBI's Uniform Crime Report statistics have historically undercounted certain serious crimes such as forcible rape. These data showed fairly stable levels of rape over the years, and were thus reliable. However, because of the crime-reporting problems associated with rape in which many women refused to report the crime to police, rape statistics understated the seriousness of the problem, and thus, to that extent, were not valid.

A diagram might help you see the relationship between reliability and validity. Figure 7.4 illustrates the relationship between the concepts by using the analogy of a target. The bull's-eye represents a fit between a measure and the definition of the construct.

Validity and *reliability* are usually complementary concepts, but in some special situations they conflict with each other. Sometimes, as validity increases, reliability is more difficult to attain, and vice versa. This occurs when the construct has a highly abstract and not easily observable definition. Reliability is easiest to achieve when the measure is precise and observable. Thus, there is a strain between the true essence of the highly abstract construct and measuring it in a concrete manner.

"Public safety," for example, is a very abstract, highly subjective construct, having to do with a person's sense of security and well-being. These feelings cut across many aspects of one's life, such as crime victimization, education, employment, and others. Highly precise quantitative data, such as the homicide rate in a given area, give reliable measures, but there is also the danger of losing the subjective essence of the concept. Criminologists from the interpretive and critical perspectives are particularly keen to keep this in mind. They believe that measurement must be precise, but also that it must be flexible and qualitative. Thus, as you can see, measurement issues ultimately return to assumptions about methodology, about how to conduct research, and about how the concepts are defined.

A Bull's-Eye = A Perfect Measure

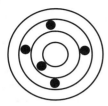  

Low Reliability
and Low Validity

High Reliability
but Low Validity

High Reliability
and High Validity

FIGURE 7.4   Illustration of Relationship between Reliability and Validity
Source: Adapted from Babbie (1995:128).

LEVELS OF MEASUREMENT

Levels of measurement is an abstract but important and widely used idea. Basically, it says that some ways a researcher measures a construct are at a higher or more refined level, and others are crude or less precisely specified. The level of measurement depends on the way in which a construct is conceptualized—that is, assumptions about whether it has particular characteristics. The level of measurement affects the kinds of indicators chosen and is tied to basic assumptions in a construct's definition. The way in which a researcher conceptualizes a variable limits the levels of measurement that he or she can use and has implications for how measurement and statistical analysis can proceed.

Continuous and Discrete Variables

Variables can be thought of as being either continuous or discrete. *Continuous variables* have an infinite number of values or attributes that flow along a continuum. The values can be divided into many smaller increments; in mathematical theory, there is an infinite number of increments. Some of continuous variables we have used in examples thus far are the homicide rate, the street price of illicit drugs, the percentage of U.S. currency held abroad, the

dollar value of seized contraband, and the violent/nonviolent prisoners ratio.

Discrete variables have a relatively fixed set of separate values or variable attributes. Instead of a smooth continuum of values, discrete variables contain distinct categories. A few discrete variables have been used as examples thus far, including the type of crime (e.g., white-collar crime, corporate crime, street crime, etc.), ethnicity, the type of smuggling (e.g., petty or commercial), and the perspectives on justice (e.g., criminal or social).

Four Levels of Measurement

Precision and Levels.   The idea of levels of measurement expands on the difference between continuous and discrete variables and organizes types of variables for their use in statistics. The four *levels of measurement* categorize the degree of precision of measurement.[13]

Deciding on the appropriate level of measurement for a construct often creates confusion. The appropriate level of measurement for a variable depends on two things: (1) how a construct is conceptualized and (2) the type of indicator or measurement that a researcher uses.

The construct itself limits the level of precision. The way a researcher conceptualizes a construct can limit how precisely it can be measured.

In working with smuggling data, for example, a researcher may decide it is wise to present continuous data on the dollar value of contraband seized in their discrete form. The data thus get analyzed as petty and noncommercial forms of smuggling. The actual dollar amount, in other words, is less important to the theoretical perspective than is the particular social structural form of a smuggling network. (See Wiegand [1993] for more discussion.)

As you can see, then, continuous variables may be put to good use as discrete variables. Yet, the opposite is not true. Discrete variables are not directly transformed into continuous variables. Let us say the researcher is now interested in looking over a set of correlation coefficients on smuggling. If he or she is driving at precise comparisons, then the discrete measurement of smuggling as either petty or commercial is not suitable. The researcher would have to use a continuous variable such as "the total annual dollar value of seized contraband per country." There would be no way of deriving the latter from the former.

To put it as a rule of thumb, it is wise to conceptualize and measure variables at the highest possible level. You can always collapse higher levels of measurement, as we have just seen, but the reverse is not true. In other words, a researcher can always choose to ignore some of the precision of the higher level of measurement. But it is impossible to take less precise information and report with more precision. To do that would be unscientific in the extreme.

The level of measurement limits the statistical measures that can be used. A wide range of powerful statistical procedures are available for the higher levels, but the types of statistics that can be used with the lowest levels are very limited.

Distinguishing among the Four Levels. The four levels from lowest to greatest or highest precision are nominal, ordinal, interval, and ratio. Each level gives a different type of information (see Table 7.2). *Nominal* measures indicate only that there is a difference among categories (e.g., type of crime: violent crime, property crime, and organizational crime). *Ordinal* measures indicate a difference, *plus* the categories can be ordered or ranked (such as the 1st, 2nd, 3rd, and 4th). Ordinal measures are often used in opinion surveys with scales such as Strongly Agree, Agree, Disagree, and Strongly Disagree.

Interval measures everything the first two do, *plus* the amount of distance between the categories can be specified. The common examples of interval measures are IQ scores and temperature, but criminologists rarely use measurement at this level. That being said, there are other measures that researchers do use, such as immigration generation (i.e., first generation, second, third, etc.) or retail price for illicit drugs.

Arbitrary zeros may be used in interval measures; they are just there to help keep score. *Ratio* measures do everything all the other levels do,

TABLE 7.2 Characteristics of the Four Levels of Measurement

LEVEL	DIFFERENT CATEGORIES	RANKED	DISTANCE BETWEEN CATEGORIES MEASURED	TRUE ZERO
Nominal	Yes			
Ordinal	Yes	Yes		
Interval	Yes	Yes	Yes	
Ratio	Yes	Yes	Yes	Yes

plus there is a true zero, which makes it possible to state relations in terms of proportion or ratios (e.g., the percentage of prisoners who are violent). In most practical situations, the distinction between interval and ratio levels makes little difference. The arbitrary zeros of some interval measures can be confusing. For example, a rise in temperature from 30 to 60 degrees is not really a doubling of the temperature, although the numbers double, because zero degrees is not the absence of all heat.

Discrete variables are nominal and ordinal, whereas continuous variables can be measured at the interval or ratio level. A ratio-level measure can be turned into an interval, ordinal, or nominal level. The interval level can always be turned into an ordinal or nominal level, but the process does not work in the opposite way.

In general, if it is necessary to use ordinal measurement, use at least five ordinal categories and obtain many observations. This is because the distortion created by collapsing a continuous construct into a smaller number of ordered categories is minimized as the number of categories and the number of observations increase.[14]

For most purposes, the ratio level of measurement is indistinguishable from interval measurement. The only difference is that ratio measurement has a "true zero." This can be confusing because some measures, like temperature, have zeros that are not true zeros. The temperature can be zero, or below zero, but zero is an arbitrary number when it is assigned to temperature. This can be illustrated by comparing zero degrees Celsius with zero degrees Fahrenheit—they are different temperatures. In addition, doubling the degrees in one system does not double the degrees in the other. Likewise, it does not make sense to say that it is "twice as warm," as is possible with ratio measurement, if the temperature rises from 2 to 4 degrees, from 15 to 30 degrees, or from 40 to 80 degrees. Another common example of arbitrary—not true—zeros occurs when measuring attitudes where numbers are assigned to statements (e.g., −1 = disagree, 0 = no opinion, +1 = agree). True zeros exist for variables such as income, age, or years of education.

Examples of the four levels of measurement are shown in Table 7.3.

INTRODUCTION TO MEASUREMENT THEORY

Measurement theory is the name for a body of mathematical and methodological theory on reliability, validity, and related topics.[15] Measurement theory gets quite technical, but a general introductory summary of its core assumption can help you understand the principles of good measurement. Measurement theory is based on the idea that an empirical measure of a concept reflects three components: (1) the true construct or an absolutely perfect measure of it, (2) systematic error, and (3) random error. People can see only the empirical measure; the three components are unobserved, hypothetical ideas about what measurement involves. The parts of measurement can be symbolically expressed as follows:

X *Observation:* The empirical indicator or observation

T *True measure:* Ideal, pure construct

S *Systematic error:* Bias; any error that is not random

R *Random error:* Nonsystematic, unavoidable, chance errors

Thus, measurement theory assumes that a specific observation is made up of the construct and of two components that are called errors because they represent deviations from the true construct. If this is put in the form of an equation, it becomes:

$$X = T + S + R$$

This equation is the core of measurement theory. In plain English, it says that an empirical observation by a researcher actually comprises three unseen sources: the construct plus two kinds of potential errors or possible sources of deviation from the true construct.

In the preceding section, you saw that perfect measurement validity is a perfect match between an empirical indicator and the construct it indi-

TABLE 7.3   Example of Levels of Measurement

VARIABLE (Level of Measurement)	HOW VARIABLE MEASURED
Ethnicity (nominal)	Ethnicity serves as an identifier. It characterizes ethnic identity such as Bosnian, Serb, Croatian, and so on, which cannot be ranked in order of importance.
Opinions about Police Behavior (ordinal)	"As far as you know, do the police in your community mostly treat African Americans worse than Whites, or both races equally?" Mostly African Americans worse than Whites Mostly equally Don't know
Immigration Generation (interval)	"Considering when your family arrived in this country, what generation are you?" First generation Second generation Third generation _____ generation
Household Income (ratio)	"How much was the total household income last year?" $ _____

cates (or its theoretical definition). The measurement theory equation says that an empirical observation and the construct are equal when there are no measurement errors—that is, when the two components that represent potential errors equal zero. Thus, using the equation and measurement theory, we can restate the definition of perfect measurement validity as $X = T$. Researchers use the equation to think about and improve validity by focusing their attention on the two possible types of errors, S and R, and how to get them to equal zero.

Let us focus on the R, or random error, part of the equation first. Probability theory from mathematics says that in the long run, over enough cases, the R becomes zero and drops out of the equation. In the language of statistical theory, the random error has an *expected value* of zero. Without getting into complex probability theory, this happens because errors that are truly random cancel each other out in the long run. Various mathematical proofs and empirical tests show that over a very large number of separate events (e.g., several million), truly random processes stabilize around a true value and errors become zero. For example, say you flip a perfectly balanced coin in a truly random way for 10 million times. The "errors"—or in this situation, getting more heads than tails or vice versa—will disappear. You can be extremely certain that your flipping will result in 50 percent heads and 50 percent tails. Another example is that of driving a car at a constant speed. Assume that you have a valid and reliable speedometer and you try to drive exactly 50 kilometers per hour, no more and no less. You will be slightly above this speed at some times and slightly below it at other times. If your errors are truly random, the speeds over and under 50 kilometers per hour will cancel each other, or the expected value of the deviations above and below the speed will be zero and your speed will be 50 kilometers per hour. Researchers do not worry a lot about random error. They assume that there is always some random error, but that, over enough replications or cases, it can be safely ignored.

Once we ignore random error, an observation *(X)* equals the true construct *(T)* and systematic or nonrandom error *(S)*. Systematic error is a potentially avoidable error that distorts results in a systematic manner. An example of a systematic error can be a poorly worded question that causes most respondents to answer in a particular way, or an interviewer's attempts to get respondents to answer in a particular way. Systematic error is at the heart of validity and reliability. It prevents indicators from measuring what they claim to measure (i.e., the true construct). Thus, another way to think about improving measurement is to eliminate systematic error or *bias*.[16]

Systematic error shows how causal inferences from empirical data can be in error. What was said earlier about measurement validity can be restated as validity when the observed measure *(X)* equals the true measure *(T)*. $X = T$ when the systematic error *(S)* is zero.

There are many possible sources of systematic error. Some have already been mentioned, such as a lack of stability reliability or a lack of construct validity, and others will be mentioned in later chapters. The point to keep in mind here is that the measurement theory equation is a way to show that any measurement bias (i.e., a nonzero value for systematic error) reduces measurement validity.

THE PRINCIPLE OF HETEROGENEOUS OBSERVATION

Another principle of good quantitative measurement is that of *heterogeneous observation*. This principle simply says that, all things being equal, many diverse or heterogeneous observations provide stronger evidence than one or very similar observations. Two applications illustrate the principle: replication and triangulation.

Replication

You are familiar with the principle of *replication*. It simply means redoing the same thing with an expectation of the same result. Ideally, the replication is conducted independently by a different researcher. The way a construct is measured, a specific finding or an entire study can be replicated. Replicating the measurement of a construct reinforces its validity, and replicating a finding increases confidence in the initial findings.

The logic of replication implies that different researchers are unlikely to make the same errors. If the same findings are reproduced, then systematic error is less likely. If the same findings cannot be reproduced, then questions are raised about the initial findings.

Although replication is a basic principle of positivist research, it occurs too infrequently in criminology or the other social sciences. Indeed, most quantitative findings are not replicated. Certain research questions, such as What are the effects of income inequality on property crime rates? do get studied by many different criminologists employing diverse conceptual definitions, research methods, operationalizations, and so on. The weight of the evidence accumulates over time, and out of it emerges often a consensus regarding the theoretical relationship in question. However, replication implies employing the identical methodology (e.g., the same level of measurement, the same operational definitions, the same research techniques, and the same sample) used by previous researchers. In this case, the failure to replicate identical research findings is usually due to one of four reasons or some combination of them (see Box 7.2).

Triangulation

Surveyors measure the distances between objects and survey the landscape by viewing points from different angles—a process called *triangulation*. They look at something from different angles or viewpoints to get a fix on its true position (see Figure 7.5). In social research, triangulation means using different types of measures, or data collection techniques, in order

Box 7.2

Reasons That Replication Fails

1. The original causal relationship is true, but the conditions of the replication differ. The original relation holds only under specific, but unstated, conditions. It is then necessary to find the conditions under which the original relationship holds. For example, research on white-collar crime in Japan suggests that it is more likely to be a collective act, whereas in the United States, research shows it tends to be an individual act (Kerbo and Inoue, 1996).

2. The original causal relationship is true, but it was not a true replication because the second test was conducted differently. This occurs when the description of the original research procedure is not specific enough or the researcher doing the replication was not careful enough. For example, a university researcher replicates a survey of tax crime that had been originally conducted by the federal tax agency (e.g., the U.S. Internal Revenue Service). The questionnaire the research is using is identical to the original, but the sample is different. Consequently, the findings were not replicated.

3. The original causal relationship is spurious. It was actually due to a different independent variable in the original situation—one that was not apparent at first. For example, the original findings in the tax crime survey are spurious because of the sample's reluctance to report his or her crimes honestly to the federal tax agency. Consequently, the findings were not replicated in the second survey that was conducted by the university researcher.

4. The original causal relationship is false. It was not reported correctly or is due to random chance. For example, a researcher analyzes his or her data poorly. Consequently, a replication of that study fails to reach the same conclusion.

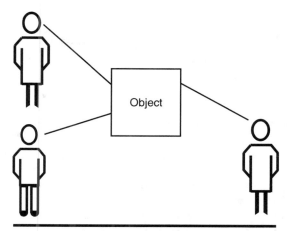

FIGURE 7.5   Triangulation: Observing from Different Viewpoints

and, more recently, ethnography to explore the relationship.

The basic idea is that measurement improves when diverse indicators are used. As the diversity of indicators gets greater, our confidence in measurement grows, because getting identical measurements from highly diverse methods implies greater validity than if a single or similar methods had been used. Simply put, it stands to reason that if the research findings from three different methods (e.g., survey, existing statistics, and ethnography) all point in the same direction, then you would feel more confident in the validity of the findings than if only one research method had been used.

SPECIALIZED MEASURES: SCALES AND INDEXES

In this section of the chapter, we will look at a number of specialized measures, including scales and indexes. Researchers have created thousands of different scales and indexes to measure social variables.[18]

Scales and indexes have been used to measure public safety, attitudes toward community policing, self-reported delinquency among various ethnic groups, the criminality of corporations, attitudes toward political corruption, the relation-

to examine the same variable. It is a special use of multiple indicators.[17]

Triangulation in criminological research is often employed to study key relationships such as that of social class and crime. Thus, researchers have used surveys, existing statistics, ship between societal development and criminality, to mention just a few. It is not important that you know these different examples, but rather that you focus on the principles of scale and index construction.

Keep two things in mind. First, virtually every social phenomenon can be measured. Some constructs can be measured directly and produce precise numerical values (e.g., family income). Other constructs require the use of surrogates or proxies that indirectly measure a variable and may not be as precise (e.g., predisposition to commit a crime). Second, a lot can be learned from measures used by other researchers. You are fortunate to have the work of thousands of researchers to draw on. It is not always necessary to start from scratch. You can use a past scale or index, or you can modify it for your own purposes. Grosof and Sardy (1985:163) have warned that creating rating scales and attitude measures "is a particularly difficult and delicate enterprise and requires a great deal of careful thought." Like the general process of knowledge creation, the process of creating measures for a construct evolves over time. Measurement is an ongoing process with constant change; new concepts are developed, theoretical definitions are refined, and scales or indexes that measure old or new constructs are improved.

Indexes and Scales

You might find the terms *index* and *scale* confusing because they are often used interchangeably. One researcher's scale is another's index. Both produce ordinal- or interval-level measures of a variable. To add to the confusion, scale and index techniques can be combined in one measure. Scales and indexes give a researcher more information about variables and make it possible to assess the quality of measurement. Scales and indexes increase reliability and validity, and they aid in data reduction; that is, they condense and simplify the information that is collected (see Box 7.3).

Mutually Exclusive and Exhaustive Attributes

Before discussing scales and indexes, it is important to review features of good measurement. The attributes of all measures, including nominal-level measures, should be mutually exclusive and exhaustive.

Mutually exclusive attributes means that an individual or unit of analysis needs to fit into one and only one attribute of a variable. For example, a variable that measures the type of crime—with the attributes of homicide, aggravated assault, forcible rape, robbery, larceny-theft, motor vehicle theft, arson, and burglary—may not be mutually exclusive if more than one crime category can be given (e.g., aggravated assault *and* robbery). If, however, only one attribute can be used at a time (e.g., aggravated assault), then the variable is mutually exclusive.

Exhaustive attributes means that all cases fit into one of the attributes of a variable. No case is without a category to fit into. When measuring type of crime, however, there are other types that do not fit into any of the categories. (These cate-

---

Box 7.3 _____

Scales and Indexes: Are They Different?

For most purposes, you can treat scales and indexes as interchangeable. Social researchers do not use a consistent nomenclature to distinguish between them.

A *scale* is a measure in which a researcher captures the intensity, direction, level, or potency of a variable construct. It arranges responses or observations on a continuum. A scale can use a single indicator or multiple indicators. Most are at the ordinal level of measurement.

An *index* is a measure in which a researcher adds or combines several distinct indicators of a construct into a single score. This composite score is often a simple sum of the multiple indicators. It is used for content and convergent validity. Indexes are often measured at the interval or ratio level.

Researchers sometimes combine the features of scales and indexes in a single measure. This is common when a researcher has several indicators that are scales (i.e., that measure intensity or direction). He or she then adds these indicators together to yield a single score, thereby creating an index.

---

gories make up the FBI's crime index.) For example, there is no category for tax evasion, smuggling, or environmental crime. The researcher must design variable attributes that correspond with the research question being asked. If he or she is interested in white-collar crime, then quite clearly the FBI's attributes for type of crime are not exhaustive.

Unidimensionality

In addition to being mutually exclusive and exhaustive, scales and indexes should also be unidimensional or one dimensional. *Unidimensionality* means that all the items in a scale or index should fit together, or measure a single construct. Unidimensionality was hinted at in the previous discussions of construct and content validity. Unidimensionality says: If you are going to combine several specific pieces of information into a single score or measure, all the pieces should be measuring the same thing. One of the more advanced techniques—factor analysis (to be discussed later in this chapter)—is often used to test for the unidimensionality of data.

There is an apparent contradiction between using a scale or index to combine parts or subparts of a construct into one measure and the criteria of unidimensionality. It is only an apparent contradiction, however, because constructs are theoretically defined at different levels of abstraction. General, higher-level or more abstract constructs can be defined as containing several subparts. Each subdimension is a part of the construct's overall content.

Let us briefly return to Donziger's (1996) study of public safety. His research question was this: How relatively safe are the various states in the United States? The most abstract construct in this study is "public safety." However, the conceptual definition Donziger used subdivided the main construct into five dimensions: level of violence, rational use of prison resources, level of poverty, violence prevention initiatives, and hope for the future. It is easy to become confused. In Donziger's study, level of violence, for instance,

is a subpart of an abstract theoretical construct that has unidimensionality. A different researcher may be interested in level of violence, not as one dimension of a more abstract construct (e.g., "public safety"), but as a measure of level of violence. This measure also has unidimensionality. This is possible because constructs can be used at different levels of abstraction. Thus, level of violence in, say, the state of Louisiana is a unidimensional construct in its own right. But it can also be thought of at a higher level of abstraction as being one factor contributing to "public safety" in Louisiana. In this instance, level of violence is a subpart of a more general and abstract unidimensional construct (i.e., "public safety").

INDEX CONSTRUCTION

The Purpose

Criminologists refer to indexes all the time. Perhaps the best known of them is the U.S. Federal Bureau of Investigation's crime index. This index is made up of police reports from some 17,000 police departments across the country. The police report information such as type of crime and arrest rates for the specific crimes mentioned earlier (homicide, aggravated assault, robbery, forcible rape, larceny-theft, motor vehicle theft, burglary, and arson). This data set contains crime data going all the way back to the 1930s (see Rosen, 1995). It is more often cited by the mass media than the National Crime Victimization Survey because the FBI crime statistics can be analyzed for particular cities, villages, towns, states, as well as for the entire country.

An *index* is a combination of items into a single numerical score. Various components or subparts of a construct are measured, then combined into a single measure. Creating indexes is so easy that it is important to be careful that every item in the index has face validity. Items without face validity should be excluded. Each part of the construct should be measured with at least one indicator. Of course, it is better to measure the subparts of an abstract construct with multiple indicators.

Since you are already familiar with Donziger's (1996) "public safety" study, the authors thought it would be useful to discuss it in greater detail (see Box 7.4). The research was conducted by a national commission of criminal justice experts, and the research method used was existing statistics. The research question was: Which state in the United States has the highest level of public safety? The commission's objective was to create a public safety index that could then be used to rank order the 50 states. The conceptual definition used had five subparts: level of violence, rational use of prison resources, level of poverty, violence prevention initiatives, and hope

---

Box 7.4 _____

Example of "Public Safety" Index*

The five dimensions of the "public safety" construct are:

1. Level of Violence
2. Rational Use of Prison Resources
3. Level of Poverty
4. Violence Prevention Initiatives
5. Hope for the Future

The respective measures for each dimension are:

1. Level of Violence
   a. Homicide rate
2. Rational Use of Prison Resources
   a. Violent/nonviolent prisoner rate
   b. Changes in incarceration rates in the past 10 years
   c. Incarceration rate
3. Level of Poverty
   a. Percentage of children in poverty
   b. Employment rate
4. Violence Prevention Initiatives
   a. Initiative number relative to homicide rate
5. Hope for the Future
   a. Percentage of high school dropouts
   b. Salary ratio (teacher:prison guard)

*Unweighted index

---

for the future. Three of the five subparts used had multiple indicators; two (i.e., level of violence and violence prevention initiatives) had only single indicators.

The measure for "level of violence" was the homicide rate, meaning the number of homicides occurring in that state in one year relative to the state's population. This produced a ratio level of measurement, which was reported at the ordinal level. The state with the lowest violence ranking was Maine; the state with the highest violence ranking was Louisiana.

The four remaining subparts were done in the same way. The rational use of state prison resources was a question of obvious policy relevance. The three measures used were closely related, although the technical appendix of the commission's book did fail to address whether these three ratio-level measures themselves were reliable. Nevertheless, the three indicators served the project's purpose. They were: (1) "the ratio of violent to nonviolent commitments to state prison"; (2) "the change in the rate of incarceration over the previous 10 years"; and (3) "the rate of incarceration of each state" (Donziger, 1996: Appendix A [n.p.]). We are assuming, of course, that *incarceration* in this instance refers only to state prison rates. The imprisonment rate is what we want to keep in mind, which is easy to find from the report's list of primary sources.

The findings are interesting. For the "rational use of state prison resources" dimension, the southern state of South Carolina sat in last place, ranked fiftieth. In fact, the eight lowest ranking states were all from the South; in order they were: South Carolina, Oklahoma, Arizona, Virginia, Texas, Alabama, Louisiana, and Mississippi.

The subpart called "level of poverty" in a state was determined by two measures: (1) the percentage of children living in poverty and (2) the employment rate. There is much more to say about measuring poverty, but these rates do approximate poverty levels. Other measures—of underemployment, in particular—would have sharpened the national commission's final report. Nebraska ranked first; Louisiana was again the worst of the 50 states.

"Violence prevention initiatives" were indicated by just one measure. Admittedly, the national commission made no effort to measure initiative efficacy. But a clever measure they did use came from a directory of federal government violence-prevention programs. From that one source *(Partnerships against Violence, Promising Programs;* United States Departments of Justice, Health and Human Services, Education, Labor, Housing and Urban Development, and Agriculture, 1994), it is a simple matter of counting the number of programs per state relative to the level of violence (as measured by the homicide rate). This is a ratio level of measurement.

North Dakota ranked first and South Carolina ranked last again. That South Carolina ranked last in violence prevention and rational use of prison resources suggests the two measures have a degree of reliability.

Trying to measure "hope for the future" was a real challenge. The national commission summoned forth a creative effort. Hope was first measured as the percentage of teens who dropped out of high school. Hope was next measured as the salary ratio between public school teachers and prison guards. There are doubtless other measures you can come up with. But on this particular scale, the state of Wisconsin was ranked most hopeful of all.

Now we are in a position to combine the five scales into a public safety index. Each scale was equally weighted. This means they all contributed equally to the index score. The state that earned the highest final grade, as the commission put it, was North Dakota. The southern states, as you might expect, ranked very poorly in the level of public safety they provide.

Weighting

An important issue in index construction is whether to weight items. Unless it is otherwise stated, assume that an index is unweighted. Likewise, unless you have a good theoretical reason for assigning different weights, use equal weights. An *unweighted index* is an index in which each item has equal weight. It involves adding up the items without modification, as if each were multiplied by 1 (or −1 for items that are negative).

In a weighted index, a researcher values or weights some items more than others. The size of weights can come from theoretical assumptions, the theoretical definition, or a statistical technique such as factor analysis (to be discussed). Weighting changes the theoretical definition of the construct.

Weighting produces different index scores, but in most cases, weighted and unweighted indexes yield similar results. Researchers are concerned with the relationship between variables, and weighted and unweighted indexes usually give similar results for the relationships between variables.[19]

Missing Data

Missing data can be a serious problem when constructing an index. Validity and reliability are threatened whenever data for some cases are missing. There are four ways to attempt to resolve the problem (see Box 7.5), but none fully solve it.

For example, let us construct an index of the degree of societal development in 1975 for 50 nations. The index contains four items: life expectancy, percentage of homes with indoor plumbing, percentage of population that is literate, and number of telephones per 100 people. We locate a source of United Nations statistics for our information. The values for Belgium are 68 + 87 + 97 + 28; for Turkey, the scores are 55 + 36 + 49 + 3; for Finland, however, we discover that literacy data are unavailable. We check other sources of information, but none has the data because they were not collected.

Rates and Standardization

You have heard of crime rates, rates of population growth, or the unemployment rate. Some indexes and single-indicator measures are expressed as rates. Rates involve standardizing the value of an item to make comparisons possible. The items in an index frequently need to be standardized before they can be combined.

Box 7.5 _____

Ways to Deal with Missing Data

1. *Eliminate all cases for which any information is missing.* If Finland is removed from the study, the index will be reliable for the nations on which information is available. This is a problem if other nations have missing information. A study of 50 nations may become a study of 20 nations. Also, the cases with missing information may be similar in some respect (e.g., all are in eastern Europe or in the Third World), which limits the generalizability of findings.

2. *Substitute the average score for cases where data are present.* The average literacy score from the other nations is substituted. This "solution" keeps Finland in the study but gives it an incorrect value. For an index with few items or for a case that is not "average," this creates serious validity problems.

3. *Insert data based on nonquantitative information about the case.* Other information about Finland (e.g., percentage of 13- to 18-year-olds in high school) is used to make an informed guess about the literacy rate. This "solution" is marginally acceptable in this situation. It is not as good as measuring Finland's literacy, and it relies on an untested assumption—that one can predict the literacy rate from other countries' high school attendance rate.

4. *Insert a random value.* This is unwise for the development index example. It might be acceptable if the index had a very large number of items and the number of cases was very large. If that were the situation, however, then eliminating the case is probably a better "solution" that produces a more reliable measure.

_____

Standardization involves selecting a base and dividing a raw measure by the base. For example, City A had 10 murders and City B had 30 murders in the same year. In order to compare murders in the two cities, the raw number of murders needs to be standardized by the city population. If the cities are the same size, City B is more dangerous. But City B may be safer if it is much larger. For example, if City A has 100,000 people and City B

has 600,000, then the murder rate per 100,000 is 10 for City A and 5 for City B.

Standardization makes it possible to compare different units on a common base. The process of standardization, also called *norming*, removes the effect of relevant but different characteristics in order to make the differences on important variables visible.

Suppose a researcher wanted to compare juvenile delinquency for two cities; one is in China and the other is in the United States. The Chinese city has many more inhabitants than the U.S. city, which would discourage the researcher from comparing the cities on the actual number of delinquents each has. However, by standardizing the number of delinquents 18 years of age or younger in each city relative to the city's population, the researcher has created a delinquency rate. This rate takes into account the population differences and thereby allows the researcher to compare the two cities.

A critical question in standardization is deciding what base to use. In the preceding example, why did the researcher use as a base the number of persons under the age of 18 years living in each city? The choice is not always obvious; it depends on the research question and the conceptual definitions being used.

Different bases can produce different rates. For example, the unemployment rate can be defined as the number of people in the work force who are out of work. The overall unemployment rate is:

$$\text{Unemployment rate} = \frac{\text{Number of unemployed people}}{\text{Total number of people working}}$$

We can divide the total population into subgroups to get rates for subgroups in the population such as White males, African American females, African American males between the ages of 18 and 28, or people with college degrees. Rates for these subgroups may be more relevant to the theoretical definition or research problem. For example, a researcher believes that unemployment is an experience that affects an entire household or family and that the base should be households, not individuals. The rate will look like this:

$$\text{New unemployment rate} = \frac{\text{Number of households with at least one unemployed person}}{\text{Total number of households}}$$

Different conceptualizations suggest different bases and different ways to standardize. When combining several items into an index, it is best to standardize items on a common base.

SCALES

The Purpose

Scaling, like index construction, creates an ordinal, interval, or ratio measure of a variable expressed as a numerical score. Scales are common in situations where a researcher wants to measure how an individual feels or thinks about something. Some call this the hardness or potency of feelings.

Scales are used for two related purposes. First, scales help in the conceptualization and operationalization processes. Scales show the fit between a set of indicators and a single construct. For example, a researcher believes that there is a single ideological dimension that underlies people's judgments about specific policies (e.g., the fairness of the tax system, privatizing public goods and utilities, or refugee resettlement). Scaling can help determine whether a single construct—for instance "conservative/liberal ideology"—underlies the positions people take on specific policies.

Second, scaling produces quantitative measures and can be used with other variables to test hypotheses. This second purpose of scaling is our primary focus because it involves scales as a technique for measuring a variable.

Logic of Scaling

As stated before, scaling is based on the idea of measuring the intensity, hardness, or potency of a variable. Graphic rating scales are an elementary

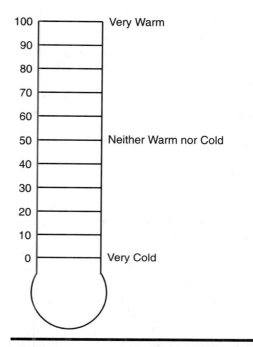

FIGURE 7.6 "Feeling Thermometer" Graphic Rating Scale

form of scaling. People indicate a rating by checking a point on a line that runs from one extreme to another. This type of scale is easy to construct and use. It conveys the idea of a continuum, and assigning numbers helps people think about quantities. Scales assume that people with the same subjective feeling mark the graphic scale at the same place.

Figure 7.6 is an example of a "feeling thermometer" scale that is used to find out how people feel about various groups in society (e.g., the National Organization of Women, the Ku Klux Klan, labor unions, physicians, etc.). This type of measure has been used by political scientists in the National Election Study since 1964 to measure attitudes toward candidates, social groups, and issues.[20]

Commonly Used Scales

Likert Scale. You have probably used *Likert scales;* they are widely used and very common in survey research. They were developed in the 1930s by Rensis Likert to provide an ordinal-level measure of a person's attitude.[21] Likert scales are called *summated-rating* or *additive scales* because a person's score on the scale is computed by summing the number of responses the person gives. Likert scales usually ask people to indicate whether they agree or disagree with a statement. Other modifications are possible; people might be asked whether they approve or disapprove, or whether they believe something is "almost always true." Box 7.6 presents several examples of Likert scales.

Likert scales need a minimum of two categories, such as "agree" and "disagree." Using only two choices creates a crude measure and forces distinctions into only two categories. It is usually better to use four to eight categories. A researcher can combine or collapse categories after the data are collected, but data collected with crude categories cannot be made more precise later.

You can increase the number of categories at the end of a scale by adding "strongly agree," "somewhat agree," "very strongly agree," and so forth. Keep the number of choices to eight or nine at most. More distinctions than that are probably not meaningful, and people will become confused. The choices should be evenly balanced (e.g., "strongly agree," "agree" with "strongly disagree," "disagree"). Nunnally (1978:521) stated:

As the number of scale steps is increased from 2 up through 20, the increase in reliability is very rapid at first. It tends to level off at about 7, and after about 11 steps, there is little gain in reliability from increasing the number of steps.

Researchers have debated about whether to offer a neutral category (e.g., "don't know," "undecided," "no opinion") in addition to the directional categories (e.g., "disagree," "agree"). A neutral category implies an odd number of categories. We will discuss this topic in Chapter 10.

A researcher can combine the items in a series of Likert scale questions into a composite index if all items measure a single construct. Consider the Likert scale example in Box 7.7. Tony is for big business and against unions. He answers the ten Likert scale questions: SD, SD, SA, A, D, SA, D, SA, SA, A. Barbara is opposed to big business and supports unions. She answers A, SA, D, D, SA, SD, A, SD, A, SD. In the example, 1 to 4 is assigned to each Likert scale answer so that a pro-union index can be formed. Questions 1, 2, 5, and 7 indicate a pro-union position and are scored SA = 4, A = 3, D = 2, SD = 1, whereas questions 3, 4, 6, 8, 9, and 10 are scored the opposite: SA = 1, A = 2, D = 3, SD = 4. Tony gets a score of $1 + 1 + 1 + 2 + 2 +$

Box 7.6 _____

Examples of Likert Scales

1. How much do you find yourself agreeing with the present position held by the United States regarding the global attempt to destroy land mines?

   ☐ Never ☐ Seldom ☐ Sometimes ☐ Often ☐ Always

2. "Many Western countries seem more concerned with striking business deals than protecting human rights." Do you

   ☐ Strongly agree ☐ Agree ☐ About 50/50 ☐ Disagree ☐ Strongly disagree ☐ Don't know

3. Do you accept or reject the recent assertion about the universality of human rights being under sustained attack?

   ☐ Strongly reject ☐ Reject ☐ Need more information to decide ☐ Accept
   ☐ Strongly accept ☐ Don't know

4. How do you feel about the slogan "African solutions to African problems"? Are you

   ☐ Strongly opposed ☐ Definitely opposed ☐ A bit of both
   ☐ Definitely unopposed ☐ Strongly unopposed

Box 7.7 _____

Example of a Likert Scale Used to Create an Index

Below are 10 statements about business and unions. Indicate your opinion by circling whether you strongly agree, agree, disagree, or strongly disagree.

	Strongly Agree	Agree	Strongly Disagree	Disagree
1. Big business has too much power today.	SA (4)	A (3)	D (2)	SD (1)
2. The gains workers have made are chiefly due to labor unions.	SA (4)	A (3)	D (2)	SD (1)
3. The profits of large companies help everyone.	SA (1)	A (2)	D (3)	SD (4)
4. Large companies are essential for a strong nation.	SA (1)	A (2)	D (3)	SD (4)
5. Labor unions are needed to protect working people.	SA (4)	A (3)	D (2)	SD (1)
6. The gains labor unions make are at the expense of other people.	SA (1)	A (2)	D (3)	SD (4)
7. Our country would be better if large companies were broken up into smaller ones.	SA (4)	A (3)	D (2)	SD (1)
8. Labor unions are too big and powerful for the good of the country.	SA (1)	A (2)	D (3)	SD (4)
9. Government regulation slows economic growth and business initiative.	SA (1)	A (2)	D (3)	SD (4)
10. Most unions are run by a tiny group of corrupt bosses and thugs.	SA (1)	A (2)	D (3)	SD (4)

Note: Values in parentheses ( ) would not be presented to a respondent answering the questionnaire but would be added later by a researcher.

_____

$1 + 2 + 1 + 1 + 2 = 14$, whereas Barbara scores $3 + 4 + 3 + 3 + 4 + 4 + 3 + 4 + 3 + 4 = 35$.

Notice that agreement suggests a probusiness opinion for some questions, whereas agreeing with other questions indicates an antibusiness opinion. The reason for switching directions in this way is to avoid the problem of the *response set*. The response set, also called *response style* and *response bias,* is the tendency of some people to answer a large number of items in the same way (usually agreeing) out of laziness or a psychological predisposition. For example, if items are worded so that saying "strongly agree" always indicates a pro-union stance, we would not know whether a person who always strongly agreed had a strong pro-union attitude or simply had a ten-

dency to agree with questions. The person might be answering "strongly agree" out of habit or a tendency to agree. Researchers word statements in alternative directions, so that anyone who agrees all the time appears to answer inconsistently or to have a contradictory opinion.

Researchers often combine many Likert-scaled attitude indicators into an index. The scale and indexes have properties that are associated with improving reliability and validity. An index uses multiple indicators, which improves reliability. The use of multiple indicators that measure several aspects of a construct or opinion improves content validity. Finally, the index scores give a more precise quantitative measure of a person's opinion. For example, each person's opinion can be measured with a number from 10 to 40, instead of in four categories: "strongly agree," "agree," "disagree," "strongly disagree."

Instead of scoring Likert items from 1 to 4, as in the previous example, the scores -2, -1, $+1$, $+2$ could be used. This scoring has an advantage in that a zero implies neutrality or complete ambiguity, whereas a high negative number means an attitude that opposes the opinion represented by a high positive number.

The numbers assigned to the response categories are arbitrary. Remember that the use of a zero does not give the scale or index a ratio level of measurement. Likert scale measures are at the ordinal level of measurement because responses indicate a ranking only. Instead of 1 to 4 or -2 to $+2$, the numbers 100, 70, 50, and 5 would have worked. Also, do not be fooled into thinking that the distances between the ordinal categories are intervals just because numbers are assigned. Although the number system has nice mathematical properties, the numbers are used for convenience only. The fundamental measurement is only ordinal.[22]

The simplicity and ease of use of the Likert scale is its real strength. When several items are combined, more comprehensive multiple indicator measurement is possible. The scale has two limitations: Different combinations of several scale items can result in the same overall score or result, and the response set is a potential danger.

Thurstone Scaling. Researchers sometimes want a measure with one numerical continuum, but the attitude variable in which they are interested has several characteristics or aspects. For example, a nongovernmental human rights organization decides it needs a public fund drive in order to carry its message to wider and more powerful circles. This is how the scale can help: The researcher conceptualizes the problem as a matter of the public's willingness to donate time and money to the issue of human rights, and identifies three dimensions. The first is the public's concern for human rights, the second is the public's knowledge of international events, and the third is the public's own financial and time

constraints. However, unless the researcher knows how the three dimensions relate to the heart of the matter—that is, the public's willingness to make a donation of time or money to the human rights organization—he or she cannot say which factor is the most important. During the late 1920s, Louis Thurstone developed scaling methods for assigning numerical values in such situations. These are now called *Thurstone scaling* or the *method of equal-appearing intervals.*[23]

Thurstone scaling is based on the *law of comparative judgment*. The law addresses the issue of measuring or comparing attitudes when each person makes a unique judgment. In other words, it anchors or fixes the position of one person's attitude relative to that of others as each makes an individual subjective judgment.

The law of comparative judgment states that it is possible to identify the "most common response" for each object or concept being judged. Although different people arrive at somewhat different judgments, the individual judgments cluster around a single-most common response. The dispersion of individual judgments around the common response follows a general statistical pattern called the *normal distribution*. From the law, it follows that, if many people agree that two objects differ, the most common responses for the two objects will be distant from each other. By contrast, if many people are confused or disagree about the differences between two objects, the common responses of the two objects will be closer to each other.

In Thurstone scaling, a researcher develops many statements (e.g., more than 100) regarding the object of interest, then uses many judges (e.g., 100) to reduce the number to a smaller set (e.g., 20) by eliminating ambiguous statements. Each judge rates the statements on an underlying continuum (e.g., favorable to unfavorable). The researcher examines the ratings and keeps those statements based on two factors: (1) agreement among the judges and (2) the statement's location on a range of possible values. The final set of statements is used to form a measurement scale that spans a range of values.

Thurstone scaling begins with a large number of evaluative statements that should be exhaustive and that cover all shades of opinion. Each should be clear and precise, and should express a single opinion. Good statements refer to the present and are not capable of being interpreted as facts. They are unlikely to be endorsed by everyone, are stated as simple sentences, and avoid words such as *always* and *never*. Researchers get ideas for writing the statements from reviewing the literature, from the mass media, from personal experience, and from asking others. The following are the sort of statements about human rights that the researcher would develop:

— I believe that human rights attracts far too little attention from governments.
— I think that the news media make too much out of the issue of human rights.
— I am not really sure where Rwanda is.
— I am well aware of the criticisms human rights groups have of the United States.
— I think that one's time is just as important as one's money in pressing for human rights.
— I do not like to donate my money to human rights causes.

A researcher next locates 50 to 300 judges. The judges do not have to be experts on the topic, but they should be familiar with the object or concept in the statements. Each judge receives a set of statement cards and instructions. Each card has one statement on it, and the judges place each card in one of several piles. The number of piles is usually 7, 9, 11, or 13. The piles represent a range of values (e.g., favorable to neutral to unfavorable) with regard to the object or concept being evaluated. Each judge places cards in rating piles independently of the other judges.

After the judges place all cards in piles, the researcher creates a chart cross-classifying the piles and the statements. For example, 100 statements and 11 piles results in an 11×100 chart, or a chart with $11 \times 100 = 1,100$ boxes. The number of judges who assigned a rating to a given statement is written into each box of the chart. Statistical measures (beyond the present discus-

sion) are used to compute the average rating of each statement and the degree to which the judges agree or disagree.

The researcher keeps the statements with the greatest between-judge agreement, or interrater reliability, as well as statements that represent the entire range of values. For example, suppose 100 statements were rated. The researcher computes the agreement score of each statement. Next, the location of the high-agreement scores across the continuum of 11 values (highly unfavorable, neutral, highly favorable) is examined. The researcher collapses the categories used by the judges into fewer categories and selects the four statements with the greatest agreement among judges for each of 3 categories to identify 12 statements.

The researcher has 12 statements, 4 for each range of the value scale. The statements are randomly mixed. The 12 statements are next presented to people who are asked whether they agree or disagree with the statement. (See Box 7.8 for another example.)

With Thurstone scaling, a researcher can construct an attitude scale or select statements from a larger collection of attitude statements. The method is seldom used today because of its limitations:

1. It measures only agreement or disagreement with statements, not the intensity of agreement or disagreement.
2. It assumes that judges and others agree on where statements appear in a rating system.
3. It is time consuming and costly.
4. It is possible to get the same overall score in several ways because agreement or disagreement with different combinations of statements can produce the same average.

Nevertheless, Thurstone scaling selects attitude items that are relatively unambiguous. It can be combined with Likert or other methods to create ordinal-level measures.

Bogardus Social Distance Scale. The *Bogardus social distance scale* measures the social distance separating ethnic or other groups from each other. It is used with one group to determine how much

Box 7.8 _____

Example of Thurstone Scaling

Variable Measured: Opinion with regard to the death penalty.

Step 1: Develop 120 statements about the death penalty using personal experience, the popular and professional literature, and listening to others.

Example Statements

1. I think that the death penalty is cruel and unnecessary punishment.
2. Without the death penalty, there would be many more violent crimes.
3. I believe that the death penalty should be used only for a few extremely violent crimes.
4. I do not think that anyone was ever prevented from committing a murder because of fear of the death penalty.
5. I do not think that people should be exempt from the death penalty if they committed a murder even if they are insane.
6. I believe that the Bible justifies the use of the death penalty.
7. The death penalty itself is not the problem for me, but I believe that electrocuting people is a cruel way to put them to death.

Step 2: Place each statement on a separate card or sheet of paper and make 100 sets of the 120 statements.

Step 3: Locate 100 persons who agree to serve as judges. Give each judge a set of the statement and instructions to place them in one of 11 piles, from 1 = highly unfavorable statement through 11 = highly favorable statement.

Step 4: The judges place each statement into one of the 11 piles (e.g., Judge #1 puts statement 1 into pile #2; Judge #2 puts the same statement into pile #1; Judge #3 also puts it into pile #2, Judge #4 puts it in pile #3, and so on).

Step 5: Collect piles from judges and create a chart summarizing their responses. See the example chart that follows.

Chart of Number of Judges Rating Each Statement Rating Pile

Statement	Unfavorable				Neutral				Favorable			Total
	_1_	_2_	_3_	_4_	_5_	_6_	_7_	_8_	_9_	_10_	_11_	
1	23	60	12	5	0	0	0	0	0	0	0	100
2	0	0	0	0	2	12	18	41	19	8	0	100
3	2	8	7	13	31	19	12	6	2	0	0	100
4	9	11	62	10	4	4	0	0	0	0	0	100

Step 6: Compute the average rating and degree of agreement by judges. For example, the average for question 1 is about 2, so there is high agreement; the average for question 3 is closer to 5, and there is much less agreement.

Step 7: Choose the final 20 statements to include in the death penalty opinion scale. Choose statements if the judges showed agreement (most placed an item in the same or a nearby pile) and ones that reflect the entire range of opinion, from favorable to neutral to unfavorable.

Step 8: Prepare a 20-statement questionnaire, and ask people in a study whether they agree or disagree with the statements.

distance it feels toward a target or "outgroup." It was developed in the 1920s by Emory Bogardus to measure the willingness of members of different ethnic groups to associate with each other. It can be used to see how close or distant people feel toward some other group (e.g., a religious minority or a deviant group).[24]

The scale has a simple logic. People respond to a series of ordered statements; those that are most threatening or most socially distant are at one end, and those that might be least threatening or socially intimate are at the other end. The logic of the scale assumes that a person who refuses contact or is uncomfortable with the socially distant items will refuse the socially closer items.

Researchers use the scale in several ways. For example, people are given a series of statements: Illegal immigrants are entering your country, are in your town, work at your place of employment, live in your neighborhood, become your personal friends, and marry your brother or sister. People are asked whether they feel comfortable with the statement or if the contact is acceptable. It is also possible to ask whether they feel uncomfortable with the relationship. People may be asked to respond to all statements, or they may keep reading statements until they are not comfortable with a relationship. There is no set number of statements required; the number usually ranges from five to nine.

A researcher can use the Bogardus scale to see how distant people feel from one outgroup versus another (see Box 7.9). The measure of social distance can be used as either an independent or a dependent variable. For example, a researcher believes that social distance from a group is greatest for people who have some other characteristic. A hypothesis might be that feelings of social distance by Whites from Vietnamese boat people is negatively associated with education; that is, the least well educated feel the most distant. Social distance from boat people is the dependent variable, and amount of education is the independent variable.

The social distance scale is a convenient way to determine how close a respondent feels toward a social group. It has two potential limitations. First, a researcher needs to tailor the categories to a specific outgroup and social setting. Second, it is not easy for a researcher to compare how a respondent feels toward several different groups unless the respondent completes a similar social distance scale for all outgroups at the same time. Of course, how a respondent completes the scale and the respondent's actual behavior in specific social situations may differ.

Semantic Differential. *Semantic Differential* was developed in the 1950s to provide an indirect measure of how a person feels about a concept, object, or other person. The technique measures subjective feelings toward something by using adjectives. This is because people communicate evaluations through adjectives in spoken and written language. Because most adjectives have polar opposites (e.g., *light/dark, hard/soft, slow/fast*), it uses polar opposite adjectives to create a rating measure or scale. The Semantic Differential captures the connotations associated with whatever is being evaluated and provides an indirect measure of it.

The Semantic Differential has been used for many purposes. In marketing research, it tells how consumers feel about a product; political advisers use it to discover what voters think about a candidate or issue; and therapists use it to determine how a client perceives himself or herself. It has considerable flexibility and usefulness that criminologists have hardly discovered.

To use the Semantic Differential, a researcher presents subjects with a list of paired opposite adjectives with a continuum of 7 to 11 points between them. The subjects mark the spot on the continuum between the adjectives that expresses their feelings. The adjectives can be very diverse and should be well mixed (e.g., positive items should not be located mostly on either the right or the left side). Studies of a wide variety of adjectives in English found that they fall into three major classes of meaning: evaluation *(good–bad)*, potency *(strong–weak)*, and activity *(active–passive)*. Of the three classes of meaning, evaluation is usually the most significant. The analysis of results is difficult, and a researcher needs to use statistical procedures to analyze a subject's feelings toward the concept.

Box 7.9 _____

Example of Bogardus Social Distance Scale

A researcher wants to find out how socially distant freshmen college students feel from illegal immigrants from two different countries: Mexico and Poland. She wants to see whether students feel more distant from students coming from Latin America or from Europe. She uses the following series of questions in an interview:

Please give me your first reaction, yes or no, whether you personally would feel comfortable having an illegal immigrant from (name of country):

_____ As a visitor to your college for a week

_____ As a full-time student enrolled at your college

_____ Taking several of the same classes you are taking

_____ Sitting next to you in class and studying with you for exams

_____ Living a few doors down the hall on the same floor in your dormitory

_____ As a same-sex roommate sharing your dorm room

_____ As someone of the opposite sex who has asked you to go out on a date

Hypothetical Results

Percentage of Freshmen Who Report Feeling Comfortable

	Mexico	Poland
Visitor	100%	100%
Enrolled	98%	100%
Same class	95%	98%
Study together	82%	88%
Same dorm	71%	83%
Roommate	50%	76%
Go on date	42%	64%

The results suggest that freshmen feel more distant from Mexican students than from Polish students. Almost all feel comfortable having the international students as visitors, enrolled in the college, and taking classes. Feelings of distance increase as interpersonal contact increases, especially if the contact involves personal living settings or activities not directly related to the classroom.

Results from a Semantic Differential tell a researcher how one person perceives different concepts or how different people view the same concept. For example, a private research firm preparing a candidate for a debate on crime policy might use this scale to discover how voters perceive the candidate on a host of criminal justice issues. It may turn out that the young voters view the candidate as leaning toward being "weak" on truth-in-sentencing legislation and "bad" on new prison construction. Elderly voters may see the candidate as leaning toward "shallow" and "unfair" on the issue of alternatives to incarceration. In Box 7.10, a voter rated the candidate on select criminal justice issues.

There are techniques for creating three-dimensional diagrams of results.[25] The three aspects are diagrammed in three-dimensional "semantic

Box 7.10_____

Example of Semantic Differential

Please read each pair of adjectives below, then place a mark on the blank space that comes closest to your first-impression feeling. There are no right or wrong answers.

How do you feel about the candidate's position on truth-in-sentencing?

Bad	____	_x_	____	____	____	____	____	____	____ Good
Deep	____	____	____	____	____	____	____	_x_	____ Shallow
Weak	____	____	_x_	____	____	____	____	____	____ Strong
Fair	____	____	____	____	____	____	____	_x_	____ Unfair
Quiet	____	____	____	____	____	____	____	____	_x_ Loud
Modern	_x_	____	____	____	____	____	____	____	____ Traditional
Simple	____	____	____	____	____	_x_	____	____	____ Complex
Fast	____	_x_	____	____	____	____	____	____	____ Slow
Dirty	____	_x_	____	____	____	____	____	____	____ Clean

How do you feel about the candiate's position on prison construction?

Bad	____	____	____	____	____	____	____	_x_	____ Good
Deep	____	_x_	____	____	____	____	____	____	____ Shallow
Weak	____	____	____	____	____	____	_x_	____	____ Strong
Fair	____	_x_	____	____	____	____	____	____	____ Unfair
Quiet	____	____	_x_	____	____	____	____	____	____ Loud
Modern	____	____	____	____	____	____	____	_x_	____ Traditional
Simple	____	____	____	____	____	_x_	____	____	____ Complex
Fast	____	____	____	____	____	____	____	_x_	____ Slow
Dirty	____	____	____	____	____	____	_x_	____	____ Clean

space." In the diagram, "good" is up and "bad" is down, "active" is left and "passive" is right, "strong" is away from the viewer and "weak" is close.

Guttman Scaling. *Guttman scaling*, or cumulative scaling, differs from the previous scales or indexes in that researchers use it to evaluate data after they are collected. This means that researchers must design a study with the Guttman scaling technique in mind. Louis Guttman developed the scale in the 1940s to determine whether a relationship existed among a set of indicators or measurement items. He used multiple indicators to document an underlying single dimension or cumulative intensity of a construct.[26]

Guttman scaling begins with measuring a set of indicators or items. These can be ques-

tionnaire items, votes, or observed characteristics. The scales can be used to measure a wide variety of criminological phenomena, such as patterns of drug use, law enforcement options, sentencing guidelines, and so on. The indicators are usually measured in a simple yes/no or present/absent fashion. From 3 to 20 indicators can be used. The researcher selects items on the belief that there is a logical relationship among them. He or she then places the results into a Guttman scale and determines whether the items form a pattern that corresponds to the relationship.

The logical relationship among items in Guttman scaling is hierarchical. Most people or cases have or agree to lower-order items. The smaller number of cases that have the higher-order items also have the lower-order ones, but not vice versa. In other words, the higher-order items build on the lower ones. The lower-order items are necessary for the appearance of the higher-order items.

An application of Guttman scaling, known as *scalogram analysis,* lets a researcher test whether a hierarchial relationship exists among the items.

Research on the popularity of the drug war in Belize, Central America, illustrates the use of hierarchical items to assess public opinion regarding a range of drug enforcement options (see Wiegand and Bennett, 1993:210). Cross-sectional data were gathered using the survey method. The random sample size was 532 heads of households living in Belize City. Interviews were face to face and lasted approximately 30 minutes.

The various drug enforcement options were conceptualized hierarchically from least obtrusive to most. Thus, the scale was as follows:

- Increase drug education.
- Increase the size of the police.
- Give police more powers.
- Increase penalties.
- Have the U.S. military train the Belizean military.
- Use U.S. DEA agents.
- Have military patrol the city.
- Have U.S. military patrol the city.

These items are *scalable,* or capable of forming a Guttman scale, if a hierarchical pattern exists.

The pattern of responses can be divided into two groups: scaled and errors (or nonscalable). If perfectly hierarchical, the scaled pattern for the Belize example would be the following:

- Not approving of any item
- Approving of only increased education
- Approving of increased education and increased size of the police force but none of the other items
- Approving of increased education, increased police force size, and giving more powers to the police but none of the other items

- Approving of increased education, increased police force size, more powers to the police, and increased penalties but none of the other items

Other combinations of answers are possible (e.g., approving of increased education and increased penalties but not approving of increased size of the police force). These, however, are not scalable. If a hierarchical relationship exists among the items, then most answers fit into the scalable patterns.

The strength or degree to which items can be scaled is measured with statistics that measure whether the responses can be reproduced based on a hierarchical pattern. Most range from zero to 100 percent. A score of zero indicates a random pattern, or no hierarchical pattern. A score of 100 percent indicates that all responses to the answer fit the hierarchical or scaled pattern. Alternative statistics to measure scalability have also been suggested.[27]

See Box 7.11 for an example of a Guttman Scale reflecting a study of drug use among high school students. The results suggest that the items are Guttman scalable; that is, there is a hierarchical pattern of drug use among the high school students. Students who use illegal drugs are likely also to use legal drugs. Few students who use illegal drugs fail to use legal drugs, but some students use only legal drugs but not illegal drugs.

SOCIAL INDICATORS

During the 1960s, some social scientists, dissatisfied with the information available to decision makers, spawned the "social indicators' movement." Its purpose was to develop indicators of social well-being. Many hoped that information about social well-being could be combined with widely used indicators of economic performance (e.g., gross national product) to better inform government and other policymaking officials. Thus, social indicator researchers wanted to measure the quality of social life so that such information could influence public policy.[28]

Box 7.11 _____

Example of Use of Guttman Scaling

A researcher wants to determine the pattern of drug use among a group of 80 high school students. He is interested in four major drug types: cigarette smoking, alcohol use, marijuana use, and cocaine use. The students were asked four separate questions (among others in a questionnaire), and the pattern of their answers could be organized into four categories:

ANSWER PATTERN	DRUG USED				NUMBER OF STUDENTS
	Cigarettes	*Alcohol*	*Marijuana*	*Cocaine*	
1	No	No	No	No	8
2	Yes	No	No	No	15
3	Yes	Yes	No	No	25
4	Yes	Yes	Yes	No	13
5	Yes	Yes	Yes	Yes	7
6	No	Yes	Yes	Yes	1
7	No	No	Yes	Yes	2
8	No	No	No	Yes	1
9	No	No	Yes	No	2
10	No	Yes	No	No	5
11	No	Yes	No	Yes	0
12	No	Yes	Yes	No	0
13	Yes	No	Yes	No	0
14	Yes	No	Yes	Yes	0
15	Yes	Yes	No	Yes	1
16	Yes	No	No	Yes	0
				Total	80

Note: Answer patterns 1 to 5 are "scaled," but 6 to 16 are not. Frequently "yes" and "no" are symbolized by + and 0, respectively.

_____

Although criminologists have been slow to explore the utility of social indicators as alternative measures for crime and justice statistics, there are many books, articles, and reports on social indicators, and even a scholarly journal, *Social Indicators Research*, devoted to the creation and evaluation of social indicators. The U.S. Census Bureau produced a report, *Social Indicators*, and the United Nations has many measures of social well-being in different nations.

A *social indicator* is any measure of social well-being used in policy. There are many specific indicators that are operationalizations of well-being. For

example, social indicators could be developed for assessing the living conditions and well-being of inmates, detainees, or refugees. They could also be used to assess the rehabilitation of inmates both inside and outside the justice system. Social indicators often entail implicit value judgments, such as which crimes are the most serious or what constitutes successful rehabilitation.

Criminologists might also lend a hand in developing quality-of-life indexes from measures of risk of victimization, policing minorities, youth crime, and so on. Quality-of-life indicators to date have tended to focus on issues of pollution, overcrowding, life expectancy, percentage of house-holds with one or more automobiles, televisions, and the like.

SPECIALIZED TECHNIQUES FOR INDEX AND SCALE CONSTRUCTION

Three sophisticated statistical techniques that social researchers use to construct or evaluate scales or indexes are presented here. The three are not an exhaustive set. There are dozens of similar techniques. Those presented here are examples of the powerful techniques professional researchers often use. You will need to acquire a background in statistics and be knowledgeable with computer programs before you will be able to use these techniques.

The purpose of introducing you to the techniques is twofold. First, you may encounter them in the methods, analysis, or results sections of scholarly journal articles. This introduction will help you understand why they are being used. Second, the logic of the techniques reinforces the basic principles of measurement and index or scale construction that you have already learned. The logic illustrates how the principles are extended to complex, sophisticated applications. Although the three techniques use advanced statistics, their logic is consistent with basic measurement principles.

Factor Analysis

Factor analysis is a group of sophisticated statistical techniques that require a computer to conduct.[29] Statistical training is necessary to use factor analysis properly. Improperly used, it creates nonsense. Factor analysis helps researchers construct indexes, test the unidimensionality of scales, assign weights to items in an index, and statistically reduce a large number of indicators to a smaller set. The statistical theory and algebra on which factor analysis is based is beyond the level of this book, but its conceptual principles are not difficult to grasp. The fundamental logic of factor analysis is based on the idea that it is possible to manipulate statistically the em-pirical relationships among several indicators to reveal a common unobserved factor or hypothetical construct.

When conducting factor analysis, a researcher begins with a number of items he or she believes to measure a single construct. At least five indicators are recommended. The indicators should be measured at the ordinal, interval, or ratio level. The interval or ratio level is preferred, and extra caution is necessary for ordinal-level measurement. The researcher gives the factor analysis computer program characteristics of the variables and technical information. The factor analysis results tell a researcher how well the items or indicators relate to an underlying factor or hypothetical construct. For example, factor analysis results tell the researcher whether the items all load, or are associated with, one or more than one factor.

Factor analysis also produces factor scores, which can be used as weights in creating an index. These scores represent how strongly each indicator is associated with the unobserved factor. For example, a researcher may be interested in conducting a cross-national victimization survey in which there are 16 Likert scale items that measure the routine activities likely to be associated with victimization. These activities include such things as working at night, carrying cash on the job, and parking one's car at an unattended lot. Factor analysis could be used to determine if the 16 items are explained by a few factors. The meaning of a factor is derived by the researcher's examination of the items that load on it. The factors can then be used to develop separate indexes of routine activities and victimization.

Let us say that a researcher ranks routine activities that place a person at risk of victimization. After choosing the top-ranked activity (e.g., working at night), no other activity can be number one. The decision about one routine activity affects or limits decisions about the other activities. This is *ipsative scoring.* By contrast with *normative scoring,* each routine activity is rated independently, such as with a Likert scale. Thus, several routine activities could have the same ranking as being "very likely to result in victimization."

Q-Sort Analysis

Q-sort analysis is a close relative of factor analysis.[30] Like factor analysis, the technique requires statistical background beyond the scope of this book. It illustrates an interesting scaling logic as well.

Q-sort methodology uses ipsative scoring, as opposed to normative scoring, which is used in most scaling or index techniques. Q-sort analysis begins with people ranking statements about a concept or object. In a manner somewhat like Thurstone scaling, people are given a large number of statements (e.g., 30 to 50) and asked to sort them. The statements are taken from popular writings on a topic, everyday conversations, television programs, and the like, and should represent diverse ways people think about a topic.

Instead of piles along one continuum, the Q-sort technique has people place statements into boxes in a grid that varies along two continua. There are as many boxes in the grid as there are statements. Each statement goes into one box. One continuum (e.g., right to left) indicates how positive or negative a person feels about the statement. The other continuum (e.g., up and down) indicates the strength of commitment to the positive or negative feelings about statements. The decision to place a statement in a box excludes placing any other statements in the same location. The raw data for Q-sort are the statements as they are organized in the grid.

In factor analysis, the researcher enters the data from many indicators, and the computer program produces a small number of factors. In Q-sort analysis, the researcher enters the grid location of statements, and the computer program identifies clusters or sets of people. Thus, Q-sort analysis shows which people organize statements in similar ways.

Q-sort analysis identifies how people organize their thinking on a topic on the basis of how they organized statements in the grid. It gives a researcher a map of major positions on an issue held by people. For example, 20 people place 45 statements about Arab-Israeli relations into a grid. The results of Q-sort analysis shows a researcher that the 20 people think about Arab-Israeli relations in one of three main ways: (1) a concern for Israeli security and fear of Arabs, (2) frustration with U.S. support for Israel and resentment toward Israel, or (3) a feeling that the world balance of power depends on what happens with Israel and its neighbors.

Cluster Analysis

As with factor and Q-sort analysis, cluster analysis is a sophisticated statistical technique that will be described only briefly and in general terms.[31] *Cluster analysis* is a technique for organizing information or items measuring a variable. It statistically organizes relationships among a large number of items and places them into groups. The grouping or classification procedure uses statistical techniques like those in factor analysis and Q-sort analysis. The technique groups items by similarity and difference.

Factor analysis results tell a researcher how each item relates to one or more unobserved factors. Results look like a list of items with a number next to each; the number is the association between an item and a factor. Results from Q-sort analysis tell a researcher how people organize statements and show that people organize statements in a small number of ways. Results consist of the list of people with a number next to each person representing the degree to which a person followed one of a few patterns for organizing statements.

Cluster analysis results, by contrast, are in the form of a graph or picture, which resembles a tree diagram because it looks like the branches of a tree. Lines extend from a trunk, to large branches, to smaller branches, and so forth to tiny twigs. There are several levels of branching. The branching diagram shows a researcher which items are similar to each other and which are different. Each item in the cluster analysis represents a tiny twig, and the pattern of connections illustrates similarity and differences. Two items that share connections to a common nearby branch are more similar than two items that share no common branch until they reach the trunk.

In the IRS Tax Practitioner Survey (United States Internal Revenue Service, 1987) mentioned earlier, a cluster analysis was used to place tax practitioners in one of several groups based on their responses to 20 survey questions. The questions dealt with so-called gray areas of tax practice that may involve unethical and illegal behavior. Based on the responses, researchers were able to array the tax practitioners into one of several clusters. The clusters differed in terms of the degree of "shady" tax practice.

CONCLUSION

In this chapter, you learned about the process of quantitative, deductive measurement. You progressed from a construct in theory through the processes of conceptualizing and operationalizing a variable to specific, concrete indicators. You also learned about two key ideas in measurement: reliability and validity. In addition,

you saw how researchers apply the principles of measurement when they create indexes and scales, and you read about some major scales they use.

Beyond the core ideas of reliability and validity, you now know principles of good measurement: Create clear definitions for concepts, use multiple indicators, employ heterogeneous observation, and, as appropriate, weigh and standardize the data. These principles hold across all fields of study and across the many quantitative research techniques (e.g., experiments, surveys, etc.).

Now that you understand how variables are measured or turned into numbers, you are ready to obtain people or units on which the variables will be measured. The next chapter explores experimental research. Experimental design illustrates how to use principles of causality and measurement.

As you are probably beginning to realize, a sound research project involves doing a good job in each phase of research. Serious mistakes or sloppiness in any one phase can do irreparable damage to the results, even if the other phases of the research project were conducted in a flawless manner.

KEY TERMS

auxiliary theory
bias
Bogardus Social Distance Scale
cluster analysis
conceptual definition
conceptual hypothesis
conceptualization
concurrent validity
construct validity
content validity
continuous variables
convergent validity
criterion validity
discrete variables
discriminant validity
empirical hypothesis

epistemic correlation
equivalence reliability
exhaustive attributes
external validity
face validity
factor analysis
Guttman scaling
heterogeneous observation
indicator
index
intercoder reliability
internal validity
interval-level measurement
law of comparative judgment
levels of measurement
Likert scale

measurement validity
multiple indicators
mutually exclusive attributes
nominal-level measurement
operational definition
operationalization
ordinal-level measurement
predictive validity
Q-sort analysis
ratio-level measurement
reliability
representative reliability
rules of correspondence
Semantic Differential
social indicator
split-half method

stability reliability
standardization
statistical validity

subpopulation analysis
test-retest method
Thurstone scaling

triangulation
unidimensionality
validity

REVIEW QUESTIONS

1. What are the three basic parts of measurement, and how do they fit together?
2. What is the difference between reliability and validity, and how do they complement each other?
3. What are ways to improve the reliability of a measure?
4. How do the levels of measurement differ from each other?
5. What are the differences between convergent, content, and concurrent validity? Can you have all three at once? Explain your answer.
6. Why are multiple indicators usually better than one indicator?
7. What is the difference between the logic of a scale and that of an index?
8. Why is unidimensionality an important characteristic of a scale?
9. What are advantages and disadvantages of weighting indexes?
10. How does standardization make comparisons easier?

NOTES

1. The terms *concept, construct*, and *idea* are used more or less interchangeably, but there are differences in meaning between them. An *idea* is any mental image, belief plan, or impression. It refers to any vague impression, opinion, or thought. A *concept* is a thought, a general notion, or a generalized idea about a class of objects. A *construct* is a thought that is systematically put together, an orderly arrangement of ideas, facts, and impressions. The term *construct* is used here because its emphasis is on taking vague concepts and turning them into systematically organized ideas.

2. Duncan (1984:220–239) presented some worthwhile cautions from a positivist approach on the issue of measuring anything.

3. See Grinnell (1987:5–18) for further discussion.

4. See Blalock (1982:25–27) and Costner (1985) on rules of correspondence or the auxiliary theories that connect abstract concept with empirical indicators. Also see Zeller and Carmines (1980:5) for a diagram that illustrates the place of the rules in the process of measurement. In his presidential address to the American Sociological Association in 1979, Hubert Blalock (1979a:882) said, "I believe that the most serious and important problems that require our immediate and concerted attention are those of conceptualization and measurement."

5. See Bailey (1984:1986) for a discussion of the three levels.

6. See Bohrnstedt (1992a) and Carmines and Zeller (1979) for discussions of reliability and various types of reliability.

7. See Sullivan and Feldman (1979) on multiple indicators. A more technical discussion can be found in Herting (1985), Herting and Costner (1985), and Scott (1968).

8. See Carmines and Zeller (1979:17). For a discussion of the many types of validity, see Brinberg and McGrath (1982).

9. The epistemic correlation is discussed in Costner (1985) and in Zeller and Carmines (1980:50–51, 137–139).

10. Kidder (1982) discussed the issue of disagreements over face validity, such as acceptance of a measure's meaning by the scientific community, but not the subjects being studied.

11. For a discussion of types of criterion validity, see Carmines and Zeller (1979:17–19) and Fiske (1982) for construct validity.

12. See Cook and Campbell (1979) for elaboration.

13. See Borgatta and Bohrnstedt (1980) and Duncan (1984:119–155) for a discussion and critique of the topic of levels of measurement.

14. Johnson and Creech (1983) examined the measurement errors that occur when variables that are conceptualized as continuous are operationalized in a series of ordinal categories. They argued that errors caused by using categories (compared to a precise continuous measure) are not serious if more than four categories and large samples are used.

15. See Blalock (1982) and Zeller and Carmines (1980) for more in-depth discussions of measurement theory in the social sciences.

16. See Carmines and Zeller (1979:13–15) and Nunally (1978).

17. For additional discussions of multiple indicators, see Blalock (1982:76–85, 265–272) and Sullivan and Feldman (1979).

18. For compilations of indexes and scales used in social research, see Brodsky and Smitherman (1983), Miller (1991), Robinson and colleagues (1972), Robinson and Shaver (1969), and Schuessler (1982).

19. For a discussion of weighted and unweighted index scores, see Nunally (1978:534).

20. Feeling thermometers are discussed in Wilcox and associates (1989).

21. For more information on Likert scales, see Anderson and associates (1983:252–255), Converse (1987:72–75), McIver and Carmines (1981:22–38), and Spector (1992).

22. Some researchers treat Likert scales as interval-level measures, but there is disagreement on this issue. Statistically, it makes little difference if the Likert scale has at least five response categories and an approximately even proportion of people answer in each category.

23. McIver and Carmines (1981:16–21) have an excellent discussion of Thurstone scaling. Also see discussions in Anderson and colleagues (1983:248–252), Converse (1987:66–77), and Edwards (1957). The example used here is partially borrowed from Churchill (1983:249–254), who described the formula for scoring Thurstone scaling.

24. The social distance scale is described in Converse (1987:62–69). The most complete discussion can be found in Bogardus (1959).

25. The Semantic Differential is discussed in Nunnally (1978:535–543). Also see Heise (1965, 1970) on the analysis of scaled data.

26. See Guttman (1950).

27. See Bailey (1987:349–351) for a discussion of an improved method for determining scalability called Minimal Marginal Reproducibility (from Edwards, 1957), which gives accurate measures of scalability. He also cited McConaghy (1975), who discussed techniques that improve upon the Minimal Marginal Reproducibility measure. Guttman scaling can involve more than yes/no choices and a large number of items, but the complexity increases quickly and computers are needed for Guttman scalogram analysis. A more elaborate and sophisticated discussion of Guttman scaling can be found in Anderson and associates (1983:256–260), Converse (1987:189–195), McIver and Carmines (1981:40–71), and Nunnally (1978:63–66). Clogg and Sawyer (1981) presented alternatives to Guttman scaling.

28. A discussion of social indicators can be found in Carley (1981). Also see Duncan (1984:233–235), Bauer (1966), Juster and Land (1981), Land (1992), Rossi and Gilmartin (1980), and Taylor (1980). Also see Ferriss (1988) on the using of social indicators for planning and social forecasting.

29. Factor analysis is discussed in Kim and Mueller (1978). For more technical discussions, see Bohrnstedt and Borgatta (1981) and Jackson and Borgatta (1981). Duncan (1984:209–216) offers a critique of factor analysis.

30. Q-sort analysis is discussed in Brown (1980, 1986), Nunnally (1978:544–558), and McKeown (1988).

31. Cluster analysis is introduced in Aldenderfer and Blashfield (1984). Also see Bailey (1975, 1983) and Lorr (1983) for social science applications.

RECOMMENDED READINGS

Anderson, Victor. (1991). *Alternative economic indicators*. New York: Routledge. This book offers a set of practical proposals for measuring the goals of sustainable and human-centered development.

Blalock, Hubert M., Jr. (1979). Measurement and conceptualization problems: The major obstacle to integrating theory and research. *American Sociological Review*, 44:881–894. Though a bit technical at times, this is a comprehensive statement about measurement from a positivist approach. It addresses the question of how theory relates to measurement. It was Blalock's presidential address to the American Sociological Association. His 1982 book (see Bibliography) expands on the ideas presented in this article.

Carley, Michael. (1981). *Social measurement and social indicators: Issues of policy and theory*.

Boston: Allen and Unwin. This is a good introduction to the history, theory, and application of social indicators. The author confronts many of the difficult issues in social indicator research. The book includes discussion of quality-of-life and national social reporting indicators. Its comparison of British and U.S. research involving social movements adds a nice comparative perspective.

Carmines, Edward G., and Richard A. Zeller. (1979). *Reliability and validity assessment.* Beverly Hills, CA: Sage. This short (70-page) book condenses an influential book by Zeller and Carmines on measurement (see Bibliography). It is a lucid introduction to measurement theory and includes excellent discussions of reliability and validity. The types and methods for measuring reliability are especially valuable.

Luger, Michael I. (1996). Quality-of-life differences and urban and regional outcomes: A review. *Housing Policy Debate*, 7(4):749–771. This review essay summarizes policy concerns arising from disparities between the quality of life among and within communities. It points up the politics surrounding the methodological assessments of social indicators.

Miller, Delbert C. (1991). *Handbook of research design and social measurement*, 5th ed. Newbury Park, CA: Sage. In addition to a short introduction to research design. Miller presents an extensive listing of scales and indexes that have been used in research. The listing includes references to where the scale or index was published and information on tests of its reliability and/or validity.

Schuessler, Karl. (1985). *Measuring social life feelings.* San Francisco: Jossey-Bass. The author surveys the multiplicity of scales and measuring instruments for concepts such as morale, alienation, life satisfaction, anomie, and social isolation. He finds many instances of the use of the same items in very different constructs. Schuessler reduced the number of different questions to 237 and used factor analysis to identify 17 factors that appear to summarize major dimensions of life satisfaction.

CHAPTER 8

EXPERIMENTAL RESEARCH

Tax Dodgers*

1. Ford Motor ($1.5 billion subsidy)
2. Chrysler ($966.2 million subsidy)
3. General Motors ($899.5 million subsidy)
4. Philip Morris ($603.1 million subsidy)
5. Berkshire Hathaway ($489.2 million subsidy)
6. GTE ($441.2 million subsidy)
7. Mobil ($439.6 million subsidy)
8. DuPont ($388.5 million subsidy)
9. Bristol-Myers-Squibb ($369.8 million subsidy)
10. Merck ($314.3 million subsidy)

—Sarah Anderson and John Cavanagh, *The Top Ten List,* p. 9.

* Calculated by the Institute for Policy Studies. Figures given are the difference between federal tax paid in 1996 and the amount the company might have paid at the statutory rate, assuming no loopholes are invoked. By law, U.S. corporations pay 35 percent of their income in taxes.

INTRODUCTION

The "Tax Dodgers" in the preceding list are among the top 30 most profitable U.S. corporations (Anderson and Cavanagh, 1997). Knowing that fact just might transform a U.S. taxpayer into someone looking for a reason to cheat, or maybe it does nothing of the sort. Under what circumstances does one decide to cheat? Can experimental research isolate the lone independent variable that pushes the taxpayer across the line? Can research tell who among us are, but for a certain set of circumstances, tax evaders?

In the previous chapters, you learned about the foundations of quantitative research. In this chapter, you will learn how to conduct a particular type of quantitative research. We begin with experimental research. It is the easiest to grasp and is used across many other fields of science.

Experimental research builds on the principles of a positivist approach more directly than do the other research techniques.[1] Researchers in the natural sciences (e.g., chemistry and physics), related applied fields (e.g., agriculture, engineering, and medicine), and the social sciences conduct experiments. The logic that guides an experiment on plant growth in biology or testing a metal in engineering is applied in experiments on human social behavior. Although it is most widely used in psychology, the experiment is found in education, criminal justice, journalism, marketing, nursing, political science, social work, and sociology. This chapter focuses first on the experiment conducted in a laboratory under controlled conditions, then looks at experiments conducted in the field.

The experiment's basic logic extends commonsense thinking. Commonsense experiments are less careful or systematic than scientifically based experiments. In commonsense language, *an experiment* means modifying something in a situation, then comparing an outcome to what existed without the modification. Imagine, for instance, not being able to start your car. You think that by cleaning off the corrosion from the battery connection perhaps the car might start. In effect, what you have formed is a hypothesis about corrosion

and battery connections. You now proceed to test the hypothesis by cleaning the connection and then trying again to start the car. It starts. You conclude that the reason why the car did not start initially was the greasy connection. Problem solved, experiment completed. All experiments, however simplistic, have three tasks: (1) form a hypothesis, (2) modify something in the situation, and (3) compare outcomes with and without modifications.

Compared to the other social research techniques, experimental research is the strongest for testing causal relationships because the three conditions for causality (temporal order, association, and no alternative explanations) are clearly met in experimental designs.

Research Questions Appropriate for an Experiment

The Issue of an Appropriate Technique. Social researchers use different research techniques (e.g., experiments and surveys) because some research questions can be addressed with certain techniques but not with others. New researchers often ask which research technique best fits which problem. This is difficult to answer because there is no fixed match between problem and technique. The answer is: Make an informed judgment.

General guidelines exist for fitting techniques to problems. Beyond guidelines, you can develop judgment from reading research reports, understanding the strengths and weaknesses of different techniques, assisting more experienced researchers with their research, and gaining practical experience.

Research Questions for Experimental Research. The logic of experimental design guides the types of research problems best addressed by experiments. A crucial factor is that in experimental design, a researcher changes a situation and has control over the setting in which the change is introduced. Only those research problems that let a researcher manipulate conditions are appropriate for experimental research. Examples of inappropriate research problems include: Did the "tong war" of 100 years ago exercise an influence in the development of Chinese organized crime in the United States? How has corporate tax crime changed in response to globalization? Has the U.S. drug war had a corrupting effect on military institutions in Latin America and the Caribbean?

The very scope of these macro-level questions make it hard to envision an appropriate experimental design. Indeed, criminologists and other social scientists are more limited than natural scientists in the degree to which they can intervene for research purposes. They are very creative in inventing treatments for independent variables, as we shall see in the next example about tax evasion experiments. Nevertheless, there are many interesting independent variables, such as globalization, that criminologists obviously cannot manipulate as independent variables of an experiment.

A researcher must decide which research design is most effective for answering his or her specific question, within practical and ethical limitations. For example, a research question is: Does fear of crime affect the behaviors of elderly people by motivating them to seek self-protection and security? An experimental researcher creates different levels of fear of crime among groups of elderly subjects. To create a fear of crime, he or she has subjects read about crimes, shows them films about crime, or places them in fear-inducing situations (e.g., in a locked room with a dangerous-looking person who makes threatening statements). Next, the researcher measures whether the subjects act in self-protective ways (e.g., push a button to create a physical barrier between themselves and the dangerous person) or answer questions about hypothetical situations involving security in certain ways (e.g., plan to buy new locks).

Other techniques (e.g., survey research) can address the same issue. A survey researcher asks elderly people questions about how much they fear crime and what they have done for self-protection and security. The researcher measures

fear by asking subjects to tell how much they already fear crime on the basis of their previous experiences.

A Short History of the Experiment in Social Research

The experimental method was borrowed by the social sciences from the natural sciences, and began in psychology. It was not widely accepted in psychology until after 1900.[2]

Wilhelm M. Wundt (1832–1920), a German psychologist and physiologist, introduced the experimental method into psychology. During the late 1800s, Germany was the center of graduate education, and leading social scientists from around the world went to Germany to study. Wundt established a laboratory for experimentation in psychology that became a model for many other social researchers. By 1900, researchers at many U.S. and other universities established psychology laboratories to conduct experimental social research. The experiment replaced a more philosophical, introspective, integrative approach that was closer to interpretive social science. For example, William James (1842–1910), the foremost U.S. philosopher and psychologist of the 1890s, did not use or embrace the experimental method.

From the turn of the century to the time of World War II, the experimental method was elaborated and became entrenched in social research. The method's widespread appeal was that it offered an objective, unbiased, scientific way to study human mental and social life at a time when the scientific study of social life was just gaining acceptance.

Four trends speeded the expansion of the experimental method in this period: the rise of behaviorism, the spread of quantification, various changes in research subjects, and practical applications.

Behaviorism is a school of psychology founded in the 1920s by the American John B. Watson (1878–1958) and extended by B. F. Skinner (1904–1990). It emphasized measuring observable behavior or outcomes of mental life and advocated the experimental method for conducting rigorous empirical tests of hypotheses. It became an influential, if not the dominant, school in American psychology.

Quantification, or measuring social phenomena with numbers, also grew between 1900 and 1940. Researchers reconceptualized social constructs so that they could be quantified, and other constructs (e.g., spirit, consciousness, will) were jettisoned from empirical research. An example is measuring mental ability by the IQ test. Originally developed by Alfred Binet (1857–1911), a Frenchman, the intelligence test was translated into English and revised by 1916. It was widely used, and the ability to express something as subjective as mental ability in a single score had public appeal as an objective way to rank and sort people. In fact, between the years of 1921 and 1936, over 5,000 articles were published on intelligence tests.[3] Many scaling and index techniques were developed in this period, and social researchers began to use applied statistics.

Early reports of empirical social research gave the names of the people who participated in research, and most early subjects were professional researchers. During the first half of the twentieth century, reports treated subjects anonymously and only reported the results of their actions. Subjects were increasingly college students or school children. These changes reflected an increasingly objective and distant relationship between the researcher and the people studied.

People increasingly used experimental methods for applied purposes. For example, intelligence testing was adopted by the U.S. Army during World War I to sort thousands of men into different positions. The leader of the "scientific management" movement, Frederick W. Taylor (1856–1915), advocated the use of the experimental method in factories and worked with management to modify factory conditions to increase worker productivity.

The experimental method began to appear in criminology in the decade of the 1960s. The basic design for experiments on taxpayer compliance,

for instance, traces back to this period, although it has been modified considerably in more recent experiments. Experiments became more logically rigorous, and by the 1970s, methodological criteria were increasingly used to evaluate research. A related trend that began in the 1960s was the increased use of deception and a concern with ethical issues. For example, a now common practice of debriefing did not come into use until the mid-1960s.[4] The experiment is still widely used because of its logical rigor and simplicity, consistency with positivist assumptions, and relatively low cost.

RANDOM ASSIGNMENT

Criminologists frequently want to compare. For example, a researcher studying tax crime probably would want to compare different groups of taxpayers with respect to the amount of money they declare (or fail to declare) to tax authorities. The cliché, "Compare apples to apples, don't compare apples to oranges," is not about fruit; it is about comparisons. It means that a valid comparison depends on comparing things that are fundamentally alike. Random assignment facilitates comparison in experiments by creating similar groups.

When making comparisons, researchers want to compare cases that do not differ with regard to variables that offer alternative explanations. Thus, to compare groups of taxpayers on their propensity to cheat, one must assume that the groups are identical, at least pertaining to key variables in the study. If, on the other hand, the groups are different at the outset of the study—say, one has a greater opportunity to cheat than another—then the researcher has great difficulty in explaining any differences he or she might find as a result of the experiment. Was it the experimental treatment (i.e., the independent variable) that caused the difference, or was it that the difference existed even before the experiment began? The researcher would have no way of knowing which of the two questions was most accurate without having comparable groups of taxpayers.

Why Randomly Assign?

Random assignment is a method for assigning cases (e.g., individuals, organizations, etc.) to groups for the purpose of making comparisons. It is a way to increase one's confidence that the groups do not differ in a systematic way. It is a mechanical method; the assignment is automatic, and the researcher cannot make assignments on the basis of personal preference or the features of specific cases.

Random assignment is random in a statistical or mathematical sense, not in an everyday sense. In everyday speech, *random* means unplanned, haphazard, or accidental, but it has a specialized meaning in mathematics. In probability theory, *random* describes a process in which each case has a known chance of being selected. Random selection lets a researcher calculate the odds that a specific case will be sorted into one group over another. Thus, the selection process obeys mathematical laws, which makes precise calculations possible. For example, a random process is one in which all cases have an exactly equal chance of ending up in one or the other group.

The wonderful thing about a random process is that over many separate random occurrences, predictable things happen. Although the process is entirely due to chance and it is impossible to predict a specific outcome at a specific time, very accurate predictions are possible over many situations.

Random assignment or randomization is unbiased because a researcher's desire to confirm a hypothesis or a research subject's personal interests do not enter into the selection process. *Unbiased* does not mean that groups with identical characteristics are selected in each specific situation of random assignment. Instead, it says something close to that: The probability of selecting a case can be mathematically determined, and, in the long run, the groups will be identical.

How to Randomly Assign

Random assignment is very simple in practice. A researcher begins with a collection of cases (individuals, organizations, or whatever the unit of analysis is), then divides it into two or more groups by a random process, such as asking people to count off, tossing a coin, or throwing dice. For example, a researcher wants to divide 32 people into two groups of 16. A random method is writing each person's name on a slip of paper, putting the slips in a hat, mixing the slips with eyes closed, then drawing the first 16 names for group 1 and the second 16 for group 2.

Because random assignment for a specific situation only gives probabilities, a specific situation can be unusual and the groups can differ. For example, it is possible, though extremely unlikely, that all cases with one characteristic will end up in one group (see the example in Box 8.1).

Matching versus Random Assignment

If the purpose of random assignment is to get two (or more) equivalent groups, would it not be simpler to match the characteristics of cases in each group? Some researchers match cases in groups on certain characteristics, such as age and sex. Matching is an alternative to random assignment, but it is an infrequently used one.

Matching presents a problem: What are the relevant characteristics to match on, and can one locate exact matches? Individual cases differ in thousands of ways, and the researcher cannot know which might be relevant. For example, suppose a researcher wants to conduct an experiment on why taxpayers cheat on their income taxes. The researcher decides to match two groups of taxpayers so they are comparable. But on which characteristics? Should the two groups be matched for age? How about occupation? Gender? Ethnicity? Opportunities to cheat? Political ideology? You get the point. True matching soon becomes an impossible task because it presumes the researcher has identified all the characteristics that are relevant to the study's dependent variable—in this case, why taxpayers cheat.

EXPERIMENTAL DESIGN LOGIC

The Language of Experiments

Experimental research has its own language or set of terms and concepts. You already encoun-

Box 8.1 _____

Example of Three Methods of Random Assignment to Two Groups

Step 1: Begin with a collection of cases with various characteristics:

Here are 30 cases in a random order with characteristics A, B, or C (A, B, and C represent any characteristic [e.g., taxpayer's age, social class, marital status, etc.]):

    A B B C A C A B C A C B A C A B C A B C A C A A B B C A B C

Step 2: Devise a mechanical procedure to select an equal number of cases into each group via a random process.

Random Selection Method #1: Assign every other name to a group:

    A B B C A C A B C A C B A C A B C A B C A C A A B B C A B C
    1 2 1 2 1 2 1 2 1 2 1 2 1 2 1 2 1 2 1 2 1 2 1 2 1 2 1 2 1 2

Outcome of Method 1

Group 1	Group 2
As 7	4
Bs 3	6
Cs 5	5

Random Selection Method #2: Assign the first half to one group, the other half to a second group:

    A B B C A C A B C A C B A C A B C A B C A C A A B B C A B C
    1 1 1 1 1 1 1 1 1 1 1 1 1 1 1 2 2 2 2 2 2 2 2 2 2 2 2 2 2 2

Outcome of Method 2

\Group 1	Group 2
As 6	5
Bs 4	5
Cs 5	5

Random Selection Method #3: Flip a fair coin. Heads goes to Group 1, tails goes to Group 2:

    A B B C A C A B C A C B A C A B C A B C A C A A B B C A B C
    H H T H T T H H T H T T T H T T H T H H H H T H T T H T T H

Outcome of Method 3

Group 1	Group 2
As 5	6
Bs 3	6
Cs 7	3

Note: Group 1 and Group 2 were arbitrarily assigned, and one could reverse the order of 1 and 2 and get equivalent results.

tered the basic ideas: random assignment and independent and dependent variables. In experimental research, the cases or people used in research projects and on whom variables are measured are called the *subjects*.

Parts of the Experiment. We can divide the experiment into seven parts. Not all experiments have all these parts, and some have all seven parts plus others. The following seven, to be discussed here, make up a true experiment:

1. Treatment or independent variable
2. Dependent variable
3. Pretest
4. Posttest
5. Experimental group
6. Control group
7. Random assignment

In most experiments, a researcher creates a situation or enters into an ongoing situation, then modifies it. The *treatment* (or the stimulus or manipulation) is what the researcher modifies. The term comes from medicine, in which a physician administers a treatment to patients; the physician intervenes in a physical or psychological condition to change it. It is the independent variable or a combination of independent variables. In earlier examples of measurement, a researcher developed a measurement instrument or indicator (e.g., a survey question), then applied it to a person or case. In experiments, researchers "measure" independent variables by creating a condition or situation. In taxpayer compliance experiments, for instance, the risk of being audited by the tax authorities is often used as an independent variable. The experimenter, in other words, creates a situation in which the subject feels the risk of audit.

Researchers go to great lengths to create treatments. Some are as minor as giving different groups of subjects different instructions. Others can be as complex as putting subjects into situations with elaborate equipment, staged physical settings, or contrived social situations to manipulate what the subjects see or feel. Researchers

want the treatment to have an impact and produce specific reactions, feelings, or behaviors.

For example, a mock jury decision is one type of a treatment. Johnson (1985) asked subjects to watch a videotape of a child-abuse trial about a man who brought his 2-year-old son to an emergency room with a skull fracture. The videotapes were the same, except that in one, the man's attorney argued that the father was a highly religious person who followed the word of God in the Bible in all family affairs. In the other videotape, no such statement was made. The dependent variable was a decision of guilty or innocent and a recommended sentence for guilty decisions. Contrary to common sense, Johnson found that subjects were more likely to find the religious defendant guilty and to recommend longer sentences.

Dependent variables or outcomes in experimental research are the physical conditions, social behaviors, attitudes, feelings, or beliefs of subjects that change in response to a treatment. Dependent variables can be measured by paper-and-pencil indicators, observation, interviews, or physiological responses (e.g., heartbeat or sweating palms). Experiments on taxpayer compliance, for instance, have used different approaches for measuring the dependent variable. Schwartz and Orleans (1967) used the subject's actual tax returns, which were obtained from the Internal Revenue Service (IRS). Having access to official tax data is desirable from a research point of view, but issues of taxpayer privacy do weigh heavy in these decisions. Other experiments have measured the dependent variable (i.e., taxpayer compliance) by simply asking the subjects how much of their income they wish to declare to tax authorities.

The examples of the types of experimental designs given here are all variations on a theme. The theme involves the use of experimental conditions to determine the factors influencing how much income the subject is willing to report to tax authorities. In these examples, the dependent variable remains the same (i.e., the subject's level of tax compliance).

Frequently, a researcher measures the dependent variable more than once during an experiment. The *pretest* is the measurement of the dependent variable prior to introduction of the treatment. The *posttest* is the measurement of the dependent variable after the treatment has been introduced into the experimental situation.

Experimental researchers often divide subjects into two or more groups for purposes of comparison. A simple experiment has two groups, only one of which receives the treatment. The *experimental group* is the group that receives the treatment or in which the treatment is present. The group that does not receive the treatment is called the *control group*. When the independent variable takes on many different values, more than one experimental group is used.

Steps in Conducting an Experiment. Following the basic steps of the research process, experimenters decide on a topic, narrow it into a testable research problem or question, then develop a hypothesis with variables. Once a researcher has the hypothesis, the steps of experimental research are clear.

A crucial early step is to plan a specific experimental design (to be discussed). The researcher decides the number of groups to use, how and when to create treatment conditions, the number of times to measure the dependent variable, and what the groups of subjects will experience from beginning to end. He or she also develops measures of the dependent variable and pilot tests the experiment (see Box 8.2).

The experiment itself begins after a researcher locates subjects and randomly assigns them to groups. Subjects are given precise, preplanned instructions. Next, the researcher measures the dependent variable in a pretest before the treatment. One group is then exposed to the treatment. Finally, the researcher measures the dependent variable in a posttest. He or she also interviews subjects about the experiment before they leave. The researcher records measures of the dependent variable and examines the results for each group to see whether the hypothesis receives support.

Control in Experiments.   Control is crucial in experimental research.[5] A researcher wants to

---

Box 8.2 _____

Steps in Conducting an Experiment

1. Begin with a straightforward hypothesis that is appropriate for experimental research.
2. Decide on an experimental design that will test the hypothesis within practical limitations.
3. Decide how to introduce the treatment or create a situation that induces the independent variable.
4. Develop a valid and reliable measure of the dependent variable.
5. Set up an experimental setting and conduct a pilot test of the treatment and dependent variable measures.
6. Locate appropriate subjects or cases.
7. Randomly assign subjects to groups (if random assignment is used in the chosen research design) and give careful instructions.
8. Gather data for the pretest measure of the dependent variable for all groups (if a pretest is used in the chosen design).
9. Introduce the treatment to the experimental group only (or to relevant groups if there are multiple experimental groups) and monitor all groups.
10. Gather data for posttest measure of the dependent variable.
11. *Debrief* the subjects by informing them of the true purpose and reasons for the experiment. Ask subjects what they thought was occurring. Debriefing is crucial when subjects have been deceived about some aspect of the experiment.
12. Examine data collected and make comparisons between different groups. Where appropriate, use statistics and graphs to determine whether or not the hypothesis is supported.

---

control all aspects of the experimental situation to isolate the effects of the treatment and eliminate alternative explanations. Aspects of an experimental situation that are not controlled by the researcher are alternatives to the treatment for change in the dependent variable and undermine his or her attempt to establish causality.

Experimental researchers use deception to control the experimental setting. *Deception* occurs when the researcher intentionally misleads subjects through written or verbal instructions, the actions of others, or aspects of the setting. It may involve the use of *confederates* or stooges—people who pretend to be other subjects or bystanders but who actually work for the researcher and deliberately mislead subjects. Through deception, the researcher tries to control what the subjects see and hear and what they believe is occurring.

For example, a researcher's instructions falsely lead subjects to believe that they are participating in a study about group cooperation. In fact, the experiment is about male/female verbal interaction, and what subjects say is being secretly tape recorded. Deception lets the researcher control the subjects' definition of the situation. It prevents them from altering their cross-sex verbal behavior because they are unaware of the true research topic. By focusing their attention on a false topic, the researcher induces the unaware subjects to act "naturally." For realistic deception, researchers may invent false treatments and dependent variable measures to keep subjects unaware of the true ones. The use of deception in experiments raises ethical issues (to be discussed).

Design Notation

Experiments can be designed in many ways. *Design notation* is a shorthand system for symbolizing the parts of experimental design.[6] Once you learn design notation, you will find it easier to think about and compare designs. For example, design notation expresses a complex, paragraph-long description of the parts of an experiment in five or six symbols arranged in two lines. It uses the following symbols: O = observation of dependent variable; X = treatment, independent variable; R = random assignment. The Os are numbered with subscripts from left to right based on time order. Pretests are O_1, posttests O_2. When the independent variable has more than two levels, the Xs are numbered with

subscripts to distinguish among them. Symbols are in time order from left to right. The R is first, followed by the pretest, the treatment, and then the posttest. Symbols are arranged in rows, with each row representing a group of subjects. For example, an experiment with three groups has an R (if random assignment is used), followed by three rows of Os and Xs. The rows are on top of each other because the pretests, treatment, and posttest occur in each group at about the same time. Table 8.1 gives the notation for many standard experimental designs.

Types of Design

Researchers combine parts of an experiment (e.g., pretests, control groups, etc.) together into an *experimental design*. For example, some designs lack pretests, some do not have control groups, and others have many experimental groups. Certain widely used standard designs have names.

You should learn the standard designs for two reasons. First, in research reports, researchers give the name of a standard design instead of describing it. When reading reports, you will be able to understand the design of the experiment if you know the standard designs. Second, the standard designs illustrate common ways to combine design parts. You can use them for experiments you conduct or create your own variations.

Classical Experimental Design.   All designs are variations of the *classical experimental design,* the type of design discussed so far, which has random assignment, a pretest and a posttest, an experimental group, and a control group. In the Schwartz and Orleans (1967) experiment, there were three randomly assigned groups of middle-income taxpayers. A month before the 1961 income tax filing date, two of the three groups were given questionnaires, which served as the treatment or independent variable. One questionnaire dealt with issues concerning the taxpayer's "social commitment." The other dealt with issues concerning deterrence, such as the likelihood of

TABLE 8.1 Summary of Experimental Designs with Notation

NAME OF DESIGN	DESIGN NOTATION
Classical experimental design	R O X O O O
Preexperimental Designs	
One-shot case study	X O
One-group pretest-posttest	O X O
Static group comparison	X O O
Quasi-Experimental Designs	
Two-group posttest only	R X O O
Interrupted time series	O O O O X O O O
Equivalent time series	O X O X O X O X O

Latin square designs	R O X_a O X_b O X_c O
	     O X_b O X_a O X_c O
	     O X_c O X_b O X_a O
	     O X_a O X_c O X_b O
	     O X_b O X_c O X_a O
	     O X_c O X_a O X_b O

Solomon four-group design	R O X O
	      O O
	           X O
	               O

Factorial designs	R X_1 Z_1 O
	     X_1 Z_2 O
	     X_2 Z_1 O
	     X_2 Z_2 O

being audited and punished. The third group acted as a control group, and responded to neither the social commitment nor the deterrence questionnaire.

After taxpayers filed their tax returns, the IRS gave the researchers access to the tax return information. The information dealt with each taxpayer's reported income and taxes paid for that year (1961) as well that for the previous year. By using two years of taxpayer information, the researchers had both a pretest and a posttest measure of reported income and taxes paid. From this, the researchers calculated the "the year-to-year average change in tax return items" (Roth et al., 1989:79). Interestingly, researchers Schwartz and Orleans found that "only the group receiving the social commitment questions was significantly higher" (i.e., reported more income and taxes paid in the second year). Thus, they concluded that normative appeals (i.e., social commitment) appear to have the stronger effect in raising levels of taxpayer compliance (i.e., the dependent variable).

Preexperimental Designs. Some designs lack random assignment and are compromises or shortcuts. These *preexperimental designs* are used in situations where it is difficult to use the classical design. They have weaknesses that make inferring a causal relationship more difficult.

One-Shot Case Study Design. Also called the one-group posttest-only design, the *one-shot case study design* has only one group, a treatment, and a posttest. Because there is only one group, there is no random assignment. In the tax experiment, for example, the researcher gives the social commitment questionnaire to a group of students, after which he or she measures their attitudes toward tax evasion (i.e., the dependent variable). A weakness of this design is that it is difficult to say for sure that the treatment caused the dependent variable. If subjects were the same before and after the treatment, the researcher would not know it.

One-Group Pretest-Posttest Design. This design has one group, a pretest, a treatment, and a posttest. It lacks a control group and random assignment. For example, the researcher measures a group of students' attitudes toward tax evasion before administering the social commitment questionnaire. This serves as a pretest. Then after the questionnaire is completed by the students, the researcher again measures their attitudes toward tax evasion, which serves as a posttest. This is an improvement over the one-shot case study because the researcher measures the dependent variable both before and after the treatment. But it lacks a control group. The researcher cannot know whether something other than the treatment occurred between the pretest and the posttest to cause the outcome.

Static Group Comparison. Also called the *posttest-only nonequivalent group design, static group comparison* has two groups, a posttest, and treatment. It lacks random assignment and a pretest. Suppose, for instance, a researcher wants to test if perceptions of tax fairness alter the subject's willingness to honestly report his or her income to tax authorities. The researcher uses his or her two criminology classes as subjects. One class is simply asked to complete a hypothetical tax return. The other group is shown a short video about the "Tax Dodgers" mentioned in the beginning of the chapter. After the video, the subjects are asked to complete the hypothetical tax return. The researcher then determines which of the two groups of students were more compliant in reporting their income. An obvious weakness in this design is that any posttest difference between the groups in reporting their income could be due to group differences prior to the experiment instead of the treatment (i.e., the "Tax Dodger" video).

Quasi-Experimental and Special Designs. These designs, like the classical design, make identifying a causal relationship more certain than do preexperimental designs. *Quasi-experimental designs* help researchers test for causal relationships in a variety of situations where the classical design is difficult or inappropriate. They are called *quasi* because they are variations of the classical experimental design. Some have randomization but lack a pretest, some use more than two groups, and others substitute many observations of one group over time for a control group. In general, the researcher has less control over the independent variable than in the classical design.

Two-Group Posttest-Only Design. This is identical to the static group comparison, with one exception: The groups are randomly assigned. It has all the parts of the classical design except a pretest. The random assignment reduces the chance that the groups differed before the treatment, but without a pretest, a researcher cannot be as certain that the groups began the same on the dependent variable.

Suppose, for example, a researcher wants to test the hypothesis that as the penalties for tax evasion increase, taxpayer compliance will increase, as well. Using a two-group posttest-only design, the researcher randomly selects three groups of university students. One group of students is simply asked to report their income on a hypothetical tax return. They are the control group. The other two groups of students are first told that the penalty rates have gone up. For one group, the penalty rate is a fine of 25 percent of unreported income; for the other group, the penalty rate is a fine of 50 percent. These two groups, too, are asked to complete a hypothetical tax return. The three groups are then compared on respective measures of the dependent variable (i.e., proportion of income not reported on hypothetical tax return). Actual experiments have shown that the net effect of increasing the penalty rate on tax noncompliance is quite small (Alm, 1996).

Interrupted Time Series. In an *interrupted time series* design, a researcher uses one group and makes multiple pretest measures before and after the treatment. Boruch (1989) discussed time series as a useful design for studying taxpayer compliance. One example would be to select a group of taxpayers and then subject them to a treatment, such as a general course about the income tax system. The hypothesis is that taxpayer education encourages subsequent compliance. Numerous pretest and posttest measures of the dependent variable are taken. Boruch pointed out that having access to "archival records" is imperative in time-series designs. So, like Schwartz and Orleans, perhaps actual IRS tax return information could be used as a measure of the dependent variable (i.e., reported income and taxes paid).

Equivalent Time Series. An *equivalent time series* is another one-group design that extends over a time period. Instead of one treatment, it has a pretest, then a treatment and posttest, then treatment and posttest, then treatment and posttest, and so on. For example, the experiment just described is slightly altered. Instead of having taxpayers attend just one educational session, they attend a series of classes about the tax system over the course of three years. After each course is completed (i.e.,

the treatment), there is an archival measure of taxpayer compliance.

Latin Square Designs. Researchers interested in how several treatments given in different sequences or time orders affect a dependent variable can use a *Latin square design.* For example, a researcher wants to test three different treatments given in different order on three groups of randomly selected taxpayers. All three groups are pretested. The treatments are (1) a general course about the income tax system, (2) a social commitment questionnaire, and (3) a video about the "Tax Dodgers." One group of taxpayers attends the course, completes the questionnaire, and views the video. Another group completes the questionnaire first, then views the video and takes the course. A third group views the video first, then takes the course and completes the questionnaire. The researcher then measures the dependent variable for each group to see which sequence of treatments had the greatest effect on taxpayer compliance.

Solomon Four-Group Design. A researcher may believe that the pretest measure has an influence on the treatment or dependent variable. A pretest can sometimes sensitize subjects to the treatment or improve their performance on the posttest (see the discussion of testing effect to come). Richard L. Solomon developed the *Solomon four-group design* to address the issue of pretest effects. It combines the classical experimental design with the two-group posttest-only design and randomly assigns subjects to one of four groups.

For example, a researcher wants to know if perceptions regarding the fairness of the tax system influence taxpayer compliance. Taxpayer compliance, the dependent variable, is measured in terms of items on a questionnaire. Because the researcher suspects the pretest questionnaire itself sensitizes and changes taxpayers, a Solomon four-group design is used.

Taxpayers are randomly selected to be in one of four groups. Two groups receive the pretest (i.e., a questionnaire measuring the dependent variable); one of them receives the treatment (i.e., views a video about tax fairness and "Tax Dodgers"), whereas the other group does not. The other two groups receive no pretest; one of them views the video on tax fairness and the other does not.

All four groups are then given a posttest (i.e., asked to complete a questionnaire measuring the dependent variable) and compared. If the two treatment groups (i.e., those who viewed the video) have similar results, and the two control groups have similar results, then the researcher knows the pretest had no effect on the posttest. However, if the two groups with a pretest (one treatment, one control) differ from the two groups without a pretest, then the researcher concludes that the pretest itself may have an effect on the dependent variable.

Factorial Designs. Sometimes, a research question suggests looking at the simultaneous effects of more than one independent variable. A *factorial design* uses two or more independent variables in combination. Every combination of the categories in variables (sometimes called *factors*) is examined. When each variable contains several categories, the number of combinations grows very quickly. The treatment or manipulation is not each independent variable; rather, it is each combination of the categories.

For example, a researcher examines taxpayer compliance, which is the dependent variable, in terms of two independent variables: audit history and perceptions of tax fairness. The research question is: Does compliance vary under different combinations of previously being audited and perceptions of fairness?

Audit history has two categories: "audited in the past" and "never audited." Perceptions of fairness has three categories: "low," "medium," and "high." There are six combinations of categories for the two variables (see Box 8.3).

The treatments in a factorial design can have two kinds of effects on the dependent variable: main effects and interaction effects. Only *main effects* are present in one-factor or single-treatment designs. In a factorial design, specific combinations of independent variable categories can also have an effect. They are called *interaction effects* because the categories in a combination interact to produce an effect beyond that of each variable alone.

A researcher measures taxpayer compliance through the use of a questionnaire made up of various compliance indexes. There is a separate group of taxpayers for each combination, so the researcher computes the number of groups by multiplying the number of categories in each variable. There are six groups in this experiment. Thus, group 1 is made up of taxpayers who have been audited *and* have low (or negative) perceptions regarding tax fairness. Group 2 is made up of taxpayers who have been previously audited *and* have medium perceptions of tax fairness, and so forth for the other four groups (see Box 8.3).

Graphing results, the researcher finds that the main effect for the never-audited groups is that their compliance levels are higher than are the previously audited groups, irrespective of perceived fairness. The main effect for perceptions of fairness is that compliance increases as perceived fairness increases, whether or not the groups have been previously audited. The left-hand graph in Box 8.3 shows these main effects.

The right-hand graph reveals some interesting interaction effects. It shows, for instance, that previously audited taxpayers, even with perceptions of low fairness, have among the highest compliance levels. It also shows that never-audited taxpayers with perceptions of high fairness have among the highest compliance levels. Curiously, however, the graph shows that previously audited taxpayers with perceptions of high fairness actually have low levels of compliance. Something about the interaction between being previously audited and having perceptions of high amounts of fairness in the tax system produces this effect. It is contrary to the researcher's theory about tax compliance, and it deserves much closer study in subsequent experiments. Thus, we see how a factorial design can produce unanticipated interaction effects, and hence spur future research.

Box 8.3 _____

Example of Factorial Design with Two Variables

TAX AUDIT EXPERIENCE	TAXPAYER'S PERCEPTIONS OF TAX FAIRNESS		
	Low	*Medium*	*High*
Previously Audited	Group 1	Group 2	Group 3
Not Previously Audited	Group 4	Group 5	Group 6

Group Number		*Design Notation*		
1		X_1	Z_1	O
2		X_1	Z_2	O
3	R	X_1	Z_3	O
4		X_2	Z_1	O
5		X_2	Z_2	O
6		X_2	Z_3	O

Where:
X_1 = previously audited, X_2 = never audited
Z_1 = low fairness, Z_2 = medium fairness, Z_3 = high fairness

GRAPHS PLOTTING HYPOTHETICAL RESULTS

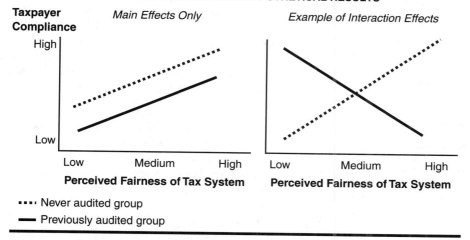

Main Effects Only   *Example of Interaction Effects*

Taxpayer Compliance

High

Low

Low   Medium   High   Low   Medium   High
Perceived Fairness of Tax System   **Perceived Fairness of Tax System**

···· Never audited group
——— Previously audited group

Researchers discuss factorial design in a shorthand way. A "two by three factorial design" is written 2 × 3. It means that there are two treatments, with two categories in one and three categories in the other. A 2 × 3 × 3 design means that there are three independent variables, one with two categories and two with three categories each.

Valentine-French and Radtke (1989) used a 2 × 2 × 3 factorial design to study the effect of victim reaction to sexual harassment blame. The subjects were 120 male and 120 female undergraduate volunteers from the University of Calgary. The researchers operationalized the independent variable as an audiotaped vignette in which a professor guaranteed a good grade to a student if she or he was willing to cooperate, permitted caressing of the student's shoulder, and let the professor kiss her or him on the cheek. The experimenters varied the situation by having the student victim be male or female and by using one of three endings: The victim blamed his or her own behavior for the incident, blamed the professor, or gave no reaction. Thus, there were six combinations of victim gender and endings.

The subjects did not know the purpose of the study and listened to the vignette alone. The experimenters measured various background characteristics of the subjects with a questionnaire, as well as the main dependent variable—attribution of blame (i.e., who was at fault). They operationalized the variable as an eight-item index measured with a 7-point Likert scale. Valentine-French and Radtke (1989) found that women were more likely to label the incident as sexual harassment and blame the professor. Both genders were more likely to blame a female victim. Male subjects, more than females, blamed the victim when the victim made a statement of self-blame. This was a $2 \times 2 \times 3$ factorial design because three independent variables were examined: the subject's gender, the victim's gender, and the victim's reactions.

INTERNAL AND EXTERNAL VALIDITY

The Logic of Internal Validity

Internal validity means the ability to eliminate alternative explanations of the dependent variable. Variables, other than the treatment, that affect the dependent variable are threats to internal validity. They threaten the researcher's ability to say that the treatment was the true causal factor producing change in the dependent variable. Thus, the logic of internal validity is to rule out variables other than the treatment by controlling experimental conditions and through experimental designs. Next, we examine major threats to internal validity.

Threats to Internal Validity

The following are 10 common threats to internal validity.[7]

Selection Bias. *Selection bias* is the threat that subjects will not form equivalent groups. It is a problem in designs without random assignment. It occurs when subjects in one experimental group have a characteristic that affects the dependent variable. For example, in our tax experiment, the treatment group, it just so happens, is made up of taxpayers who are retired and thus tend to have little opportunity to cheat on their income taxes. The control group, on the other hand, is mainly made up of younger taxpayers who have more opportunities to underreport income. Random assignment of subjects easily solves the problem of selection bias.

History. This is the threat that an event unrelated to the treatment will occur during the experiment and influence the dependent variable. *History effects* are more likely in experiments that continue over a long time period. During the course of the tax experiment, for instance, there is a major scandal in which the vice president of the country is arrested for tax evasion. The controversy surrounding his arrest has a powerful effect on the subjects over and above any effect the independent variable (or treatment) may have had. Moreover, the experimental design gives the researcher no way to assess this effect.

Maturation. This is the threat that some biological, psychological, or emotional process within the subjects and separate from the treatment will change over time. *Maturation* is more common in experiments over long time periods. Suppose, for example, the researcher is using an interrupted time-series design to study the experimental effects of a new law that lowers income tax rates. The researcher hypothesizes that the new law will improve taxpayer compliance. The experiment spans a three-year period. However, in that time, some subjects mature in their political outlook, in that they begin to appreciate the need for government. Their maturing leads them to be more compliant taxpayers, which is quite apart from the lower tax rates brought about by the new law. Designs with a pretest and control group help researchers determine whether maturation or history effects are present, because both experimental and control groups will show similar changes over time.

Testing. Sometimes, the pretest measure itself affects an experiment. This *testing effect* threatens internal validity because more than the treatment alone affects the dependent variable. Information on the Solomon four-group design specifically dealt with this. To reiterate, the pretest itself creates the change in the dependent variable. In asking subjects how well they comply with tax laws, the researcher is exposing subjects to ideas about how well they *should* comply, which is implicitly a testing effect. Consequently, there is no way of telling what independent role a treatment, such as viewing a video on tax dodgers, has played.

Instrumentation. This threat is related to stability reliability. It occurs when the *instrument* or dependent variable measure changes during the experiment. For example, suppose a tax experiment measured taxpayer compliance, the dependent variable, from questionnaire items. If the subject pool happens to be made up of different language groups, the researcher is faced with having to have questionnaires in those languages. To minimize instrumentation bias, the researcher must be very careful that the language is consistent and comparable for all versions of the questionnaire.

Mortality. *Mortality,* or attrition, arises when some subjects do not continue throughout the experiment. Although the word *mortality* means death, it does not necessarily mean that subjects have died. If a subset of subjects leaves partway through an experiment, a researcher cannot know whether the results would have been different if the subset had stayed.

Social scientists have criticized the Schwartz and Orleans experiment on issues of subject mortality. The problem stems from their not collecting data from all subjects, as some had dropped out of the study. As Roth and associates (1989:79) stated, "If those who refused interviews differed systematically from those who were interviewed

in terms of their responsiveness to deterrence- and commitment-based appeals, the validity of findings may have been affected." As a rule of thumb, researchers should notice and report the number of subjects in each group during pretests and posttests to detect this threat to internal validity.

Statistical Regression. *Statistical regression* is not easy to grasp intuitively. It is a problem of extreme values or a tendency for random errors to move group results toward the average. It can occur in two ways.

One situation arises when subjects are unusual with regard to the dependent variable. Because they begin as unusual or extreme, subjects are unlikely to respond further in the same direction. For example, a group of hardened white-collar criminals from a nearby federal prison completed a pretest about their attitudes toward tax fairness. The pretest revealed that they believe the tax system is extremely unfair. The criminals are then shown a video that criticizes tax-dodger corporations. Surprisingly, the posttest indicates that their attitudes have become less extreme—that is, they think the tax system is more fair after seeing the video. This confuses the researcher because a control group of university students had just the opposite response to the video (i.e., it made them think that the tax system is unfair). The researcher cannot understand the different reactions to the video, but then considers that perhaps random chance alone has made the white-collar criminals appear less extreme when measured the second time.[8]

A second situation involves a problem with the measurement instrument. If many subjects score very high (at the ceiling) or very low (at the floor) on a variable, random chance alone will produce a change between the pretest and the posttest. For example, a researcher gives 80 subjects a test, and 75 get perfect scores. He or she then gives a treatment to raise scores. Because so many subjects already had perfect scores, random errors will reduce the group average because those who got perfect scores can randomly move in only one direction—to get some answers wrong. An examination of scores on pretests will help researchers detect this threat to internal validity.

Diffusion of Treatment or Contamination.
Diffusion of treatment is the threat that subjects in different groups will communicate with each other and learn about the other's treatment. Researchers avoid it by isolating groups or having subjects promise not to reveal anything to others who will become subjects. Say, for example, the researcher is experimenting on whether increasing the probability of tax audit reduces income underreporting. The researcher decides to audit the treatment group at high probabilities and the control group at normal probabilities. Diffusion would threaten internal validity if the treatment group were to tell the control group about the high audit probabilities, which could in turn cause the control group to alter its behavior in the experiment. A researcher needs outside information such as postexperimental interviews with subjects to detect this threat.

Compensatory Behavior. Some experiments provide something of value to one group of subjects but not to another, and the difference becomes known. The inequality may produce pressure to reduce differences, competitive rivalry between groups, or resentful demoralization. All these types of *compensatory behavior* can affect the dependent variable in addition to the treatment. For example, one group of subjects is helped in completing a task, whereas the control group receives no help. The latter group might resent having no help and simply stop trying, or the group may work extra hard to overcome the lack of help. It is difficult to detect this threat unless outside information is used (see the earlier discussion of diffusion of treatment).

Experimenter Expectancy. Although it is not always considered a traditional internal validity problem, the experimenter's behavior, too, can threaten causal logic.[9] A researcher may threaten internal validity, not by purposefully unethical behavior but by indirectly communicating *experimenter expectancy* to subjects. Researchers

may be highly committed to the hypothesis and indirectly communicate the hypothesis or desired findings to subjects. For example, a researcher might unwittingly communicate to a group of subjects that he or she disapproves of income tax evasion. This impression is conveyed through eye contact, tone of voice, pauses, and other nonverbal cues. Thus, a similar disapproval on the part of subjects might be hardly more than the subjects "telling the experimenter what he or she wants to hear."

The *double-blind experiment* is designed to control researcher expectancy. In it, people who have direct contact with subjects do not know the details of the hypothesis or the treatment. It is *double* blind because both the subjects and those in contact with them are blind to details of the experiment (see Figure 8.1). For example, a researcher wants to see if a new drug is effective. Using pills of three colors—green, yellow, and pink—the researcher puts the new drug in the yellow pill, puts an old drug in the pink one, and makes the green pill a *placebo*—a false treatment that appears to be real (e.g., a sugar pill without any physical effects). Assistants who give the pills and record the effects do not know which color contains the new drug. Only another person who does not deal with subjects directly knows which colored pill contains the drug and examines the results.

External Validity and Field Experiments

Even if an experimenter eliminates all concerns about internal validity, external validity remains a potential problem. *External validity* is the ability to generalize experimental findings to events and settings outside the experiment itself. If a study lacks external validity, its findings hold true only in experiments, making them useless to both basic and applied science. In this section, we look at types of external validity and factors that influence it.

Realism. Are experiments realistic? There are two types of realism to consider.[10] *Experimental realism* is the impact of an experimental treatment or setting on subjects; it occurs when subjects are

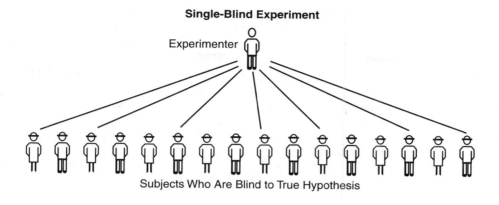

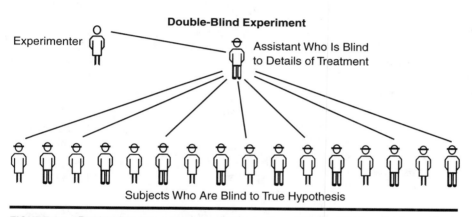

FIGURE 8.1   Double-Blind Experiments: An Illustration of Single-Blind, or Ordinary, and Double-Blind Experiments

caught up in the experiment and are truly influenced by it. It is weak if subjects remain unaffected by the treatment, which is why researchers go to great lengths to create realistic conditions. Aronson and Carlsmith (1968:25) noted:

> All experimental procedures are "contrived" in the sense that they are invented. Indeed, it can be said that the art of experimentation rests primarily on the skill of the investigator to judge the procedure which is the more accurate realization of his conceptual variable and has the greatest impact and the more credibility for the subject.

Mundane realism asks: Is the experiment like the real world? It is a concern that tax experiments,

for example, do not entirely capture the realistic reactions taxpayers have to the threat of audit, changes in the tax rates, tax penalties, and so on. Alm (1996:116) has framed the point nicely:

> A decision to report $2 in an experiment is clearly different from a decision to report actual income on an annual tax return, even if laboratory incentives are salient. In particular, the laboratory setting cannot capture a catastrophic loss such as jail, and it cannot capture the social stigma that some surveys suggest is an important factor in taxpayer reporting.

Mundane realism would be stronger if the experimenter had subjects learn factual information used in real life instead of something invented for an experiment alone.

Mundane realism most directly affects external validity—the ability to generalize from experiments to the real world.[11] Two aspects of experiments can be generalized. One is from the subjects to other people. Can experimental findings on groups of subjects who are university students, for example, be generalized to the entire population of taxpayers, most of whom are not university students? A related aspect is generalizing from an artificial setting to everyday life. How can watching a 15-minute video of the unfairness of the corporate tax dodgers be equated with a lifetime of experiencing a regressive tax burden?

Reactivity.   Subjects may react differently in an experiment than they would in real life because they know they are part of a study; this is called *reactivity.* The *Hawthorne effect* is a specific kind of reactivity.[12] The name comes from a series of experiments by Elton Mayo at the Hawthorne, Illinois, plant of Westinghouse Electric during the 1920s and 1930s. Researchers modified many aspects of working conditions (e.g., lighting, time for breaks, etc.) and measured productivity. They discovered that productivity rose after each modification, no matter what it was. This curious result occurred because the workers did not respond to the treatment but to the additional attention they received from being part of the experiment and knowing that they were being watched. Later research questioned whether this occurred, but the name is still used for an effect from the attention of researchers. A related effect is the effect of something new, which may wear off over time. Smith and Glass (1987:148) have called this the *novelty effect.*

Demand characteristics are another type of reactivity. Subjects may pick up clues about the hypothesis or goal of an experiment, and they may change their behavior to what they think is demanded of them (i.e., support the hypothesis) in order to please the researcher.

A last type of reactivity is the *placebo effect,* observed when subjects are given the placebo but respond as if they had received the real treatment. For example, in an experiment on stopping smoking, subjects are given either a drug to reduce their dependence on nicotine or a placebo. If subjects who received the placebo also stop smoking, then participating in an experiment and taking something that subjects believed would help them quit smoking had an effect. The subjects' belief in the placebo alone affected the dependent variable.

Boruch (1989:363) found reactivity to be an issue of concern in many of the tax experiments:

> *For instance, a randomized test of the effect of amnesty programs on tax delinquents may engender distress or anger among control group members who have not been afforded amnesty or who regarded amnesty as unfair to honest taxpayers. That distress may lead individuals to resist further, to seek remedies to perceived unfairness in the courts, or to take some other action.*

Boruch (1989:363–364) recommended that researchers "design a side experiment whenever possible to determine whether and how awareness [i.e., reactivity] influences behavior. This requires that at least one subsample be unaware of the experiment and that awareness be measured."

Field Experiments.   This chapter has focused on experiments conducted under the highly controlled conditions of a laboratory. Experiments are also conducted in real-life or field settings. In field settings, a researcher has less control over the experimental conditions. The amount of control varies on a continuum. At one end is the highly controlled *laboratory experiment,* which takes place in a specialized setting or laboratory; at the opposite end is the *field experiment,* which takes place in the "field"—in natural settings such as a subway car, a liquor store, or a public sidewalk. Subjects in field experiments are usually unaware that they are involved in an experiment and react in a natural way. For example, researchers have had a confederate fake a heart attack on a subway car to see how the bystanders react.[13]

A dramatic example is a field experiment by Harari and colleagues (1985) on whether a male passerby will attempt to stop an attempted rape. In this experiment, conducted at San Diego State University, an attempted rape was staged on a somewhat isolated campus path in the evening. The staged attack was clearly visible to unsuspecting male subjects who approached alone or in groups of two or three. In the attack, a female student was grabbed by a large man hiding in the bushes. As the man pulled her away and tried to cover her mouth, the woman dropped her books. She struggled and screamed. "No, no! Help, help, please help me!" and "Rape!" Hidden observers told the actors when to begin to stage the attack and noted the actions of subjects. Assistance was measured as movement toward the attack site or movement toward a police officer visible across a nearby parking lot. The study found that 85 percent of men in groups and 65 percent of men walking alone made a detectable move to assist the woman.

The amount of experimenter control is related to internal and external validity. Laboratory experiments tend to have greater internal validity but lower external validity; that is, they are logically tighter and better controlled, but less generalizable. Field experiments tend to have greater external validity but lower internal validity; that is, they are more generalizable but less controlled. Quasi-experimental designs are more common. For example, in the experiment involving the staged attempted rape, the experimenters recreated a very realistic situation with high external validity. It had more external validity than putting people in a laboratory setting and asking them what they would do hypothetically. Yet, subjects were not randomly assigned. Any man who happened to walk by became a subject. The experimenters could not precisely control what the subject heard or saw. The measurement of subject response was based on hidden observers who may have missed some subject responses.

PRACTICAL CONSIDERATIONS

Every research technique has informal tricks of the trade. They are pragmatic and based on common sense but account for the difference between the successful research projects of an experienced

researcher and the difficulties a novice researcher faces. Three are discussed here.

Planning and Pilot Tests

All social research requires planning, and most quantitative researchers use pilot tests. During the planning phase of experimental research, a researcher thinks of alternative explanations or threats to internal validity and how to avoid them. The researcher also develops a neat and well-organized system for recording data. In addition, he or she should devote serious effort to pilot testing any apparatus (e.g., computers, video cameras, tape recorders, etc.) that will be used in the treatment situation, and he or she must train and pilot test confederates. After the pilot tests, the researcher should interview the pilot subjects to uncover aspects of the experiment that need refinement.

Instructions to Subjects

Most experiments involve giving instructions to subjects to set the stage. A researcher should word instructions carefully and follow a prepared script so that all subjects hear the same thing. This ensures reliability. The instructions are also important in creating a realistic cover story when deception is used. Aronson and Carlsmith (1968:46) noted, "One of the most common mistakes the novice experimenter makes is to present his instructions too briefly."

Postexperiment Interview

At the end of an experiment, the researcher should interview subjects, for three reasons. First, if deception was used, the researcher needs to *debrief* the subjects, telling them the true purpose of the experiment and answering questions. Second, he or she can learn what the subjects thought and how their definitions of the situation affected their behavior. Finally, he or she can explain the importance of not revealing the true nature of the experiment to other potential subjects.

RESULTS OF EXPERIMENTAL RESEARCH: MAKING COMPARISONS

Comparison is the key to all research. By carefully examining the results of experimental research, a researcher can learn a great deal about threats to internal validity, and whether the treatment has an impact on the dependent variable.

Table 8.2 compares the results from a series of five tax experiments using the classical experimental design. In all cases, the dependent variable is the subject's level of tax compliance. Tax compliance is measured as the amount of income reported. The independent variable is the tax rate on declared or reported income. The hypothesis being tested is that tax rates are inversely related to reported income (i.e., as tax rates go up, reported income goes down). The experiments were conducted in a laboratory and the subjects were university students. The subjects played a game in which they "earned" money and determined how much of their earnings to report to the tax authority.

The 30 subjects in the experimental group of Experiment 1 reported an average of $50 less, whereas the 30 subjects in the control group reported the same amount of income. Only one person dropped out of the experiment. Experiment 2 had similar results, although 11 people from the experimental group dropped out. This indicates a problem with subject mortality. The experimental group in Experiment 3 reported on average $8 less compared to $2 in the control group. However, the experimental and control groups began with an average of $31 difference (i.e., $160 vs. $191). This suggests a problem with selection bias. Experiment 4 had no selection bias or experimental mortality. However, those in the experimental group reported practically the same amount of income as did those in the control group. It appears that the treatment (i.e., higher tax rates) had no effect on income reporting. Experiment 5 also avoided selection bias and experimental mortality problems. Subjects in the experimental group on average reported $32 less, as did the subjects in the control group. This suggests that the maturation, history, or diffusion of treatment effects may have occurred. To explore these in detail, the researcher must interview the subjects after Experiment 5 ends.

A WORD ON ETHICS

Ethical considerations are a significant issue in experimental research because experimental research is intrusive (i.e., it interferes). Treatments may involve placing people in contrived social settings and manipulating their feelings or behaviors. Dependent variables may be what subjects say or do. The amount and type of intrusion is limited by ethical standards. Researchers must be careful, for example, that their tax experiments do not contribute to the subject's likelihood of evading income taxes. To do this, they must painstakingly monitor all stages of the experiment and then debrief subjects afterward so as not to convey the message that tax evasion is approved behavior.

Deception is common in social experiments, but it involves misleading or lying to subjects. Such dishonesty is not condoned as acceptable in itself and is acceptable only as the means to achieve a goal that cannot be achieved otherwise. Even for a worthy goal, deception can be used only with restrictions. The amount and type of deception should not go beyond what is minimally necessary, however. Subjects should be debriefed and informed of the true purpose of the research.

Ethics is discussed in detail in the last chapter. The important thing to remember is that the major responsibility for what happens to subjects directly or indirectly as a consequence of their involvement in research rests with the researcher. Social researchers should always treat subjects with respect and dignity. They should not lose their sensitivity to other people and should never treat subjects as inanimate objects or mere guinea pigs who exist only for the researcher's needs.

CONCLUSION

In this chapter, you learned about random assignment and the methods of experimental research.

TABLE 8.2 Comparisons of Results, Classical Experimental Design, Tax Compliance Experiments

EXPERIMENT 1				EXPERIMENT 4		
	Pretest	*Posttest*			*Pretest*	*Posttest*
Experimental	190 (30)	140 (29)	Experimental		190 (30)	188 (29)
Control group	189 (30)	189 (30)	Control group		192 (29)	189 (28)

EXPERIMENT 2				EXPERIMENT 5		
	Pretest	*Posttest*			*Pretest*	*Posttest*
Experimental	190 (30)	141 (19)	Experimental		190 (30)	158 (30)
Control group	189 (30)	189 (28)	Control group		191 (29)	159 (28)

EXPERIMENT 3				SYMBOLS FOR COMPARISON PURPOSES		
	Pretest	*Posttest*			*Pretest*	*Posttest*
Experimental	160 (30)	152 (29)	Experimental		A (A)	C (C)
Control group	191 (29)	189 (29)	Control group		B (B)	D (D)

COMPARISONS

	A–B	*C–D*	*A–C*	*B–D*	*(A)–(C)*	*(B)–(D)*
Experiment 1	1	49	−50	0	−1	0
Experiment 2	1	48	−49	0	−11	0
Experiment 3	31	37	−8	−2	−1	0
Experiment 4	2	1	−2	−3	−1	−1
Experiment 5	1	1	−32	−32	0	−1

A–B Do the two groups begin the same? If not, selection bias may be possibly occurring.
C–D Do the two groups end the same? If not, the treatment may be ineffective, or there may be strong history, maturation, or diffusion or treatment effects.
A–C Did the experimental group change? If not, treatment may be ineffective.
(A)–(C) Did the number of subjects in the experimental group or control group change?
and If a large drop occurs, experimental mortality may be a threat to internal
(B)–(D) validity.

INTERPRETATION

Experiment 1 No internal validity threats evident, treatment effects
Experiment 2 Experimental mortality threat likely problem
Experiment 3 Selection bias likely problem
Experiment 4 No internal validity threat evident, no treatment effects
Experiment 5 History, maturation, diffusion of treatment threats are a likely problem

Note: Numbers are average reported income. Numbers in parentheses ( ) are number of subjects per group. Random assignment is made to the experimental or control group.

Random assignment is an effective way to create two (or more) groups, which can be treated as equivalent and hence compared. In general, experimental research provides precise and relatively unambiguous evidence for a causal relationship. It follows the positivist approach and produces quantitative results that can be analyzed with statistics.

This chapter also examined the parts of an experiment and how they can be combined to produce different experimental designs. In addition to the classical experimental design, you learned about preexperimental and quasi-experimental designs. You also learned how to express them using design notation.

You learned that internal validity—the internal logical rigor of an experiment—is a key idea in experimental research. Threats to internal validity are possible alternative explanations to the treatment. You also learned about external validity and how field experiments maximize external validity.

The real strength of experimental research is its control and logical rigor in establishing evidence for causality. In general, experiments tend to be easier to replicate, less expensive, and less time consuming than the other techniques. Experimental research also has limitations. First, some questions cannot be addressed using experimental methods because control and experimental manipulation are impossible. Another limitation is that experiments usually test one or a few hypotheses at a time. This fragments knowledge and makes it necessary to synthesize results across many research reports. External validity is another potential problem because many experiments rely on small nonrandom samples of college students.[14]

You learned how a careful examination and comparison of results can alert you to potential problems in research design. Finally, you saw some practical and ethical considerations in experiments. Deception, in particular, is an issue in experimental research.

In the next chapters, you will examine survey research and other research techniques. The logic of the nonexperimental methods differs from that of the experiment. Experimenters focus narrowly on a few hypotheses. They usually have one or two independent variables, a single dependent variable, a few small groups of subjects, and an independent variable that the researcher induces. By contrast, other social researchers test many hypotheses at once. They measure a large number of independent and dependent variables and use a larger number of randomly sampled subjects. Their independent variables are usually preexisting conditions in subjects.

KEY TERMS

classical experimental design
compensatory behavior
control group
debrief
deception
demand characteristics
dependent variable
design notation
diffusion of treatment
double-blind experiment
equivalent time series
experimental design
experimental group
experimental realism

experimenter expectancy
external validity
factorial design
field experiment
Hawthorne effect
history effects
internal validity
interrupted time series
laboratory experiment
Latin square design
maturation
mortality
mundane realism
novelty effect

one-shot case study
placebo
placebo effect
posttest
preexperimental designs
pretest
quasi-experimental designs
random assignment
reactivity
selection bias
Solomon four-group design
static group comparison
subjects
treatment

REVIEW QUESTIONS

1. What are the seven elements or parts of an experiment?
2. What distinguishes preexperimental designs from the classical design?
3. Which design permits the testing of different sequences of several treatments?
4. What does a "two by three factorial design" mean? Write it in design notation, assuming that random assignment with posttest only was used.
5. How do the interrupted and the equivalent time series designs differ?
6. What is the logic of internal validity and how does the use of a control group fit into that logic?
7. How does the Solomon four-group design show the testing effect?
8. What is the double-blind experiment and why is it used?
9. Do field or laboratory experiments have greater internal validity? External validity? Explain.
10. What is the difference between experimental and mundane realism?

NOTES

1. Cook and Campbell (1979:9–36, 91–94) argued for a modification of a more rigid positivist approach to causality for experimental research. They suggested a "critical-realist" approach, which shares some features of the critical approach outlined in Chapter 4.

2. For discussions of the history of the experiment, see Danziger (1988), Gillespie (1988), Hornstein (1988), O'Donnell (1985), and Scheibe (1988).

3. See Hornstein (1988:11).

4. For events after World War II, see Harris (1988) and Suls and Rosnow (1988). For a discussion of the increased use of deception, see Reynolds (1979:60).

5. For a discussion of control in experiments, see Cook and Campbell (1979:7–9) and Spector (1981: 15–16).

6. The notation for research design is discussed in Cook and Campbell (1979:95–96), Dooley (1984: 132–137), and Spector (1981:27–28).

7. For additional discussions of threats to internal validity, see Cook and Campbell (1979:51–68),

Kercher (1992), Spector (1981:24–27), Smith and Glass (1987), and Suls and Rosnow (1988).

8. This example is borrowed from Mitchell and Jolley (1988:97).

9. Experimenter expectancy is discussed in Aronson and Carlsmith (1968:66–70), Dooley (1984:151–153), and Mitchell and Jolley (1988:327–329).

10. Also see Aronson and Carlsmith (1968:22–25).

11. For a discussion of external validity, see Cook and Campbell (1979:70–80).

12. The Hawthorne effect is described in Roethlisberger and Dickenson (1939), Franke and Kaul (1978), and Lang (1992). Also see the discussion in Cook and Campbell (1979:123–125) and Dooley (1984:155–156). Gillespie (1988, 1991) discussed the political context of the experiments and how it shaped them.

13. See Piliavin and associates (1969).

14. See Graham (1992).

RECOMMENDED READINGS

Boruch, Robert F. (1989) Experimental and quasi-experimental designs in taxpayer compliance research. In *Taxpayer Compliance,* edited by John Scholz Roth and Anne Witte, pp. 339–379. Philadelphia: University of Pennsylvania Press. This chapter is a concise summary of tax experi-

ments. It describes the basic experimental designs used in terms of their relative strengths and weaknesses. It also summarizes their results.

Campbell, Donald T., and Julian C. Stanley. (1963). *Experimental and quasi-experimental designs for research.* Chicago: Rand McNally. This is the classic of experimental design. The basic ideas about threats to internal validity are presented in detail. The discussion of experimental validity (internal and external) and design issues is still valuable.

Cook, Thomas D., and Donald T. Campbell. (1979). *Quasi-experimental design: Design and analysis issues for field settings*. Chicago: Rand McNally. If there were only one book to read on experimental design, this would be it. The authors cover the basics of experimental logic and causality and advance thinking on experimental design. They explore many potential threats to internal and external validity and present alternative designs.

Huck, Schuyler W., and Howard M. Sandler. (1979). *Rival hypotheses: Alternative interpretations of data based conclusions*. New York: Harper & Row. This is an unusual book, with two sections. The first has short summaries of 100 published research reports on many different topics. The second section is a discussion of internal validity threats or other possible problems that may exist in each report and limit ability of a researcher to draw conclusions about causal relations.

Spector, Paul E. (1981). *Research designs*. Beverly Hills, CA: Sage. This is a short (80-page) introduction to the basic concepts of research design. It includes discussions of threats to internal validity and different experimental designs. The discussion of different types of interaction effects is especially useful.

SAMPLING

> *The National Crime Victimization Survey (NCVS) obtains information about crimes from an ongoing, nationally representative sample of households in the United States. . . . In 1996 approximately 45,400 households and 94,000 people age 12 years of older were interviewed.*
> —Cheryl Ringel, *Criminal Victimization 1996*, p. 9

INTRODUCTION

The use of sampling has indeed fortified criminology's scientific status. Without an advanced appreciation of sampling, criminologists would have great difficulty transcending legal and political definitions of crime and justice. Our research would, in such cases, be frustrated by a lack of alternatives to official crime statistics, such as those gathered by the police. This in turn narrows the field of criminological research, while compromising the discipline's ability to conduct independent scientific inquiry, as Sellin (1938) and others have long recognized.

One of the biggest advances in criminological science occurred in the United States in the early 1970s with the advent of the National Crime Victimization Survey (NCVS). The victimization survey liberated the research agenda by giving criminologists for the first time a way to analyze "hidden crimes"—that is, those crimes not reported to the police. Thus, criminologists can now interpret official statistics in light of victimization data. Having a source of data independent of the police strengthens the discipline's critique of the criminal justice system. Of course, without sophisticated sampling techniques, there would be no national victimization survey.

Yet there is much more to be accomplished, particularly in the area of corporate crime. As Coleman (1998:9) has pointed out, "Neither of the two major sources of data on street crime— the Uniform Crime Reports and the National Crime Victimization Survey—gives us much useful information about most types of white-collar crime." Thus, it is especially incumbent on criminologists to apply sampling techniques to the study of white-collar crime. For this reason, many of the examples in this chapter deal with sampling in the area of corporate crime.

In this chapter, you will learn about sampling. Sampling is based on statistical theories that are not explored in depth here. Instead, emphasis is on giving you an understanding of sampling concepts and how to apply them in practice. Sampling is a powerful technique with wide applications in criminology. It is used primarily in survey research, content analysis, and nonreactive research—the three types of quantitative research techniques we will examine in the upcoming chapters.

TYPES OF SAMPLING

Why Sample?

Sampling, like random assignment, is a process of systematically selecting cases for inclusion in a research project. When a researcher randomly assigns, he or she sorts a collection of cases into two or more groups using a random process. By contrast, in random sampling, he or she selects a smaller subset of cases from a larger pool of cases (see Figure 9.1). A researcher can both sample and randomly assign. He or she can first sample to obtain a smaller set of cases (e.g., 150 people out of 20,000) and then use random assignment to divide the smaller set into groups (e.g., divide the 150 people into three groups of 50).

A researcher gets a set of cases, or a *sample*, from sampling that is more manageable and cost effective to work with than the pool of all cases. For example, it would be much less costly and time consuming to measure variables on 150 than on 20,000 people. The difficulty with using the smaller subset instead of the entire pool is that the

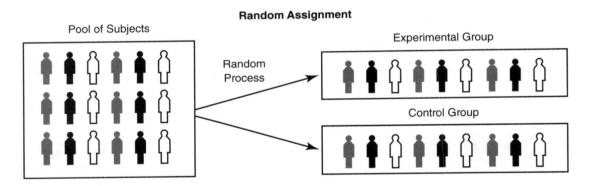

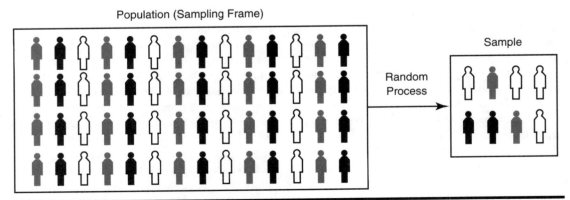

FIGURE 9.1   Random Assignment and Random Sampling

researcher is not interested in a small subset of cases alone. Instead, he or she wants to generalize to the entire pool. If well done, sampling lets a researcher measure variables on the smaller set of cases but generalize results accurately to all cases.

Your first reaction to the claim that a researcher can use a small subset to generalize accurately to a much larger pool of cases may be one of disbelief. It sounds too good to be true. But sampling is powerful, and it works. With a well-conducted sample, a researcher can measure variables with 2,000 cases, generalize to 200 million, and not be off by more than 2 to 4 percent from the results that would be obtained if all 200 million were used.

How is it possible to use so few cases to generalize accurately to so many? It is not based on trickery or magic but on logical statistical reasoning that has been tested repeatedly with empirical evidence. Moreover, a researcher cannot use just any sample to generalize accurately. The sample must be selected according to precise procedures, and statements made about it are subject to limitations.

Populations, Elements, and Sampling Frames

A researcher draws a sample from a larger pool of cases, or *elements*. A *sampling element* is the unit of analysis or case in a population. It can be a person, a group, an organization, a written document or symbolic message, or even a social action (e.g., an arrest, a court case, or newspaper articles) that is being measured. The large pool is the *population,* which has an important role in sampling. Sometimes, the term *universe* (defined in Chapter 6) is used interchangeably with *population.* To define the population, a researcher specifies the unit being sampled, the geographical location, and the temporal boundaries of populations. Consider the examples of populations in Box 9.1. All the examples include the elements to be sampled (CEOs, criminal investigations, tax returns, corporations, etc.) and geographical and time boundaries.

A researcher begins with an idea of the population (e.g., all people in a city) but defines it more precisely. The term *target population* refers to the specific pool of cases that he or she wants to

---

Box 9.1 _____

Examples of Populations

1. All chief executive officers (CEOs) of U.S.-based multinational corporations living in the United States on April 15, 1999
2. All criminal investigations conducted by the U.S. Securities and Exchange Commission (SEC) from 1980 through 1999
3. All criminal violations committed by large manufacturing and wholesale, retail, and service corporations in the United States during 1998–99
4. All persons arrested for insider trading in the United States from 1995 through 1999
5. All corporations exporting goods manufactured by Chinese prison labor in 1999

---

study. The ratio of the size of the sample to the size of the target population is the *sampling ratio.* For example, the population has 50,000 people, and a researcher draws a sample of 150 from it. Thus, the sampling ratio is 150/50,000 = 0.003, or 0.3 percent. If the population is 500 and the researcher samples 100, then the sampling ratio is 100/500 = 0.20, or 20 percent.

A population is an abstract concept. How can population be an abstract concept, when there are a given number of people at a certain time? Except for specific small populations, one can never truly freeze a population to measure it.

Suppose, for example, a criminologist wanted to study corporate crime. Defining the population of all corporations in a particular country is perhaps easier said than done. At any given moment, there are many new corporations being formed and many others filing bankruptcy. Corporate mergers and breakups are also regular occurrences, and then there is the issue of domestic and multinational corporations. These are just a few of the complications in the population. Thus, although one can conceive of the population of corporations in the abstract, it is extremely difficult to identify concretely.

Because a population is an abstract concept, except for small specialized populations (e.g., all employees in a corporation), a researcher needs to estimate the population. As an abstract concept, the population needs an operational definition. This process is similar to developing operational definitions for constructs that are measured.

A researcher operationalizes a population by developing a specific list that closely approximates all the elements in the population. This list is a *sampling frame.* He or she can choose from many types of sampling frames: telephone directories, tax records, driver's license records, and so on. Listing the elements in a population sounds simple. It is often difficult because there may be no good list of elements in a population.

A good sampling frame is crucial to good sampling. A mismatch between the sampling frame and the conceptually defined population can be a major source of error. Just as a mismatch between the theoretical and operational definitions of a variable creates invalid measurement, so a mismatch between the sampling frame and the population causes invalid sampling. Researchers try to minimize mismatches.

For example, research into the structure of the foreign-exchange black market in Belize, Central America, used two different sampling frames to get a complete listing of businesses in Belize City (see Wiegand, 1994). "The first was a listing of licensed businesses obtained from the Belize Board of Trade" (p. 149). Since this particular list also contained businesses outside the city, it had to be edited down so as to include only those businesses within the city limits. In and of itself, however, the Board of Trade sampling frame was not sufficiently complete. It omitted small, casual businesses in the so-called informal sector (e.g., street vendors and curbside stands). A second sampling frame was thus obtained from the "city's weekly register of informal street vendors."

Any characteristic of a population (e.g., the percentage of businesses purchasing currency on the black market) is a *parameter.* It is the true characteristic of the population. Parameters are determined when all elements in a population are measured. The parameter is never known with absolute accuracy for large popu-

lations (e.g., the population of a nation), so researchers must estimate it on the basis of samples. Researchers use information from the sample, called a *statistic,* to estimate population parameters.

A famous case in the history of sampling illustrates the limitations of the technique. The *Literary Digest,* a major U.S. magazine, sent postcards to people before the 1920, 1924, 1928, and 1932 U.S. presidential elections. The magazine took the names for the sample from automobile registrations and telephone directories—the sampling frame. People returned the postcards indicating whom they would vote for. The magazine correctly predicted all four election outcomes. The magazine's success with predictions was well known, and in 1936, it increased the sample to 10 million. The magazine predicted a huge victory for Alf Landon over Franklin D. Roosevelt. But the *Literary Digest* was wrong; Franklin D. Roosevelt won by a landslide.

The prediction was wrong for several reasons, but the most important were mistakes in sampling. Although the magazine sampled a large number of people, its sampling frame did not accurately represent the target population (i.e., all voters). It excluded people without telephones or automobiles, a sizable percentage of the population in 1936, during the worst of the Great Depression of the 1930s. The frame excluded as much as 65 percent of the population and a segment of the voting population (lower income) that tended to favor Roosevelt.[1] The magazine had been accurate in earlier elections because people with higher and lower incomes did not differ in how they voted. Also, during earlier elections, before the Depression, more lower-income people could afford to have telephones and automobiles.

You can learn two important lessons from the *Literary Digest* mistake. First, the sampling frame is crucial. Second, the size of a sample is less important than whether or not it accurately represents the population. A representative sample of 2,500 can give more accurate predications about the U.S. population than a nonrepresentative sample of 10 million or 50 million.

TABLE 9.1 Types of Samples

NONPROBABILITY	PROBABILITY
Haphazard: Select anyone who is convenient.	*Simple:* Select people based on a true random procedure.
Quota: Select anyone in predetermined groups.	
Purposive: Select anyone in a hard-to-find target population.	*Systematic:* Select every *k*th person (quasi-random).
Snowball: Select people connected to one another.	*Stratified:* Randomly select people in predetermined groups.
	Cluster: Take multistage random samples in each of several levels.

Nonprobability Sampling

Samples can be divided into two groups: those that are based on the principles of randomness from probability theory and those that are not. (See Table 9.1 for a summary.) Sampling based on probability theory lets a researcher say precise things about sampling and use powerful statistics. Samples that are not based on probability theory are more limited. A researcher uses them out of ignorance, because of a lack of time, or in special situations. Except for special situations, quantitative researchers prefer probability samples.

Haphazard, Accidental, or Convenience. *Haphazard sampling* can produce ineffective, highly unrepresentative samples and is not recommended. When a researcher haphazardly selects cases that are convenient, he or she can easily get a sample that seriously misrepresents the population. Such samples are cheap and quick; however, the bias and systematic errors that easily occur make them worse than no sample at all.[2] The person-on-the-street interview conducted by television programs is an example of a haphazard sample. Television interviewers go out on the street with camera and microphone to talk to a few people who are convenient to interview. The people walking past a television studio in the middle of the day do not represent everyone (e.g., homemakers, people in rural areas, etc.). Likewise, television interviewers often select people who look "normal" to them and avoid people who are unattractive, poor, very old, or inarticulate.

Another common example of haphazard sampling is when politicians send out a questionnaire to people in their district. Not everyone who receives the questionnaire is motivated to fill it out and mail it back to the politician. Although the number who do return the questionnaire may be quite large (e.g., 5,000), there is no precise way to generalize their responses to the population. Newspapers, magazines, and television programs often do similar haphazard sampling. They may ask the public to call in with their opinion regarding a particular issue (e.g., their personal opinion regarding capital punishment). Such samples may have entertainment value, but they can give a distorted view and seriously misrepresent the population.

Quota. *Quota sampling* is an improvement over haphazard sampling, but it, too, is a weak type of sampling.[3] In quota sampling, a researcher first identifies relevant categories then decides how many to get in each category. Thus, the number in various categories of the sample is fixed. For example, a researcher may wish to sample corporations of differing size. He or she selects five small corporation (e.g., having less than 100 employees), 10 medium-sized corporations (e.g., having 100 to 250 employees), and 15 large corporations (e.g., having over 250 employees). As with matching in random assignment, it is difficult to represent all population characteristics accurately.

Quota sampling is an improvement because the researcher can ensure that some population differences are in the sample. In haphazard sampling, all those interviewed might be of the same age, sex, or race. But once the quota sampler fixes the categories and number of cases in each category, he or she uses haphazard sampling. Not only is misrepresentation possible because haphazard sampling is used within the categories, but nothing prevents the researcher from selecting corporations, for instance, that he or she likes best or can contact easily.

Another example of quota sampling is found in Aguilar's (1989) study of the informal economy of Manila. The researcher conducted three "street counts," which revealed the various types of street traders (e.g., type of commodity) in the city. A quota sample was then drawn with elements for each trader type. Of course, the researcher made "no claims as to representativeness of the sample" (p. 8). Nevertheless, the researcher found that "bribery to secure protection has become part of the everyday life in street trading" (p. 24).

Despite its problems, quota sampling is easier, cheaper, and quicker than probability sampling. In probability sampling, a researcher must create a sampling frame, then locate specific individuals in the frame. Specific people may be unavailable, several attempts to contact them are required, and people who are contacted might still refuse.

Purposive or Judgmental.   Serious quantitative researchers avoid the aforementioned nonprobability samples. *Purposive sampling* is an acceptable kind of sampling for special situations. It uses the judgment of an expert in selecting cases or it selects cases with a specific purpose in mind. It is inappropriate if it is used to pick the "average corporation" or the "typical CEO." With purposive sampling, the researcher never knows whether the cases selected represent the population. It is used in exploratory research or in field research.[4]

Purposive sampling is appropriate in three situations. First, a researcher uses it to select unique cases that are especially informative. For example, a researcher wants to study the role financial corporations play in the crime of money laundering. He or she decides to select a bank in a country known to be active in the transshipment of cocaine.

Second, a researcher may use purposive sampling to select members of a difficult-to-reach, specialized population. For example, the researcher wants to study prostitutes. It is impossible to list all prostitutes and sample randomly from the list. Instead, he or she uses subjective information (e.g., locations where prostitutes solicit, social groups with whom prostitutes associate, etc.) and experts (e.g., police who work on vice units, other prostitutes, etc.) to identify a "sample" of prostitutes for inclusion in the research project. The researcher uses many different methods to identify the cases, because his or her goal is to locate as many cases as possible. For example, Harper (1982) formed the sample in his field research study of U.S. tramps and hoboes in the 1970s by befriending "experts" (i.e., tramps) and living with them on trains and in skid row areas.

Another situation for purposive sampling occurs when a researcher wants to identify particular types of cases for in-depth investigation. The purpose is less to generalize to a larger population than it is to gain a deeper understanding of types. For example, in the first major study of corporate crime in the United States, Sutherland (1949) purposively sampled 70 of the 200 largest nonfinancial corporations. He then analyzed the sample in terms of the respective criminal sanctions brought against each corporation over about a 45-year period.

In his study of the political influence of corporate elites, Useem (1984) used a type of quota and purposive sampling. He interviewed 72 directors of major British corporations and 57 officials from large U.S. firms. He chose the sample to include both U.S. and British firms and to include some directors who sat on the boards of more than one firm. In addition, he matched firms by industry and size, and limited geographical locations in order to reduce travel costs.

Clinard and Yeager's pivotal study of corporate crime (1980) likewise took a purposive approach to sampling U.S. corporations. Acknowledging the difficulty in assembling data on corporate violations, the authors conducted

> *a systematic analysis of federal administrative, civil, and criminal actions either initiated or completed by 25 federal agencies against the 477 largest publicly owned manufacturing (Fortune 500) corporations in the United States during 1975 and 1976. In addition, a more limited study was made of the 105 largest wholesale, retail, and service corporations, for a total of 582 corporations. The 1975 sales of the corporations studied ranged from $300 million to more than $45 billion, with an average of $1.7 billion for all 582 firms. (pp. 110–111)*

Their sample purposively excluded "banking, insurance, transportation, communication, and utilities corporations," however, given the special regulations pertaining to the nature of these industries.

Snowball Sampling. Social researchers are often interested in an interconnected network of people or organizations.[5] The network could be criminologists around the world investigating the same problem, the social structure of a smuggling network, the process of money laundering, illegal bribes paid by a multinational corporation to a military junta, or the movement of small-arms weaponry into war zones, to name just a few. The crucial feature is that each person or unit is connected with another through a direct or indirect linkage. This does not mean that each person directly knows, interacts with, or is influenced by every other person in the network. Rather, it means that, taken as a whole, with direct and indirect links, most are within an interconnected web of linkages.

Consider the example of small-arms smuggling. Perhaps a researcher has interviewed a weapons importer in Africa who has received weapons from an arms supplier in the Middle East. The supplier also has a client state in Central America. All three are part of the same

trading network. Researchers represent such networks by drawing a *sociogram*—a diagram of circles connected with lines. In Figure 9.2, the circles represent each corporate supplier or government buyer, and the lines represent business linkages for a small-arms trading network.

The small-arms sociogram reveals that Corporation A (CA) and Government A (GA) have an exclusive linkage. It also shows that Corporation B (CB) has a direct linkage with Government B (GB) and an indirect linkage with Government C (GC), Government D (GD), and Government E (GE).

Snowball sampling (also called *network, chain referral,* or *reputational sampling*) is a method for identifying and sampling (or selecting) the cases in a network. It is based on an analogy to a snowball, which begins small but becomes larger as it is rolled on wet snow and picks up additional snow. Snowball sampling is a multistage technique. It begins with one or a few

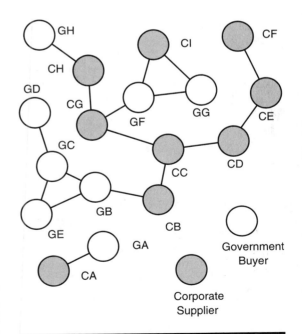

FIGURE 9.2 Sociogram of a Small-Arms Trading Network

people or cases and spreads out on the basis of links to the initial cases.

Wright and colleagues (1996) provided a good example of a snowball sampling strategy. Their study attempted to contact active residential burglars in St. Louis, Missouri, to learn about the factors that go into targeting a house to burglarize. As they pointed out, "The most difficult aspect of using a snowball sampling technique is locating an initial contact or two" (p. 2). They solved the problem in this way:

> Fortunately, we were able to short-cut that process [i.e., frequenting known criminal hangouts] by hiring an ex-offender (who, despite committing hundreds of serious crimes, had few arrests and no felony convictions) with high status among several groups of black street criminals in St. Louis. This person retired from crime after being shot and paralyzed in a gangland-style execution attempt. He then attended a university and earned a bachelor's degree, but continued to live in his old neighborhood, remaining friendly, albeit superficially, with local criminals. We initially met him when he attended a colloquium in our department and disputed the speaker's characterization of street criminals. (pp. 2–3)

Sometimes a combination of snowball sampling and quota sampling can be used to shed light on complex criminological relationships. Consider the approach taken by Inciardi and colleagues (1996) in their research on the relationship of crime and crack cocaine:

> Selection of street and [drug] treatment respondents was guided by subsample quotas for gender, age, and ethnicity to ensure a demographically diverse sample. In the treatment programs, this generally meant returning repeatedly to interview every new client in the hard-to-fill subsamples (younger and white or Hispanic). On the street, subsample targets meant conducting the interview process in several selected neighborhoods to get the required race-ethnic diversity. Street respondents were located through standard multiple-starting-point "snowball sampling" techniques in the neighborhoods with high rates of cocaine use

> by street interviewers familiar with and well known in the target area. (pp. 61–62)

Probability Sampling

Why Random?   The area of applied mathematics called probability theory relies on random processes. The word *random* has a special meaning in mathematics. It refers to a process that generates a mathematically random result; that is, the selection process operates in a truly random method (i.e., no pattern), and a researcher can calculate the probability of outcomes. In a true random process, each element has an equal probability of being selected.

Probability samples that rely on random processes require more work than nonrandom ones. A researcher must identify specific sampling elements (e.g., person) to include in the sample. For example, if conducting a telephone survey, the researcher needs to try to reach the specific sampled person, by calling back four or five times, to get an accurate random sample.[6]

Random samples are most likely to yield a sample that truly represents the population. In addition, random sampling lets a researcher statistically calculate the relationship between the sample and the population—that is, the size of the *sampling error*. A nonstatistical definition of the sampling error is the deviation between sample results and a population parameter due to random processes.

This chapter does not cover the technical and statistical details of random sampling. Instead, it focuses on the fundamentals of how sampling works, the difference between good and bad samples, how to draw a sample, and basic principles of sampling in social research. This does not mean that random sampling is unimportant. Random sampling is crucial, and it is essential to learn the fundamentals. If you plan to pursue a career using quantitative research, you should get more statistical background than space permits here.

Types of Probability Samples
Simple Random.   The *simple random sample* is both the easiest random sample to understand and

the one on which other types are modeled. In simple random sampling, a researcher develops an accurate sampling frame, selects elements from the sampling frame according to a mathematically random procedure, then locates the exact element that was selected for inclusion in the sample.

After numbering all elements in a sampling frame, a researcher uses a list of random numbers to decide which elements to select. He or she needs as many random numbers as there are elements to be sampled; for example, for a sample of 100, 100 random numbers are needed. The researcher can get random numbers from a *random-number table,* a table of numbers chosen in a mathematically random way. Random-number tables are available in most statistics and research methods books, including this one (see Appendix A). The numbers are generated by a pure random process so that any number has an equal probability of appearing in any position. Computer programs can also produce lists of random numbers.

You may ask, "Once I select an element from the sampling frame, do I then return it to the sampling frame or do I keep it separate?" The common answer is that it is not returned. Unrestricted random sampling is random sampling with replacement—that is, replacing an element after sampling it so it can be selected again. In simple random sampling without replacement, the researcher ignores elements already selected into the sample.

The logic of simple random sampling can be illustrated with an elementary example—sampling marbles from a jar. We have a large jar with 5,000 red and white marbles in it. The 5,000 marbles are our population, and the parameter we want to estimate is the percentage of red marbles in it. We randomly select 100 marbles. (We close our eyes, shake the jar, pick one marble, and repeat the procedure 100 times.) We now have a random sample of marbles. We count the number of red marbles in our sample to estimate the percentage of red versus white marbles in the population. This is a lot easier than counting all 5,000 marbles. My sample has 52 white and 48 red marbles.

Does this mean that the population parameter is 48 percent red marbles? Maybe not. Because of random chance, our specific sample might be off. We can check our results by dumping the 100 marbles back in the jar, mixing the marbles, and drawing a second random sample of 100 marbles. On the second try, our sample has 49 white marbles and 51 red ones. Now we have a problem. Which is correct? How good is this random sampling business if different samples from the same population can yield different results? We repeat the procedure over and over until we have drawn 130 different samples of 100 marbles each (see Box 9.2 for results). Most people might empty the jar and count all 5,000, but we want to see what is going on. The results of our 130 different samples reveal a clear pattern. The most common mix of red and white marbles is 50/50. Samples that are close to that split are more frequent than those with more uneven splits. The population parameter appears to be 50 percent white and 50 percent red marbles.

Mathematical proofs and empirical tests demonstrate that the pattern found in Box 9.2 always appears. The set of many different samples is our *sampling distribution.* It is a distribution of different samples that shows the frequency of different sample outcomes from many separate random samples. The pattern will appear if the sample size is 1,000 instead of 100; if there are ten colors of marbles instead of two; if the population has 100 marbles or 10 million marbles instead of 5,000; and if the population is people, automobiles, or colleges instead of marbles. In fact, the pattern will become clearer as more and more independent random samples are drawn from the population.

The pattern in the sampling distribution suggests that over many separate samples, the true population parameter (i.e., the 50/50 split in the preceding example) is more common than any other result. Some samples deviate from the population parameter, but they are less common. When many different random samples are plotted as in the graph in Box 9.2, then the sampling distribution looks like a normal or bell-shaped curve. Such a curve is theoretically important and is used throughout statistics.

Box 9.2

Example of Sampling Distribution

Red	White	Number of Samples
42	58	1
43	57	1
45	55	2
46	54	4
47	53	8
48	52	12
49	51	21
50	50	31
51	49	20
52	48	13
53	47	9
54	46	5
55	45	2
57	43	1
	Total	130

Number of red and white marbles that were randomly drawn from a jar of 5,000 marbles with 100 drawn each time, repeated 130 times for 130 independent random samples.

Number of Samples

```
31                                        *
30                                        *
29                                        *
28                                        *
27                                        *
26                                        *
25                                        *
24                                        *
23                                        *
22                                        *
21                                    *   *
20                                    *   *   *
19                                    *   *   *
18                                    *   *   *
17                                    *   *   *
16                                    *   *   *
15                                    *   *   *
14                                    *   *   *
13                                    *   *   *   *
12                                *   *   *   *   *
11                                *   *   *   *   *
10                                *   *   *   *   *
 9                                *   *   *   *   *   *
 8                            *   *   *   *   *   *   *
 7                            *   *   *   *   *   *   *
 6                            *   *   *   *   *   *   *
 5                            *   *   *   *   *   *   *   *
 4                        *   *   *   *   *   *   *   *   *
 3                        *   *   *   *   *   *   *   *   *
 2                    *   *   *   *   *   *   *   *   *   *   *
 1        *   *       *   *   *   *   *   *   *   *   *   *   *       *
         42  43  44  45  46  47  48  49  50  51  52  53  54  55  56  57
```

Number of Red Marbles in a Sample

The *central limit theorem* from mathematics tells us that as the number of different random samples in a sampling distribution increases toward infinity, the pattern of samples and the population parameter become more predictable. With a huge number of random samples, the sampling distribution forms a normal curve, and the midpoint of the curve approaches the population parameter as the number of samples increases.

Perhaps you want only one sample because you do not have the time or energy to draw many different samples. You are not alone. A researcher rarely draws many samples. He or she usually draws only one random sample, but the central limit theorem lets him or her generalize from one sample to the population. The theorem is about many samples, but lets the researcher calculate the probability of a particular sample being off from the population parameter.

Random sampling does not guarantee that every random sample perfectly represents the population. Instead, it means that most random samples will be close to the population most of the time, and that one can calculate the probability of a particular sample being inaccurate. A researcher estimates the chance that a particular sample is off or unrepresentative (i.e., the size of the sampling error) by using information from the sample to estimate the sampling distribution. He or she combines this information with knowledge of the central limit theorem to construct *confidence intervals.*

The confidence interval is a relatively simple but powerful idea. When television or newspaper polls are reported, you may hear about something called the margin of error being plus or minus 2 percentage points. This is a version of confidence intervals. A confidence interval is a range around a specific point. It is used to estimate a population parameter. A range is used because the statistics of random processes do not let a researcher predict an exact point, but they let the researcher say with a high level of confidence (e.g., 95 percent) that the true population parameter lies within a certain range.

The calculations for sampling errors or confidence intervals are beyond the level of this discussion. The sampling distribution is the key idea that lets a researcher calculate the sampling error and confidence interval. Thus, he or she cannot say, "This sample gives a perfect measure of the population parameter," but can say, "I am 95 percent certain that the true population parameter is no more than 2 percent different from what I have found in my sample."

For example, we cannot say, "There are precisely 2,500 red marbles in the jar based on a random sample." We can say, "We are 95 percent certain that the population parameter lies between 2,450 and 2,550." We can combine characteristics of the sample (e.g., its size, the variation in it) with the central limit theorem to predict specific ranges around the parameter with a great deal of confidence.

Systematic Sampling. Systematic sampling is simple random sampling with a shortcut for random selection. Again, the first step is to number each element in the sampling frame. Instead of using a list of random numbers, a researcher calculates a *sampling interval,* and the interval becomes his or her quasi-random selection method. The sampling interval (i.e., 1 in k, where k is some number) tells the researcher how to select elements from a sampling frame by skipping elements in the frame before selecting one for the sample.

Qouta and associates (1997) studied prison experiences and coping styles by sampling from a frame of 200 freed Palestinian prisoners from two refugee camps in the West Bank. They systematically sampled every second name. The sampling ratio was 100/200 = .50 = 50 percent. The sampling interval was 200/100 = 2. Indeed, you can think of the sampling interval as the inverse of the sampling ratio.

In most cases, a simple random sample and a systematic sample yield virtually equivalent results. One important situation in which systematic sampling cannot be substituted for simple random sampling occurs when the elements in a sample are organized in some kind of cycle or pattern. Suppose the sampling frame of 200 prisoners in the West Bank included both men and women. If it listed the husband's name before the wife's, in those cases in which both husband and wife were prisoners, then the sampling frame had a systematic bias. The result of this is an unrepresentative sample that favors the selection of one spouse over the other. When a sampling frame is organized as couples, even-numbered sampling intervals result in samples with either all husbands or all wives.

Table 9.2 illustrates simple random sampling and systematic sampling. Notice that different names were drawn in each sample. For example, H. Adams appears in both samples, but C. Droullard is only in the simple random sample. This is because it is rare for any two random samples to be identical.

The sampling frame contains 20 males and 20 females (gender is in parenthesis after each name). The simple random sample yielded 3 males and 7 females, and the systematic sample yielded 5 males and 5 females. Does this mean that systematic sampling is more accurate? No. To check this, draw a new sample using different random numbers; try taking the first two digits and beginning at the end (e.g., 82 from 82752, then 23 from 23912). Also draw a new systematic sample with a different random start. The last time the random start was 18. Try a random start of 11 (the last underlined number of the top half of the second column). What did you find? How many of each sex?[7]

Stratified Sampling.   In *stratified sampling,* a researcher first divides the population into subpopulations (strata) on the basis of supplementary information.[8] After dividing the population into strata, the researcher draws a random sample from each subpopulation. He or she can sample randomly within strata using simple random or systematic sampling. In stratified sampling, the researcher controls the relative size of each stratum, rather than letting random processes control it. This guarantees representativeness or fixes the proportion of different strata within a sample. Of course, the necessary supplemental information about strata is not always available.

In general, stratified sampling produces samples that are more representative of the population than simple random sampling if the stratum information is accurate. A simple example illustrates why this is so. Imagine a population that is 51 percent female and 49 percent male; the population parameter is a sex ratio of 51 to 49. With stratified sampling, a researcher draws random samples among females and among males so that the sample contains a 51 to 49 percent sex ratio. If the researcher had used simple random sampling, it would be possible for a random sample to be off from the true sex ratio in the population. Thus, he or she makes fewer errors representing the population and has a smaller sampling error with stratified sampling.

Stratified sampling is used to ensure that interesting strata are included in the sample, even though they comprise only a small percentage of the population. With simple random sampling, on the other hand, there is always a possibility that these strata might not be sampled. This possibility does not exist with a stratified approach. In some situations, a researcher wants the proportion of a stratum to differ from its true proportion in the population. A good illustration of stratified sampling is the Taxpayer Compliance Measurement Program (TCMP) conducted by the U.S. Internal Revenue Service (IRS).

The TCMP is "an important statistical instrument for measuring compliance for the vast number of U.S. taxpayers" (United States Internal Revenue Service, 1979:56). The basic approach involves the IRS conducting a thorough, line-by-line audit of a sample of individual taxpayers. Given there are over 100 million taxpayers in the United States, it is necessary that the IRS draw a random sample to represent the entire population. In principle, all U.S. taxpayers have a chance of being selected in the TCMP sample. However, the IRS is particularly interested in sampling taxpayers who, because of their source of income (e.g., self-employment), have a greater opportunity to cheat than other types of taxpayers (e.g., wage earners). Using a simple random approach, chances are the sample might underrepresent low-compliance taxpayers. To deal with this, stratified sampling is used.

The population of taxpayers is stratified in terms of level of income and type of income, and

TABLE 9.2   How to Draw Simple Random and Systematic Samples

1. Number each case in the sampling frame in sequence. The list of 40 names is in alphabetical order, numbered from 1 to 40.
2. Decide on a sample size. We will draw two 25 percent (10-name) samples.
3. For a *simple random sample*, locate a random-number table (see excerpt; a fuller table appears in Appendix A). Before using random-number table, count the largest number of digits needed for the sample (e.g., with 40 names, two digits are needed; for 100 to 999, three digits; for 1,000 to 9,999, four digits). Begin anywhere on the random number table (we will begin in the upper left) and take a set of digits (we will take the last two). Mark the number on the sampling frame that corresponds to the chosen random number to indicate that the case is in the sample. If the number is too large (over 40), ignore it. If the number appears more than once (10 and 21 occurred twice in the example), ignore the second occurrence. Continue until the number of cases in the sample (10 in our example) is reached.
4. For a *systematic sample*, begin with a random start. The easiest way to do this is to point blindly at the random number table, then take the closest number that appears on the sampling frame. In the example, 18 was chosen. Start with the random number, then count the sampling interval, or 4 in our example, to come to the first number. Mark it, and then count the sampling interval for the next number. Continue to the end of the list. Continue counting the sampling interval as if the beginning of the list was attached to the end of the list (like a circle). Keep counting until ending close to the start, or on the start if the sampling interval divides evenly into the total of the sampling frame.

No.	Name (Gender)	Simple Random	Systematic	No.	Name (Gender)	Simple Random	Systematic
01	Abrams, J. (M)			21	Hjelmhaug, N. (M)	Yes*	
02	Adams, H. (F)	Yes	Yes (6)	22	Huang, J. (F)	Yes	Yes (1)
03	Anderson, H. (M)			23	Ivono, V. (F)		
04	Arminond, L. (M)			24	Jaquees, J. (M)		
05	Boorstein, A. (M)			25	Johnson, A. (F)		
06	Breitsprecher, P. (M)	Yes	Yes (7)	26	Kennedy, M. (F)		Yes (2)
07	Brown, D. (F)			27	Koschoreck, L. (F)		
08	Cattelino, J. (F)			28	Koykkar, J. (M)		
09	Cidoni, S. (M)			29	Kozlowski, C. (F)	Yes	
10	Davis, L. (F)	Yes*	Yes (8)	30	Laurent, J. (M)		Yes (3)
11	Droullard, C. (M)	Yes		31	Lee, R. (F)		
12	Durette, R. (F)			32	Ling, C. (M)		
13	Elsnau, K. (F)	Yes		33	McKinnon, K. (F)		
14	Falconer, T. (M)		Yes (9)	34	Min, H.	Yes	Yes (4)
15	Fuerstenberg, J. (M)			35	Moini, A. (F)		
16	Fulton, P. (F)			36	Navarre, H. (M)		
17	Gnewuch, S. (F)			37	O'Sullivan, C. (M)		
18	Green, C. (M)		START, Yes (10)	38	Oh, J. (M)		Yes (5)
19	Goodwanda, T. (F)	Yes		39	Olson, J. (M)		
20	Harris, B. (M)			40	Ortiz y Garcia, L. (F)		

*Numbers that appeared twice in random numbers selected.

(continued)

TABLE 9.2   (continued)

Excerpt from a Random-Number Table (for Simple Random Sample)

150<u>10</u>	18590	001<u>02</u>	94174	22099	422<u>10</u>
901<u>22</u>	382<u>21</u>	215<u>29</u>	047<u>34</u>	60457	000<u>13</u>
67256	13887	941<u>19</u>	01061	27779	11007
13761	23390	12947	445<u>06</u>	36457	21210
81994	666<u>11</u>	16597	076<u>21</u>	51949	44417
79180	25992	46178	62108	43232	23912
07984	47169	88094	15318	01921	82752

some 50,000 tax returns are selected for TCMP examination. The stratification procedure is as follows:

> The sampling procedure was designed to construct a stratified sample consisting of returns in each of ten examination classes. These examination classes ... were designed to cluster the taxpaying population into groups, each of which presents a distinct compliance profile. First, there is the subpopulation of Form 1040A filers, a numerous group whose [tax] returns are of highly simplified type. Next, there are three separate subpopulations of "nonbusiness" taxpayers (low income, medium income, high income). These are Form 1040 filers who append neither a Schedule C [i.e., for self-employment income] nor a Schedule F [i.e., for farm income] to their return. "Non-farm business returns," i.e., Schedule C filers showing at least some self-employment income, are similarly clustered into low, medium, and high income classes. Finally, "Farm business returns," i.e., returns with Schedule F attached are low, medium, and high income types. TCMP sampling rates vary across the ten examination classes [or strata]. For example, the sampling rates in the Form 1040A class are low while those in the high-income farm class are quite high. These TCMP sampling rates are designed to reflect sampling needs consistent with compliance patterns of different classes. (p. 54)

Designing, sampling, auditing, and analyzing data from a sample of 50,000 taxpayers necessitates a considerable investment of time and money. A TCMP cycle, from beginning to end, likely takes three years to complete, and costs in the tens of millions. It is a huge investment, but it brings an even far bigger value to the public. The Taxpayer Compliance Measurement Program provides the "mathematical procedure [i.e., DIF—discriminant function formulae] used by the IRS to select returns having a high examination potential for its regular field and office examinations" (p. 54). In other words, TCMP sharpens the IRS's aim in targeting individual taxpayers likely to be cheating on their taxes. It is what Alpern (1978) called "the backbone of the audit selection system" (see Box 9.3).

Cluster Sampling.   Cluster sampling addresses two problems: Researchers lack a good sampling frame for a dispersed population and the cost to reach a sampled element is very high.[9] For example, there is no single list of all households in the United States. Even if a researcher had access to a fairly complete listing, the cost of trying to reach a sample of households widely dispersed across the country would be very expensive. Instead of using a single sampling frame, researchers use a sampling design that involves multiple stages and clusters.

A *cluster* is a unit that contains final sampling elements but can be treated temporarily as a sampling element itself. A researcher first samples clusters, each of which contains elements, then draws a second sample from within the clusters selected in the first stage of sampling. In other words, the researcher randomly samples clusters, then randomly samples elements from within the selected clusters. This has a big practical advan-

Box 9.3 _____

Illustration of Stratified Sampling: Sample of 100 Individual Taxpayers, Stratified by Type and Amount of Income

AUDIT CLASS	POPULATION		SIMPLE RANDOM SAMPLE	STRATIFIED SAMPLE	ERRORS COMPARED TO THE POPULATION
	N	*Percent*	*n*	*n*	
I	15	2.88	1	3	−2
II	25	4.81	2	5	−3
III	25	4.81	6	5	+1
IV	100	19.23	22	19	+3
V	100	19.23	21	19	+2
VI	75	14.42	9	14	+5
VII	50	9.62	8	10	−2
VIII	75	14.42	5	14	+1
IV	30	5.77	3	6	−3
X	25	4.81	3	5	−2
Total	520	100.00	100	100	

Randomly select 3 of 15 I, 5 of 25 II, and so on.

Note: Traditionally, *N* symbolizes the number in the population and *n* represents the number in the sample. The simple random sample overrepresents III, IV, and V, but underrepresents I, II, VI, VII, VIII, IX, X, and taxpayers.

The stratified sample gives an accurate representation of each type of position.

Taxpayer Audit Classes Used by the Internal Revenue Service:

I   = Simple/Low-income taxpayers (e.g., IRS 1040 EZ)
II   = Nonbusiness/Low-income taxpayers
III = Nonbusiness/Medium-income taxpayers
IV   = Nonbusiness/High-income taxpayers
V   = Business/Low-income taxpayers
VI   = Business/Medium-income taxpayers
VII = Business/High-income taxpayers
VIII = Farm/Low-income taxpayers
IX   = Farm/Medium-income taxpayers
X   = Farm/High-income taxpayers

_____

tage. He or she may be able to get a sampling frame of clusters even if a sampling frame of elements is not available. Once clusters are chosen, a sampling frame of elements for the sampled clusters may be created. A second advantage is that the elements within each cluster are close to one another, so there may be savings in reaching the elements.

A researcher draws several samples in stages in cluster sampling. In a three-stage sample, stage 1 is random sampling of big clusters; stage 2 is random sampling of small clusters within each selected big cluster; and the last stage is sampling of elements from within the sampled small clusters. For example, a researcher wants a sample of individuals from Mapleville. First, he or she randomly samples city blocks, then households within blocks, then individuals within households (see Box 9.4). Although there is no accurate list of all residents of Mapleville, there is an accurate list

Box 9.4 _____

Illustration of Cluster Sampling

Goal: Draw a random sample of 240 people in Mapleville.

Step 1: Mapleville has 55 districts. Randomly select 6 districts.

1 2 3* 4 5 6 7 8 9 10 11 12 13 14 15* 16 17 18 19 20 21 22 23 24 25 26
27* 28 29 30 31* 32 33 34 35 36 37 38 39 40* 41 42 43 44 45 46 47 48
49 50 51 52 53 54* 55

* = Randomly selected.

Step 2: Divide the selected districts into blocks. Each district contains 20 blocks. Randomly select 4 blocks from the district.

Example of District 3 (selected in step 1):

1 2 3 4* 5 6 7 8 9 10* 11 12 13* 14 15 16 17* 18 19 20

* = Randomly selected.

Step 3: Divide blocks into households. Randomly select households.

Example of Block 4 of District 3 (selected in step 2):

Block 4 contains a mix of single-family homes, duplexes, and four-unit apartment buildings. It is bounded by Oak Street, River Road, South Avenue, and Greenview Drive. There are 45 households on the block. Randomly select 10 households from the 45.

1	#1 Oak Street	16	"	31	"*
2	#3 Oak Street	17*	#154 River Road	32	"*
3*	#5 Oak Street	18	#156 River Road	33	"
4	"	19*	#158 River Road	34	#156 Greenview Drive
5	"	20*	"	35	"*
6	"	21	#13 South Avenue	36	"
7	#7 Oak Street	22	"	37	"
8	"	23	#11 South Avenue	38	"
9*	#150 River Road	24	#9 South Avenue	39	#158 Greenview Drive
10	"*	25	#7 South Avenue	40	"
11	"	26	#5 South Avenue	41	"
12	"	27	#3 South Avenue	42	"
13	#152 River Road	28	#1 South Avenue	43	#160 Greenview Drive
14	"	29*	"	44	"
15	"	30	#152 Greenview Drive	45	"

* = Randomly selected.

Step 4: Select a respondent within each household.

Summary of cluster sampling:

1 person randomly selected per household
10 households randomly selected per block
4 blocks randomly selected per district
6 districts randomly selected in the city
1 × 10 × 4 × 6 = 240 people in sample

of blocks in the city. After selecting a random sample of blocks, the researcher counts all households on the selected blocks to create a sample frame for each block. He or she then uses the list of households to draw a random sample at the stage of sampling households. Finally, the researcher chooses a specific individual within each sampled household.

Cluster sampling is usually less expensive than simple random sampling, but it is less accurate. Each stage in cluster sampling introduces sampling errors, so a multistage cluster sample has more sampling errors than a one-stage random sample.[10]

A researcher who uses cluster sampling must decide the number of clusters and the number of elements within clusters. For example, in a two-stage cluster sample of 240 people from Mapleville, the researcher could randomly select 120 clusters and select 2 elements from each, or randomly select 2 clusters and select 120 elements in each. Which is best? The general answer is that a design with more clusters is better because elements within clusters (e.g., people living on the same block) tend to be similar to each other (e.g., people on the same block tend to be more alike than those on different blocks). If few clusters are chosen, many similar elements could be selected, which would be less representative of the total population. For example, the researcher could select two blocks with relatively wealthy people and draw 120 people from each. This would be less representative than a sample with 120 different city blocks and 2 individuals chosen from each.

When a researcher samples from a large geographical area and must travel to each element, cluster sampling significantly reduces travel costs. As usual, there is a trade-off between accuracy and cost.

For example, Alan, Ricardo, and Barbara each plan to visit and personally interview a sample of 1,500 students who represent the population of all college students in North America. Alan obtains an accurate sampling frame of all students and uses simple random sampling. He travels to 1,000 different locations to interview one or two students at each. Ricardo draws a random sample of three colleges from a list of all 3,000 colleges, then visits the three and selects 500 students from each. Barbara draws a random sample of 300 colleges. She visits the 300 and selects 5 students at each. If travel costs average $250 per location, Alan's travel bill is $250,000, Ricardo's is $750, Barbara's is $75,000. Alan's sample is highly accurate, but Barbara's is only slightly less accurate for one-third the cost. Ricardo's sample is the cheapest, but it is not representative at all.

Within-household sampling. Once a researcher samples a household or similar unit (e.g., family or dwelling unit) in cluster sampling, the question arises: Whom should the researcher choose? A potential source of bias is introduced if the first person who answers the telephone, the door, or the mail is used in the sample. The first person who answers should be selected only if his or her answering is the result of a truly random process. This is rarely the case. Certain people are unlikely to be at home, and in some households one person (e.g., a husband) is more likely than another to answer the telephone or door. Researchers use within-household sampling to ensure that after a random household is chosen, the individual within the household is also selected randomly.

Researchers can randomly select a person within a household in several ways.[11] The most common method is to use a selection table specifying who is to be chosen (e.g., oldest male, youngest female, etc.) after the size and composition of the household are known (see Table 9.3). This removes any bias that might arise from choosing the first person to answer the door or telephone, or from the interviewer's selecting the person who appears to be friendliest.

Probability proportionate to size (PPS). There are two ways to cluster sample. The method just described is proportionate or unweighted cluster sampling. It is proportionate because the size of each cluster (or number of elements at

TABLE 9.3 Within-Household Sampling

Selecting individuals within sampled households. Number selected is the household chosen in Box 9.4.

Number	Last Name	Adults (over Age 18)	Selected Respondent
3	Able	1 male, 1 female	Female
9	Bharadwaj	2 females	Youngest female
10	DiPiazza	1 male, 2 females	Oldest female
17	Wucivic	2 males, 1 female	Youngest male
19	Cseri	2 females	Youngest female
20	Taylor	1 male, 3 females	Second oldest female
29	Velu	2 males, 2 females	Oldest male
31	Wong	1 male, 1 female	Female
32	Gray	1 male	Male
35	Mall-Krinke	1 male, 2 females	Oldest female

Example Selection Table (Only Adults Counted)

Males	Females	Whom to Select	Males	Females	Whom to Select
1	0	Male	2	2	Oldest male
2	0	Oldest male	2	3	Youngest female
3	0	Youngest male	3	2	Second oldest male
4+	0	Second oldest male	3	3	Second oldest female
0	1	Female	3	4	Third oldest female
0	2	Youngest female	4	3	Second oldest male
0	3	Second oldest female	4	4	Third oldest male
0	4+	Oldest female	4	5+	Youngest female
1	1	Female	5+	4	Second oldest male
1	2	Oldest female	5+	5+	Fourth oldest female
1	3	Second oldest female			
2	1	Youngest male			
3	1	Second oldest male			

+ = or more

each stage) is the same. Unfortunately, the more common situation is for the cluster groups to be of different sizes. When this is the case, the researcher must adjust the probability or sampling ratio at various stages in sampling.

The foregoing cluster sampling example with Alan, Barbara, and Ricardo illustrates the problem with unweighted cluster sampling. Barbara drew a simple random sample of 300 colleges from a list of all 3,000 colleges, but she made a mistake—unless every college has an identical number of students. Her method gave each college an equal chance of being selected—a 300/3,000 or 10 percent chance. But colleges have different numbers of students, so each student does not have an equal chance to end up in her sample.

Barbara listed every college and sampled from the list. A large university with 40,000 students and a small college with 400 students had an equal chance of being selected. But if she chose the large university, the chance of a given student at that college being selected was 5 in 40,000 (5/40,000 = 0.0125 percent), whereas a student at the small college had a 5 in 400 (5/400 = 1.25 percent) chance of being selected. The small-college student was 100 times more likely to be in her sample. The total probability of being selected for a student from the large university was 0.125 percent (10 × 0.0125), while it was 12.5 percent (10 × 1.25) for the small-college student. Barbara violated a principle of random sampling—that each element has an equal chance to be selected into the sample.

If Barbara uses probability proportionate to size (PPS) and samples correctly, then each final sampling element or student will have an equal probability of being selected. She does this by adjusting the chances of selecting a college in the first stage of sampling. She must give large colleges with more students a greater chance of being selected and small colleges a smaller chance. She adjusts the probability of selecting a college on the basis of the proportion of all students in the population who attend it. Thus, a college with 40,000 students will be 100 times more likely to be selected than one with 400 students.

Random-Digit Dialing. *Random-digit dialing (RDD)* is a special sampling technique used in research projects in which the general public is interviewed by telephone.[12] It differs from the traditional method of sampling for telephone interviews because a published telephone directory is not the sampling frame.

Three kinds of people are missed when the sampling frame is a telephone directory: people without telephones, people who have recently moved, and people with unlisted numbers. Those without phones (e.g., the poor, the uneducated, and transients) are missed in any telephone interview study, but the proportion of the general public with a telephone has grown to nearly 95 percent in advanced industrialized nations. As the percentage of the public with telephones has increased, the percentage with unlisted numbers has also grown. Several kinds of people have unlisted numbers: people who want to avoid collection agencies; the very wealthy; and those who want privacy and want to avoid obscene calls, salespeople, and prank calls. In some urban areas, the percentage of unlisted numbers is as high as 40 percent. In addition, people change their residences, so directories that are published

annually or less often have numbers for people who have left and do not list those who have recently moved into an area. A researcher using RDD randomly selects telephone numbers, thereby avoiding the problems of telephone directories. The population is telephone numbers, not people with telephones. RDD is not difficult, but it takes time and can frustrate the person doing the calling.

Here is how RDD works in the United States. Telephone numbers have three parts: a three-digit area code, a three-digit exchange number or central office code, and a four-digit number. For example, the area code for Madison, Wisconsin, is 608, and there are many exchanges within the area code (e.g., 221, 993, 767, 455); but not all of the 999 possible three-digit exchanges (from 001 to 999) are active. Likewise, not all of the 9,999 possible four-digit numbers in an exchange (from 0000 to 9999) are being used. Some numbers are reserved for future expansion, are disconnected, or are temporarily withdrawn after someone moves. Thus, a possible U.S. telephone number consists of an active area code, an active exchange number, and a four-digit number in an exchange.

In RDD, a researcher identifies active area codes and exchanges, then randomly selects four-digit numbers. A problem is that the researcher can select any number in an exchange. This means that some selected numbers are out of service, disconnected, pay phones, or numbers for businesses; only some numbers are what the researcher wants—working residential phone numbers. Until the researcher calls, it is not possible to know whether the number is a working residential number. This means spending a lot of time getting numbers that are disconnected, for businesses, and so forth. For example, Groves and Kahn (1979:45) found that only about 22 percent of the numbers called were working residential numbers. Research organizations often use computers to select random digits and dial the phone automatically. This speeds the process, but a human must still listen and find out whether the number is a working residential one.

Remember that the sampling element in RDD is the phone number, not the person or the household. Several families or individuals can share the same phone number, and in other situations each person may have a separate phone number or more than one phone number. This means that after a working residential phone is reached, a second stage of sampling is necessary, within household sampling, to select the person to be interviewed.

Box 9.5 presents an example of how the many sampling terms and ideas can be used together in a specific real-life situation.

Consider the sampling problem that Martin and Dean (1993) faced. For a survey on reactions to the AIDs epidemic, they wanted a sample of 700 gay men from New York City. The men had to live in the city, be over age 18, not be diagnosed as having AIDS, and engage in sex with other men. The sample was to represent all areas of the city, diverse lifestyles, and various ethnic backgrounds. The authors began with a purposive sample using five diverse sources to recruit 291 respondents. They first contacted 150 New York City organizations with predominately homosexual or bisexual members. They

Box 9.5

A Detailed Look at the U.S. National Crime Victimization Survey Sample

Criminologists are increasingly relying on self-reported survey data to study criminal behavior, victimization, delinquency and drug consumption, fear of crime, and routine activities, among other topics. These surveys typically cover national and international populations and span large geographical areas. Because of the cost of random sampling in such studies and the difficulty in obtaining a comprehensive sampling frame, criminologists and other social scientists favor cluster sampling.

As already mentioned, the National Crime Victimization Survey (NCVS) is a very important survey in the United States for obtaining national estimates of crime victimization. The NCVS's cluster sampling is complex, involving three stages of sampling: counties or groups of counties, enumeration district, and housing unit. The methodology is described in fine detail here:

Survey estimates are derived from a stratified, multistage cluster sample. The primary sampling units (PSU) composing the first stage of the sample were counties, groups of counties, or large metropolitan areas. Large PSUs were included in the sample automatically and are considered to be self-representing (SR) since all of them were selected. The remaining PSUs, called non-self-representing (NSR) because only a subset of them was selected, were combined into strata by grouping PSUs with similar geographic and demographic characteristics, as determined by the 1980 census.

The 1994 NCVS sample households were drawn from the 1980-based sample design. The 1980 design consists of 84 SR PSUs and 153 NSR strata, with one PSU per stratum selected with probability proportionate to population size. The NCVS sample design has been revised to take advantage of the availability of data from the 1990 census. However, the 1990-based sample will not start contributing to the NCVS estimates until 1995.

The two remaining stages of sampling were designed to ensure a self-weighting probability sample of housing units and group-quarter dwellings within each of the selected areas. . . . This involved a systematic selection of enumeration districts (geographical areas used for the 1980 census), with a probability of selection proportionate to their 1980 population size, followed by the selection of segments (clusters of approximately four housing units each) from within each enumeration district. To account for units built within each of the sample units after the 1980 Census, a sample was drawn of permits issued for the construction of residential housing. Jurisdictions that do not issue building permits were sampled using small land-area segments. These supplementary procedures, though yielding a relatively small portion of the total sample, enabled persons living in housing units built after 1980 to be properly represented in the survey.

Approximately 58,060 housing units and other living quarters were designed for the sample. (Maguire and Pastore, 1997:624–627)

next screened these to 90 organizations that had eligible men for the study. From the 90, they drew a stratified random sample of 52 organizations by membership size. They randomly selected five members from each of the organizations. Reports of Martin and Dean's study appeared in local news sources. This brought calls from which they got 41 unsolicited volunteers. Another source of 32 men were referrals from respondents who had participated in a small pilot study. In addition, 72 men were identified at an annual New York City Gay Pride Parade. And 15 eligible men were contacted at a New York City clinic and asked to participate.

The researchers next used snowball sampling. They asked each of the 291 respondents to give a recruitment packet to three gay male friends. Each friend who agreed to participate was also asked to give packets to three friends. This continued until it had gone five levels out from the initial 291 men. Eventually, 746 men were recruited into the study. Martin and Dean checked their sample against two random samples of gay men in San Francisco, a random digit dialing sample of 500, and a cluster sample of 823 using San Francisco census tracts. Their sample paralleled those from San Francisco on race, age, and the percent being "out of the closet."

HOW LARGE SHOULD A SAMPLE BE?

Students and new researchers often ask, "How large does my sample have to be?" The best answer is, "It depends." It depends on the kind of data analysis the researcher plans, on how accurate the sample has to be for the researcher's purposes, and on population characteristics. As you have seen, a large sample size alone does not guarantee a representative sample. A large sample without random sampling or with a poor sampling frame is less representative than a smaller one with random sampling and an excellent sampling frame.

The question of sample size can be addressed in two ways. One is to make assumptions about the population and use statistical equations about random sampling processes. The calculation of sample size by this method requires a statistical

discussion that goes beyond the level of this text.[13] The researcher must make assumptions about the degree of confidence (or number of errors) that is acceptable and the degree of variation in the population.

A second and more frequently used method is a rule of thumb—a conventional or commonly accepted amount. Researchers use it because they rarely have the information required by the statistical method and because it gives sample sizes close to those of the statistical method. Rules of thumb are not arbitrary but are based on past experience with samples that have met the requirements of the statistical method.

One principle of sample sizes is, the smaller the population, the bigger the sampling ratio has to be for an accurate sample (i.e., one with a high probability of yielding the same results as the entire population). Larger populations permit smaller sampling ratios for equally good samples. This is because as the population size grows, the returns in accuracy for sample size shrink.

For small populations (under 1,000), a researcher needs a large sampling ratio (about 30 percent). For example, a sample size of about 300 is required for a high degree of accuracy. For moderately large populations (10,000), a smaller sampling ratio (about 10 percent) is needed to be equally accurate, or a sample size of around 1,000. For large populations (over 150,000), smaller sampling ratios (1 percent) are possible, and samples of about 1,500 can be very accurate. To sample from very large populations (over 10 million), one can achieve accuracy using tiny sampling ratios (0.025 percent) or samples of about 2,500. The size of the population ceases to be relevant once the sampling ratio is very small, and samples of about 2,500 are as accurate for populations of 200 million as for 10 million. These are approximate sizes, and practical limitations (e.g., cost) also play a role in a researcher's decision.

A related principle is that for small samples, small increases in sample size produce big gains in accuracy. Equal increases in sample size produce more of an increase in accuracy for small than for large samples. For example, an increase in sample size from 50 to 100 reduces errors from

7.1 percent to 2.1 percent, but an increase from 1,000 to 2,000 only decreases errors from 1.6 percent to 1.1 percent (Sudman, 1976a:99).

A researcher's decision about the best sample size depends on three things: (1) the degree of accuracy required, (2) the degree of variability or diversity in the population, and (3) the number of different variables examined simultaneously in data analysis. Everything else being equal, larger samples are needed if the population has a great deal of variability or heterogeneity, or if one wants to examine many variables in the data analysis simultaneously. Smaller samples are sufficient when less accuracy is acceptable, when the population is homogeneous, or when only a few variables are examined at a time.

The analysis of data on subgroups also affects a researcher's decision about sample size. If the researcher wants to analyze subgroups in the population, he or she needs a larger sample. For example, we want to analyze four variables for males between the ages of 30 and 40 years old. If this sample is of the general public, then only a small proportion (e.g., 10 percent) of sample cases will be males in that age group. A rule of thumb is to have about 50 cases for each subgroup to be analyzed. Thus, if we want to analyze a group that is only 10 percent of the population, then we should have 10 × 50 or 500 cases in the sample to be sure we get enough for the subgroup analysis.

DRAWING INFERENCES

A researcher samples so he or she can draw inferences from the sample to the population. In fact, a subfield of statistical data analysis that concerns drawing accurate inferences is called *inferential statistics* (discussed in Chapter 12). The researcher directly observes variables using units in the sample. The sample stands for or represents the population. Researchers are not interested in samples in themselves; they want to infer to the population. Thus, a gap exists between what the researcher concretely has (a sample) and what is of real interest (a population) (see Figure 9.3).

In previous chapters, you saw how the logic of measurement could be stated in terms of a gap between abstract constructs and concrete indicators. Measures of concrete, observable data are approximations for abstract constructs. Researchers use the approximations to estimate what is of real interest (i.e., constructs and causal laws). Conceptualization and operationalization bridge the gap in measurement just as the use of sampling frames, the sampling process, and inference bridge the gap in sampling.

Researchers put the logic of sampling and the logic of measurement together by directly observing measures of constructs and empirical relationships in samples (see Figure 9.3). They infer or generalize from what they can observe empirically in samples to the abstract causal laws and constructs in the population.

Validity and sampling error have similar functions, as can be illustrated by the analogy between the logic of sampling and the logic of measurement—that is, between what is observed and what is discussed. In measurement, a researcher wants valid indicators of constructs—that is, concrete indicators that accurately represent abstract constructs. In sampling, he or she wants samples that have little sampling error—concrete collections of cases that accurately represent unseen and abstract populations. A valid measure is one that deviates little from the construct it represents. A sample with little sampling error permits estimates that deviate little from population parameters.

Researchers try to reduce sampling errors. The calculation of the sampling error is not presented here, but it is based on two factors: the sample size and the amount of diversity in the sample. Everything else being equal, the larger the sample size, the smaller the sampling error. Likewise, the greater the homogeneity (or the less the diversity) in a sample, the smaller its sampling error.

Sampling error is also related to confidence intervals. If two samples are identical except that one is larger, the one with more cases will have a smaller sampling error and narrower confidence intervals. Likewise, if two samples are identical except that the cases in one are more similar to

A Model of the Logic of Sampling

What You Would Like to Talk About

Population

Sampling Frame

Sampling Process

What You Actually Observe in the Data

Sample

A Model of the Logic of Measurement

Theoretical Concepts and Causal Laws

What You Would Like to Talk About

Operationalization

What You Actually Observe in the Data

Measures and Empirical Relationships

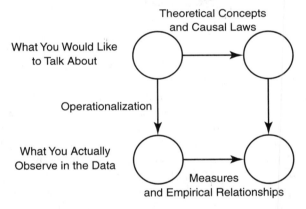

A Model Combining Logics of Sampling and Measurement

Population

Concepts

What You Would Like to Talk About

Causal Laws

Sample

Measures and Empirical Relationships

What You Actually Observe in the Data

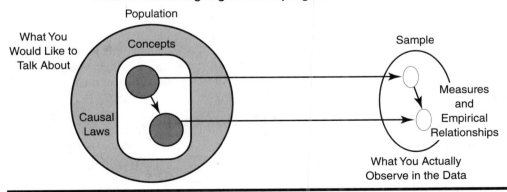

FIGURE 9.3 Model of the Logic of Sampling and of Measurement

each other, the one with greater homogeneity will have a smaller sampling error and narrower confidence intervals. A narrow confidence interval means more precise estimates of the population parameter for a given level of confidence. For example, a researcher wants to estimate average annual family income. He or she has two samples. Sample 1 gives a confidence interval of $30,000 to $36,000 around the estimated population parameter of $33,000 for an 80 percent level of confidence. For a 95 percent level of confidence, the range is $23,000 to $43,000. A sample with a smaller sampling error (because it is larger or is more homogeneous) might give a $30,000 to $36,000 range for a 95 percent confidence level.

CONCLUSION

In this chapter, you learned about sampling. Sampling is widely used in social research, especially in survey research and nonreactive research techniques. You learned about four types of sampling that are not based on random processes: haphazard, quota, snowball, and purposive. Only the last two are acceptable, and even then their use depends on special circumstances.[14] In general, probability sampling is preferred because it produces a sample that represents the population and enables the researcher to use powerful statis-

tical techniques. In addition to simple random sampling, you learned about systematic, stratified, and cluster sampling. Although this book does not cover the statistical theory used in random sampling, from the discussion of sampling error, the central limit theorem, and sample size, it should be clear that random sampling produces more accurate and precise sampling.

Before moving on to the next chapter, it may be useful to restate a fundamental principle of social research: Do not compartmentalize the steps of the research process; rather, learn to see the interconnections between the steps. Research design, measurement, sampling, and specific research techniques are interdependent. Unfortunately, the constraints of presenting information in a course or textbook necessitate presenting the parts separately, in sequence. In practice, researchers think about data collection when they design research and develop measures for variables. Likewise, sampling issues influence research design, measurement of variables, and data collection strategies. As you will see in future chapters, good social research depends on simultaneously controlling quality at several different steps—research design, conceptualization, measurement, sampling, and data collection and handling. The researcher who makes major errors at any one stage may make an entire research project worthless.[15]

KEY TERMS

central limit theorem	purposive sampling	sampling interval
cluster sampling	quota sampling	sampling ratio
confidence intervals	random-digit dialing (RDD)	simple random sampling
haphazard sampling	random-number table	snowball sampling
inferential statistics	sample	sociogram
parameter	sampling distribution	statistic
population	sampling element	stratified sampling
probability proportionate to	sampling error	systematic sampling
size (PPS)	sampling frame	target population

REVIEW QUESTIONS

1. When is purposive sampling used?
2. When is the snowball sampling technique appropriate?

3. What is a sampling frame and why is it important?

4. Which sampling method is best when the population has several groups and a researcher wants to ensure that each group is in the sample?

5. How can you get a sampling interval from a sampling ratio?

6. When should a researcher consider using probability proportionate to size?

7. What is the population in random-digit dialing? Are sampling frame problems avoided? Explain.

8. How do researchers decide how large a sample to use?

9. How are the logic of sampling and the logic of measurement related?

10. When is random-digit dialing used, and what are its advantages and disadvantages?

NOTES

1. For a discussion of the *Literary Digest* sampling mistake, see Babbie (1995:188–190), Dillman (1978:9–10), Frey (1983:18–19), and Singleton and colleagues (1988:132–133).

2. See Stern (1979:77–81) on biased samples. He also discusses ways to identify problems with samples in published reports.

3. Quota sampling is discussed in Kalton (1983:91–93) and Sudman (1976a:191–200).

4. For further discussion on purposive sampling, see Grosof and Sardy (1985:172–173) and Singleton and associates (1988:153–154; 306). Bailey (1987:94–95) describes "dimensional" sampling, which is a variation of purposive sampling.

5. For additional discussion of snowball sampling, see Babbie (1995:287), Bailey (1987:97), and Sudman (1976a:210–211). Also see Bailey (1987:366–367), Dooley (1984:86–87), Kidder and Judd (1986:240–241), Lindzey and Byrne (1968:452–525), and Singleton and associates (1988:372–373) for discussions of sociometry and sociograms. Network sampling issues are discussed in Galaskiewicz (1985), Granovetter (1976), and Hoffmann-Lange (1987).

6. See Traugott (1987) on the importance of persistence in reaching sampled respondents for a representative sample. Also see Kalton (1983:63–69) on the importance of nonresponse.

7. Only one name appears in both. The stratified sample has 6 males and 4 females; the simple random sample has 5 males and 5 females. (Complete the lower block of numbers, then begin at the far right of the top block.)

8. Stratified sampling techniques are discussed in more detail in Frankel (1983:37–46), Kalton (1983:19–28), Mendenhall and colleagues (1971:53–88), Sudman (1976a:107–130), and Williams (1978:162–175).

9. Cluster sampling is discussed in Frankel (1983: 47–57), Kalton (1983:28–38), Kish (1965), Mendenhall and colleagues (1971:121–141, 171–183), Sudman (1976a:69–84), and Williams (1978:144–161).

10. For a discussion, see Frankel (1983:57–62), Kalton (1983:38–47), Sudman (1976a:131–170), and Williams (1978:239–241).

11. Within-household sampling is discussed in Czaja and colleagues (1982) and in Groves and Kahn (1979:32–36).

12. For more on random-digit dialing issues, see Dillman (1978:238–242), Frey (1983:69–77), Glasser and Metzger (1972), Groves and Kahn (1979:20–21, 45–63), Kalton (1983:86–90), and Waksberg (1978). Kviz (1984) reported that telephone directories can produce relatively accurate sampling frames in rural areas, at least for mail questionnaire surveys. Also see Keeter (1995).

13. See Kraemer and Thiemann (1987) for a technical discussion of selecting a sample size.

14. Berk (1983) argued that sampling that is nonrandom or a sampling process that excludes a nonrandom subset of cases can create seriously inaccurate estimates of causal relations.

15. For a further discussion of sample size calculation, see Grosof and Sardy (1985:181–185), Kalton (1983:82–90), Sudman (1976a:85–105), and Williams (1978:211–227).

RECOMMENDED READINGS

Henry, Gary T. (1990) *Practical sampling.* Newbury Park, CA: Sage. This is a relatively nontechnical introduction to sampling. Henry focuses on practical, applied issues in carrying out a sample. He also discusses different sampling designs, sampling error, and the calculation of sample size. His concept of total error in samples is very useful.

Kalton, Graham. (1983). *Introduction to survey sampling.* Beverly Hills, CA: Sage. This short (96-page) paperback provides a condensed overview of major sampling techniques and issues. Although it is not written for the sampling statistician, the author assumes that readers have a background of one or two courses in elementary statistics. The author includes practical concerns in the discussion.

Mendenhall, William, Lyman Ott, and Richard L. Scheaffer. (1971). *Elementary survey sampling.* Belmont, CA: Duxbury Press. Readers who have had at least one course in statistics and who would like to build on that knowledge to better understand the applied aspects of sampling concepts will find this book useful. Although the authors do not focus on the practical aspects of sampling, they provide a clearly written, step-by-step introduction to statistical issues that arise in different sampling designs.

Sudman, Seymour. (1976). *Applied sampling.* New York: Academic Press. Sudman provides an excellent overview of sampling for the reader who has some statistical background but whose primary interest is in using sampling techniques in the social sciences. The book covers the major sampling issues most researchers will encounter, with practical and elementary statistical discussions of the issues.

Williams, Bill. (1978). *A sampler on sampling.* New York: Wiley. As the title suggests, this book is a sampler, packed with examples and exercises. The examples come from many different fields and show the importance of good sampling. Readers without at least one course in elementary statistics will have difficulty with several of the chapters.

CHAPTER 10

SURVEY RESEARCH

> *The claim that national security is endangered by a vaguely defined
> threat to Western cultures opens up the way to justifications for granting
> extraordinary powers to military and police forces. The portrayal of the
> drug problem as one of survival of Western society removes policy
> makers from normal legal restraints. It justifies the argument that the
> problem is too urgent to submit to domestic and international debates.*
> —Dr. Jaime Malmud Goti, former chair of the Presidential Commission on Drug Control in
> Argentina, as quoted in Scott and Marshall, *Cocaine Politics*, p. 6

INTRODUCTION

Crime, as you know, is becoming increasingly international in scope, as is law enforcement. Consequently, more and more criminological research is adopting an international perspective. At the heart of this perspective is the researcher's desire to consider cross-national comparisons of crime and justice. So vital is this to the research agenda of criminologists that the U.S. Department of Justice's research institute recently issued a call for proposals on this very topic. In stemming the tide of transborder crime, the institute has solicited proposals for research into crime's "common and different causes . . . across many nations, and [for] developing responses that can be applied" (U.S. National Institute of Justice, 1998:2).

An often overlooked dimension of comparative research relates crime to the broader issues of foreign policy and international relations. Perhaps nowhere is the interplay between crime and international politics more evident than in the research on U.S. drug control policy. Criminologists are keen to study the political and social implications of drug policy, and have found the survey method to be an excellent way to gather data.

This chapter focuses on survey research. You will learn the main elements of good survey research, as well as some limitations in the method itself. Moreover, in an effort to nurture a comparative research perspective, the chapter contains examples of surveys conducted in different countries, relating the discussion to drug policy and crime victimization, among other things. Keep in mind, however, that irrespective of where a survey is conducted, the same methodological principles and scientific norms apply.

Research Questions Appropriate for a Survey

Survey research developed within the positivist approach to social science.[1] Surveys produce quantitative information about the social world and describe features of people or the social world. They are also used to explain or explore. The survey asks many people (called *respondents*) about their beliefs, opinions, characteristics, and past or present behavior.

Surveys are appropriate for research questions about self-reported beliefs or behaviors. They are strongest when the answers people give to questions measure variables. Researchers usually ask about many things at one time in surveys, measure many variables (often with multiple indicators), and test several hypotheses in a single survey.

The following are examples of research questions criminologists might ask in a survey:

1. *Behavior.* Have you used cocaine one or more times in the last 30 days? Have you carried a weapon (e.g., gun, knife, or club) on one or more of the 30 days preceding the survey? Did you report the crime to the police?

2. *Attitudes/beliefs/opinions.* How safe would you feel being alone and outside in your area of town at night? In your opinion, how much of the illegal drug problem in your country is caused by the demand for drugs in the United States?

3. *Characteristics.* What country were you born in? What is the highest level of education that you completed? Are you presently employed?

4. *Expectations.* Do you plan to purchase any home security devices in the next 12 months? Do you plan to alter any of your routine activities because of your fear of crime?

5. *Self-classification.* Into which social class would you put you and your family? Do you consider yourself to be a target of hate crime?

6. *Knowledge.* How much have you heard about the U.S. War on Drugs? Is there a "crack house" in your neighborhood?

A History of Survey Research

The modern survey can be traced back to ancient forms of the census.[2] A *census* includes information on characteristics of the entire population in a territory. It is based on what people tell officials or what officials observe. Surveys, on the other hand, focus on a sample of the population. As pointed out in the previous chapter, if the sampling is done correctly, the survey results can be more accurate than those of the census.

The survey has a long and varied history. Its use for social research in the United States and Great Britain began with social reform movements and social service professions documenting the conditions of urban poverty that followed early industrialization. At first, surveys were overviews of an area based on questionnaires and other data. Scientific sampling and statistics were absent. For example, between 1851 and 1864, Henry Mayhew published the 4-volume *London Labour and the London Poor,* based on conversations with street people and observations of daily life. Charles Booth's 17-volume (1889–1902) *Labour and Life of the People of London* and B. Seebohm Rowntree's *Poverty: A Study of Town Life* (1906) also examined the extent of urban poverty. Similar work appeared in the United States in *Hull House Maps and Papers of 1895* and in W. E. B. DuBois's *Philadelphia Negro* (1899).

Four forces greatly reshaped the social survey into modern quantitative survey research in the United States from 1920 to World War II. First, researchers applied statistically based sampling techniques and precise measurement to the survey, especially after the *Literary Digest* debacle (see Chapter 9). Second, researchers created scales and indexes to gather systematic quantitative data on attitudes, opinions, and subjective aspects of social life. Third, many others found uses for the survey and adapted it to a variety of applied areas. Market research emerged as a distinct field and adapted surveys to study consumer behavior. Journalists used surveys to measure public opinion and the impact of the radio. Religious organizations and charities used surveys to identify areas of need. Government agencies used surveys to improve services for agricultural and social programs. Also, more social scientists began to use the survey as a source of empirical data for their basic research.

In addition, there was a major reorientation of most empirical social research, especially the survey, away from a mix of methods used by nonacademics to focus on local social problems. The reorientation created respectable, "scientific" methods modeled after the natural sciences. Social research became more professional, objective, and non-political.[3]

Survey research expanded and matured during World War II, especially in the United States.

Academic social researchers and practitioners from industry converged in Washington, DC, to work in the war effort. Survey researchers studied morale, consumer demand, production capacity, enemy propaganda, and black markets. The wartime cooperation helped academic social researchers and applied practitioners learn from each other and gain experience in conducting many large-scale surveys. Academic researchers helped practitioners appreciate precise measurement, sampling, and statistical analysis, while practitioners helped academics learn the practical side of organizing and conducting large-scale surveys.

After World War II, officials dismantled the extensive government survey research establishment. This was, in part, a cost-cutting move. Also, some members of the U.S. Congress feared that others might use survey results to advance social policies, such as helping the unemployed or promoting equal rights for African Americans who lived in racially segregated southern states.

Many researchers returned to universities and created new social research organizations. At first, the universities were hesitant to embrace expanded survey research. Survey research was expensive and involved many people. In addition, traditional social researchers were wary of quantitative research and skeptical of a technique used in private industry. The culture of applied researchers and business-oriented poll takers clashed with that of traditional basic researchers who lacked statistical training. Yet, surveys grew in use. This growth was not limited to the United States. Within three years of the end of World War II, national survey research institutes had been established in France, Norway, Germany, Italy, the Netherlands, Czechoslovakia, and Britain (Scheuch, 1990).

Survey research has grown immensely important to social scientists in the last three decades or so. During this period, criminologists have become regular producers and consumers of such research. The following five factors contributed to the rapid growth in survey research:[4]

1. *Computers.* Computer technology that became available to social scientists by the 1960s made the sophisticated statistical analysis of large-scale survey data sets feasible for the first time. Today, the computer is an indispensable tool for analyzing data from most surveys.

2. *Organizations.* New social research centers with an expertise and interest in quantitative research were established at major and regional universities in the industrialized world. Today, survey centers are also popping up in developing countries, as well.

3. *Data storage.* By the 1970s, data archives were created to store and permit the sharing of the large-scale survey data for secondary analysis (discussed in Chapter 11). The collection, storage, and sharing of information on hundreds of variables for thousands of respondents expanded the use of surveys.

4. *Funding.* The 1960s brought increases in federal support for survey research in the social sciences. Criminologists were often the beneficiaries of this trend. Federal funding in the United States, for instance, attracted criminologists working in universities and nonprofit institutes. The extent of funding fluctuated, first rising in the 1960s, to only drop back in the 1970s. The 1980s and 1990s witnessed the trend to commercialize survey research. The government's involvement in survey research is being privatized or contracted out to private research companies. Commercialization is likely to continue in the future. In the years ahead, survey research will surely continue to cross borders toward a full international perspective.

5. *Methodology.* By the 1970s, substantial research was being conducted on ways to improve the validity of surveys. The survey technique advanced as errors were identified and corrected.[5] In addition, researchers created improved statistics for analyzing quantitative data and taught them to a new generation of researchers.

Today, quantitative survey research is a major industry both within and outside universities. Many organizations conduct surveys. The professional survey industry probably employs over 60,000 people in the United States alone. Most of these are part-time workers, assistants, or semiprofessionals. About 6,000 full-time professional survey researchers design and analyze surveys.[6]

Researchers use surveys for basic research in universities and research centers. Researchers in many fields (communication, education, economics, political science, social psychology, and sociology) conduct and analyze surveys. Many U.S. universities have centers for survey research. Major centers include the Survey Research Center at the University of California at Berkeley, the National Opinion Research Center (NORC) at the University of Chicago, and the Institute for Social Research (ISR) at the University of Michigan.

Several applied areas rely heavily on the survey: government, marketing, private policy research, and mass media. Governments around the world at the national and local levels regularly conduct surveys to inform policy decisions. Private-sector survey research can be divided into three types of organizations: opinion polling organizations (e.g., Gallup, Harris, Roper, Yankelovich and Associates, etc.), marketing firms (e.g., Nielsen, Market Facts, Market Research Corporation, etc.), and nonprofit research organizations (e.g., Mathematica Policy Research, Rand Corporation, etc.).[7]

Major television and newspaper organizations regularly conduct surveys. Rossi and associates (1983:14), who found 174 polls sponsored by media organizations, stated, "Polling is as much a feature of the media as comics and the horoscope!" In addition, there are many ad hoc or in-house surveys. Businesses, schools, and other organizations conduct small-scale surveys of employees, clients, students, and the like to address specific applied questions.

Survey researchers have formed separate professional organizations. The American Association for Public Opinion Research, founded in 1947, sponsors a scholarly journal devoted to survey research called *Public Opinion Quarterly*. The Council of American Survey Research Organization is an organization for commercial polling firms. There is also an international survey research organization—the World Association of Public Opinion Research.[8]

In the past three decades, the quantitative survey has become a widely used technology for social research both inside and outside universities. Although knowledge about how to conduct a good survey has grown significantly, the explosion of survey applications has outpaced developments in the survey technique as a method to quantitatively measure human social life.

THE LOGIC OF SURVEY RESEARCH

What Is a Survey?

In experiments, researchers place people in small groups and test one or two hypotheses with a few variables. Subjects respond to a treatment created by the researcher. Causality is shown by the timing of the treatment, by observing associations between the treatment and the dependent variable, and by controlling for alternative explanations.

By contrast, survey researchers sample many respondents who answer the same questions. They measure many variables, test multiple hypotheses, and infer temporal order from questions about past behavior, experiences, characteristics, and so on. For example, in a survey conducted in Belize, Central America, researchers found that the public's willingness to wage a war on drugs rested most heavily on two independent variables: the respondent's level of education and gender (Wiegand and Bennett, 1993). Obviously, the respondent's gender and educational level are prior to current public opinion.

Experimenters physically control for alternative explanations. Survey researchers measure variables that represent alternative explanations (i.e., control variables), then statistically examine their effects to rule out alternative explanations. They think of alternative explanations when planning a survey and measure the alternatives with control variables.

Survey research is often called correlational. Survey researchers use control variables and correlations in statistical analysis. They approximate the rigorous test for causality that experimenters achieve with their physical control over temporal order and alternative explanations.

Steps in Conducting a Survey

The survey researcher follows a deductive approach. He or she begins with a theoretical or applied research problem and ends with empirical measurement and data analysis. Once a researcher decides that the survey is an appropriate method, two basic steps in a research project—the research design and data collection—can be divided into the substeps outlined in Figure 10.1.

In the first phase, the researcher develops an instrument—a survey questionnaire or interview schedule—that he or she uses to measure variables. Respondents read the questions themselves and mark answers on a *questionnaire*. An *interview schedule* is a set of questions read to the respondent by an interviewer, who also records responses. To simplify the discussion, the authors will use only the term *questionnaires*.

A survey researcher conceptualizes and operationalizes variables as questions. He or she writes and rewrites questions for clarity and completeness, and organizes questions on the questionnaire based on the research question, the respondents, and the type of survey. (The types of surveys are discussed later.)

When preparing a questionnaire, the researcher thinks ahead to how he or she will record and organize data for analysis. He or she pilot tests the questionnaire with a small set of respondents similar to those in the final survey. If interviewers are used, the researcher trains them with the questionnaire. He or she asks respondents in the pilot test whether the questions were clear and explores their interpretations to see whether his or her intended meaning was clear.

In the survey of attitudes toward the drug war in Belize, for instance, the researchers conducted a pilot test, not in Belize itself, but in Washington, DC, with Belizeans referred to them by the Belize Embassy (Wiegand and Bennett, 1993). This increased the likelihood that survey respondents in

FIGURE 10.1   Details of Two Research Steps in Survey Research

DESIGN AND PLANNING PHASE

1. Decide on type of survey (e.g., mail, telephone interview), type of respondent, and the population.
2. Develop the survey instrument/questionnaire:
   a. Write questions to measure variables.
   b. Decide on response categories.
   c. Organize question sequence.
   d. Design questionnaire layout.
3. Plan a system for recording answers.
4. Pilot test the instrument and train interviewers if necessary.
5. Draw the sample:
   a. Define target population.
   b. Decide on type of sample.
   c. Develop sampling frame.
   d. Decide on sample size.
   e. Select sample.

DATA COLLECTION PHASE

1. Locate and contact the respondents.
2. Make introductory statements or provide instructions.
3. Ask questions and record answers.
4. Thank respondent and continue to next respondent.
5. End data collection and organize data.

Belize would be able to relate to the research questions being asked of them. Once the researchers finalize the questionnaire, they can then set out to draw a sample, as discussed in the previous chapter.

After the planning phase, the researcher is ready to collect data. This phase is usually shorter than the planning phase. He or she locates sampled respondents in person, by telephone, or by mail. Respondents are given information and instructions on completing the questionnaire or interview. The questions follow, and there is a simple stimulus/response or question/answer pattern. The researcher accurately records answers or responses immediately after they are given. After all respondents complete the questionnaire and are thanked, he or she organizes the data and prepares them for statistical analysis.

Conducting a survey inevitably involves coordinating many people and steps. This becomes even more of a challenge when in a country different from your own. Coordinating the social networks and contacts, while respecting local traditions and culture, is difficult to do and requires wide cooperation for the survey to succeed. In the Belize survey, the researchers gained access into the local community by way of contacts at the University College of Belize.

The administration of survey research requires organization and accurate record keeping.[9] The researcher keeps track of each respondent, questionnaire, and interviewer. For example, he or she gives each sampled respondent an identification number, which also appears on the questionnaire. He or she then checks completed questionnaires against a list of sampled respondents. Next, the researcher reviews responses on individual questionnaires, stores original questionnaires, and transfers information from questionnaires to a format for statistical analysis. Meticulous bookkeeping and labeling are essential. Otherwise, the researcher may find that valuable data and effort are lost through sloppiness.

CONSTRUCTING THE QUESTIONNAIRE

Principles of Good Question Writing

A good questionnaire forms an integrated whole. The researcher weaves questions together so they flow smoothly. He or she includes introductory remarks and instructions for clarification and measures each variable with one or more survey questions.

There are two key principles for good survey questions: Avoid confusion and keep the respondent's perspective in mind. Good survey questions give the researcher valid and reliable measures. They also help respondents feel that they understand the question and that their answers are meaningful. Questions that do not mesh with a respondent's viewpoint or that respondents find confusing are not good measures. A survey researcher exercises extra care if the respondents are heterogeneous or come from different life situations than his or her own.

Researchers face a dilemma. They want each respondent to hear exactly the same question, but will the questions be equally clear, relevant, and meaningful to all respondents? If respondents have diverse backgrounds and frames of reference, exactly the same wording may not have the same meaning. Yet, tailoring question wording to each respondent makes comparisons almost impossible. A researcher would not know whether the wording of the question or differences in respondents accounted for different answers.

Question writing is more of an art than a science. It takes skill, practice, patience, and creativity. The principles of question writing are illustrated in the 10 things to avoid when writing survey questions. The list does not include every possible error, only the more frequent problems.[10]

1. *Avoid jargon, slang, and abbreviations.* The technical terms and jargon criminologists use—terms such as *incarceration, stick up, deterrence, insider trading,* and so many others—may have little meaning to the average person. To use them in a survey of criminologists is one thing, but to use the jargon with the general public is probably not advisable. Indeed, one should avoid slang, jargon, and overly technical terms unless a specialized population is being surveyed. Target the vocabulary and grammar to the respondents sampled. Thus, for example, a crime victimization survey conducted in the United States would be written with about an eighth-grade reading vocabulary. That level of literacy, however, would probably be too high if the same victimization survey were also being conducted in a poor country where illiteracy is common.

2. *Avoid ambiguity, confusion, and vagueness.* Ambiguity and vague wording pose one of the biggest problems for survey question writers. Part of the problem can be solved through the use of specific cues that make it easier for a respondent to identify and recall past experiences.

An illustration of the importance of using unambiguous wording is the redesigned U.S. National Crime Victimization Survey (NCVS). The old design (i.e, the National Crime Survey or NCS) was changed in 1992 in the hope of getting a better reporting of victimization (Kindermann et al., 1997). In particular, cues were added for certain questions as a means of probing deeper into "nonstereotypic crimes, such as those that involve offenders who are not strangers. There was good reason to believe that these types of events were not recounted in the old design" (p. 4). Indeed, the cues did improve the recounting of victimizations to the interviewer, especially "for respondents with traditionally lower rates of victimization than it did for those with traditionally higher rates" (p. 5) (see Box 10.1).

3. *Avoid emotional language and prestige bias.* Words have implicit connotative as well as explicit denotative meanings. Likewise, titles or positions in society (e.g., president, expert, etc.) carry prestige or status. Words with strong emotional connotations and stands on issues linked to people with high social status can color how respondents hear and answer survey questions.

Use neutral language. Avoid words with emotional "baggage," because respondents may react to the emotionally laden words rather than to the issue. For example, the question, "What do you think about a policy to pay murderous terrorists who threaten to steal the freedoms of peace-loving people?" is full of emotional words—such as *murderous, freedoms, steal,* and *peace.*

Also avoid *prestige bias*—associating a statement with a prestigious person or group. Respondents may answer on the basis of their feelings toward the person or group rather than addressing the issue. Using, for example, the name of a popular (or unpopular) politician in a survey question will most likely bias the survey responses. Suppose a criminologist wanted to do a survey of public opinion in Central America toward drug enforcement policy. Phrasing the question as "Do you approve or disapprove of U.S. President Clinton's drug enforcement policies?" forces the respondent to consider drug policy in terms of President Clinton. Given the

Box 10.1 _____

Improving Crime Victimization Questions

OLD DESIGN (NCS, used from 1972 to 1992)

1. Did anyone take something directly from you by using force, such as by a stickup, mugging, or threat?
2. Did anyone TRY to rob you by using force or threatening to harm you?
3. Did anyone beat you up, attack you, or hit you with something, such as a rock or bottle?
4. Were you knifed, shot at, or attacked with some other weapon by anyone else?
5. Did anyone THREATEN to beat you up or THREATEN you with a knife, gun, or some other weapon, NOT including telephone threats?
6. Did anyone TRY to attack you in some other way?

NEW DESIGN (NCVS, beginning 1992)

1. Has anyone attacked or threatened you in any of these ways—
   a. With any weapon, for instance, a gun or knife—
   b. With anything like a baseball bat, frying pan, scissors, or stick—
   c. By something thrown, such as a rock or bottle—
   d. Include any gabbing, punching, or choking—
   e. Any rape, attempted rape, or other type of sexual assault—
   f. Any face-to-face threats—OR
   g. Any attack or threat or use of force by anyone at all?
   Please mention it even if you were not certain it was a crime.

2. Incidents involving forced or unwanted sexual acts are often difficult to talk about. Have you been forced or coerced to engage in unwanted sexual activity by—
   a. Someone you didn't know before
   b. a casual acquaintance OR
   c. Someone you know well.

The clues used in the new design are much clearer and often take into account situations that may not fit into popular conceptions of crime. For example, the new design specifically refers to common household items _(baseball bat, frying pan, scissors)_ as being potential weapons. By the same token, there are cues to encourage respondents to report victimization more fully (e.g., _Please mention it even if you were not certain it was a crime_); and specific cues to probe for nonstereotypic crimes of sexual assault (e.g., _a casual acquaintance OR someone you know well_).

The effects of the new design were impressive. Higher estimates of victimization reporting were generally found for most crime categories. For instance, rape victimization was much more likely to be reported with the new design (e.g., 157 percent increase). As predicted, the greatest increase occurred for "nonstereotypic" crime categories. Thus, the new design has the greatest impact on "nonstranger" crimes, attempted crimes, and crimes not reported to the police, as summarized here:

	New Design*	_Old Design*_
Victim-Offender Relationship		
Stranger	26.5	19.5
Nonstranger	22.5	12.8
Completed	15.8	11.7
Attempted	33.5	20.4

Box 10.1   Continued

	New Design*	Old Design*
Crime Reporting to the Police		
Reported	21.0	16.0
Not reported	27.5	15.7

*Estimated victimization rates per 1,000 persons.
Source: Adapted from Kindermann, Lynch, and Cantor (1997).

political influence U.S. presidents wield in that part of the world, the respondents may be reacting more to their opinion of the U.S. presidency than to U.S. drug policy.

4. *Avoid double-barreled questions.* Make each question about one and only one topic. A *double-barreled question* consists of two or more questions joined together. It makes a respondent's answer ambiguous. Asking a person to respond to two questions at once makes no sense. Thus, it would not be a good idea to ask a survey question such as "Do you agree or disagree with U.S. drug policy and trade policy in Central America?" The respondent may not be able to give just one answer. On the other hand, it may be perfectly appropriate to ask this question, which is not double barreled: "Do you agree or disagree with the United States linking its trade policy in Central America with its drug policy?" Labaw (1980:154) noted, "Perhaps the most basic principle of question wording, and one very often ignored or simply unseen, is that only one concept or issue or meaning should be included in a question." A researcher who wants to ask about the joint occurrence of two things—for example, attitudes towards drug policy and attitudes towards trade policy—should ask two separate questions.

Also, be careful not to confuse a respondent's belief that a relationship exists between two variables with the empirical relationship itself. Consider, for example, a question asked in a national survey in the United States (Johnson, 1997). The question read: "As far as you know, do the police in your community mostly treat Blacks

worse than Whites, or both races equally?" The results (see Box 10.2) reveal that Black respondents were much more likely to believe that the police act in a biased way toward them. One should not take that to mean that the police are therefore biased. Rather, the question is tapping levels of perceived police behavior.

5. *Avoid leading questions.* Make respondents feel that all responses are legitimate. Do not let them become aware of an answer that the researcher wants. A *leading* (or *loaded*) *question* is one that leads the respondent to choose one response over another by its wording. There are many kinds of leading questions.

Also, respondents can be led to give either positive or negative answers, depending on how the survey question is worded. For example, respondents would tend to agree with this question: "Because of the extent of illegal drug trafficking in Central America, wouldn't you agree that the military should be used to help out with drug enforcement?" Respondents would tend to disagree with a question asking: "People who favor using the military for drug enforcement probably do not care about the potential for corruption. How do you feel about the matter?"

An interesting related matter is that survey researchers have compared public opinions about militarizing drug enforcement. The comparative data suggest that the level of opposition is much greater in Latin America than in the United States. For example, "Whereas fifty percent (50%) of the Americans opposed the use of U.S. troops in Colombia, around two-thirds (64%) of the

Box 10.2_____

Perceptions of Police Behavior

"As far as you know, do the police in your community mostly treat Blacks worse than Whites, or both races about equally?"

	General Public (%)	Blacks (%)	Whites (%)
Mostly Blacks worse than Whites	14	42	11
Mostly equally	74	47	76
Mixed	2	11	1
Don't know	10	0	12

Source: Adapted from Johnson (1997).

Colombians opposed this tactic." Nonetheless, U.S. President Clinton has asked Congress "for increased funds to combat drug trafficking in Colombia, setting a goal to rid America's streets of Colombian cocaine and heroin over the next three years . . . [even though] there was no evidence of political will in Colombia to eliminate drug trafficking" (*Crime & Justice International,* 1998:22–23). "In Belize, seventy-two percent (72%) opposed any direct U.S. military involvement in the drug war" (Wiegand and Bennett, 1993:210).

6. *Avoid asking questions that are beyond respondents' capabilities.* Asking something that few respondents know frustrates respondents and produces poor-quality responses. Respondents cannot always recall past details and may not know specific factual information. For example, few respondents in the general population would be in a position to answer: "How involved are youth gangs in the sale and trafficking of illegal drugs?" Asking respondents to make a choice about something they know nothing about may result in an answer, but one that is unreliable and meaningless. When many respondents are unlikely to know about an issue, use a full-filter question form (to be discussed).

Phrase questions in the terms in which respondents think. For example, instead of asking how involved in drug trafficking youth gangs are, the researcher could ask: "In the past three months, how often, if ever, have you personally seen young people selling or using drugs in your neighborhood?"

7. *Avoid false premises.* Do not begin a question with a premise with which respondents may not agree, then ask about choices regarding it. Respondents who disagree with the premise will be frustrated and not know how to answer. For example, the question about perceptions of police behavior (see Box 10.2) contains the implicit assumption that the police either "treat Blacks worse than Whites, or both races equally." Obviously, it precludes the possibility of police treating Whites worse than Blacks.

8. *Avoid asking about future intentions.* Avoid asking people about what they might do under hypothetical circumstances. Responses are poor predictors of behavior. Questions such as, "Suppose you were from Colombia, South America. How do you think you would feel about U.S. drug enforcement efforts in your country?" are usually a waste of time. It is better to ask about current or recent attitudes and behavior. In general, respondents answer specific, concrete questions that relate to their experiences more reliably than they do those about abstractions that are beyond their immediate experiences.

9. *Avoid double negatives.* Double negatives in ordinary language are grammatically incorrect

and confusing. For example, "I ain't got no job" logically means that the respondent does have a job, but the second negative is used in this way for emphasis. Such blatant errors are rare, but more subtle forms of the double negative are also confusing. They arise when respondents are asked to agree or disagree with a statement. For example, respondents who disagree with the statement, "The United States should not tie U.S. foreign aid to a country's success in fighting against illegal drugs" are logically stating a double negative because they *disagree* with *not* doing something.

10. *Avoid overlapping or unbalanced response categories.* Make response categories or choices mutually exclusive, exhaustive, and balanced. *Mutually exclusive* means that response categories do not overlap. Overlapping categories that are numerical ranges (e.g., 5–10, 10–20, 20–30) can be easily corrected (e.g., 5–9, 10–19, 20–29). *Exhaustive* means that every respondent has a choice—a place to go. For example, asking respondents, "Are you working or unemployed?" leaves out respondents who are not working but do not consider themselves unemployed (e.g., full-time homemakers, people on vacation, students, the disabled, retired persons, etc.). A researcher first thinks about what he or she wants to measure and then considers the circumstances of respondents. When asking about a respondent's employment, for instance, does the researcher want information on the primary job or on all jobs? On full-time work only or both full- and part-time work? On jobs for pay only or on unpaid or volunteer jobs as well?

Keep response categories *balanced* so as not to lead a respondent. An example of an unbalanced set of categories would be: "In your opinion, how important is it to sign a treaty with the United States to extradite drug criminals to the United States? Is it very important, important, or not important?"

Aiding Respondent Recall

Survey researchers have recently examined a respondent's ability to accurately recall past behavior and events when answering survey questions.[12] This always has been a critical issue in oral history and recollections for historical research (see Chapter 15), but it is also an significant issue for survey questions about recent events. Recalling events accurately takes more time and effort than the dozen seconds that respondents have to answer survey questions. Also, one's ability to recall accurately declines over time. Studies in crime victimization show that although most respondents can recall significant events that occurred in the past several weeks, half are inaccurate a year later.

The validity of the U.S. National Crime Victimization Survey, for example, depends in large measure on the respondent's ability to recall past victimizations (see Figure 10.2):

> *Major sources of nonsampling error are related to the ability of the respondents to recall in detail the crimes that occurred during the six months prior to the interview. . . . Another source of nonsampling error is the inability of some respondents to recall the exact month a crime occurred, even though it was placed in the correct reference period. This error source is partially offset by interviewing monthly. (Maguire and Pastore, 1997:625)*

Survey researchers recognize that memory is less trustworthy than once assumed. It is affected by many factors—the topic (threaten-

FIGURE 10.2 Recalling Assault Victimization

Research based on interviews of victims shows that assault is recalled with the least accuracy of any crime measured by the NCVS. This may be related to the tendency of victims not to report crimes committed by offenders who are not strangers, especially if they are relatives. In addition, for certain groups, crimes involving assault could be a part of its culture, and are therefore considered normal or at least considered not important enough to report to a survey interviewer. These recall problems may contribute to an underestimate of the actual rate of assault.

Source: Adapted from Maguire and Pastore (1997).

ing or socially desirable), events occurring simultaneously and subsequently, the significance of an event for a person, situational conditions (question wording and interview style), and the respondent's need to have internal consistency. "Evidence now accumulating suggests that the task of recalling if and when events occur is far more difficult than survey researchers typically assumed. Real world events appear to be forgotten rapidly" (Turner and Martin, 1984: 296).

The complexity of respondent recall does not mean that survey researchers cannot ask about past events; rather, they need to customize questions and interpret results cautiously. Researchers should provide respondents with special instructions and extra thinking time. They should also provide aids to respondent recall, such as a fixed time frame or location references.

Many respondents will *telescope*—compress time when asked about frequency, tending to overreport recent events. Two techniques reduce telescoping: situational framing (e.g., ask the respondent to recall a specific situation and then ask about it) and decomposition (e.g., ask several specifics and add them up). The following passage reveals how telescoping is specifically dealt with in the NCVS:

> *Telescoping is another problem in which incidents that occurred before the reference period are placed within the period. The effect of telescoping is minimized by using the bounding procedure previously described [i.e., bounding establishes a time frame to avoid duplication of crimes on subsequent interviews]. The interviewer is provided with a summary of the incidents reported in the preceding interview and, if a similar incident is reported, it can be determined whether or not it is a new one by discussing it with the victim. Events that occurred after the reference period are set aside for inclusion with the data from the following interview. (Maguire and Pastore, 1997:624–625)*

To be sure, survey researchers who ask about past events or behavior, even within a bounded period (e.g., six months) need to do so with great care.

Types of Questions and Response Categories

Threatening versus Nonthreatening Questions.
Researchers sometimes ask about sensitive issues or ones that respondents find threatening.[13] Many respondents find questions about sexual behavior, drug or alcohol use, deviant behavior, mental health, illegal activity, or controversial public issues to be threatening. Researchers who ask such questions must do so with extra care.

Threatening questions are part of a broader issue. Respondents may try to present a positive image of themselves to interviewers or researchers instead of giving true answers. Respondents may be ashamed, embarrassed, or afraid to give a truthful answer. Instead, they give what they believe to be the normative or socially desirable answer. This is the *social desirability bias*. This social pressure can cause an overreporting or underreporting of the true situation. As a general rule of thumb, criminologists must realize that "the more value-laden the behavior, the more reluctant the respondents may be to give an honest answer. For example, the data generated would be meaningless if people were asked whether they had raped or committed some other sexual offense against a child" (Martens, 1997:235).

Criminologists interested in conducting comparative survey research must also keep in mind that "persons from different cultures have different frames of reference about what is a sensitive topic, and they have higher or lower thresholds concerning the disclosure of criminal and antisocial acts" (Martens, 1997:235). This point is well illustrated in the following:

> *An interesting contrast emerges when the data from the CEIFO [Swedish Center for Immigration Research] are compared with Ahlberg's study of Iranian female offenses of theft in [Swedish] shops and department stores. In Ahlberg's study, nearly 10 percent of Iranian women had been suspected of such an offense during the period studied. Not one Iranian women in the CEIFO survey self-reported committing such an offense. Police records show Iranian women to have the highest participation rate for thefts in shops and department stores of any group, but they had the lowest rate according to the self-report study. (Martens, 1997:235)*

Researchers can increase truthful answers to questions by offering explicit guarantees of confidentiality and by telling respondents that truthful answers are wanted and that any answer is acceptable. They should ask questions on sensitive topics after respondents have developed trust in an interviewer. They can also wait until after asking less threatening warm-up material and providing a meaningful context. They can phrase questions to make it easy for a respondent to admit engaging in the threatening behavior. For example, instead of asking whether a respondent masturbates, they ask, "About how frequently do you masturbate: once a week, once a month, every day, or never?" Another method is to have an introductory statement that states that many people engage in the behavior. Also, by embedding a threatening response within more serious activities, it may be made to seem less deviant. For example, respondents may hesitate to admit shoplifting if it is asked first, but after being asked about armed robbery or burglary, they may admit to shoplifting because it appears less serious.

Survey methods that permit greater anonymity are better for threatening issues. Thus, it may be better to use a mail or self-administered questionnaire. In face-to-face interview situations, respondents can be given a card with responses and just report a letter or number corresponding to their answer.

The techniques to survey sensitive behavior may differ across groups in society. For example, Aquilino and Losciuto (1990) examined the use of legal and illegal drugs among 18- to 34-year-olds using *random digit dialing (RDD)* telephone interviews and self-administered questionnaires with special procedures to protect anonymity (e.g., sealing answers in a locked box). They found little difference between the two survey methods for White respondents. For African American respondents, the self-administered questionnaire was more likely to reveal the use of illegal drugs. (Also see Johnson and colleagues, 1989.)

A complicated invention for asking threatening questions in face-to-face interview situations

is the *randomized response technique (RRT)*. The technique uses statistics beyond the level of this book, but the basic idea is to use known probabilities to estimate unknown proportions. Here is how RRT works. An interviewer gives the respondent two questions: One is threatening (e.g., "Do you use heroin?"), the other not threatening (e.g., "Were you born in September?"). A random method (e.g., toss of coin) is used to select the question to answer. The interviewer does not see which question was chosen but records the respondent's answer. The researcher uses knowledge about the probability of the random outcome and the frequency of the nonthreatening behavior to estimate the frequency of the sensitive behavior. Researchers have found, for instance, that for measuring self-reported tax cheating, "the results were promising for the randomized response relative to the locked-box method. Perceived anonymity was higher and admission of tax cheating was consistently higher" (Boruch, 1989:343).

Knowledge Questions. Studies suggest that a large majority of the public cannot correctly answer elementary geography questions or identify important political documents (e.g., the Declaration of Independence). Researchers sometimes want to find out whether respondents know about an issue or topic, but knowledge questions can be threatening because respondents do not want to appear ignorant.[15]

Surveys may measure opinions better if they first ask about factual information, because many people have inaccurate factual knowledge. For example, Nadeau and colleagues (1993) found that most Americans seriously overestimate the percent of racial minorities in the population. Only 15 percent of U.S. adults accurately report (plus or minus 6 percent) that 12.1 percent of the U.S. population is African American. Over half believe it is above 30 percent. Similarly, Jews make up about 3 percent of the U.S. population, but a majority (60 percent) of Americans believe the proportion to be 10 percent.

Other studies have shown that many Americans have little factual knowledge about criminal sentencing. Donziger (1996:59) has addressed this issue in detail:

> Consider the following polling question, which for years has been used to gauge public attitudes toward sentencing: "Are sentences too harsh, about right or not harsh enough?" Most people consistently respond to this question by saying that sentences are not harsh enough. . . .
>
> This interpretation of the polling data fails to consider three additional findings from more in-depth polls. First, when answering a question like this, most of us automatically think of violent offenders who have criminal histories. Second, the public has little idea of the actual severity of sentencing practices. Most of us underestimate the length of sentences for crimes, especially for non-violent offenders. Finally, this question fails to take into account limited public awareness of punishments other than prison—punishments that are often more effective at preventing crime and less costly to implement.

First, a researcher pilot tests questions so that questions are at an appropriate level of difficulty. Little is gained if 99 percent of respondents cannot answer the question. Knowledge questions can be worded so that respondents feel comfortable saying they do not know the answer—for example, "How much, if anything, have you heard about. . . ."

Respondents may overstate their knowledge or recognition of people or events. One way to check this is to use a *sleeper question*—a question or response choice about which a respondent could not possibly know. For example, in a study to assess public support for alternatives to incarceration, the researcher may decide to list a fictitious alternative (e.g., the "trying harder" alternative). If, say, 15 percent of the respondents said they knew of this alternative, then the researcher can assume that knowledge about actual alternatives have been likewise overstated.

Skip or Contingency Questions. Researchers avoid asking questions that are irrelevant for a respondent. Yet, some questions apply only to specific respondents. A *contingency question* is a two- (or more) part question.[16] The answer to

the first part of the question determines which of two different questions a respondent next receives. Contingency questions select respondents for whom a second question is relevant. Sometimes they are called *screen* or *skip questions*. On the basis of the answer to a first question, the respondent or an interviewer is instructed to go to another or to skip certain questions. The following set of contingency questions could be used to explore the dynamics of crime reporting:

Q84. Did you report this crime to the police?
___ Yes
___ No (If "no," skip to Q87.)
___ Don't know

Q85. When you reported the crime to the police, were they
___ Very helpful
___ Somewhat helpful
___ Not very helpful
___ Not helpful at all
___ Don't know

Q86. Did the police ever catch the criminal and bring him or her to justice?
___ No
___ Yes
___ Don't know

Q87. Why didn't you report this crime to the police? Was it because you
___ Didn't think the police would do any- thing
___ Didn't want to get involved with the police
___ Thought the person who committed the crime might hurt you if reported
___ Didn't want the person arrested
___ Didn't think the crime was serious
___ Other (_____)
___ Don't know

Open versus Closed Questions

There has been a long debate about open versus closed questions in survey research.[17] An *open-ended* (unstructured, free response) *question* asks a question to which respondents can give any answer (e.g., "What was the most serious crime committed against you in the last year?"). A *closed-ended* (structured, fixed response) *question* both asks a question and gives the respondent fixed responses from which to choose (e.g., "In your opinion, during the past 12 months have ille-

gal drugs (1) become a bigger problem, (2) stayed about the same, (3) become less of a problem, or (4) don't know?").

Each form has advantages and disadvantages (see Box 10.3). The crucial issue is not which form is best. Rather, it is under what conditions a form is most appropriate. A researcher's

---

Box 10.3 _____

Closed versus Open Questions

ADVANTAGES OF CLOSED

- It is easier and quicker for respondents to answer.
- The answers of different respondents are easier to compare.
- Answers are easier to code and statistically analyze.
- The response choices can clarify question meaning for respondents.
- Respondents are more likely to answer about sensitive topics.
- There are fewer irrelevant or confused answers to questions.
- Less articulate or less literate respondents are not at a disadvantage.
- Replication is easier.

DISADVANTAGES OF CLOSED

- They can suggest ideas that the respondent would not otherwise have.
- Respondents with no opinion or no knowledge can answer anyway.
- Respondents can be frustrated because their desired answer is not a choice.
- It is confusing if many (e.g., 20) response choices are offered.
- Misinterpretation of a question can go unnoticed.
- Distinctions between respondent answers may be blurred.
- Clerical mistakes or marking the wrong response is possible.
- They force respondents to give simplistic responses to complex issues.
- They force people to make choices they would not make in the real world.

ADVANTAGES OF OPEN

- They permit an unlimited number of possible answers.
- Respondents can answer in detail and can qualify and clarify responses.
- Unanticipated findings can be discovered.
- They permit adequate answers to complex issues.
- They permit creativity, self-expression, and richness of detail.
- They reveal a respondent's logic, thinking process, and frame of reference.

DISADVANTAGES OF OPEN

- Different respondents give different degrees of detail in answers.
- Responses may be irrelevant or buried in useless detail.
- Comparisons and statistical analysis become very difficult.
- Coding responses is difficult.
- Articulate and highly literate respondents have an advantage.
- Questions may be too general for respondents who lose direction.
- Responses are written verbatim, which is difficult for interviewers.
- A greater amount of respondent time, thought, and effort is necessary.
- Respondents can be intimidated by questions.
- Answers take up a lot of space in the questionnaire.

choice to use an open- or closed-ended question depends on the purpose and the practical limitations of a research project. The demands of using open-ended questions, with interviewers writing verbatim answers followed by time-consuming coding, may make them impractical for a specific project.

Large-scale surveys have closed-ended questions because they are quicker and easier for both respondents and researchers. Yet, something important may be lost when an individual's beliefs and feelings are forced into a few fixed categories that a researcher created. To learn how a respondent thinks, to discover what is really important to him or her, or to get an answer to a question with many possible answers (e.g., age), open questions may be best. In addition, sensitive topics may be more accurately measured with closed questions.

The disadvantages of a question form can be reduced by mixing open-ended and closed-ended questions in a questionnaire. Mixing them also offers a change of pace and helps interviewers establish rapport. Periodic probes (i.e., follow-up questions by interviewers) with closed-ended questions can reveal a respondent's reasoning. Researchers also use *partially open questions* (i.e., a set of fixed choices with a final open choice of "other"), which allows respondents to offer an answer that the researcher did not include.

A total reliance on closed questions can distort results. For example, a study compared open and closed versions of the question, "What is the major problem facing the nation?" Respondents ranked different problems as most important depending on the form of the question. As Schuman and Presser (1979:86) reported, "Almost all respondents work within the substantive framework of the priorities provided by the investigators, *whether or not it fits their own priorities*" (emphasis added). In another study, respondents were asked open and closed questions about what was important in a job. Half of the respondents who answered the open-ended version gave answers that were outside closed-question responses.

Open-ended questions are especially valuable in early or exploratory stages of research. For large-scale surveys, researchers use open questions in pilot tests, then develop closed-question responses from the answers given to the open questions. Glock (1987:50) noted:

> *A major source of data in survey research is the qualitative interview conducted during the planning phases of a project. Such interviews, with a small but roughly representative sample of the population to be surveyed subsequently, afford an indispensable way to learn about the nature of variation and how to go about operationalizing it.*

Researchers writing closed questions have to make many decisions. How many response choices should be given? Should they offer a middle or neutral choice? What should be the order of responses? What types of response choices? How will the direction of a response be measured?

Answers to these questions are not easy. For example, two response choices are too few, but more than five response choices are rarely a benefit. Researchers want to measure meaningful distinctions and not collapse them. More specific responses yield more information, but too many specifics create confusion. For example, rephrasing the question, "Are you satisfied with your local police department?" (which has a yes/no answer) to "How satisfied are you with your local police department—very satisfied, somewhat satisfied, somewhat dissatisfied, or not satisfied at all?" gives the researcher more information and a respondent more choices.

Nonattitudes and the Middle Positions. Survey researchers debate whether to include choices for neutral, middle, and nonattitudes (e.g., "not sure," "don't know," or "no opinion").[18] Two types of errors can be made: accepting a middle choice or "no attitude" response when respondents hold a nonneutral opinion, or forcing respondents to choose a position on an issue when they have no opinion about it. Researchers also try to avoid both false positives (falsely stating an opinion when one does not know) and false negatives (falsely stating "don't know" when one has an opinion) with more attention given to false positives (Gilljam and Granberg, 1993).

Many fear that respondents will chose nonattitude choices to evade making a choice. Yet, it is usually best to offer a nonattitude choice, because people will express opinions on fictitious issues, objects, and events. By offering a nonattitude (middle or no opinion) choice, researchers identify those holding middle positions or those without opinions.

The issue of nonattitudes can be approached by distinguishing among three kinds of attitude questions: standard-format, quasi-filter, and full-filter questions (see Box 10.4). The *standard-format question* does not offer a "don't know" choice; a respondent must volunteer it. A *quasi-filter question* offers respondents a "don't know" alternative. A *full-filter question* is a special type of contingency question. It first asks if respondents have an opinion, then asks for the opinion of those who state that they do have an opinion.

Many respondents will answer a question if a "no opinion" choice is missing, but they will choose "don't know" when it is offered, or say that they do not have an opinion if asked. Such respondents are called *floaters* because they "float" from giving a response to not knowing. Their responses are affected by minor wording changes, so researchers screen them out using quasi-filter or full-filter questions. Filtered questions do not eliminate all answers to nonexistent issues, but they reduce the problem.

Box 10.4_____

Standard-Format, Quasi-Filter, and Full-Filter Questions

STANDARD FORMAT

Q106. Do you support or not the U.S. program to spray marijuana crops in Belize?

QUASI-FILTER

Q106. Do you support, oppose, or have no opinion on the U.S. program to spray marijuana crops in Belize?

FULL FILTER

Q106. Not everyone has an opinion about the U.S. program to spray marijuana crops in Belize. Do you have an opinion on this or not? [For those answering yes only]

Q107. How strongly do you support or oppose the U.S. program to spray marijuana crops in Belize?

☐ Strongly support ☐ Support ☐ Oppose ☐ Strongly oppose

Example of Results from Different Question Forms

	Standard Form (%)	Quasi-Filter (%)	Full Filter (%)
Support	48.2	27.7	22.9
Oppose	38.2	29.5	20.9
No opinion	13.6*	42.8	56.3

* Volunteered

Middle alternative floaters chose a middle position when it is offered, or another alternative if it is not. They have less intense feelings about an issue. There is also a slight *recency effect;* that is, respondents are more likely to choose the last alternative offered. The recency effect suggests that it is best to present responses on a continuum, with the middle or neutral position stated in the middle.

Researchers have two choices: offering a middle position for those who are truly ambiguous or moderate, or omitting the middle choice and forcing respondents to choose a position but following it immediately with a question asking how strongly they feel about the choice. This latter choice is preferred because attitudes have two aspects: direction (for or against) and intensity (strongly held or weakly held). For example, two respondents may both support U.S. marijuana eradication programs in Belize, Central America. But one may hold the opinion more fiercely and be more committed than the other. This involves intensity of attitude.

Agree/Disagree, Rankings or Ratings?   Survey researchers who measure values and attitudes have debated two issues about the responses offered.[19] Should questionnaire items make a statement and ask respondents whether they agree or disagree with it, or should it offer respondents specific alternatives? Should the questionnaire include a set of items and ask respondents to rate them (e.g., approve, disapprove), or should it give them a list of items and force them to rank-order items (e.g., from most favored to least favored)?

It is best to offer respondents explicit alternatives. For example, instead of asking, "Do you agree or disagree with the statement, 'Men are better suited to . . . ,' " ask, "Do you think men are better suited, women are better suited, or both are equally suited?" Less well educated respondents are more likely to agree with a statement, whereas forced-choice alternatives encourage thought and avoid the *response set* bias—a tendency of some respondents to agree and not really decide.

Researchers create bias if question wording gives respondents a reason for choosing one alternative. For example, respondents were asked whether they supported or opposed a law on energy conservation. The results changed when respondents heard, "Do you support the law or do you oppose it because the law would be difficult to enforce?" instead of simply, "Do you support or oppose the law?"

It is better to ask respondents to choose among alternatives by ranking instead of rating items along an imaginary continuum (see Figure 10.3). Respondents can rate several items equally high but will place them in a hierarchy if asked to rank them.[20]

Schwarz and associates (1991) found that respondents use the numbers assigned to response scales as a clue to how to think about a survey question. They suggest that researchers attach positive and negative numbers to response categories (e.g., −5 to +5) only when they conceptualize a variable in clear bipolar terms and use positive numbers (e.g., 0 to 10) when they con-

FIGURE 10.3   Public Confidence in Selected Institutions

"I am going to read you a list of institutions in American society. Would you tell me how much respect and confidence you, yourself, have in each one: a great deal, quite a lot, some, or very little?"

Institution	Percent with "A Great Deal" or "Quite a Lot"
Military	64
Police	58
Presidency	45
Supreme Court	44
Banks	43
Public schools	40
Television news	33
Organized labor	26
Congress	21
Big business	21
Criminal justice system	20

Source: Adapted from Johnson (1997).

ceptualize it along a single continuum. Both positive and negative numbers may be appropriate for a question such as, "How do you feel about the U.S program to spray marijuana plants in Belize?" but positive numbers alone may be better for a question such as, "How successful would you say that program is?"

Wording Issues

Survey researchers face two wording issues. The first, discussed earlier, is to use simple vocabulary and grammar to minimize confusion. The second issue involves effects of specific words or phrases. It is trickier because it is not possible to know in advance whether a word or phrase affects responses.[21]

The well-documented difference between *forbid* and *not allow* illustrates the problem of wording differences. Both terms have the same meaning, but many more people are willing to "not allow" something than to "forbid" it. In general, less well educated respondents are most influenced by minor wording differences.

Certain words seem to trigger an emotional reaction, and researchers are just beginning to learn of them. For example, Smith (1987) found large differences (e.g., twice as much support) in U.S. survey responses depending on whether a question asked about spending "to help the poor" or "for welfare." He suggested that the word *welfare* has such strong negative connotations for Americans (lazy people, wasteful and expensive programs, etc.) that it is best to avoid it.

Possible *wording effects* are illustrated by what appears to be a noncontroversial question. Peterson (1984) examined four ways to ask about age: "How old are you?" "What is your age?" "In what year were you born?" and "Are you . . . 18–24, 25–34, . . . ?" He checked responses against birth certificate records and found that from 98.7 to 95.1 percent of respondents gave correct responses depending on the form of question used. He also found that the form of question that had the fewest errors had the highest percentage of refusals to answer, and the form with the most errors had the lowest refusal rate. This example

suggests that errors in a noncontroversial factual question vary with minor wording changes and that increasing the respondent's willingness to answer may increase errors in responses.

Many respondents are confused by words or their connotations. For example, respondents were asked whether they thought television news was impartial. Researchers later learned that large numbers of respondents had ignored the word *impartial*—a term the middle-class, educated researchers assumed everyone would know. Less than half the respondents had interpreted the word as intended with its proper meaning. Over one-fourth ignored it or had no idea of its meaning. Others gave it unusual meanings, and one-tenth thought it was directly opposite to its true meaning (Foddy, 1993). Presser (1990) found that wording effects in surveys may not change over time. He compared the impact of filter-form questions, wording changes (e.g., *forbid* versus *not allow*), and open versus closed answers in 1976 and 1986. He found that, overall, answers changed during the decade, but the difference between question forms stayed the same. For example, in 1976, 59 percent of Americans said the government is too powerful in a standard-form question and 50 percent in a filter-form question. In 1986, it was 50 percent for the standard form and 40 percent for the filter form.

Questionnaire Design Issues

Length of Survey or Questionnaire. How long should a questionnaire be or an interview last?[22] Researchers prefer long questionnaires or interviews because they are more cost effective. The cost for extra questions—once a respondent has been sampled, has been contacted, and has completed other questions—is small. There is no absolute proper length. The length depends on the survey format (to be discussed) and on the respondent's characteristics. A 10-minute telephone interview is rarely a problem and can usually be extended to 20 minutes. A few researchers stretched this to beyond 30 minutes. Mail questionnaires are more variable. A short (3- or 4-page) questionnaire is appropriate for the general population. Some researchers have had success with questionnaires as long as 10 pages (about 100 items) with the general public, but responses drop significantly for longer questionnaires. For highly educated respondents and a salient topic, using questionnaires of 15 pages may be possible. Face-to-face interviews lasting an hour are not uncommon. In special situations, face-to-face interviews as long as three to five hours have been conducted.

Question Order or Sequence. A survey researcher faces two question sequence issues.[23] The first is how to organize items in the overall questionnaire. The second involves context effects of answering specific questions before others.

In general, you should sequence questions to minimize the discomfort and confusion of respondents. A questionnaire has opening, middle, and ending questions. After an introduction explaining the survey, it is best to make opening questions pleasant, interesting, and easy to answer so that they help a respondent to feel comfortable about the questionnaire. Avoid asking many boring background questions or threatening questions first. Organize questions in the middle into common topics. Mixing questions on different topics causes confusion. Orient respondents by placing questions on the same topic together and introduce the section with a short introductory statement (e.g., "Now I would like to ask you questions about your attitude toward police"). Make question topics flow smoothly and logically, and organize them to assist respondents' memory or comfort levels. Do not end with highly threatening questions, and always end with a "thank you."

Researchers are concerned that the order in which questions are presented may influence respondents' answers. These *order effects* are strongest for respondents who lack strong opinions or who are less well educated. They use previous questions as a context to help them answer later questions. You can do two things about specific question order effects: Use a *funnel sequence* of questions—that is, ask more general

questions before specific ones (e.g., ask about crime in general before asking about specific types of crime). Or, divide the number of respondents in half and give half the questions in one order and the other half the alternative order, then examine the results to see whether question order mattered. If question order effects are found, which order tells you what the respondents really think? The answer is that you cannot know for sure.

For example, a few years ago, the authors' students conducted a telephone survey on two topics: concern about crime and attitudes toward a new antidrunk driving law. A random half of the respondents heard questions about the drunk-driving law first; the other half heard about crime first. The results were examined to see whether there was any *context effect*—a difference by topic order. The respondents who were asked about the drunk-driving law first expressed less fear about crime than did those who were asked about crime first. Likewise, they were more supportive of the drunk-driving law than were those who first heard about crime. The first topic created a context within which respondents answered questions on the second topic. After they were asked about crime in general and thought about violent crime, drunk driving may have appeared to be a less important issue. By contrast, after they were asked about drunk driving and thought about drunk driving as a crime, they may have expressed less concern about crime in general.

Nonresponse, Refusals, and Response Rates. Have you ever refused to answer a survey? The likelihood that people will agree to a request to complete a questionnaire varies for different types of contact. Charities expect a 1 percent response rate, whereas the census expects a 95 percent rate. Response rates are a big concern in survey research. If a high proportion of the sampled respondents do not respond, researchers become cautious about generalizing from the results. If the nonresponders differ from those who respond (e.g., are less educated), low response rates can create bias and weaken validity.

Failure to get a response from a sampled respondent can take several forms: The respondent could not be contacted, he or she was contacted but was unable to complete the survey (e.g., spoke another language, had no time, was ill, etc.), he or she refused to complete a questionnaire or refused to be interviewed, or he or she refused to answer some questions.[24]

One report notes that as many as 38 percent of Americans refuse to participate in surveys. This is a disturbing trend for survey researchers. It is due to many factors—a fear of strangers and crime, social isolation, an overload of surveys, and, most important,

> *people who refuse to participate in surveys appear to be more negative about surveys in general, more withdrawn and isolated from their environment and more concerned about maintaining their privacy free of any intrusion by strangers. (Sudman and Bradburn, 1983:11)*

In addition to privacy concerns, an unfavorable past experience with surveys is a major cause of nonresponse. Legitimate survey research is impeded by misused survey techniques, insensitive interviewers, poorly designed or written questionnaires, and inadequate explanations of surveys to respondents.

Comparative criminologists must hope that the trend toward less public participation in survey research evident in the United States since the 1950s does not spread to other countries.[25] Evidence of higher rates of nonresponse for ethnic minorities and others has already begun to appear in the scholarly literature (see Box 10.5).

Survey researchers disagree about what constitutes an adequate response rate. *Adequate* is a judgment call that depends on the population, practical limitations, the topic, and the response with which specific researchers feel comfortable. Most researchers consider anything below 50 percent to be poor and over 90 percent as excellent.

If response rates are below 75 percent, the survey results can differ significantly from what they would be if everyone responded. For example, a survey reports that a majority of respondents support crime policy, when in fact a majority of the population actually oppose it. This is likely when the response rate is low and those who do not respond have different views from those who do.

To complicate matters, researchers calculate response rates in different ways. The same survey can have a 50 to 75 percent rate depending on the formula used. For example, response rates for telephone or face-to-face interviews are usually based on the percentage responding of the number who were located and contacted, not of the number who were sampled.

Response rates for self-administered questionnaires (e.g., those distributed to a class) are close to 100 percent and present little problem. Rates are high for face-to-face interviews (about 90 percent), followed by telephone interviews (about 80 percent). Response rates are a major concern for mail questionnaires. A response rate of 10 to 50 percent is common for a mail survey.

A researcher can increase response rates in several ways. In telephone interview surveys, interviewers can make five callbacks before dropping a respondent. They can keep a record of each call so that they do not always call back at the

---

Box 10.5

Victimization Rates of Dutch and Non-Dutch Residents in 1992

	Dutch (%) (N = 4,341)	Non-Dutch (%) (N = 107)*
Bicycle theft	5.9	12.0
Theft from car	3.7	5.7
Theft of car	3.7	8.1
Theft of purse	2.5	4.4
Burglary	2.8	7.2
Total rate	34.8	47.4

* The low number of non-Dutch respondents is related to a high level of nonresponse among minority members.
Source: Adapted from Junger-Tas (1997).

same time. Ideal times to call vary, but from 6:00 through 9:00 P.M. on Sunday through Thursday is usually a good period of time.

Even with several callbacks, noncontact rates of 20 percent are common. Once interviewers contact a respondent, he or she must be persuaded to cooperate. Refusal rates for telephone interviews are often about 20 percent. Although it is impossible with random digit dialing, cooperation rates on telephone interviews are usually higher if the researcher sends a letter three to five days in advance telling the respondent to expect the interview call. Interviewers give their name, the organization conducting the survey, the general topic of the survey, and the approximate amount of time the interview will take.

Face-to-face interviewers first have the task of locating a respondent. An advance letter or telephone call to arrange an appointment is wise, but repeat visits may be necessary. Even with an appointment, respondents may hesitate or refuse. Interviewers should have a photo identification card and should explain who is interviewing the respondent and why. Once a respondent is contacted and a well-trained, pleasant interviewer is at the doorstep, most respondents cooperate.

Getting survey responses from some populations, such as low-income, inner-city minorities, poses a special challenge. Pottick and Lerman (1991) used a journalistic-style letter introducing the survey and a personal telephone call reminding respondents of an interview. They compared this approach with a standard method using an academic-style letter and a follow-up letter. Their approach produced a more rapid response and more respondents. For example, their technique resulted in 65 pecent participation, compared to 39 percent for the standard method. Their approach also brought in respondents who were more generally pessimistic and those who felt less well understood by government and social service agencies.

There is a large body of literature on ways to increase response rates for mail questionnaires (see Box 10.6).[26] Heberlein and Baumgartner (1978) reported 71 factors affecting mail questionnaire response rates.

Box 10.6

Ten Ways to Increase Mail Questionnaire Response

1. Address the questionnaire to a specific person, not "Occupant," and send it first class.
2. Include a carefully written, dated cover letter on letterhead stationery. In it, request respondent cooperation, guarantee confidentiality, explain the purpose of the survey, and give the researcher's name and phone number.
3. *Always* include a postage-paid, addressed return envelope.
4. The questionnaire should have a neat, attractive layout and reasonable page length.
5. The questionnaire should be professionally printed and easy to read, with clear instructions.
6. Send two follow-up reminder letters to those not responding. The first should arrive about one week after sending the questionnaire, the second a week later. Gently ask for cooperation again and offer to send another questionnaire.
7. Do not send questionnaires during major holiday periods.
8. Do not put questions on the back page. Instead, leave a blank space and ask the respondent for general comments.
9. Sponsors that are local and are seen as legitimate (e.g., government agencies, universities, large firms, etc.) get a better response.
10. Include a small monetary inducement ($1) if possible.

A meta-analysis of 115 articles on mail survey responses taken from 25 journals published between 1940 and 1988 revealed that cover letters, questionnaires of four pages or less, a return envelope with postage, and a small monetary reward all increase returns (Yammarino et al., 1991). Many of the techniques suggested follow the Total Design Method (to be discussed) and help to make the task easy as well as interesting for respondents.

Format and Layout. There are two format or layout issues: the overall physical layout of the questionnaire and the format of questions and responses.

Questionnaire Layout.   Layout is important, whether a questionnaire is for an interviewer or for the respondent.[27] Questionnaires should be clear, neat, and easy to follow. Give each question a number and put identifying information (e.g., name of organization) on questionnaires. Never cramp questions together or create a confusing appearance. A few cents saved in postage or printing will ultimately cost more in terms of lower validity due to a lower response rate or of confusion of interviewers and respondents. Make a *cover sheet* or face sheet for each interview, for administrative use. Put the time and date of interview, the interviewer, the respondent identification number, and the interviewer's comments and observations on it. A professional appearance with high-quality graphics, space between questions, and good layout improves accuracy and completeness and helps the questionnaire flow.

Give interviewers or respondents instructions on the questionnaire. Print instructions in a different style from the questions (e.g., in a different color or font or in all capitals) to distinguish them. This is important for interview surveys so that an interviewer can distinguish between questions for respondents and instructions intended for the interviewer alone.

Layout is crucial for mail questionnaires because there is no friendly interviewer to interact with the respondent. Instead, the questionnaire's appearance persuades the respondent. In mail surveys, include a polite, professional cover letter on letterhead stationery, identifying the researcher and offering a telephone number for questions. Details matter. Respondents will be turned off if they receive a bulky brown envelope with bulk postage addressed to Occupant or if the questionnaire does not fit into the return envelope. Always end with "Thank you for your participation." Interviewers and questionnaires should leave respondents with a positive feeling about the survey and a sense that their participation is appreciated.

Question Format.   Survey researchers decide on a format for questions and responses. Should respondents circle responses, check boxes, fill in dots, or put an × in a blank? The principle is to make responses unambiguous. Boxes or brackets to be checked and numbers to be circled are usually clearest. As mentioned before, use arrows and instructions for contingency questions. Visual aids are also helpful. For example, hand out thermometer-like drawings to respondents when asking about how warm or cool they feel toward someone. A *matrix question* (or grid question) is a compact way to present a series of questions using the same response categories (see Box 10.7). It saves space and makes it easier for the respondent or interviewer to note answers for the same response categories.

Sanchez (1992) examined the effect of two questionnaire layouts on questions about religion asked by experienced interviewers. She found that a clearer layout reduced "not ascertained" responses from 8.8 to 2.04 percent. In addition, when she changed the format for a contingency question to make it clearer, the percentage of interviewers who probed for specific religious denomination increased from about 91 percent to over 99 percent.

Total Design Method.   Dillman (1978) developed the *total design method (TDM)* to improve mail and telephone surveys. The method has both theoretical and practical parts. The theory says that a survey is a social interaction in which respondents act on the basis of what they expect to receive in exchange for their cooperation. They cooperate when social costs are low, when the expected benefit exceeds the perceived costs, and when researchers create a feeling of trust. The practical part repeats the advice given here about good question wording and questionnaire design. Thus, a good survey design has pilot tests, minimizes personal costs to respondents, and requires minimal effort and time from respondents. It creates intangible rewards, such as a feeling of doing something of value or being important. It also builds trust between the respondent and the interviewer or survey organization through a profes-

Box 10.7 _____

Example of a Matrix Question

SECTION I: ANTIDRUG OPTIONS IN BELIZE, CENTRAL AMERICA

I would like to ask you some questions concerning what you think should be done about the drug problem. Do you think it is *Very Important, Somewhat Important, Not Very Important,* or *Not at All Important* to do the following:

	Very Important	Somewhat Important	Not Very Important	Not at All Important	Don't Know
Q94. Increase the number of Belize police to patrol and arrest drug dealers in your area of town.	☐	☐	☐	☐	☐
Q95. Use undercover intelligence to penetrate financial networks of money launderers.	☐	☐	☐	☐	☐
Q96. Give the Belize police greater power to stop and search people suspected of dealing drugs.	☐	☐	☐	☐	☐
Q97. Have the U.S. military train Belizean paramilitary police units.	☐	☐	☐	☐	☐
Q98. Have the Government of Belize (GOB) provide cover for Central Intelligence Agency (CIA) operations in Central America.	☐	☐	☐	☐	☐

Source: Adapted from Wiegand and Bennett (1993).

---

sional-looking questionnaire, evidence of a legitimate sponsor, and return postage in advance.

TYPES OF SURVEYS: ADVANTAGES AND DISADVANTAGES

Mail and Self-Administered Questionnaires

Advantages. Researchers can give questionnaires directly to respondents or mail them to respondents who read instructions and questions, then record their answers. This type of survey is by far the cheapest, and it can be conducted by a single researcher. A researcher can send questionnaires to a wide geographical area. The respondent can complete the questionnaire when it is convenient and can check personal records if necessary. Mail questionnaires offer anonymity and avoid interviewer bias. They are very effective, and response rates may be high for a target population that is well educated or that has a strong interest in the topic or the survey organization.

Disadvantages. Since people do not always complete and return questionnaires, the biggest problem with mail questionnaires is a low response rate. Most questionnaires are returned within two weeks, but others trickle in up to two months later. Researchers can raise response rates by sending nonrespondents reminder letters, but this adds to the time and cost of data collection.

A researcher cannot control the conditions under which a mail questionnaire is completed. A questionnaire completed during a drinking party by a dozen laughing people may be returned along with one filled out by an earnest respondent. Also, no one is present to clarify questions or to probe for more information when respondents give incomplete answers. Someone other than the sampled respondent (e.g., spouse, new resident, etc.) may open the mail and complete the questionnaire without the researcher's knowledge. Different respondents can complete the questionnaire weeks apart or answer questions in a different order than that intended by researchers. Incomplete questionnaires can also be a serious problem.

Researchers cannot visually observe the respondent's reactions to questions, physical characteristics, or the setting. For example, an impoverished 70-year-old White woman living alone on a farm could falsely state that she is a prosperous 40-year-old Asian male doctor living in a nearby town with three children. Such extreme intentional lies are rare, but serious errors can go undetected.

The mail questionnaire format limits the kinds of questions that a researcher can use. Questions requiring visual aids (e.g., look at this picture and tell me what you see), open-ended questions, many contingency questions, and complex questions do poorly in mail questionnaires.

It is particularly important that criminologists conducting comparative survey research take into account the differing levels of literacy around the world. To put it bluntly, questionnaires mailed to an illiterate population are unlikely to be completed correctly and returned. Even those that are completed and returned to the researcher were probably only poorly understood, hence conveying sketchy information at best (see Table 10.1).

Telephone Interviews

Advantages. The telephone interview is a popular survey method because about 95 percent of the population can be reached by telephone. An interviewer calls a respondent (usually at home), asks questions, and records answers. Researchers sample respondents from lists or telephone directories, or use RDD, and can quickly reach many people across long distances. A staff of interviewers can interview 1,500 respondents across a nation within a few days and, with several callbacks, response rates can reach 90 percent. Although this method is more expensive than a mail questionnaire, special reduced long distance phone rates help. In general, the telephone interview is a flexible method with most of the strengths of face-to-face interviews but for about half the cost. Interviewers control the sequence of questions and can use some probes. A specific respondent is chosen and is likely to answer all the questions alone. The researcher knows when the questions were answered and can use contingency questions effectively, especially with computer-assisted telephone interviewing (CATI) (to be discussed).

Disadvantages. Relatively high cost and limited interview length are disadvantages of telephone interviews. In addition, respondents without telephones are impossible to reach, and the call may come at an inconvenient time. The use of an interviewer reduces anonymity and introduces potential interviewer bias. Open-ended questions are difficult to use, and questions requiring visual aids are impossible. Interviewers can only note serious disruptions (e.g., background noise) and respondent tone of voice (e.g., anger or flippancy) or hesitancy.

Face-to-Face Interviews

Advantages. Face-to-face interviews have the highest response rates and permit the longest questionnaires. They have the advantages of the telephone interview, and interviewers also can observe the surroundings and can use nonverbal communication and visual aids. Well-trained interviewers can ask all types of questions, can ask complex questions, and can use extensive probes.

TABLE 10.1   Types of Surveys and Their Features

FEATURES	TYPE OF SURVEY		
	Mail Questionnaire	*Telephone Interview*	*Face-to-Face Interview*
Administrative Issues			
Cost	Cheapest	Moderate	Expensive
Speed	Slowest	Fastest	Slow to moderate
Length (number of questions)	Moderate	Short	Longest
Response rate	Lowest	Moderate	Highest
Research Control			
Probes possible	No	Yes	Yes
Specific respondent	No	Yes	Yes
Question sequence	No	Yes	Yes
Only one respondent	No	Yes	Yes
Visual observation	No	No	Yes
Success with Different Questions			
Visual aids	Limited	None	Yes
Open-ended questions	Limited	Limited	Yes
Contingency questions	Limited	Yes	Yes
Complex questions	Limited	Limited	Yes
Sensitive questions	Some	Some	Some
Sources of Bias			
Social desirability	No	Some	Worse
Interviewer bias	No	Some	Worse
Respondent's reading skill	Yes	No	No

Disadvantages.   High cost is the biggest disadvantage of face-to-face interviews. The training, travel, supervision, and personnel costs for interviews can be high. Interviewer bias is also greatest in face-to-face interviews. The appearance, tone of voice, question wording, and so forth of the interviewer may affect the respondent. In addition, interviewer supervision is less than for telephone interviews, which supervisors monitor by listening in.[28]

Special Situations

Certain situations will require a researcher to survey entire organizations, such as government agencies. For example, recently the U.S. Office of National Drug Control Policy put into place a measurement system to certify the political will of different countries to wage war on illegal drugs. This will necessitate a comparative surveying of law enforcement agencies in source and transit countries. In the phraseology of the U.S. government, the system is "an architecture for assessing the performance of national counterdrug activities" (Office of National Drug Control Policy, 1997:38).

Surveying white-collar elites requires special techniques.[29] Powerful leaders in business, government, and so on are difficult to reach. Assistants may intercept mail questionnaires, and restricted access can present a formidable obstacle to face-to-face or telephone interviewing.

Access is facilitated when a prestigious source calls or sends a letter of introduction. Once the researcher makes an appointment, the researcher, not a hired interviewer, conducts the interviews. Personal interviews with a high percentage of open-ended questions are usually more successful than all closed-ended questions. Confidentiality is a crucial issue and should be guaranteed, since elites often have information that few others do.

The focus group is a special kind of interview situation that is largely nonquantitative.[30] In *focus groups,* a researcher gathers together 6 to 12 people in a room with a moderator to discuss one or more issues for one to two hours. The issue can be a public concern, a product, a television program, a political candidate, or a policy. The moderator introduces issues and ensures that no one person dominates. The moderator is flexible, keeps people on the topic, and encourages discussion. Responses are tape recorded or recorded by a secretary who assists the moderator. The group members should be homogeneous enough to reduce conflict but should not include friends or relatives. Focus groups are useful in exploratory research or to generate new ideas for hypotheses, questionnaire items, and the interpretation of results.

Costs

Professional-quality survey research can be expensive if all costs are considered. The cost varies according to the type of survey used. A simple formula is that for every $1 in cost for mail survey, a telephone interview survey costs about $5 and a face-to-face interview about $15. For example, Dillman (1983) estimated that a 12-page mail survey of 450 respondents costs over $3,000 in 1980 dollars. This estimate is low because the labor to develop and pretest questions and costs associated with data analysis are not included. Groves and Kahn (1979:188–212) estimated the cost of a nationwide, half-hour telephone interview survey of 1,500 respondents at about $40,000 in 1980 dollars. Professional interviewing firms may charge $50 per completed 20-minute interview

just for the telephone call and interviewer time. Backstrom and Hursh-Cesar (1981:42) estimated the full costs for a professional survey project at $60,000 in 1980 dollars. Their project has 20-minute face-to-face interviews of 600 respondents in a nearby area. Most of the costs are personnel related. This is not high for professional research, and a comparable project today would exceed $150,000.

The Belize Crime and Justice Survey mentioned in this chapter involved a cross-sectional random sample of 532 households in Belize City (Wiegand and Bennett, 1993). The sampling frame listed households that were hooked up to the electricity board; the sample size was 532 households. The questionnaire had 107 items and the face-to-face interviews lasted about 30 minutes. Around a dozen student interviewers from the University College of Belize completed the interviews in two weeks. The cost to field the survey was approximately $5,000 in 1990.

INTERVIEWING

The Role of the Interviewer

Interviews to gather information occur in many settings. Employers interview prospective employees, medical personnel interview patients, mental health professionals interview clients, social service workers interview the needy, reporters interview politicians and others, police officers interview witnesses and crime victims, and talk-show hosts interview celebrities (see Box 10.8). Survey research interviewing is a specialized kind of interviewing. As with most interviewing, its goal is to obtain accurate information from another person.[31]

The survey interview is a social relationship. Like other social relationships, it involves social roles, norms, and expectations. The interview is a short-term, secondary social interaction between two strangers with the explicit purpose of one person's obtaining specific information from the other. The social roles are those of the interviewer and the interviewee or respondent. Information is obtained in a structured conversation in which the

Box 10.8 _____

Example of Probes and Recording Full Responses to Closed Questions

Interviewer question: Have you been the victim of a crime in the last six months?

Respondent answer: Well, I'm not quite sure.
  Probe: Please mention it even if you are not sure it is a crime.

Interviewer question: Have you had anything stolen from you in the last six months?

Respondent answer: Not that I can remember.
  Probe: Does this include incidents committed by someone you know?

Record Response to a Closed Question

Interviewer question: On a scale of 1 to 7, how do you feel about capital punishment or the death penalty, where 1 is strongly in favor of the death penalty, and 7 is strongly opposed to it?
(Favor) 1 _ 2 _ 3 _ 4 _ 5 _ 6 _ 7 _ (Oppose)

Respondent's answer: About a 4. I think that all murderers, rapists, and violent criminals should get death, but I don't favor it for minor crimes like stealing a car.

---

interviewer asks prearranged questions and records answers, and the respondent answers. It differs in several ways from ordinary conversation (see Table 10.2).

An important problem for interviewers is that many respondents are unfamilar with the survey respondents' role and "respondents often do not have a clear conception of what is expected of them" (Turner and Martin, 1984:282). As a result, they substitute another role that may affect their responses. Some believe the interview is an intimate conversation or thearpy session, some see it as a bureaucratic exercise in completing forms, some view it as a citizen referendum on policy choices, some view it as a testing situation, and some see it as a form of deceit in which interviewers are trying to trick or entrap respondents (Turner and Martin, 1984:262–269). Even in a well-designed, professional survey, follow-up research found that only about half the respondents understand questions exactly as intended by researchers. Respondents reinterpreted questions to make them applicable to their ideosynactic,

personal situations or to make them easy to answer (Turner and Martin, 1984:282).

The role of interviewers is difficult. They obtain cooperation and build rapport, yet remain neutral and objective. They encroach on the respondents' time and privacy for information that may not directly benefit the respondents. They try to reduce embarrassment, fear, and suspicion so that respondents feel comfortable revealing information. They may explain the nature of survey research or give hints about social roles in an interview. Good interviewers monitor the pace and direction of the social interaction as well as the content of answers and the behavior of respondents.

Survey interviewers are nonjudgmental and do not reveal their opinions, verbally or nonverbally (e.g., by a look of shock). If a respondent asks for an interviewer's opinion, he or she politely redirects the respondent and indicates that such questions are inappropriate. For example, if a respondent asks, "What do you think?" the interviewer may answer, "Here, we are inter-

TABLE 10.2   Differences between a Structured Survey Interview and Ordinary Conversation

ORDINARY CONVERSATION	THE SURVEY INTERVIEW
1. Questions and answers from each participant are relatively equally balanced.	1. Interviewer asks and respondent answers most of the time.
2. There is an open exchange of feelings and opinions.	2. Only the respondent reveals feelings and opinions.
3. Judgments are stated and attempts are made to persuade the other of a particular point of view.	3. Interviewer is nonjudgmental and does not try to change respondent's opinions or beliefs.
4. A person can reveal deep inner feelings to gain sympathy or as a therapeutic release.	4. Interviewer tries to obtain direct answers to specific questions.
5. Ritual responses are common (e.g., "Uh huh," shaking head, "How are you?" "Fine").	5. Interviewer avoids making ritual responses that influence a respondent and also seeks genuine answers, not ritual responses.
6. The participants exchange information and correct the factual errors that they are aware of.	6. Respondent provides almost all information. Interviewer does not correct a respondent's factual errors.
7. Topics rise and fall and either person can introduce new topics. The focus can shift directions or digress to less relevant issues.	7. Interviewer controls the topic, direction, and pace. He or she keeps the respondent "on task," and irrelevant diversions are contained.
8. The emotional tone can shift from humor, to joy, to affection, to sadness, to anger, and so on.	8. Interviewer attempts to maintain a consistently warm but serious and objective tone throughout.
9. People can evade or ignore questions and give flippant or noncommittal answers.	9. Respondent should not evade questions and should give truthful, thoughtful answers.

Source: Adapted from Gorden (1980:19–25) and Sudman and Bradburn (1983:5–10).

ested in what *you* think; what I think doesn't matter." Likewise, if the respondent gives a shocking answer (e.g., "I was arrested three times for beating my infant daughter and burning her with cigarettes"), the interviewer does not show shock, surprise, or disdain but treats the answer in a matter-of-fact manner. He or she helps respondents feel that they can give any truthful answer.

You might ask, "If the survey interviewer must be neutral and objective, why not use a robot or machine?" Machine interviewing has not been very successful because it lacks the human warmth, sense of trust, and rapport that an interviewer creates. An interviewer helps define the situation and ensures that respondents have the information sought, understand what is expected, give relevant answers, are motivated to cooperate, and give serious answers. The interview is a social interaction in which "the

behavior of both interviewer and respondent stems from their attitudes, motives, expectations, and perceptions" (Cannell and Kahn, 1968:538).

Interviewers do more than interview respondents. For example, Moser and Kalton (1972:273) reported that face-to-face interviewers spend only about 35 percent of their time interviewing. About 40 percent is spent in locating the correct respondent, 15 percent in traveling, and 10 percent in studying survey materials and dealing with administrative and recording details.

Stages of an Interview

The interview proceeds through stages, beginning with an introduction and entry. The interviewer gets in the door, shows authorization, and reassures and secures cooperation from the respondent. He or she is prepared for reactions such as,

"How did you pick me?" "What good will this do?" "I don't know about this." "What's this about, anyway?" The interviewer can explain why the specific respondent is interviewed and not a substitute.

The main part of the interview consists of asking questions and recording answers. The interviewer uses the exact wording on the questionnaire—no added or omitted words and no rephrasing. He or she asks all applicable questions in order, without returning to or skipping questions unless the directions specify this. He or she goes at a comfortable pace and gives nondirective feedback to maintain interest.

In addition to asking questions, the interviewer accurately records answers. This is easy for closed-ended questions, where interviewers just mark the correct box. For open-ended questions, the interviewer's job is more difficult. He or she listens carefully, must have legible writing, and must record what is said verbatim without correcting grammar or slang. More important, the interviewer never summarizes or paraphrases because this causes a loss of information or distorts answers. For example, the respondent in a study of the adaptation of war refugees to their host nation might tell the interviewer, "Me too damn scared to leave apartment. Bad trouble in the street with guns; innocent people gettin' killed." The interviewer writes, "Respondent somewhat fears being victimized." Obviously, much valuable data are lost in the process.

The interviewer knows how and when to use probes. A *probe* is a neutral request to clarify an ambiguous answer, to complete an incomplete answer, or to obtain a relevant response. Interviewers recognize an irrelevant or inaccurate answer and use probes as needed.[32] There are many types of probes. A three- to five-second pause is often effective. Nonverbal communication (e.g., tilt of head, raised eyebrows, or eye contact) also works well. The interviewer can repeat the question or repeat the reply and then pause. She or he can ask a neutral question, such as, "Any other reasons?" "Can you tell me more about that?" "How do you mean?" "Could you explain more for me?" (see Box 10.8).

The last stage is the exit, when the interviewer thanks the respondent and leaves. He or she then goes to a quiet, private place to edit the questionnaire and record other details while they are fresh. Other details include the date, time, and place of the interview; a thumbnail sketch of the respondent and interview situation; the respondent's attitude (e.g., serious, angry, or laughing); and any unusual circumstances (e.g., "Telephone rang at question 27 and respondent talked for four minutes before the interview started again"). He or she notes anything disruptive that happened during the interview (e.g., "Teenage son entered room, sat at opposite end, turned on television with the volume loud, and watched a baseball game"). The interviewer also records personal feelings and anything that was suspected (e.g., "Respondent became nervous and fidgeted when questioned about his marriage"). Converse and Schuman (1974) provided colorful examples of face-to-face interviewing events from such sketches.

Training Interviewers

A large-scale survey requires hiring several interviewers.[33] Few people other than professional survey researchers appreciate the difficulty of the interviewer's job. A professional-quality interview requires the careful selection of interviewers and good training. As with any employment situation, adequate pay and good supervision are important for consistent high-quality performance.

Unfortunately, professional interviewing has not always paid well or provided regular employment. In the past, interviewers were largely drawn from a pool of middle-aged women willing to accept irregular part-time work. Good interviewers are pleasant, honest, accurate, mature, responsible, moderately intelligent, stable, and motivated. They have a nonthreatening appearance, have experience with many types of people, and possess poise and tact. If the survey involves interviewing in high-crime areas, interviewers need extra protection. Researchers may consider interviewers' physical appearance, age, race, sex, languages spoken, and even the voice. For example, in a study using trained female telephone interviewers from homogeneous social backgrounds, Oksenberg and colleagues (1986) found fewer refusals for interviewers whose voices had higher pitch and greater pitch variation, and who spoke louder, faster, with clear pronunciation and sounded more pleasant and cheerful.

Researchers train professional interviewers in a one- to two-week training course, which usually includes lectures and reading, observation of expert interviewers, mock interviews in the office and in the field that are recorded and critiqued, many practice interviews, and role playing. The interviewers learn what survey research is about and the role of the interviewer. They become familiar with the questionnaire and the purpose of questions, although not with the answers expected.

Although interviewers largely work alone, researchers use an interviewer supervisor in large-scale surveys with several interviewers. Supervisors are familiar with the area, assist with problems, oversee the interviewers, and ensure that work is completed on time. For telephone interviewing, this includes helping with calls, checking when interviewers arrive and leave, and monitoring interview calls. In face-to-face interviews, supervisors check to find out whether the interview actually took place. This means calling back or sending a confirmation postcard to a sample of respondents. They can also check the response rate and incomplete questionnaires to see whether interviewers are obtaining cooperation, and they may reinterview a small subsample, analyze answers, or observe interviews to see whether interviewers are accurately asking questions and recording answers.

Interviewer Bias

Survey researchers proscribe interviewer behavior to reduce bias. Ideally, the actions of a particular interviewer will not affect how a respondent answers, and responses will not vary from what they would be if asked by any other interviewer. This goes beyond reading each question exactly as worded: "Strictly speaking, interviewer distortion exists whenever there is any deviation from the 'true' response (defined in terms of the purpose of the study) in the response elicited and recorded by the interviewer" (Hyman, 1975:226).

Interview bias falls into six categories:

1. Errors by the respondent—forgetting, embarrassment, misunderstanding, or lying because of the presence of others
2. Unintentional errors or interviewer sloppiness—contacting the wrong respondent, misreading a question, omitting questions, reading questions in the wrong order, recording the wrong answer to a question, or misunderstanding the respondent
3. Intentional subversion by the interviewer—purposeful alteration of answers, omission or rewording of questions, or choice of an alternative respondent
4. Influence due to the interviewer's expectations about a respondent's answers based on the respondent's appearance, living situation, or other answers
5. Failure of an interviewer to probe or to probe properly
6. Influence on the answers due to the interviewer's appearance, tone, attitude, reactions to answers, or comments made outside of the interview schedule

Survey researchers are still learning about the factors that influence survey interviews. They know that interviewer expectations can create significant bias. Interviewers who expect difficult interviews have them, and those who expect certain answers are more likely to get them. Proper interviewer behavior and exact question reading may be difficult, but the issue is larger.

The social setting in which the interview occurs can affect answers, including the presence of other people. For example, students answer differently depending on whether they are asked questions at home or at school (Zane and Matsoukas, 1979). In general, survey researchers do not want others present because they may affect respondent answers. It may not always make a difference, however, especially if the others are small children.[34] For example, Aquilino (1993) found that when a spouse is present, respondents are more likely to indicate that a divorce or separation will make them worse off. Also, wives report greater husband contributions to housework when the husband is present. Respondents are also more likely to report fights and premarital cohabitation if the spouse is present.

The interviewer's race or gender may influence the interview. Bradburn (1983:314) noted:

> *The principal conclusion one draws from the available studies of interviewer-respondent characteristics is that interviewer characteristics which are clearly perceivable by respondents, such as sex and race, may make a substantial difference for attitude questions related to these characteristics.*

An interviewer's race or ethnic group can affect how respondents answer race or ethnic group questions.[35] For example, African Americans express greater closeness to Whites when interviewed by a White as opposed to an African American interviewer. The race of the interviewer may also affect answers to some policy issues, such as support for civil rights leaders and government programs. For instance, Hispanic and White-Anglo respondents in Texas answered questions on bilingualism and Hispanic culture differently depending on whether their telephone interviewer was Hispanic or Anglo (Reese et al., 1986).

Race or ethnicity may affect attitudes and self-reports of behavior because of social distance, power differences, or ingroup/outgroup relations. In general, interviewers of the same race or cultural heritage get more accurate responses to sensitive questions. In a multicultural society, researchers should always record the racial-ethnic heritage of both interviewers and respondents.

Gender may also affect interview responses. For example, Kane and MacAulay (1993) found that male repondents were more likely to support work-related gender equality with a woman interviewer. Female respondents were more likely to support gender-related collective action and group policy stands when with a woman interviewer. If the same question asked by the same interviewer is answered differently by men and women, representative reliability is threatened.

Cultural Meanings and Survey Interviews

Research into survey errors and interview bias has advanced thinking about larger issues of how people create social meaning and achieve cultural understanding.[36] Survey researchers are troubled when the same words have different meanings and implications depending on the social situation, who speaks them, how they are spoken, and the social distance between the speaker and listener. Also, respondents do not always understand the social situation of the survey interview, may misinterpret the nature of survey research, and may seek clues for how to answer in the wording of questions or subtle actions of the interviewer. Moreover, "it is important not to lose sight of the fact that the interview setting is itself distinct from other settings in which attitudes are expressed, and hence we should not expect to find complete congruence between attitudes expressed in interviews and in other social contexts" (Turner and Martin, 1984:276).

Criminologists have found that victimization surveys conducted by the government often differ significantly from victimization surveys conducted by criminologists not associated with the government. Research on victimization of ethnic minorities in Holland, for example, serves as a good example of this (see Box 10.9). A small, nongovernmental survey of victimization among Surinamese, Turks, and Moroccans in Amsterdam and Rotterdam produced considerably different results than did the official victimization survey. Junger-Tas (1997:284–285) commented:

> *The study was meant to provide a "first impression" of minority victimization. About 75 percent of respondents were long-term residents (ten years or more). Two-thirds were men. Education and employment were somewhat above average*

Box 10.9_____

Victimization of Three Ethnic Groups in Amsterdam and Rotterdam in 1992, Compared with General Population Rates

	Surinamese (%) (N = 100)	Turkish (%) (N = 98)	Moroccan (%) (N = 99)	General Population Rate (%)
Total property	66	68	47	43
Bicycle theft	22	28	20	17
Vandalism of car	22	25	12	9
Total violence	14	12	34	9
Physical threats	13	12	11	7
Assault	2	7	29	2

Source: Adapted from Junger-Tas (1997).

for both groups. *Results were compared with the standardized population survey on victimization, fear of crime, and police services—the "politiemonitor"—which is regularly held in most Dutch cities. Comparisons were made with the police monitor's results in Amsterdam and Rotterdam.*

Initially, survey research was based on a "naive assumption model" (Foddy, 1993:13). Researchers try to improve survey research by reducing the gap between actual experience in conducting surveys and the ideal survey expressed as the model's assumptions. The model's assumptions include the following:

1. Researchers have clearly conceptualized all variables being measured.
2. Questionnaires have no wording, question order, or related effects.
3. Respondents are motivated and willing to answer all the questions asked.
4. Respondents possess complete information and can accurately recall events.
5. Respondents understand each question exactly as the researcher intends it.
6. Respondents give more truthful answers if they do not know the hypotheses.
7. Respondents give more truthful answers if they receive no hints or suggestions.
8. The interview situation and specific interviewers have no effects on answers.
9. The process of the interview has no impact on the respondents' beliefs or attitudes.
10. Respondents' behaviors match perfectly their verbal responses in an interview.

Some survey researchers are questioning the assumptions of this model. For example, as an interviewer strives to act in a more neutral and uniform way, he or she reduces the type of bias that causes unreliability because of individual interviewer behavior. Yet, such attempts to reduce bias cause other problems according to interpretive or critical social science researchers (see Box 10.10; also see Devault, 1990).[37] Researchers argue that meaning is created in social context; therefore, standard wording will not produce the same meaning for all respondents. For example, some respondents express their values and feelings by telling stories instead of answering straightforward questions with fixed answers. Standard interviewer behavior may actually lower validity, especially for respondents from

Box 10.10 _____

Interviewing: Positivist and Feminist Approaches

In this chapter you have learned the positivist approach to survey research interviewing. In the ideal survey interview, the interviewer withholds her or his own feelings and beliefs. The interviewer should be so objective and neutral that it should be possible to substitute another interviewer and obtain the same responses.

Feminist researchers approach interviewing very differently. Feminist interviewing is similar to qualitative interviewing (to be discussed in Chapter 14). Oakley (1981) criticized positivist survey interviewing as being part of a masculine paradigm. It is a social situation in which the interviewer exercises control and dominance while suppressing the expression of personal feelings. It is manipulative and instrumental. The interviewer and the respondent become merely the vehicles for obtaining the objective data.

The goals of feminist research vary, but two common goals are to give greater visibility to the subjective experience of women and to increase the involvement of the respondent in the research process. Features of feminist interviewing include the following:

- A preference for an unstructured and open-ended format
- A preference for interviewing a person more than once
- Creation of social connections and building a trusting social relationship
- Disclosure of personal experiences by the interviewer
- Drawing on female skills of being open, receptive, and understanding
- Avoiding control and fostering equality by downplaying professional status
- Exhibiting careful listening, interviewers become emotionally engaged with respondents
- Respondent-oriented direction, not researcher oriented or questionnaire oriented
- Encouragement of respondents to express themselves in ways they are most comfortable—for example, by telling stories or following digressions
- Creation of a sense of empowerment and an esprit de corps among women

---

social groups outside the middle-class world of most survey researchers.

In complex human interaction, people invariably add interpretative meaning to simple questions. The dilemma is that ordinary conversations contain organizational features that are designed to detect and correct misinterpretation and build shared understanding. Many of these very features are controlled in the survey interview situation to ensure that each respondent is treated in a standard way. Standardizing words does not automatically produce standardized meaning. Paradoxically, "the validity of survey data is potentially undermined by the same prohibition against interaction that is intended to ensure reliability" (Suchman and Jordan, 1992:242).

Social meaning does not reside in the words alone. It resides in the social context and interaction among people, and in cultural frames (sometimes divided by gender, race, region, etc.) in which people live. For example, men and women think differently about their health, and they will report the same health status differently (Groves et al., 1992). Does this mean that far more men are in excellent health than women? Even so-called objective categories in survey research, such as race or ethnicity, can vary greatly in how respondents think subjectively and answer (Smith, 1984). Human responses in interviews are more complex and vary more by situations than outlined by the naive assumption model. For example, "Inaccurate reporting is not a response tendency or a predisposition to be untruthful. Individuals who are truthful on one occasion or in response to particular questions may not be truthful at other times or to other questions" (Wentworth, 1993:130).

Given this complexity and possible distortion, what should the diligent survey researcher do? The issues of social meaning suggest that a survey researcher should at least supplement closed-ended questionnaires with open-ended questions and probes. This takes more time, requires better-trained interviewers, and produces responses that may be less standardized and more difficult to quantify. Fixed-answer questionnaires based on the naive assumption model imply a more simple and mechanical way of responding than occurs in many situations. The inquiry into interviewer bias, cultural meanings, and the interview as a social situation provides a lesson in how qualitative and quantitative styles of social research complement one another. As quantitative survey researchers strived to eliminate sources of interviewer bias and respondent confusion, they discovered that qualitative researchers offered valuable insights into how people construct meaning in various social settings.

Computer-Assisted Telephone Interviewing

Advances in computer technology and lower computer prices have enabled many professional survey research organizations to install *computer-assisted telephone interviewing (CATI)* systems.[38] With CATI, the interviewer sits in front of a computer terminal (screen with a keyboard) and manually makes calls or has the computer automatically call. Wearing a headset and microphone, the interviewer reads the questions from a computer screen for the specific respondent who is called, then enters the answer via the keyboard. Once he or she enters an answer, the computer shows the next question on the screen.

CATI speeds interviewing and reduces interviewer errors. It also eliminates the separate step of entering information into a computer and speeds data processing. Of course, CATI requires an investment in computer equipment and some knowledge of computers. CATI is valuable for contingency questions because the computer can show the questions appropriate for a specific respondent; interviewers do not have to turn pages looking for the next question. In addition,

the computer can check an answer immediately after the interviewer enters it. For example, if an interviewer enters an answer that is impossible or clearly an error (e.g., an *H* instead of an *M* for "Male"), the computer will beep and send a message requesting another answer.

The National Crime Victimization Survey uses a CATI technique with about 30 percent of the some 48,000 households sampled in 1994 (Maguire and Pastore, 1997). It employs three levels of CATI usage with "concern toward an optimal workload for the field interviewers" (p. 624). However much these computer programs may speed the more technical aspects of survey research, they cannot substitute for a good understanding of the survey method or an appreciation of its limitations. The researcher must still clearly conceptualize variables, prepare well-worded questions, design the sequence and forms of questions and responses, and pilot test questionnaires. Communicating unambiguously with respondents and eliciting credible responses remain the most important parts of survey research (see Figure 10.4).

FIGURE 10.4   Ten Items to Include When Reporting Survey Research

1. The sampling frame used (e.g., telephone directories)
2. The dates on which the survey was conducted
3. The population that the sample represents (e.g., U.S. adults, Australian college students, etc.)
4. The size of the sample for which information was collected
5. The sampling method (e.g., random)
6. The exact wording of the questions asked
7. The method of the survey (e.g., face to face, telephone, etc.)
8. The organizations that sponsored the survey (paid for it and conducted it)
9. The response rate or percentage of those contacted who actually completed the questionnaire
10. Any missing information or "don't know" responses when results on specific questions are reported

THE ETHICAL SURVEY

Like all social research, people can conduct surveys in ethical or unethical ways. A major ethical issue in survey research is the invasion of privacy.[39] Survey researchers can intrude into a respondent's privacy by asking about intimate actions and personal beliefs. People have a right to privacy. Respondents decide when and to whom to reveal personal information. They are likely to provide such information when it is asked for in a comfortable context with mutual trust, when they believe serious answers are needed for legitimate research purposes, and when they believe answers will remain confidential. Researchers should treat all respondents with dignity and reduce anxiety or discomfort. They are also responsible for protecting the confidentiality of data.

A second issue involves voluntary participation by respondents. Respondents agree to answer questions and can refuse to participate at any time. They give "informed consent" (see Chapter 17) to participate in research. Researchers depend on respondents' voluntary cooperation, so researchers need to ask well-developed questions in a sensitive way, treat respondents with respect, and be very sensitive to confidentiality.

A third ethical issue is the exploitation of surveys and pseudosurveys. Because of its popularity, some people use surveys to mislead others. A *pseudosurvey* is when someone uses the survey format in an attempt to persuade someone to do something and has little or no real interest in learning information from a respondent. Charlatans use the guise of conducting a survey to invade privacy, gain entry into homes, or "suggle" (sell in the guise of a survey). An example of a pseudosurvey occurred in the 1994 U.S. election campaign as "suppression polls." In this situation, an unknown survey organization telephoned a potential voter and asked whether the voter supported a given candidate. If the voter supported the candidate, the interviewer asked whether the respondent would still support the candidate if he or she knew that the candidate had an unfavorable characteristic (e.g., had been arrested for drunk driving, used illegal drugs, raised the wages of convicted criminals in prison, etc.). The goal of the interview was not to measure candidate support; rather, it was to identify a candidate's supporters then attempt to sway them by giving negative information. One of the authors received such a call, as did an unsuccessful candidate for governor who was the object of the suppression poll. No one has been prosecuted for this using campaign tactic.

Another ethical issue is when people misuse survey results or use poorly designed or purposely rigged surveys. People may demand answers from surveys that surveys cannot provide or may not understand a survey's limitations. Those who design and prepare surveys may lack sufficient training to conduct a legitimate survey. Policy decisions made based on careless or poorly designed surveys may result in waste and human hardship. Such misuse makes it important that legitimate researchers conduct methodologically rigorous survey research. Researchers should be aware of and report the limitations of survey results. "It is untenable to confront survey data as if they were error free" (Alwin, 1977:132). Researchers also need to combat unscrupulous politicians, businesspeople, and others who rig surveys to produce deceptive results.

Mass media reporting of survey results and the quality of surveys being reported permits abuse.[40] Few people reading survey results may appreciate it, but researchers should include details about the survey (see Figure 10.4) to reduce the misuse of survey research and increase questions about surveys that lack such information. Survey researchers urge the media to include such information, but it is rarely included. Over 88 percent of reports on surveys in the mass media fail to reveal the researcher who conducted the survey, and only 18 percent provide details on how the survey was conducted (Singer, 1988). This occurs while the media report more surveys than other types of social research.

Currently, there are no quality-control standards to regulate the opinion polls or surveys reported in the U.S. media. Researchers have made unsuccessful attempts since World War II to require adequate samples, interviewer training and supervision, satisfactory questionnaire design, public availability of results, and controls on the integrity of survey organizations (Turner and Martin, 1984:62). As a result, the mass media report both biased and misleading survey results and rigorous, professional survey results without distinction. The media report "the commonly cited margins of error . . . [that] promote overconfidence in survey estimates. These figures commonly account only for sampling variations and do not take into account other sources of variation in survey estimates" (Turner and Martin, 1984:107). It is not surprising that public confusion and a distrust of all surveys occurs.

CONCLUSION

In this chapter, you learned about survey research. Survey research is the most widely used research technique in criminology. It has a long history, but it has undergone dramatic expansion and maturation in the past three decades. You also learned some principles of writing good survey questions. There are many things to avoid and to include when writing questions. You also learned about the advantages and disadvantages of three types of survey research: mail, telephone interviews, and face-to-face interviews. You saw that interviewing, especially face-to-face interviewing, can be difficult.

Although this chapter focused on survey research, researchers use questionnaires to measure variables in other types of quantitative research (e.g., experiments). The survey, often called the sample survey because random sampling is usually used with it, is a distinct technique. It is a process of asking many people the same questions and examining their answers.

The survey is a process in which researchers translate a research problem into questionnaires, then use these with respondents to create data. Survey researchers involve other people—respondents—who answer questions. From the answers, the researcher creates quantitative data that he or she analyzes to address the research problem. Survey researchers try to minimize errors, but survey data often contain them. Errors in surveys can compound each other. For example, errors can arise in sampling frames, from nonresponse, from question wording or order, and from interviewer bias. Do not let the existence of errors discourage you from using the survey, however. Instead, learn to be very careful when designing survey research and cautious about generalizing from the results of surveys.

KEY TERMS

census
closed-ended question
computer-assisted telephone
    interviewing (CATI)
context effect
contingency question
cover sheet
double-barreled question
floaters
focus groups
full-filter question
funnel sequence

interview schedule
matrix question
open-ended question
order effects
partially open question
prestige bias
probe
quasi-filter question
questionnaire
randomized response
    technique (RRT)
recency effect

respondents
response set
sleeper question
social desirability bias
standard-format question
telescoping
threatening questions
total design method (TDM)
wording effects

REVIEW QUESTIONS

1. What are the six types of things surveys often ask about? Give an example of each that is different from the examples in the book.

2. Why are surveys called *correlational,* and how do they differ from experiments?

3. What five changes occurred, beginning in the 1960s, that dramatically affected survey research?

4. Identify 5 of the 10 things to avoid in question writing.

5. What topics are threatening to respondents, and how can a researcher ask about them?

6. What are advantages and disadvantages of open-ended versus closed-ended questions?

7. What are filtered, quasi-filtered, and standard-format questions? How do they relate to floaters?

8. How does ordinary conversation differ from a survey interview?

9. Under what conditions are mail, telephone interviews, or face-to-face interviews best?

10. What is CATI and when might it be useful?

NOTES

1. The use of a strict positivist approach within survey research is a source of criticism by those who adopt an interpretative approach. For such criticism, see Denzin (1989), Mishler (1986), and Phillips (1971). Also see Carr-Hill (1984b) for a similar criticism from the critical social science approach.

2. The history of survey research is discussed in Converse (1987), Hyman (1991), Rossi and colleagues (1983), Marsh (1982:9–47), Miller (1983:19–125), Moser and Kalton (1972:6–15), Sudman (1976b), and Sudman and Bradburn (1987).

3. See Blumer (1991a, 1991b), Blumer and colleagues (1991), Bannister (1987), Camic and Xie (1994), Cohen (1991), Deegan (1988), Ross (1991), Sklar (1991), Turner (1991), and Yeo (1991).

4. See Converse (1987:383–385), *Statistical Abstract of the United States,* and Rossi and colleagues (1983:8).

5. As Hyman (1975:4) remarked, "Let it be noted that the demonstration of error marks an advanced stage of a science. All scientific inquiry is subject to error, and it is far better to be aware of what it is, to study the sources in an attempt to reduce it, and to estimate the magnitudes of errors in our findings, than to be ignorant of errors concealed in the data." Examples of research on survey methodology include Bishop and colleagues

(1983, 1984, 1985), Bradburn (1983), Bradburn and Sudman (1980), Cannell and colleagues (1981), Converse and Presser (1986), Groves and Kahn (1979), Hyman (1991), Schuman and Presser (1981), Sudman and Bradburn (1983), and Tanur (1992).

6. See Rossi and associates (1983:10).

7. See Bayless (1981) on the Research Triangle Institute.

8. For a list of survey organizations, see Bradburn and Sudman (1988).

9. The administration of survey research is discussed in Backstrom and Hursh-Cesar (1981:38–45), Dillman (1978:200–281;1983), Frey (1983:129–169), Groves and Kahn (1979:40–78, 186–212), Prewitt (1983), Tanur (1983), and Warwick and Lininger (1975:20–45, 220–264).

10. Similar lists of prohibitions can be found in Babbie (1990:127–132), Backstrom and Hursh-Cesar (1981: 140–153), Bailey (1987:110–115), Bradburn and Sudman (1988:145–153), Converse and Presser (1986:13–31), deVaus (1986:71–74), Dillman (1978: 95–117), Frey (1983:116–127), Fowler (1984:75–86), Moser and Kalton (1972:318–341), Sheatsley (1983:216–217), Sudman and Bradburn (1983: 132–136), and Warwick and Lininger (1975: 140–148).

11. Sudman and Bradburn (1983:39) suggest that even simple questions (e.g., "What brand of soft drink do you usually buy?") can cause problems. Respondents who are highly loyal to one brand of traditional carbonated sodas can answer the question easily. Other respondents must implicitly address the following questions to answer the question as it was asked: (a) What time period is involved—the past month, the past year, the last 10 years? (b) What conditions count—at home, at restaurants, at sporting events? (c) Buying for oneself alone or for other family members? (d) What is a "soft drink"? Do lemonade, iced tea, mineral water, or fruit juices count? (e) Does "usually" mean a brand purchased as 51 percent or more of all soft drink purchases, or the brand purchased more frequently than any other? Respondents rarely stop and ask for clarification; they make assumptions about what the researcher means.

12. See Abelson and colleagues (1992), Auriat (1993), Bernard and colleagues (1984), Croyle and Loftus (1992), Krosnick and Abelson (1992), Loftus and colleagues 1990), Loftus and colleagues (1992), and Pearson and Dawes (1992).

13. See Bradburn (1983), Bradburn and Sudman (1980), and Sudman and Bradburn (1983) on threatening or sensitive questions. Backstrom and Hursh-Cesar (1981:219) and Warwick and Lininger (1975:150–151) provide useful suggestions as well. See Fox and Tracy (1986) for a discussion on the randomized response technique. Also see DeLamater and MacCorquodale (1975) on measuring sexual behavior with survey research and see Herzberger (1993) for general design issues when examining sensitive topics.

14. See DeMario (1984) and Sudman and Bradburn (1983:59).

15. For a discussion of knowledge questions, see Converse and Presser (1986:24–31), Backstrom and Hursh-Cesar (1981:124–126), Sudman and Bradburn (1983:88–118), and Warwick and Lininger (1975: 158–160).

16. Contingency questions are discussed in Babbie (1990:136–138), Bailey (1987:135–137), de Vaus (1986:78–80), Dillman (1978:144–146), and Sudman and Bradburn (1983:250–251).

17. For a further discussion of open and closed questions, see Bailey (1987:117–122), Converse (1984), Converse and Presser (1986:33–34), de Vaus (1986:74–75), Geer (1988), Moser and Kalton (1972: 341–345), Sudman and Bradburn (1983:149–155), Schuman and Presser (1979; 1981:79–111), and Warwick and Lininger (1975:132–140).

18. For a discussion of the "don't know," "no opinion," and middle positions in response categories, see Backstrom and Hursh-Cesar (1981:148–149), Bishop (1987), Bradburn and Sudman (1988:154), Brody (1986), Converse and Presser (1986:35–37), Duncan and Stenbeck (1988), Poe and associates (1988), and Sudman and Bradburn (1983:140–141). The most extensive discussion is found in Schuman and Presser (1981:113–178). For more on filtered questions, see Bishop and colleagues (1983, 1984) and Bishop and colleagues (1986).

19. The disagree/agree versus specific alternatives debate is discussed in Bradburn and Sudman (1988:149–151), Converse and Presser (1986:38–39), Schuman and Presser (1981:179–223), and Sudman and Bradburn (1983:119–140). Backstrom and Hursh-Cesar (1981:136–140) discuss forms of asking Likert agree/disagree questions.

20. The ranking versus ratings issue is discussed in Alwin and Krosnick (1985), Krosnick and Alwin (1988), and Presser (1984). Also see Backstrom and Hursh-Cesar (1981:132–134) and Sudman and Bradburn (1983:156–165) for formats of asking rating and ranking questions.

21. For a discussion of wording effects in questionnaires, see Bradburn and Miles (1979), Peterson (1984), Schuman and Presser (1981:275–296), Sheatsley (1983), and Smith (1987). Hippler and Schwarz (1986) found the same difference between *forbid* and *not allow* in the Federal Republic of Germany, suggesting that the distinction is not unique to the United States or to the English language.

22. The length of questionnaires is discussed in Dillman (1978:51–57; 1983), Frey (1983:48–49), Herzog and Bachman (1981), and Sudman and Bradburn (1983:226–227).

23. For a discussion of the sequence of questions or question order effects, see Backstrom and Hursh-Cesar (1981:154–176), Bishop and colleagues (1985), Bradburn (1983:302–304), Bradburn and Sudman (1988:153–154), Converse and Presser (1986:39–40), Dillman (1978:218–220), McFarland (1981), McKee and O'Brien (1988), Moser and Kalton (1972:346–347), Schuman and Ludwig (1983), Schuman and Presser (1981:23–74), Schwartz and Hippler (1995), and Sudman and Bradburn (1983:207–226).

24. For additional discussion of nonresponse and refusal rates, see Backstrom and Hursh-Cesar (1981:140–141, 274–275), DeMaio (1980), Frey

(1983:38–41), Groves and Kahn (1979:218–223), Martin (1985:701–706), Nederhof (1986), Oksenberg and colleagues (1986), Schuman and Presser (1981:331–336), Sigelman (1982), Stech (1981), Sudman and Bradburn (1983), and Yu and Cooper (1983). Also see Fowler (1984:46–52) on calculating response rates and bias due to nonresponse. For a discussion of methods for calculating response rates, see Bailey (1987:169), Dillman (1978:49–51), and Frey (1983:38). Bailar and Lanphier (1978:13) noted that improper calculation of response rates is not uncommon, and in a review of surveys found nonresponse rates of 4 to 75 percent.

25. See "Surveys Proliferate, but Answers Dwindle," *New York Times,* October 5, 1990, p. 1, and "Fewer Americans Talking to Research Firms," *Capital Times* (Madison, WI), January 31, 1986, p. 5. Sudman (1976b:114–116) also discusses a growing refusal rate.

26. More extensive discussions of how to increase mail questionnaire return rates can be found in Bailey (1987:153–168), Church (1993), Dillman (1978, 1983), Fox and colleagues (1988), Goyder (1982), Heberlein and Baumgartner (1978, 1981), Hubbard and Little (1988), Jones (1979), and Willimack and colleagues (1995). Bailey (1987) has given a useful summary of experiments on return rates. Dillman (1978) has given practical advice on sending out a mailing, including examples of follow-up letters and instructions on folding letters into envelopes with questionnaires.

27. For a discussion of general format and the physical layout of questionnaires, see Babbie (1990), Backstrom and Hursh-Cesar (1981:187–236), Dillman (1978, 1983), Mayer and Piper (1982), Sudman and Bradburn (1983:229–260), Survey Research Center (1976), and Warwick and Lininger (1975:151–157).

28. For additional discussion of comparing types of surveys, see Backstrom and Hursh-Cesar (1981:16–23), Bradburn and Sudman (1988:94–110), Dillman (1978:39–78), Fowler (1984:61–73), and Frey (1983:27–55). For specific details on telephone interviews, see Blankenship (1977), Frey (1983), and Groves and Kahn (1979).

29. Elite interviewing is discussed in Dexter (1970). Also see Galaskiewicz (1987), Useem (1984), Verba and Orren (1985), and Zuckerman (1972). Also see Chapter 13.

30. For additional discussion of focus groups, see Churchill (1983:179–184), Krueger (1988), and Labaw (1980:54–58).

31. For more on survey research interviewing, see Brenner and associates (1985), Cannell and Kahn (1968), Converse and Schuman (1974), Dijkstra and van der Zouwen (1982), Foddy (1993), Gorden (1980), Hyman (1975), Moser and Kalton (1972:270–302), and Survey Research Center (1976). For a discussion of telephone interviewing in particular, see Frey (1983), Groves and Mathiowetz (1984), Jordan and colleagues (1980), and Tucker (1983).

32. The use of probes is discussed in Backstrom and Hursh-Cesar (1981:266–273), Gorden (1980:368–390), and Hyman (1975:236–241).

33. For a discussion of interviewer training and interview expectations, see Backstrom and Hursh-Cesar (1981:237–307), Billiet and Loosveldt (1988), Bradburn and Sudman (1980), Oksenberg and colleagues (1986), Singer and Kohnke-Aguirre (1979), and Tucker (1983). Sudman (1976b:115) noted that middle-class women are less likely nowadays to want to work as interviewers.

34. See Bradburn and Sudman (1980).

35. The race or ethnicity of interviewers is discussed in Anderson and associates (1988), Cotter and associates (1982), Finkel and associates (1991), Gorden (1980:168–172), Reese and associates (1986), Schaffer (1980), Schuman and Converse (1971), and Weeks and Moore (1981).

36. See Bateson (1984), Clark and Schober (1992), Foddy (1993), Lessler (1984), and Turner (1984).

37. See Briggs (1986), Cicourel (1982), and Mishler (1986) for critiques of survey research interviewing.

38. CATI is discussed in Bailey (1987:201–202), Bradburn and Sudman (1988:100–101), Frey (1983: 24–25, 143–149), Groves and Kahn (1979:226), Groves and Mathiowetz (1984), and Karweit and Meyers (1983). Also see Freeman and Shanks (1983).

39. For a discussion of ethical concerns specific to survey research, see Backstrom and Hursh-Cesar (1981:46–50), Fowler (1984:135–144), Frey (1983:177–185), Kelman (1982:79–81), and Reynolds (1982:48–57). Marsh (1982:125–146) and Miller (1983:47–96) provided useful discussions for and against the use of survey research. The use of informed consent is discussed in Singer and Frankel (1982) and in Sobal (1984).

40. On reporting survey results in the media, see Channels (1993) and MacKeun (1984).

RECOMMENDED READINGS _____

Bradburn, Norman M., and Seymour Sudman. (1988). *Polls and surveys: Understanding what they tell us.* San Francisco: Jossey-Bass. This is an easy-to-read, nontechnical introduction to the variety of polls and surveys. It is less about how to conduct a survey than about what surveys can and cannot tell us. It has an informal style and is written for a lay audience.

Converse, Jean M., and Stanley Presser. (1986). *Survey questions: Handcrafting the standardized questionnaire.* Beverly Hills, CA: Sage. This is a short (74-page) book covering many critical issues in writing questionnaires. It discusses much of the recent research on improving questionnaires in a nontechnical way. It describes the difficult decisions involved in designing questionnaires and has good advice on improving questionnaire writing.

Dillman, Don A. (1978). *Mail and telephone surveys.* New York: Wiley. Although it is now a bit dated, Dillman's book has become a classic in survey research with its discussion of the Total Design Method. It is a comprehensive treatment of mail and telephone surveys. There are many practical hints and suggestions for successful survey research practice.

Fowler, Floyd J., Jr. (1993). *Survey research methods,* 2nd ed. Beverly Hills, CA: Sage. This is a solid, short introduction that summarizes the basics of survey research. It covers the steps in survey research and is a good starting place for the beginning researcher.

Rossi, Peter H., James D. Wright, and Andy B. Anderson (1983). *Handbook of survey research.* New York: Academic. Many of the articles in this book are rather technical for the beginner. Nevertheless, it is a rich source of information on current developments about the full range of survey research methods.

Tanur, Judith M. (Ed.) (1992). *Questions about questions: Inquiries into the cognitive bases of surveys.* New York: Russell Sage Foundation. This excellent collection of 12 articles examines how respondents recall, think, and answer in a survey situation. The articles grapple with the most serious issues in survey interviewing. Theories of how respondents recall and answer, as well as empirical research, are included.

CHAPTER 11

NONREACTIVE RESEARCH AND AVAILABLE DATA

> *In short, the outcome of the current struggle over tobacco is very much in doubt. That makes it all the more urgent for us to analyze the behavior of the cigarette companies and figure out what to do about a product that kills an estimated 473,000 Americans a year.*
> —Michael Massing, "How to Win the Tobacco War," p. 32

INTRODUCTION

To speak about the "behavior of cigarette *companies*" is to suggest an organizational perspective. Quite distinct from individualistic conceptions of crime, this perspective explores the extent to which a corporation or government organization "encourages and in some cases even requires illegal behavior by some of its members" (Coleman, 1998:12). In a sense, an organizational perspective views organizations as humans, capable of forming criminal intent and of behaving illegally.

With respect to the tobacco companies, the organizational crime perspective raises research questions concerning corporate strategies to conceal the truth about nicotine, addiction, and lung cancer from the public, as well as to market tobacco products to minors (Massing, 1996). These questions in turn raise others: Are there criminogenic elements in the cultural structure and processes of the tobacco companies? Are executives and staff socialized in ways that encourage them to turn a "blind eye" to corporate crime? To what extent are tobacco executives, companies, or perhaps the entire industry, criminally liable? And, relatedly, how is corporate crime treated by the mass media? Do the media point blame or excuse it?

Such questions represent the cutting edge of the organizational perspective on crime. They also represent an excellent application of a set of quantitative research techniques collectively referred to as *nonreactive research.*

Experiments and survey research are both *reactive;* that is, the people being studied are aware of that fact. The techniques in this chapter address a limitation of reactive measures. You will learn about four quantitative research techniques that are *nonreactive;* that is, those being studied are not aware that they are part of a research project. Nonreactive techniques are largely based on positivist principles but are also used by interpretive and critical researchers.

The first technique you will learn about is not really a distinct technique but a loose collection of inventive nonreactive measures. It is followed by content analysis, which builds on the fundamentals of quantitative research design and is a well-developed research technique in criminology. Existing statistics and secondary analysis, the last two techniques, refer to the collection of existing information from government documents or previous surveys. Researchers examine the data in new ways to address new questions. Although the data may have been reactive when first collected, a researcher can address new questions without reactive effects.

NONREACTIVE MEASUREMENT

The Logic of Nonreactive Research

Nonreactive measurement begins when a researcher notices something that indicates a variable of interest. The critical thing about nonreactive or *unobtrusive measures* (i.e., measures that are not obtrusive or intrusive) is that the people being studied are not aware of it but leave evidence of their social behavior or actions "naturally." The observant researcher infers from the evidence to behavior or attitudes without disrupting those being studied. Unnoticed observation is also a type of nonreactive measure.

One might notice, for instance, as Hilts (1996) did, that tobacco executives, "normally full of easy confidence, [would] 'bristle defensively, or else fall into silence,' whenever children were mentioned" (as quoted in Massing, 1996:34). An untrained observer, of course, might miss the executive's shift in demeanor, and hence underestimate the connection between young smokers and corporate profits.

Varieties of Nonreactive or Unobtrusive Observation

Nonreactive measures are varied, and researchers have been creative in inventing indirect ways to measure social behavior (see Box 11.1 for examples). Because the measures have little in common except being nonreactive, they are best learned through examples. Some are *erosion measures,* where selective wear is used as a measure, and some are *accretion measures,* where the measures are deposits of something left behind.[1]

Researchers have examined family portraits in different historical eras to see how gender relations within the family are reflected in seating patterns. Urban anthropologists have examined the contents of garbage dumps to learn about lifestyles from what is thrown away (e.g., liquor bottles indicate level of alcohol consumption). Based on garbage, people underreport their liquor consumption by 40 to 60 percent (Rathje and Murphy, 1992:71). Researchers have studied the listening habits of drivers by checking what stations their radios are tuned to when cars are repaired. They have measured interest in different exhibits by noting worn tiles on the floor in different parts of a museum. They have studied differences in graffiti in male versus female high school restrooms to show gender differences in themes. Some have examined high school yearbooks to compare the high school activities of

Box 11.1 _____

Content Analysis in Criminology: A Summary of Some Recent Findings

A study of TV crime shows by the Media Institute in Washington, DC, indicates that, although the fictional criminals portrayed on television are, on the average, both older and wealthier than the real criminals who figure in the FBI's Uniform Crime Reports, "TV crimes are almost 12 times as likely to be violent as crimes committed in the real world." A review of several decades of research confirms that violent crimes are overrepresented on TV news and fictional crime shows, and that "young people, black people and people of low socioeconomic status are underrepresented as offenders or victims in television programs"—exactly opposite from the real world in which nonviolent property crimes far outnumber violent crimes, and young, poor, and African Americans predominate as offenders and victims. As a result, TV crime shows broadcast the double-edged message that one-on-one crimes of the poor are the typical crimes of all and thus not uniquely caused by the pressures of poverty, *and* that the criminal justice system pursues rich and poor alike.

Reiman (1998) further stated:

In addition to the steady diet of fictionalized TV violence and crime, there has been an increase in the graphic display of crime on many TV news programs. Crimes reported on TV news are also far more frequently violent than real crimes are. . . . Here, too, the focus is on one-on-one violence, rather than, say, corporate pollution.

Source: Reiman (1998:62–63).

those who had psychological problems in later life versus those who did not. Researchers have noted bumper stickers in support of different political candidates to see if one candidate's supporters are more likely than another's to obey traffic laws. Some have even measured television-watching habits by noting changes in water pressure due to the use of toilets during television commercials.[2]

In criminal justice sciences, in particular, nonreactive measures are very important. They appear chiefly in the form of crime scene forensics. Using biochemical evidence to reconstruct the crime incident and determine guilt, criminal justice professionals have come to rely heavily on DNA typing. This process, like matching fingerprints, maps and compares unique individual patterns of, in this case, genetic information (or DNA). Its applications are "a powerful criminal justice tool that helps to establish, with a high degree of certitude, the guilt or innocence of suspects. . . . For example, a forensic scientist might compare a semen sample retrieved from a rape victim to a DNA sample taken from a suspect. If fragments appear in both samples, a match is declared" (Hammond and Caskey, 1997:1–2).

Recording and Documentation

Creating nonreactive measures follows the logic of quantitative measurement, although qualitive researchers also use nonreactive observation. A researcher first conceptualizes a construct, then links the construct to nonreactive empirical evidence, which is its measure. The operational definition of the variable includes how the researcher systematically notes and records observations.

CONTENT ANALYSIS

What Is Content Analysis?

Content analysis is a technique for gathering and analyzing the content of text. The *content* refers to words, meanings, pictures, symbols, ideas, themes, or any message that can be communicated. The *text* is anything written, visual, or spoken that serves as a medium for communication. It includes books, newspaper or magazine articles, advertisements, speeches, official documents, films or videotapes, musical lyrics, photographs, articles of clothing, or works of art. For example, nearly a thousand tobacco industry documents were recently released to the public (Meier, 1997). These materials touch on delicate matters, including the marketing to minors and the funneling of money to finance scientific projects.

These papers would make an excellent text for criminologists interested in using content analysis method to study corporate fraud from an organizational perspective.

Content analysis goes back nearly a century and is used in many fields—literature, history, journalism, political science, education, psychology, and so on. At the first meeting of the German Sociological Society, in 1910, Max Weber suggested using it to study newspapers.[3]

In content analysis, a researcher uses objective and systematic counting and recording procedures to produce a quantitative description of the symbolic content in a text.[4] In fact, Markoff and colleagues (1974) suggested that "textual coding" might be a better name than content analysis. There are qualitative or interpretive versions of content analysis. The emphasis here is on quantitative data about a text's content.

Qualitative content analysis is not highly respected by most positivist researchers. Nonetheless, feminist researchers and others adopting more critical or interpretative approaches favor it. The criticisms largely reflect the differences among approaches to criminology presented in Chapter 4. Quantitative content analysis researchers sometimes include a qualitative evaluation of the content for exploratory purposes, out of sympathy for qualitative approaches, or to give them greater confidence that the quantitative measures are valid.

Content analysis is nonreactive because the process of placing words, messages, or symbols in a text to communicate to a reader or receiver occurs without influence from the researcher who analyzes its content. Returning to the tobacco industry documents recently released, one can be sure that the tobacco executives who wrote internal memoranda did so with no intention of them ever being read, let alone content analyzed, by anyone outside the tobacco industry.

An initial step in conducting a content analysis involves sorting themes or subject categories that appear in the text. For example, a criminologist might decide to sort tobacco industry documents into subject categories corresponding to potential areas of criminal fraud, such as the following:

1. Documents about industry- or company-sponsored research on health effects of smoking
2. Documents about the funding of research
3. Documents reflecting public statements by tobacco executives on the risks of smoking
4. Documents reflecting on the marketing of tobacco products to youth under age 18

Content analysis lets a researcher reveal the content (i.e., messages, meanings, symbols, etc.) in a source of communication (i.e., a book, article, movie, etc.). It lets him or her probe into and discover content in a different way from the ordinary way of reading a book or watching a television program.

With content analysis, a researcher can compare content across many texts and analyze it with quantitative techniques (e.g., charts and tables). In addition, he or she can reveal aspects of the text's content that are difficult to see. Content analysis can document—in objective, quantitative terms—whether your vague feelings based on unsystematic observation are true. It yields repeatable, precise results about the text.

Content analysis involves random sampling, precise measurement, and operational definitions for abstract constructs. The content of the text is then analyzed or coded so as to produce quantitative data. After a researcher gathers the data, he or she enters them into computers and analyzes them with statistics in the same way an experimenter or survey researcher would.

Topics Appropriate for Content Analysis

Criminologists are certainly no strangers to the content analysis method. Much of the existing research centers on characterizations the media are apt to make. Examples include the overrepresentation of minorities as offenders (Smith, 1984), exaggerating the extent of stranger-based crimes (Chermak, 1994), and misportraying the operations of the criminal justice system (Gorelick, 1989).

The analysis of mass media coverage of corporate crime occurs less often in comparison.

Nevertheless, criminologists have used content analysis to substantiate the editorial biases toward minimizing corporate liability (Wright et al., 1995), the reluctance to call corporate wrongdoing "crime" (Lofquist, 1997), and the fixing of blame on noncorporate causes (Wright et al., 1995). Box 11.1 cites Reiman's potent summary of these research findings.

But researchers have also applied content analysis to topics such as war crimes. In one particular study, a researcher (Smith, 1984) was interested in studying local responses to the Japanese war crimes trial in Malaysia and Singapore. Using editorials, news stories, and letters to the editor from a local newspaper (i.e., *New Straits Times*) as the text, Smith was able to document how quickly the "news" of war crimes fades and is forgotten by the press. Aside from mentions of the Chinese concern for the war crimes trial, the newspaper virtually ignored the topic, so that by 1947, press interest had almost entirely turned to other postwar issues such as food shortages.

Content analysis is useful for three types of research problems. First, it is helpful for problems involving a large volume of text. A researcher can measure large amounts of text (e.g., years of newspaper articles) with sampling and multiple coders. Second, it is helpful when a topic must be studied "at a distance." For example, content analysis can be used to study historical documents, the writings of someone who has died, or broadcasts in a hostile foreign country. Finally, content analysis can reveal messages in a text that are difficult to see with casual observation. The creator of the text or those who read it may not be aware of all its themes, biases, or characteristics.

Measurement and Coding

General Issues.   Careful measurement is crucial in content analysis because a researcher takes diffuse and murky symbolic communication and turns it into precise, objective, quantitative data. He or she carefully designs and documents procedures for coding to make replication possible.

Constructs in content analysis are operationalized with a *coding system,* a set of instructions or rules on how to systematically observe and record content from text. A researcher tailors it to the type of text or communication medium being studied (e.g., television drama, novels, photos in magazine advertisements, etc.). It also depends on the researcher's unit of analysis.

Units.   The unit of analysis can vary a great deal in content analysis. It can be a word, a phrase, a theme, a plot, a newspaper article, a character, and so forth. For example, a content analysis of the tobacco papers might have a corporate memoranda as the unit of analysis.

What Is Measured?   Measurement in content analysis uses *structured observation*: systematic, careful observation based on written rules. The rules explain how to categorize and classify observations. As with other measurement, categories should be mutually exclusive and exhaustive. Written rules make replication possible and improve reliability. Although researchers begin with preliminary coding rules, they often conduct a pilot study and refine coding on the basis of it.

Coding systems identify one or more of four characteristics of text content: frequency, direction, intensity, and space. A researcher measures from one to all four characteristics in a content analysis research project. Each will be briefly explained.

Frequency.   *Frequency* simply means counting whether or not something occurs and, if it occurs, how often (e.g., counting how many different sources were cited in a newspaper article about corporate crime).

Direction.   *Direction* is noting the direction of messages in the content along some continuum (e.g., noting if the news source cited in the corporate crime article supported or opposed the criminal liability of the corporation in question).

Intensity.   *Intensity* is the strength or power of a message in a direction (e.g., noting how strongly the news source cited in the corporate crime article supported or opposed corporate criminal liability).

Space.   A researcher can record the size of a text message or the amount of space or volume allocated to it. *Space* in written text is measured by counting words, sentences, paragraphs, or space on a page (e.g., square inches). For video or audio text, space can be measured by the amount of time allocated. For example, a TV character may be present for a few seconds or continuously in every scene of a two-hour program.

Coding, Validity, and Reliability

Manifest Coding.   Coding the visible, surface content in a text is called *manifest coding*. For example, a researcher counts the number of times a phrase or word appears in written text, or whether a specific action appears in a photograph or video scene. The coding system lists terms or actions that are then located in text. A researcher can use a computer program to search for words or phrases in text and have a computer do the counting work. To do this, he or she learns about the computer program, develops a comprehensive list of relevant words or phrases, and puts the text into a form that computers can read.[5]

Manifest coding is highly reliable because the phrase or word either is or is not present. Unfortunately, manifest coding does not take the connotations of words or phrases into account. The same word can take on different meanings depending on the context. The possibility that there are multiple meanings of a word limits the measurement validity of manifest coding.

Latent Coding.   A researcher using *latent coding* (also called *semantic analysis*) looks for the underlying, implicit meaning in the content of a text. For example, a researcher reads a newspaper article about corporate crime and decides if it contains themes regarding corporate criminal liability. The coding system must thus have general rules to guide the researcher's effort to identify these themes in the text, and then to assign them a quantitative value.

Latent coding tends to be less reliable than manifest coding. It depends on a coder's knowledge of language and social meaning.[6] Training, practice, and written rules improve reliability, but still it is difficult to consistently identify themes, opinions, and the like. Yet, the validity of latent coding can exceed that of manifest coding because people communicate meaning in many implicit ways that depend on context, not just in specific words.

A researcher can use both manifest and latent coding. If the two approaches agree, the final result is strengthened; if they disagree, the researcher may want to reexamine the operational and theoretical definitions.

Intercoder Reliability.   Content analysis often involves coding information from a very large number of units. A research project might involve observing the content in dozens of books, hundreds of hours of television programming, or thousands of newspaper articles. In addition to coding the information personally, a researcher may hire assistants to help with the coding. He or she teaches coders the coding system and trains them to fill out a recording sheet. Coders should understand the variables, follow the coding system, and ask about ambiguities. A researcher records all decisions he or she makes about how to treat a new specific coding situation after coding begins so that he or she can be consistent.

A researcher who uses several coders must *always* check for consistency across coders. He or she does this by asking coders to code the same text independently and then checking for consistency across coders. The researcher measures *intercoder reliability,* a type of equivalence reliability, with a statistical coefficient that tells the degree of consistency among coders.[7] The coefficient is *always* reported with the results of content analysis research.

When the coding process stretches over a considerable time period (e.g., more than three months), the researcher also checks stability reliability by having each coder independently code samples of text that were previously coded. He or she then checks to see whether the coding is stable or changing. For example, six months of newspaper articles are coded in April and coded again in July without the coders looking at their original coding decisions. Large deviations in coding necessitate retraining and coding the text a second time.

How to Conduct Content Analysis Research

Question Formulation. As in most research, content analysis researchers begin with a research question. When the question involves variables that are messages or symbols, content analysis may be appropriate. For example, Lofquist (1997) was interested in media bias and crime. He did a content analysis that compared how a local newspaper treated two stories, one having to do with the abduction of a small girl and the other having to do with the collapse and flooding of a large salt mine owned by a multinational corporation.

Units of Analysis. A researcher decides on the units of analysis (i.e., the amount of text that is assigned a code). For example, for a political campaign, each issue (or day) of a newspaper is the unit of analysis.

Sampling. Researchers may choose to use probability or nonprobability sampling, depending largely on the specifics of the research question. A probability sampling would require the same process mentioned in Chapter 9. It would involve a sampling frame, a table of random numbers, and perhaps stratified subsamples, among other things.

Comparing news magazine coverage of individual and corporate crime, for example, may lend itself to probability sampling. First, the researcher decides which weekly news magazines are most interesting to analyze based on the research question. Then, he or she randomly selects articles from those magazines spanning a set period of time (see Table 11.1). One way to select specific articles is to list all articles published by the weekly magazines between, say, 1976 and 1998. This sampling frame of articles is then used, along with a table of random numbers, to draw the probability sample of news stories. Another way to go about probability sampling is to select random weeks of the year and then analyze relevant articles contained in those corresponding issues of the news magazines. In other words, the researcher decides whether to sample by news story or by week of the year.

Lofquist's (1997) study on this topic, on the other hand, used nonprobability purposive sampling. He selected "every relevant story published [in a local newspaper] in the three-month period following the event" (p. 247). He chose to limit his content analysis to three months of text "because it seemed to provide ample time for developments in each story [i.e., the abduction and the collapse of the mine] and for consideration of their causes (p. 247).

Variables and Constructing Coding Categories. Lofquist (1997) compared what the local newspaper wrote about two widely reported "crimes" that took place in Rochester, New York, in 1994. As mentioned earlier, one crime was the case of a 4-year-old girl who disappeared from in front of her own home; the other was the collapse and flooding of a mine owned by a multinational company. Lofquist coded how the cause of events was described in the newspaper articles. The cause of events was simply categorized as being either "an accident," "negligence," or "a crime." He then simply coded the entire sample of newspaper stories, using manifest and latent coding.

With manifest coding, the researcher could create a list of specific words used to denote whether the event was an accident, due to negligence, or a crime. Words describing the event as an "accident" would include: *natural disaster, an act of God, beyond control,* and so on. The researcher could then literally count the number of times one of the words was used in a news story.

TABLE 11.1 Excerpt from Sampling Frame Worksheet

MAGAZINE	ISSUE	ARTICLE	NUMBER	ARTICLE In Sample?[a]	SAMPLED Article ID
Time	January 1–7, 1976	pp. 2–3	000001	No	
Time	"	p. 4, bottom	000002	No	
Time	"	p. 4, top	000003	Yes—1	0001
.					
.					
.					
Time	March 1–7, 1995	pp. 2–5	002101	Yes—10	0454
Time	"	p. 6, right column	002102	No	
Time	"	p. 6, left column	002103	No	
Time	"	p. 7	002104	No	
.					
.					
.					
Time	December 24–31, 1995	pp. 4–5	002201	Yes—22	0467
Time	"	p. 5, bottom	002202	No	
Time	"	p. 5, top	002203	Yes—23	0468
Newsweek	January 1–7, 1976	pp. 1–2	010030	No	
Newsweek	"	p. 3	010031	Yes—1	0469
.					
.					
U.S. News	December 25–31, 1995	p. 62	140401	Yes—23	1389

[a]"Yes" means the number was chosen from a random number table. The number after the dash is a count of the number of articles selected for a year.

With latent coding, the process is more subtle. The researcher must create rules or guidelines to follow when the meaning of the text becomes implicit, ironic, or in doubt. The rules spell out the criteria for judging the intended meaning of the text. Thus, the word *accident* may appear in the text. But to grasp its intended meaning, the researcher needs to examine the context in which the word or phrase appears. The context will give the researcher clues as to its meaning. This is why latent coding is just as important to researchers as manifest coding. The point is, the meaning of a text must be understood in the context of other words and phrases in the text (see Box 11.2).

In addition to written rules for coding decisions, a content analysis researcher creates a *recording sheet* (also called a *coding sheet*) on which to record information. Each unit should have a separate recording sheet. The sheets do not have to be pieces of paper; they can be 3″ × 5″ or 4″ × 6″ file cards, or lines in a computer record or file. When a lot of information is recorded for

Box 11.2_____

Example of Blank Coding Sheet

**A CONTENT ANALYSIS OF TV
TRUE CRIME SHOWS**

Background Information

1. Coder's name:_____
2. Case number:_____
3. Date of broadcast:_____
4. Length of episode:_____(in minutes:seconds)
5. Location of episode:_____

Portrayal of Suspect

6. Number of suspects (code up to 3 suspects):

Age   Race   Sex   Social Class

——   ——   ——   ——

——   ——   ——   ——

——   ——   ——   ——

7. Does the suspect show remorse (code up to 3 suspects):

Yes   No

——   ——

——   ——

——   ——

8. Suspected crime (code only primary offense for up to 3 suspects):

Violent   Nonviolent

——   ——

——   ——

——   ——

Portrayal of Arresting Officer

9. Number of officers (code up to 3 officers):

Age   Race   Sex   Social Class

——   ——   ——   ——

——   ——   ——   ——

——   ——   ——   ——

10. Does officer use physical force against suspect (code up to 3 officers):

Yes   No

——   ——

——   ——

——   ——

_____

each recording unit, more than one sheet of paper can be used.

Each recording sheet has a place to record the identification number of the unit and spaces for information about each variable. The researcher should also put identifying information about the research project on the sheet in case her or she wants to go back to it. Finally, in multiple coders, the sheet notes the coder to check intercoder reliability and, if necessary, makes it possible to recode information for inaccurate coders. After completing all recording sheets and checking for accuracy, one can begin data analysis.

Inferences

The inferences a researcher can or cannot make on the basis of results is critical in content analysis. Content analysis describes what is in the text. It cannot reveal the intentions of those who created the text or the effects that messages in the text have on those who receive them.

For example, the content analysis method cannot indicate whether the media's coverage of corporate crime has a particular effect on the way the public views corporate crime. To pursue this line of thinking would require additional research methods, such as the survey. Nevertheless, content analysis will continue to play a major role in criminological research on issues related to "the social control functions of the news media" (Chermak, 1997:716).

EXISTING STATISTICS/DOCUMENTS AND SECONDARY ANALYSIS

Topics Appropriate for Exisiting Statistics Research

It is difficult to specify topics that are appropriate for existing statistics research because they are so varied. Any topic on which information has been collected and is publicly available can be studied. In fact, existing statistics projects may not fit neatly into a deductive model of research design. Rather, researchers creatively reorganize the existing information into the variables for a research question after first finding what data are available.

You learned that experiments are best for topics where the researcher controls a situation and manipulates an independent variable. You saw that survey research is best for topics where the researcher asks questions and learns about reported attitudes or behavior. Earlier, you found that content analysis is for topics that involve the content of messages in cultural communication.

Existing statistics research is best for topics that involve information that has been collected by large bureaucratic organizations. Public or private organizations systematically gather many types of information. Such information is gathered for policy decisions or as a public service. It is rarely collected for purposes directly related to a specific research question. Thus, existing statistics research is appropriate when a researcher wants to test hypotheses involving variables that are also in official reports of social, economic, and political conditions. These include descriptions of organizations or the people in them. Often, such information is collected over long time periods.

Citing just several of the many research topics criminologists have addressed using ex-

isting statistics method gives one a sense of how versatile this method is. Criminologists have long been interested in the relationship of unemployment and crime. In an study of this nature mentioned earlier, Carlson and Michalowski (1997:224) developed a set of hypotheses about the unemployment/crime relationship and tested the hypotheses using large government data sets. The crime data they analyzed were the Uniform Crime Reports annual estimates of crime, beginning in 1933. The unemployment data also came from the U.S. government and was likewise longitudinal. It consisted of the official annual average unemployment rates for the U.S. civilian labor force. These statistics are compiled by the Bureau of the Census in the *Statistical Abstracts of the United States.*

Curry and colleagues (1996) also used existing statistics to analyze the national scope of gang crime in the United States. In particular, the criminologists used longitudinal survey data collected previously by the National Institute of Justice. The data represented law enforcement information on gang-related crime drawn from a sample of law enforcement agencies in over 125 municipalities across the country.

To cite one more example, Manson and Gilliard (1997) analyzed data from the Firearm Inquiries Statistics (FIST) program administered by the U.S. Bureau of Justice Statistics. The FIST program was set up by the U.S. government in 1994 "to describe presale background checks of applicants to buy a handgun from a Federal firearm licensee" (p. 1). Their findings revealed that these background checks result in around a 2 to 3 percent rejection rate due to, among other things, the potential buyer of the firearm having a prior felony conviction.

As you will see, the opportunities for criminologists to analyze existing statistics are almost limitless. Existing statistics will become increasingly valuable for comparative criminological research, as well. Every year, more and more data sets become available to researchers around the world, as countries and international agencies improve their research capabilities.

Locating Data

Locating Existing Statistics.   The main sources of existing statistics are government or international agencies and private sources. An enormous volume and variety of information exists. If you plan to conduct existing statistics research, it is wise to discuss your interests with an information professional—in this case, a reference librarian, who can point you in the direction of possible sources.

Many existing documents are "free"—that is, publicly available at libraries—but the time and effort it takes to search for specific information can be substantial. Researchers who conduct existing statistics research spend many hours in libraries. After the information is located, it is recorded on cards, graphs, or recording sheets for later analysis. Often, it is already available in a format for computers to read. For example, the U.S. National Institute of Justice (NIJ) has gathered such data sets from its previously funded research. These data sets are available from the *National Archive of Criminal Justice Data (NACJD)* at the Inter-university Consortium for Political and Social Research (ICPSR) at the University of Michigan.

There are so many sources that only a small sample of what is available is discussed here. The single-most valuable source of statistical information about the United States is the *Statistical Abstract of the United States,* which has been published annually (with a few exceptions) since 1878. The *Statistical Abstract* is available in all public libraries and can be purchased from the U.S. Superintendent of Documents. It is a selected compilation of the many official reports and statistical tables produced by U.S. government agencies. It contains the most significant statistical information from hundreds of more detailed government reports. You may want to examine more specific government documents. (The detail of what is available in government documents is mind boggling. For example, you can learn that there were two African American females over the age of 75 in Tucumcari City, New Mexico, in 1980.)

The *Statistical Abstract* has 1,400 charts, tables, and statistical lists from over 200 govern-ment and private agencies. It is hard to grasp all that it contains (see Figure 11.1) until you sit down with the *Abstract* and skim through the tables. A two-volume set summarizes similar information across many years; it is called *Historical Statistics of the U.S.: Colonial Times to 1970.*

Most governments publish similar statistical yearbooks. Australia's Bureau of Statistics produces *Yearbook Australia*, Statistics Canada produces *Canada Yearbook,* New Zealand's Department of Statistics publishes *New Zealand Official Yearbook,* and in the United Kingdom the Central Statistics Office publishes *Annual Abstract of Statistics.*[8] Many nations publish books with historical statistics, as well.

Locating government statistical documents is an art in itself. Some publications exist solely to assist the researcher. For example, the *American Statistics Index: A Comprehensive Guide* and *Index to the Statistical Publications of the U.S. Government and Statistics Sources: A Subject Guide to Data on Industrial, Business, Social Education, Financial and Other Topics for the U.S. and Internationally* are two helpful guides for the United States.[9] The United Nations and international agencies such as the World Bank have their own publications with statistical information for various countries (e.g., literacy rates, percentage of the labor force working in agriculture, birth rates)—for example, the *Demographic Yearbook, UNESCO Statistical Yearbook,* and *United Nations Statistical Yearbook.*

Perhaps the single-most indispensable source of existing statistics from criminologists in the United States is the annual *Sourcebook of Criminal Justice Statistics* (Maguire and Pastore, 1997). Statistical data are available either in hard copy or on CD-ROM technology. The variety of statistical data sets that are published in the *Sourcebook* are simply amazing (see Figure 11.2). It is important to point out, however, that corporate crime data sets still tend to be quite uncommon.

In typical stages of research (see Chapter 1), researchers design a project and collect data to address a research question. Yet, large-scale data collection is expensive and difficult. The cost and time required for a major national survey that uses

FIGURE 11.1   A Selected List of the Types of Information in the *Statistical Abstract of the United States* (represents only a tiny percentage of what is available)

Divorce rate by state by year

Number of burglary arrests resulting in a conviction

Deaths from motor vehicle accidents

State government expenditures for water pollution control

Average monthly temperature for cities of over 50,000 population

Number of votes for political candidates, by state

Tons of salt mined, by state

Number of employees in the farm machinery industry

Federal government spending for law enforcement

Number of aliens expelled from the country

Number of banks suspended or bankrupt per year

Average teacher salaries and spending per pupil in each state

Number of handguns legally imported per year

Housing units without indoor plumbing occupied by different races

Millions of feet of plywood imported and exported per year

Billions of dollars in profits for 170 largest corporations, by year

Number of new books published in history in a year

Number of hunting licenses in South Dakota or any other state

Party composition of each state legislature in the United States by year

Average dollars in sales per employee in motor vehicle companies

Number of overnight camping stays in Yosemite National Park

Number of master's degrees granted in sociology in a year by gender

Military pay for a staff sergeant for various years

Death rates by race for different states

Number of public executions by state and race for different years

Millions of dollars in revenue for television networks

Number of hogs in Arkansas or in any other state

Average cost for a dozen eggs in various years

Number of submarines France or other nations have

Electricity production of Hungary or other nations

Number of juvenile delinquents per 1,000 population per year

Average net corporate profit for different sizes of firms

Percentage of city government revenue coming from liquor store taxes

Percentage of all retail sales that tobacco products represent

Number of square miles of water in each state

Acres of federally owned land in each state

Percentage of households with a color television, by family income

Average farm size and farm value by state

Average amount spent on newspaper advertising for real estate, by year

Average number of local telephone calls per day in various years

Total annual sales of vacuum cleaners per year

Average residential rent in selected major metropolitan areas

Number of physicians per 1,000 population in various nations

Number of barrels of oil imported to United States from Canada per year

Number of successful and unsuccessful space craft launches by United States and USSR (Russia) each year since 1957

---

rigorous techniques are prohibitive for most researchers. Fortunately, the organization, preservation, and dissemination of major survey data sets have improved. Today, there are archives of past surveys that are open to researchers.

The ICPSR at the University of Michigan is the world's major archive of social science data. Over 17,000 survey research and related sets of information are stored and made available to researchers at modest costs. Other centers hold survey data in the United States and other nations.[10]

A widely used source of survey data for the United States is the *General Social Survey (GSS),* which has been conducted annually in most years by the National Opinion Research Center at the University of Chicago. In recent years, it has cov-

FIGURE 11.2   Selected Contents of the Annual *Sourcebook of Criminal Justice Statistics*

A. Statistics on Characteristics of the Criminal Justice System
1. Expenditures for criminal justice activities
2. Federal drug control funding
3. Salaries for police officers and other law enforcement personnel
4. Criminal cases filed per judgeship in U.S. District Courts
5. Statutory provisions on firearms

B. Statistics on Public Attitudes toward Crime and Criminal Justice-Related Topics
1. Most important problems for country and communities
2. Public confidence in social institutions
3. Perceptions of crime and safety
4. Police officials' attitudes toward efforts to reduce the drug problem
5. Pornography, prostitution, and homosexuality

C. Statistics on Nature and Distribution of Known Offenses
1. Victim-offender relationship in violent victimization
2. Reasons for reporting and not reporting crime victimization to the police
3. Bias-motivated (hate) crimes

4. Offenses known to the police
5. Terrorist incidents

D. Statistics on Characteristics and Distribution of Persons Arrested
1. Number and rate of arrests, national estimates
2. Arrest rate trends
3. Drug and property seizure by the U.S. Customs Service
4. Offenses cleared by arrest
5. Aliens deported from the United States

E. Statistics on Judicial Processing of Defendants
1. Requests for immunity by federal prosecutors
2. Cases filed, terminated, and pending in U.S. District Courts
3. Time served in prison for offenders sentenced in U.S. District Courts
4. Criminal tax fraud cases
5. U.S. Army court-martial cases

F. Statistics on Persons under Correctional Supervision
1. Adults on probation
2. Jail inmates with HIV/AIDS
3. State and federal prisoners executed
4. Escapes from correctional facilities
5. Noncitizens in U.S. federal prisons

Source: Adapted from Maguire and Pastore (1997).

ered other nations, as well. The data are made publicly available for secondary analysis at a low cost.[11]

For example, backlash hypothesis—that White males who work in companies with affirmative action policies are very resentful of programs to aid minorities—was tested with a secondary analysis of GSS data by Taylor (1995). She analyzed already gathered GSS data on White males and looked at their answers to whether affirmative action policies were operating at their workplace and examined their attitudes toward programs to assist racial minorities. Contrary to the backlash hypothesis, Taylor discovered that such men were actually more supportive of programs for minorities than other men.

Reliability and Validity

Existing statistics and secondary data are not trouble free just because a government agency or other source gathered the original data. Researchers must be concerned with validity and reliability, as well as with some problems unique to this research technique. Maier (1991) has an entire book on existing statistics in social research and potential problems with their use.

A common error is the *fallacy of misplaced concreteness*. It occurs when someone gives a false impression of accuracy by quoting statistics in greater detail than warranted by how the statistics are collected and by overloading detail (Horn, 1993:18). For example, to cite statistical correlations between unemployment and crime without really knowing how the data were collected (i.e., the research design) might, if one is not cautious, cause a researcher to rush to conclusions (i.e., premature closure). In short, secondary data are useful provided the researcher understands the underlying research design.

Units of Analysis and Variable Attributes. A common problem in existing statistics is finding the appropriate units of analysis. Many statistics are published for aggregates, not the individual. For example, a table in a government document has information (e.g., unemployment rate, crime rate, etc.) for a state, but the unit of analysis for the research question is the individual (e.g., "Are unemployed people more likely to commit property crimes?"). The potential for committing the ecological fallacy is very real in this situation. It is less of a problem for secondary survey analysis because researchers can obtain raw information on each respondent from archives.

A related problem involves the categories of variable attributes used in existing documents or survey questions. This is not a problem if the initial data were gathered in many highly refined categories. The problem arises when the original data were collected in broad categories or ones that do not match the needs of a researcher.

It would be entirely inappropriate, for example, for a criminologist interested in the relationship of unemployment and crime among Asian Americans to use existing data that categorize ethnicity in terms of "Black," "White," and "Other." The "Other" category includes Asian Americans as well as other ethnic/racial groups. It takes a special effort on the part of researchers to discover existing statistical data that suits the research question being asked.

Validity. Validity problems can occur when using existing statistics. One type of problem occurs when the researcher's theoretical definition does not match that of the government agency or organization that collected the information. Official policies and procedures specify definitions for official statistics, but often criminologists change these definitions to suit their own research purposes. Carlson and Michalowski (1997:224), for example, chose a definition of *serious crime* that included "crimes which generate the greatest fear in the general public (homicide, robbery, aggravated assault, and burglary)."

Deciding on a definition of *unemployment* is also a thorny issue for criminologists. Carlson and Michalowski (1997:24) adopted the official definition: "Since most of the research that has led to ambiguous results concerning the unemployment-crime relationship has used the U.S. civilian labor force as a whole, we also use this measure to maintain comparability." The official definition of *unemployment* regards only those who are now actively seeking work (full or part time) as unemployed. The official statistics exclude those who have stopped looking, who work part time out of necessity, or who do not look because they believe no work is available. Box 11.3 further teases out comparative definitions of *unemployment.*

A second validity problem arises when official statistics are a surrogate or proxy for a construct in which a researcher is really interested. This is often unavoidable, however, because the researcher cannot collect original data. Criminologists interested in quantifying the extent of smuggling might decide to make use of official trade data as a proxy for smuggling. Junguito and Caballero (1982), for example, analyzed illegal trade transactions of Colombia, South America, using official statistics: "A recent study compared the figures of various countries' importation of goods coming from Colombia with Colombian exports statistics, finding that, for the whole group of OECD countries, Colombia was 'under-invoicing' its exports by 14 percent, while those sent to the United States and Canada were under-invoiced by 9 percent" (p. 293).

A third validity problem arises because the researcher lacks control over how information is collected. All information, even that in official government reports, is originally gathered by people in bureaucracies as part of their jobs. A researcher depends on them for collecting, organizing, reporting, and publishing data accurately. Systematic errors in collecting the initial information (e.g., census people who avoid poor neighborhoods and make up information, or people who put a false age on a driver's license); errors in organizing and reporting information (e.g., a police department that is sloppy about filing crime reports and loses some); and errors in publishing information (e.g., a typographical error in a table) all reduce measurement validity.

Box 11.3 _____

Unemployment Rates versus the Nonemployed

In most countries, the official unemployment rate measures only the unemployed (see below) as a percent of all working people. It would be 50 percent higher if two other categories of nonemployed people were added: involuntary part-time workers and discouraged workers (see below). In some countries (e.g., Sweden and United States), it would be nearly double if it included these people. This does not consider other nonworking people, transitional self-employed, or the underemployed (see below). What a country measures is a theoretical and conceptual definition issue: What construct should an unemployment rate measure and why measure it?

An economic policy or labor market perspective says the rate should measure those ready to enter the labor market immediately. It defines nonworking people as a supply of high-quality labor, an input for use in the economy available to employers. By contrast, a social policy or human resource perspective says the rate should measure those who are not currently working to their fullest potential. The rate should represent people who are not or cannot fully utilize their talents, skills, or time to the fullest. It defines nonworking people as a social problem of individuals unable to realize their capacity to be productive, contributing members of society.

CATEGORIES OF NONEMPLOYED/FULLY UTILIZED

Unemployed people	People who meet three conditions: lack a paying job outside the home, are taking active measures to find work, can begin work immediately if it is offered.
Involuntary part-time workers	People with a job, but who work irregularly or fewer hours than they are able and willing.
Discouraged workers	People able to work and who actively sought it for some time, but being unable to find it, have given up looking.
Other nonworking	Those not working because they are retired, on vacation, temporarily laid off, semidisabled, homemakers, full-time students, or in the process of moving.
Transitional self-employed	Self-employed who are not working full time because they are just starting a business or are going through bankruptcy.
Underemployed	Persons with a temporary full-time job for which they are seriously overqualified. They seek a permanent job in which they can fully apply their skills and experience.

Source: Adapted from _The Economist,_ July 22, 1995, p. 74.

Reliability. Problems with reliability can plague existing statistics research. Stability reliability problems develop when official definitions or the method of collecting information changes over time. Official definitions of crime, unemployment, and the like change periodically. Even if a researcher learns of such changes, consistent measurement over time is impossible. For example, during the early 1980s, the method for calculating the U.S. unemployment rate changed. Previously, the unemployment rate was calculated as the number of unemployed persons divided by the number in the civilian work force. The new method divided the number of unemployed by the civilian work force plus the number of people in the military. Likewise, when police departments computerize their records, there is an apparent increase in crimes reported, not because crime increases but due to improved record keeping.

Equivalence reliability can also be a problem. For example, a measure of crime across a nation depends on each police department's providing accurate information. If departments in one region of a country have sloppy bookkeeping, the measure loses equivalence reliability. Likewise, studies of police departments suggest that political pressures to increase arrests are closely related to the number of arrests. For example, political pressure in one city may increase arrests (e.g., a crackdown on crime), whereas pressures in another city may decrease arrests (e.g., to show a drop in crime shortly before an election in order to make officials look better).

Representative reliability is also a problem in official statistics. For example, if the poorly dressed or non-White law offender is more likely to be arrested, then crime statistics are not reliable estimates across subpopulations.

Missing Data. One problem that plagues researchers who use existing statistics and documents is that of missing data. Sometimes, the data were collected but have been lost. More frequently, the data were never collected. The decision to collect official information is made within government agencies. The decision to ask questions on a survey whose data are later made publicly available is made by a group of researchers. In both cases, those who decide what to collect may not collect what another researcher needs in order to address a research question. Government agencies start or stop collecting information for political, budgetary, or other reasons.

For example, the IRS's Taxpayer Compliance Measurement Program (TCMP), which was mentioned in previous chapters, is a case in point. Due to funding considerations and the politics of tax administration (see Wiegand, 1987), the government has decided to discontinue TCMP research. This is particularly problematic for criminologists interested in doing basic research on tax crime in the United States, not to mention the applied uses for the TCMP data.

Example of Existing Statistics/Documents Research

In some sense, we are back to where we began this chapter. Criminologists have a very powerful research technique at their disposal in existing statistics method. This method, as well as other nonreactive techniques, including content analysis, are particularly well suited for studying crime from an organizational perspective.

As suggested at the outset of the chapter, there is great research potential for criminologists wishing to analyze existing statistics and documents. One example to consider was mentioned: the tobacco industry documents recently released to the public. But, of course, there are many others open to criminologists. Consider the crime of money laundering (see Chapter 2).

Money laundering involves "washing dirty money" by disguising the illicit cash as legal income (Wray, 1993). It facilitates an array of cash-generating criminal activities, most especially illicit drug trafficking and organized crime. In just the United States alone, federal law enforcement officials estimate that between $100 and $300 billion in U.S. currency is laundered each year.

From the law enforcement perspective, money laundering is most readily detected during the "placement" stage of the process. Placement involves either depositing the ill-gotten cash into a bank directly or converting it to a less suspicious medium of exchange, such as money orders or cashier's checks. In either case, detection is a risk. The Bank Secrecy Act of 1970 armed law enforcement with a way to trace the movement of large sums of cash. Federal documents, such as the currency transaction report (CRT), are now required to be completed and sent to the Treasury Department whenever business or banking transactions exceed $10,000 in currency. The Bank Secrecy Act (BSA) requires "individuals as well as banks and other institutions, such as check cashing, currency exchanges, and money transmitters, to report large foreign and domestic financial transactions" (p. 2).

This mountain of government documents, approaching some 90 million in number, represents a full challenge to researchers fascinated with an organizational perspective on financial crimes. It also represents a wealth of financial intelligence for federal and state law enforcement agencies (see Table 11.2)

ISSUES OF INFERENCE AND THEORY TESTING

Inferences from Nonreactive Data

A researcher's ability to infer causality or test a theory on the basis of nonreactive data is limited. It is difficult to use unobtrusive measures to establish temporal order and eliminate alternative explanations. In content analysis, a researcher cannot generalize from the content to its effects on those who read the text, but can only use the correlation logic of survey research to show an association among variables. Unlike the ease of survey research, a researcher does not ask respondents direct questions to measure variables, but relies on the information available in the text.

Ethical Concerns

Ethical concerns are not at the forefront of most nonreactive research because the people being studied are not directly involved. The primary ethical concern is the privacy and confidentiality of using information gathered by someone else. Another ethical issue is that official statistics are social and political products. Implicit theories and value assumptions guide which information is collected and the categories used when gathering it. Measures or statistics that are defined as official and collected on a regular basis are objects of political conflict and guide the direction of policy. By defining one measure as official, public policy is shaped to lead to outcomes that would be different if an alternative, but equally valid, measure had been used.

The collection of official statistics stimulates public opinion and raises a concern that often generates further data collection. For example, the construction of "drunken driving as a social problem" was prompted by official figures on automobile fatalities and the like. Likewise, organizational crime will loom larger in the minds of people as better data are collected and disseminated to researchers.

TABLE 11.2 Requests for Bank Secrecy Act (BSA) Data, 1992

SOURCE	NUMBER OF REQUESTS
Treasury Department	831
Justice Department	801
State agencies	677
Postal Inspection Service	340
Interpol	113
Defense Department	103
Financial regulatory agencies	90
Other	253
Total	3,208

Source: Adapted from Wray (1993).

CONCLUSION

This chapter reviews some very important nonreactive (or unobtrusive) research methods. Suggestions of specific criminological topics were discussed that related to the organizational perspective on crime that seem particularly well-suited to these nonreactive techniques. The authors believe that as the disciplines of criminology and criminal justice mature, more and more researchers will employ these techniques in the study of organizational crime.

KEY TERMS

accretion measures
coding system
content
erosion measures
fallacy of misplaced
    concreteness

General Social Survey (GSS)
intercoder reliability
latent coding
manifest coding
nonreactive
recording sheet

Statistical Abstract of the
    United States
structured observation
text
unobtrusive measures

REVIEW QUESTIONS

1. For what types of research questions is content analysis appropriate?
2. What are the four characteristics of content that are observed and recorded in coding systems?
3. Of what reliability problems should the researcher using existing statistical data be aware?
4. What are the advantages and disadvantages of secondary data analysis?
5. Why do content analysis researchers use multiple coders, and what is the possible problem with doing this?
6. How are inferences limited in content analysis?
7. What units of analysis are used in content analysis?
8. What is the aggregation problem in existing statistics?
9. What are the three validity problems in content analysis?
10. Of what limitations of using existing statistics should researchers be aware?

NOTES

1. See Webb and colleagues (1981:7–11).
2. For an inventory of nonreactive measures, see Bouchard (1976) and Webb and associates (1981).
3. See Krippendorff (1980:13).
4. For definitions of content analysis, see Holsti (1968:597), Krippendorff (1980:21–24), Markoff and associates (1974:5–6), Stone and Weber (1992), and Weber (1985:81, note 1).
5. Weber (1984, 1985) and Stone and Weber (1992) provided a summary of computerized content analysis techniques.
6. See Andren (1981:58–66) for a discussion of reliability and latent or semantic analysis. Coding categorization in content analysis is discussed in Holsti (1969:94–126).
7. See Krippendorff (1980) for various measures of intercoder reliability. Also see Fiske (1982) for the related issue of convergent validity.
8. Many non-English yearbooks are also produced; for example, *Statistiches Jahrbuch* for the Federal Republic of Germany, *Annuaire Statistique de la*

France for France, and Denmark's *Statiskisk Ti Arsoversigt*. Japan produces an English version of its yearbook called the *Statistical Handbook of Japan*.
9. Guides exist for the publications of various governments—for example, the *Guide to British Government Publications, Australian Official Publications,* and *Irish Official Publications*. Similar publications exist for most nations. For example, *DOD's Parliamentary Companion for the United Kingdom* and the *Parliamentary Handbook of the Commonwealth of Australia* are both similar to the *Almanac of American Politics*.
10. Other major U.S. archives of survey data include the National Opinion Research Center, University of Chicago; the Survey Research Center, University of California–Berkeley; the Behavioral Sciences Laboratory, University of Cincinnati; Data and Program Library Service, University of Wisconsin–Madison; the Roper Center, University of Connecticut–Storrs; and the Institute for Research in Social Science, University

of North Carolina–Chapel Hill. Also see Kiecolt and Nathan (1985) and Parcel (1992).

11. The General Social Survey is described in Alwin (1988) and in Davis and Smith (1986).

12. See Block and Burns (1986), Carr-Hill (1984a), Hindess (1973), Horn (1993), Maier (1991), and Van den Berg and Van der Veer (1985). Discussions by Norris (1981) and Starr (1987) are also very helpful.

RECOMMENDED READINGS

Jacob, Herbert. (1984). *Using published data: Errors and remedies*. Beverly Hills, CA: Sage. This short (55-page) book is valuable. As the title suggests, it is about using existing data and focusing on possible errors. The chapters on validity and reliability are very helpful.

Rathje, William, and Cullen Murphy. (1992). *Rubbish: The archaeology of garbage*. New York: Harper. This is a fun but thoughtful look at how researchers have studied garbage to understand human behavior. Written for a lay audience, it reviews many of the studies and techniques used to study what we leave behind.

Stewart, David W. (1984). *Secondary research: Information sources and methods*. Beverly Hills, CA: Sage. Stewart's book is valuable for discovering sources of existing statistics. It contains an introduction to basic issues in secondary research and lists many sources of social science data.

Webb, Eugene J., Donald Campbell, R. Schwartz, L. Sechrest, and J. Grove. (1981). *Nonreactive measures in the social sciences*, 2nd ed. Boston: Houghton Mifflin. This is an update of the social science classic *Unobtrusive Measures* by several of the authors. In addition to a wealth of examples of nonreactive measures, the book includes discussions of ethics in covert measurements, nonreactive observation, the use of archival (existing statistics) data, and limitations on the use of nonreactive measures.

Weber, Robert Philip. (1985). *Basic content analysis*. Beverly Hills, CA: Sage. There are many books on content analysis. Weber provides a moderately sophisticated introduction to the technique, including different content analysis techniques and computer programs to assist the researcher. New as well as experienced researchers who have not used content analysis extensively can learn much from this book.

CHAPTER 12

ANALYZING QUANTITATIVE DATA

This . . . is an invitation to all students to explore a social science of crime that is both numerate and accessible.

—John Hagan, A. R. Gillis, and David Brownfield, *Criminological Controversies*, p. xx

INTRODUCTION

The fact is, criminologists work with numbers. There is no getting around it. As social *scientists,* we possess a skeptical appreciation for crime statistics, an appreciation for how they are collected, and an appreciation for how they are analyzed. Quantitative analysis is the bread and butter of basic research in criminology and applied research in criminal justice. One would have little more than a pedestrian point of view about the core questions of class, gender, race, age, and the environment without referencing quantitative research.

The proper way to think about scattergrams, pie charts, correlations, multiple regressions, tables of numbers—that is, the stuff of quantitative criminology—is as tools. Principally, they are easy tools to learn to use. Do not be intimidated by them. By the time you finish reading this chapter, you will have acquired the foundation to comprehend and critique quantitative research. This is like opening a door to "an exciting topic where the facts may be even more interesting than fiction" (Hagan et al., 1996:xx).

DEALING WITH DATA

Coding Data

Before a researcher examines quantitative data to test hypotheses, he or she needs to put them in a different form. You encountered the idea of coding data in the last chapter. Here, data *coding* means systematically reorganizing raw data into a format that is machine readable (i.e., easy to analyze using computers). As with coding in content analysis, researchers create and consistently apply rules for transferring information from one form to another.[1]

Coding can be a simple clerical task when the data are recorded as numbers on well-organized recording sheets, but it is very difficult when, for example, a researcher wants to code answers to open-ended survey questions into numbers in a process similar to latent content analysis.

Researchers use a coding procedure and a codebook for data coding. The *coding procedure* is a set of rules stating that certain numbers are assigned to variable attributes. For example, a researcher codes males as 1 and females as 2. Each category of a variable and missing information needs a code. A *codebook* is a document (i.e., one or more pages) describing the coding procedure and the location of data for variables in a format that computers can use.

When you code data, it is very important to create a well-organized, detailed codebook and make multiple copies of it. If you do not write down the details of the coding procedure, or if you misplace the codebook, you have lost the key to the data and will have to recode the raw data all over again.

Researchers begin thinking about a coding procedure and codebook before they collect data. Survey researchers, for example, often precode their questionnaires before collecting the data. *Precoding* means actually writing the code categories directly on the questionnaire. The codes are contained within the codebook. Figure 12.1 gives an example of a precoded survey question, and Table 12.1 shows an excerpt from the corresponding codebook.

If a researcher does not precode, his or her first step after collecting data is to create a codebook. He

FIGURE 12.1 Precoded Survey Question

"Are there any situations you can imagine in which you would approve of a policeman striking an adult female citizen?"

Yes	1
No	2
Not sure (volunteered)	3
No response	9

Source: Adapted from a General Social Survey question asked of a national sample of Americans, as cited in Johnson (1997:14).

or she also gives each case an identification number to keep track of the cases. Next, the researcher transfers the information from each questionnaire into a format that computers can read.

Entering Data

Most computer programs designed for data analysis need the data in a grid format. In the grid, each row represents a respondent, subject, or case. In computer terminology, these are called *data records*. Each is the record of data for a single case. A column or set of columns represents specific variables. It is possible to go from a column and row location (e.g., row 7, column 5) back to the original source of data (e.g., a questionnaire item on police behavior for respondent 8). A column or set of columns assigned to a variable is called a *data field* or just a *field*.

A researcher transfers information from questionnaires, recording sheets, or similar raw data forms into a format for computers in four ways: code sheets, direct entry, optical scan sheets, and computer-assisted telephone interviewing (CATI). First, he or she can use graph paper or special grid forms for computers (called *transfer* or *code sheets*) by writing code numbers in squares that correspond to a row and column location, then typing it into a computer. Second, the researcher can sit at a computer and directly type in the data. This *direct-entry method* is easiest if information is already in a similar format, as with content analysis

TABLE 12.1 Excerpt from Codebook

COLUMN	VARIABLE NAME	DESCRIPTION
1–4	ID	Respondent identification number
5–8	Date	Month/Day (e.g., 0525)
9	Interviewer	Interviewer who collected the data: 1 = Jasmine 2 = Teddy 3 = Juan 4 = Sharon 5 = Jason
10	Sex	Interviewer report of respondent's sex 1 = Male, 2 = Female
11	Striking	Approve police striking 1 = Yes 2 = No 3 = Not Sure (volunteered) 4 = No Response Blank = Missing Information

recording sheets. Otherwise, it can be very time consuming and error prone. Third, he or she can put data on an *optical scan sheet*. Special machines—optical scanners—read the information from the sheets into a computer. You may have used optical scan sheets, which are used for scoring multiple-choice tests. They are specially printed forms on which a person fills in boxes or circles using a pencil to indicate a response. The researcher can use the last method if his or her project involved telephone interviewing. Computer-assisted telephone interviewing was described in Chapter 10. Interviewers wearing telephone headsets sit at a computer keyboard and enter data directly as respondents answer questions during the interview.

Cleaning Data

Accuracy is extremely important when coding data. Errors made when coding or entering data into a computer threaten the validity of measures and cause misleading results. A researcher who has a perfect sample, perfect measures, and no errors in gathering data, but who makes errors in the coding process or in entering data into a computer, can ruin a whole research project.

After very careful coding, the researcher checks the accuracy of coding, or "cleans" the data. He or she may code a 10 to 15 percent random sample of the data a second time. If no coding errors appear, the researcher proceeds; if he or she finds errors, the researcher rechecks all coding.

Researchers verify coding after the data are in a computer in two ways. *Possible code cleaning* (or *wild code checking*) involves checking the categories of all variables for impossible codes. For example, respondent sex is coded 1 = Male, 2 = Female. Finding a 4 for a case in the field for the sex variable indicates a coding error. A second method, *contingency cleaning* (or *consistency checking*), involves cross-classifying two variables and looking for logically impossible combinations. For example, education is cross-classified by occupation. If a respondent is recorded as never having passed the eighth grade and also is recorded as being a legitimate medical doctor, the researcher checks for a coding error.

A researcher can modify data after they are in a computer. He or she may not use more refined categories than were used when collecting the original data, but may combine or group information. For example, the researcher may group ratio-level income data into five ordinal categories. Also, he or she can combine information from several indicators to create a new variable or add the responses to several questionnaire items into an index score.

RESULTS WITH ONE VARIABLE

Frequency Distributions

The word *statistics* has several meanings. It can mean a set of collected numbers (e.g., numbers of homicides in a city) as well as a branch of applied mathematics used to manipulate and summarize the features of numbers. Criminologists use both types of statistics. Here, we focus on the second type—ways to manipulate and summarize numbers that represent data from a research project.

Descriptive statistics describe numerical data. They can be categorized by the number of variables involved: univariate, bivariate, or multivariate (for one, two, and three or more variables). *Univariate statistics* describe one variable (*uni*- refers to one; *-variate* refers to variable). The easiest way to describe the numerical data of one variable is with a *frequency distribution*. It can be used with nominal-, ordinal-, interval-, or ratio-level data and takes many forms. For example, O'Toole and colleagues (1994) conducted a survey of 447 business and public-sector organizations in Victoria, Australia, to identify crimes of fraud against them. Table 12.2 summarizes the types of fraud using frequency distribution.

Besides frequency distributions, criminologists often use graphs and charts to summarize univariate statistics. Some common types of graphic representations are the *histogram*, *bar chart*, and *pie chart*. Most people have seen these. The terminology is not exact, but histograms are usually upright bar graphs for interval or ratio data.[2]

For interval- or ratio-level data, a researcher often groups the information into categories. The grouped categories should be mutually exclusive. Interval- or ratio-level data are often plotted in a *frequency polygon*. In it the number of cases or frequency is along the vertical axis, and the values of the variable or scores are along the horizontal axis. A polygon appears when the dots are connected (see Figure 12.2).

TABLE 12.2 Raw Count and Percentage Frequency Distribution

TYPE OF FRAUD	FREQUENCY	%
Misappropriation of stock or equipment	251	25
Misappropriation of cash	162	16
False expense account claims	113	11
Unauthorized use of equipment	79	8
False invoices	50	5
Kickbacks/bribes	45	4
Supplier overcharging	42	4
False claims to obtain credit	41	4
Passing off worthless checks	38	4
Unauthorized use of organization credit cards	30	3
Misuse by employees of organization checks	30	3
Other	129	12
Total	1010	100 (rounded)

Source: Adapted from O'Toole and colleagues (1994).

Measures of Central Tendency

Researchers often want to summarize the information about one variable into a single number. They use three measures of central tendency, or measures of the center of the frequency distribution: mean, median, and mode, which are often called *averages* (a less precise and less clear way of saying the same thing).

The *mode* is the easiest to use and can be used with nominal, ordinal, interval, or ratio data. It is simply the most common or frequently occurring number. For example, the mode of the following list is 5: 6 5 7 10 9 5 3 5. A distribution can have more than one mode. For example, the mode of this list is both 5 and 7: 5 6 1 2 5 7 4 7. If the list gets long, it is easy to spot the mode in a frequency distribution—just look for the most frequent score. There will always be at least one case with a score that is equal to the mode.

The *median* is the middle point. It is also the 50th percentile, or the point at which half the cases are above it and half below it. It can be

Frequency

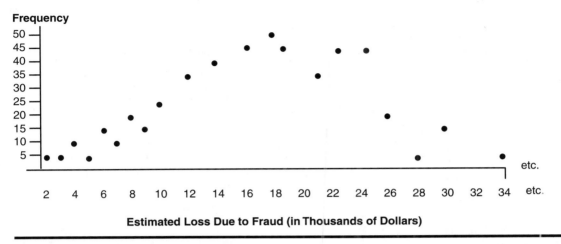

Estimated Loss Due to Fraud (in Thousands of Dollars)

FIGURE 12.2 Example of Frequency Polygon

used with ordinal-, interval-, or ratio-level data (but not nominal level). You can "eyeball" the mode, but computing a median requires a little more work. The easiest way is first to organize the scores from highest to lowest, then count to the middle. If there is an odd number of scores, it is simple. Seven people are waiting for a bus; their ages are 12 17 20 27 30 55 80. The median age is 27. Note that the median does not change easily. If the 55-year-old and the 80-year-old both got on one bus, and the remaining people were joined by two 31-year-olds, the median remains unchanged. If there is an even number of scores, things are a bit more complicated. For example, six people have the following ages: 17 20 26 30 50 70. The median is somewhere between 26 and 30. Compute the median by adding the two middle scores together and dividing by 2, or 26 + 30 = 56/2 = 28. The median age is 28, even though no person is 28 years old. Note that there is no mode in the list of six ages because each person has a different age.

The *mean,* also called the arithmetic average, is the most widely used measure of central tendency. It can be used *only* with interval- or ratio-level data.[3] Compute the mean by adding up all scores, then divide by the number of scores. For example, the mean age in the previous example is 17 + 20 + 26 + 30 + 50 + 70 = 213; 213/6 = 35.5.

No one in the list is 35.5 years old, and the mean does not equal the median.

The mean is strongly affected by changes in extreme values (very large or very small). For example, the 50- and 70-year-old left and were replaced with two 31-year-olds. The distribution now looks like this: 17 20 26 30 31 31. The median is unchanged: 28. The mean is 17 + 20 + 26 + 30 + 31 + 31 = 155; 155/6 = 25.8. Thus, the mean dropped a great deal when a few extreme values were removed.

If the frequency distribution forms a "normal" or bell-shaped curve, the three measures of central tendency equal each other. If the distribution is a *skewed distribution* (i.e., more cases are in the upper or lower scores), then the three will not be equal. If most cases have lower scores with a few extreme high scores, the mean will be the highest, the median in the middle, and the mode the lowest. If most cases have higher scores with a few extreme low scores, the mean will be the lowest, the median in the middle, and the mode the highest. In general, the median is best for skewed distributions, although the mean is used in most other statistics (see Figure 12.3).

Measures of Variation

Measures of central tendency are a one-number summary of a distribution; however, they give

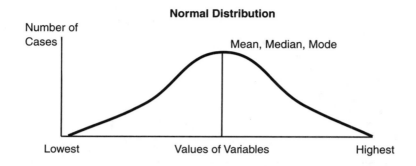

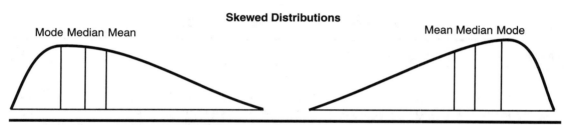

FIGURE 12.3   Measures of Central Tendency

only its *center*. Another characteristic of a distribution is its spread, dispersion, or variability
around the center. Two distributions can have
identical measures of central tendency but differ
in their spread about the center. For example,
seven people are these ages: 25 26 27 30 33 34
35. Both the median and the mean are 30.
Another seven people have the identical median
and mean, but their ages are 5 10 20 30 40 50
55. The ages of the second group are spread
more from the center, or the distribution has
more variability.

Variability has important social implications. For example, in city X, the median and
mean family income is $25,600 per year, and it
has zero variation. *Zero variation* means that
every family has an income of exactly $25,600.
City Y has the same median and mean family
income, but 95 percent of its families have
incomes of $8,000 per year and 5 percent have
incomes of $300,000 per year. City X has perfect
income equality, whereas there is great inequality
in city Y. A researcher who does not know the

variability of income in the two cities misses very
important information.

Researchers measure variation in three ways:
range, percentile, and standard deviation. *Range*
is the simplest. It consists of the largest and small-
est scores. For example, the range for the first
group is from 25 to 35, or 35 − 25 = 10 years. If
the 35-year-old was replaced by a 60-year-old,
the range would change to 60 − 25 = 45 years.
Range has limitations. For example, here are two
groups of six with a range of 35 years: 30 30 30 30
30 65 and 20 45 46 48 50 55.

Percentiles tell the score at a specific place
within the distribution. One percentile you
already learned is the median, the 50th percentile.
Sometimes the 25th and 75th percentiles or the
10th and 90th percentiles are used to describe a
distribution. For example, the 25th percentile is
the score at which 25 percent of the distribution
have either that score or a lower one. The computation of a percentile follows the same logic as the
median. If you have 100 people and want to find
the 25th percentile, you rank the scores and count

up from the bottom until reaching number 25. If the total is not 100, simply adjust the distribution to a percentage basis.

Standard deviation is the most difficult to compute measure of dispersion; it is also the most comprehensive and widely used. The range and percentile are for ordinal-, interval-, and ratio-level data, but the standard deviation requires an interval or ratio level of measurement. It is based on the mean and gives an "average distance" between all scores and the mean. People rarely compute the standard deviation by hand for more than a handful of cases because computers and calculators can do it in seconds.

Look at the calculation of the standard deviation in Figure 12.4. If you add up the absolute difference between each score and the mean (i.e., subtract each score from the mean), you get zero. This is because the mean is equally distant from all scores. Also notice that the scores that differ the most from the mean have the largest effect on the sum of squares and on the standard deviation.

The standard deviation is of limited usefulness by itself. It is used for comparison purposes. For example, suppose a researcher was interested in the causal effects of parental education on self-reported delinquency. The researcher has collected data from three classes of students, and parental education was operationalized as parents' years of schooling. The standard deviation for class A is 3.317 years. (The calculations are presented in Figure 12.4.) The respective standard deviations for class B and class C are 0.812 and 6.239.

The standard deviation tells a researcher that the parents of children in class B are very similar, whereas those for class C are very different. In fact, in class B, the schooling of an "average" parent is less than a year above or below than the mean for all parents, so the parents are very homogeneous. In class C, however, the "average" parent is more than six years above or below the mean, so the parents are very heterogeneous.

The standard deviation and the mean are used to create z-scores. *Z-scores* let a researcher compare two or more distributions or groups.

The z-score, also called a *standardized score,* expresses points or scores on a frequency distribution in terms of a number of standard deviations from the mean. Scores are in terms of their relative position within a distribution, not as absolute values.

Z-scores are easy to calculate from the mean and standard deviation (see Box 12.1). For example, an employer interviews students from Kings College and Queens College. She learns that the colleges are similar and that both grade on a 4.0 scale. Yet, the mean grade-point average at Kings College is 2.62 with a standard deviation of .50, whereas the mean grade-point average at Queens College is 3.24 with a standard deviation of .40. The employer suspects that grades at Queens College are inflated. Suzette from Kings College has a grade-point average of 3.62, while Jorge from Queens College has a grade-point average of 3.64. Both students took the same courses. The employer wants to adjust the grades for the grading practices of the two colleges (i.e., create standardized scores). She calculates z-scores by subtracting each student's score from the mean, then dividing by the standard deviation. For example, Suzette's z-score is $3.62 - 2.62 = 1.00/.50 = 2$, whereas Jorge's z-score is $3.64 - 3.24. = .40/.40 = 1$. Thus, the employer learns that Suzette is two standard deviations above the mean in her college, whereas Jorge is only one standard deviation above the mean for his college. Although Suzette's absolute grade-point average is lower than Jorge's, relative to the students in each of their colleges Suzette's grades are much higher than Jorge's.

RESULTS WITH TWO VARIABLES

A Bivariate Relationship

Univariate statistics describe a single variable in isolation. *Bivariate statistics* are much more valuable. They let a researcher consider two variables together and describe the relationship between variables. Even simple hypotheses require two variables.

FIGURE 12.4 The Standard Deviation

STEPS IN COMPUTING THE STANDARD DEVIATION

1. Compute the mean.
2. Subtract the mean from each score.
3. Square the resulting difference for each score.
4. Total up the squared differences to get the sum of squares.
5. Divide the sum of squares by the number of cases to get the variance.
6. Take the square root of the variance, which is the standard deviation.

EXAMPLE OF COMPUTING THE STANDARD DEVIATION

[8 respondents, variable = years of schooling]

Score	Score – Mean	Squared (Score – Mean)
15	15 – 12.5 = 2.5	6.25
12	12 – 12.5 = –0.5	.25
12	12 – 12.5 = –0.5	.25
10	10 – 12.5 = –2.5	6.25
16	16 – 12.5 = 3.5	12.25
18	18 – 12.5 = 5.5	30.25
8	8 – 12.5 = 4.5	20.25
9	9 – 12.5 = –3.5	12.25

Mean = 15 + 12 + 12 + 10 + 16 + 18 + 8 + 9 = 100, 100/8 = 12.5
Sum of squares = 6.25 + .25 + .25 + 6.25 + 12.25 + 30.25 + 20.25 + 12.25 = 88
Variance = Sum of squares/Number of cases = 88/8 = 11
Standard deviation = Square root of variance = $\sqrt{11}$ = 3.317 years.
Here is the standard deviation in the form of a formula with symbols.

Symbols:
X = SCORE of case Σ = Sigma (Greek letter) for sum, add together
$\overline{X}$ = MEAN N = Number of cases

*Formula:**

$$\text{Standard deviation} = \sqrt{\frac{\Sigma (X - \overline{X})^2}{N}}$$

---

* There is a slight difference in the formula depending on whether one is using data for the population or a sample to estimate the population parameter.

Bivariate statistical analysis shows a *statistical relationship* between variables—that is, things that appear together. For example, "a frequently tested proposition at the core of a control theory of crime asserts that parental supervision reduces delinquent behavior" (Hagan, 1996:17). This is a statistical relationship between two variables: the amount of parental supervision and delinquency.

Statistical relationships are based on two ideas: covariation and independence. *Covariation* means that things go together or are associated. To covary means to vary together; cases with certain values on one variable are likely to have certain values on the other one. The previous example suggests that as the amount of parental supervision increases, there is a corresponding decrease in the amount of delinquent behavior (see Figure 12.5). To put it differently, knowing one's level of parental supervision reveals the probability of that person engaging in delinquent behavior.

Box 12.1_____

Calculating Z-Scores

Personally, the authors do not like the formula for z-scores, which is:

Z-score = (Score – Mean)/Standard Deviation, or in symbols:

$$z = \frac{X - \bar{X}}{\delta}$$

where: X = score, $\bar{X}$ = mean, δ = standard deviation

The authors usually rely on a simple conceptual diagram that does the same thing and that shows what z-scores really do. Consider data on the ages of school children with a mean of 7 years and a standard deviation of 2 years. How does one compute the z-score of 5-year-old Miguel, or what if Yashohda's z-score is a + 2, but one needs to know her age in years? First, draw a little chart from –3 to +3 with zero in the middle. Put the mean value at zero, because a z-score of zero is the mean and z-scores measure distance above or below it. Stop at 3 because virtually all cases fall within 3 standard deviations of the mean in most situations. The chart looks like this:

```
|____|____|____|____|____|____|
-3   -2   -1   0   +1   +2   +3
```

Now, label the values of the mean and add or subtract standard deviations from it. One standard deviation above the mean (+1) when the mean is 7 and standard deviation is 2 years is just 7 + 2, or 9 years. For a –2 z–score, put 3 years. This is because it is 2 standard deviations, of 2 years each (or 4 years), lower than the mean of 7. The diagram now looks like this:

```
1    3   5   7   9    11    13   age in years
|____|___|___|___|____|____|
-3   -2  -1  0   +1   +2   +3
```

It is easy to see that Miguel, who is 5 years old, has a z-score of –1, whereas Yashohda's z-score of +2 corresponds to 11 years old. One can read from z-score to age, or age to z-score. For fractions, such as a z-score of –1.5, just apply the same fraction to age to get 4 years. Likewise, an age of 12 is a z-score of +2.5.

Independence is the opposite of covariation. It means there is no association or no relationship between variables. If two variables are independent, cases with certain values on one variable do not have any particular value on the other variable. Consider, for example, perhaps the most controversial bivariate relationships in criminology: the relationship between social class and crime. Researchers have operartionalized the two variables in a variety of ways to explore the causal effect of social class. Some research, indeed, has shown no

statistical relationship between the two variables. Hagan (1996:15) has addressed this point:

> This is . . . an ideologically charged area of debate that is further complicated by the frequent failure of scientific efforts that use self-report surveys of adolescents to find substantial associations between parental status and delinquency. However, we have argued that when appropriate measures of unemployment are used both among individuals and at higher levels of aggregation [i.e., neighborhoods], consistent relationships are found.

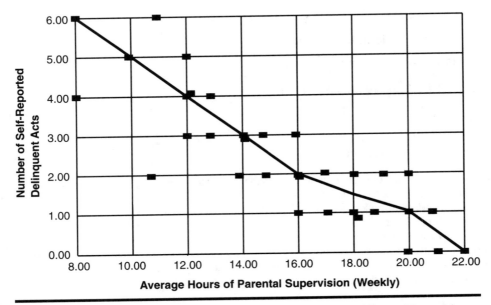

FIGURE 12.5 Example of a Scattergram: Self-Reported Delinquency and Parental Supervision

Most researchers state hypotheses in terms of a causal relationship or expected covariation; if they use the null hypothesis, the hypothesis is that there is independence. It is used in formal hypothesis testing and is frequently found in inferential statistics (to be discussed).

Three techniques help researchers decide whether a relationship exists between two variables: (1) a scattergram, or a graph or plot of the relationship; (2) cross-tabulation, or a percentaged table; and (3) measures of association, or statistical measures that express the amount of covariation by a single number (e.g., correlation coefficient). Also see Box 12.2 on graphing data.

Seeing the Relationship: The Scattergram

What Is a Scattergram (or Scatterplot)? A *scattergram* is a graph on which a researcher plots each case or observation, where each axis represents the value of one variable. It is used for variables measured at the interval or ratio level, rarely for ordinal variables, and never if either variable is nominal. There is no fixed rule for which variable (independent or dependent) to place on the horizontal or vertical axis, but usually the independent variable

(symbolized by the letter X) goes on the horizontal axis and the dependent variable (symbolized by Y) on the vertical axis. The lowest value for each should be the lower left corner and the highest value should be at the top or to the right.

How to Construct a Scattergram. Begin with the range of the two variables. Draw an axis with the values of each variable marked and write numbers on each axis (graph paper is helpful). Next, label each axis with the variable name and put a title at the top.

You are now ready for the data. For each case, find the value of each variable and mark the graph at a place corresponding to the two values.

For example, a researcher makes a scattergram of the parental supervision/delinquency relationship for 33 young people. The dependent variable (i.e., self-reported delinquency) forms the vertical (or Y) axis, and the independent variable (i.e., hours of parental supervision) forms the horizontal (or X) axis. The points are plotted accordingly; thus, the first case has four self-reported delinquent acts and eight average hours of parental supervision per week. The second case has six self-reported delinquent acts and eight

Box 12.2

Graphing Accurately

The pattern in graph A shows drastic change. A steep drop in 1980 is followed by rapid recovery and instability. The pattern in graph B is much more constant. The decline from 1979 to 1980 is smooth, and the other years are almost level. Both graphs are for identical data, the U.S. business failure rate from 1975 to 1992. The X axis (bottom) for years is the same. The scale of the Y axis is 60 to 160 in graph A and 0 to 400 in graph B. The pattern in graph A only looks more dramatic because of the Y axis scale. When reading graphs, be careful to check the scale. Some people purposely choose a scale to minimize or dramatize a pattern in the data.

Graph A

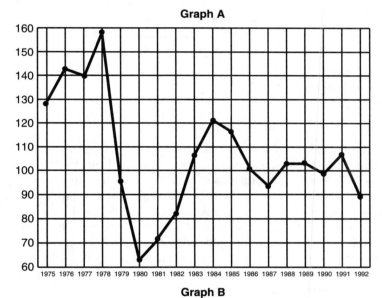

Graph B

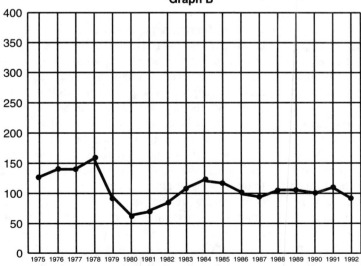

average hours of supervision, and so on (refer to Figure 12.5).

The scattergram in Figure 12.5 is a plot of data for all 33 young people in the survey. As you can see, it shows a *negative relationship* between delinquency and parental supervision. In other words, as the number of hours of parental supervision increases, the self-reported incidences of delinquency decreases.

The scattergram is complete after all the cases have been plotted, which can take some time if there are many cases. Also, some types of computer software can plot a scattergram after the data are in the computer.

What Can You Learn from the Scattergram? A researcher can see three aspects of a bivariate relationship in a scattergram: form, direction, and precision.

Form. Relationships can take three forms: independence, linear, and curvilinear. *Independence* or no relationship is the easiest to see. It looks like a random scatter with no pattern, or a straight line that is exactly parallel to the horizontal or vertical axis. A *linear relationship* means that a straight line can be visualized in the middle of a maze of cases running from one corner to another. A *curvilinear relationship* means that the center of a maze of cases would form a U curve, right side up or upside down, or an S curve.

Direction. Linear relationships can have a positive or negative direction. The plot of a *positive* relationship looks like a diagonal line from the lower left to the upper right. Higher values on X tend to go with higher values on Y, and vice versa.

A *negative* relationship looks like a line from the upper left to the lower right. It means that higher values on one variable go with lower values on the other. For example, people with more education are less likely to have been arrested. If we look at a scattergram of data on a group of males where years of schooling (X axis) are plotted by number of arrests (Y axis), we see that most cases (or men) with many arrests are in the lower right, because most of them completed few years of school. Most cases

with few arrests are in the upper left because most have had more schooling. The imaginary line for the relationship can have a shallow or a steep slope. More advanced statistics provide precise numerical measures of the line's slope.

Precision. Bivariate relationships differ in their degree of precision. *Precision* is the amount of spread in the points on the graph. A high level of precision occurs when the points hug the line that summarizes the relationship. A low level occurs when the points are widely spread around the line. Researchers can "eyeball" a highly precise relationship. They can also use advanced statistics to measure the precision of a relationship in a way that is analogous to the standard deviation for univariate statistics.

Bivariate Tables

What Is a Bivariate Table? The bivariate percentaged table is widely used. It presents the same information as a scattergram in a more condensed form. The data can be measured at any level of measurement, although interval and ratio data must be grouped if there are many different values. The table is based on *cross-tabulation;* that is, the cases are organized in the table on the basis of two variables at the same time. Bivariate tables usually contain percentages.

Constructing Percentaged Tables. It is easy to construct a percentaged table, but there are ways to make it look professional. We will first review the steps for constructing a table by hand. The same principles apply if a computer makes the table. We begin with the raw data, which can be organized into a format for computers. They might look like data from an imaginary survey in Box 12.3.

The next step is to create a *compound frequency distribution (CFD)*. This is similar to the frequency distribution, except that it is for each combination of the values of two variables. Suppose, for example, a criminologist wants to see the relationship between age and attitude toward the legalization of marijuana. Since age is measured at the ratio level, it must be grouped into ordinal categories. Ratio- or interval-level

Box 12.3_____

Raw Data and Frequency Distributions

EXAMPLE OF RAW DATA

Case	Age	Gender	Schooling	Attitude toward Legalizing Marijuana
01	21	F	14	1
02	36	M	8	1
03	77	F	12	2
04	41	F	20	2
05	29	M	22	3
06	45	F	12	3
07	19	M	13	2
08	64	M	12	3
09	53	F	10	3
10	44	M	21	1
etc.				

(Attitude scoring, 1 = Agree, 2 = No Opinion, 3 = Disagree)

TWO FREQUENCY DISTRIBUTIONS:
AGE AND ATTITUDE TOWARD LEGALIZING MARIJUANA

Age Group	Number of Cases	Attitude	Number of Cases
Under 30	26		
30–45	30	Agree	38
46–60	35	No Opinion	26
61 and older	15	Disagree	40
Missing	3	Missing	5
Total	109	Total	109

COMPOUND FREQUENCY DISTRIBUTION:
AGE GROUP AND ATTITUDE TOWARD LEGALIZING MARIJUANA

Age	Attitude	Number of Cases
Under 30	Agree	20
Under 30	No Opinion	3
Under 30	Disagree	3
30–45	Agree	10
30–45	No Opinion	10
30–45	Disagree	5
46–60	Agree	4
46–60	No Opinion	10
46–60	Disagree	21
61 and older	Agree	3
61 and older	No Opinion	2
61 and older	Disagree	10
	Subtotal	101
Missing on either variable		8
Total		109

data are converted to the ordinal level for percentaged tables. Otherwise, there could be too many categories for a variable, making the table virtually impossible to interpret.

The CFD has every combination of categories. Age has four categories and attitude has three, so there are $3 \times 4 = 12$ rows. The steps to create a CFD are as follows:

1. Figure all possible combinations of variable categories.
2. Make a mark next to the combination category into which each case falls.
3. Add up the marks for the number of cases in a combination category.

If there is no missing information problem, add up the numbers of categories (e.g., all the "Agree"s, or all the "61 and Older"s). In the example, missing data are an issue. The four "Agree" categories in the CFD add up to 37 (20 + 10 + 4 + 3), not 38, as in the univariate frequency distribution, because one of the 38 cases has missing information for age.

The CFD is an intermediate step that makes table construction easier. Computer programs give you the completed table right away.

The next step is to set up the parts of a table (see Figure 12.6) by labeling the rows and columns. The independent variable usually is placed in the columns, but this convention is not always followed. Next, each number from the CFD is placed in a cell in the table that corresponds to the combination of variable categories. For example, the CFD shows that 20 of the under-30-year-olds agree (top number), and so does Figure 12.6 (upper left cell).

Figure 12.6 is a raw count or frequency table. Its cells contain a count of the cases. It is easy to make, but interpreting a raw count table is difficult because the rows or columns can have different totals, and what is of real interest is the relative size of cells compared to others.

Researchers convert raw count tables into percentaged tables to see bivariate relationships. There are three ways to percentage a table: by row, by column, and for the total. The first two are often used and show relationships.

Is it best to percentage by row or column? Either can be appropriate. Let us first review the mechanics of percentaging a table. When calculating column percentages, compute the percentage each cell is of the column total. This includes the total column or marginal for the column variable. For example, the first column total is 26 (there are 26 people under age 30), and the first cell of that column is 20 (there are 20 people under age 30 who agree). The percentage is $20/26 = 0.769$ or 76.9 percent. Or, for the first number in the marginal, $37/101 = 0.366 = 36.6$ percent (see Table 12.3). Except for rounding, the total should equal 100 percent.

Computing row percentages is similar. Compute the percentage of each cell as a percentage of the row total. For example, using the same cell with 20 in it, we now want to know what percentage it is of the row total of 37, or $20/37 = 0.541 = 54.1$ percent. Percentaging by row or column gives different percentages for a cell unless the marginals are the same.

The column and row percentages serve to address different research questions. *Column percentages* answer questions concerning the distribution of attitudes for a given age group. Thus, of respondents under 30 years of age, 76.9 percent agree with the notion of legalizing marijuana (see Table 12.3). *Row percentages,* on the other hand, answer questions about the age distribution among those holding a certain attitude. Of respondents agreeing to marijuana legalization, 54.1 percent are under 30 years of age So, it depends on which question the researcher is asking as to whether he or she should percentage by column or row. One way of percentaging emphasizes people's attitudes at a given age; the other emphasizes people's ages for a given attitude.

A researcher's hypothesis may imply looking at row percentages or the column percentages. When beginning, calculate percentages each way and practice interpreting, or figuring out, what each says. For example, our hypothesis is that age affects attitude, so column percentages are most helpful. However, if our interest was in describing the age make-up of groups of people with different attitudes, then row percentages are appropriate. As Zeisel (1985:34) noted, whenever one factor in a

FIGURE 12.6   Age Group by Attitude about Legalizing Marijuana Raw Count Table (a)

RAW COUNT TABLE

ATTITUDE (b)	Under 30	30–45	46–60	61 and Older	TOTAL (c)
		AGE GROUP			
Agree	20	10	4	3	37
No opinion	3 (e)	10	10	2	25
Disagree	3	5	21	10	39
Total (c)	26	25	35	15	101

Missing cases (f) = 8

(d)

THE PARTS OF A TABLE

(a) Give each table a *title*, which names variables and provides background information.

(b) Label the row and column variable and give a name to each of the variable categories.

(c) Include the totals of the columns and rows. These are called the *marginals*. They equal the univariate frequency distribution for the variable.

(d) The numbers with the labeled variable categories and the totals are called the *body of a table*.

(e) Each number or place that corresponds to the intersection of a category for each variable is a *cell of a table*.

(f) If there is missing information (cases in which a respondent refused to answer, ended interview, said "don't know," etc.), report the number of missing cases near the table to account for all original cases.

cross-tabulation can be considered the cause of the other, percentage will be most illuminating if they are computed in the direction of the causal factor.

Reading a Percentaged Table.   Once you understand how a table is made, reading it and figuring out what it says are much easier. To read a table, first look at the title, the variable labels, and any sources of background information. Next, look at the direction in which percentages have been computed—in rows or columns. Notice that the percentaged tables in Table 12.3 have the same title. This is because the same variables are used. It would have helped to note how the data were percentaged in the title, but this is rarely done. Sometimes, researchers present abbreviated tables and omit the 100 percent total or the marginals, which adds to the confusion. It is best to include all the parts of a table and clear labels.

Researchers read percentaged tables to make comparisons. Comparisons are made in the opp-

osite direction from that in which percentages are computed. A rule of thumb is to compare across rows if the table is percentaged down (i.e., by column) and to compare up and down in columns if the table is percentaged across (i.e., by row).

When reading column-percentaged tables, compare across rows. In Table 12.3, for instance, over three-fourths (76.9 percent) of the youngest group agree, and they are the only group in which a majority agree. Only 11.5 percent disagree, compared to 60 and 66.7 percent, respectively, for the two oldest groups. In row-percentaged tables, compare columns or age groups. In Table 12.3, most of those who agree are in the youngest group, with the proportion declining as age increases. Most no-opinion people are in the middle-age groups. Those who disagree are older, especially in the 46–60 group (53.8 percent).

It takes practice to see a relationship in a percentaged table. If there is no relationship in a table, the cell percentages look approximately

TABLE 12.3   Age Group by Attitude about Legalizing Marijuana

COLUMN-PERCENTAGED TABLE

| | AGE GROUP | | | | |
ATTITUDE	*Under 30*	*30–45*	*46–60*	*61 and Older*	**TOTAL**
Agree	76.9%	40%	11.4%	20%	36.6%
No opinion	11.5	40	28.6	13.3	24.8
Disagree	<u>11.5</u>	<u>20</u>	<u>60</u>	<u>66.7</u>	<u>38.6</u>
Total	99.9	100	100	100	100
(N)	(26)*	(25)*	(35)*	(15)*	(101)*
Missing cases = 8					

ROW-PERCENTAGED TABLE

| | AGE GROUP | | | | | |
ATTITUDE	*Under 30*	*30–45*	*46–60*	*61 and Older*	**TOTAL**	*(N)*
Agree	54.1%	27%	10.8%	8.1%	100%	(37)*
No opinion	12	40	40	8	100	(25)*
Disagree	<u>7.7</u>	<u>12.8</u>	<u>53.8</u>	<u>25.6</u>	<u>99.9</u>	<u>(39)*</u>
Total	25.7	24.8	34.7	14.9	100.1	(101)*
Missing cases = 8						

*For percentaged tables, provide the number of cases or *N* on which percentages are computed in parentheses near the total of 100%. This makes it possible to go back and forth from a percentaged table to a raw count table and vice versa.

equal across rows or columns. A linear relationship looks like larger percentages in the diagonal cells. If there is a curvilinear relationship, the largest percentages form a pattern across cells. For example, the largest cells might be the upper right, the bottom middle, and the upper left. It is easiest to see a relationship in a moderate-sized table (9 to 16 cells) where most cells have some cases (at least five cases are recommended) and the relationship is strong and precise.

Principles of reading a scattergram can help you see a relationship in a percentaged table. Imagine a scattergram that has been divided into 12 equal-sized sections. The cases in each section correspond to the number of cases in the cells of a table that is superimposed onto the scattergram. The table is a condensed form of the scattergram. The bivariate relationship line in a scattergram corresponds to the diagonal cells in a percentaged table. Thus, a simple way to see strong relationships is to circle the largest percentage in each row (for row-percentaged tables) or column (for column-percentaged tables) and see if a line appears.

The circle-the-largest-cell rule works—with one important caveat. The categories in the percentages table *must* be ordinal or interval and in the same order as in a scattergram. In scattergrams, the lowest variable categories begin at the bottom left. If the categories in a table are not ordered the same way, the rule does not work.

Bivariate Tables without Percentages.   Very often, researchers present bivariate tables displaying information other than percentages. A measure of central tendency (usually the mean) is reported when one variable is nominal or ordinal (e.g., attitude toward legalizing marijuana) and the other is ordinal- or ratio-level (e.g., age of the

TABLE 12.4 Attitude toward Legalizing Marijuana by Mean Age of Respondent

LEGALIZING MARIJUANA	MEAN AGE	(*N*)
Agree	26.2	(37)
No opinion	44.5	(25)
Disagree	61.9	(39)

Missing cases = 8

respondent). The mean age of those stating the various attitudes is shown in Table 12.4. Such tables are not constructed from the cumulative frequency distribution (CFD). Instead, all cases are divided into the ordinal variable categories (i.e., Agree, No opinion, Disagree); then the mean is calculated from the raw data for the cases in each variable category.

Statistical data are commonly reported in tables as rates. Table 12.5 gives an example. Note that "Black/White ratio" is the ratio of the two incarceration rates.

Measures of Association

A measure of association is a single number that expresses the strength, and often the direction, of a relationship. It condenses information about a bivariate relationship into a single number.

There are many measures of association. The correct one depends on the level of measurement. Many measures are called by letters of the Greek alphabet. Lambda, gamma, tau, chi (squared), and rho are commonly used measures. The emphasis here is on interpreting the measures, not on their calculation. In order to understand each measure, you will need to complete a beginning statistics course. See Box 12.4 on the correlation.

Most of the elementary measures discussed here follow a *proportionate reduction in error (PRE)* logic. The logic asks: How much does knowledge of one variable reduce the errors that are made when guessing the values of the other variable? Independence means that knowledge of one variable does not reduce the chance of errors on the other variable. Measures of association equal zero if the variables are independent.

If there is a strong association or relationship, then few errors are made predicting a second variable on the basis of knowledge of the first, or the proportion of errors reduced is large. A large number of correct guesses suggests that the measure of association is a nonzero number if an association exists between the variables. Figure 12.7 describes five commonly used bivariate measures of association. Notice that most range from –1 to +1, with negative numbers indicating a negative relationship and positive numbers a positive relationship. A measure of 1.0 means a 100 percent reduction in errors, or perfect prediction.

MORE THAN TWO VARIABLES

Statistical Control

Showing an association or relationship between two variables is not sufficient to say that an independent

TABLE 12.5 International Comparison of Rates of Imprisonment (per 100,000 persons) by Race, 1990

	COUNTRY		
RACE	*United States*	*United Kingdom*	*Australia*
All	474.3	89.3	83.9
"Black" or Aboriginal	1,860.0	547.0	754.6
"White" or non-Aboriginal	284.4	80.9	72.7
Black/White ratio	6.5	6.8	18.6

Source: Adapted from Broadhurst (1997:452).

Box 12.4

Correlation

The formula for a correlation coefficient (rho) looks awesome to most people. Calculating it by hand, especially if the data have multiple digits, can be a very long and arduous task. Nowadays, computers do the calculation. However, the problem with relying on computers to do the work is that a researcher may not understand what the coefficient means. Here is a short, simplified example to show how it is done.

The purpose of a correlation coefficient is to show how much two variables "go together" or covary. Ideally, the variables have a ratio level of measurement (some use variables at the interval level). To calculate the coefficient, we first convert each score on a variable into its z-score. This "standardizes" the variable based on its mean and standard deviation. Next, we multiply the z-scores for each case together. This tells us how much the variables for a case vary together—cases with high z-scores on both variables get much bigger, while those low on both are much smaller. Finally, we

divide the sum of the multiplied z-scores by the number of cases. It yields a type of "average" covariation that has been standardized. In short, a correlation coefficient is the product of z-scores added together, then divided by the number of cases. It is always between +1.0 and −1.0 and summarizes scattergram information about a relationship into a single number.

Let us look at the correlation between the unemployment rate and price for a gram of cocaine for five different cities. First, anyone who is brave or lacks math-symbol phobia can look at one of the frequently used formulas for a correlation coefficient:

$$(\Sigma\,[z\text{-score}_1][z\text{-score}_2])/N$$

where: Σ = sum, z-score$_1$ = z-score for 1st variable (see Box 12.1), z-score$_2$ = z-score for 2nd variable, N = number of cases

Here is how to calculate a correlation coefficient without directly using the formula:

CITY	UNEMPLOY- MENT RATE	PRICE	(DIFFERENCE) Unemploy- ment	Price	SQUARED DIFF. Unemploy- ment	Price	Z-SCORES Unemploy- ment	Price	Z-SCORE PRODUCT
A	2	$10	−2	−5	4	25	−1.43	−.70	1.0
B	3	$ 5	−1	−10	1	100	−.71	−1.41	1.0
C	5	$20	+1	+5	1	25	.71	+.70	.50
D	6	$25	+2	+10	4	100	+1.43	+1.41	2.0
E	4	$15	0	0	0	0	0	0	0
Total	20	$75			10	250			4.50

Mean: Unemployment = 4; Price = $15
Variance: Unemployment = 10/5 = 2; Price = 250/5 = 50.
Stnd. Dev.: Unemployment = square root of 2 = 1.4; Price = square root of 50 = 7.1
Correlation: 4.50/5 = .90

Step 1: Calculate the mean and standard deviation for each variable. (For the standard deviation, first subtract each score from its mean, next square the difference, now sum squared differences, then divide the sum by the number of cases for the variance. Then take the square root of the variance.)
Step 2: Convert each score for the variables into their z-scores. (Just subtract each score from its mean and divide by its standard deviation.)
Step 3: Multiply the z-scores together for each case.
Step 4: Sum the products of z-scores, then divide by the number of cases.

FIGURE 12.7   Five Measures of Association

Lambda is used for nominal-level data. It is based on a reduction in errors based on the mode and ranges between 0 (independence) and 1.0 (perfect prediction or the strongest possible relationship).

Gamma is used for ordinal-level data. It is based on comparing pairs of variable categories and seeing whether a case has the same rank on each. Gamma ranges from -1.0 to $+1.0$, with 0 meaning no association.

Tau is also used for ordinal-level data. It is based on a different approach than gamma and takes care of a few problems that can occur with gamma. Actually, there are several statistics named tau (it is a popular Greek letter), and the one here is Kendall's tau. Kendall's tau ranges from -1.0 to $+1.0$, with 0 meaning no association.

Rho is also called Pearson's product moment correlation coefficient (named after the famous statistician Karl Pearson and based on a product moment statistical procedure). It is the most commonly used measure of correlation, the correlation statistic people mean if they use the term *correlation* without identifying it further. It can be used only for data measured at the interval or ratio level. Rho is used for the mean and standard deviation of the variables and tells how far cases are from a relationship (or regression) line in a scatterplot. Rho ranges from -1.0 to $+1.0$, with 0 meaning no association. If the value of rho is squared, sometimes called *R*-squared, it has a unique proportion reduction in error meaning. *R*-squared tells how the percentage in one variable (e.g., the dependent) is accounted for, or explained by, the other variable (e.g., the independent). Rho measures linear relationships only. It cannot measure nonlinear or curvilnear relationships. For example, a rho of zero can indicate either no relationship or a curvilinear relationship (see Box 12.4).

Chi-squared has two different uses. It can be used as a measure of association in descriptive statistics like the others listed here, or in inferential statistics. Inferential statistics are briefly described next. As a measure of association, chi-squared can be used for nominal and ordinal data. It has an upper limit of infinity and a lower limit of zero, meaning no association (see Box 12.7).

SUMMARY OF MEASURES OF ASSOCIATION

Measure	Greek Symbol	Type of Data	High Association	Independence
Lambda	λ	Nominal	1.0	0
Gamma	γ	Ordinal	$+1.0, -1.0$	0
Tau (Kendall's)	τ	Ordinal	$+1.0, -1.0$	0
Rho	ρ	Interval, ratio	$+1.0, -1.0$	0
Chi-square	χ^2	Nominal, ordinal	Infinity	0

variable *causes* a dependent variable. In addition to temporal order and association, a researcher must eliminate alternative explanations—explanations that can make the hypothesized relationship spurious. Experimental researchers do this by choosing a research design that physically controls potential alternative explanations for results (i.e., that threaten internal validity).

In nonexperimental research, a researcher controls for alternative explanations with statistics. He or she measures possible alternative explanations with *control variables*, then examines the control variables with multivariate tables and statistics that help him or her decide whether a bivariate relationship is spurious. They also show the relative size of the effect of multiple independent variables on a dependent variable.

A researcher controls for alternative explanations in multivariate (more than two variables) analysis by introducing a third (or sometimes a fourth or fifth) variable. Table 12.6, for example, explores the relationship between gender and self-reported smoking behavior. The bivariate relationship is shown. Table 12.7 adds "Type of Family" as a control variable. In other words, the effects of family type are controlled or statistically removed from the analysis. Hagan (1996:37–38) has summarized these tables:

> Smoking is a form of deviant behavior where women today overall have a rough parity with men. This is reflected in a survey undertaken in 1989 of adolescents in a wealthy section of Toronto called Forest Hill. . . . [However], while there is only a 1 percent difference by gender in smoking in [Table 12.6], more notable percentage differences appear in [Table 12.7], and the differences are in opposite directions: sons are more likely than daughters to smoke in more patriarchal families (24.6 percent versus 16 percent), while daughters are now more likely to smoke in less patriarchal families (29.9 percent versus 22.5 percent). The increase in female smoking in less patriarchal families is pronounced, nearly doubling from 16 percent to 30 percent.
>
> The pattern of percentage differences is a form of interaction effect often called "suppression." It suggests that there is a relationship between gender and smoking that is suppressed in [Table 12.6], which becomes apparent in [Table 12.7] when differences in parental power relationships (i.e., patriarchal relationships) are taken into account.

Statistical control is a key idea in advanced statistical techniques. A measure of association like the correlation coefficient only suggests a relationship. Until a researcher considers control variables, the bivariate relationship could be spurious. Researchers are cautious in interpreting bivariate relationships until they have considered control variables.

TABLE 12.6 Gender and Self-Reported Smoking Behavior

	NO	**YES**	**N**
Male	77.5 (110)	22.5 (32)	100% (142)
Female	76.5 (104)	23.5 (32)	100% (136)

Source: Adapted from Hagan (1997).

TABLE 12.7 Gender and Self-Reported Smoking Behavior, Controlling for Family Type

	MORE PATRIARCHAL		
	No	*Yes*	*N*
Male	84.0 (63)	16.0 (12)	100% (75)
Female	75.4 (49)	24.6 (16)	100% (65)
	LESS PATRIARCHAL		
	No	*Yes*	*N*
Male	70.1 (147)	29.9 (20)	100% (67)
Female	77.5 (55)	22.5 (16)	100% (71)

Source: Adapted from Hagan (1997).

After they introduce control variables, researchers talk about the *net effect* of an independent variable—the effect of the independent variable "net of," or in spite of, the control variable. There are two ways to introduce control variables: trivariate percentaged tables and multiple regression analysis. Each will be briefly discussed next.

The Elaboration Model of Percentaged Tables

Constructing Trivariate Tables. In order to meet all the conditions needed for causality, researchers want to "control for" or see whether an alternative explanation explains away a causal relationship. If an alternative explanation explains a relationship, then the bivariate relationship is spurious. Alternative explanations are operationalized as third variables, which are called *control variables* because they control for alternative explanation.

One way to take such third variables into consideration and see whether they influence the bivariate relationship is to statistically introduce control variables using trivariate or three-variable tables. Trivariate tables differ slightly from bivariate tables; they consist of multiple bivariate tables.

A trivariate table has a bivariate table of the independent and dependent variable for each category of the control variable. These new tables are called *partials*. The number of partials depends on the number of categories in the control variable. Partial tables look like bivariate tables, but they use a subset of the cases. Only cases with a specific value on the control variable are in the partial. Thus, it is possible to break apart a bivariate table to form partials or combine the partials to restore the initial bivariate table.

Trivariate tables have three limitations. First, they are difficult to interpret if a control variable has more than four categories. Second, control variables can be at any level of measurement, but interval or ratio control variables must be grouped (i.e., converted to an ordinal level), and how cases are grouped can affect the interpretation of effects. Finally, the total number of cases is a limiting factor because the cases are divided among cells in partials. The number of cells in the partials equals the number of cells in the bivariate relationship multiplied by the number of categories in the control variable. For example, a control variable has three categories, and a bivariate table has 12 cells, so the partials have $3 \times 12 = 36$ cells. An average of five cases per cell is recommended, so the researcher will need $5 \times 36 = 180$ cases at minimum.

Like bivariate table construction, a trivariate table begins with a compound frequency distribution (CFD), but it is a three-way instead of a two-way CFD. The age/marijuana legalization relationship can again serve as our example. We found that younger people were more likely to agree with legalization, whereas older people tended to hold just the opposite opinion. Does gender make a difference? Table 12.8 looks at this trivariate relationship between age, attitude, and gender.

As with the bivariate tables, each combination in the CFD represents a cell in the final (here the partial) table. Each partial table has the variables in an initial bivariate table.

For three variables, three bivariate tables are logically possible. In the example, the combinations are: (1) gender by attitude, (2) age group by attitude, and (3) gender by age group. The partials are set up on the basis of the initial bivariate relationship. The independent variable in each is "age group" and the dependent variable is "attitude." "Gender" is the control variable. Thus, the trivariate table consists of a pair of partials, each showing the age/attitude relationship for a given gender.

A researcher's theory suggests the hypothesis in the initial bivariate relationship; it also tells him or her which variables provide alternative explanations, (i.e., the control variables). Thus, the choice of the control variable is based on theory.

As with bivariate tables, the CFD provides the raw count for cells (partials here). A researcher converts them into percentages in the same way as for a bivariate table (i.e., divide cells by the row or column total). For example, in the partial table for females, the upper left cell has a 10. The row percentage for that cell is $10/17 = 58$ percent.

The *elaboration paradigm* is a system for reading percentaged trivariate tables.[4] It describes the pattern that emerges when a control variable is introduced. Five terms describe how the partial tables compare to the initial bivariate table, or how the original bivariate relationship changes after the control variable is considered (see Box 12.5). The examples of patterns presented here show strong cases. More advanced statistics are needed when the differences are not as obvious.

The *replication pattern* is the easiest to understand. It is when the partials replicate or reproduce the same relationship that existed in the bivariate table before considering the control variable. It means that the control variable has no effect.

The *specification pattern* is the next easiest pattern. It occurs when one partial replicates the initial bivariate relationship but other partials do not. For example, research may suggest that as the unemployment rate in a community rises, the lar-

TABLE 12.8   CFD and Tables for a Trivariate Analysis

COMPOUND FREQUENCY DISTRIBUTION FOR TRIVARIATE TABLE

MALES			FEMALES		
Age	*Attitude*	*Number of Cases*	*Age*	*Attitude*	*Number of Cases*
Under 30	Agree	10	Under 30	Agree	10
Under 30	No Opinion	1	Under 30	No Opinion	2
Under 30	Disagree	2	Under 30	Disagree	1
30–45	Agree	5	30–45	Agree	5
30–45	No Opinion	5	30–45	No Opinion	5
30–45	Disagree	2	30–45	Disagree	3
46–60	Agree	2	46–60	Agree	2
46–60	No Opinion	5	46–60	No Opinion	5
46–60	Disagree	11	46–60	Disagree	10
61 and older	Agree	3	61 and older	Agree	0
61 and older	No Opinion	0	61 and older	No Opinion	2
61 and older	Disagree	5	61 and older	Disagree	5
	Subtotal	51		Subtotal	50
Missing on either variable		4	Missing on either variable		4
Number of males		55	Number of females		54

PARTIAL TABLE FOR MALES

	AGE GROUP				
ATTITUDE	*Under 30*	*30–45*	*46–60*	*61 and Older*	**TOTAL**
Agree	10	5	2	3	20
No Opinion	1	5	5	0	11
Disagree	2	2	11	5	20
Total	13	12	18	8	51

Missing cases = 4

PARTIAL TABLE FOR FEMALES

	AGE GROUP				
ATTITUDE	*Under 30*	*30–45*	*46–60*	*61 and Older*	**TOTAL**
Agree	10	5	2	0	17
No Opinion	2	5	5	2	14
Disagree	1	3	10	5	19
Total	13	13	17	7	50

Missing cases = 4

Box 12.5_____

Summary of the Elaboration Paradigm

Pattern Name	Pattern Seen When Comparing Partials to the Original Bivariate Table
Replication	Same relationship in both partials as in bivariate table.
Specification	Bivariate relationship is only seen in one of the partial tables.
Interpretation	Bivariate relationship weakens greatly or disappears in the partial tables (control variable is intervening).
Explanation	Bivariate relationship weakens greatly or disappears in the partial tables (control variable is before independent variable).
Suppressor variable	No bivariate relationship; relationship appears in partial tables only.

EXAMPLES OF ELABORATION PATTERNS

Replication

	BIVARIATE TABLE			PARTIALS			
				Control = Low		Control = High	
	Low	High		Low	High	Low	High
Low	85%	15%	Low	84%	16%	86%	14%
High	15%	85%	High	16%	84%	14%	86%

Interpretation or Explanation

	BIVARIATE TABLE			PARTIALS			
				Control = Low		Control = High	
	Low	High		Low	High	Low	High
Low	85%	15%	Low	45%	55%	55%	45%
High	15%	85%	High	55%	45%	45%	55%

Specification

	BIVARIATE TABLE			PARTIALS			
				Control = Low		Control = High	
	Low	High		Low	High	Low	High
Low	85%	85%	Low	95%	5%	50%	50%
High	15%	15%	High	5%	95%	50%	50%

Suppressor Variable

	BIVARIATE TABLE			PARTIALS			
				Control = Low		Control = High	
	Low	High		Low	High	Low	High
Low	54%	46%	Low	84%	16%	14%	86%
High	46%	54%	High	16%	84%	86%	14%

ceny theft rate also goes up. By controlling for gender, however, you now have evidence that this bivariate relationship holds for the 15- to 24-year-olds but not for the 65- to 85-year-olds. In other words, the control variable *specified* the unemployment/larceny/theft relationship.

The control variable has a large impact in both the interpretation and explanation patterns. In both, the bivariate table shows a relationship that disappears in the partials. In other words, the relationship appears to be independence in the partials. The two patterns cannot be distinguished by looking at the tables alone. The difference between them depends on the location of the control variable in the causal order of variables. Theoretically, a control variable can be in one of two places, either between the original independent and dependent variables (i.e., the control variable is intervening), or before the original independent variable.

The *interpretation pattern* describes the situation in which the control variable intervenes between the original independent and dependent variables. For example, the relationship between age and attitude toward the legalization of marijuana may be interpreted by adding a control variable that intervenes between these independent and dependent variables. Political ideology is one possibility. A general political ideology forms prior to the formation of a specific attitude on the legalization issue. Hence, political ideology is formed as one matures, and out of one's political ideology comes specific attitudes toward issues such as legalization. In this example of the interpretation pattern, the control variable is an intervening variable, which helps you interpret the meaning of the complete relationship.

The *explanation pattern* looks the same as interpretation. The difference is the temporal order of the control variable. In this pattern, a control variable comes before the independent variable in the initial bivariate relationship. For instance, gender can be used as a control variable to help explain the relationship between unemployment and violent crime. Since gender precedes unemployment in time, it is an antecedent variable, as opposed to an intervening variable. The explanation pattern changes when the control variable (gender) is added. The unemployment/violent crime relationship disappears, suggesting it to be spurious.

The *suppressor variable pattern* occurs when the bivariate tables suggest independence but a relationship appears in one or both of the partials. You saw an example of a suppressor variable earlier (Tables 12.6 and 12.7). The relationship between gender and self-reported smoking behavior was hidden (or suppressed) until the control variable (i.e., type of family) was added. The true relationship became apparent in the partials when controlled for family type.

Multiple Regression Analysis

Multiple regression is a statistical technique whose calculation is beyond the level in this book. Although it is quickly computed by the appropriate statistics software, a background in statistics is needed to prevent making errors in its calculation and interpretation. It requires interval- or ratio-level data. It is discussed here for two reasons. First, it controls for many alternative explanations and variables simultaneously (it is rarely possible to use more than one control variable at a time using percentaged tables). Second, it is widely used in criminology, and you are likely to encounter it when reading research reports or articles.

Multiple regression results tell the reader two things. First, the results have a measure called R-squared (R^2), which tells how well a set of variables explains a dependent variable. *Explain* means reduced errors when predicting the dependent variable scores on the basis of information about the independent variables. A good model with several independent variables might account for, or explain, a large percentage of variation in a dependent variable. For example, an R^2 of .50 means that knowing the independent and control variables improves the accuracy of predicting the dependent variable by 50 percent, or half as many errors are made as would be made without knowing about the variables.

Second, the regression results measure the direction and size of the effect of each variable on a dependent variable. The effect is measured precisely and given a numerical value. For example, a researcher can see how five independent or control variables simultaneously affect a dependent variable, with all variables controlling for the effects of one another. This is especially valuable for testing theories that state that multiple independent variables cause one dependent variable (see Chapter 3 for examples of causal diagrams).

The effect on the dependent variable is measured by a standardized regression coefficient or the Greek letter beta (β). It is similar to a correlation coefficient. In fact, the beta coefficient for two variables equals the r correlation coefficient.

Researchers use the beta regression coefficient to determine whether control variables have an effect. For example, the bivariate correlation between X and Y is .75. Next, the researcher statistically considers four control variables. If the beta remains at .75, then the four control variables have no effect. However, if the beta for X and Y gets smaller (e.g., drops to .20), it indicates that the control variables have an effect.

Suppose a criminologist is interested in studying money laundering. He or she may want to know what explains increases or decreases in the number of currency transaction reports (CTRs) sent to the federal government. Multiple regression analysis would be a suitable technique. For sake of argument, five independent variables are included in the regression model: (1) the number of banks in the country, (2) the amount of currency in the economy, (3) the size of enforcement staff, (4) the retail price of cocaine, and (5) the gross domestic product (GDP). All independent variables together have a 38 percent accuracy in predicting the number of CTRs (see Box 12.6).[5]

The example suggests that enforcement and GDP have the strongest effects of the five independent variables. Curiously, these are negatively related to the number of currency transaction reports. The price variable has a positive relationship with the dependent variable, but its effect is about half as strong as the enforcement variable.

Box 12.6

Example of Multiple Regression Results

DEPENDENT VARIABLE IS NUMBER OF CURRENCY TRANSACTION REPORTS

Independent Variable	Standardized Regression Coefficients
Banks	−.19
Currency	.01
Enforcement	−.44
Price	.23
Gross domestic product	−.39
	$R^2 = .38$

INFERENTIAL STATISTICS

The Purpose of Inferential Statistics

The statistics discussed so far in this chapter are descriptive statistics. But researchers often want to do more than describe; they want to test hypotheses, know whether sample results hold true in a population, and decide whether differences in results (e.g., between the mean scores of two groups) are big enough to indicate that a relationship really exists. Inferential statistics use probability theory to test hypotheses formally, permit inferences from a sample to a population, and test whether descriptive results are likely to be due to random factors or to a real relationship.

This section explains the basic ideas of inferential statistics but does not deal with inferential statistics in any detail. This area is more complex than descriptive statistics and requires a background in statistics.

Inferential statistics rely on principles from probability sampling, where a researcher uses a random process (e.g., a random number table) to select cases from the entire population. Inferential statistics are a precise way to talk about how confident a researcher can be when inferring from the results in a sample to the population.

You have already encountered inferential statistics if you have read or heard about "statistical significance" or results "significant at the .05 level." Researchers use them to conduct various statistical tests (e.g., a *t*-test or an *F*-test). Statistical significance is also used in formal hypothesis testing, which is a precise way to decide whether to accept or to reject a null hypothesis.[6]

Statistical Significance

Statistical significance means that results are not likely to be due to chance factors. It indicates the probability of finding a relationship in the sample when there is none in the population. Because probability samples involve a random process, it is always possible that sample results will differ from a population parameter. A researcher wants to estimate the odds that sample results are due to a true population parameter or to chance factors of random sampling. Statistical significance uses probability theory and specific statistical tests to tell a researcher whether the results (e.g., an association, a difference between two means, a regression coefficient) are produced by random error in random sampling.

Statistical significance only tells what is likely. It cannot prove anything with absolute certainty. It states that particular outcomes are more or less probable. Statistical significance is *not* the same as practical, substantive, or theoretical significance. Results can be statistically significant but theoretically meaningless or trivial. For example, two variables can have a statistically significant association due to coincidence, with no logical connection between them (e.g., length of fingernails and ability to speak French).

Levels of Significance

Researchers usually express statistical significance in terms of levels (e.g., a test is statistically significant at a specific level) rather than giving the specific probability. The *level of statistical significance* (usually .05, .01, or .001) is a way of talking about the likelihood that results are due to chance factors—that is, that a rela-

tionship appears in the sample when there is none in the population. If a researcher says that results are significant at the .05 level, this means the following:

— Results like these are due to chance factors only 5 in 100 times.
— There is a 95 percent chance that the sample results are not due to chance factors alone, but reflect the population accurately.
— The odds of such results based on chance alone are .05, or 5 percent.
— One can be 95 percent confident that the results are due to a real relationship in the population, not chance factors.

These all say the same thing in different ways. This may sound like the discussion of sampling distributions and the central limit theorem in the chapter on sampling. It is not an accident. Both are based on probability theory, which researchers use to link sample data to a population. Probability theory lets us predict what happens in the long run over many events when a random process is used. In other words, it allows precise prediction over many situations in the long run, but not for a specific situation. Since we have one sample and we want to infer to the population, probability theory helps us estimate the odds that our particular sample represents the population. We cannot know for certain unless we have the whole population, but probability theory lets us state our confidence—how likely it is that the sample shows one thing while something else is true in the population.

Take, for example, a study of some 1,600 court dispositions in Australia that showed Aborigines are relatively more likely to be sentenced to prison (Broadhurst, 1997). The question is: Does the sample of 1,600 represent all court dispositions? Is it discrimination? Or is it just chance finding? Using a Chi-square statistic (see Box 12.7), the researcher can state his or her findings with much more confidence (see Table 12.9). And, given the probability of 1 out of 1,000, one can confidently say that there is a relationship between Aboriginality and court dispositions.

Box 12.7_____

Chi-Square

The chi-square (χ^2) is used in two ways. This creates confusion. As a *descriptive statistic*, it tells us the strength of the association between two variables; as an *inferential statistic*, it tells us the probability that any association we find is likely to be due to chance factors. The chi-square is a widely used and powerful way to look at variables measured at the ordinal level. It is a more precise way to tell whether there is an association in a bivariate percentaged table than by just "eye balling" it.

Logically, we first figure out "expected values" in a table. We do this based on information from the marginals alone. Recall that marginals are frequency distributions of each variable alone. An expected value can be thought of as our "best guess" without looking at the body of the table. Next, we look at the data to see how much differs from the "expected value." If it differs by a lot, then there may be an association between the variables. If the data in a table are identical or very close to the expected values, then the variables are not associated; they are independent. In other words, *independence* means "what is going on" in a table is what we would expect based on the marginals alone. Chi-square is zero if there is independence and gets bigger as the association gets stronger. If the data in the table greatly differ from the expected values, then we know something is "going on" beyond what we would expect from the marginals alone (i.e., an association between the variables). See the example of an association between race and court disposition.

RAW OR OBSERVED DATA TABLE

	COURT DISPOSITION			
RACE	*Acquitted*	*Prison*	*Noncustodial*	**TOTAL**
White	30	10	10	50
Black	10	30	10	50
Other	30	20	50	100
Total	70	60	70	200

EXPECTED VALUES TABLE

Expected value = (Column total × Row total)/Grand total). EXAMPLE (70 × 50)/200 = 17.5

	COURT DISPOSITION			
RACE	*Acquitted*	*Prison*	*Noncustodial*	**TOTAL**
White	17.5	15	17.5	50
Black	17.5	15	17.5	50
Other	35	30	35	100
Total	70	60	70	200

DIFFERENCE TABLE

Difference = (Observed − Expected). EXAMPLE (30 − 17.5) = 12.5

	COURT DISPOSITION			
RACE	*Acquitted*	*Prison*	*Noncustodial*	**TOTAL**
White	12.5	−5	−7.5	0
Black	−7.5	15	−7.5	0
Other	−5	−10	15	0
Total	0	0	0	0

(continued)

Box 12.7 (continued)

Chi-square = Sum of each difference squared, then divided by the expected value of the cell. Example: 12.5 squared = 156.25, divided by 17.5 = 8.93.

Chi-square = 1st row (8.93 + 1.67 + 3.21) +
2nd row (3.21 + 15 + 3.21) +
3rd row (.71 + 3.33 + 6.43) = 45.7

Since chi-squared is not zero, the data are not independent; there is an association. The chi-square coefficient cannot tell us the direction (e.g., negative) of the association. For inferential statistics, we need to use a chi-square table or computer program to evaluate the association (i.e., to see how likely such a large chi-square is to occur by chance alone). Without going into all the details about the chi-square table, this association is rare; it occurs by chance less than 1 in 1,000 times. For a table with nine cells, a chi-square of 45.7 is significant at the .001 level.

Type I and Type II Errors

If the logic of statistical significance is based on stating whether chance factors produce results, why use the .05 level? It means a 5 percent chance that randomness could cause the results. Why not use a more certain standard—for example, a 1 in 1,000 probability of random chance? This gives a smaller chance that randomness versus a true relationship caused the results.

There are two answers to this way of thinking. The simple answer is that the scientific community has informally agreed to use .05 as a rule of thumb for most purposes. Being 95 percent confident of results is the accepted standard for explaining the social world.

A second, more complex answer involves a trade-off between making Type I and Type II errors (see Table 12.10). A researcher can make two kinds of logical errors. A *Type I error* occurs when the researcher says that a relationship exists when in fact none exists. It means falsely rejecting

TABLE 12.9   Example of Chi-Square

	HIGHER COURT DISPOSITIONS BY ABORIGINALITY, 1990 (IN PERCENT)		
	N	*Noncustodial*	*Prison*
Aborigine	298	40.3	59.7
Non-Aborgine	1,177	54.8	45.2
Unknown	125	58.4	41.6

Note: Chi-square = 22.1, *df* = 2; *p* < 0.0001.
Source: Adapted from Broadhurst (1997:441).

TABLE 12.10   Type I and Type II Errors

WHAT THE RESEARCHER SAYS	TRUE SITUATION IN THE WORLD	
	No Relationship	*Causal Relationship*
No relationship	No error	Type II error
Causal relationship	Type I error	No error

a null hypothesis. A *Type II error* occurs when a researcher says that a relationship does not exist, when in fact it does. It means falsely accepting a null hypothesis. Of course, researchers want to avoid both errors. They want to say that there is a relationship in the data only when it does exist and that there is no relationship only when there really is none, but they face a dilemma: As the odds of making one type of error decline, the odds of making the opposite error increase.

The idea of Type I and Type II errors may seem difficult at first, but the same logical dilemma appears outside research settings. For example, a jury can err by deciding that an accused person is guilty when in fact he or she is innocent. Or the jury can err by deciding that a person is innocent when in fact he or she is guilty. The jury does not want to make either error. It does not want to jail the innocent or to free the guilty, but the jury must make a judgment using limited information. Likewise, a pharmaceutical company has to decide whether to sell a new drug. The company can err by stating that the drug has no side effects when, in fact, it has the side effect of causing blindness. Or it can err by holding back a drug because of fear of serious side effects when in fact there are none. The company does not want to make either error. If it makes the first error, the company will face lawsuits and injure people. The second error will prevent the company from selling a drug that may cure illness and produce profits.

Let us put the ideas of statistical significance and the two types of error together. An overly cautious researcher sets a high level of significance and is likely to make one kind of error. For example, the researcher might use the .0001 level. He or she attributes the results to chance unless they are so rare that they would occur by chance only 1 in 10,000 times. Such a high standard means that the researcher is most likely to err by saying results are due to chance when in fact they are not. He or she may falsely accept the null hypothesis when there is a causal relationship (a Type II error). By contrast, a risk-taking researcher sets a low level of significance, such as .10. His or her results indicate a relationship would occur by chance 1 in 10 times. He or she is likely to err by saying that a causal rela-

tionship exists, when in fact random factors (e.g., random sampling error) actually cause the results. The researcher is likely to falsely reject the null hypothesis (Type I error). In sum, the .05 level is a compromise between Type I and Type II errors.

This section outlines the basics of inferential statistics. The statistical techniques are precise and rely on the relationship between sampling error, sample size, and central limit theorem. The power of inferential statistics is their ability to let a researcher state, with specific degrees of certainty, that specific sample results are likely to be true in a population.

Tests for inferential statistics are useful but limited. The data must come from a random sample, and tests only take into account sampling errors. Nonsampling errors (e.g., a poor sampling frame or a poorly designed measure) are not considered. Do not be fooled into thinking that such tests offer easy, final answers.

CONCLUSION

In this chapter, you learned how to organize and analyze quantitative data. You now have the foundation for understanding quantitative criminology.

You know how data must first be coded before being analyzed by univariate, bivariate, and, finally, multivariate statistics. You also know that bivariate relationships might be spurious, thus requiring the use of control variable. Beginning researchers sometimes feel as though they have done something wrong if the data do not support their hypothesis. *There is nothing wrong with rejecting a hypothesis.* Hypotheses are educated guesses based on limited knowledge; they need to be tested. Good research depends on high-quality methodology, not on supporting a pet hypothesis.

Good criminologists must guard against possible errors in research. Errors can occur throughout the research process: research design, measurement, data collection, coding, calculating statistics, assembling tables, or interpreting results. All of this must be accounted for as the criminologist asks himself or herself what the research means. The only way to assign meaning to tables, charts, and statistics is with the use of criminological theory.

The facts do not speak for themselves. It is the scientist's understanding of concepts and their relationships that unlocks the meaning of quantitative data. This is not to say, however, that you should not be open to new ideas that will inevitably result from you doing the research. Consider these new ideas and reflect on how they might fit into the research at hand.

This is what top scientists do in every field of study.

We turn now to the fascinating topic of qualitative research. Criminology has an extremely rich tradition when it comes to qualitative research. For decades, criminologists have strived to study the world of deviants and criminals from the inside, so to speak. This requires a completely different approach to research, as mentioned in an earlier discussion of positivist and interpretive approaches to criminology.

KEY TERMS

bar chart
bivariate statistics
body of a table
cell of a table
code sheets
codebook
coding
coding procedure
compound frequency
   distribution
computer programs
contingency cleaning
control variable
covariation
cross-tabulation
curvilinear relationship
data records
descriptive statistics

direct entry method
elaboration paradigm
explanation pattern
field
frequency distribution
frequency polygon
histogram
independence
interpretation pattern
level of statistical significance
linear relationship
marginals
mean
median
mode
net effect
optical scan sheet
partials

percentile
pie chart
possible code cleaning
proportionate reduction in
   error (PRE)
range
replication pattern
scattergram
skewed distribution
specification pattern
standard deviation
statistical relationship
statistical significance
suppressor variable pattern
Type I error
Type II error
univariate statistics
z-score

REVIEW QUESTIONS

1. What is a codebook and how is it used in research?
2. How do researchers clean data and check their coding?
3. Describe how interval- and ratio-level variables can be used in tables.
4. In what ways can a researcher display frequency distribution information?
5. Describe the differences between mean, median, and mode.
6. What three features of a relationship can be seen from a scattergram?
7. What is a compound frequency distribution and how is it used?
8. When can a researcher generalize from a scattergram to a percentaged table to find a relationship among variables?

9. Discuss the concept of control as it is used in trivariate analysis.

10. What does it mean to say "statistically significant at the .001 level," and what type of error is more likely: Type I or Type II?

NOTES

1. Some of the best practical advice on coding and handling quantitative data come from survey research. See discussions in Babbie (1995:366–372), Backstrom and Hursh-Cesar (1981:309–400), Fowler (1984:127–133), Sonquist and Dunkelberg (1977:210–215), and Warwick and Lininger (1975:234–291).

2. For discussions of many different ways to display quantitative data, see Fox (1992), Henry (1995), Tufte (1983, 1991), and Zeisel (1985:14–33).

3. There are other statistics to measure a special kind of mean for ordinal data and for other special situations, which are beyond the level of discussion in this book.

4. For a discussion of the elaboration paradigm and its history, see Babbie (1995:400–409) and Rosenberg (1968).

5. Beginning students and people outside criminology are sometimes surprised at the low (10 to 50 percent) predictive accuracy in multiple regression results.

There are three responses to this. First, a 10 to 50 percent reduction in errors is really not bad compared to purely random guessing. Second, positivist criminology is still developing. Although the levels of accuracy may not be as high as those of the physical sciences, they are much higher than for any explanation of crime possible 10 or 20 years ago. Finally, the theoretically important issue in most multiple regression models is less than the accuracy of overall prediction than the effects of specific variables. Most hypotheses involve the effects of specific independent variables on dependent variables.

6. In formal hypothesis testing, researchers test the *null hypothesis.* They usually want to reject the null because rejection of the null indirectly supports the alternative hypothesis to the null, the one they deduced from theory as a tentative explanation. The null hypotheis was discussed in Chapter 6.

RECOMMENDED READINGS

Bohrnstedt, George, and David Knoke. (1994). *Statistics for social data analysis,* 3rd ed. Itasca, IL: Peacock. This is a favorite among the dozens of statistics books for social researchers. It covers both descriptive and inferential statistics from the basics to the advanced. It is clearly written and real data and real theories are used in the examples. In it you will find discussed most of the statistics that are used in recent articles of the major scholarly journals.

Henry, Gary T. (1995). *Graphing data: Techniques for display and analysis.* Thousand Oaks, CA: Sage. This is an accessible, short introduction to graphing quantitative social science data. Unlike the very sophisticated books on graphing by Edward Tufte (1983, 1991), Henry is for beginners and has many practical tips. For example, Henry notes that certain charts (three-dimensional charts, stacked bar charts) are confusing or misleading.

Seltzer, Richard A. (1996). *Mistakes that social scientists make.* New York: St. Martin's. This one is fun but very useful. Seltzer has collected short, real-life examples of typical problems researchers encounter. By learning about problems other researchers have had, you will be able to anticipate and avoid many of them.

Zeisel, Hans. (1985). *Say it with figures,* 6th ed. New York: Harper & Row. This standard has been used since 1947. It discusses solutions to important data analysis issues in nontechnical language. It clearly discusses ways to present data analysis in the form of tables and elementary statistics. For example, there are three chapters on using percentages.

QUALITATIVE RESEARCH DESIGN

Crime was an important source of income for poor townsmen, but its history has not yet been studied and statistics chiefly illustrate the changing sizes and preoccupations of police forces.

—John Iliffe, *The African Poor*, p. 175

INTRODUCTION

Iliffe's words were written about urban crime in colonial Nigeria, but they also underscore the significance of the qualitative perspective. They do that, first and foremost, by contextualizing crime, or connecting it to its social context. Block and Chambliss (1981:228) emphasized the importance of a contextual perspective:

> *We suggest not only adopting the historical methodology that we have employed in this work (including contemporary history), but also carefully and relentlessly emphasizing the lives of people in the context of a political economy viewed "from the bottom up" as a necessary palliative to conventional viewpoints.*

Thus, to grasp the causes and consequences of urban crime in the preceding example, one must explore the political economy of Nigerian colonialism. This leads to a critique of the colonial order that impoverished many people, and suggests that urban crime be understood, in large measure, as an economic survival strategy. Again, according to Block and Chambliss (1981:221), "By grounding studies in notions of political economy, the symbiotic relationships at the center of criminality, law creation, and law enforcement within particular historical epochs are illuminated."

If historical/comparative context is important to a qualitative perspective, so too is a grounded understanding of the social meaning actors attribute to their own criminal behavior. Polsky (1997:229) has criticized criminologists for not getting an up-close view of crime, criminals, and the justice system:

> Their misplaced morality leads them [i.e., criminologists], in practice, to pass up the field study of criminals, to invent various rationalizations for avoiding it, to exaggerate its difficulties, and to neglect some fairly obvious techniques for avoiding these difficulties.

His advice to criminologists wanting "to build a real science" is to imitate what Malinowski called "open-air anthropology":

> The anthropologist must relinquish his comfortable position in the long chair on the veranda of the missionary compound, Government station, or planter's bungalow. . . . He must go out into the villages, and see the natives at work in gardens, on the beach, in the jungle. . . . Information must come to him full-flavored from his own observations of native life. (as quoted in Polsky, 1997:229)

The point is, qualitative criminologists must not be satisfied with the "preoccupations of police forces" and official statistics, but rather must have an empathetic understanding of the "poor townsmen." Simply put, qualitative criminologists are duty bound to do fieldwork to learn about their subjects firsthand. Interestingly, a growing trend in qualitative research combines historical analysis with fieldwork. This approach is being termed *historical ethnography* (Hutchinson, 1996).

Some criminologists falsely think that qualitative research is easier to do than quantitative research. They believe all the criminologist does is "hang around," keeping his or her ears open, waiting for something to happen. While it is true that qualitative criminologists do not rely on statistics and rarely begin with a formal theory and hypothesis to test, the belief that qualitative research is easy is a myth. The triumph of qualitative criminology is due more to the dedication, hard work, sensitivity, courage, and writing skills of the individual researcher than to anything intrinsic in the methodology itself.[1]

Consequently, this chapter cannot give specific rules for doing qualitative criminology. Instead, we will look at the underlying characteristics of qualitative research design and discuss tips on how researchers can combine qualitative and quantitative methods effectively.

THE QUALITATIVE ORIENTATION

In this section, you will learn some ways in which a qualitative research orientation differs from that of quantitative research—approaches to data, reliance on nonpositivist perspectives to criminology, the greater use of *logic in practice,* and the following of a more cyclical research path (see Table 13.1).

Approaching Data

A qualitative research style involves more than looking at qualitative data. Positivists often try to convert the data into a quantitative form or analyze it using quantitative techniques. For positivists, qualitative data are mental states or conditions that cause measurable behavior. The issue is how to capture it with precise, reliable quantitative measurement. By contrast, qualitative researchers view qualitative data as intrinsically meaningful, not as deficient. For them, the central issues are not how to convert qualitative data into reliable, objective numbers; rather, "they concern such matters as the accessibility of other (sub)cultures, the relativity of actor's accounts of their social worlds, and the relation between sociological descriptions and actors' conceptions of their actions" (Halfpenny, 1979:803). The qualitative research style values qualitative data. Its entire orientation is organized around theorizing, collecting, and analyzing qualitative data. Qualitative researchers may have different concerns about data. Often, they may be concerned more with generating new concepts than with testing existing ones.

Some people believe that qualitative data are "soft," intangible, and immaterial. Such data are so fuzzy and elusive that researchers cannot really capture them. This is not necessarily the case.

TABLE 13.1   Differences between Quantitative and Qualitative Research

QUANTITATIVE	QUALITATIVE
▪ Test hypothesis that the researcher begins with.	▪ Capture and discover meaning once the researcher becomes immersed in the data.
▪ Concepts are in the form of distinct variables.	▪ Concepts are in the form of themes, motifs, generalizations, and taxonomies.
▪ Measures are systematically created before data collection and are standardized.	▪ Measures are created in an ad hoc manner and are often specific to the individual setting or researcher.
▪ Data are in the form of numbers from precise measurement.	▪ Data are in the form of words from documents, observations, and transcripts.
▪ Theory is largely causal and is deductive.	▪ Theory can be causal or noncausal and is often inductive.
▪ Procedures are standard, and replication is assumed.	▪ Research procedures are particular, and replication is very rare.
▪ Analysis proceeds by using statistics, tables, or charts and discussing how what they show relates to hypotheses.	▪ Analysis proceeds by extracting themes or generalizations from evidence and organizing data to present a coherent, consistent picture.

Qualitative data are empirical. They involve documenting real events, recording what people say (with words, gestures, and tone), observing specific behaviors, studying written documents, or examining visual images. These are all concrete aspects of the world. For example, McNamara (1986) used a qualitative approach to explore the social process of bribing police officers in Bolivia. His evidence was empirical—that is, it was based on real-life observation and experience, not make-believe. It was just as "hard" as any data quantitative criminologists might use. Indeed, given the research question, it is difficult to imagine how he could have even employed a quantitative technique.

A Nonpositivist Perspective

Qualitative criminology relies largely on the interpretive and critical approaches to social science. The two approaches differ from each other in important ways, but both are alternatives to positivism, which is the foundation of quantitative research. Quantitative research is contrary to most of the core assumptions and goals of inter-

pretive social science (see Chapter 4). In contrast to interpretive researchers, critical researchers use quantitative techniques. When they do so, however, critical criminologists diverge from strict positivism. They apply theory in a different way, give the historical context a major role, critique social conditions, and reveal deep structures of social relations.

There is no one-to-one correspondence between research techniques and the approaches to criminology. Nevertheless, historical-comparative research is most compatible with a critical approach. Sometimes, it is also used by researchers who adopt the interpretive or the positivist approach. Field research is suited to the assumptions of an interpretive approach, but some critical researchers also use it.

The significance of the three approaches is evident in how a researcher sees data. A quantitative researcher assumes that he or she can conceptualize criminological concepts as variables, and that he or she can develop objective, precise measures with numbers that capture important features of the social world. By contrast, a qualitative researcher focuses on subjective meanings, definitions, metaphors, symbols, and descriptions of specific cases. He or she attempts to capture aspects of the social world (e.g., sights, odors, atmosphere, etc.) for which it is difficult to develop precise measures expressed as numbers.

We can see how the three approaches relate to research techniques by considering the contrast between the technocratic and transcendent perspectives to research.[2] The *technocratic perspective* fits better with positivism, and, although unknowingly, quantitative researchers more frequently fall into it. In it, the researcher is the expert, and research questions often originate with the sponsors of the research (i.e., those who supply funds). The goal of research is to discover and document lawlike generalizations oriented toward increasing efficiency. Thus, this is the perspective of a technician who serves bureaucratic needs.

By contrast, the *transcendent perspective* more closely fits the interpretive and critical approaches. In it, research questions originate with the standpoint of the people being studied, not that of outsiders. Its goal is to remove false beliefs held by those being studied and to treat people as creative, compassionate living beings, not as objects. It often raises questions about power or inequality and views social relations more as the outcome of willful actions than as laws of human nature. It tries to help people grow, take charge of their lives, and engage in social change—that is, to transcend current social conditions.

The transcendent perspective is particularly evident in the emerging body of research on human rights issues. Some of this new research appears as documentary films. A case in point is the 1994 film entitled "Solo, The Law of the *Favela*" by Jos de Putter. It portrays everyday life in the slums of Rio de Janeiro, and the young boys whose passion for soccer helps them adjust to a situation of violence, crime, and abject poverty.

A Logic in Practice

According to Kaplan (1964:3–11), statements about how to do social research follow two logics: reconstructed logic and logic in practice. All research mixes both types, although the propor-

tion of each type of logic varies. Statements about quantitative research are likely to be "reconstructed," whereas qualitative research arises more "in practice."

Reconstructed logic means that the logic of how to do research is highly organized and restated in an idealized, formal, and systematic form. It is reconstructed into logically consistent rules and terms. It is a cleansed model of how good research should proceed. This logic appears in textbooks and in published research reports. For example, the rules for conducting a simple random sample are very straightforward and follow a step-by-step procedure.

Logic in practice is the logic of how research is actually carried out. It is relatively messy, with more ambiguity, and is tied to specific cases and oriented toward the practical completion of a task. It has fewer set rules. The logic is based on judgment calls or norms shared among experienced researchers. It depends on an informal folk wisdom passed among researchers when they get together over lunch or coffee and discuss doing research.

Quantitative research is usually described as using reconstructed logic. This makes it easier to define and learn from books or formal instruction. Quantitative researchers describe the technical research procedures they use (e.g., a systematic random sample of 300 drawn from a telephone directory; Likert scaling). The procedures are shared, explicit methods.

Qualitative research uses more of a logic in practice. It relies on the informal wisdom that has developed from the experiences of researchers. Qualitative research reports may not discuss method (common for historical-comparative research) or may have a personal autobiographical account tailored to a particular study (common for field research). Few procedures or terms are standardized and there is a debate among qualitative researchers about whether they ever should be. Many qualitative researchers learned how to do research by reading many reports, by trial and error, and by working in an apprentice role with an experienced researcher. This does not mean that qualitative research is less valid, but it may be more difficult for someone learning about it for the first time to grasp.

A Nonlinear Path

Researchers follow a path when conducting research. The path is a metaphor for the sequence of things to do: what is finished first or where a researcher has been, and what comes next or where he or she is going. The path may be one that is well worn and marked with signposts where many other researchers have trod. Alternatively, it may be a new path into unknown territory where few others have gone, and without signs marking the direction forward.

In general, quantitative researchers follow a more linear path than do qualitative researchers. A *linear research path* follows a fixed sequence of steps. It is like a staircase leading in one clear direction. It is a way of thinking and a way of looking at issues—the direct, narrow, straight path that is most common in western European and North American culture.

Qualitative research is more nonlinear and cyclical. Rather than moving in a straight line, a *cyclical research path* makes successive passes through steps, sometimes moving backward and sideways before moving on. It is more of a spiral, moving slowly upward but not directly. With each cycle or repetition, a researcher collects new data and gains new insights.

People who are used to the direct, linear approach may be impatient with a less direct cyclical path. From a strict linear perspective, a cyclical path looks inefficient and sloppy. But the diffuse cyclical approach is not merely disorganized, undefined chaos. It can be highly effective for creating a feeling for the whole, for grasping subtle shades of meaning, for pulling together divergent information, and for switching perspectives. It is not an excuse for doing poor-quality research, and it has its own discipline and rigor. It borrows devices from the humanities (e.g., metaphor, analogy, theme, motif, and irony) and is oriented toward constructing meaning. A cyclical path is suited for tasks such as translating languages, where delicate shades of meaning, subtle

connotations, or contextual distinctions can be important.

CHARACTERISTICS OF QUALITATIVE RESEARCH

In this section, we look at six characteristics of a qualitative style of research: importance of the context, the case study method, the researcher's integrity, grounded theory, process, and interpretation.

The Context Is Critical

Qualitative researchers emphasize the importance of social context for understanding the social world. They hold that the meaning of a social action or statement depends, in an important way, on the context in which it appears. When a researcher removes an event, social action, answer to a question, or conversation from the social context in which it appears, or ignores the context, social meaning and significance are distorted.

Attention to social context means that a qualitative researcher notes what came before or what surrounds the focus of study. It also implies that the same events or behaviors can have different meanings in different cultures or historical eras. The example at the beginning of this chapter serves as a good illustration of this (see Box 13.1). Urban crime in colonial Nigeria can be perceived in various ways. To colonial authorities, it is individual lawlessness that must not go unpunished. But to the poor townspeople, crime represents an acceptable way to deal with the vicissitudes of colonial rule. Perceiving themselves as victims of an unwanted system of exploitation, the townspeople may feel no recourse but to commit property crime. Perhaps in some situations, the criminal might be viewed as a hero—something of a Robin Hood—who challenges the property rights of colonial masters. Indeed, this is the perspective Eric Hobsbawm adopted in his historical analysis of "social bandits":

> *Underworld robbers and raiders regard the peasants as their prey and know them to be hostile; the robbed in turn regard the attackers as criminals in their sense of the term and not merely by official*

Box 13.1 _____

Example of the Importance of Context for Meaning

The meaning of "urban crime in colonial Nigeria" is different in different social contexts.

PERSPECTIVE OF COLONIAL AUTHORITIES	PERSPECTIVE OF POOR TOWNSPEOPLE
1. The colonial system of rule in Nigeria is desirable. It helps modernize the country and brings educational, social, and economic opportunities to most of the population of the country.	1. The colonial system of rule in Nigeria is imposed by England through military means. Colonial authority is inherently illegitimate. It is a system that favors the privileged few and exploits the masses. People migrate to the city because of the destruction of the traditional (precolonial), rural economy and way of life.
2. Crime is a direct challenge to legitimate colonial authority. It is the individual lawlessness of a relatively few, bad people in Lagos and other urban areas of the country.	2. Most forms of urban (property) crime are the direct consequence of economic marginalization of townspeople. Criminals are ordinary folks who are forced to break the colonial (illegitimate) law. Some "social criminals" are considered folk heroes who rob from the rich and give to the poor.
3. Punishment of criminal behavior must be certain and severe, so as to deter future lawlessness. If left unchecked, the spread of crime will undermine the political and economic foundations of colonial rule.	3. The colonial police and justice system are established to protect the property rights of colonial masters. Popular cultural norms support the social criminals rather than the police.

law. It would be unthinkable for a social bandit to snatch the peasants' (though not the lord's) harvest in his own territory, or perhaps even elsewhere. Those who do therefore lack the peculiar relationship which makes banditry "social." (quoted in Block and Chambliss, 1981:224)

The Value of the Case Study

A quantitative researcher usually gathers specific information on a great many cases (e.g., respondents, subjects, etc.). By contrast, a qualitative researcher may use a case study approach. He or she might gather a large amount of information on one or a few cases, go into greater depth, and get more details on the cases being examined. He or she gathers a range of information about a few selected cases.

The case study researcher also goes about data analysis differently. Whereas a quantitative researcher looks for patterns in the variables on many cases, a case study researcher faces an overwhelming amount of data but has been immersed in it. Immersion gives the researcher an intimate familiarity with people's lives and culture. He or she looks for patterns in the lives, actions, and words of people in the context of the complete case as a whole.

Take the example of Mercer Sullivan's (1989) case study of three New York City neighborhoods. The researcher compared the relative effects of deindustrialization in a White working-class neighborhood, an Hispanic American neighborhood, and an African American neighborhood. He found that in the White neighborhood, informal employment networks made up of friends and family helped the youth find jobs, despite the deindustrialization. The same was not true, however, of the other two. There were no such networks for the youth to tap into in either the Hispanic American or the African American neighborhoods. In this context, "getting paid" was a slang term the minority youth used to describe their petty theft (e.g., muggings and purse snatchings) and drug dealing, which served as employment alternatives.

Researcher Integrity

A Question of Trust. Researchers who adopt a positivist, quantitative approach ask: How can qualitative research be objective or unbiased? There are many opportunities for a researcher's personal influence to affect qualitative research. A field researcher hangs around and observes a social group for an extended period. He or she gets to know the people being studied, and his or her presence in the setting can affect what occurs. A field researcher sees, hears, remembers, and records only some of what occurs, and puts only some of what is in his or her field notes into a final report. Likewise, a historical-comparative researcher sorts through and reads many sources. The evidence about the past is incomplete, and he or she selects some available material for emphasis. Replication is rare in qualitative research, and researchers usually work alone.

Researcher integrity is a real issue. In fact, Collins (1984:339) argued that an important reason for an increased reliance on quantitative methods, replication, and statistics in social research is a lack of trust: "We set stringent statistical criteria not because logically they are crucial for establishing the truth of a theory but *because our intellectual community is socially distrustful of the honesty of investigators*" (emphasis added).

Checks. Qualitative researchers ensure that their research accurately reflects the evidence and have checks on their evidence.[3] For field researchers, this involves a thorough and often time-consuming process of checking the veracity of what he or she has been told or has observed. The researcher seeks confirming evidence by talking to and observing a wide circle of individuals in the field. Even if the researcher believes there may be some inaccuracy in what is being reported, this itself is evidence of the informant's perspective and vested interests. Similarly, the researcher examining historical evidence uses techniques for verifying the authenticity of sources (see Chapter 16).

Another check is the great volume of detailed written notes that qualitative researchers record. Researchers vary the amount of detail they record, but they may have hundreds or thousands of pages of notes. Besides a detailed verbatim description of the evidence, notes include references to the sources, commentaries by the researcher, and key terms to help organize the notes. They also include quotes, maps, diagrams, paraphrasing, and counts. Field notes and the subsequent analysis can be cross-checked by reading them to subjects who have personally experienced the specific issues in question. Hutchinson's (1996:29–30) ethnographic study of the effects of prolonged civil war on the Nuer of southern Sudan provides a good illustration of this:

> *Last, this book is unusual, I suspect, in the degree to which it was composed in active collaboration with the Nuer not only as informants but as critical commentators. While in the field I discussed many of the book's main themes with numerous Nuer men and women living deep in the countryside. All six core chapters were also read by a diverse group of university-educated Nuer located in Sudan, England, and the United States. Thanks to their cooperation and assistance, I am confident that the ethnographic materials presented here are not only nuanced and accurate but, more important, successful in conveying an experientially resonant interpretation of the historical themes examined.*

The most important way that a qualitative researcher creates trust in readers is the way he or she presents evidence. A qualitative researcher does not present all of his or her detailed notes in a report; rather, he or she spins a web of interlocking details, providing sufficient texture and detail so that the readers feel that they are there. A qualitative researcher's firsthand knowledge of events, people, and situations cuts two ways. It raises questions of bias, but it also provides a sense of immediacy, direct contact, and intimate knowledge.

Different Kinds of Bias. The debate over researcher integrity involves opposing assumptions about the proper role of a researcher. A positivist, quantitative approach says that the influence of an individual researcher is a bias. It contaminates objective facts and should be eliminated.

Qualitative researchers assume it is impossible to eliminate the effect of the researcher completely. Although a reliance on mechanical techniques and fixed standards may appear to eliminate the human factor, it introduces its own form of bias: the bias of mechanical techniques. Smith (1988:5) warned, "Without firsthand information about the research setting, it is difficult for quantitative researchers to develop adequate conceptual frameworks for their studies."

Recognizing the human factor does not mean that a qualitative researcher arbitrarily interjects personal opinions or selects evidence to support personal prejudices. Instead, a researcher's presence is always an explicit issue. A qualitative researcher takes advantage of personal insight, feelings, and perspective as a human being to understand the social life under study, but is aware of his or her values or assumptions. He or she takes measures to guard against the influence of prior beliefs or assumptions when doing research. Rather than hiding behind "objective" techniques, the qualitative researcher is forthright and makes his or her values explicit in a report. Qualitative researchers tell readers how they gathered data and how they see the evidence.

Grounded Theory

A quantitative researcher gathers data after he or she theorizes, develops hypotheses, and creates measures of variables. By contrast, a qualitative researcher begins with a research question and little else. Theory develops during the data collection process. This more inductive method means that theory is built from data or grounded in the data. Moreover, conceptualization and operationalization occur simultaneously with data collection and preliminary data analysis. Many researchers use *grounded theory*. It makes qualitative research flexible and lets data and theory interact (see Box 13.2). Qualitative researchers remain open to the unexpected, are willing to change the direction or focus of a research project, and may abandon their original research question in the middle of a project.

A qualitative researcher builds theory by making comparisons. For example, when a researcher observes an event (e.g., a police officer confronting a speeding motorist), he or she immediately ponders questions and looks for similarities and differences. When watching a police officer stop a speeder, a qualitative researcher asks: Does the police officer always radio in the car's license number before proceeding? After radioing the car's location, does the officer ask the motorist to get out of the car sometimes, but in others casually walk up to the car and talk to the seated driver? When data collection and theorizing are interspersed, theoretical questions arise that suggest future observations, so new data are tailored to answer theoretical questions that came from thinking about previous data.

Process and Sequence

The passage of time is an integral part of qualitative research. Qualitative researchers look at the sequence of events and pay attention to what happens first, second, third, and so on. Because qualitative researchers examine the same case or set of cases over time, they can see an issue evolve, a conflict emerge, or a social relationship develop. The researcher can detect process and causal relations.

In historical research, the passage of time may involve years or decades. In field research, the passage of time is shorter. Nevertheless, in both types of research, a researcher notes what is occurring at different points in time and recognizes that *when* something occurs is often important.

Interpretation

The word *interpretation* means the assignment of significance or coherent meaning. Reports of quan-

Box 13.2 _____

What Is Grounded Theory?

Grounded theory is a widely used approach in qualitative research. It is not the only approach and it is not used by all qualitative researchers. *Grounded theory* is "a qualitative research method that uses a systematic set of procedures to develop an inductively derived theory about a phenomenon" (Strauss and Corbin, 1990:24). The purpose of grounded theory is to build a theory that is faithful to the evidence. It is a method for discovering new theory. In it, the researcher compares unlike phenomena with a view toward learning similarities. He or she sees micro-level events as the foundation for a more macro-level explanation. Grounded theory shares several goals with more positvist-oriented theory. It seeks theory that is comparable with the evidence that is precise and rigorous, capable of replication, and generalizable. A grounded theory approach pursues generalizations by making comparisons across social situations.

Qualitative researchers use alternatives to grounded theory. Some qualitative researchers offer an in-depth depiction that is true to an informant's worldview. They excavate a single social situation to elucidate the micro processes that sustain stable social interaction. The goal of other researchers is to provide a very exacting depiction of events or a setting. They analyze specific events or settings in order to gain insight into the larger dynamics of a society. Still other researchers apply an existing theory to analyze specific settings that they have placed in a macro-level historical context. They show connections among micro-level events and between micro-level situations and larger social forces for the purpose of reconstructing the theory and informing social action (see Burawoy, 1991:271–287 and Hammersley, 1992 for a summary of several alternatives).

___

titative research usually include tables and charts with numbers. Quantitative research is expressed in numbers (e.g., percentages or statistical coefficients), and a researcher gives meaning to the numbers and tells how they relate to hypotheses.

In qualitative research, interpretation is different. Qualitative research reports rarely include tables with numbers. The only visual presentations of data may be maps, photographs, or diagrams showing how ideas are related. A researcher weaves the data into discussions of their significance. The data are in the form of words, including quotes or descriptions of particular events. Any numerical information is supplementary to the textual evidence.

A qualitative researcher interprets data by giving them meaning, translating them, or making them understandable. However, the meaning he or she gives begins with the point of view of the people being studied. He or she interprets data by finding out how the people being studied see the world, how they define the situation, or what it means for them. As Geertz (1979:228) remarked, "The trick is to figure out what the devil they think they are up to."

Thus, the first step in qualitative interpretation, whether a researcher is examining historical documents or the text of spoken words or human behavior, is to learn about its meaning for the people being studied.[4] The people who created the social behavior have personal reasons or motives for their actions. This is first-order interpretation. A researcher's discovery and reconstruction of this *first-order interpretation* is a *second-order interpretation,* because the researcher comes in from the outside to discover what occurred. In a second-order interpretation, the researcher elicits an underlying coherence or sense of meaning in the data. Because meaning develops within a set of other meanings, not in a vacuum, a second-order interpretation places the human action being studied in the "stream of behavior" or events to which it is related—its context.

A researcher who adopts a strict interpretive approach may stop at a second-order interpretation—that is, once he or she understands the significance of the action for the people being studied. Many qualitative researchers go further to generalize or link the second-order interpretation to general theory. They move to a broader level of interpretation, or *third-order interpretation,* where a researcher assigns general theoretical significance.

COMPLEMENTARY EVIDENCE

Most researchers adopt either qualitative or quantitative research expertise and are often opponents on issues. However, it is a mistake to take this antagonism too far. Instead of observing a strict either or dichotomy, many researchers try to combine quantitative and qualitative research. The logic of qualitative research does not forbid the use of numbers, statistics, and precise quantitative measurement; such quantitative data can be a source of information, which supplements or complements qualitative data. Sprague and Zimmerman (1989:82) remarked:

> We do not have to reject quantitative methods to approve of qualitative methods. Posing one against the other is presenting a false choice, especially from the perspective of feminist and other sociologies of knowledge which recognize that each way of doing research is a construction and has its biases.

In Chapter 7, you encountered the concept of triangulation, combining different methodological techniques to overcome weaknesses in specific techniques. The quantitative researcher uses triangulation to get a better fix on the objective truth when testing hypotheses and to reduce method effects.

Qualitative researchers also advocate triangulation, but for different reasons.[5] First, it increases the sophisticated rigor of their data collection and analysis; that is, it makes their methods more public or open to scrutiny. Second, triangulation helps reveal the richness and diversity of social settings. Qualitative researchers do not assume there is a single view of reality, but believe that different methods reveal different perspectives. Finally, data on the same social event collected by different methods, different researchers, or at different times may not converge into one consistent picture. For quantitative researchers, such differences are so-called errors or biases to be eliminated. Qualitative researchers anticipate such differences and treat them as a valuable source of information about social life. They are themselves an aspect of social life to be analyzed. Lever (1981:200)

noted, "Variation in results yielded by different methods, far from being an unwanted source of error or bias, can be an additional source of data."

Qualitative data give quantitative researchers rich information about the social processes in specific settings. They may also give critical researchers the potential to break through assumptions implicit in quantitative approaches. Criminologists doing quantitative analysis of official crime statistics, for example, are invariably locked into the underlying assumptions embedded in these data. Official statistics assume the "official" perspective of the legal order and the justice system, which may or may not be the same perspective held by members of the community. In other words, official crime statistics tend to assume a value consensus rather than value conflict (Reiman, 1998).

Short Departure to Look at Elite Studies

Most criminological research is focused on "the average person," "the typical criminal," minorities, or the poor and powerless urban underclass. Criminologists since Sutherland have, of course, acknowledged the need to study powerful elites in society. Yet, "few social researchers study elites because elites are by their very nature difficult to penetrate. Elites establish barriers that set their members apart from the rest of society" (Hertz and Imber, 1993:3).

Nevertheless, there is a growing number of criminologists and other social scientists who have conducted valuable research on issues of corporate power, "elite deviance," and white-collar crime (e.g., Coleman, 1998; Domhoff, 1974; Benson, 1985; Sharp, 1995; Jesilow et al., 1993). But the difficulties in doing this sort of criminological research is certainly not for the neophyte researcher.

The first difficulty involves gaining access to elite networks, which are protected by "gatekeepers." Criminologists interested in studying corporate elites may face security guards, secretaries, and others whose official job is to prevent access. Thomas (1993:83) reported, "It took me nearly two years of phone calls, screening meetings with executive assistants, and networking to interview executives." Also, time pressures are great. Elites are very busy, or give that appearance. Researchers will have to schedule meetings and may have limited time. Techniques to improve access include informal settings (meals, waiting in airports, travel time, etc.) and a willingness to adjust to an elite schedule. Issues of access are more common in qualitative than quantitative research.

Second, social contacts and connections are essential for gaining access and establishing trust. A researcher's personal social background or pedigree is an important resource. If the researcher is not from a wealthy family or was not socialized under privileged conditions, he or she may need to cultivate appropriate sponsors with the so-called right connections. He or she will need an ability to display proper form. Elites will use who you know, who talked to you, and who introduced whom as signs of approval or endorsement. The researcher who lacks a good sponsor or prestigious credentials or affiliations will seldom be treated seriously, even he or she gains access.

Elites are often highly educated and knowledgeable. This has several implications. It means that the researcher is expected to have conducted extensive library and background work prior to direct contact. It also means that the elite member may be aware of social research techniques and read studies. This can increase cooperation or it can have the opposite effect. Elites may try to dominate or manipulate the research situation. Most elites are used to being in charge and having others defer to them. Most are adept at detecting subtle shifts in the flow events and skilled at controlling social situations. This may include where people sit, the direction of a conversation, and so on. Elite members may direct conversation away from what the researcher finds of interest and use up the time, while the researcher must be cautious not to create offense. The reseacher needs to gain sufficient control to accomplish his or her purpose. He or she needs refined social skills and diplomacy, and wants to get the elite member to let down his or her guard without creating tension or distress. The researcher can do this, but only with great delicacy and dexterity. Researchers may use their poise and discretion in a formal survey or when dealing with experimental subjects, but for some qualitative research, such skills are an essential research tool.

A related concern in elite studies is sensitivity to frontstage and backstage performances. *Frontstage social settings* are public, outward settings and situations in which people know others may be observing and therefore display specific social performances. *Backstage social settings* are private and intimate settings where people let their guard down and feel comfortable and trusting. When studying elites, frontstage events are often intentional and highly managed to create specific impressions. Thus, a researcher may be ushered into a large plush office, with a beautiful view, original art on the walls, sofas along the wall and a huge, clean desk. A elite member, highly experienced in dealing with others, may smile and give a researcher the official, public relations version of events. This "front" may not correspond to the backstage of private clubs, home, and other informal discussions of the elite member. The researcher may not get beyond the official, visible role. In backstage situations and settings, the elite member may reveal his or her true prejudices or feelings and may expose personal values or beliefs. Access to backstage situations is often very difficult. It may require developing a long-term relationship with the elite member. In quantitative studies, researchers rarely penetrate beyond the frontstage, while many qualitative studies are designed to go beyond public, surface relations.

A next set of differences involves gaining trust and handling an elite's settings or interview situations. The researcher needs to master the appropriate language and demeanor. All subcultures share ways of acting and speaking. Such informal customs and folkways contain assumptions and understandings of key events or situations. Using the proper phrases and adhering to subtle social rituals will signal that a researcher shares the outlook and assumptions of the elite subculture. The researcher who uses improper phases or who behaves unsuitably may signal that he or she is not to be trusted. For example, elite subcultures are built on an assumption of material security and inclusion. Many elites can bridge the social distance between themselves in others by managing an outward appearance of composure, radiating self-confidence, and expressing social graces and manners. Some researchers find this demeanor intimidating and may feel that they are being subtly "put in their place," but in a warm, friendly, and open manner. Qualitative researchers often find that they need to create trust and reduce interpersonal social distance when gathering data.

A last issue is protecting the integrity of research process. A degree of secrecy, or seclusion for privacy, if not physical protection, is common in elite settings. A researcher must exercise discretion. He or she needs to be sensitive to elite concerns about public exposure or fears of an exposé. Elites may be suspicious and demand a review of a research report, or only reveal things off the record. In addition, they may have the knowledge to detect subtle violations of agreed-upon limits or hire experts to review research reports. In addition, if a researcher violates trust, elites have the resources to bring lawsuits. At the same time, a researcher wants to learn as much as possible and uphold principles of good, unimpeded research. Qualitative researchers often find that they must stimultaneously balance protecting the confidentiality of subjects and ensuring the honesty of the research process itself.

EXAMPLE STUDIES

Examples of two specific qualitative research studies show how researchers apply the principles of qualitative research in practice, how qualitative researchers do not always follow a strict interpretive approach, and how they combine a qualitative method with quantitative principles.

Example of Field Research

Recently, qualitative criminologists have begun to tackle the thorny problem of studying corporate crime. The problems associated with studying corporate elites have been dealt with in different ways. Benson (1985) and Jesilow and colleagues (1993) remedied the problems by conducting interviews with white-collar criminals who had been already convicted of a crime (e.g., tax evasion, insider trading, and insurance fraud). The fact that their criminality was a matter of public knowledge improved their willingness to cooperate with the researchers.

Sharp (1995), on the other hand, took a different approach. She was interested in documenting the decisions and events leading up to crimes of corporate fraud, as opposed to interviewing the criminals after the fact. Thus, it was necessary for her to conduct fieldwork within a corporation. The corporation she choose to study was Prudential-Bache, a subsidiary of Prudential Life Insurance Company ("the Rock").

The sophisticated investment fraud Sharp examined involved the marketing of limited partnerships. Limited partnerships were a very popular tax shelter in the late 1970s and early 1980s. Prudential-Bache made huge profits selling and managing them for the public (generally the affluent and the middle class). In reality, however, the company was paid very much for doing very little. The U.S. Congress closed the limited partnership tax loophole in the 1980s, yet Prudential-Bache still continued to market them.

Sharp focused her fieldwork on documenting the corporate culture at Prudential-Bache. Like any anthropologist learning the ways of a new culture, Sharp studied the socialization process that introduced new members into this criminogenic setting. She conducted personal interviews with corporate executives and provided readers with an insider's view of corporate meetings, social events, and the day-to-day routines at the company. By recreating personal conversations she had had with corporate executives, Sharp communicated to readers a sense of the norms and values governing Prudential-Bache. Management imbued their employees with an almost blind commitment to the "bottom line" (i.e., corporate profits). Even at social events, parties, and company trips, as Sharp described in detail, the culture's emphasis on profit making was dominant over ethics.

Sharp's research reveals the power of qualitative criminology. From reading her book, one comes away with an understanding of the systemic and cultural dimensions that contribute to corporate fraud.

Example of Historical-Comparative Study

Light's (1977) study of ethnic vice industries serves as a good example of historical-comparative research. He was interested in explaining the different forms of prostitution found in ethnic communities in the United States. In order to make the issue more manageable, Light concentrated on the period from 1880 to 1944, and looked at two ethnic groups in particular: Chinese Americans and African Americans. His research also illustrates how qualitative and quantitative research complement each other. Thus, while drawing heavily from historical archives, Light also used demographic data to make his argument.

The main question is this: Why did prostitution in African American areas take the form of streetwalking, whereas in Chinatowns the brothel system was in effect? The answer has little to do with issues of consumer demand, or, as Light put it,

The historical comparison of blacks and Chinese confirms the claim that American society channeled disadvantaged minorities into illegal industries. But a close review also shows that no purely demand theory can account entirely for style, organization or succession in illegal enterprise because socio-cultural and demographic characteristics of minorities also affected these outcomes. (1977:475)

There were two main factors that contributed to the Chinese American form of prostitution. The first had to do with the surplus of Chinese men relative to Chinese women. Light (1977:470) argued that "the shortage of women in Chinatowns encouraged brothel prostitution and eliminated streetwalking. All Chinese prostitutes were full-time professionals." In African American communities, on the other hand, there was an abundance of women. Thus, "the least organized but largest class of black prostitutes

was independent streetwalkers. In nearly all cases, these were unemployed women who turned to prostitution until marriage or a regular job provided alternative support" (pp. 470–471).

The other factor was the presence in Chinatowns of ethnic organized crime syndicates (or "tongs"). To quote Light, "The vice industry consisted entirely of resorts owned by or affiliated with a Chinese secret society" (1977:472). Contrast that with African Americans, however, which had no functional equivalent. Again, quoting Light, "Black migrants of the lower class did not arrive with a culturally-provided framework around which to organize a syndicated vice industry" (p. 472).

Thus, we see that the historical-comparative perspective is able to account for organizational differences in ethnic prostitution. Indeed, it is hard to imagine finding a more appropriate perspective for analyzing this particular criminological topic.

CONCLUSION

Little of this chapter discussed specific ways to design research, although there was a lot of information about qualitative research. This was not an oversight. This chapter is a necessary background to practical design issues in qualitative research. More practical design issues are found in the next two chapters. As the discussion of logic in practice and a cyclical research path suggest, such issues are difficult to separate from doing the research itself.

This chapter focused on the differences between quantitative and qualitative research and the general characteristics of qualitative research. Its primary purpose has been to acquaint you with the point of view of qualitative research. It is important to make the transition from the mindset of quantitative research before examining specific ways to conduct qualitative research.

As stated before, the qualitative and quantitative distinction is often overdrawn and presented as a false, rigid dichotomy. It is nevertheless important to understand and appreciate the strengths of each on its own terms. It is too easy to apply the assumptions, standards, and orientation of a positivist, quantitative approach and find qualitative research wanting.

KEY TERMS

cyclical research path
first-order interpretation
grounded theory
linear research path

logic in practice
reconstructed logic
second-order interpretation

technocratic perspective
third-order interpretation
transcendent perspective

REVIEW QUESTIONS

1. How do the three approaches to science provide a guide for researchers?

2. What are the implications of saying that qualitative research uses more of a logic in practice than a reconstructed logic?

3. What does it mean to say that qualitative research follows a nonlinear path? In what ways is a more cyclical path valuable?

4. Why is the context of social events important for qualitative researchers?

5. What are the characteristics of the case study and why can it yield important information?

6. Compare the ways quantitative and qualitative researchers deal with personal bias and the issue of trusting the researcher.

7. How do qualitative researchers use theory?

8. Explain how qualitative researchers approach the issue of interpreting data. Refer to first-, second-, and third-order interpretations.

9. What are the three reasons qualitative researchers advocate triangulation that differ from the main reason given by quantitative researchers?

10. Identify five things survey research can do for field research and vice versa.

NOTES

1. Ward and Grant (1985) and Grant and colleagues (1987) analyzed research in sociology journals and suggested that journals with a higher proportion of qualitative research articles addressed gender topics, but that studies of gender are not themselves more likely to be qualitative.

2. See Lofland and Lofland (1984:118–121).

3. For examples of checking, see Agar (1980) and Becker (1970c).

4. See Blee and Billings (1986), Ricoeur (1970), and Schneider (1987) on the interpretation of text in qualitative research.

5. For additional discussion of triangulation, see Denzin (1989:234–247).

6. See Carr-Hill (1984b) on praxis and introducing qualitative features into survey research.

RECOMMENDED READINGS

Berger, Peter L., and Thomas Luckmann. (1967). *The social construction of reality: A treatise in the sociology of knowledge.* New York: Doubleday. This is a classic work in sociology on what is called a constructionist view—that people define and socially construct meaning. It is recommended for anyone unfamiliar with the view or interested in better understanding the background of qualitative research, especially field research.

Marshall, Catherine, and Gretchen B. Rossman. (1989). *Designing qualitative research.* Beverly Hills, CA: Sage. This unusual book includes some of the nuts and bolts of developing a proposal for qualitative research. It is especially valuable for beginning field researchers and includes discussions of managing time and framing a research question. An unusual feature of the book is its use of numerous vignettes containing concrete examples.

FIELD RESEARCH

Experience with adult, unreformed, "serious" criminals in their natural environment . . . has convinced me that if we are to make a major advance in our scientific understanding of criminal lifestyles, criminal subculture, and their relation to larger society, we must undertake genuine field research on these people. I am also convinced that this research can be done by many sociologists, and much more easily, than the criminology textbooks lead us to suppose.

—Ned Polsky, "Research Method, Morality and Criminology," p. 217

INTRODUCTION

Relatively few criminologists have ever conducted field research. There are various reasons as to why this is so. For one, criminologists tend to be most deeply influenced by positivism. Advances in computer technology, computer software, and the availability of huge data sets have all served to convince most criminologists to put their efforts into quantitative research. Polsky (1997:218), among others, has criticized mainstream criminology on this point:

> That is just where criminology falls flat on its face. Especially in the study of adult career criminals, we over-depend on a skewed sample, studies in non-natural surroundings (anti-crime settings), providing mostly data recollected long after the event.

It has also been argued that criminologists are apt to avoid field research "out of fear of being caught with their anti-criminal values down" (Polsky, 1997:229). That is to say, there is an underlying morality in the discipline that warns researchers not to get too close to criminals. As one criminologist put it, an intense interest in the criminal's life "really constitutes a romantic encouragement of the criminal" (quoted in Polsky, 1997:226). However, if this were the case, then, as Polsky has stated,

> the great majority of criminologists are social scientists only up to a point—the point usually being the start of the second, "control of crime," half of the typical criminology course—and beyond that point they are really social workers in disguise or else correction officers manqué. For them a central task of criminology, often the central task, is to find more effective ways to reform lawbreakers and to keep other people from becoming lawbreakers.

These are complex issues having to do with the ethics of criminological research, which will be discussed in Chapter 17. But at this point, suffice it to say that the science of crime and justice will not advance by ignoring field research techniques. Moreover, as this chapter will discuss, doing field research is not as difficult as you

might think. It simply depends on the researcher's "trained abilities to look at people, listen to them, think and feel with them, talk with them rather than at them" (Polsky, 1997:219).

Research Questions Appropriate for Field Research

Criminologists are most likely to employ field research to shed light on the perspectives and points of view of their subjects. Said differently, field research exemplifies the interpretive paradigm that was discussed at length in Chapter 4. Through sustained interaction with subjects in their natural setting, researchers begin to see the world through the eyes of their subjects. It thus lends itself very well to criminological studies emphasizing *verstehen* or the empathetic understanding of these research subjects. Field research, for example, would be an appropriate method for understanding the feelings of a crime victim or for understanding the feelings of the perpetrator.[1]

For the sake of consistent terminology, this text refers to the people who are studied in a field setting as *members*. They are the insiders belonging to a social group, subculture, or natural setting that the "outsider" (i.e., field researcher) wishes to penetrate and whose perspective the researcher wants to understand.

Field research has been used to study a wide range of subjects, subcultures, and settings. As a research method, it has been employed in the study of professional fences (Cromwell et al., 1993; Klockars, 1974), youth crime (Sullivan, 1989), police officers (Hunt, 1984; Pepinsky, 1980; Skolnick, 1994; Van Maanen, 1973; Waegel, 1984), coca leaf farm villages (Weatherford, 1986), burglars (Wright et al., 1996), drug gangs (Hagedorn, 1988), skid rows (Fowler, 1998), prostitutes (Prus and Vassilakopoulos, 1979), and skid-row tramps (Spradley, 1970), to cite just a few. Indeed, criminologists have only begun to scratch the surface in their adoption of field research techniques.

A Short History of Field Research

Early Beginnings. Field research has its early roots in the written journals provided by traders, travelers, government officials, explorers, and missionaries.[2] Their writings described distant lands and exotic cultures but were, for the most part, more anecdotal than scientific. However, field research became more rigorous in the hands of European anthropologists in the late nineteenth century. They used a field-based method, which they called *ethnography,* to get inside the perspective of their subjects. To get this insider's perspective, ethnographers recognized the importance of firsthand experience. Thus, they immersed themselves in these cultures, living among their subjects, learning their ways, and speaking their language. The subjects and cultures they chose to study could not have been more removed from the industrial reality wrenching North America and Europe. But, to their credit, the good ethnographers were able to see the connections between industrial development, colonialism, and the preindustrial peoples they studied.

By the 1920s, cultural anthropologist Bronislaw Malinowski was already arguing for the separation of the direct observation and native statements from the ethnographer's inferences. Perhaps the standard reference in ethnographic research is Sir E. E. Evans-Pritchard's work among the Nuer of southern Sudan (see Evans-Pritchard, 1940).

Chicago School of Sociology. Shortly after the turn of the twentieth century, a group of urban sociologists centered in Chicago set out to document the social consequences of industrial development. They used a field-based method, which came to be called *participant observation.* Participant observation requires sociologists to "get their hands dirty" by collecting data through direct observation, personal interaction with subjects, and informal interviews. Their research site was the city of Chicago: on street corners, in barrooms and railroad cars, in hotel lobbies and coffee shops, and so on.

In the first phase of field research, lasting from the 1910s to the 1930s, the Chicago sociologists published superb field studies of tramps, delinquents, deviants, maladjusted girls, and others. Early studies such as *The Hobo* (Anderson, 1923), *The Jack Roller* (Shaw, 1930), and *The Gang* (Thrasher, 1927) established the "Chicago school's" reputation for first-rate descriptive studies of street life.

Early on, the Chicago school adopted elements of muckraking journalism. One of its central figures, Robert E. Park (1864–1944), had been a newspaper reporter. His concern was that a sociologist should be like "a good reporter" (Polsky, 1997:219). Park urged researchers to get behind fronts, use informants, look for conflict, and expose what was "really happening." This approach resembled ethnography to the extent that it required the researcher to enter into the lives and culture of his or her subjects. It differed, however, in that ethnography tended to stress a more thorough immersion in the culture being studied, and generally examined preindustrial, rather than urban, settings.

In the second phase, from the 1940s to the 1960s, the Chicago school developed participant observation as a distinct technique. It applied an expanded anthropological model to groups and settings in the researcher's society. Three principles emerged:

1. Study people in their natural settings, or in situ.
2. Study people by directly interacting with them.
3. Gain an understanding of the social world and make theoretical statements about the members' perspective.

Over time, the method moved from strict description to theoretical analyses based on involvement by the researcher in the field.

After World War II, field research faced increased competition from survey and quantitative research. Field research declined as a proportion of all social research from World War II to the 1970s. In the 1970s and 1980s, however, several changes rejuvenated field research. First, field researchers borrowed ideas and techniques from cognitive psychology, cultural anthropology, folklore, and linguistics. Second, researchers reexamined the epistemological roots and philosophical assumptions of social science (see Chapter 4) that justified their method. Finally, field researchers became more self-conscious about their techniques and methods. They wrote about methodology and became more systematic about it as a research technique.

Today, field research has a distinct set of methodologies. Field researchers directly observe and interact with members in natural settings to get inside their perspective. They embrace an activist or social constructionist perspective on social life. They do not see people as a neutral medium through which social forces operate, nor do they see social meanings as something "out there" to observe. Instead, they hold that people create and define the social world through their interactions. Human experiences are filtered through a subjective sense of reality, which affects how people see and act on events. Thus, they replace the positivist emphasis on "objective facts" with a focus on the everyday, face-to-face social processes of negotiation, discussion, and bargaining to construct social meaning.

Field researchers see research as simultaneously a description of the social world and a part of it. As part of a socially created setting, a researcher's presence in the field cannot be just neutral data gathering.

Ethnography and Filmmaking.   Field research in criminology will continue to evolve in two directions. Borrowing heavily from cultural anthropology, criminologists will likely become even more steeped in the ethnographic tradition. Also, the new technology of filmmaking will prove invaluable to criminologists wishing to document their subject matter visually and experientially. Let us briefly examine these two emerging developments.

Ethnography.   *Ethnography* comes from cultural anthropology.[3] *Ethno* means people or folk, and *graphy* refers to describing something. Thus *ethnography* means describing a culture and understanding another way of life from the native point of view. As Franke (1983:61) stated, "Culture, the object of our description, resides within the thinking of natives." Ethnography assumes that people make inferences—that is, go beyond what is explicitly seen or said to what is meant or implied. People display their culture (what people think, ponder, or believe) through behavior (e.g., speech and actions) in specific social contexts. Displays of behavior do not give meaning; rather, meaning is inferred, or someone figures out meaning. Moving from what is heard or observed to what is actually meant is at the center of ethnography. Cultural knowledge includes symbols, songs, sayings, facts, ways of behaving, and objects (e.g., telephones, newspapers, etc.). We learn the culture by watching television, listening to parents, observing others, and the like.

Cultural knowledge includes both explicit knowledge, what we know and talk about, and tacit knowledge, what we rarely acknowledge. For example, *explicit knowledge* of bribery involves an experiential understanding of corruption as a social process (e.g., the process of paying off an unethical police officer). But having *tacit knowledge* of bribery goes beyond the surface meaning to include such things as the alerting phrases and body language that suggest one's willingness to enter into a bribery agreement. There are cultural norms surrounding every social behavior, including criminal behavior such as bribery and corruption. Ethnographers have firsthand experience with both the explicit and the tacit cultural knowledge that members use.

Somewhat related to ethnography is *ethnomethodology.*[4] Quite simply, it is the study of commonsense knowledge. Operating on the assumption that social meaning is fragile and fluid, and constantly being created and recreated, ethnomethodologists examine ordinary social interaction to identify the tacit rules for constructing social meaning and common sense.[5]

Anthropologist Clifford Geertz stated that a critical part of ethnography is *thick description,*[6] a rich, detailed description of specifics (as opposed to summary, standardization, generalization, or variables). A thick description of a three-minute event may go on for pages. It captures the sense of what occurred and the drama of events, thereby permitting multiple interpretations. It places events in a context so that the reader of an ethnographic report can infer cultural meaning.

Filmmaking. Field research in criminology is beginning to benefit from the new technology of filmmaking. Since the 1960s, filmmaking has changed tremendously, owing to the invention of portable and affordable recording equipment. This new equipment allows filmmakers to synchronize both picture and sound while in the field. Prior to this time, only massive and extremely expensive equipment could perform this task. But with the new filmmaking technology (e.g., handheld video recorders, magnetic sound stock, etc.), ethnographic and documentary filmmakers "no longer had to bring their subjects into a studio and interview them on a set; they could go anywhere in the world and record people speaking in their own words" (Barbash and Taylor, 1997:27).

The advantages of the new filmmaking technology are only just now being recognized by criminologists. Having portable equipment opens "new arenas of human experience—in particular people's private and domestic lives" (Barbash and Taylor, 1997:28). If it is true what Barbash and Taylor contend—that "film offers possibilities of its own, such as the portrayal of living experience, in ways that are unavailable to writing" (p. 35)— then one can only imagine the even greater impact classic criminological field studies would have as documentary films. For instance, the contemporary criminologist could personally observe Sutherland's (1937) "professional thief" or Klockars's (1974) "fence" every time he or she watched the film. The ability to communicate the nuance of lived experience, which lies at the heart of criminological field research, is thus greatly enhanced. Again, citing Barbash and Taylor (1997:1): "More than any other medium or art form, film uses experience to express experience."

Besides this, the new technology holds the promise of reaching wider audiences than most criminologists could ever imagine. The political and sociological effects of reaching an expanded audience can only strengthen the discipline of criminology. For example, in the early 1980s, one of your authors (Professor Wiegand) conducted an ethnography of urban homelessness. As part of that project, he put together a short video (entitled "Living") to convey the images and sounds of homelessness in one city in the United States. This video was then used to introduce the topic to a national funding agency, which in turn resulted in that city receiving a large grant to construct a new homeless shelter. Perhaps more than speeches and statistical data, it was the video's images that convinced the agency to fund the city's proposed homeless shelter.

Criminologists still lag behind anthropologists in filmmaking experience. Yet, the subject matter of criminology so readily lends itself to film that it seems only a matter of time before ethnographic and documentary films will be commonplace in the discipline.

THE LOGIC OF FIELD RESEARCH

What Is Field Research?

It is difficult to pin down a specific definition of *field research* because it is more of an orientation toward research than a fixed set of techniques to apply.[7] A field researcher uses various methods to obtain information. As Schatzman and Strauss (1973:14) said, "Field method is more like an umbrella of activity beneath which any technique may be used for gaining the desired knowledge, and for processes of thinking about this information." A *field researcher* is a "methodological pragmatist" (Schatzman and Strauss, 1973:7), a resourceful, talented individual who has ingenuity, and an ability to think on her feet while in the field.

Field research is based on naturalism, which is also used to study other phenomena (e.g., oceans, animals, plants, etc.). *Naturalism* involves observing ordinary events in natural settings, not in contrived, invented, or researcher-created settings. Research occurs in the field and outside the safe settings of an office, laboratory, or classroom. Reiss (1992) has said that a researcher's direct observation of events in natural settings is central to sociology's status as a science, and that this status is threatened if sociology turns from naturalism.

A field researcher examines social meanings and grasps multiple perspectives in natural social settings. He or she gets inside the meaning system of members and then goes back to an outside or research viewpoint. As Van Maanen (1982:139) noted, "Fieldwork means involvement and detachment, both loyalty and betrayal, both openness and secrecy, and most likely, love and hate." The researcher switches perspectives and sees the setting from multiple points of view simultaneously: "Researchers maintain membership in the culture in which they were reared while establishing membership in the groups which they are studying; they are socialized into another culture" (Burgess, 1982a:1).

Let us look at what practicing field researchers do (see Box 14.1). Research is usually conducted by a single individual, although small teams have been effective. A researcher is directly involved in and part of the social world studied, so his or her personal characteristics are relevant in research. Wax (1979:509) noted:

Informal and quantitative methods, the peculiarities of the individual tend to go unnoticed. Electronic data processing pays no heed to the age, gender, or ethnicity of the research director or programmer. But, in fieldwork, these basic aspects of personal identity become salient; they drastically affect the process of field research.

The researcher's direct involvement in the field often has an emotional impact. Field research can be fun and exciting, but it can also disrupt one's personal life, physical security, or mental well-being. More than other types of social research, it reshapes friendships, family life, self-identity, or personal values:

The price of doing fieldwork is very high, not in dollars (field work is less expensive than most other kinds of research) but in physical and mental effort. It is very hard work. It is exhausting to live two lives simultaneously. (Bogdan and Taylor, 1975:vi)

Box 14.1

What Do Field Researchers Do?

A field researcher does the following:

1. Observes ordinary events and everyday activities as they happen in natural settings, in addition to any unusual occurrences
2. Becomes directly involved with the people being studied and personally experiences the process of daily social life in the field setting
3. Acquires an insider's point of view while maintaining the analytic perspective or distance of an outsider
4. Uses a variety of techniques and social skills in a flexible manner as the situation demands
5. Produces data in the form of extensive written notes, as well as diagrams, maps, or pictures to provide very detailed descriptions
6. Sees events holistically (e.g., as a whole unit, not in pieces) and individually in their social context
7. Understands and develops empathy for members in a field setting, and does not just record "cold" objective facts
8. Notices both explicit (recognized, conscious, spoken) and tacit (less recognized, implicit, unspoken) aspects of culture
9. Observes ongoing social processes without upsetting, disrupting, or imposing an outside point of view
10. Copes with high levels of personal stress, uncertainty, ethical dilemmas, and ambiguity

Steps in a Field Research Project

Naturalism and direct involvement mean that field research is more flexible or less structured than quantitative research. This makes it essential for a researcher to be well organized and prepared for the field. It also means that the steps of a project are not entirely predetermined but serve as an approximate guide or road map (see Figure 14.1).

Flexibility.   Field researchers rarely follow fixed steps. In fact, flexibility is a key advantage of field research, which lets a researcher shift

FIGURE 14.1   Steps in Field Research

1. Prepare oneself, read the literature, and defocus.
2. Select a field site and gain access to it.
3. Enter the field and establish social relations with members.
4. Adopt a social role, learn the ropes, and get along with members.
5. Watch, listen, and collect quality data.
6. Begin to analyze data and to generate and evaluate working hypotheses.
7. Focus on specific aspects of the setting and use theoretical sampling.
8. Conduct field interviews with member informants.
9. Disengage and physically leave the setting.
10. Complete the analyses and write the research report.

Note: There is no fixed percentage of time needed for each step. For a rough approximation, Junker (1960:12) suggested that, once in the field, the researcher should expect to spend approximately one-sixth of his or her time observing, one-third recording data, one-third of the time analyzing data, and one-sixth reporting results. Also see Denzin (1989:176) for eight steps of field research.

direction and follow leads. Good field researchers recognize and seize opportunities, "play it by ear," and rapidly adjust to fluid social situations. Douglas (1976:14–16) argued that the techniques of field research share much in common with those of other types of investigative inquiry such as investigative journalism and detective work.

A field researcher does not begin with a set of methods to apply or explicit hypotheses to test. Rather, he or she chooses techniques on the basis of their value for providing information. In the beginning, the researcher expects little control over data and little focus. Once socialized to the setting, however, he or she focuses the inquiry and asserts control over the data.

Getting Organized in the Beginning.   Human and personal factors can play a role in any research project, but they are crucial in field research. Field projects often begin with chance occurrences or a personal interest. Field researchers can begin with their own experiences,

such as working at a job, having a hobby, or being a patient or an activist.[8]

Field researchers use the skills of careful looking and listening, short-term memory, and regular writing. Before entering the field, a new researcher practices observing the ordinary details of situations and writing them down. Attention to details and short-term memory can improve with practice. Likewise, keeping a daily diary or personal journal is good practice for writing field notes.

As with all social research, reading the scholarly literature helps the researcher learn concepts, potential pitfalls, data collection methods, and techniques for resolving conflicts. In addition, a field researcher finds diaries, novels, journalistic accounts, and autobiographies useful for gaining familiarity and preparing emotionally for the field.

Field research begins with a general topic, not specific hypotheses. A researcher does not get locked into any initial misconceptions. He or she needs to be well informed but open to discovering new ideas. Finding the right questions to ask about the field takes time.

A researcher first empties his or her mind of preconceptions and defocuses. There are two types of *defocusing*.[9] The first is casting a wide net in order to witness a broad range of situations, people, and settings—getting a feel for the overall setting before deciding what to include or exclude. The second type of defocusing means not focusing exclusively on the role of researcher. As Douglas (1976:122) noted, it is important to extend one's experience beyond a strictly professional role. The researcher should move outside his or her comfortable social niche to experience as much as possible in the field without betraying a primary commitment to being a researcher.

Another preparation for field research is self-knowledge. A field researcher needs to know himself or herself and reflect on personal experiences. He or she can expect anxiety, self-doubt, frustration, and uncertainty in the field. Especially in the beginning, the researcher may feel that he or she is collecting the wrong data and may suffer emotional turmoil, isolation, and confusion. He or she often feels doubly marginal: an outsider in the field setting and also distant from friends, family, and other researchers.[10] The relevance of a researcher's emotional make-up, personal biography, and cultural experiences makes it important to be aware of his or her personal commitments and inner conflicts (see the later section on stress).

Fieldwork can have a strong impact on a researcher's identity and outlook. Researchers may be personally transformed by the field experience. Some adopt new values, interests, and moral commitments, or change their religion or political ideology.[11] Hayano (1982:148) remarked from his study on gambling,

> *By this time I felt more comfortable sitting at a poker table than I did at faculty meetings and in my classes. Most of my social life focused on poker playing, and often, especially after a big win, I felt the desire to give up my job as a university professor in order to spend more time in the cardroom.*

CHOOSING A SITE AND GAINING ACCESS

Although a field research project does not proceed by fixed steps, some common concerns arise in the early stages. These include selecting a site, gaining access to the site, entering the field, and developing rapport with members in the field.

Selecting a Site

Where to Observe.   Field researchers talk about doing research on a setting, or *field site,* but this term is misleading. A site is the context in which events or activities occur, a socially defined territory with shifting boundaries. A social group may interact across several physical sites. For example, Polsky's (1997) fieldwork with heroin users and dealers illustrates the shifting boundaries of his field site: "During the summer of 1960 . . . I spent much time with people involved in heroin use and distribution, in their natural settings: on rooftops, in apartments, in tenement hallways, on stoops, in streets, in automobiles, in parks and taverns" (p. 224).

The field site and research question are bound up together, but choosing a site is not the same as focusing on a *case* for study. A case is a social relationship or activity; it can extend beyond the boundaries of the site and have links to other social settings. A researcher selects a site, then identifies cases to examine within it—for example, how police interrogate suspects.

Selecting a field site is an important decision, and researchers take notes on the site selection processes. Three factors are relevant when choosing a field research site: richness of data, unfamiliarity, and suitability.[12] Some sites are more likely than others to provide rich data. Sites that present a web of social relations, a variety of activities, and diverse events over time provide richer, more interesting data. Beginning field researchers should choose an unfamiliar setting. It is easier to see cultural events and social relations in a new site. Bogdan and Taylor (1975: 28) noted, *"We would recommend that researchers choose settings in which the subjects are strangers and in which they have no particular professional knowledge or expertise"* (emphasis in original). When "casing" possible field sites, one must consider such practical issues as the researcher's time and skills, serious conflicts among people in the site, the researcher's personal characteristics and feelings, and access to parts of a site.

A researcher's ascriptive characteristics can limit access. For example, an African American researcher cannot hope to study the Ku Klux Klan or neo-Nazis, although some researchers have successfully crossed some ascriptive lines.[13] Sometimes "insider" and "outsider" teams can work together.

Skolnick's (1994:35) participant observation of the Westville police serves as a good example of this:

> *I could walk into a bar looking for a dangerous armed robber who was reportedly there without undergoing much danger myself because I would not be recognized as a police officer. Similarly, I could drive a disguised truck, with a couple of officers hidden in the rear, up to a building without the lookout recognizing me.*

Physical access to a site can be an issue. Sites are on a continuum, with open and public areas (e.g., public restaurants, airport waiting areas, etc.) at one end and closed and private settings (e.g., private firms, clubs, activities in a person's home, etc.) at the other. A researcher may find that he or she is not welcome or not allowed on the site, or there are legal and political barriers to access. Laws and regulations in institutions (e.g., public schools, hospitals, prisons, etc.) restrict access. In addition, institutional review boards (see Chapter 17) may limit field research on ethical grounds.

Gatekeepers.   A *gatekeeper* is someone with the formal or informal authority to control access to a site.[14] It can be the thug on the corner, an administrator of a hospital, or the owner of a business. Informal public areas (e.g., sidewalks, public waiting rooms, etc.) rarely have gatekeepers; formal organizations have authorities from whom permission must be obtained.

Field researchers expect to negotiate with gatekeepers and bargain for access. The gatekeepers may not appreciate the need for conceptual distance or ethical balance. The researcher must set nonnegotiable limits to protect research integrity. If there are many restrictions initially, a researcher can often reopen negotiations later, and gatekeepers may forget their initial demands as trust develops. It is ethically and politically astute to call on gatekeepers. Researchers do not expect them to listen to research concerns or care about the findings, except insofar as these findings might provide evidence for someone to criticize them.

Dealing with gatekeepers is a recurrent issue as a researcher enters new levels or areas. In addition, a gatekeeper can shape the direction of research:

> Even the most friendly and co-operative gatekeepers or sponsors will shape the conduct and development of research. To one degree or another, the ethnographer will be channeled in line with existing networks of friendship and enmity, territory, and equivalent boundaries. (Hammersley and Atkinson, 1983:73)

In some sites, gatekeeper approval creates a stigma that inhibits the cooperation of members.

For example, prisoners may not be cooperative if they know that the prison warden gave approval to the researcher. As West (1980:35) remarked regarding juvenile delinquents, "I am convinced that such access routes almost always retard—or in some cases prevent—the establishment of rapport with delinquents."

Strategy for Entering

Entering a field site requires having a flexible strategy or plan of action, negotiating access and relations with members, and deciding how much to disclose about the research to field members or gatekeepers.

Planning.   Entering and gaining access to a field site is a process that depends on commonsense judgment and social skills. Field sites usually have different levels or areas, and entry is an issue for each. Entry is more analogous to peeling the layers of an onion than to opening a door. Moreover, bargains and promises of entry may not remain stable over time. A researcher needs fallback plans or may have to return later for renegotiation. Because the specific focus of research may not emerge until later in the research process or may change, it is best to avoid being locked into specifics by gatekeepers.

Entry and access can be visualized as an *access ladder* (see Figure 14.2). A researcher begins at the bottom rung, where access is easy and where he or she is an outsider looking for public information. The next rung requires increased access. Once close on-site observation begins, he or she becomes a passive observer, not questioning what members say. With time in the field, the researcher observes specific activities that are potentially sensitive or seeks clarification of what he or she sees or hears. Reaching this access rung is more difficult. Finally, the researcher may try to shape interaction so that it reveals specific information, or he or she may want to see highly sensitive material. This highest rung of the access ladder is rarely attained and requires deep trust.[15]

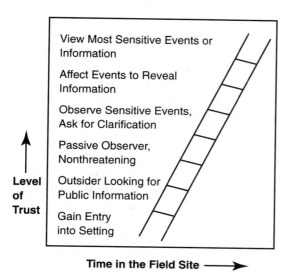

View Most Sensitive Events or
Information

Affect Events to Reveal
Information

Observe Sensitive Events,
Ask for Clarification

Passive Observer,
Nonthreatening

Outsider Looking for
Public Information

Gain Entry
into Setting

Level
of
Trust

Time in the Field Site ⟶

FIGURE 14.2 The Access Ladder

Negotiation. Social relations are negotiated and formed throughout the process of fieldwork.[16] Negotiation occurs with each new member until a stable relationship develops to gain access, develop trust, obtain information, and reduce hostile reactions. The researcher expects to negotiate and explain what he or she is doing over and over in the field (see the discussion of normalizing social research, to follow).

Deviant groups and elites often require special negotiations for gaining access. To gain access to deviant subcultures, field researchers have used contacts from the researcher's private life, gone to social welfare or law enforcement agencies where the deviants are processed, advertised for volunteers, offered a service (e.g., counseling) in exchange for access, or gone to a location where deviants hang out and joined a group.

Criminologists wanting to make initial contact with active criminals often reject working through official channels (i.e., the criminal justice system). Instead, they may frequent locales, such as bars, where criminals are known to go (Wright et al., 1996). But this often entails a long waiting period. Another approach is to work through ex-

offenders who have maintained criminal contacts, as Wright and Donmoon (1992) did in their field study of residential burglars.[17]

Polsky (1997:222) suggested a rather novel technique:

> Getting an initial introduction or two is not nearly so difficult as it might seem. Among students whom I have had perform the experiment of asking their relatives and friends to see if any could provide an introduction to a career criminal, fully a third reported that they could get such introductions.

Disclosure. A researcher must decide how much to reveal about himself or herself and the research project. Disclosing one's personal life, hobbies, interests, and background can build trust and close relationships, but the researcher will also lose privacy, and he or she needs to ensure that the focus remains on events in the field.

A researcher also decides how much to disclose about the research project. Disclosure ranges on a continuum from fully covert research, in which no one in the field is aware that research is taking place, to the opposite end, where everyone knows the specifics of the research project. The degree and timing of disclosure depends on a researcher's judgment and particulars in the setting. Disclosure may unfold over time as the researcher feels more secure.

Researchers disclose the project to gatekeepers and others unless there is a good reason for not doing so, such as the presence of gatekeepers who would seriously limit or inhibit research for illegitimate reasons (e.g., to hide graft or corruption). Even in these cases, a researcher may disclose his or her identity as a researcher, but may pose as one who seems submissive, harmless, and interested in nonthreatening issues.

Entering the Field

After a field site is selected and access obtained, researchers must learn the ropes, develop rapport with members, adopt a role in the setting, and maintain social relations. Before confronting such issues, the researcher should ask: How will I present myself? What does it mean for me to be a "measurement instrument"? How can I assume an "attitude of strangeness"?

Presentation of Self. People explicitly and implicitly present themselves to others. We display who we are—the type of person we are or would like to be—through our physical appearance, what we say, and how we act. The presentation of self sends a symbolic message. It may be, "I'm a serious, hard-working student," "I'm a warm and caring person," "I'm a cool jock," or "I'm a rebel and party animal." Many selves are possible, and presentations of selves can differ depending on the occasion.

A field researcher is conscious of the presentation of self in the field. Take, for example, Skolnick's (1994:35) presentation of self in his study of the Westville police: "My appearance, unlike the stereotype of the police officer, proved to be an advantage because I could sometimes aid the police in carrying out some of their duties."

Polsky (1997:224) dealt with the issue as follows:

> I did not dress as I usually do (suit, shirt and tie), because that way of dressing in the world which I was investigating would have made it impossible for many informants to talk to me, e.g., would have made them worry about being seen with me because others might assume I represented the law. But on the other hand, I took care always to wear a short-sleeved shirt or T-shirt and an expensive wristwatch, both of which let any newcomer who walked up know immediately that I was not a junkie.

Perhaps the rule of thumb is this: Do not overdress so as to stand out, but exactly copying the dress of those being studied is not necessary, either. Thus, a professor studying police need not dress like one, but would probably want to dress informally or casually. By the same token, doing an ethnography of corporate executives may require the researcher to dress more formally, depending on his or her particular field role.[18]

A researcher must be aware that self-presentation will influence field relations to some degree. It is difficult to present a highly deceptive front or to present oneself in a way that deviates sharply from the person one is ordinarily. Sullivan (1989:7), for example, adopted a straightforward presentation of self by telling subjects the following: "My job is only to do research. I am not a cop or a social worker. I am only trying to get information. Any questions that I ask you that you think are too personal, you don't have to answer."

Researcher as Instrument. The researcher is the instrument for measuring field data. This has two implications. First, it puts pressure on the researcher to be alert and sensitive to what happens in the field and to be disciplined about recording data. Second, it has personal consequences. Fieldwork involves social relationships and personal feelings. Field researchers are flexible about what to include as data and admit their own subjective insights and feelings, or "experiential data."[19] Personal, subjective experiences are part of field data. They are valuable both in themselves and for interpreting events in the field. Instead of trying to be objective and eliminate personal reactions, field researchers treat their feelings toward field events as data. The following quote reveals the researcher's ability to reflect on his personal feeling:

> On that date, I was, by prearrangement, to interview a black drug pusher at his home. I was assisted in making the arrangements by his probation officer (also black) who got to know me during my probation research and offered to help me with my fencing research. Now, generally speaking, I am not a very "groovy" person. I cannot use hip language, and if I do, it is quite apparent that I am out of my element. Fortunately, I knew myself well enough to know that I really had no alternative but to be what I am—a young college professor in his twenties. With tape recorder in one hand and an entire brief case full of questionnaires in the other, my probation officer friend and I entered the pusher's home on June 2. (Klockars, 1974:206)

The researcher's own surprise, anxiety, or doubt may become an opportunity for reflection and insight.[20]

An Attitude of Strangeness.   It is hard to recognize what we are very close to. The everyday world we inhabit is filled with thousands of details. If we paid attention to everything all the time, we would suffer from severe information overload. We manage by ignoring much of what is around us and by engaging in habitual thinking. Unfortunately, we fail to see the familiar as distinctive, and assume that others experience reality just as we do. We tend to treat our own way of living as natural or normal.

Field research in familiar surroundings is difficult because of a tendency to be blinded by the familiar. In fact, "intimate acquaintance with one's own culture can create as much blindness as insight" (McCracken, 1988:12). By studying other cultures, researchers encounter dramatically different assumptions about what is important and how things are done. This confrontation of cultures, or culture shock, has two benefits: It makes it easier to see cultural elements and it facilitates self-discovery. Researchers adopt the attitude of strangeness to gain these benefits. The *attitude of strangeness* means questioning and noticing ordinary details or looking at the ordinary through the eyes of a stranger. Strangeness helps a researcher overcome the boredom of observing ordinary details. It helps him or her see the ordinary in a new way, one that reveals aspects of the setting of which members are not consciously aware.

For example, one customarily thinks the phrase *getting paid* refers to income from legal employment. However, Sullivan's (1989) field study of youth crime reveals a different meaning in which the phrase refers to committing property crime. Thus, the attitude of strangeness helps make the tacit meaning of the culture visible to the researcher. A field researcher adopts both a stranger's and an insider's point of view. The stranger sees events as specific social processes, whereas to an insider, they seem natural. Davis (1973) called this the Martian and the convert: The Martian sees everything as strange and questions assumptions, whereas the convert accepts everything and wants to become a believer. Researchers need both views, as well as the ability to switch back and forth.[21]

Strangeness also encourages a researcher to reconsider his or her own social world. Immersion in a different setting breaks old habits of thought and action. He or she finds reflection and introspection easier and more intense when encountering the unfamiliar, whether it is a different culture or a familiar culture seen through a stranger's eyes.

Building Rapport

A field researcher builds rapport by getting along with members in the field. He or she forges a friendly relationship, shares the same language, and laughs and cries with members. This is a step toward obtaining an understanding of members and moving beyond understanding to empathy—that is, seeing and feeling events from another's perspective.

It is not always easy to build rapport. The social world is not all in harmony, with warm, friendly people. A setting may contain fear, tension, and conflict. Members may be unpleasant, untrustworthy, or untruthful; they may do things that disturb or disgust a researcher. An experienced researcher is prepared for a range of events and relationships. He or she may find, however, that it is impossible to penetrate a setting or get really close to members. Settings where cooperation, sympathy, and collaboration are impossible require different techniques.[22] Also, the researcher accepts what he or she hears or sees at face value, but without being gullible. As Schatzman and Strauss (1973:69) remarked, "The researcher believes 'everything' and 'nothing' simultaneously."

Charm and Trust.   A field researcher needs social skills and personal charm to build rapport. Trust, friendly feelings, and being well liked facilitate communication and help him or her to understand the inner feelings of others. There is no magical way to do this. Showing a genuine concern for and interest in others, being honest, and sharing feelings are good strategies, but they are not foolproof. It depends on the specific setting and members.

Many factors affect trust and rapport—how a researcher presents himself or herself; the role he or she chooses for the field; and the events that encourage, limit, or make it impossible to achieve trust. Trust is not gained once and for all. It is a developmental process built up over time through many social nuances (e.g., sharing of personal experiences, story telling, gestures, hints, facial expressions). It is constantly re-created and seems easier to lose once it has been built up than to gain in the first place.

Establishing trust is important, but it does not ensure that all information will be revealed. It may be limited to specific areas of inquiry. Trust is also often tested in the field and must be constantly reaffirmed, as the following quote suggests:

> A number of offenders tested us by asking what a criminal associate said about a particular matter. We declined to discuss such issues, explaining that the promise of confidentiality extended to all those participating in our research. (Wright et al., 1996:5)

Freeze Outs.   Some members may not be open and cooperative. *Freeze outs* are members who express an uncooperative attitude or an overt unwillingness to participate. Field researchers may never gain the cooperation of everyone, or a warm relationship may develop only after prolonged persistence.

Understanding.   Rapport helps field researchers understand members, but understanding is a precondition for greater depth, not an end in itself. It slowly develops in the field as the researcher overcomes an initial bewilderment with a new or unusual language and system of social meaning. Once he or she attains an understanding of the member's point of view, the next step is to learn how to think and act within a member's perspective. This is *empathy,* or adopting another's perspective. Empathy does not necessarily mean sympathy, agreement, or approval; it means feeling things as another does.[23]

RELATIONS IN THE FIELD

You play many social roles in daily life—daughter/son, student, customer, sports fan—and maintain social relations with others. You choose some roles and others are structured for you. Few have a choice but to play the role of son or daughter. Some roles are formal (e.g., bank teller, police chief, etc.), others are informal (flirt, elder states person, buddy, etc.). You can switch roles, play multiple roles, and play a role in a particular way. Field researchers play roles in the field. In addition, they learn the ropes and maintain relations with members.

Roles in the Field

Preexisting versus Created Roles.   At times, a researcher adopts an existing role. Some existing roles provide access to all areas of the site, the ability to observe and interact with all members, the freedom to move around, and a way to balance the requirements of researcher and member. At other times, a researcher modifies an existing role or even creates a new role. Wright and associates (1996), for example, played the role of a helper, which fostered rapport with their subjects (i.e., currently active residential burglars):

> We took subjects to job interviews or work, helped some enroll in school, and gave others advice on legal matters. We even assisted a juvenile offender who was injured while running away from the police, to arrange for emergency surgery when his parents, fearing that they would be charged for the operation, refused to give their consent. (p. 5)

The adoption of a field role takes time and will probably evolve during the course of the fieldwork. Let it happen.

Limits on the Role Chosen.   The field roles open to a researcher are affected by ascriptive factors and physical appearance. He or she can change some aspects of appearance, such as dress or hairstyle, but not ascriptive features such as age, race, gender, and attractiveness. Nevertheless, such factors can be important in gaining access and can restrict the available roles.

Since many roles are sex-typed, gender is an important consideration. Female researchers often have more difficulty when the setting is perceived as dangerous or seamy and where males are in control (e.g., police work, drug dealing, etc.). They may be shunned or pushed into limiting gender stereotypes (e.g., "sweet kid," "mascot," "loud mouth," etc.). Male researchers have more problems in routine and administrative sites where males are in control (e.g., courts, large offices, etc.). They may not be accepted in female-dominated territory. In sites where both males and females are involved, both sexes may be able to enter and gain acceptance.[24]

Level of Involvement.   Field roles can be arranged on a continuum by the degree of detachment or involvement a researcher has with members. At one extreme are roles of a detached outsider; at the other extreme are roles of an intimately involved insider. The range of field roles is described in three systems developed by Junker, Gans, and the Adlers (see Box 14.2). Junker's system is from the old Chicago school and that by Gans is a simplification of Junker's system. The Adlers's system moves beyond the Chicago school to incorporate insights from ethnography.

A researcher's involvement depends on negotiations with members, specifics of the setting, the researcher's comfort, and the particular field role adopted. Many move from the outsider to the insider end of the continuum with time in the field.

Each level of involvement has advantages and disadvantages. Different field researchers advocate different levels of involvement. For example, the Adlers's complete member role is criticized by some for overinvolvement and loss of a researcher's perspective. Others argue that it is the only way to really understand a member's social world.

Roles at the outsider end of the continuum reduce the time needed for acceptance, make overrapport less an issue, and can sometimes help members open up. They facilitate detachment and

protect the researcher's self-identity. A researcher feels marginal. Although there is less risk of "going native," he or she is also less likely to know an insider's experience and misinterpretation is more likely.

To really understand social meaning for those being studied, the field researcher must participate in the setting, as others do. Holy (1984: 29–30) observed:

> The researcher does not participate in the lives of subjects in order to observe them, but rather observes while participating fully in their lives . . . through living with the people being studies. . . . She comes to share the same meanings with them in the process of active particpation in their social life. . . . Research means, in this sense, socialization to the culture being studied.

By contrast, roles at the insider end of the continuum facilitate empathy and sharing of a member's experience. The goal of fully experiencing the intimate social world of a member is achieved. Nevertheless, a lack of distance from, too much sympathy for, or overinvolvement with members is likely. A researcher's reports may be questioned, data gathering is difficult, there can be a dramatic impact on the researcher's self, and the distance needed for analysis may be hard to attain.[25]

Other Considerations.   Most field sites contain informal groups, hierarchies, and rivalries. The researcher must therefore take heed in the relations he or she is forming that they do not unnecessarily close off other parts of the field site. Again, the field study of burglars by Wright and colleagues (1996) is instructive. The following passage points to the delicate negotiations that field researchers must do to keep rapport and channels of communication open and free flowing:

> Over the course of the research, numerous disputes arose between offenders and informants over the payment of referral fees. We resisted becoming involved in these disputes, reckoning that such involvement could only result in the alienation of one or both parties. Instead, we made it clear that our funds were intended as

Box 14.2 _____

Three Systems of Role Involvement by Field Researchers

JUNKER[a]

Complete observer	The researcher is behind a one-way mirror or in an "invisible role" (e.g., janitor) that permits undetected and unnoticed observation and eavesdropping.
Observer as participant	The researcher is a known, overt observer from the beginning, who has more limited or formal contact with members.
Participant as observer	The researcher and members are aware of the research role, but the researcher is an intimate friend who is a pseudomember.
Complete participant	The researcher acts as a member and shares the secret information of insiders because the researcher's identity is not known to members.

GANS[b]

Total researcher	The researcher has little personal involvement and is a passive observer, "on the sidelines," who does not influence events in the field.
Researcher participant	The researcher participates but is only partially involved or committed to a member's perspective.
Total participant	The researcher is completely emotionally involved while in the field, and becomes a detached researcher only after leaving.

THE ADLERS[c]

Peripheral membership	The researcher maintains distance between self and members; membership is limited by the researcher's beliefs, ascriptive characteristics, or discomfort with member activities.
Active membership	The researcher assumes a membership role and goes through the same induction as other members; participation in core activities produces high levels of trust and acceptance, but researchers retain a researcher identity and can periodically withdraw from the field.
Complete membership	The researcher converts and "goes native" but later becomes an ex-member researcher. By "surrendering" to membership and becoming an equal, fully committed member, the researcher experiences the same emotions as others. He or she needs to leave the field and undergo reorientation to return to being a researcher.

[a]See Junker (1960). Also see Denzin (1989), Gold (1969), Pearsall (1970), and Roy (1970).
[b]See Gans (1982).
[c]See Adler and Adler (1987).

interview payments and thus would be given only to interviewees. (p. 4)

In short, the researcher needs to be aware that by adopting a role, he or she may be forming allies and enemies who can assist or limit the fieldwork.

Learning the Ropes

As a researcher learns the ropes on the field site, he or she learns how to cope with personal stress, how to normalize the social research, and how to act like an "acceptable incompetent."

Stress. Fieldwork can be highly rewarding, exciting, and fulfilling, but it also can be difficult:

> Fieldwork must certainly rank with the more disagreeable activities that humanity has fashioned for itself. It is usually inconvenient, to say the least, sometimes physically uncomfortable, frequently embarrassing, and, to a degree, always tense. (Shaffir et al., 1980:3)

New researchers face embarrassment, experience discomfort, and are overwhelmed by the details in the field. For example, in her study of U.S. relocation camps for Japanese Americans during World War II, respected field researcher Rosalie Wax (1971) reported that she endured the discomfort of 120-degree Fahrenheit temperatures, filthy and dilapidated living conditions, dysentery, and mosquitoes. She felt isolated, she cried a lot, and she gained 30 pounds from compulsive eating. After months in the field, she thought she was a total failure; she was distrusted by members and got into fights with the camp administration.

Maintaining a "marginal" status is stressful; it is difficult to be an outsider who is not fully involved, especially when studying settings full of intense feelings. The loneliness and isolation of fieldwork may combine with the desire to develop rapport and empathy to cause overinvolvement. A researcher may "go native" and drop the professional researcher's role to become a full member of the group being studied. Or the researcher may feel guilt about learning intimate details as members drop their guard, and may come to overidentify with members.[26]

Some emotional stress is inevitable in field research. Instead of suppressing emotional responses, the field researcher is sensitive to emotional reactions. He or she copes in the field by keeping a personal diary, emotional journal, or written record of inner feelings, or by having sympathetic people outside the field site in which to confide.[27]

Normalizing Social Research.

A field researcher not only observes and investigates members in the field but is observed and investigated by members as well:

> In studying a criminal it is important to realize that he will be studying you, and to let him study you. Don't evade or shut off any questions he might have about your personal life, even if those questions are designed to "take you down," for example, designed to force you to admit that you too have knowingly violated the law. He has got to define you satisfactorily to himself and his colleagues if you are to get anywhere, and answering his questions frankly helps this process along. (Polsky, 1997:223)

In overt field research, members are usually initially uncomfortable with the presence of a researcher. Most are unfamiliar with field research and fail to distinguish between sociologists, criminologists, and social workers. They may see the researcher as an outside critic or spy, or as a savior or all-knowing expert.

An overt field researcher must *normalize social research*—that is, help members redefine social research from something unknown and threatening to something normal and predictable. He or she can help members manage research by presenting his or her own biography, explaining field research a little at a time, appearing nonthreatening, or accepting minor deviance in the setting (e.g., minor violations of official rules).[28]

Another way to normalize research is to explain it in terms members understand. Sometimes, members' excitement about being written up in a book is useful. And sometimes it is not, as Klockars (1974:201–202) found out when trying to convince "Knuckles," a professional fence, to cooperate in the field research:

> My strategy in trying to convince Knuckles to talk to me was to offer him a kind of anonymous immortality in exchange for information. To have someone want to write a book about you is for most people, I suspect, flattering. I hoped to convince Knuckles that he could have a book written about him even if the details had to be changed to protect his true identity. The day after I talked to Knuckles on the phone I visited him at the hospital.
> I brought a copy of Sutherland's The Professional Thief with me. . . . I hoped it would serve as a precedent—as evidence that another criminal had seen fit to work with a college professor in recounting the details of his occupation. . . .

Although I think the strategy was sound, it did not work.

Acceptable Incompetent. A researcher is in the field to learn, not to be an expert. Depending on the setting, he or she appears to be a friendly but naive outsider, an acceptable incompetent who is interested in learning about the social life of the field. An *acceptable incompetent* is someone who is partially competent (skilled or knowledgeable) in the setting but who is accepted as a nonthreatening person who needs to be taught.[29] As Schatzman and Strauss (1973:25) noted, "The researcher should play down any expertise or profound knowledge he may have on the subject on which the hosts may claim to be expert; the researcher is and should act the learner, indicating no inclination to evaluate the host's activities."

A field researcher may know little about the setting or subculture at first. He or she may be seen as a fool who is hoodwinked or short-changed, and may be the butt of jokes for his or her lack of adeptness in the setting. Even when the researcher is knowledgeable, he or she displays less than full information to draw out a member's knowledge. Of course, the researcher can overdo this and appear so ignorant that he or she is not taken seriously.

Maintaining Relations

Social Relations. With time, a field researcher develops and modifies social relationships. Members who are cool at first may warm up later. Or they may put on a front of initial friendliness, and their fears and suspicions surface only later. A researcher is in a delicate position. Early in a project, when not yet fully aware of everything about a field site, the researcher does not form close relationships because circumstances may change. Yet, if he or she does develop close friends, they can become allies who will defend the researcher's presence and help him or her gain access.

A field researcher monitors how his or her actions or appearance affects members. For example, a physically attractive researcher who interacts with members of the opposite sex may encounter crushes, flirting, and jealousy. He or she develops an awareness of these field relations and learns to manage them.[30]

In addition to developing social relationships, a field researcher must be able to break or withdraw from relationships as well. Ties with one member may have to be broken in order to forge ties with others or to explore other aspects of the setting. As with the end of any friendly relationship, the emotional pain of social withdrawal can affect both the researcher and the member. The researcher must balance social sensitivity and the research goals.

Small Favors. *Exchange relationships* develop in the field, in which small tokens or favors, including deference and respect, are exchanged.[31] A researcher may gain acceptance by helping out in small ways. Exchange helps when access to sensitive issues is limited. A researcher may offer small favors but not burden members by asking for return favors. As the researcher and members share experiences and see each other again, members recall the favors and reciprocate by allowing access. For example, Klockars (1974:219) described the small gifts and favors he would do for his informant "Vincent," a professional fence:

> *I ate with him, drank with him, learned from him, invited him to my home, brought him cakes my wife had baked, brought my family to his store, drove him in my car, visited him in the hospital, sent him birthday cards, and showed him my son's baby pictures.*

Indeed, the social relationship the two men formed was in many ways one of friendship and warmth.

Conflicts in the Field. Fights, conflict, and disagreements can erupt in the field, or a researcher may study groups with opposing positions. In such situations, the researcher will feel pressure to take sides and will be tested to see if he or she can be trusted. In such occasions, a researcher usually stays on the neutral sidelines and walks a tightrope between opposing sides. This is because once he or she becomes aligned with one side, the researcher will cut off access to the other side.[32] In addition, he or she will see the situation from only one point of view. Nevertheless, some (e.g., Van Maanen, 1982:115) argue that true neutrality is illusory. As a researcher becomes involved with members and embroiled in webs of relationships and commitments, neutrality becomes almost impossible.

Appearing Interested. Field researchers maintain an *appearance of interest* in the field. An experienced researcher appears to be interested in and involved with field events by statements and behaviors (e.g., facial expression, going for coffee, organizing a party, etc.) even if he or she is not truly interested. This is because field relations may be disrupted if the researcher appears to be bored or distracted. Putting up such a temporary front of involvement is a common small deception in daily life and is part of being polite.[33]

Of course, selective inattention (i.e., not staring or appearing not to notice) is also part of acting polite. If a person makes a social mistake (e.g., accidentally uses an incorrect word, passes gas, etc.), the polite thing to do is to ignore it. Selective inattention is used in fieldwork, as well. It gives an alert researcher an opportunity to learn by casually eavesdropping on conversations or observing events not meant to be public.

Social Breakdowns. A social breakdown occurs when different cultural expectations or social assumptions collide in the course of fieldwork. These breakdowns can be detrimental to the field researcher's objective of establishing trust with members. Indeed, the social breakdown might lead to a "freeze-out" of the researcher.

Social breakdowns highlight social meanings in conflict. When they occur, they often produce an awkward embarrassment for the researcher. They may also give cause for insiders to exclude the field researcher's penetration into the field site.

Consider, for example, Henry's (1978:35–36) micro-level analysis of the fencing of stolen goods. He wrote that "it is necessary to know as much as possible about a newcomer before suggesting that he become part of the [illegal] trading

network." Citing Ditton's (1977a:38) ethnography of pilferers, Henry went on to say:

> *Once the members of a trading network have decided that a person is "all right" and that he shares the same attitude to life as themselves, they may test him out with an offer for "cheap" goods. . . . This often takes the form of a particularly loaded question which he [Ditton] described as the "alerting phrase."*

If the ethnographer fails in answering the loaded question to the satisfaction of the insiders, he or she will have, in effect, created a social breakdown. In this particular instance, such a breakdown might well prevent the researcher from gaining deeper access into the illegal trading network.

OBSERVING AND COLLECTING DATA

This section looks at how to get good qualitative field data. Field data are what the researcher experiences and remembers, and what are recorded in field notes and become available for systematic analysis.

Watching and Listening

Observing. A great deal of what researchers do in the field is to pay attention, watch, and listen carefully. They use all the senses, noticing what is seen, heard, smelled, tasted, or touched. The researcher becomes an instrument that absorbs all sources of information.

A field researcher carefully scrutinizes the physical setting to capture its atmosphere. He or she asks: What is the color of the floor, walls, ceiling? How large is a room? Where are the windows and doors? How is the furniture arranged, and what is its condition (e.g., new or old and worn, dirty or clean)? What type of lighting is there? Are there signs, paintings, plants? What are the sounds or smells?

For example, a field researcher studying the fencing of stolen goods might write this into his or her field notes: "Four of us had breakfast this morning at 7 o'clock. The conversation, as usual, centered on last night's basketball game. Everyone was laughing and loud. I was then quietly asked what I thought about government's meddling in people's businesses. Suddenly, the mood dropped, as the others got serious, stopped talking, and waited for my answer. I answered that government is too nosey. There was an almost imperceptible sigh of relief, as the mood lightened and the conversation returned to basketball. Perhaps this question was loaded to test my trustworthiness."

A field researcher notes aspects of physical appearance such as neatness, dress, and hairstyle because they express messages that can affect social interactions. People spend a great deal of time and money selecting clothes, styling and combing hair, grooming with makeup, shaving, ironing clothes, and using deodorant or perfumes. These are part of their presentation of self. Even people who do not groom, shave, or wear deodorant present themselves and send a symbolic message by their appearance. No one dresses or looks "normal." Such a statement suggests that a researcher is not seeing the social world through the eyes of a stranger or is insensitive to social signals.

What people do is also significant. A field researcher notices where people sit or stand, the pace at which they walk, and their nonverbal communication. People express social information, feelings, and attitudes through nonverbal communication, including gestures, facial expressions, and how one stands or sits (standing stiffly, sitting in a slouched position). People express relationships by how they position themselves in a group and through eye contact. A researcher may read the social communication of people by noting that they are standing close together, looking relaxed, and making eye contact.

A field researcher also notices the context in which events occur: Who was present? Who just arrived or left the scene? Was the room hot and stuffy? Such details may help the researcher assign meaning and understand why an event occurred. If they are not noticed, the details are lost, as is a full understanding of the event.

Listening.   A field researcher listens carefully to phrases, accents, and incorrect grammar, listening both to *what* is said and *how* it is said or what was implied. For example, people often use phrases such as "you know" or "of course" or "et cetera." A field researcher knows the meaning behind such phrases. He or she can try to hear everything, but listening is difficult when many conversations occur at once or when eavesdropping. Luckily, significant events and themes usually recur.

Argot.   People who interact with each other over a time period develop shared symbols and terminology. They create new words or assign new meanings to ordinary words. New words develop out of specific events, assumptions, or relations. Knowing and using the language can signal membership in a distinct subculture. A field researcher learns the specialized language, or *argot*.[34]

> *Researchers must start with the premise that words and symbols used in their world may have different meaning in the world of their subjects. They must also be attuned to new words and words used in contexts other than those with which they are familiar. (Bogdan and Taylor, 1975:53)*

A field researcher discovers how the argot fits into social relations or meanings. The argot gives a researcher clues to what is important to members and how they see the world. In Sutherland's classic field study, *The Professional Thief* (1937), slang terms are used to refer to amateur thiefs. A few of them are "snatch-and-grab thief," "boot-and-shoe thief," and "raw-jaw" method. These terms clearly convey the low opinion professionals have of amateurs.

Wright and colleagues (1996:5) familiarized themselves with the field argot of burglars before conducting the fieldwork, as indicated here:

> *We made an effort to "fit in" by learning the distinctive terminology and phrases used by the offenders. Here again, the assistance of the ex-offender proved invaluable. Prior to entering the field, he suggested ways in which questions might be asked so that the subjects would better under-*

stand them, and provided us with a working knowledge of popular street terms (e.g., "boy" for heroin, "girl" for cocaine) and pronunciations (e.g., "hair ron" for heroin).

Taking Notes

Most field research data are in the form of field notes. Good notes are the bricks and mortar of field research (Fetterman, 1989). Full field notes can contain maps, diagrams, photographs, interviews, tape recordings, videotapes, memos, objects from the field, notes jotted in the field, and detailed notes written away from the field. A field researcher expects to fill many notebooks or file cabinets, or the equivalent in computer memory. He or she spends more time writing notes than being in the field. Some researchers produce 40 single-spaced pages of notes for three hours of observation. With practice, even a new field researcher can produce several pages of notes for each hour in the field.

Writing notes is often boring, tedious work that requires self-discipline. The notes contain extensive descriptive detail drawn from memory. A researcher makes it a daily habit or compulsion to write notes immediately after leaving the field. The notes must be neat and organized because the researcher will return to them over and over again. Once written, the notes are private and valuable. A researcher treats them with care and protects confidentiality. Members have the right to remain anonymous, and researchers often use *pseudonyms* (false names) in notes. Field notes may be of interest to hostile parties, blackmailers, or legal officials, so some researchers write field notes in code.

A researcher's state of mind, level of attention, and conditions in the field affect note taking. He or she will usually begin with relatively short one- to three-hour periods in the field before writing notes. Johnson (1975:187) remarked:

The quantity and quality of the observational records vary with the field worker's feelings of restedness or exhaustion, reactions to particular events, relations with others, consumption of alcoholic beverages, the number of discrete observations, and so forth.

Types of Field Notes. Field researchers take notes in many ways.[35] The recommendations here (also see Box 14.3) are suggestions. Full field notes have several types or levels. Five levels will be described. It is usually best to keep all the notes for an observation period together and to distinguish types of notes by separate pages. Some researchers include inferences with direct observations if they are set off by a visible device such as brackets or colored ink. The quantity of notes varies across types. For example, six hours in the field might result in 1 page of jotted notes, 40 pages of direct observation, 5 pages of researcher inference, and 2 pages total for methodological, theoretical, and personal notes.

Jotted Notes. It is nearly impossible to take good notes in the field. Even a known observer in a public setting looks strange when furiously writing. More important, when looking down and writing, the researcher cannot see and hear what is happening. The attention given to note writing is taken from field observation where it belongs. The specific setting determines whether any notes in the field can be taken. The researcher may be able to write, and members may expect it, or he or she may have to be secretive (e.g., go to the restroom).

Jotted notes are written in the field. They are short, temporary memory triggers such as words, phrases, or drawings taken inconspicuously, often scribbled on any convenient item (e.g., napkin, matchbook). They are incorporated into direct observation notes but are never substituted for them.

Direct Observation Notes. The basic source of field data are notes a researcher writes immediately after leaving the field, which he or she can add to later. The notes should be ordered chronologically with the date, time, and place on each entry. They serve as a detailed description of what the researcher heard and saw in concrete, specific terms. To the extent possible, they are an exact recording of the particular words, phrases, or actions.

A researcher's memory improves with practice. A new researcher can soon remember exact phrases from the field. Verbatim statements should be written with double quote marks to dis-

Box 14.3

Recommendations for Taking Field Notes

1. Record notes as soon as possible after each period in the field, and do not talk with others until observations are recorded.
2. Begin the record of each field visit with a new page, with the date and time noted.
3. Use jotted notes only as a temporary memory aid, with key words or terms, or the first and last things said.
4. Use wide margins to make it easy to add to notes at any time. Go back and add to the notes if you remember something later.
5. Plan to type notes and keep each level of notes separate so it will be easy to go back to them later.
6. Record events in the order in which they occurred, and note how long they last (e.g., a 15-minute wait, a one-hour ride).
7. Make notes as concrete, complete, and comprehensible as possible.
8. Use frequent paragraphs and quotation marks. Exact recall of phrases is best, with double quotes; use single quotes for paraphrasing.
9. Record small talk or routines that do not appear to be significant at the time; they may become important later.
10. "Let your feelings flow" and write quickly without worrying about spelling or "wild ideas." Assume that no one else will see the notes, but use pseudonyms.
11. Never substitute tape recordings completely for field notes.
12. Include diagrams or maps of the setting, and outline your own movements and those of others during the period of observation.
13. Include the researcher's own words and behavior in the notes. Also record emotional feelings and private thoughts in a separate section.
14. Avoid evaluative summarizing words. Instead of "The sink looked disgusting," say, "The sink was rust-stained and looked as if it had not been cleaned in a long time. Pieces of food and dirty dishes looked as if they had been piled in it for several days."
15. Reread notes periodically and record ideas generated by the rereading.
16. Always make one or more backup copies, keep them in a locked location, and store the copies in different places in case of fire.

---

tinguish them from paraphrases. Dialogue accessories (nonverbal communication, props, tone, speed, volume, gestures) should be recorded as well. A researcher records what was actually said and does not clean it up; notes include ungrammatical speech, slang, and misstatements (e.g., write, "Uh, I'm goin' home, Sal," not "I am going home, Sally").

Researcher Inference Notes. A field researcher listens to members in order to "climb into their skin" or "walk in their shoes."[36] This involves a three-step process. The researcher listens without applying analytical categories; he or she compares what is heard to what was heard at other times and to what others say; then the researcher applies his or her own interpretation to infer or figure out what it means. In ordinary interaction, we do all three steps simultaneously and jump quickly to

our own inferences. A field researcher learns to look and listen without inferring or imposing an interpretation. His or her observations without inferences go into *direct observation notes.*

A researcher records inferences in a separate section that is keyed to direct observations. People never see social relationships, emotions, or meaning. They see specific physical actions and hear words; then they use background cultural knowledge, clues from the context, and what is done or said to assign social meaning. For example, one does not see *love* or *anger;* one sees and hears specific actions (red face, loud voice, wild gestures, obscenities) and draw inferences from them (the person is angry).

A researcher learns to keep inferred meaning separate from direct observations. Direct observation notes, being descriptive in nature, are presented without going into the social meaning of the observation. Researchers, in other words, refrain from making any inferences as to theoretical or symbolic meaning. Inference notes, on the other hand, reflect on the observation in an attempt to assign social meaning to it. It is the *separation of inference* that allows multiple meanings to arise when reading and rereading direct observation notes. If a researcher records inferred meaning without separation, he or she loses other possible meanings. (See Box 14.4 for excerpts of actual direct observation field notes.)

Analytic Notes.   Researchers make many decisions about how to proceed while in the field. Some acts are planned (e.g., to conduct an interview, to observe a particular activity, etc.) and others seem to occur almost out of thin air.. Field researchers keep methodological ideas in analytic notes to record their plans, tactics, ethical and procedural decisions, and self-critiques of tactics.

Theory emerges in field research during data collection and is clarified when a researcher reviews field notes. Analytic notes have a running account of a researcher's attempts to give meaning to field events. He or she thinks out loud in the notes by suggesting links between ideas, creating hypotheses, proposing conjectures, and developing new concepts.

Analytic memos are part of the theoretical notes. They are systematic digressions into theory, where a researcher elaborates on ideas in depth, expands on ideas while still in the field, and modifies or develops more complex theory by rereading and thinking about the memos.

Box 14.4 _____

Excerpts of Direct Observation Field Notes Taken from Sullivan's (1989) Ethnography Entitled *Getting Paid*

EXCERPT #1

I talked to a female member of one of the youth crews. She was talking to one of her friends by the benches and didn't seem to be working, although she said that she was. She said that she was hired as a junior counselor in the manpower center, but she has never performed those duties. Instead, she is asked to pick up paper and sweep. She insists that she wants to work under her job title and not as an orderly.

She boasts about getting paid and not showing at all. No one checks the time cards. She said that no one enjoys working there because it's boring and disorganized. No one knows who is responsible for what. She says that it is known to the individual that he or she can't get fired from the job because the purpose is to keep them out of trouble and off the streets. She said that summer jobs should have a full seven-hour day doing something worthwhile, getting experience, and, most of all, doing something interesting. (pp. 78–79)

EXCERPT #2

I ran into two of the guys. They offered to sell me a pair of leather gloves. They had at least ten pairs of the gloves. I told them I didn't want them so one of them asked me for a quarter to buy a soda. He entered the store and bought a bottle of juice and stole another one which he hid under his coat. The owner of the store saw the lump under his jacket and asked what it was. Sammy said "a gun" and walked out. The owner came outside but Sammy had already hidden the bottle. Then Sammy offered to sell the gloves to the store owner's wife. She said she didn't want them because she couldn't sell them. She then said, "If you get me Duracell batteries I'll buy them from you, or anything that I can sell here." (p. 129)

EXCERPT #3

Wilson began to describe the after-hours place. "When I say after-hours, I mean some of these places don't even open up until three o'clock in the morning." He said that a lot of what goes on in these places has to do with cocaine. People go there to buy, sell, and take cocaine, mostly to take it. Given the hours of these places, most of the clientele are hustlers. I asked, "What kind of hustles are we talking about: gambling, prostitution, organized theft, drugs?" He said, "All kinds of drugs. These places are like trade schools in the drug business." (p. 168)

Personal Notes.   As discussed earlier, personal feelings and emotional reactions become part of the data and color what a researcher sees or hears in the field. A researcher keeps a section of notes that is like a personal diary. He or she records personal life events and feelings in it ("I'm tense today, I wonder if it's because of the fight I had yesterday with . . ."; "I've got a headache on this gloomy, overcast day").

Personal notes serve three functions: They provide an outlet for a researcher and a way to cope with stress; they are a source of data about personal reactions; they give him or her a way to evaluate direct observation or inference notes when the notes are later reread. For example, if the researcher was in a good mood during observations, it might color what he or she observed.

Maps and Diagrams.   Field researchers often make maps and draw diagrams or pictures of the features of a field site.[37] This serves two purposes: It helps a researcher organize events in the field and it helps convey a field site to others. Field researchers find three types of maps helpful: spatial, social, and temporal. The first helps orient the data; the latter two are preliminary forms of data analysis. A *spatial map* locates people, equipment, and the like in terms of geographical physical space to show where activities occur. A *social map* shows the number or variety of people and the arrangements among them in terms of power, influence, friendship, division of labor, a so on. A *temporal map* shows the ebb and flow of people, goods, services, communications, and so forth.

Machine Recordings to Supplement Memory. Tape recorders and videotapes can be helpful supplements in field research. They never substitute for field notes or a researcher's presence in the field. They cannot be introduced into all field sites, and can be used only after a researcher develops rapport. Recorders and videotapes provide a close approximation to what occurred and a permanent record that others can review. They help a researcher recall events and observe what does not happen, or nonresponses, which are easy

to miss. Nevertheless, these items create disruption and an increased awareness of surveillance. Researchers who rely on them must address associated problems (e.g., ensure that batteries are fresh and there are enough blank tapes). Also, relistening to or viewing tapes can be time consuming. For example, it may take over 50 hours to listen to 50 hours recorded in the field. Transcriptions of tape are expensive and not always accurate; they do not always convey subtle contextual meanings or mumbled words.[38]

Of course, ethnographic and documentary filmmaking especially bring the issue of machine-assisted observation to the foreground. Barbash and Taylor (1997:77) offered this general advice:

> *Research footage does itself contain some interpretation: the filmmaker and/or anthropologist employs standards of significance in selecting when and what to shoot. (That does not mean that they can always articulate or even know exactly what those criteria are.) Nonetheless, the essential point of research footage is that it be as unselective and unstructured as possible—in other words, that it provide less discourse about social life than an objective record of it. As far as possible, the interpretation should come later and should focus, not on the filmic discourse, but on the reality of which it ostensibly provides a record. The camera is deployed as an impartial instrument in the service of science, fixing all that is fleeting for infinite future analysis. (pp. 77–78, emphasis added)*

Interview Notes.   If a researcher conducts field interviews (to be discussed), he or she keeps the interview notes separate.[39] In addition to recording questions and answers, he or she creates a *face sheet.* This is a page at the beginning of the notes with information such as the date, place of interview, characteristics of interviewee, content of the interview, and so on. It helps the interviewer when rereading and making sense of the notes.

Data Quality

The Meaning of Quality.   What does the term *high-quality data* mean in field research, and what does a researcher do to get such data?[40] For a quantitative researcher, high-quality data are reliable and valid; they give precise, consistent measures of the same "objective" truth for all researchers. An interpretive approach suggests a different kind of data quality. Instead of assuming one single, objective truth, field researchers hold that members subjectively interpret experiences within a social context. What a member takes to be true results from social interaction and interpretation. Thus, high-quality field data capture such processes and provide an understanding of the member's viewpoint.

A field researcher does not eliminate subjective views to get quality data; rather, quality data include his or her subjective responses and experiences. Quality field data are detailed descriptions from the researcher's immersion and authentic experiences in the social world of members.[41]

Reliability in Field Research. The reliability of field data addresses the question: Are researcher observations about a member or field event internally and externally consistent? *Internal consistency* refers to whether the data are plausible given all that is known about a person or event, eliminating common forms of human deception. In other words, do the pieces fit together into a coherent picture? For example, are a member's actions consistent over time and in different social contexts?

External consistency is achieved by verifying or cross-checking observations with other, divergent sources of data. In other words, does it all fit into the overall context? For example, can others verify what a researcher observed about a person? Does other evidence confirm the researcher's observations? Reliability in field research also includes what is not said or done, but is expected or anticipated. Such omissions or null data can be significant but are difficult to detect.

Reliability in field research depends on a researcher's insight, awareness, suspicions, and questions. He or she looks at members and events from different angles (legal, economic, political, personal) and mentally asks questions: Where does the money come from for that? What do those people do all day?

Field researchers depend on what members tell them. This makes the credibility of members and their statements part of reliability. To check member credibility, a researcher asks: Does the person have a reason to lie? Is she in a position to know that? What are the person's values and how might that shape what she says? Is he just saying that to please me? Is there anything that might limit his spontaneity?

Field researchers take subjectivity and context into account as they evaluate credibility. They know that a person's statements or actions are affected by subjective perceptions. Statements are made from a particular point of view and colored by an individual's experiences. Instead of evaluating each statement to see if it is true, a field researcher finds statements useful in themselves. Even inaccurate statements and actions can be revealing from a researcher's perspective.

Other obstacles to reliability include behaviors that can mislead a researcher: misinformation, evasions, lies, and fronts.[42] *Misinformation* is an unintended falsehood caused by the uncertainty and complexity of life.

Evasions are intentional acts of avoiding or not revealing information. Common evasions include not answering questions, answering a different question than was asked, switching topics, or answering in a purposefully vague and ambiguous manner.

Lies are untruths intended to mislead or to give a false view. Douglas (1976:73) noted, "In all other research settings I've known about in any detail, lying was common, both among members and to researchers, especially about the things that were really important to the members."

Fronts are shared and learned lies and deceptions. They can include the use of physical props and collaborators. For example, a bar is really a place to make illegal bets. The bar appears legitimate and sells drinks, but its true business is revealed only by careful investigation.

Validity in Field Research. Validity in field research is the confidence placed in a researcher's analysis and data as accurately representing the social world in the field. Replicability is not a criterion because field research is virtually impossible to replicate. Essential aspects of the field change: The social events and context change, the members are different, the individual researcher differs, and so on. There are four kinds of validity or tests of research accuracy: ecological validity, natural history, member validation, and competent insider performance.

Ecological validity is the degree to which the social world described by a researcher matches the world of members. It asks: Is the natural setting described relatively undisturbed by the researcher's presence or procedures? A project has ecological validity if events would have occurred without a researcher's presence.

Natural history is a detailed description of how the project was conducted. It is a full and candid disclosure of a researcher's actions, assumptions, and procedures for others to evaluate. A project is valid in terms of natural history if outsiders see and accept the field site and the researcher's actions.

Member validation occurs when a researcher takes field results back to members, who judge their adequacy. A project is member valid if members recognize and understand the researcher's description as reflecting their intimate social world. Member validation has limitations because conflicting perspectives in a setting produce disagreement with researcher's observations, and members may object when results do not portray their group in a favorable light. In addition, members may not recognize the description because it is not from their perspective or does not fit with their purposes.[43]

Competent insider performance is the ability of a nonmember to interact effectively as a member or pass as one. This includes the ability to tell and understand insider jokes. A valid field project gives enough of a flavor of the social life in the field, and sufficient detail so that an outsider can act as a member. Its limitation is that it is not possible to know the social rules for every situation. Also, an outsider might be able to pass simply because members are being polite and do not want to point out social mistakes.[44]

Focusing and Sampling

Focusing. The field researcher first gets a general picture, then focuses on a few specific problems or issues (see Figure 14.3).[45] A researcher decides on specific research questions and develops hypotheses only after being in the field and experiencing it firsthand. At first, everything seems relevant; later, however, selective attention focuses on specific questions and themes.

Sampling. Field research sampling differs from survey research sampling, although sometimes both use snowball sampling (see Chapter 9).[46] A field researcher samples by taking a smaller, selective set of observations from all possible observations. It is called *theoretical sampling* because it is guided by the researcher's developing theory. Field researchers sample times, situations, types of events, locations, types of people, or contexts of interest.

For example, a researcher samples time by observing a setting at different times. He or she observes at all times of the day, on every day of the week, and in all seasons to get a full sense of how the field site stays the same or changes. It is often best to overlap when sampling (e.g., to have sampling times from 7:00 A.M. to 9:00 A.M., from 8:00 A.M. to 10:00 A.M., from 9:00 A.M. to 11:00 A.M., etc.).

A researcher samples locations because one location may give depth, but a narrow perspective. Sitting or standing in different locations helps the researcher get a sense of the whole site.

Field researchers sample people by focusing their attention or interaction on different kinds of people (old-timers and newcomers, old and young, males and females, leaders and followers). As a researcher identifies types of people, or people with opposing outlooks, he or she tries to interact with and learn about all types.

For example, a researcher samples three kinds of field events: routine, special, and unanticipated. Routine events (e.g., opening up a store for business) happen every day and should not be considered unimportant simply because they are routine.

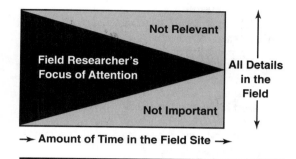

FIGURE 14.3 Focusing in Field Research

Special events (e.g., annual office party) are announced and planned in advance. They focus member attention and reveal aspects of social life not otherwise visible. Unanticipated events are those that just happen to occur while a researcher is present.

THE FIELD RESEARCH INTERVIEW

So far, you have learned how field researchers observe and take notes. They also interview members, but field interviews differ from survey research interviews. This section introduces the field interview.

The Field Interview

Field researchers use unstructured, nondirective, in-depth interviews, which differ from formal survey research interviews in many ways (see Table 14.1).[47] The field interview involves asking questions, listening, expressing interest, and recording what was said.

The field interview is a joint production of a researcher and a member. Members are active participants whose insights, feelings, and cooperation are essential parts of a discussion process that reveals subjective meanings. "The interviewer's presence and form of involvement—how she or he listens, attends, encourages, interrupts, digresses, initiates topics, and terminates responses—is in-

tegral to the respondent's account" (Mishler, 1986:82).

Field research interviews go by many names: unstructured, depth, ethnographic, open ended, informal, and long. Generally, they involve one or more people being present, occur in the field, and are informal and nondirective (i.e., the respondent may take the interview in various directions) (see Fontana and Frey, 1994).

A field interview involves a mutual sharing of experiences. A researcher might share his or her background to build trust and encourage the informant to open up, but does not force answers or use leading questions. She or he encourages and guides a process of mutual discovery.

In field interviews, members express themselves in the forms in which they normally speak, think, and organize reality. A researcher retains members' jokes and narrative stories in their natural form and does not repackage them into a standardized format. The focus is on the member's perspective and experiences. In order to stay close to the member's experience, the researcher asks questions in terms of concrete examples or situations—for example, "Could you tell me things that led up to your quitting in June?" instead of "Why did you quit your job?"

Field interviews occur in a series over time. A researcher begins by building rapport and steering conversation away from evaluative or highly sensitive topics. He or she avoids probing inner feelings until intimacy is established, and even then, the researcher expects apprehension. After several meetings, he or she may be able to probe more deeply into sensitive issues and seek clarification of less sensitive issues. In later interviews, he or she may return to topics and check past answers by restating them in a nonjudgmental tone and asking for verification—for example. "The last time we talked, you said that you started taking things from the store after they reduced your pay. Is that right?"

The field interview is a "speech event," closer to a friendly conversation than the stimulus/response model found in a survey research interview (see Chapter 10). You are familiar with a

TABLE 14.1 Survey Interviews versus Field Search Interviews

TYPICAL SURVEY INTERVIEW	TYPICAL FIELD INTERVIEW
1. It has a clear beginning and end.	1. The beginning and end are not clear. The interview can be picked up later.
2. The same standard questions are asked of all respondents in the same sequence.	2. The questions and the order in which they are asked are tailored to specific people and situations.
3. The interviewer appears neutral at all times.	3. The interviewer shows interest in responses, encourages elaboration.
4. The interviewer asks questions, and the respondent answers.	4. It is like a friendly conversational exchange, but with more interviewer questions.
5. It is almost always with one respondent alone.	5. It can occur in group setting or with others in the area, but varies.
6. It has a professional tone and businesslike focus; diversions are ignored.	6. It is interspersed with jokes, asides, stories, diversions, and anecdotes, which are recorded.
7. Closed-ended questions are common, with rare probes.	7. Open-ended questions are common, and probes are frequent.
8. The interviewer alone controls the pace and direction of interview.	8. The interviewer and member jointly control the pace and direction of the interview.
9. The social context in which the interview occurs is ignored and assumed to make little difference.	9. The social context of the interview is noted and seen as important for interpreting the meaning of responses.
10. The interviewer attempts to mold the communication pattern into a standard framework.	10. The interviewer adjusts to the member's norms and language usage.

Source: Adapted from Briggs (1986), Denzin (1989), Douglas (1985), Mishler (1986), Spradley (1979a).

friendly conversation, which has its own informal rules and the following elements: (1) a greeting ("Hi, it's good to see you again"); (2) the absence of an explicit goal or purpose (we don't say, "Let's now discuss what we did last weekend"); (3) avoidance of repetition (we don't say, "Could you clarify what you said about . . ."); (4) question asking ("Did you see the race yesterday?"); (5) expressions of interest ("Really? I wish I could have been there!"); (6) expressions of ignorance ("No, I missed it. What happened?"); (7) turn taking, so the encounter is balanced (one person does not always ask questions and the other only answer); (8) abbreviations ("I missed the Derby, but I'm going to the Indy," not "I missed the Kentucky Derby horse race but I will go to the Indianapolis 500 automotive race"); (9) a pause or brief silence when neither person talks is acceptable; (10) a closing (we don't say, "Let's end this

conversation"; instead, we give a verbal indicator before physically leaving—"I've got to get back to work now. See ya tomorrow.").

The field interview differs from a friendly conversation. It has an explicit purpose—to learn about the informant and setting. A researcher includes explanations or requests that diverge from friendly conversations. For example, he or she may say, "I'll like to ask you about . . . ," or "Could you look at this and see if I've written it down right?" The field interview is less balanced. A higher proportion of questions come from the researcher, who expresses more ignorance and interest. Also, it includes repetition, and a researcher asks the member to elaborate on unclear abbreviations.[48]

Field research interviewers watch for markers. A *marker* in a field interview is "a passing reference made by a respondent to an important event or feeling state" (Weiss, 1994:77). Suppose, for example, you are interviewing a corporate executive about how her company disposes of its toxic waste. She responds that the company has a regular contract with another company to do that job. But she also mentions in passing that sometimes they must "cut a special contract" with a smaller company. The researcher should pick up on this reference to the smaller company and be sure to return to it later for further questioning. Most importantly, the interviewer listens. He or she does not interrupt frequently, repeatedly finish the respondent's sentences, offer associations (e.g., "Oh, that is just like X"), insist on finishing asking a question that the respondent has begun to answer, fight for control over the interview process, or stay with a line of thought and ignore new leads (see Weiss, 1994:78).

Life History

Life history or a biographical interview is a special type of field interviewing. It overlaps with oral history (see Chapter 15).[49] There are multiple purposes for stories of the past and these may shape the forms of interview (see Smith, 1994). In a life history interview, researchers interview and gather documentary material about a particular individual's life, usually someone who is old. "The concept of *life story* is used to designate the retrospective information itself without the corroborative evidence often implied by the term *life history*" (Tagg, 1985:163). Researchers ask open-ended questions to capture how the person understands his or her own past. Exact accuracy in the story is less critical than the story itself. Researchers recognize that the person may reconstruct or add present interpretations to the past; the person may "rewrite" his or her story. The main purpose is to get at how the respondent sees/remembers the past, not just some kind of objective truth.

Researchers sometimes use a life story grid in which they ask the person what happened at various dates and in several areas of life. A grid may consist of categories such as migration, occupation, education, or family events for each of a dozen ages in the person's life. Researchers

often supplement the interview information with artifacts (e.g., old photos) and may present them during the interview to stimulate discussion or recollection. "Life writing as an empirical exercise feeds on data: letters, documents, interviews" (Smith, 1994:290). McCraken (1988:20) gave an example of how objects aided the interview by helping him understand how the person being interviewed saw things. When interviewing a 75-year-old woman in her living room, McCraken initially thought the room just contained a lot of cluttered physical objects. After having the woman explain the meaning of each item, it was clear that she saw each as a memorial or a memento. The room was a museum to key events in her life. Only after the author looked at the objects in this new way did he begin to see the furniture and objects not an inanimate things but as objects that radiated meaning.

Klockars's (1974) field study of fencing stolen goods is, to be more precise, an oral history. For a period of nearly a year and a half, Klockars got well acquainted with "Vincent." They met once or twice a week, usually over dinner in an Italian restaurant, and "Vincent would recount the events and deals he had participated in since last I [the researcher] saw him" (p. 218). Over the months, their conversations first revolved around "his [Vincent's] prefencing years: his family, his school, his years in the orphanage, his street hustling, his marriage, and his years in Mid-City" (p. 219). By the end of the period, the conversations between the two had moved well beyond biographical details to the "working principles of his world." Thus, Vincent's life history served as a vehicle which led the criminologist to a general knowledge of the stolen goods market.

Types of Questions in Field Interviews

Field researchers ask three types of questions in a field interview: descriptive, structural, and contrast questions. All are asked concurrently, but each type is more frequent at a different stage in the research process (see Figure 14.4). During the early stage, a researcher primarily asks descriptive questions. He or she gradually adds

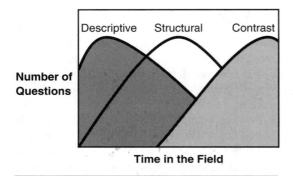

FIGURE 14.4   Types of Questions in Field Research

structural questions until, in the middle stage after analysis has begun, they make up a majority of the questions. Contrast questions appear in the middle of a field research study and increase until, by the end, they are asked more than any other type.[50]

Descriptive questions are asked to explore the setting and learn about the background of members. Recall that Klockars's early conversations with Vincent focused on Vincent's prefencing days. This gave Klockars biographical information about his subject. After some weeks in the field, the researcher began to incorporate more *structural questions* into their conversations. For example, the criminologist began to ask Vincent to explain how stolen goods are fenced. The two also began to discuss not only fencing, in general, but also particular situations and deals in which Vincent was involved.

The interview then often turns to *contrast questions*. It is at this point in the interview process that the researcher asks questions that force the subject "to stop and think," to make comparisons and contrasts, and to reflect on his or her own comments. The interviews are detailed at this point and require the researcher to be well acquainted with the jargon and tacit meaning being expressed.

Informants

An informant or key actor in field research is a member with whom a field researcher develops a relationship and who tells about, or informs on, the field.[51] Who makes a good informant? The ideal informant has four characteristics:

1. The informant is totally familiar with the culture and is in position to witness significant events makes a good informant. He or she lives and breathes the culture and engages in routines in the setting without thinking about them. The individual has years of intimate experience in the culture; he or she not a novice.

2. The individual is currently involved in the field. Ex-members who have reflected on the field may provide useful insights, but the longer they have been away from direct involvement, the more likely it is that they have reconstructed their recollections.

3. The person can spend time with the researcher. Interviewing may take many hours, and some members are simply not available for extensive interviewing.

4. Nonanalytic individuals make better informants. A nonanalytic informant is familiar with and uses native folk theory or pragmatic common sense. This is in contrast to the analytic member, who preanalyzes the setting, using categories from the media or education. Even members educated in the social sciences can learn to respond in a nonanalytic manner, but only if they set aside their education and use the member perspective.

A field researcher may interview several types of informants. Contrasting types of informants who provide useful perspectives include rookies and old-timers, people in the center of events and those on the fringes of activity, people who recently changed status (e.g., through promotion) and those who are static, frustrated or needy people and happy or secure people, the leader in charge and the subordinate who follows. A field researcher expects mixed messages when he or she interviews a range of informants.

Interview Context

Field researchers recognize that a conversation in a private office may not occur in a crowded lunchroom.[52] Often, interviews take place in the member's home environment so that he or she is comfortable. This is not always best. If a member is preoccupied or there is no privacy, a researcher will move to another setting (e.g., restaurant or university office).

The interview's meaning is shaped by its Gestalt or whole interaction of a researcher and a member in a specific context. For example, a researcher notes nonverbal forms of communication (e.g., shrugs, gestures, etc.) that add meaning:

> The investigator should note important facts that will not appear on the record of the interview itself, be it a tape recording or a video recording or a set of notes. Detailed notes on the setting, the participants, time of day, ongoing social or ritual events, and so forth should be complemented by the researcher's perceptions of the interaction: (Briggs, 1986:104)

LEAVING THE FIELD

Work in the field can last for a few weeks to a dozen years.[53] In either case, at some point work in the field ends. Some researchers (e.g., Schatzman and Strauss) suggest that the end comes naturally when theory building ceases or reaches a closure; others (e.g., Bogdan and Taylor) feel that fieldwork could go on without end and that a firm decision to cut off relations is needed.

Experienced field researchers anticipate a process of disengaging and exiting the field. Depending on the intensity of involvement and the length of time in the field, the process can be disruptive or emotionally painful for both the researcher and the members. A researcher may experience the emotional pain of breaking intimate friendships when leaving the field. He or she may feel guilty and depressed immediately before and after leaving. He or she may find it difficult to let go because of personal and emotional entanglements. If the involvement in the field was intense and long, and the field site differed from his or her native culture, the researcher may need months of adjustment before feeling at home with his or her original cultural surroundings.

Once a researcher decides to leave—because the project reaches a natural end and little new is being learned, or because external factors force it to end (e.g., end of a job, gatekeepers order the researcher out, etc.)—he or she chooses a method of exiting. The researcher can leave by a quick exit (simply not return one day) or slowly withdraw, reducing his or her involvement over weeks. He or she also needs to decide how to tell members and how much advance warning to give.

The exit process depends on the specific field setting and the relationships developed. In general, a researcher lets members know a short period ahead of time. He or she fulfills any bargains or commitments that were built up and leaves with a clean slate. Sometimes, a ritual or ceremony, such as a going-away party or shaking hands with everyone, helps signal the break for members. Maintaining friendships with members is also possible and is preferred by feminist researchers.

A field researcher is aware that leaving affects members. Some members may feel hurt or rejected because a close social relationship is ending. They may react by trying to pull a researcher back into the field and make him or her more of a member, or they may become angry and resentful. They may grow cool and distant because of an awareness that the researcher is really an outsider. In any case, fieldwork is not finished until the process of disengagement and exiting is complete.

ETHICAL DILEMMAS OF FIELD RESEARCH

The direct personal involvement of a field researcher in the social lives of other people raises many ethical dilemmas. The dilemmas arise when a researcher is alone in the field and has little time to make a moral decision. Although he or she may be aware of general ethical issues before entering the field, they arise unexpectedly in the course of observing and interacting in the field. We will look at five ethical issues in field research: deception, confidentiality, involvement with deviants, the powerful, and publishing reports.[54]

Deception

Deception arises in several ways in field research: The research may be covert; or may assume a false role, name, or identity; or may mislead members in some way. The most hotly debated of the ethical issues arising from deception is that of covert versus overt field research.[55] Some support it (Douglas, 1976; Johnson, 1975) and see it as necessary for entering into and gaining a full knowledge of many areas of social life. Others oppose it (Erikson, 1970) and argue that it undermines a trust between researchers and society. Although its moral status is questionable, there are some field sites or activities that can only be studied covertly.

Covert research is never preferable and never easier than overt research because of the difficulties of maintaining a front and the constant fear of getting caught. As Lofland and Lofland (1995:35) noted, "As in all other ethical dilemmas of naturalistic research, we believe that the ethically sensitive, thoughtful and knowledgeable investigator is the best judge of whether covert research is justified."

Confidentiality

A researcher learns intimate knowledge that is given in confidence. He or she has a moral obligation to uphold the confidentiality of data. This includes keeping information confidential from others in the field and disguising members' names in field notes. Much more is said on this in the material on research ethics in Chapter 17. For now, a brief discussion on a common approach in ensuring confidentiality will suffice. Take, for instance, Sullivan's (1989) fieldwork on youth crime and employment in three neighborhoods in Brooklyn, New York. Sullivan stated:

> The neighborhoods we studied are referred to here by pseudonyms. . . . [My] descriptions of the neighborhoods are written so as to convey what needs to be known about them without making them precisely identifiable. . . .
>
> La Barriada is a mixed Latino and white neighborhood, though all the youths we studied here were Latino, either first- or second-generation migrants to New York from Puerto Rico. . . .
>
> Projectville is a predominantly black neighborhood in which there is a large concentration of public housing. . . .
>
> Hamilton Park is a predominantly white neighborhood in which most families are supported by relatively high-paying blue-collar jobs. (pp. 18–20)

In Skolnick's (1994:23–25) fieldwork, he explained:

> Data for this book were drawn from a study of criminal law officials conducted by the author mainly in Westville [pseudonym], a city of approximately four hundred thousand with a nonwhite population of about 30 percent. . . .
>
> First, Westville is a "real" city. It is neither a college town where the role of a researcher might be limited by a connection with the university nor a megalopolis like New York or London that dominates the surrounding country. . . .
>
> Along with being a real city, Westville is reputed to have an exemplary machinery for administering criminal justice.

Involvement with Deviants

Researchers who conduct field research on deviants who engage in illegal behavior face additional dilemmas. They know of and are sometimes involved in illegal activity. Fetterman (1989) called this *guilty knowledge*. Having guilty knowledge is perhaps an inevitability for field researchers studying criminal behavior, as Polsky (1997:225) indicated in the following passage:

> If sociologists are effectively to study adult criminals in their natural settings, they must make the moral decision that in some ways they will break the law themselves. They need not be a "participant" observer and commit the criminal acts under study, yet they have to witness such acts or be taken into confidence about them and not blow the whistle. That is, investigators have to decide that when necessary they will "obstruct justice" or have "guilty knowledge" or ban an "accessory" before or after the act, in the full legal sense of those terms.

The Powerful

Field researchers tend to study those without power in society (e.g., street people, the poor, children, and lower-level workers in bureaucracies). Powerful elites can block access and have effective gatekeepers. Researchers are criticized for ignoring the powerful, and they are also criticized by the powerful for being biased toward the less powerful. Becker (1970c) explained this by the *hierarchy of credibility,* which says that those who study deviants or low-level subordinates in an organization are viewed as biased, whereas those with authority are assumed to be credible. In groups with hierarchies or organizations, most people assume that those at or near the top have the right to define the way things are going to be, that they have a broader view and are in a position to do something. Thus, "the sociologist who favors officialdom will be spared the accusation of bias" (Becker, 1970c:20). When field researchers become immersed in the world of the less powerful and understand that point of view, they are expressing a rarely heard perspective. They may be accused of bias because they give a voice to parts of society that are not otherwise heard.

Publishing Field Reports

The intimate knowledge that a researcher obtains and reports creates a dilemma between the right of privacy and the right to know. A researcher does not publicize member secrets, violate privacy, or harm reputations. Yet, if he or she cannot publish anything that might offend or harm someone, some of what the researcher learned will remain hidden, and it may be difficult for others to believe general statements if critical details are omitted.

Some researchers suggest asking members to look at a report to verify its accuracy and to approve of their portrayal in print. For marginal groups (e.g., addicts, prostitutes, crack users, etc.), this may not be possible, but researchers still have to respect member privacy. On the other hand, censorship or self-censorship can be a danger. A compromise position is that truthful but unflattering material may be published only if it is essential to the researchers' larger arguments.[56]

CONCLUSION

In this chapter, you learned that field research is very important to the advancement of criminology. The subject matter criminologists study naturally lends itself to field research. Moreover, doing field research is not as frightening or difficult as the new researcher might think. Although the specific steps for doing fieldwork cannot be laid out, it is important to remember that good field research stems from experience. Some of the insights that other criminologists have gained from their field research experience have been presented in considerable detail. You should take these lessons to heart, but there is no substitute for the actual experience of doing fieldwork.

Field research necessarily focuses on micro-level interactions in the present. However, this technique is not particularly useful for studying past events. Historical/comparative research, as you shall see in the next chapter, is better suited for this.

KEY TERMS

acceptable incompetent	competent insider performance	face sheet
access ladder	contrast question	field site
analytic memos	defocusing	freeze outs
appearance of interest	descriptive question	fronts
argot	direct observation notes	gatekeeper
attitude of strangeness	ecological validity	go native
breakdown	ethnography	guilty knowledge
case	external consistency	hierarchy of credibility

jotted notes   naturalism   structural question
marker   normalize social research   theoretical sampling
member validation   pseudonyms   thick description
natural history   separation of inference

REVIEW QUESTIONS

1. What were the two major phases in the development of the Chicago school, and what are the journalistic and anthropological models?

2. List 5 of the 10 things the "methodological pragmatist" field researcher does.

3. Why is it important for a field researcher to read the literature before beginning fieldwork? How does this relate to defocusing?

4. Identify the characteristics of a field site that make it a good one for a beginning field researcher.

5. How does the "presentation of self" affect a field researcher's work?

6. What is the attitude of strangeness, and why is it important?

7. What are relevant considerations when choosing roles in the field, and how can the degree of researcher involvement vary?

8. Identify three ways to ensure quality field research data.

9. Compare differences between a field research and a survey research interview, and between a field interview and a friendly conversation.

10. What are the different types or levels of field notes, and what purpose does each serve?

NOTES

1. See Lofland and Lofland (1995:6,18–19).

2. For a background in the history of field research, see Adler and Adler (1987:8–35), Burgess (1982a), Douglas (1976:39–54), Holy (1984), and Wax (1971:21–41). For additional discussion of the Chicago school, see Blumer (1984) and Faris (1967).

3. Ethnography is described in Agar (1986), Franke (1983), Hammersley and Atkinson (1983), Sanday (1983), and Spradley (1979a:3–12; 1979b:3–16).

4. For more on ethnomethodology, see Cicourel (1964), Denzin (1970), Leiter (1980), Mehan and Wood (1975), and Turner (1974). Also see Emerson (1981:357–359) and Lester and Hadden (1980) on the relationship between field research and ethnomethodology. Garfinkel (1974a) discussed the origins of the term *ethnomethodology*.

5. The misunderstandings of people resulting from disjuncture of different cultures is a common theme.

6. See Geertz (1973, 1979) on "thick description." Also see Denzin (1989:159–160) for additional discussion.

7. For a general discussion of field research and naturalism, see Adler and Adler (1994), Georges and Jones (1980), Holy (1984), and Pearsall (1970). For discussions of contrasting types of field research, see Clammer (1984), Gonor (1977), Holstein and Gubrium (1994), Morse (1994), Schwandt (1994), and Strauss and Corbin (1994).

8. See Georges and Jones (1980:21–42) and Lofland and Lofland (1995:11–15).

9. Johnson (1975:65–66) has discussed defocusing.

10. See Lofland (1976:13–23) and Shaffir and colleagues (1980:18–20) on feeling marginal.

11. See Adler and Adler (1987:67–78).

12. See Hammersley and Atkinson (1983:42–45) and Lofland and Lofland (1995:16–30).

13. Jewish researchers have studied Christians (Kleinman, 1980), Whites have studied African Americans (Liebow, 1967), and adult researchers have become intimate with youngsters (Fine, 1987; Fine and Glassner, 1979; Thorne and Luria, 1986). Also see Eichler (1988), Hunt (1984), and Wax (1979) on the role of race, sex, and age in field research.

14. For more on gatekeepers and access, see Beck (1970:11–29), Bogdan and Taylor (1975:30–32), and Wax (1971:367).

15. Adapted from Gray (1980:311). See also Hicks (1984) and Schatzman and Strauss (1973:58–63).

16. Negotiation in the field is discussed in Gans (1982), Johnson (1975:58–59, 76–77), and Schatzman and Strauss (1973:22–23).

17. Entering and gaining access to field sites with deviant groups is discussed in Becker (1970a:31–38), Lofland and Lofland (1995:31–41), and West (1980). Elite access is discussed by Hoffman (1980) and Spencer (1982). Also see Hammersley and Atkinson (1983:54–76).

18. For more on roles in field settings, see Barnes (1970:241–244), Emerson (1981:364), Hammersley and Atkinson (1983:88–104), Warren and Rasmussen (1977), and Wax (1979). On dress, see Bogdan and Taylor (1975:45) and Douglas (1976).

19. See Strauss (1987:10–11).

20. See Georges and Jones (1980:105–133) and Johnson (1975:159). Clarke (1975) noted that it is not necessarily "subjectivism" to recognize this in field research.

21. See Gurevitch (1988), Hammersley and Atkinson (1983), and Schatzman and Strauss (1973:53) on "strangeness" in field research.

22. See Douglas (1976), Emerson (1981:367–368), and Johnson (1975:124–129) on the question of whether the researcher should always be patient, polite, and considerate.

23. See Wax (1971:13) for a discussion of understanding in field research.

24. For discussions of ascribed status (and, in particular, gender) in field research, see Adler and Adler (1987), Ardener (1984), Ayella (1993), Denzin (1989:116–118), Douglas (1976), Easterday and associates (1982), Edwards (1993), Lofland and Lofland (1995:23), and Van Maanen (1982).

25. Roy (1970) argued for the "Ernie Pyle" role based on his study of union organizing in the southern United States. In this role, named after a World War II battle journalist, the researcher "goes with the troops" as a type of participant as observer. Trice (1970) discussed the advantages of an outsider role. Schwartz and Schwartz (1969) gave a valuable discussion of roles in participant observation and the effects of various roles.

26. See Gans (1982), Goward (1984b), and Van Maanen (1983b:282–286).

27. See Douglas (1976:216) and Corsino (1987).

28. For discussion of "normalizing," see Gans (1982:57–59), Georges and Jones (1980:43–164), Hammersley and Atkinson (1983:70–76), Harkens and Warren (1993), Johnson (1975), and Wax (1971). Mann (1970) discussed how to teach members about a researcher's role.

29. The acceptable incompetent or learner role is discussed in Bogdan and Taylor (1975:46), Douglas (1976), Hammersley and Atkinson (1983:92–94), and Lofland and Lofland (1995:56).

30. See Warren and Rasmussen (1977) for a discussion of cross-sex tension.

31. Also see Adler and Adler (1987:40–42), Bogdan and Taylor (1975:35–37), Douglas (1976), and Gray (1980:321).

32. See Bogdan and Taylor (1975:50–51), Lofland and Lofland (1995:57–58), Shupe and Bromley (1980), and Wax (1971).

33. See Johnson (1975:105–108).

34. See Becker and Geer (1970), Spradley (1979a, 1979b), and Schatzman and Strauss (1973) on argot.

35. For more on ways to record and organize field data, see Bogdan and Taylor (1975:60–73), Hammersley and Atkinson (1983:144–173), and Kirk and Miller (1986:49–59).

36. See Schatzman and Strauss (1973:69) on inference.

37. See Denzin (1989:87), Lofland and Lofland (1995:197–201), Schatzman and Strauss (1973:34–36), and Stimson (1986) for discussions of maps in field research.

38. See Albrecht (1985), Bogdan and Taylor (1975:109), Denzin (1989:210–233), and Jackson (1987) for more on taping in field research.

39. See Burgess (1982b), Lofland and Lofland (1995:89–98), and Spradley (1979a, 1979b) on notes for field interviews.

40. For additional discussion of data quality, see Becker (1970b), Dean and Whyte (1969), Douglas (1976:7), Kirk and Miller (1986), and McCall (1969).

41. Douglas (1976:115) argued that it is easier to "lie" with "hard numbers" than with detailed observations of natural settings, especially if the field data were collected with others and have extensive quotes presented in context.

42. Adapted from Douglas (1976:56–104).

43. See Bloor (1983) and Douglas (1976:126).

44. For more on validity in field research, see Briggs (1986:24), Bogdan and Taylor (1975), Douglas (1976), Emerson (1981:361–363), and Sanjek (1990).

45. See Lofland (1976) and Lofland and Lofland (1995:99–116) for an especially valuable discussion of

focusing. Spradley (1979b:100–111) also provides helpful discussion.

46. See Denzin (1989:71–73, 86–92), Glaser and Strauss (1967), Hammersley and Atkinson (1983: 45–53), Honigmann (1982), and Weiss (1994:25–29) on sampling in field research.

47. Discussion of field interviewing can be found in Banaka (1971), Bogdan and Taylor (1975:95–124), Briggs (1986), Burgess (1982c), Denzin (1989:103–120), Douglas (1985), Lofland and Lofland (1995:78–88), Spradley (1979a), and Whyte (1982).

48. For more on comparisons with conversations, see Briggs (1986:11), Spradley (1979a:56–68), and Weiss (1994:8).

49. See Denzin (1989:182–209), Nash and McCurdy (1989), Smith (1994), and Tagg (1985) on biographical or life history interviews.

50. The types of questions are adapted from Spradley (1979a, 1979b).

51. Field research informants are discussed in Dean and associates (1969), Kemp and Ellen (1984), Schatzman and Strauss (1973), Spradley (1979a:46–

54), and Whyte (1982).

52. Interview contexts are discussed in Hammersley and Atkinson (1983:112–126) and in Schatzman and Strauss (1973:83–87). Briggs (1986) argued that nontraditional populations and females communicate better in unstructured interviews than with standardized forms of expression.

53. Altheide (1980), Bogdan and Taylor (1975: 75–76), Lofland and Lofland (1995:61), Maines and colleagues (1980), and Roadburg (1980) discuss leaving the field.

54. Ethical issues are discussed further in Chapter 17. Also see Lofland and Lofland (1995:26, 63, 75, 168–177), Miles and Huberman (1994:288–297), and Punch (1986).

55. Covert, sensitive study is discussed in Ayella (1993), Edwards (1993), and Mitchell (1993).

56. See Barnes (1970), Becker (1969), Fichter and Kolb (1970), Goward (1984a), Lofland and Lofland (1995:204–230), Miles and Huberman (1994:298–307), and Wolcott (1994) on publishing field research results.

RECOMMENDED READINGS

Barbash, Ilisa, and Lucien Taylor. (1997). *Cross-cultural filmmaking.* Berkeley: University of California Press. This book is the best available text on ethnographic and documentary filmmaking.

Cromwell, Paul. (1996). *In their own words: Criminals on crime.* Los Angeles: Roxbury. This little book is a selection of readings that exemplify field research. A wide variety of different field sites and fieldwork issues are revealed in these excerpts of actual criminological field research.

Denzin, Norman K., and Yvonna S. Lincoln (Eds.). (1994). *Handbook of qualitative research.* Thousand Oaks, CA: Sage. This is a comprehensive collection of essays on qualitative research, with

special attention to various forms of field research. It is not a "how-to" book like Lofland and Lofland (1995), but social researchers interested in understanding field research should study this overview of modern qualitative research.

Lofland, John, and Lyn H. Lofland. (1995). *Analyzing social settings: A guide to qualitative observation and analysis,* 3rd ed. Belmont, CA: Wadsworth. This is a brief introduction to conducting field research for the beginner. The book is short, clearly written, and assumes very little prior knowledge of field research. It includes many practical suggestions for doing field research.

CHAPTER 15

HISTORICAL-COMPARATIVE RESEARCH

> *Most social scientists view history as "just one damn thing after another."*
>
> —A. R. Gillis, "Urbanization, Sociohistorical Context, and Crime," p. 76

INTRODUCTION

Unfortunately, criminologists are as just guilty as other social scientists in their failure to adopt a historical-comparative perspective. The power of this perspective derives from its ability to make comparisons either across time (i.e., historical) or across place (i.e., comparative). By emphasizing the historical-comparative method, one is able to expand the generalizability of criminological theory. Gillis (1996:77) addressed this point: "Propositions derived from theory are typically seen to apply across time as well as across space, and continually testing hypotheses with data from the same place and period can give a false sense of credibility to these generalizations." Thus, for criminologists to advance general explanations that have wide validity, it

359

is imperative that they do historical-comparative research.

Indeed, there has been a longstanding tradition in criminology of such research. Sociologists Emile Durkheim, Max Weber, and Karl Marx, whose writings were influential in the founding of criminology, were deeply committed to the historical-comparative perspective. Yet today, there are entire subfields within criminology woefully lacking in this particular research perspective. Much of the research on organized crime, corporate crime, and transnational crime, for example, really has little or no appreciation for the historical and comparative dimensions of crime.

The historical-comparative (H-C) method, as you shall see, is really a collection of different techniques and approaches. The method incorporates into the analysis not only quantitative data but also draws from qualitative sources as well as the discipline of history. Often, a case study is chosen for a particular theoretical reason, and then the researcher applies these different techniques in constructing an historical-comparative perspective.

A Short History of Historical-Comparative Research

The H-C method came to criminology by way of sociology. As mentioned, classical sociological thought was steeped in the tradition. The comparative element in sociology finds its parallel in anthropological theory. One would expect as much, however, in view of the huge emphasis given to ethnographic research. Historians, particularly social historians, have also influenced sociology, and in turn criminology.

Yet, despite this rich tradition, social scientists relied very little on it until the 1960s in the United States, although with notable exceptions.[1] Disciplinary lines had began to meld in the social sciences, and new specializations took form, among them criminology, criminal justice, police studies, and corrections. This had the effect of renewing scholarly interest in the historical-comparative method. With the translations of Marx and Weber generally available and read in univer-

sities, the 1960s and the 1970s saw the beginning of a sustained wave of nuanced studies in the historical-comparative tradition.[2]

Pearson's (1993:136–137) work serves as an outstanding example of criminological research:

> *I have offered a comparative historical account of outbreaks of machine-breaking and hooliganism in the 1960s when migrant workers were attacked by youths in the same Lancashire cotton towns. In the postwar period the British cotton industry entered a rapid decline, involving profound dislocations in the working class life of cotton towns. Migrant workers—principally from India and Pakistan—were employed in increasing numbers in the textile industry in order to facilitate the technological changeover to more intensive forms of shift-working which were introduced to fight off competition from foreign cotton imports. Ironically, these low-cost cotton imports often came from the same countries as the low-cost migrant labor. Intense conflicts and rivalries emerged between local people and the migrant workers over housing, jobs, and—as far as young working class men were concerned—girls. The phenomenon of "paki-bashing," as it was called, which was condemned on all sides as an irrational hooliganism, emerges as a rational (if primitive) form of resistance to the dislocations within the cotton towns when it is set in its social and historical context. "From below" the migrant workers appeared to be the cause of much of the distress in the cotton towns in the late 1950s and 1960s; just as the machines appeared as the enemy of working people in the earlier historical dislocations of the industrial revolution. I have argued that it is much more useful to think of "paki-bashing" in these terms, rather than to conjure with such dubious criminological ephemera as "criminal psychopath" or "chromosome defect" or "unsocialized youth" who are allegedly the products of "broken homes." It is necessary, in other words, to reconnect the fractured political and historical contexts of criminology where it is customary to make an unnecessarily severe distinction between "crime" on the one hand and "politics" on the other.*

Historical-comparative research has continued to gain popularity in the social sciences.[3] Similarly, the method is also being put to good use by contemporary criminologists, social historians, sociologists, and anthropologists.[4]

Research Questions Appropriate for Historical-Comparative Research

The historical-comparative method is perhaps best suited for the big questions that address macro-level social change (see Barkey, 1991; Beisel, 1990; Blee, 1991; Brown and Warner, 1992; Tolnay and Beck, 1992). There are any number of such questions begging to be taken up by criminologists. These are just three of the many: What are the effects of globalization on corporate crime? What role do so-called Asian values play in lowering crime rates? What historical parallels can be drawn from traditional organized crime syndicates (e.g., Chinese Triads) and contemporary forms of organized crime?[5]

Relatedly, the historical-comparative method is well suited for questions that have the state as a unit of analysis. Evans and colleagues (1985:348) emphasized this point in their historical-comparative analysis of revolutionary movements: "Comparisons across countries and time periods and an emphasis on historical depth, the tracing out of processes over time, are optimal strategies for research on states."

The historical-comparative method can also serve to strengthen criminological theory. By framing one's research question in historical-comparative terms, the researcher is able to generate new concepts, expand existing concepts, and see theoretical relationships in a new light. Indeed, it is wise for criminologists to formulate theories that span a single historical epoch, culture, or nation.[6]

Another advantage associated with the H-C method is that it establishes a relative context within which a topic of interest can be analyzed. In a word, the historical-comparative method contextualizes the research question. It addresses the question relative to a given time and place.

At the same time, however, this may create problems for other researchers who have no real grasp of the H-C context, and hence no framework for judging the significance of the research findings. Take, for example, Pearson's (1993:136) analysis of "paki-bashing." At one level, it is an analysis of scapegoating. It describes the hooliganism ("the vandalism, fights between rival gangs of youth, attacks on migrant labor, street crime, and muggings") perpetrated by the Lancashire working class on ethnic Indians and Pakistanis who worked there in the textile mills in the 1960s. But at another level, the author is drawing certain parallels between "paki-bashing" and the machine-bashing carried out by the Luddites in those same mills 150 years earlier. Unless one is familiar with the social history of the Luddites—a group of unemployed textile workers who smashed to pieces the very machinery that had taken their jobs—one does not fully appreciate how a hate-motivated crime such as "paki-bashing" relates to the broader issues of technological change, alienation, and property crime.

THE LOGIC OF HISTORICAL-COMPARATIVE RESEARCH

Confusion over terms reigns in H-C research. Researchers call what they do historical, comparative, or historical-comparative, but mean different things. The key question is: Is there a distinct historical-comparative method and logic, or is there just social research that happens to examine social life in the past or in several societies? "There has been a long dispute in society as to whether 'comparative' studies should be distinguished as a special category of research" (Nowak, 1989:37).

The Logic of Historical-Comparative Research and Quantitative Research

Quantitative versus Historical-Comparative Research.   A source of the confusion is that some researchers use a positivist, quantitative approach to study historical or comparative issues. Others rely on the qualitative, interpretative, or critical approaches. According to Ragin and Zaret (1983), a Durkheimian (or positivist) approach and a Weberian (or interpretative) approach to H-C research use different logics. Ragin (1987:2) argued, "The most distinctive aspect of comparative social science is the wide gulf between qualitative and quantitative work."[7]

Positivist researchers reject the idea that there is a distinct H-C method. They measure variables, test hypotheses, analyze quantitative data, and replicate research to discover generalizable laws that hold across time and societies. They see no fundamental difference between quantitative social research and historical-comparative research. They apply quantitative research techniques, with some minor adjustments, to study the past or other cultures.

This confusion is summarized by Øyen (1990:7):

> The vocabulary for distinguishing between different kinds of comparative research is redundant and not very precise. Concepts such as cross-country, cross-national, cross-societal, cross-systemic, cross-institutional, as well as trans-national, trans-societal, trans-cultural, and comparisons on the macro-level, are used both as synonymous with comparative research in general and as denoting specific kinds of comparisons.

Most social research examines social life in the present in a single nation—that of the researcher. All possible H-C research can be organized along three dimensions. First, does the researcher focus on what occurs in one nation or a small set of nations, or does the researcher attempt to study many nations? Second, how does the researcher involve time or history? Does he or she focus on a single time period in the past, examine events across many years, or study the present or a recent time period? Finally, is the researcher's analysis based primarily on quantitative or qualitative data? If we cross-classify the three dimensions, we get a typology of 18 logically possible kinds of H-C research (see Table 15.1). No wonder there is so much confusion over what constitutes H-C research.

The H-C research currently being conducted does not fall evenly across all possible kinds. A large majority of criminological research fits into 11 kinds. Most research is in cells 1, 4, 5, 7, 8, 10, 11, 13, 14, 15, and 16. This includes all of the single-nation columns. Researchers who examine small sets of nations over long time periods tend to use qualitative data. Those looking at the present tend to use quantitative data. This includes research on many nations. Gurr (1976) conducted an historical-comparative study of crime rates in three cities: London, Stockholm, and Sydney. He focused first on the period from the 1840s to the 1930s, and found that crime rates had decreased in all three cities. He then expanded his time frame by examining crime rates from the 1930s to the 1970s. In this period, he found crime increased in all three cities in roughly the same magnitude that it had decreased in the previous period. Gurr interpreted this to mean that, although improvements in crime reporting no doubt accounted for some of the increase, most of increase in crime indeed reflected underlying changes in the rates of criminal behavior.

Ditton (1977b), for example, used the historical-comparative method to explain the historical context of employee theft. He began by reviewing historical studies on the "common" rights held by peasant farmers in seventeenth-century England. These common rights permitted individuals "the right to take or use some portion of the profit that another's soil brings" (p. 40). In exchange for fealty to one's feudal lord, the peasants had a set of tradition rights, including the right to graze animals on common (uncultivated) lands; the right to collect herbs, nuts, wood, gravel, clay, and so on from the commons; and the right to hunt and fish on the land.

In time, the common rights eroded; and, as common property evolved into private property, these rights became forbidden. Forced off the land, the farm workers migrated to urban areas where they found dangerous, difficult work in factories. "As one might expect, and empirical evidence supports this, a major source of irritation to factory owners who took on such 'idle' rural laborers was their penchant for making off with parts of the workplace or the fruits of their labor, in addition to their wages" (Ditton, 1977b:43). Ditton concluded his historical-comparative analysis with a general, theoretical statement about employee theft: "[Workers] situated

TABLE 15.1 Logically Possible Kinds of Historical-Comparative Research

TIME DIMENSION AND KIND OF DATA	COMPARATIVE DIMENSION		
	Single Nation*	Few Nations	Many Nations
One Time in Past			
Quantitative	1	2	3
Qualitative	4	5	6
Across Time			
Quantitative	7	8	9
Qualitative	10	11	12
Present			
Quantitative	13	14	15
Qualitative	16	17	18

*Nation different than researcher's and audience of results for present time.

at structurally disadvantaged parts receive large segments of their wages 'invisibly'—as tips or fiddles from customers, or pilferage and perks from employers" (p. 57).

Rum-Running in Belize, Central America, 1920 to 1933. Ashdown (1980) conducted historical-comparative research on the little-known role the country of Belize (formerly British Honduras) played in smuggling illegal alcohol into the United States during Prohibition. The port of Belize City, with its prominent British-Creole businessmen and "cooperative" Customs Department, was the focal point of a thriving reexport trade. Scotch whiskey was shipped into Belize from the United Kingdom, and held there in bond until it could be reloaded aboard schooners owned by local businessmen for reexport. The whiskey was actually "transhipped on the high seas to U.S. 'rumrunners' before it reached its ostensible destination, the Bahamas" (p. 15).

The existing trade data from that period tell the story: In 1920, Belize imported some 6,000 gallons of whiskey from the United Kingdom. Most of it never left the port and was reexported to Central America "as part of the old entrepot trade" (Ashdown, 1980:15). By 1923, around 85,000 gallons passed was imported with "77,000 leaving it [Belize] for the Bahamas." By the 1930, over 220,000 gallons of Scotch whiskey was being reexported each year.

Having such a lucrative smuggling operation in the port city was a mixed blessing for the colonial government. Export tariffs on alcohol were doubled in 1923 (to $1 per gallon). Although officially denouncing the trade as "a dubious commerce," the colonial governor did make good use of the extra tax revenue—some $25,000 per year, which was used for the construction of schools. By the end of the decade, whisky duties contributed around 10 percent of the country's revenues. In short, it had become a fiscal mainstay of Belize budget, particularly given the decline in export revenues from mahogany and chicle. Thus, the governor wrote to the colonial office in England that to enforce port regulations "would involve a sacrifice" which he was "extremely reluctant to impose on a penurious and struggling Colony" (Ashdown, 1980:16). The governor was then reminded by the colonial office in England that "the preservation of friendly relations between the [British] Empire and the U.S.A. was a matter of greater importance [than the tax revenues of Belize]" (p. 16).

As political pressure from above increased, the Belize City businessmen became threatened that a crackdown on their reexport trade would lead to a "political crisis culminating perhaps in such grave disorder that armed force would be necessary to contain it" (Ashdown, 1980:17).

As luck would have it, the spreading political crisis was short-lived. Not only did the smuggling market begin to disappear as anti-Prohibition forces in the United States gained ground but also the hurricane of 1931 virtually leveled Belize City. The local manager of United Fruit Company summarized the situation in 1931: "[Belize City port] was virtually empty of bootleggers, sixteen had left with cargoes of liquor, evidently for Christmas trade" (p. 17). Within 12 months, some 2,000,000 gallons of unsaleable whiskey lay in "Rum Row" off New York, and "Belize schooners were engaged in carrying any cargo they could obtain" (Ashdown, 1980:17).

Ashdown's (1980) research exemplified a case study of official complicity in economic crime. Tax revenues were generated for a short while, but not without cost in political legitimacy. The merchant houses were on the verge of rising up in demonstrated opposition. The government was trapped but for unique historical occurrences. The violent weather in 1931, a fate suffered again in 1961, blew Belize City nearly out of existence. This eased pressure for the moment, as did the Americans growing call for a legal drink. Prohibition ended in 1933 and the colonial government in Belize held on.

The Logic of Historical-Comparative Research and Interpretive Research

A distinct, qualitative historical-comparative type of social research differs from the positivist approach. It also differs from an extreme interpretive approach, which some field researchers, cultural anthropologists, and historians advocate.

Historical-comparative researchers who use case studies and qualitative data may depart from positivist principles. Their research is an intensive examination of a limited number of cases in which social meaning and context are critical. An

example of how positivist researchers view such an approach is illustrated by Lieberson's (1991) criticism of the wave of H-C research that uses a small number of comparative cases. Adopting a positivist approach to social science, Lieberson found the H-C research inadequate. He did not believe that it could find a probabilistic causal effect of an independent variable on a dependent variable, which he assumed to be the proper model for social science. He claimed that the comparative methods many H-C researchers adopt "frequently lead to erroneous conclusions."

Like interpretive field research, H-C research focuses on culture, tries to see through the eyes of those being studied, reconstructs the lives of the people studied, and examines particular individuals or groups.

An extreme interpretive position goes beyond a desire to see the world through the eyes of others. It says that an empathic understanding of the people being studied is the primary goal of social research. It takes a strict ideographic, descriptive approach and avoids causal statements, systematic concepts, or theoretical models. An extreme interpretive approach assumes that each social setting is unique and that compari-sons are impossible. It recreates specific subjective experiences and describes particulars. As Stone (1987:31) noted, traditional history "deals with a particular problem and a particular set of actors at a particular time and a particular place." Gadamer (1979:116) suggested this position when he said:

> Historical consciousness is interested in knowing, not how men, people, or states develop in general, but, quite on the contrary, how this man, this people, or this state became what it is: how each of these particulars could come to pass and end up specifically there. (emphasis in original)

A distinct H-C approach borrows from ethnography and cultural anthropology, and some varieties of H-C are close to "thick description" in their attempt to recreate the reality of another time or place. Yet, borrowing from the strengths of ethnography does not require adopting the extreme interpretive approach.[8]

A Distinct Historical-Comparative Approach

The distinct historical-comparative research method avoids the excesses of the positivist and interpretive approaches. It combines a sensitivity to specific historical or cultural contexts with theoretical generalization. Historical-comparative researchers may use quantitative data to supplement qualitative data and analysis. The logic and goals of H-C research are closer to those of field research than to those of traditional positivist approaches. The following discussion describes six similarities between H-C research and field research, and six more unique features of historical-comparative research (see Table 15.2).

Similarities to Field Research. First, both H-C research and field research recognize that the researcher's point of view is an unavoidable part of research. Both types of research involve interpretation, which introduces the interpreter's location in time, place, and world view. Historical-comparative research does not try to produce a single, unequivocal set of objective facts. Rather, it is a confrontation of old with new or of different world views. It recognizes that a researcher's reading of historical or comparative evidence is influenced by an awareness of the past and by living in the present. "Our present-day consciousness of history is fundamentally different from the manner in which the past appeared to any foregoing people" (Gadamer, 1979:109–110).

Second, both field and H-C research examine a great diversity of data. In both, the researcher becomes immersed in data to gain an empathic understanding of events and people. Both capture subjective feelings and note how everyday, ordinary activities signify important social meaning.

The researcher inquires, selects, and focuses on specific aspects of social life from the vast array of events, actions, symbols, and words. An H-C researcher organizes data and focuses attention on the basis of evolving concepts. He or she examines rituals and symbols that dramatize culture (e.g., parades, clothing, placement of objects, etc.) and investigates the motives, rea-

sons, and justifications for behaviors. For example, Burrage and Corry (1981) used records of the official order of appearance of guilds at major public events (parades, pageants, feasts, royal visits, etc.) as a way to measure changes in occupation status in London between the fourteenth and seventeenth centuries.[9]

Third, both field and H-C researchers often use *grounded theory*. Theory usually emerges during the process of data collection. Both examine the data without beginning with fixed hypotheses. Instead, they develop and modify concepts and theory through a dialogue with the data, then apply theory to reorganize the evidence. Zaret (1978:118) remarked, "Historically grounded theory means that concepts emerge from the analytic problem of history: ordering the past into structures, conjunctures and events. History and theory can thus be simultaneously constructed." Thus, data collection and theory building interact. Thompson (1978:39) called this "a dialogue between concept and evidence, a dialogue conducted by successive hypotheses, on the one hand, and empirical research on the other."[10]

Next, both field and H-C research involve a type of translation. The researcher's meaning system usually differs from that of the people he or she studies, but he or she tries to penetrate and understand their point of view. Once the life, language, and perspective of the people being studied have been mastered, the researcher "translates" it for others who read his or her report.

Fifth, both field and H-C researchers focus on action, process, and sequence and see time and process as essential. Both say that people construct a sense of social reality through actions that occur over time. Both are sensitive to an ever-present tension between agency, the fluid-social action and changing social reality, and structure, the fixed regularities and patterns that shape social actions and perceptions. Both see social reality simultaneously as something created and changed by people and as imposing a restriction on human choice.[11]

Sixth, generalization and theory are limited in field and H-C research. Historical and cross-cultural knowledge is incomplete and provisional,

TABLE 15.2   Summary of a Comparison of Approaches to Research: The Qualitative versus Quantitative Distinction

TOPIC	BOTH FIELD AND H-C	QUANTITATIVE
Researcher's perspective	Include as an intergral part of the research process	Remove from research process
Approach to data	Immersed in many details to acquire understanding	Precisely operationalize variables
Theory and data	Grounded theory, dialogue between data and concepts	Deductive theory versus empirical data
Present findings	Translate a meaning system	Test hypotheses
Action/structure	People construct meaning but within structures	Social forces shape behavior
Laws/generalization	Limited generalizations that depend on context	Discover universal, context-free laws

FEATURES OF DISTINCT H-C RESEARCH APPROACH

TOPIC	HISTORICAL-COMPARATIVE RESEARCHER'S APPROACH
Evidence	Reconstructs from fragments and incomplete evidence
Distortion	Guards against using own awareness of factors outside the social or historical context
Human role	Includes the consciousness of people in a context and uses their motives as causal factors
Causes	Sees cause as contingent on conditions, beneath the surface, and due to a combination of elements
Micro/macro	Compares whole cases and links the micro to macro levels or layers of social reality
Cross-contexts	Moves between concrete specifics in a context and across contexts for more abstract comparisons

based on selective facts and limited questions. Neither deduces propositions or tests hypotheses in order to uncover fixed laws. Likewise, replication is unrealistic because each researcher has a unique perspective and assembles a unique body of evidence. Instead, researchers offer plausible accounts and limited generalizations.

Unique Features of Historical-Comparative Research. Despite its many similarities to field research, some important differences distinguish H-C research. As the title to David Lowenthal's *The Past Is a Foreign Country* (1985) suggests, research on the past and on an alien culture share much in common with each other, and what they share distinguishes them from other approaches.

First, the evidence for H-C research is usually limited and indirect. Direct observation or involvement by a researcher is often impossible. An H-C researcher reconstructs what occurred from the evidence, but he or she cannot have absolute confidence in his reconstruction.

Historical evidence in particular depends on the survival of data from the past, usually in the form of documents (e.g., letters and newspapers). The researcher is limited to what has not been destroyed and what leaves a trace, record, or other evidence behind.

Historical-comparative researchers interpret the evidence. Different people looking at the same evidence often ascribe different meanings to it, so a researcher must reflect on evidence. An understanding of it based on a first glance is rarely possible. The researcher also becomes immersed in and absorbs details about a context. For example, a researcher examining the family in the past or a distant country needs to be aware of the full social context (e.g., the nature of work, forms of communication, transportation technology, etc.). He or she looks at maps and gets a feel for the laws in effect, the condition of medical care, and common social practices. For example, the meaning of "a visit by a family member" is affected by conditions such as roads of dirt and mud, the inability to call ahead of time, and the lives of people who work on a farm with animals that need constant watching.

Another feature is that a researcher's reconstruction of the past or another culture is easily distorted. Compared to the people being studied, a historical-comparative researcher is usually more aware of events occurring prior to the time studied, events occurring in places other than the location studied, and events that occurred after the period studied. This awareness gives the researcher a greater sense of coherence than was experienced by those living in the past or in an isolated social setting. "In short, historical explanation surpasses any understanding while events are still occurring. The past we reconstruct is more coherent than the past when it happened" (Lowenthal, 1985:234). A researcher's broader awareness can create the illusion that things happened because they had to, or that they fit together neatly.

A researcher cannot easily see through the eyes of those being studied. Knowledge of the present and changes over time can distort how events, people, laws, or even physical objects are perceived. For example, the old buildings that survive into the present are more permanent and solid than those that did not survive. Moreover, a surviving building looks different in 2000 than it did in 1800 because of the context in which it appears. When the 1800 building was newly built and standing among similar buildings, the people living at the time saw it differently than people do in the dawn of the twenty-first century. They experienced various building styles differently, and the building did not appear as something preserved in an old style in the context of newer buildings from the subsequent two hundred years.

Historical-comparative researchers recognize the capacity of people to learn, make decisions, and act on what they learn to modify the course of events. When conscious people are involved, lawlike generalizations that hold across societies are limited.[12] For example, if a group of people are aware of or gain consciousness of their own past history and avoid the mistakes of the past, they may act consciously to alter the course of events. Of course, people will not necessarily learn or act on what they have learned, and if they do act they will not necessarily be successful. Nevertheless, people's capacity to learn introduces indeterminacy into historical-comparative explanations.

An H-C researcher wants to find out whether various courses of action were viewed as plausible by the people involved. Thus, the world view and knowledge of those people is a conditioning factor, shaping what the people being studied saw as possible or impossible ways to achieve goals. The researcher asks whether people were conscious of certain things. For example, if an army knew an enemy attack was coming and so decided to cross a river in the middle of the night, the action "crossing the river" would have a different meaning than in the situation where the army did not know the enemy was approaching.

Historical-comparative research takes an approach to causality that is more contingent than determinist. An H-C researcher often uses combinational explanations. They are analogous to a chemical reaction in which several ingredients (chemicals, oxygen) are added together under specified conditions (temperature, pressure) to produce an outcome (explosion). This differs from a linear causal explanation. The logic is more "A, B, and C appeared together in time and place, then D resulted" than "A caused B, and B caused C, and C caused D." Ragin (1987:13) summarized:

> Most comparativists, especially those who are qualitatively oriented, are interested in specific historical sequences or outcomes and their causes across a set of similar cases. Historical outcomes often require complex, combinational explanations, and such explanations are very difficult to prove in a manner consistent with the norms of mainstream quantitative social science.

For example, sociologist Max Weber used a fundamentally multicausal approach in his H-C research. His explanations gave cultural factors equal weight to economic, demographic, or social structural factors. His approach employed a combination of causal factors through the ideal type, which was neither a deductive formal theory to test, nor an inductive, problem-specific theory (see Kalberg, 1994).

Historical-comparative research focuses on whole cases and on comparisons of complex wholes versus separate variables across cases. A researcher approaches the whole as if it has multiple layers. He or she grasps surface appearances as well as reveals the general, hidden structures, unseen mechanisms, or causal processes.

A historical-comparative researcher integrates the micro (small-scale, face-to-face interaction) and macro (large-scale social structures) levels. Instead of describing micro-level or macro-level processes alone, the researcher describes both levels or layers of reality and links them to each other.[13] For example, an H-C researcher examines the details of individual biographies by reading diaries or letters to get a feel for the individuals: the food they ate, their recreational pursuits, their clothing, their sicknesses, their relations with friends, and so on. He or she links this micro-level view of individuals

to macro-level processes: increased immigration, mechanization of production, proletarianization, tightened labor markets, and the like.

A sixth feature of H-C research is its ability to shift between a specific context and a general comparison. A researcher examines several specific contexts, notes similarities and differences, then generalizes. He or she then looks again at the specific contexts using the generalizations.

Comparative researchers compare across cultural-geographic units (e.g., urban areas, nations, societies, etc.).[14] Historical researchers investigate past contexts, usually in one culture (e.g., periods, epochs, ages, eras, etc.), for sequence and comparison.[15] Of course, a researcher can combine both to investigate multiple cultural contexts in one or more historical contexts. Yet, each period or society has its unique causal processes, meaning systems, and social relations, which may lack equivalent elements across the units. This produces a creative tension between the concrete specifics in a context and the abstract ideas a researcher uses to make links across contexts.

The use of transcultural concepts in comparative analysis is analogous to the use of transhistorical ones in historical research.[16] In comparative research, a researcher translates the specifics of a context into a common, theoretical language. In historical research, theoretical concepts are applied across time. "The comparative investigator can thus be regarded as fighting a continuous struggle between the 'culture-boundness' of system-specific categories and the 'contentlessness' of system-inclusive categories" (Smelser, 1976:178).

The Annales School. Discussions of H-C research frequently refer to the *Annales school,*[17] a research method associated with a group of French historians (e.g., Marc Bloch, Fernand Braudel, Lucien Febvre, and Emmanuel Le Roy Ladurie), and named after the scholarly journal *Annales: Économies, Sociétés, Civilisations,* founded in 1929. The school's orientation can be summarized by four interrelated characteristics used by some H-C researchers.

One characteristic is the school's synthetic, totalizing, holistic, or interdisciplinary approach. Annales researchers combine geography, ecology, economics, and demography with cultural factors to give a total picture of the past. They blend together the diverse conditions of material life and collective beliefs or culture into a comprehensive reconstruction of the past civilization.

A second characteristic is illustrated by a French term of the school, the *mentalities* of an era. This term is not directly translatable into English. It means a distinctive world view, perspective, or set of assumptions about life—the way that thinking was organized, or the overall pattern of conscious and unconscious cognition, belief, and values that prevailed in an era. Thus, researchers try to discover the overall arrangement of thought in a historical period that shaped subjective experience about fundamental aspects of reality: the nature of time, the relationship of humans to the physical environment, how truth is created, and the like.

The Annales approach mixes concrete historical specificity and abstract theory. Theory takes the form of models or deep underlying structures, which are causal or organizing principles that account for everyday events: "There is the geographical, economic, and social current which examines the long-run structural processes and continuities underlying observable events of history. This current is broadly synonymous with the Annales School of historians" (Lloyd, 1986:241). Annales historians look for both the deep-running currents that shape the surface events and the individual actions that are examined by traditional historians.

A last characteristic is an interest in long-term structures or patterns. In contrast to traditional historians who focus on particular individuals or events over short time spans, from several years to a few decades, Annales historians examine long-term changes, over periods of a century or more, in the fundamental way that social life is organized. To describe the long time span they study, they use the term *longue durée*. It means a long duration or a historical era in geographic space (e.g., feudal-

ism in western Europe, or the fifteenth to eighteenth centuries in the Mediterranean region). To do this, a researcher must adopt a unique orientation toward history. As Braudel (1980:33) noted, "For the historian, accepting the *longue durée* entails a readiness to change his style, his attitudes, a whole reversal in his thinking, a whole new way of conceiving of social affairs."

The Annales school has influenced H-C research in several ways. It challenges the prevailing focus on short time spans and puts events in a broader context. It also reinforces the building of theory about underlying structures and emphasizes a sensitivity to the different subjective consciousness of the past. Finally, it encourages a holistic integration of diverse types of historical data.

STEPS IN A HISTORICAL-COMPARATIVE RESEARCH PROJECT

Earlier, you saw how H-C research compares with other types of social research. In this section, we turn to the process of doing H-C research. Conducting historical-comparative research does not involve a rigid set of steps and, with only a few exceptions, it does not use complex or specialized techniques.

Conceptualizing the Object of Inquiry

An H-C researcher begins by becoming familiar with the setting and conceptualizes what is being studied. He or she may start with a loose model or set of preliminary concepts and apply them to a specific setting. The provisional concepts contain implicit assumptions or organizing categories that he or she uses to see the world, "package" observations, and search through evidence.

If a researcher is not already familiar with the historical era or comparative settings, he or she conducts an orientation reading (reading several general works). This will help the researcher grasp the specific setting, assemble organizing concepts, subdivide the main issue, and develop lists of questions to ask.[18] Concepts and evidence interact to stimulate research. For example,

Skocpol (1979) began her study of revolution with puzzles in macro-sociological theory and the histories of specific revolutions. The lack of fit between histories of revolutions and existing theories stimulated her research.

It is impossible to begin serious research without a framework of assumptions, concepts, and theory. Whether or not a researcher is conscious and explicit about it, he or she organizes specific details into analytic categories. Researchers find it best to recognize this process explicitly and avoid the *Baconian fallacy*. Named for Francis Bacon, it is assuming that a researcher operates without preconceived questions, hypotheses, ideas, assumptions, theories, paradigms, postulates, prejudices, or presumptions of any kind.

Locating Evidence

Next, a researcher locates and gathers evidence through extensive bibliographic work. A researcher uses many indexes, catalogs, and reference works that list what libraries contain. For comparative research, this means focusing on specific nations or units and on particular kinds of evidence within each. The researcher frequently spends weeks searching for sources in libraries, travels to several different specialized research libraries, and reads dozens (if not hundreds) of books and articles. Comparative research often involves learning one or more foreign languages.

As the researcher masters the literature and takes numerous detailed notes, he or she completes many specific tasks: creating a bibliography list (on cards or computer) with complete citations, taking notes that are neither too skimpy nor too extensive (i.e., more than one sentence but less than dozens of pages of quotes), leaving margins on note cards for adding themes later on, taking all notes in the same format (e.g., on cards, paper, etc.), and developing a file on themes or working hypotheses.

A researcher adjusts initial concepts, questions, or focus on the basis of what he or she discovers in the evidence. New issues and questions arise as he or she reads and considers a range of research reports at different levels of analysis (e.g., general context and detailed narratives on specific topics) and multiple studies on a topic, crossing topic boundaries.

Evaluating Quality of Evidence

As an H-C researcher gathers evidence, he or she asks two questions: How relevant is the evidence to emerging research questions and evolving concepts? How accurate and strong is the evidence?

The question of relevance is a difficult one. As Tilly (1981:13) remarked, "All documents are not equally valuable in reconstructing the past." As the focus of research shifts, evidence that was not relevant can become relevant. Likewise, some evidence may stimulate new avenues of inquiry and a search for additional confirming evidence.

Concerns about the accuracy of evidence will be discussed. An H-C researcher reads evidence for three things: the implicit conceptual framework, particular details, and empirical generalizations (factual statements on which there is agreement). He or she evaluates alternative interpretations of evidence and looks for "silences," or cases where the evidence fails to address an event, topic, or issue. Ashdown's (1980) work on rum-running (discussed earlier) is a case in point. He made it clear that "the Official Correspondence (between the Governor and the colonial office in England) is, understandably, sketchy on this matter." His information came mainly from "the chance survival of the fragmentary correspondence of a Belize business house" (p. 18).

Researchers try to avoid possible fallacies in the evidence. Fischer (1970) provided an extensive list of such fallacies. For example, the fallacy of *pseudoproof* is a failure to place something into its full context. The evidence might state that there was a 50 percent increase in income taxes, but its impact is not meaningful outside of a context. The researcher must ask: Did other taxes decline? Did income increase? Did the tax increase apply to all income? Was everyone affected equally? Another fallacy to avoid with historical evidence is *anachronism,* when an event appears to have occurred before or after the time it actually did. A researcher should be precise about the sequence of events and note discrepancies in dating events in evidence.

Organizing Evidence

As a researcher gathers evidence and locates new sources, he or she begins to organize the data. Obviously, it is unwise to take notes madly and let them pile up haphazardly. A researcher usually begins a preliminary analysis by noting low-level generalizations or themes. For example, in a study of revolution, a researcher develops a theme: The rich peasants supported the old regime. He or she can record this theme in his or her notes and later assign it significance.

The interaction of data and theory means that a researcher goes beyond a surface examination of the evidence to develop new concepts by critically evaluating the evidence based on theory. Keat and Urry (1975:113) suggested this process: "Any process of concept formation which is based on the way society presents itself will be inadequate, misleading and ideological." The H-C researcher must be able to read accounts with a grain of skepticism. When the colonial governor of Belize, for example, goes on record that "no attempt has been made within my experience to encourage or in any way facilitate the operations of persons engaged in the liquor smuggling traffic," the researcher must immediately detect the tone of false piety (Ashdown, 1980:16).

Synthesizing

The next step is the process of synthesizing evidence. The researcher refines concepts and moves toward a general explanatory model after most of the evidence is in. Old themes or concepts are discussed or revised, and new ones are created. Concrete events are used to give meaning to concepts. The researcher looks for patterns across time or units, and draws out similarities and differences with analogies. He or she organizes divergent events into sequences and groups them together to create a larger picture. Plausible expla-

nations are then developed that subsume both concepts and evidence as he or she organizes the evidence into a coherent whole. The researcher then reads and rereads notes and sorts and resorts them into piles or files on the basis of organizing schemes. He or she looks for and writes down the links or connections he or she sees while looking at the evidence in different ways.

A researcher often looks for new evidence to verify specific links that appear only after an explanatory model is developed. He or she evaluates how well the model approximates the evidence and adjusts it accordingly. He or she goes back and forth from the abstract to the concrete. At each stage, the researcher asks: If this model is true, would it produce the whole of the evidence I found?

The major task for the H-C researcher is organizing and giving new meaning to evidence. Skocpol (1979:xiv) argued:

> The comparative historian's task—and potential distinctive scholarly contribution—lies not in revealing new data about particular aspects of the large time periods and distinctive places surveyed, but rather in establishing the interest and prima facie validity of an overall argument about causal regularities across various historical cases.

Historical-comparative researchers also identify critical indicators and supporting evidence for themes or explanations. A *critical indicator* is unambiguous evidence, which is usually sufficient for inferring a specific theoretical relationship. Researchers seek these indicators for key parts of an explanatory model. Indicators critically confirm a theoretical inference and occur when many details suggest a clear interpretation. For example, a critical indicator of hostility between two nations is a formal declaration of war. A critical indicator of the rising political power of a social group is the formation of formal organizations with a large membership identified with the group and advocating its position. *Supporting evidence* is evidence for less central parts of a model. It can be evidence that builds the overall background or context, evidence that is less abundant or weaker, and evidence for which a clear and unambiguous theoretical interpretation is lacking.

Writing a Report

The last step is to combine evidence, concepts, and synthesis into a research report. (The report is discussed in detail in Appendix B.) The way in which the report is written is key in H-C research. Assembling evidence, arguments, and conclusions into a report is always a crucial step; but more than in quantitative approaches, the careful crafting of evidence and explanation makes or breaks H-C research. A researcher distills mountains of evidence into exposition and prepares extensive footnotes. She or he weaves together evidence and arguments to communicate a coherent, convincing picture to readers.

DATA AND EVIDENCE IN HISTORICAL CONTEXT

Types of Historical Evidence

First, some terms need clarification. *History* has several meanings: It means the events of the past (e.g., it is *history* that the French withdrew troops from Vietnam), a record of the past (e.g., a *history* of French involvement in Vietnam), and a discipline that studies the past (e.g., a department of *history*).[19] *Historiography* is the method of doing historical research or of gathering and analyzing historical evidence.

Researchers draw on four types of historical evidence or data: primary sources, secondary sources, running records, and recollections.[20] Traditional historians rely heavily on primary sources. H-C researchers often use secondary sources or the different data types in combination.

Primary Sources.   The letters, diaries, newspapers, movies, novels, articles of clothing, photographs, and so forth of those who lived in the past and have survived to the present are *primary sources*. They are found in archives (a place where documents are stored), in private collections, in family closets, or in museums (see Box 15.1). Today's documents and objects (our letters, television programs, commercials, clothing, automobiles, etc.) will be primary sources for future historians.

For example, McIllwain (1997:37) used primary source material in his study of the war between "two rival tongs, the On Leong and the Hip Sing" in New York's Chinatown a century or so ago. He reached widely for his historical evidence, finding newspaper accounts, government reports and correspondence, and firsthand accounts of the politics, personalities, and institutions of Chinatown. He had the extreme good fortune of stumbling upon the "District Attorney's closed case files, the Magistrates Court papers, the Court of General Sessions papers, and the Supreme Court papers" (p. 31).

Published and unpublished written documents are the most important type of primary source. Researchers find them in their original form or preserved in microfiche or on film. They are often the only surviving record of the words, thoughts, and feelings of people in the past. Written documents are helpful for studying societies and historical periods with writing and literate people. A frequent criticism of written sources is that they were largely written by elites or those in official organizations; thus, the views of the illiterate, the poor, or those outside official social institutions may be overlooked.

The written word on paper was the main medium of communication prior to the wide spread use of telecommunications, computers, and video technology to record events and ideas. In fact, the spread of forms of communication that do not leave a permanent physical record (e.g., telephone conversations, computer records, and television or radio broadcasts), and that have largely replaced letters, written ledgers, and newspapers, may make the work of future historians more difficult.

Secondary Sources.   Primary sources have realism and authenticity, but the practical limitation of time can restrict research on many primary sources to a narrow time frame or location. To get

Box 15.1_____

Using Archival Data

The archive is the main source for primary historical materials. Archives are accumulations of documentary materials (papers, photos, letters, etc.) in private collections, museums, libraries, or formal archives.

LOCATION AND ACCESS

Finding whether a collection exists on a topic, organization, or individual can be a long, frustrating task of many letters, phone calls, and referrals. If the material on a person or topic does exist, it may be scattered in multiple locations. Gaining access may depend on an appeal to a family member's kindness for private collections or traveling to distant libraries and verifying one's reason for examining many dusty boxes of old letters. Also, the researcher may discover limited hours (e.g., an archive is open only four days a week from 10 A.M. to 5 P.M., but the researcher needs to inspect the material for 40 hours).

SORTING AND ORGANIZATION

Archive material may be unsorted or organized in a variety of ways. The organization may reflect criteria that are unrelated to the researcher's interests. For example, letters and papers may be in chronological order, but the researcher is interested only in letters to four professional colleagues over three decades, not daily bills, family correspondence, and so on.

TECHNOLOGY AND CONTROL

Archival materials may be in their original form, on microforms, or, more rarely, in an electronic form.

Researchers may be allowed only to take notes, not make copies, or they may be allowed only to see select parts of the whole collection. Researchers become frustrated with the limitations of having to read dusty papers in one specific room and being allowed only to take notes by pencil for the few hours a day the archive is open to the public.

TRACKING AND TRACING

One of the most difficult tasks in archival research is tracing common events or persons through the materials. Even if all material is in one location, the same event or relationship may appear in several places in many forms. Researchers sort through mounds of paper to find bits of evidence here and there.

DRUDGERY, LUCK, AND SERENDIPITY

Archival research is often painstaking slow. Spending many hours pouring over partially legible documents can be very tedious. Also, researchers will often discover holes in collections, gaps in a series of papers, or destroyed documents. Yet, careful reading and inspection of previously untouched material can yield startling new connections or ideas. The researcher may discover unexpected evidence that opens new lines of inquiry (see Elder et al., 1993, and Hill, 1993).

---

a broader picture, many H-C researchers use *secondary sources,* the writings of specialist historians who have spent years studying primary sources. For example, Raudzens (1997) consulted six major references in an attempt to develop a better quantitative understanding of war. In particular, he focused on one-day battles occurring in wars from 1490 through 1780.

Running Records.   *Running records* consist of files or existing statistical documents maintained

by organizations. Most of the sources Ashdown (1980) incorporated into his study of whiskey smuggling were the running records of business transactions and correspondence obtained from an import-export business in Belize.

Recollections.   The words or writings of individuals about their past lives or experiences based on memory are *recollections*. These can be in the form of memoirs, autobiographies, or interviews. Because memory is imperfect, recollections are often distorted in ways that primary sources are not.

Oral history is an especially useful type of recollection.[21] It involves conducting unstructured interviews with people about their lives or events they personally witnessed. This approach is especially valuable for gathering data from illiterate populations. Ashdown (1980:18) suggested the use of oral history in order to fill out the historical details of the whiskey smuggling in Belize:

> *Even less information is to be gleaned from the pages of the* Clarion *[a Belize newspaper] and in the circumstances, therefore, it would be valuable to have the oral testimony of those persons still living who, as employees of the government or the merchants, had some part in this unusual commerce.*

Research with Secondary Sources

Uses and Limitations. Social researchers often use secondary sources, the books and articles written by specialist historians, as evidence of past conditions.[22] As Skocpol (1984:382) remarked, the use of such materials is not systematized, and "comparative historical sociologists have not so far worked out clear, consensual rules and procedures for the valid use of secondary sources as evidence." Secondary sources have limitations and need to be used with caution.

The limitations of secondary historical evidence include problems of inaccurate historical accounts and a lack of studies in areas of interest. Such sources cannot be used to test hypotheses. Post facto (after-the-fact) explanations cannot meet positivist criteria of falsifiability, because few statistical controls can be used and replication is impossible.[23] Yet, historical research by others plays an important role in developing general explanations, among its other uses.[24]

Potential Problems. The many volumes of secondary sources present a maze of details and interpretations for an H-C researcher. He or she must transform the mass of specialized descriptive studies into an intelligible picture. This picture needs to be consistent with and reflective of the richness of the evidence. It also must bridge the many specific time periods or locales. The researcher faces potential problems with secondary sources.

One problem is in reading the works of historians.[25] Historians do not present theory-free, objective "facts." They implicitly frame raw data, categorize information, and shape evidence using concepts. The historian's concepts are a mixture drawn from journalism, the language of historical actors, ideologies, philosophy, everyday language in the present, and social science. Most lack a rigorous definition, are vague, are applied inconsistently, and are not mutually exclusive nor exhaustive. For example, a historian may describe in detail common eighteenth-century business practices in England, but fails in linking these described practices to a general theory of commercial crime. Thus, for a criminologist to rely on the historian's research, he or she runs the risk of not being able to distinguish between business practices that were considered acceptable and those that were considered unacceptable (or even criminal).

A second problem is that the historian's selection procedure is not transparent. Historians select some information from all possible evidence. As Carr (1961:138) noted, "History therefore is a process of selection in terms of historical significance . . . from the infinite oceans of facts the historian selects those which are significant for his purpose." Yet, the H-C researcher does not know how this was done. Without knowing the selection process, a historical-comparative researcher must rely on the historian's judgments, which can contain biases.[26] For example, a historian reads 10,000 pages of newspapers, letters, and diaries, then boils down this information into summaries and selected quotes in a 100-page book. An H-C researcher does not know whether information that the historian left out is relevant for his or her purposes.

The typical historian's research practice also introduces an individualist bias. A heavy reliance on primary sources and surviving artifacts combines with an atheoretical orientation to produce a narrow focus on the actions of specific people. This particularistic, micro-level view directs a reader's attention away from integrating themes or patterns. Despite the typical historian's aversion to theory or models, this emphasis on the documented activities of specific individuals is itself a type of theoretical orientation.[27]

A third problem is in the organization of the evidence. Historians organize evidence as they write works of history. They often write *narrative history* (see Box 15.2). This compounds problems of undefined concepts and the selection of evidence. Jones (1976) argued that historians reconstruct events from the residues of the past and assign significance to some of these events.

In the historical narrative, the writer organizes material chronologically around a single coherent "story." The logic is that of a sequence of unfolding action. Thus, each part of the story is connected to each other part by its place in the time order of events. Together, all the parts form a unity or whole. Conjuncture and contingency are key elements of the narrative form—that is, if X (or X plus Z) occurred, then Y would occur, and if X (or X plus Z) had not occurred, something else would have followed. The contingency creates a logical interdependency between an earlier and later events.

With its temporal logic, the narrative organization differs from how sociologists create explanations. It differs from quantitative explanation in which the researcher identifies statistical patterns to infer causes. It also differs from most qualitative data analysis (see Chapter 16) in which researchers compare a model to specific cases (ideal-type analysis or illustrative method), compare similarities and differences in a collection of cases (analytic comparison), or abstract from a set of cases to theoretical statements (successive approximation).

A major difficulty of the narrative is that the organizing tool—time order or position in a sequence of events—does not alone denote theo-

Box 15.2

The Narrative in History

Many historians write in the traditional narrative form, which can be a secondary source for the H-C researcher.

CHARACTERISTICS OF THE NARRATIVE FORM

1. It tells a story or tale, with a plot and subplots, watersheds, and climaxes.
2. It follows a chronological order and sequence of events.
3. It focuses on specific individuals, not on structures or abstract ideas.
4. It is primarily particular and descriptive, not analytic and general.
5. It presents events as unique, unpredictable, and contingent.

STRENGTHS OF THE NARRATIVE FORM

1. It is colorful, interesting, and entertaining to read.
2. It gives an overall feel for life in a different era, so that readers get the sense that they were there.
3. It communicates the way people in the past subjectively experienced reality and helps readers identify emotionally with people in the past.
4. It surrounds individuals and specific events with a mix of many aspects of social reality.

WEAKNESSES OF THE NARRATIVE FORM

1. It hides causal theories and concepts or leaves them implicit.
2. It uses rhetoric, ordinary language, and commonsense logic to persuade, and therefore is subject to logical fallacies of semantic distortion and various rhetorical devices.
3. It tends to ignore the normal or ordinary for the unique, dramatic, extraordinary, or unusual.
4. It rarely builds on previous knowledge and does little to create general knowledge.
5. It tends to be overly individualistic, overstating the role of particular people and their ability to shape events voluntarily.

retical or historical causality. In other words, the narrative meets only one of the three criteria for establishing causality (see Chapter 3)—that of temporal order. Moreover, narrative writing obscures any underlying causal models or processes. This occurs when a historian includes events in the narrative that have no causal significance. He or she adds them to enrich the background or context, to add color. Likewise, he or she presents events that have no immediate causal impact, but that may have a causal effect later in the process. In other words, narratives may include events with a delayed causal impact or that are temporarily "on hold."

Also, few narrative historians explicitly state how combination or interaction effects operate. For example, the historian discusses three conditions for an event. Yet, rarely do readers know whether all three conditions must operate together to have a causal impact, but no two conditions alone, or no single condition alone, creates the same impact.[28]

The narrative organization creates difficulties for the researcher using secondary sources and creates conflicting findings. H-C researchers must read though weak concepts, unknown selection criteria, and unclear casual logic. Beneath the narrative may reside the historian's social theory, but it remains implicit and hidden. Burke (1980:35) noted, "Traditional historians often deny having anything to do with models, but in practice many of them use models. . . . Using models in this way without being aware of their logical status has sometimes landed historians in needless difficulties."

A last problem is that a historian is influenced by historiographic schools, personal beliefs, social theories, and current events at the time the research is conducted.

Historians writing today examine primary materials differently from how those writing in the 1920s did. In addition, there are various schools of historiography (e.g., diplomatic, demographic, ecological, psychological, Marxist, intellectual, etc.) that have their own rules for seeking evidence and asking questions. Carr (1961:54) warned, "Before you study history,

study the historian. . . . Before you study the historian, study his historical and social environment."

Research with Primary Sources

The historian is the major issue when a researcher uses secondary sources. When using primary sources, the key issue is that only a fraction of everything written or used in the past has survived into the present. Moreover, what survived is a nonrandom sample of what once existed. Lowenthal (1985:191–192) observed, "The surviving residues of past thoughts and things represent a tiny fraction of previous generations' contemporary fabric."

Historical-comparative researchers attempt to read primary sources with the eyes and assumptions of a contemporary who lived in the past. This means "bracketing," or holding back knowledge of subsequent events and modern values. Cantor and Schneider (1967:46) stated, "If you do not read the primary sources with an open mind and an intention to get inside the minds of the writings and look at things the way *they* saw them, you are wasting your time.")

Another problem is that locating primary documents is a time-consuming task. A researcher must search through specialized indexes and travel to archives or specialized libraries. Primary sources are often located in a dusty, out-of-the-way room full of stacked cardboard boxes containing masses of fading documents. These may be incomplete, unorganized, and in various stages of decay. Once the documents or other primary sources are located, the researcher evaluates them by subjecting them to external and internal criticism (see Figure 15.1).

External criticism means evaluating the authenticity of a document itself to be certain that it is not a fake or a forgery. Criticism involves asking: Was the document created when it is claimed to have been, in the place where it was supposed to be, and by the person who claims to be its author? Why was the document produced to begin with, and how did it survive?

External Criticism

Internal Criticism

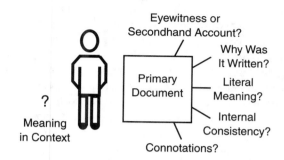

FIGURE 15.1 External and Internal Criticism

Once the document passes as being authentic, a researcher uses *internal criticism,* an examination of the document's contents to establish credibility. A researcher evaluates whether what is recorded was based on what the author directly witnessed or is secondhand information. This requires examining both the literal meaning of what is recorded and the subtle connotations or intentions. The researcher notes other events, sources, or people mentioned in the document and asks whether they can be verified. He examines implicit assumptions or value positions, and the relevant conditions under which the document was produced is noted (e.g., during wartime or under a totalitarian regime). He or she also considers language usage at the time and the context of statements within the document to distill a meaning.

Many types of distortions can appear in primary documents. One is *bowdlerization* (Shafer, 1980:163)—a deliberate distortion designed to protect moral standards or furnish a particular image. For example, if a criminologist wanted to study the history of vice crimes (e.g., prostitution) in a given community, he or she must be able to sort out the idealized portrayal of community that is apt to be contained in certain types of primary documents, such as church or family records.[29]

In addition to primary and secondary sources, historical researchers use what Topoloski (1976)

called *nonsource-based knowledge.* This is knowledge available to a researcher about the past that does not originate in a specfic primary document or secondary source. It can be based on logical reasoning. For example, suppose a criminologist knew that a particular ethnic group had had very poor relations with the police historically. That piece of background information would logically suggest related insights. One might infer that the poor relations with the police leads to, among other things, a reluctance to report crime. Hence, official police statistics may well systematically underestimate levels of crime in that ethnic community.

COMPARATIVE RESEARCH

Types of Comparative Research

A Comparative Method. Problems in other types of research are magnified in a comparative study.[30] Holt and Turner (1970:6) said, "In principle, there is no difference between comparative cross-cultural research and research conducted in a single society. The differences lie, rather, in the magnitude of certain types of problems." Comparative research is more of a perspective or orientation than a separate research technique. In this section, we consider its strengths.

A comparative perspective exposes weaknesses in research design and helps a researcher improve the quality of research. The focus of comparative research is on similarities and differences between units, and "comparison is central to the very acts of knowing and perceiving" (Warwick and Osherson, 1973:7).

Comparative research helps a researcher identify aspects of social life that are general across units (e.g., cultures), as opposed to being limited to one unit alone. All researchers want to generalize to some degree. Positivist researchers are interested in discovering general laws or patterns of social behavior that hold across societies. But most positivist research is not comparative. Ragin (1994:107) observed:

> Comparative researchers examine patterns of similarities and differences across cases and try to come to terms with their diversity. . . . Quantitative researchers also examine differences among cases, but with a different emphasis, the goal is to explain the covariation of one variable with another, usually across many cases. . . . The quantitative researcher typically has only broad familiarity with the cases.

The comparative orientation improves measurement and conceptualization. Concepts developed by researchers who conduct research across several social units or settings are less likely to apply only to a specific culture or setting. It is difficult for a researcher to detect hidden biases, assumptions, and values until he or she applies a concept in different cultures or settings. Different social settings provide a wider range of events or behavior, and the range in one culture is usually narrower than for human behavior in general. Thus, research in a single culture or setting focuses on a restricted range of possible social activity.

The way comparative research raises new questions and stimulates theory building is a major strength. Suppose, for example, a criminologist was interested in comparing the determinants of "fear of crime" in two different countries: a rich country and a poor country. He or she may find that illegal aliens in poor countries have a distinctive pattern in that they do not fear violent crime as much as they fear property crime. This is counterintuitive to what is generally known about fear of crime. It thus forces the criminologist to refine his or her theory in order to address this comparative difference.

Comparative research also has limitations. It is more difficult, more costly, and more time consuming than research that is not comparative. The types of data that can be collected and problems with equivalence (to be discussed) are also frequent problems.

Another limitation is the number of cases. Comparative researchers can rarely use random sampling. Sufficient information is not available for all of the approximately 150 nations in the world. It is unavailable for a nonrandom subset (poor countries, nondemocratic countries, etc.). In addition, can a researcher treat all nations as equal units when some have over a billion people and others only 100,000? The small number of cases creates a tendency for researchers to particularize and see each case as unique, limiting generalization. For example, a researcher examines five cases (e.g., countries), but the units differ from each other in 20 ways. It is difficult to test theory or determine relationships when there are more different characteristics than units.

A third limitation is that comparative researchers can apply, not test, theory, and can make only limited generalizations. Despite the ability to use combinational theory and to consider cases as wholes in H-C research, rigorous theory testing or experimental research is rarely possible. A criminologist interested in explaining the lower levels of crime in Asian countries, for example, would not be able to use an experimental method that requires the comparison of a test group (e.g., China) and a control group (e.g., the United States). Simply put, with the nation-state being the unit of analysis, the researcher has no real control over experimental conditions (e.g., the independent variable).

Four Types.   Kohn (1987) has discussed four types of comparative research. The first two fit into a distinct H-C approach, the third is an extension of a positivist approach, and the last is a unique approach.[31]

The primary focus of *case study comparative research* is to compare particular societies or cultural units, not to make broad generalizations. Examples of questions addressed by this type are as follows: How does informal social control in China differ from social control in the United States? To what extent do minorities in Australia display similar or different levels and types of criminal behavior as minorities in the United States? How do the social-psychological rationalizations of corporate criminals in Japan compare with such rationalizations in the United States? A researcher intensively examines a limited number of cases, where the "case" is a culturally defined group. By examining in depth a small number of cases, usually less than half a dozen, there is relatively little need to be concerned about the equivalence of units. This method is helpful for identifying factors that are constant or that vary among a few cases (Ragin, 1987).

A researcher uses *cultural-context research* to study cases that are surrogates for types of societies or units. For example, a criminologist may do a comparative study of hate crime among the youth in the United States and the former German Democratic Republic (GDR) in order to identify similarities between capitalist and former communist societies. Thus, the researcher is interested in these two cases not in and of themselves, but rather because they represent types of societies. In other words, the researcher could have perhaps just as well chosen Canada and Poland to compare.

In the third type of comparative research, the nation is the unit of analysis. In *cross-national research,* researchers measure variables across many nations. Nations are not mentioned by name, but a researcher measures variation across nations, converting unique features of nations into variables. For statistical analysis, the cross-national researcher needs information on at least 50 nations. Although there are nearly 150 independent nation-states, data are rarely available for more than 50 nations.

Transnational research is a type of comparative research in which a researcher uses a multi-nation unit (e.g., a region of the globe such as the Third World) and focuses on the relations among blocs of nations as units. He or she does not see nations as isolated entities but as parts of an international system.

The Units Being Compared

Culture versus Nation. For convenience, comparative researchers often use the nation-state as their unit of analysis. The nation-state is the major unit used in thinking about the divisions of people across the globe today. Although it is a dominant unit in current times, it is neither an inevitable nor a permanent one; in fact, it has been around for only about 300 years.

The nation-state is a socially and politically defined unit. In it, one government has sovereignty (i.e., military control and political authority) over populated territory. Economic relations (e.g., currency, trade, etc.), transportation routes, and communication systems are integrated within territorial boundaries. The people of the territory usually share a common language and customs, and there is usually a common educational system, legal system, and set of political symbols (e.g., flag, national anthem, etc.). The government claims to represent the interests of all people in the territory under its control.

The nation-state is not the only unit for comparative research. It is frequently a surrogate for culture, which is more difficult to define as a concrete, observable unit. *Culture* refers to a common identity among people based on shared social relations, beliefs, and technology. Cultural differences in language, custom, traditions, and norms often follow national lines. In fact, sharing a common culture is a major factor causing the formation of distinct nation-states.

The boundaries of a nation-state may not match those of a culture. In some situations, a single culture is divided into several nations; in other cases, a nation-state contains more than one culture. Over the past centuries, boundaries between cultures and distinct vibrant cultures have been destroyed, rearranged, or diffused as territory around the world was carved into colonies or nation-states by wars and conquest. For example, European empires imposed arbitrary boundaries over several cultural groups in nations that were once colonies.[32] Likewise, new immigrants or ethnic minorities are not always assimilated into the dominant culture in a nation. For example, one region of a nation may have people with a distinct ethnic background, language, customs, religion, social institutions, and identity (e.g., the province of Quebec in Canada). Such intranational cultures can create regional conflict, since ethnic and cultural identities are the basis for nationalism.[33]

The nation-state is not always the best unit for comparative research. A researcher should ask: What is the relevant comparative unit for my research question—the nation, the culture, a small region, or a subculture? For example, a criminologist may be interested in knowing if crime rates for Asian immigrants in the United States are higher or lower than crime rates for Chicano/Chicana immigrants. The researcher may conduct longitudinal comparative research to see if these crime rates differ for subsequent generations of Asian and Chicano/Chicana immigrants to the United States.

Nevertheless, boundaries between cultures or subcultures are difficult to operationalize. Cultures are hard to define, are constantly evolving, and have boundaries that blend into each other. Except for cases of border disputes, boundaries between nations are less ambiguous, but they, too, change over time. There is no easy answer. The issue of the appropriate unit to use remains a serious one.

Galton's Problem. The issue of the units of comparison is related to a problem named after Sir Francis Galton, who raised an issue at the Royal Anthropological Institute in 1889 regarding a paper by E. B. Taylor. When researchers compare units or their characteristics, they want the units to be distinct and separate from each other. If the units are not really different but are actually the subparts of a larger unit, then researchers will find spurious relationships. For example, the units are the states and provinces in Canada, France, and the United States; a re-

searcher discovers a strong association between speaking English and having the dollar as currency, or speaking French and using the franc as currency. Obviously, the association exists because the units of analysis (i.e., states or provinces) are actually subparts of larger units (i.e., nations). The features of the units are due to their being parts of larger units and not to any relationship among the features. Social geographers also encounter this because many social and cultural features diffuse across geographic space.

Galton's problem is an important issue in comparative research because cultures rarely have fixed boundaries.[34] It is hard to say where one culture ends and another begins, whether one culture is distinct from another, or whether the features of one culture have diffused to another over time. Galton's problem occurs when the relationship between two variables in two different units is actually due to a common origin, and they are not truly distinct units (see Figure 15.2).

Galton's problem originated with regard to comparisons across cultures, but it applies to historical comparisons also. It arises when a researcher asks whether units are really the same or different in different historical periods. For example, is the Cuba of 1875 the same country as the Cuba of 1975? Do 100 years since the end of Spanish colonialism, the rise of U.S. influence, independence, dictatorship, and a communist revolution fundamentally change the unit?

Data in Cross-Cultural Research

Comparative Field Research. Comparative researchers use field research and participant observation in cultures other than their own. Anthropologists are specially trained and prepared for this type of research. The exchange of methods between anthropological and field research suggests that there are small differences between field research in one's own society and in another culture. Field research in a different culture is usually more difficult and places more requirements on the researcher.

A   B   C

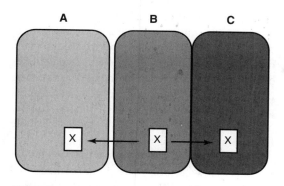

FIGURE 15.2 Galton's Problem. *Galton's problem* occurs when a researcher observes the same social relationship (represented by X) in different settings or societies (represented as A, B, and C) and falsely concludes that the social relationship arose independently in these different places. The researcher may believe he or she has discovered a relationship in three separate cases. But the actual reason for the occurrence of the social relation may be a shared or common origin that has diffused from one setting to others. This is a problem because the researcher who finds a relationship (e.g., crime pattern) in distinct settings or units of analysis (e.g., societies) may believe it arose independently in different units. This belief suggests that the relationship is a human universal. The researcher may be unaware that in fact it exists because people have shared the relationship across units.

Existing Sources of Qualitative Data. Comparative researchers can use secondary sources. For example, a researcher who conducts a comparative study of the Brazilian, Canadian, and Japanese criminal justice systems can read studies by researchers from many countries, including Brazil, Canada, and Japan, which describe the criminal justice systems in the three nations.

There may have been 5,000 different cultures throughout human history; about 1,000 of them have been studied by social researchers. A valuable source of ethnographic data on different cultures is the *Human Relations Area Files (HRAF)* and the related *Ethnographic Atlas.*[35] The HRAF is a collection of field research reports that anthropologist George

Murdock began to gather and organize in 1938. It brings together information from ethnographic studies on various cultures, most of which are primitive or small tribal groupings. Extensive information on nearly 300 cultures has been organized by social characteristics or practices (e.g., infant feeding, suicide, childbirth, etc.). A study on a particular culture is divided up, and its information on a characteristic is grouped with that from other studies. This makes it easy to compare many cultures on the same characteristic. For example, a researcher interested in inheritance can learn that of 159 different cultures in which it has been studied, 119 have a patrilineal form (father to son), 27 matrilineal (mother to daughter), and 13 mixed inheritance.

Researchers can use the HRAF to study relationships among several characteristics of different cultures. For example, to find out whether sexual assault against women, or rape, is associated with patriarchy (i.e., the holding of power and authority by males), a researcher can examine the presence of sexual assault and the strength of patriarchy in many cultures to determine whether the two are associated.

There are limitations to using the HRAF, however. First, the quality of the original research reports varies. The quality of original information depends on the initial researcher's length of time in the field, familiarity with the language, and prior experience, as well as on the explicitness of the research report. In addition, the range of behavior observed by the initial researcher and the depth of inquiry can vary. Another limitation involves the cultures that have been studied. Western researchers have made contact with and conducted field research on a limited number of cultures prior to these cultures' contact with the outside world. The cultures studied are not a representative sample of all the human cultures that existed. In addition, Galton's problem (discussed earlier) can be an issue.

Cross-National Survey Research. Survey research was discussed in a previous chapter. This section examines issues that arise when a researcher uses the survey technique in other cultures.[36] The problems or limitations of a cross-cultural survey are not different in principle from those of a survey within one culture. Nevertheless, they are usually so much greater in magnitude and severity that a researcher must carefully consider whether the survey is the best method in a setting.

A cardinal precondition for survey research in a different culture is that the researcher must possess an in-depth knowledge of its norms, practices, and customs. Without such an in-depth knowledge, it is easy to make serious errors in procedure and interpretation. Knowing another language is not enough. A researcher needs to be multicultural and thoroughly know the culture in addition to being familiar with the survey method. Substantial advance knowledge about the other culture is needed prior to entering it or planning the survey. Close cooperation with the native people of the other culture is also essential.

A researcher's choice of the cultures or nations to include in a cross-cultural survey should be made on both substantive (e.g., theoretical, research question) and practical grounds. Each step of survey research (question wording, data collection, sampling, interviewing, etc.) must be tailored to the culture in which it is conducted. One critical issue is how the people from the other culture experience the survey. In some cultures, the survey and interviewing itself may be a strange, frightening experience, analogous to a police interrogation. For example, conducting a crime victimization survey in a country with a repressive military regime (e.g., Burma) would be very, very difficult. Most likely, the respondents would be reluctant to be seen talking to "an outsider" (i.e., the researcher), for fear this might get him or her in trouble with the Burmese government.

Sampling for a survey is also affected by the cultural context. Comparative survey researchers must consider whether accurate sampling frames are available, the quality of mail or telephone service, and transportation to remote rural areas.

They need to be aware of such factors as how often people move, the types of dwellings in which people live, the number of people in a dwelling, the telephone coverage, or typical rates of refusal. Researchers must tailor the sampling unit to the culture and consider how basic units, such as the family, are defined in that culture. Special samples or methods for locating people for a sample may be required.

Questionnaire writing problems in the researcher's own culture are greatly magnified when studying a different culture. A researcher needs to be especially sensitive to question wording, questionnaire length, introductions, and topics included. He or she must be aware of local norms and of the topics that can and cannot be addressed by survey research. For example, open discussions of political issues can be life threatening in some societies; elsewhere, discussions of religion or sexuality are taboo. In addition to these cultural issues, translation and language equivalency pose problems (see the later discussion of equivalence). Techniques such as back translation (to be discussed) and the use of bilingual people are helpful, but there may be situations in which it is impossible to ask a question of interest in a different language.

Interviewing requires special attention in cross-cultural situations. Selection and training of interviewers depends on the education, norms, and etiquette of the other culture. The interview situation raises issues such as norms of privacy, ways to gain trust, beliefs about confidentiality, and differences in dialect. For example, in some cultures, an interviewer must spend a day in informal discussion before achieving the rapport needed for a short formal interview.

Comparative researchers need to be aware of a version of social desirability bias—the *courtesy bias*. It occurs when strong cultural norms cause respondents to hide anything unpleasant or give answers that the respondent thinks that the interviewer wants. Respondents may seriously understate or overstate some characteristics (e.g., self-reported criminality) because of cultural norms. In addition, the manner in which answers are given (e.g., tone of voice, situation, etc.) may change their meaning.

Access can be a serious issue in cultures where cultural norms limit openness or protect privacy. In addition, the researcher's origin from another country or culture may be a significant barrier in itself. Specific problems involve knowing what agencies and individuals to contact, the appropriate procedures for making contacts (e.g., a formal letter of introduction), how to maintain goodwill (e.g., gift giving), and the effects of such arrangements on the quality and comparability of research. In some cultures, bribery, family connections, or the approval of local political authorities are required for access to sampling frames, certain sections of a town, or specific respondents. In addition, a researcher may have to take special precautions to protect the confidentiality and integrity of data once they have been collected.

Existing Sources of Quantitative Data. Quantitative data for many variables are available for different nations (see also Chapter 11). In addition, large collections of quantitative data have been assembled. They gather information on many variables from other sources (e.g., newspaper articles, official government statistics, United Nations reports, etc.).

One vital source of comparative data is the United Nations Interregional Crime and Justice Research Institute (UNICRI). In addition to sponsoring periodic seminars on topics of interest to criminologists, such as the 1997 seminar on "Anti-Corruption Strategies for Central and Eastern European and CIS Countries," and making these seminar reports available to researchers, the Institute is a clearinghouse for primary research material. The UNICRI has a Documentation Server that "handles the collection, analysis and dissemination of legislative, statistical and bibliographical documents contained in the UNICRI Library has completed the transfer of 18,000 documents which are now on-line" (*Crime & Justice International,* 1998a:11).

The UNICRI has been responsible, since 1991, for managing the International Crime

Victimization Survey (ICVS) in developing countries and countries in transition. Longitudinal comparative survey data from the ICVS are currently available to criminologists and other social science researchers. And from time to time, the UNICRI also makes available technical reports and quantitative data on select comparative topics, such as United Nations peacekeeping operations, firearms regulations, crimes against the environment, juvenile justice, and domestic violence. The United Nations also publishes an annual *Demographic Year Book* that contains a plethora of quantitative data, including comparative homicide rates and war casualties.

Another source, the *World Handbook of Political and Social Indicators* (Taylor and Jodice, 1983), has dozens of indicators for 156 countries for 35 years. Indicators include such variables as the literacy rate, the number of medical doctors, the degree of urbanization, and the number of protest demonstrations. There are many notes on how data were gathered and classified because of the complexity of using data from different countries.

There are significant limitations on existing cross-national data, many of which are shared by other existing statistics. The theoretical definition of variables and the reliability of data collection can vary dramatically across nations. Missing information is a frequent limitation. Intentional misinformation in the official data from some governments can be a problem. Another limitation involves the nations on which data is collected. For example, during a 35-year period, new nations come into existence and others change their names or change their borders.

Despite recent improvements in the quality of comparative crime statistics, most notably perhaps the international crime victimization surveys, the quantitative data are still plagued with the same problems Clinard and Abbott (1973:22) identified more than 25 years ago:

> *Some of the important questions raised are whether official statistics reflect the actual amount of crime, whether changes in law enforcement and methods of recording affect an analysis*

of crime trends, and whether the characteristics of arrested offenders are really representative of those actually committing crimes.

Western Cultural Bias

Most social research is conducted by people who live, work, or have been educated in any one of a handful of societies in which advanced Western culture is dominant. This creates a danger of a Western cultural bias and ethnocentrism. As Myrdal (1973:89) concluded, "A Western approach must be regarded as a biased approach."

Each culture has its own assumptions, modes of thought, orientation toward time, and fundamental values about human life. All these influence thinking and social relations. If criminologists were totally free of culture or had a unique professional culture apart from any specific culture, then cultural bias would not be an issue. But this is unrealistic. It is too easy for researchers to believe that their assumptions, concepts, findings, and values—which are colored by Western culture—apply universally to all people in the world.

Much social research has some cultural bias. Although this is not desirable, it does not mean that social science research is false or impossible to conduct. It means that researchers need to be aware of such a bias and constantly combat it. They can do this in two ways: by becoming aware of how their own culture influences thinking and by becoming familiar with a diverse range of cultures.

The strong suit of comparative criminology is that it forces researchers to challenge their own preconceived cultural notions.[37] This plays out in a wide variety of ways in criminological research. (See Box 15.3 for select examples of this.) The Western bias, for example, presumes the existence of formal institutional means for meting out justice. In other words, it implicitly assumes the primary importance of the criminal justice system, as opposed to more indigenous approaches to crime and justice. Clinard and Abbott (1973:23) embellished this point in their classic study of crime in developing societies:

In more traditional areas, crime is often handled informally within groups, without involving law enforcement agencies. Only in the case of serious offenses such as homicide is a crime likely to be reported to the police.

Unfortunately, researchers have yet to delve into the effect of these informal mediation structures, such as "elder courts," which still hold sway in regions of Africa and Asia.

EQUIVALENCE IN HISTORICAL-COMPARATIVE RESEARCH

The Importance of Equivalence

Equivalence is a critical issue in all research.[38] It is the issue of making comparisons across divergent contexts, or whether a researcher, living in a specific time period and culture, correctly reads, understands, or conceptualizes data about people from a different historical era or culture. Without equivalence, a researcher cannot use the same concepts or measures in different cultures or historical periods, and this makes comparison difficult, if not impossible. It is similar to the problems that arise with measurement validity in quantitative research.

The equivalence issue varies on a continuum. At one extreme, a researcher discovers something that is totally foreign to his or her experience (e.g., infant children were treated harshly by their parents and frequently killed) or that is unique to a particular time or culture. At the opposite extreme, there are subtle differences, which are easily overlooked but could affect comparisons. For example, the social meaning of crime varies from one culture to the next. What may be considered a serious criminal offense, such as domestic assault, in one culture might be considered a "husband's right" in another culture.

Types of Equivalence

The equivalence issue has implications for H-C research. A researcher might misunderstand or misinterpret events in a different era or culture. Assuming that the interpretation is correct, a researcher may find it difficult to conceptualize

Box 15.3 _____

Two Examples of Western Bias in Comparative Criminological Research

EXAMPLE 1: Bias in Assuming the Public Has Easy Access to the Police

The convenience of the police station to the injured party is important. . . . Central Government police stations [in Uganda, Africa] are concentrated in the principal townships and are situated on the main roads. Large areas are without policing in the sense of permanently resident police and there appears to be little regular patrolling outside towns and industrial areas because of staff shortages and problems of cost. A minor theft ten miles from a police station would not be reported but a similar offense at a distance of 200 yards would. The Uganda police have stated that the immediate consequence of the erection of a new police station is a substantial increase in reported crime. The physical convenience of reporting is of paramount importance as there are no other means of getting information to the police—in the absence of a rural telephone system they cannot be rung up and information by letter except for very serious offenses will not receive quick attention. (Clinard and Abbott, 1973:23–24)

EXAMPLE 2: Bias in Assuming the Public Can Afford to Attend Criminal Court

There are also high costs of attendance at court [in Uganda], when there may be prolonged delays before giving evidence, involving both loss of time which cannot be retrieved by an agriculturalist at planting or harvesting, and money because he may have to pay for accommodation as well as food during the hearing. The more serious the case, the more distant the court of hearing will be from the site of the crime; even though the Judges of the High Court tour to provisional centers where there are also Resident Magistrates, with power to try most cases other than those involving capital punishment, the witness in any case of rural crime will have to sleep away from home which is a worrying experience for both farmers and cattlemen. (Clinard and Abbott, 1973:24)

and organize the events to make comparisons across times or places. If he or she fully grasps another culture, a researcher may still find it difficult to communicate with others from his or her own time and culture. The equivalence issue can be divided into four subtypes: lexicon equivalence, contextual equivalence, conceptual equivalence, and measurement equivalence.

**Lexicon Equivalence.**   _Lexicon equivalence_ is the correct translation of words and phrases, or finding a word that means the same thing as another word. This is clearest between two languages. Comparative researchers often use a technique called _back translation_ to achieve lexicon equivalence.[39] In back translation, a phrase or question is translated from one language to another and then back again. For example, a phrase in English is translated into Korean and

then independently translated from Korean back into English. A researcher then compares the first and second English versions. Back translation does not help much when words or concepts are foreign and do not exist in a different language and cultural setting. For example, the notion of "hate-motivated crime" is not directly translatable into the Malay language. This does not imply that hate crimes do not happen in, say, Indonesia or Malaysia. They certainly do, as evidenced by the victimization of Chinese businessmen during the recent uprisings in these countries. Rather, it suggests that "hate crime," as an analytical category or conceptualization, does not exist in the minds of the public. Translations in these instances may require complex explanations.

Lexicon equivalence can also entail a change in the meaning of a word over time. For example, the word _rape_ today carries connotations (e.g., spousal sexual assault) that were not conceived of historically. Nonetheless, a sensitivity to subtle changes in the meaning of words is imperative to comparative criminologists. Unfortunately, as Jones (1983:24) noted, "Harnessing elementary insights derived from theories of language to problems of substantive historical interpretation is in . . . an extremely primitive state."

Contextual Equivalence. *Contextual equivalence* is the correct application of terms or concepts in different social or historical contexts. It is an attempt to achieve equivalence within specific contexts. Of course, social and historical contexts are inextricably tied to specific historical periods. Take, for instance, the contextual meaning of being a criminal (i.e., being convicted and officially labeled as such by the criminal justice system). In traditional context, being labeled a "criminal" completely altered one's social interactional patterns. That person was often ostracized from the community body and shunned from participating in cultural activities (e.g., marriage, employment, etc.). In the context of contemporary U.S. underclass culture, on the other hand, being labeled a criminal carries a totally different meaning and set of consequences for the person. Culturally, some have even argued that having this experience constitutes a sort of rite of passage to adulthood (see Donziger, 1996).

Conceptual Equivalence. The ability to use the same concept across divergent cultures or historical eras is *conceptual equivalence*. Researchers live within specific cultures and historical eras. Their concepts are based on their experiences and knowledge from their own culture and era. Researchers may try to stretch their concepts by learning about other cultures or eras, but their views of other cultures or eras are colored by their current life situations. This creates a persistent tension and raises the question: Can a researcher create concepts that are simultaneously true reflections of life experiences in different cultures or eras and that also make sense to him or her?

The issue of a researcher's concept is a special case of a larger issue, because concepts can

be incompatible across different time periods or cultures. Is it possible to create concepts that are true, accurate, and valid representations of social life in two or more cultural or historical settings that are very different? For example, Thompson (1967) argued that the subjective experience of time and its measurement were radically different in the preindustrial period. Thus, as we saw in Ditton's (1977b) historical analysis of employee theft, the act of "stealing" something from one's employer has had different cultural meanings over time. To the displaced rural population, taking things home from work for personal use was not seen as a crime at all. Indeed, in the feudal context, such behavior was considered by the factory workers to be part of their "common right." Obviously, the factory owners have arrived at a different interpretation of this behavior.

Measurement Equivalence. The term *measurement equivalence* means measuring the same concept in different settings. If a researcher develops a concept appropriate to different contexts, the question remains: Are different measures necessary in different contexts for the same concept? Armer (1973:52) defined this idea as follows: "Conceptual equivalence with respect to measurement refers to whether the instruments used in separate societies in fact measure the same concept, regardless of whether the manifest content and procedures are identical or not." He argued that it may be necessary to use different indicators in different contexts. A researcher might measure a concept using an attitude survey in one culture but field research in another. The issue then becomes: Can a researcher compare results based on different indicators?

ETHICS

Ethical problems are less intense in H-C research than in other types of criminological research because a researcher is less likely to have direct contact with the people being studied. Historical-comparative research shares the ethical concerns found in other nonreactive research techniques.

The use of primary historical sources occasionally raises special ethical issues. First, it is difficult to replicate research based on primary material. The researcher's selection criteria for use of evidence and external criticism of documents places a burden on the integrity of the individual researcher. Novick (1988:220) suggested:

> The historian has seen, at first hand, a great mass of evidence, often unpublished. The historian develops an interpretation of this evidence based on years of immersion in the material—together, of course, with the perception apparatus and assumptions he or she brings to it. Historians employ devices, the footnote being the most obvious example, to attain for their work something approaching "replicability," but the resemblance is not all that close.

Errors in documentation or the failure to document primary sources sufficiently may create an accusation of fraud against historians, especially from opposing historiographic schools.[40]

Second, the right to protect one's privacy may interfere with the right to gather evidence. A person's descendants may want to destroy or hide private papers or evidence of scandalous behavior. Even major political figures (e.g., presidents) want to hide embarrassing official documents.

Comparative researchers must be sensitive to cultural and political issues of cross-cultural interaction. They need to learn what is considered offensive within a culture. Sensitivity means showing respect for the traditions, customs, and meaning of privacy in a host country. For example, it would be taboo for a male criminologist to interview a married woman in Muslim cultures without her husband being present.

In general, a researcher who visits another culture wants to establish good relations with the host country's government. He or she will not take data out of the country without giving something (e.g., results) in return. The military or political interests of the researcher's home nation or the researcher's personal values may conflict with official policy in the host nation. A researcher may be suspected of being a spy or may be under pressure from his or her home country to gather covert information.

CONCLUSION

In this chapter, you have learned methodological principles for organizing an inquiry into historical and comparative materials. The H-C approach has gained renewed attention in recent decades. It is appropriate when asking big questions about macro-level change, or for understanding social processes that operate across time or are universal across several societies. Historical-comparative research can be carried out in several ways, but a distinct qualitative H-C approach is similar to that of field research in important respects.

Historical-comparative research involves a different orientation toward research more than it means applying a specialized set of techniques. Some specialized techniques are used, such as the external criticism of primary documents. Nevertheless, the most vital feature of H-C research is how a researcher approaches a question, probes data, and moves toward explanations.

Historical-comparative research is more difficult to conduct than research that is neither historical nor comparative, but the difficulties are due to issues that are present to a lesser degree in other types of social research. For example, issues of equivalence exist to some degree in all social research. In H-C research, however, the problems cannot be treated as secondary concerns. They are at the forefront of how research is conducted and determine whether a research question can be answered.

We have examined qualitative data collection and research in the past two chapters. Both included some discussion of data analysis because data analysis occurs simultaneously with data collection. In the next chapter, we look more closely at the issue of qualitative data analysis and theoretical explanations.

KEY TERMS

anachronism
Annales school
back translation
Baconian fallacy
bowdlerization
case study comparative
    research
conceptual equivalence
contextual equivalence
courtesy bias
critical indicator

cross-national research
cultural-context research
external criticism
Galton's problem
grounded theory
historiography
Human Relations Area Files
    (HRAF)
internal criticism
lexicon equivalence
longue durée

measurement equivalence
mentalities
narrative history
oral history
primary sources
recollections
running records
secondary sources
transnational research

REVIEW QUESTIONS

1. What are some of the unique features of historical-comparative research?

2. What are the similarities between field research and H-C research?

3. What is the Annales school, and what are three characteristics or terms in its orientation toward studying the past?

4. What is the difference between a critical indicator and supporting evidence?

5. What questions are asked by a researcher using external criticism?

6. What are the limitations of using secondary sources?

7. What was Galton's problem and why is it important in comparative research?

8. What strengths or advantages are there to using a comparative method in social research?

9. In what ways is cross-national survey research different from survey research within one's own culture?

10. What is the importance of equivalence in H-C research, and what are the four types of equivalence?

NOTES

1. The early works include the following: Marc Bloch, *Feudal society,* transl. L. A. Manyon (Chicago: University of Chicago Press, 1961; original 1939–1940); George Homans, *English villagers of the thirteenth century* (Cambridge, MA: Harvard University Press, 1941); Robert K. Merton, *Science, technology and society in seventeenth century England* (New York: Harper & Row, 1970; originally published in 1938); and Karl Polanyi, *The great transformation,* revised ed. (Boston: Beacon, 1957; originally published in 1957).

2. Some influential works of this period include Anderson (1974a, 1974b), Hector (1975), Paige (1975), Skocpol (1979), Tilly and colleagues (1975), and Wallerstein (1974).

3. Of 193 articles published in the *American Sociological Review (ASR)* between 1989 and 1991, 82 were broadly historical or comparative. Of 101 articles in the *American Journal of Sociology (AJS)* in the same time period, 32 were historical or comparative. They represent 114 of 294 articles, or 38.8 percent of articles. Between 1986 and 1988, approximately 174 articles appeared in the *ASR* and 105 in the *AJS*. Of all *ASR* articles 46 (26.4 percent) and of all *AJS* articles, 31 (29.5 percent) were either historical or comparative. In the period 1976 to 1978, H-C articles were 34 of the 165 appearing in the *ASR* (20.6 perent) and 18 of 126 in the *AJS* (14.3 percent).

4. Additional information on the history of historical-comparative research can be found in Johnson (1982),

Kohn (1987, especially footnote 1), Lipset (1968), Novick (1988), Roy (1984), Skocpol (1984), Smith (1991), Warwick and Osherson (1973), and Zaret (1978).

5. For a discussion of differences between generalizations and analysis across temporal units and cultural units, see Firebaugh (1980) and Smelser (1976).

6. See McDaniel (1978), Przeworski and Teune (1970), and Stinchcombe (1978) for additional discussion.

7. Brown (1978), Johnson (1982), Lloyd (1986), and McLennan (1981:66–71) provided discussions of the relationship between positivist and nonpositivist approaches to historical-comparative research, and the turn toward a realist philosophy of science. See Murphey (1973) with regard to historical research. For comparative research, articles by Hymes (1970) and Mehan (1973) show the implications when nonpositivist approaches are taken seriously.

8. For more on borrowing from anthropology, see Biersack (1989), Desan (1989), Johnson (1982), Sewell (1980), Stone (1987), and Walters (1980).

9. See also Desan (1989), Griswold (1983), and Ryan (1989) for discussions of ritual and cultural symbolism.

10. Also see Carr (1961:35, 69), McDaniel (1978), Novick (1988:604), and Ragin (1987:164–166) on the dialogue metaphor for the relationship between theory and evidence in historical-comparative research.

11. For additional discussion, see Sewell (1987).

12. See Roth and Schluchter (1979:205).

13. For an additional discussion of the penetration of surface events, see Bloch (1953:13), Lloyd (1986), McLennan (1981:42–44), and Sewell (1987).

14. See Naroll (1968) for a discussion of difficulties in creating distinctions. Also see Whiting (1968). Sociologists often use the term *society* without realizing the theoretical-classificatory processes involved.

15. See the discussion on periodization in the next chapter.

16. Transhistorical concepts are discussed by others, such as Bendix (1963), Przeworski and Teune (1970), and Smelser (1976).

17. For more on the Annales school, see Braudel (1980), Darnton (1978), Hunt (1989), Lloyd (1986), and McLennan (1981).

18. Orientation reading is discussed in Shafer (1980:46–48).

19. Shafer (1980:2) discussed this in greater depth.

20. See Lowenthal (1985:187).

21. For additional information on oral history, see Dunaway and Baum (1984), Sitton and associates

(1983), and Thompson (1978). Also see Prucha (1987:78–80) for a guide to major collections of oral histories in the United States.

22. Bendix (1978:16) distinguished between the *judgments* of historians and the *selections* of sociologists. Sociologists are seen as restricted to selecting illustrative materials, deferring to expert historians who, despite their different purposes, possess far greater knowledge of specific historical materials.

23. Merton (1957:93–94) discussed the limitation of post-facto interpretations.

24. For a discussion of law versus tendency in historical social theory, see Applebaum (1978b) and McLennan (1981:75). Murphey (1973:86) provided a useful discussion of the issues.

25. The word *read,* as used here, means to bring a theoretical framework and analytic purpose to the text. Specific details and the historian's interpretations are read "through" (i.e., passed, but not without notice) in order to discover patterns of relations in underlying structures. See Sumner (1979) for discussion. This relates to the objectivity question in historiography, which is a current debate. See Novick (1988) and Winkler (1989).

26. Bonnell (1980:161), Finley (1977:132), and Goldthorpe (1977:189–190) discussed how historians use concepts. Selection in this context is discussed by Abrams (1982:194) and Ben-Yehuda (1983).

27. For introductions to how historians see their method, see Barzun and Graff (1970), Braudel (1980), Cantor and Schneider (1967), Novick (1988), or Shafer (1980). Most focus on the assembly of historical details that are documented in artifacts, including those of collective biography. This focuses attention on specific historical actors, their actions and motives, so it takes on an individualistic-voluntaristic slant, and studies become ideographic accounts of micro behavior. See also Block (1977), Laslett (1980), and MacIver (1968).

28. The narrative is discussed in Gallie (1963), Griffin (1993), McLennan (1981:76–87), Runciman (1980), and Stone (1987:74–96).

29. For more on the use and evaluation of primary sources, see Barzun and Graff (1970:63–128), Cantor and Schneider (1967:22–91), Dibble (1963), Mariampolski and Hughes (1978), Milligan (1979), Platt (1981), Shafer (1980:127–170), and Topolski (1976). Bloch's (1953:79–137) general discussion of the nature of historical criticism is still valuable today.

30. For more on the strengths and limitations of comparative research, see Anderson (1973), Holt and Turner (1970), Kohn (1987), Ragin (1987), Smelser

(1976), Vallier (1971a, 1971b), Walton (1973), and Whiting (1968).

31. Similar classifications are provided in Bollen and associates (1993), Chase-Dunn (1989:309–333), and Ragin (1994). Also see Ragin (1989) for a critique of Kohn's typology.

32. For example, Eric Wolf's (1982) study of the cultures or civilizations around the world between 1400 and 1900 illustrates the existence of many separate cultures and civilizations prior to European colonization and the rise of nation-states.

33. For examples, see Hector (1975) and See (1986).

34. See Elder (1973) and Whiting (1968) on Galton's problem.

35. For more on the *Human Relations Area File* and the *Ethnographic Atlas,* see Murdock (1967, 1971) and Whiting (1968).

36. For more on comparative survey research, see Burton and White (1987), Elder (1973), Frey (1970), Verba (1971), Warwick and Lininger (1975), and Williamson and colleagues (1982:315–319). For an additional discussion of access issues, see Armer (1973:59) and Form (1973).

37. See Frey (1970), Grimshaw (1973), and McDaniel (1978).

38. For additional discussions of equivalence, see Anderson (1973), Armer (1973), Frey (1970), Holt and Turner (1970), Przeworski and Teune (1970, 1973), and Warwick and Osherson (1973).

39. For more on back translation, see Anderson (1973), Grimshaw (1973), and Hymes (1970).

40. See Novick (1988:612–622) for an extensive discussion of the David Abraham case.

RECOMMENDED READINGS

Greenberg, David F. (1993). *Crime and capitalism.* Philadelphia: Temple University Press. Many of the research articles in this edited collection exemplify the best in historical criminology.

Griswold, Wendy. (1994). *Cultures and societies in a changing world.* Thousand Oaks, CA: Pine Forge Press. This short book builds on a series of essays and articles on historical and comparative issues by the author. The central idea in the book is cultural meaning. The reader is treated to a fascinating discussion on the creation, production, and distribution of cultural meanings, artifacts, or practices across time and nations.

Skocpol, Theda (Ed.). (1984). *Vision and method in historical sociology.* New York: Cambridge University Press. This collection of essays discusses the works of nine major H-C researchers. The essays examine the lives, research, and thinking of those who shaped twentieth-century H-C research. In addition, the editor provides an informative essay on historical sociology and a useful annotated bibliography on the methods of H-C research.

Smelser, Neil. (1976). *Comparative methods in the social sciences.* Englewood Cliffs, NJ: Prentice-Hall. Smelser surveys issues in comparative research and examines the works of Alexis de Tocqueville, Emile Durkheim, and Max Weber to distill their comparative method. He argues that the basic logic of comparative research differs little from that of quantitative research, but that it has special problems because of the small number of cases involved.

Thomson, Janice E. (1994). *Mercenaries, pirates, and sovereigns.* Princeton, NJ: Princeton University Press. This is a historical analysis of "nonstate violence in the international system." By examining the historical record about pirates, corsairs, mercenaries, and such, the author is able to develop a theory about the state's emerging control over these nonstate forms of violence. Her analysis also details how states have historically benefitted from these "nonstate" crimes.

Tilly, Charles. (1981). *As sociology meets history.* New York: Academic Press. These essays give us a sense of how this major H-C researcher approaches his work. It has three major themes: that historians and sociologists talk past one another, that serious historical work can be rigorous and quantitative, and that a solid grounding in historical evidence is required for any discussion of macro-level social change.

Yow, Valerie Raleigh. (1994). *Recording oral history: A practical guide for social scientists.* Thousand Oaks, CA: Sage. The central contribution of this book is expressed in the subtitle. It is a practical, "how-to" guide. The reader learns how to conduct an oral history interview and is given many examples. Included in an appendix are the standards of the Oral History Association.

ANALYZING QUALITATIVE DATA

> *When she [Lucia Barrera de Cerna] refers in this declaration to camouflaged uniforms she refers to various colors that she has seen soldiers in the street wearing. The headgear [cachuchas] that she refers to had a short visor. When Father Nachito yelled she could tell from the sound that he was located in the house of the Fathers. She is not able to say whether said screams were inside or outside the house.*
>
> —Lawyers Committee for Human Rights, *The Jesuit Murders: A Report on the Testimony of a Witness*, p. 15

INTRODUCTION

The preceding quote is from a translated interview of an eyewitness to a killing. Six Jesuit priests, their cook, and her 15-year-old daughter were shot dead in cold blood on the grounds of the University of Central America in San Salvador, El Salvador. The killings occurred on November 16, 1989, sometime between 2:30 and 3:00 in the morning. Sra. Lucia Barrera de Cerna was the lone eyewitness willing to give testimony. The testimony was taken by a judge in El Salvador. Distrustful of the justice system and fearing for her safety, Lucia nevertheless made her public declaration. In the flat terms of El Salvadoran legal documents, Lucia's declaration described the murderous events that transpired that night. By the light of the moon, Lucia stated she saw two armed men in military fatigues. In this one statement of fact, Lucia had, in effect, publicly intimated that the El Salvadoran military was behind the murders.

This excerpt is qualitative data. Qualitative data come in the form of text, written words, phrases, or symbols representing people and events in real life. In this case, the data are words: Lucia's official testimony before an El Salvadoran judge (as well as the Fiscal General, which is El Salvador's equivalent to the U.S. Attorney General). The data are from a primary source, which is important from an historical-comparative perspective, as we saw in the last chapter. The fact that a high-ranking El Salvadoran politician was present during the interview suggests the gravity of Lucia's testimony and the intense pressure she was under. As researchers, we are always concerned about the validity and reliability of data. We would therefore be particularly interested in the possible biasing effects that the politician's presence might have had on the data.

These are the sort of issues that go into analyzing qualitative data. Typically, qualitative data analysis is criticized for being unsystematic. Admittedly, qualitative analysis cannot be entirely learned in cookbook fashion. Still, there is much that can be done about making the process of analyzing qualitative data more explicit and systematic.[1] Keep in mind that no single analytic plan will work in all cases. But there are techniques for analyzing qualitative data that work better with field research, and others that work better with historical-comparative research. You will learn these techniques in this chapter.

QUANTITATIVE AND QUALITATIVE ANALYSIS

Qualitative and quantitative forms of data analysis have similarities and differences.

Similarities

First, the form of analysis for both types of data in both styles of research involves inference.

Researchers infer from the empirical details of social life. To *infer* means to pass a judgment, to use reasoning, and to reach a conclusion based on evidence. In both forms of data analysis, the researcher carefully examines empirical information to reach a conclusion. The conclusion is reached by reasoning and simplifies the complexity in the data. There is some abstraction or distance from the data, but this varies by the style of research. Both forms of data analysis anchor statements about the social world in a inquiry that has adequacy (i.e., it is faithful to the data). "In qualitative research, *adequacy* refers to the amount of data collected, rather than to the number of subjects as in quantitative research. Adequacy is attained when sufficient data has been collected that saturation occurs" (Morse, 1994:230, emphasis in original).

A second similarity is that both forms of analysis involve a public method or process. Researchers systematically record or gather data and in so doing make accessible to others what they did. Both types of researchers collect large amounts of data. They describe the data and document how they collected and examined it. The degree to which the method is standardized and visible may vary, but all researchers reveal their study design in some way. "Research designs in qualitative research are not always made explicit, but they are at least implicit in every piece of research" (King et al., 1994:118).

Next, comparison is a central process to all data analysis, qualitative or quantitative. All social researchers compare features of the evidence they have gathered internally or with related evidence. Researchers identify multiple process, causes, properties, or mechanisms within the evidence. They then look for patterns—similarities and differences, aspects that are alike and unlike:

> [Qualitative] researchers examine patterns of similarities and differences across cases and try to come to terms with their diversity. . . . Quantitative researchers also examine differences among cases, but with a different emphasis, the goal is to explain the covariation of one variable with another, usually across many cases. . . . The

quantitative researcher typically has only broad familiarity with the cases. (Ragin, 1994:107)

Fourth, in both qualitative and quantitative forms of data analysis, researchers strive to avoid errors, false conclusions, and misleading inferences. Researchers are also alert for possible fallacies or illusions. They sort through various explanations, discussions, and descriptions, and evaluate merits of rivals, seeking the more authentic, valid, true, or worthy among them.

Differences

Qualitative data analysis differs from quantitative analysis in four ways. First, quantitative researchers choose from a specialized, standardized set of data analysis techniques. Hypothesis testing and statistical methods vary little across different social research projects or across the natural and social sciences. Quantitative analysis is highly developed and builds on applied mathematics. By contrast, qualitative data analysis is less standardized. The wide variety in possible approaches to qualitative research is matched by the many approaches to data analysis. Qualitative research is often inductive. Researchers rarely know the specifics of data analysis when they begin a project. Schatzman and Strauss (1973:108) remarked, "Qualitative analysts do not often enjoy the operational advantages of their quantitative cousins in being able to predict their own analytic processes; consequently, they cannot refine and order their raw data by operations built initially into the design of research."

A second difference is that quantitative researchers do not begin data analysis until they have collected all of the data and condensed them into numbers. They then manipulate the numbers in order to see patterns or relationships. Qualitative researchers can look for patterns or relationships, but they begin analysis early in a research project, while they are still collecting data. The results of early data analysis guide subsequent data collection. Thus, analysis is less a distinct final stage of research than a dimension of research that stretches across all stages.

Another difference is the relation to social theory. Quantitative researchers manipulate

numbers that represent empirical facts in order to test an abstract hypothesis with variable constructs. By contrast, qualitative researchers create new concepts and theory by blending together empirical evidence and abstract concepts. Instead of testing a hypothesis, a qualitative analyst may illustrate or color in evidence showing that a theory, generalization, or interpretation is plausible.

The fourth difference is the degree of abstraction or distance from the details of social life. In all data analysis, a researcher places raw data into categories that he or she manipulates in order to identify patterns and arrive at generalizations. In quantitative analysis, this process is clothed in statistics, hypotheses, and variables. Quantitative researchers use the symbolic language of statistical relationships between variables to discuss causal relations. They assume that social life can be measured by using numbers. When they manipulate the numbers according to the laws of statistics, the numbers reveal features of social life.

Qualitative analysis is less abstract than statistical analysis and closer to raw data. Qualitative analysis does not draw on a large, well-established body of formal knowledge from mathematics and statistics. The data are in the form of words, which are relatively imprecise, diffuse, and context-based, and can have more than one meaning:

> *Words are not only more fundamental intellectually; one may also say that they are necessarily superior to mathematics in the social structure of the discipline. For words are a mode of expression with greater open-endedness, more capacity for connecting various realms of argument and experience, and more capacity for reaching intellectual audiences. (Collins, 1984:353)*

Explanations and Qualitative Data

Qualitative explanations take many forms. A qualitative researcher does not have to choose between a rigid ideographic/nomothetic dichotomy—that is, between describing specifics and verifying universal laws. Instead, a researcher develops explanations or generalizations that are close to concrete data and contexts but are more than simple descriptions. He or she usually uses a lower level, less abstract theory, which is grounded in concrete details. He or she may build new theory to create a realistic picture of social life and stimulate understanding more than to test a causal hypothesis. Explanations tend to be rich in detail, sensitive to context, and capable of showing the complex processes or sequences of social life. The explanations may be causal, but this is not always the case. The researcher's goal is to organize a large quantity of specific details into a coherent picture, model, or set of interlocked concepts.

A qualitative researcher rarely tries to document universal laws; rather, he or she divides explanations into two categories: highly unlikely and plausible. The researcher is satisfied by building a case or supplying supportive evidence. He or she may eliminate some theoretical explanations from consideration while increasing the plausibility of others because only a few explanations will be consistent with a pattern in the data. Qualitative analysis can eliminate an explanation by showing that a wide array of evidence contradicts it. The data might support more than one explanation, but *all* explanations will not be consistent with it. In addition to eliminating less plausible explanations, qualitative data analysis helps to verify a sequence of events or the steps of a process. This temporal ordering is the basis of finding associations among variables, and it is useful in supporting causal arguments.

The form of analysis and theorizing in qualitative research sometimes makes it difficult to see generalizations. Some qualitative researchers are almost entirely descriptive and avoid theoretical analysis. In general, it is best to make theories and concepts explicit. Without an analytic interpretation or theory provided by the researcher, the readers of qualitative research may use their own everyday, taken-for-granted ideas. Their commonsense framework is likely to contain implicit assumptions, biases, ethnocentrism, and ill-defined concepts from dominant cultural values.[2]

CONCEPT FORMATION

In this section, you will learn about themes or concepts, coding qualitative data, and analytic memo writing. Qualitative researchers sometimes use variables, but more often they use general ideas, themes, or concepts as analytic tools for making generalizations. Qualitative analysis often uses nonvariable concepts or simple nominal-level variables.

Conceptualization in Qualitative Research

Quantitative researchers conceptualize variables and refine concepts as part of the process of measuring variables that comes before data collection or analysis. By contrast, qualitative researchers form new concepts or refine concepts that are grounded in the data. Concept formation is an integral part of data analysis and begins during data collection. Thus, conceptualization is one way that a qualitative researcher organizes and makes sense of data.

A qualitative researcher analyzes data by organizing it into categories on the basis of themes, concepts, or similar features. He or she develops new concepts, formulates conceptual definitions, and examines the relationships among concepts. Eventually, he or she links concepts to each other in terms of a sequence, as oppositional sets (*X* is the opposite of *Y*), or as sets of similar categories that he or she interweaves into theoretical statements. Qualitative researchers conceptualize or form concepts as they read through and ask critical questions of data (e.g., field notes, historical documents, secondary sources, etc.).

Questions instigate conceptualization. For example, reading over Lucia's excerpt, one might ask: Are these murders an example of "crime by government" (Hagan, 1997)? What means of military socialization are used to prepare soldiers to commit crimes by government? What are the social class backgrounds of death squad members? These questions force us to expand our criminological concepts—to think more broadly in terms of crime *by* government, military socialization and political crime, death squad rationalizations of guilt, and so on. Thus, qualitative analysis involves the formation of new and expanded concepts by asking theory-based questions of the data. [3]

In qualitative research, ideas and evidence are mutually interdependent. This applies particularly to case study analysis. Cases are not given preestablished empirical units or theoretical categories apart from data; they are defined by data and theory. By analyzing a situation, the researcher organizes data and applies ideas simultaneously to create or specify a case. Making or creating a case, called *casing,* brings the data and theory together. Determining what to treat as a case resolves a tension or strain between what the researcher observes and his or her ideas about it. "Casing viewed as a methodological step, can occur at any phase of the research process, but occurs especially at the beginning of the project and at the end" (Ragin, 1992b:218).

Coding Qualitative Data

A quantitative researcher codes after all the data have been collected. He or she arranges measures of variables, which are in the form of numbers, into a machine-readable form for statistical analysis.

Coding data has a different meaning and role in qualitative research. A researcher organizes the raw data into conceptual categories and creates themes or concepts, which he or she then uses to analyze data. Instead of a simple clerical task, qualitative coding is an integral part of data analysis. It is guided by the research question and leads to new questions. It frees a researcher from entanglement in the details of the raw data and encourages higher-level thinking about them. It also moves him or her toward theory and generalizations:

> Codes are tags or labels for assigning units of meaning to the descriptive or inferential information complied during a study. Codes usually are attached to "chunks" of varying size—words, phases, sentences or whole paragraphs, connected or unconnected to a specific setting. (Miles and Huberman, 1994:56)

Coding is two simultaneous activities: mechanical data reduction and analytic categorization of data. The researcher imposes order on the data. "Contrasted with the weeks and weeks in which she will be engaged in mechanical processing, the truly analytic moments will occur during bursts of insight or pattern recognition" (Wolcott, 1994:24). Coding data is the hard work of reducing mountains of raw data into manageable piles. In addition to making a large mass of data manageable, coding allows a researcher to quickly retrieve relevant parts of it. Between the moments of thrill and inspiration, a great deal of coding qualitative data, or filework, can be wearisome and tedious. Plath (1990:375) remarked, it has "all the dramatic tension of watching paint dry." She also stated:

> The task of shifting through much material can become daunting. For weeks, even months, you may have nothing to show as proof of effort expended. . . . Filework is the outward manifestation of an inward pledge that most of us make to continue striving to understand a particular people. (Plath, 1990:374)

Strauss (1987) defined three kinds of qualitative data coding, which are described next. The researcher reviews the data on three occasions, using a different coding each time, and codes the same raw data in three passes. Strauss (1987:55) warned, "Coding is the most difficult operation for inexperienced researchers to understand and to master." Others have suggested similar types of coding (see Lofland and Lofland, 1995:192–193; Miles and Huberman, 1994:57–71; and Sanjek, 1990:388–392).

Open Coding. *Open coding* is performed during a first pass through recently collected data. The researcher locates themes and assigns initial codes or labels in a first attempt to condense the mass of data into categories. He or she slowly reads field notes, historical sources, or other data, looking for critical terms, key events, or themes, which are then noted. Next, he or she writes a preliminary concept or label at the edge of a note card or computer record and highlights it with brightly colored ink or in some similar way. The researcher is open to creating new themes and to changing these initial codes in subsequent analysis. A theoretical framework helps if it is used in a flexible manner.

Open coding brings themes to the surface from deep inside the data. The themes are at a low level of abstraction and come from the researcher's initial research question, concepts in the literature, terms used by members in the social setting, or new thoughts stimulated by immersion in the data. As Schatzman and Strauss (1973:121) warned, it is important for researchers to see abstract concepts in concrete data and to move back and forth between abstract concepts and specific details:

> Novices occasionally, if not characteristically, bog down in their attempts to utilize substantive levers [i.e., concepts of a discipline] because they view them as real forms. Experienced researchers and scholars more often see through these abstract devices to the ordinary, empirical realities they represent; they are thereby capable of considerable conceptual mobility. Thus, we urge the novice in analysis to convert relatively inert abstractions into stories—even with plots.

For example, Lucia's description of the murders was specific in detail. She described "camouflaged uniforms . . . [of] various colors that she has seen soldiers in the street wearing." Good qualitative researchers are able to identify abstract concepts based on concrete details. Concepts such as *political crime, paramilitary crime, civil war,* and so on, come to mind from reading Lucia's declaration.

Historical-comparative researchers also use open coding. For example, the concepts that emerge from coding Lucia's eyewitness account of the murders can be easily combined together into interesting substantive relationships: What is the relationship between death squad activity and religion? What role do the military and police play in the death squad activity? Is there a relationship between U.S. foreign aid to El Salvador and the death squads? What political and eco-

nomic interests in El Salvador perceive the Jesuits as a threat? As this example illustrates, axial coding helps make related theme and concepts buried in the qualitative data more explicit.

Although some researchers (e.g., Miles and Huberman, 1994:58) suggest that a researcher begins coding with a list of concepts, researchers generate most coding themes while reading data notes. Regardless of whether he or she begins with a list of themes, a researcher makes a list of themes *after* open coding. Such a list serves three purposes:

1. It helps the researcher see the emerging themes at a glance.
2. It stimulates the researcher to find themes in future open coding.
3. The researcher uses the list to build a universe of all themes in the study, which he or she reorganizes, sorts, combines, discards, or extends in further analysis.

Qualitative researchers vary in how completely and in how much detail they code. Some code every line or every few words; others code paragraphs and argue that much of the data are not coded and are dross or left over. The degree of detail in coding depends on the research question, the "richness" of the data, and the researcher's purposes.

Open-ended coding extends to analytic notes or memos that a researcher writes to himself or herself while collecting data. Researchers should write memos on their codes (see the later discussion of analytic memo writing).

Axial Coding. This is a "second pass" through the data. During open coding, a researcher focuses on the actual data and assigns code labels for themes. There is no concern about making connections among themes or elaborating the concepts that the themes represent. By contrast, in *axial coding,* the researcher begins with an organized set of initial codes or preliminary concepts. In this second pass, he or she focuses on the initial coded themes more than on the data. Additional codes or new ideas may emerge during this pass, and the researcher notes them; but his or her primary task is to review and examine initial codes. He or she moves toward organizing ideas or themes and identifies the axis of key concepts in analysis.

Miles and Huberman (1994:62) have warned,

Whether codes are created and revised early or late is basically less important than whether they have some conceptual and structural order. Codes should relate to one another in coherent, study-important ways; they should be part of a governing structure.

During axial coding, a researcher asks about causes and consequences, conditions and interactions, strategies and processes, and looks for categories or concepts that cluster together. He or she asks questions such as: Can I divide existing concepts into subdimensions or subcategories? Can I combine several closely related concepts into one more general one? Can I organize categories into a sequence (i.e., A, then B, then C), or by their physical location (i.e., where they occur), or their relationship to a major topic of interest?

A criminologist doing research on paramilitary death squads, for example, may decide to make the concept of *social class* a major theme. In selective coding he or she would go back through the qualitative data and look for information regarding the social class of the victims, the social class of the death squad murders, the social class interests that challenge the death squad worldview, and so on. The array of themes and concepts identified in axial coding helps the researcher discover interesting new research questions and conceptual relationships to explore.

During selective coding, major concepts, themes, and relationships emerge and ultimately guide the researcher's analysis. Researchers organize and reorganize specific themes and relate them to other major themes. This is fundamentally important in the formation of new concepts and grounded theory.

Axial coding not only stimulates thinking about linkages between concepts or themes but it also raises new questions. It can suggest dropping some themes or examining others in more depth.

In addition, it reinforces the connections between evidence and concepts. As a researcher consolidates codes and locates evidences, he or she finds evidence in many places for core themes and builds a dense web of support in the qualitative data for them. This is analogous to the idea of multiple indicators described with regard to reliability and measuring variables. The connection between a theme and data is strengthened by multiple instances of empirical evidence.[4]

Selective Coding.   By the time a researcher is ready for this last pass through the data, he or she has identified the major themes of the research project. *Selective coding* involves scanning data and previous codes. Researchers look selectively for cases that illustrate themes and make comparisons and contrasts after most or all data collection is complete. They begin after they have well-developed concepts and have started to organize their overall analysis around several core generalizations or ideas. During selective coding, major themes or concepts ultimately guide the researcher's search. He or she reorganizes specific themes identified in earlier coding and elaborates more than one major theme.

Analytic Memo Writing

Qualitative researchers are always writing notes. Their data are recorded in notes, they write comments on their method or research strategy in notes, and so on. They are compulsive note-takers, keep their notes organized in files, and often have many files with different kinds of notes: a file on methodological issues (e.g., locations of sources or ethical issues), a file of maps or diagrams, a file on possible overall outlines of a final report or chapter, a file on specific people or events, and so on.

The *analytic memo* is a special type of note.[5] It is a memo or discussion of thoughts and ideas about the coding process that a researcher writes to himself or herself. Each coded theme or concept forms the basis of a separate memo, and the memo contains a discussion of the concept or theme. The rough theoretical notes form the beginning of analytic memos.

The analytic memo forges a link between the concrete data or raw evidence and more abstract, theoretical thinking (see Figure 16.1). It contains a researcher's reflections on and thinking about the data and coding. The researcher adds to the memo and uses it as he or she passes through the data with each type of coding. The memos form the basis for analyzing data in the research report. In fact, rewritten sections from good-quality analytic memos can become sections of the final report.

The technology involved in writing analytic memos is simple: pen and paper, a few notebooks, a stack of file folders, and photocopies of notes. Some researchers use computers, but it is not necessary (see Appendix C). There are many ways to write analytic memos; each researcher develops his or her own style or method. Some concrete suggestions based on the experience of other researchers are provided in Box 16.1. Some

researchers make multiple copies of notes, then cut them and place parts of a copy into an analytic memo file. This works well if the physical files are large and analytic memos are kept distinct within the file (e.g., on different-colored paper or placed at the beginning). Other researchers list within the analytic memo file locations in the data notes where a theme appears. Then it is easy to move between the analytic memo and the data. Because data notes contain highlighted or marked themes, it is easy to find specific sections in the data. An intermediate strategy is to keep a running list of locations where a major theme appears in the data, but also include copies of a few key sections of the notes for easy reference.[6]

As a researcher reviews and modifies analytic memos, he or she discusses ideas with colleagues and returns to the literature with a focus on new issues. Analytic memos may help to generate potential hypotheses, which can be added and dropped as needed, and to develop new themes or coding systems.

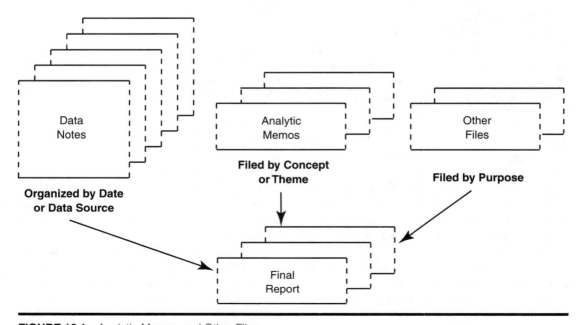

FIGURE 16.1   Analytic Memos and Other Files

Box 16.1 _____

Suggestions for Analytic Memo Writing

1. Start to write memos shortly after you begin data collection, and continue memo writing until just before the final research report is completed.
2. Put the date on memo entries so that you can see progress and the development of thinking. This will be helpful when rereading long, complicated memos, since you will periodically modify memos as research progresses and add to them.
3. Interrupt coding or data recording to write a memo. Do not wait and let a creative spark or new insight fade away—write it down.
4. Periodically read memos and compare memos on similar codes to see whether they can be combined, or whether differences between codes can be made clearer.
5. Keep a separate file for memos on each concept or theme. All memo writing on that theme or concept is kept together in one file, folder, or notebook. Label it with the name of the concept or theme so it can be located easily. It is important to be able to sort or reorganize memos physically as analysis progresses, so you should be able to sort the memos in some way.
6. Keep analytic memos and data notes separate because they have different purposes. The data are evidence. The analytic memos have a conceptual, theory-building intent. They do not report data, but comment on how data are tied together or how a cluster of data is an instance of a general theme or concept.
7. Refer to other concepts within an analytic memo. When writing a memo, think of similarities to, differences between, or causal relationships to other concepts. Note these in the analytic memo to facilitate later integration, synthesis, and analysis.
8. If two ideas arise at once, put each in a separate memo. Try to keep each distinct theme or concept in a separate memo and file.
9. If nothing new can be added to a memo and you have reached a point of saturation in getting any further data on a theme or concept, indicate that in the memo.
10. Keep a list of codes or labels for the memos that will let you look down the list and see all the memos. When you periodically sort and regroup memos, reorganize this list of memo labels to correspond to the sorting.

Source: Adapted from Miles and Huberman (1994:72–76), Lofland and Lofland (1995:193–194), and Strauss (1987:127–129). Also see Lester and Hadden (1980).

METHODS OF QUALITATIVE DATA ANALYSIS

The coding and memo-writing techniques discussed in the previous section are generic and can be used in most types of analyses. There are also more specific methods of qualitative data analysis. In this section, you will learn about four such methods selected from the all possible methods: successive approximation, the illustrative method, analytic comparison, and ideal types. Qualitative researchers sometimes combine the methods or use them with quantitative analysis.

In general, *data analysis* means a search for patterns in data—recurrent behaviors, objects, or a body of knowledge. Once a pattern is identified, it is interpreted in terms of a criminological theory or the setting in which it occurred. The qualitative researcher moves from the description of a historical event or social setting to a more general interpretation of its meaning.

A potential source of confusion is the multiple forms that data take in various stages of qualitative research. For example, field research data are raw sense data that a researcher experiences, recorded data in field notes, and selected or processed data that appear in a final report (see Figure 16.2). Data analysis involves examining, sorting, categorizing, evaluating, comparing, synthesizing, and contemplating the coded data as well as reviewing the raw and recorded data.

Successive Approximation

This method involves repeated iterations or cycling through steps, moving toward a final analysis. Over time, or after several iterations, a researcher moves from vague ideas and concrete details in the data toward a comprehensive analysis with generalizations. This is similar to three kinds of coding discussed earlier.

A researcher begins with research questions and a framework of assumptions and concepts. He or she then probes into the data, asking questions of the evidence to see how well the concepts fit the evidence and reveal features of the data. He or she also creates new concepts by abstracting from the

evidence and adjusts concepts to fit the evidence better. The researcher then collects additional evidence to address unresolved issues that appeared in the first stage, and repeats the process. At each stage, the evidence and the theory shape each other. This is called *successive approximation* because the modified concepts and the model approximate the full evidence and are modified over and over to become successively more accurate.

Each pass through the evidence is provisional or incomplete. The concepts are abstract, but they are rooted in the concrete evidence and reflect the context. As the analysis moves toward generalizations that are subject to conditions and contingencies, the researcher refines generalizations and linkages to reflect the evidence better.[7]

Take the concept of *death squad,* for instance. In the abstract, it connotes a clandestine

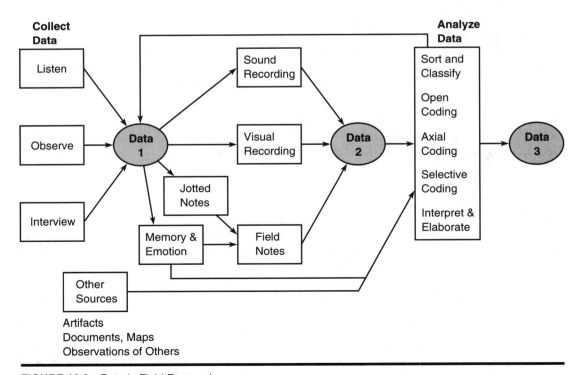

FIGURE 16.2   Data in Field Research

Note: (Data 1 = Raw sense data, experiences of researcher; Data 2 = Recorded data, physical record of experiences; Data 3 = Selected, processed data in a final report)

Source: Adapted from Ellen (1984a:214).

paramilitary unit with veiled connections to individuals in government. These units terrorize those who question prevailing political-economic arrangements. In the concrete, Lucia's words "camouflaged uniforms . . . that she has seen *soldiers in the street wearing* (emphasis added)" are clear qualitative evidence of our concept of *death squad.*

As the qualitative analysis moves toward generalizations that are subject to conditions and contingencies, the researcher continues to strengthen the linkage connecting concept to data. The concept of *death squad* is still too general. It can be refined by asking Where? and When? Thus, the concept is being sharpened so that we must consider similarities and differences between, say, a death squad in El Salvador today and one of 30 years ago. Or we might compare it with similar phenomenon in Colombia, Guatemala, and Argentina. Or the comparison may bring in other regions of the world in addition to Latin America. Specifying the concept in historical-comparative terms brings new meaning to the data. Lucia is speaking about a specific type of death squad within the context of her country and her life. As Carr (1961:76) so aptly put it, "The division of history into periods is not a fact, but a necessary hypothesis."

The Illustrative Method

Another method of analysis uses empirical evidence to illustrate or anchor a theory. With the *illustrative method,* a researcher applies theory to a concrete historical situation or social setting, or organizes data on the basis of prior theory. Preexisting theory provides the *empty boxes.* The researcher sees whether evidence can be gathered to fill them.[8] The evidence in the boxes confirms or rejects the theory, which he or she treats as a useful device for interpreting the social world. The theory can be in the form of a general model, an analogy, or a sequence of steps.[9]

There are two variations of the illustrative method. One is to show that the theoretical model illuminates or clarifies a specific case or single situation. A second is the parallel demonstration of a model in which a researcher juxtaposes multiple cases (i.e., units or time periods) to show that the theory can be applied in multiple cases. In other cases, the researcher illustrates theory with specific material from multiple cases. An example of parallel demonstration would be if a researcher were to develop an elaborate theoretical model of conditions that give rise to death squad activities, and then supply evidence from various countries (e.g., El Salvador, Indonesia, and Guatemala) that illustrate the model. This demonstrates the applicability of the theoretical model in several different cases.

Analytic Comparison

British philosopher and social thinker John Stuart Mill (1806–1873) developed logical methods for making comparisons that are still used today. His *method of agreement* and *method of difference* form the basis of *analytic comparison* in qualitative data analysis.[10] Aspects of this logic are also used when making comparisons in experimental research. This differs from the illustrative method in that a researcher does not begin with an overall model consisting of empty boxes to fill with details. Instead, he or she develops ideas about regularities or patterned relations from preexisting theories or induction. The researcher then focuses on a few regularities and makes contrasts with alternative explanations, then looks for regularities that are not limited to a specific setting (time, place, group, etc.). He or she is not seeking universal laws, only regularities within a social context. For example, the researcher looks for patterns in death squad activity occurring in many different countries and time periods. This would not lead to causal laws that apply to all death squads anywhere and anytime, but it would draw out consistencies and patterns that are commonly related to such political crimes. Therefore, it would allow the researcher to make generalizations beyond any single case.

Method of Agreement.   The method of agreement focuses a researcher's attention on what is common across cases. The researcher establishes that cases have a common outcome, then tries to locate a common cause, although other features of the cases may differ. The method of agreement proceeds by a process of elimination. He or she eliminates features as possible causes if they are not shared across cases that have a common outcome.

Suppose, for instance, that a criminologist has qualitative data in the form of eyewitness accounts of death squad assassinations for four different countries. He or she would carefully review the four cases for features they have in common. One feature might be that death squads occur to terrorize those in support of land reform. Of course, the four cases will differ in many respects, but the researcher can argue that, despite differences, the critical similarities exist.

Method of Difference.   Researchers can use the method of difference alone or in conjunction with the method of agreement. The method of difference is usually stronger and is a "double application" of the method of agreement. A researcher first locates cases that are similar in many respects but differ in a few crucial ways. He or she pinpoints features whereby a set of cases is similar with regard to an outcome and causal features, and another set whereby the cases differ on outcomes and causal features. The method of difference reinforces information from positive cases (e.g., cases that have common causal features and outcomes) with negative cases (e.g., cases lacking the outcome and causal features). Thus, a researcher looks for cases that have many of the causal features of positive cases but lack a few key features and have a different outcome.

An Example.   The method of agreement and method of difference are difficult to grasp in the abstract. Ragin (1987) provided a system for using the methods of agreement and difference. Look at Box 16.2 for an example of each method. In the method of agreement chart, note that *a* and *b* are common in all four cases and are crucial similarities despite the many differences (*c–q*). Suppose

cases 1 through 4 represent four nations that have all experienced death squad activity within the past five years, and that the letters represent structural features of their respective societies. Thus, *a* is the experience of having death squad murders within the past five years, *b* is a large propertied class, *c* is a military junta form of government, and so on through *x*.

Using the method of agreement, a criminologist interested in explaining outcome *a* (i.e., a nation with death squad murders) notes the close pattern it has with *b* (i.e., the concentration of property into the hands of the few). It exists for all four cases. This gets the criminologist to thinking: Is there some connection between having a powerful landowning class and death squad murders? He or she then hypothesizes that *b* is a critical causal factor for the development of *a*.

Box 16.2 also shows the method of difference. It shows that cases 1 and 2 are similar on five features (*a, b, c, f,* and *o*). It also shows that cases 1 and 2 are different from either case 5 or case 6 or both on all other features except *f*. The researcher uses cases 5 and 6, two nations not having death squad murders, to help explain why cases 1 and 2 have them. The researcher is now in a position to identify some of the features that are probably not critical to *a* (i.e., death squad murders). For example, feature *c* (i.e., a military junta) is probably not critical to a society's having death squad murders. Features *o* (i.e., receiving U.S. military assistance) and *f* (i.e., fighting a civil war) are similarly probably not critical to whether a nation has death squad murders. Again, it appears that *b* (i.e., concentration of property among the few) is the key feature in that it is the only feature that both cases 1 and 2 have in common and that neither cases 5 nor 6 have. It is the critical difference between cases 1 and 2, on the one hand, and cases 5 and 6, on the other hand.

Ideal Types

Max Weber's *ideal type* is used by many qualitative researchers. Ideal types are models or mental

Box 16.2

Example of Method of Agreement and Method of Difference

METHOD OF AGREEMENT

Case 1	Case 2	Case 3	Case 4
a	a	a	a
b	b	b	b
c	c	d	e
f	f	g	h
i	j	k	k
l	m	l	n
o	o	p	q

METHOD OF DIFFERENCE

Case 1	Case 2	Case 5	Case 6
a	a	x	x
b	b	z	q
c	c	d	c
f	f	f	f
i	j	k	k
l	m	l	n
o	o	o	q

Key: Each letter represents a characteristic of a society.

a = Society has death squad murders in the past five years.

b = Society has a propertied class owning over three-fourths of the land.

c = Society has a military junta.

d = Society has a negative trade balance.

e = Society has corrupt national police.

f = Society is fighting a civil war.

g = Society has a steady supply of imported weapons.

h = Society has a tiny, elite-only public education system.

i = Society has a large indigenous class.

j = Society has a free press.

k = Society has a communist insurgency.

l = Society has a plantation economy.

m = Society has an established tourism industry.

n = Society transships cocaine.

o = Society receives U.S. military aid.

p = Society has a budget deficit.

q = Society has a professional civil service.

x = Society has a high homicide rate (over 10 per 100,000 persons) abstractions of social relations or processes. They are pure standards against which the data or "reality" can be compared. An ideal type is a device used for comparison, because no reality ever fits an ideal type. For example, a criminologist may want to construct a mental model of the key features of a death squad murder. This ideal type model does not make reference to any particular death squad murder. Rather, the ideal type is an abstraction that lists the essential structures and process of such murders in general. Historical and comparative differences are not taken into account in the ideal type. Nevertheless, the ideal type is useful when applied to specific cases to see how closely the case approximates the ideal type.

Weber's method of ideal types also complements Mills's method of agreement. Recall that with the method of agreement, a researcher's attention is focused on what is common across cases, and he or she looks for common causes in cases with a common outcome. By itself, the method of agreement implies a comparison against actual cases. This comparison of cases could also be made against an idealized model.

Qualitative researchers have used ideal types in two ways: to contrast the impact of contexts and as analogy.

Contrast Contexts.   Researchers who adopt a strongly interpretive approach may use ideal types to interpret data in a way that is sensitive to the context and cultural meanings of members. They do not test hypotheses or create a generalizable theory, but use the ideal type to bring out the specifics of each case and to emphasize the impact of the unique context.[11]

Researchers making contrasts between contexts often choose cases with dramatic contrasts or distinctive features. A criminologist might wish to compare criminal justice systems, for instance. He or she could begin by constructing an ideal type of system. This ideal type would lay out in general terms the essential structures (e.g., the institution of law enforcement) and process (e.g., punishment of offenders) of any criminal justice system. The ideal type is then used to gain insight

into the cultural differences related to specific criminal justice systems that the researcher happens to be interested in, such as People's Republic of China, the United States, Australia, and Saudi Arabia.

When comparing contexts, researchers do not use the ideal type to illustrate a theory in different cases or to discover regularities. Instead, they accentuate the specific and the unique. For example, the analysis would show that China's criminal justice system has some very unique features—one of them being "reeducation through labor" (Lawyers Committee for Human Rights, 1996). This term refers to the state's authority to punish "minor offenses not meriting a trial" by sending people to work camps for indefinite lengths of time (p. 176). This feature of the Chinese criminal justice system is usually reserved for dissidents who challenge state authority. It provides a way for the Chinese government to rid themselves of dissidents without having to parade them through a public trial.

Other methods of analysis focus on the general and ignore peculiarities. By contrast, a researcher who uses ideal types can show how unique features shape the operation of general processes. As Skocpol and Somers (1980:178) explained:

> *Above all, contrasts are drawn between or among individual cases. Usually such contrasts are developed with the aid of references to broad themes or orienting questions or ideal type concepts. Themes and questions may serve as frameworks for pointing out differences among cases. Ideal types may be used as sensitized devices—benchmarks against which to establish the particular features of each case.*

Analogies.   Ideal types are used as analogies to organize qualitative data. An *analogy* is a statement that two objects, processes, or events are similar to each other. Researchers use them to communicate ideas and to facilitate logical comparisons. Analogies transmit information about patterns in data by referring to something that is already known or an experience familiar to the reader. Analogies can describe relationships buried deep within many details and are a short-hand method for seeing patterns in a maze of specific events. They make it easier to compare social processes across different cases or settings.[12]

For example, a researcher may find it illuminating to think of private prisons as analogous to hotels. After all, both are first and foremost commercial enterprises in which making a profit is the key consideration. Consequently, there is an abiding interest to have "no vacancies." Researchers might begin thinking about the political influence wielded by prison corporations. Unlike hotels, prisons are not able to advertise in the popular media. Thus, an interesting research question, one prompted by the analogy, is this: How do prison corporations "advertise," which is to say, how do they attract customers? As you can see, thinking in terms of analogies usually suggests a line of inquiry that the criminologist can follow in an effort to formulate new ideas and questions.

The use of analogies to analyze qualitative data serves as a heuristic device (i.e., a device that helps one learn or see). It can represent something that is unknown and is especially valuable when researchers attempt to make sense of or explain data by referring to a deep structure or an underlying mechanism.[13] Ideal types do not provide a definitive test of an explanation. Rather, they guide the conceptual reconstruction of the mass of details into a systematic format.

Other Techniques

Qualitative researchers use many other analysis techniques. Here, we briefly look at four of the many other techniques to illustrate the variety (see Miles and Huberman [1994] for an extensive list). Some also stimulate researchers to gather data in new ways.

Network Analysis. The idea of social networks was discussed in Chapter 3 with network theory and in Chapter 9 with snowball sampling. Qualitative researchers often "map" the connections among a set of people, organizations, events, or places. Using sociograms and similar

mapping techniques, they can discover, analyze, and display sets of relations.

It would be very interesting, for example, to do a network analysis of death squad murderers who have been brought to justice. A criminologist might wish to see if the social networks of these murderers have in them any ties to the power elite, such as politicians, government officials, corporate leaders, or foreign military officers. Politically, this study would be extremely sensitive, as one might imagine, but methodologically it is quite doable and illustrates the usefulness of network analysis.[14]

Time Allocation Analysis. Time is an important resource. Researchers examine the way people or organizations spend or invest time to reveal implicit rules of conduct or priorities. Researchers document the duration or amount of time devoted to various activities. Often, people are unaware of or do not explicitly acknowledge the importance of an activity on which they spent time. For example, time allocation analysis is a qualitative technique particularly well suited for studying issues dealing with the nature of police work, the time-related determinants of delinquency, and the daily routines of criminals and victims.[15]

Flowchart and Time Sequence. In addition to the amount of time devoted to various activities, researchers analyze the order of events or decisions. Historical researchers have traditionally focused on documenting the sequence of events, but comparative and field researchers also look at flow or sequence. In addition to when events occur, researchers use the idea of a decision tree or flowchart to outline the order of decisions, to understand how one event or decision is related to others.

Many criminal justice students are probably familiar with the various flowcharts commonly used to identify the sequence of events occurring within a particular criminal justice system. In the United States, for example, the elaborate flowchart is built around five main processes. In sequence, they are (1) entry into the criminal justice system, including crime reporting, investigation, arrest, and booking; (2) prosecution and pre-trial services, including initial appearance, preliminary hearing, and bail; (3) adjudication, including grand jury, arraignment, plea bargaining, and trial; (4) sentencing and sanctions, including sentencing, appeal, and probation; and (5) corrections, including penitentiary, pardon, capital punishment, and parole (see U.S. Department of Justice, 1988).[16]

Multiple Sorting Procedure.   Multiple sorting is a technique that a researcher can use in field research or oral history. Its purpose is to discover how people categorize their experiences or classify items into systems of similar or different. Multiple sorting procedure has been adopted by cognitive anthropologists and psychologists. It can be used to collect, verify, or analyze data. Here is how it works. The researcher gives those being studied a list of terms, photos, places, names of people, and so on, and asks them to organize the lists into categories or piles. The subjects or members use categories of their own devising. Once sorted, the researcher asks about the criteria used. The subjects are then given the items again and asked to sort them in other ways they may think of them. There is a similarity to Thurstone scaling in that people sort items, but here, the number of piles and type of items differ. More significantly, the purpose of the sorting is not to create a uniform scale but to discover the variety of ways people understand the world.

Suppose, for example, one is doing research on the ways in which the public perceives the criminal justice system. The researcher could begin by providing subjects with a complete set of terms referring to the different parts of the criminal justice system. The terms, in the context of the United States, would include *arrest, grand jury, indictment, trial, sentencing, appeals,* and so on. The subject is then asked to sort the terms into, say, three or four piles based on different criteria. The first sorting of terms might be based on "how biased" each part of the system is. The second sorting could be based on "how expensive" each part is. The researcher could continue doing this

sorting-and-resorting exercise. Then, by examining the various ways the criminal justice terms were sorted, the researcher begins to understand how subjects understand and make sense out of the system.[17]

WHAT IS MISSING, OR THE IMPORTANCE OF NEGATIVE EVIDENCE

You have seen some of the ways that qualitative researchers analyze data. The emphasis has been on finding patterns, analyzing events, and using models to present what is found in the data. In this section, we look at how things that are *not* in the data can be important for analysis.

Negative Evidence

It may seem strange to look for things that did not happen, but the nonappearance of something can reveal a great deal and provide valuable insights. Many researchers emphasize positive data and ignore what is not explicitly in the data, but being alert to absences is also important.

For example, a field researcher doing an ethnography of corporate crime may take notice that the topic of conversation within the company depends on who is involved and who is not. It would be extremely rare to find top management standing around in the hall talking with employees about corporate fraud. Yet, that topic might receive quite a lot of attention among the employees whenever management is *not* around.

Take another example. The field researcher doing an ethnography of a police department perhaps notices that the police officers never mention the name of one particular informant whenever a certain police officer is in the group. This should get the researcher thinking about the informal relationships that have been formed and how these relationships might foster police corruption.

Historical-comparative researchers can use the same approach. Criminologists might want to understand, for example, why historically an anti-corporate crime movement never really gained momentum in the United States or why such a movement is relatively absent in the United States compared to other industrialized countries.

When rereading notes and coding data, it is easy to forget about things that do not appear, and it is hard to learn how to think about things that are not evident in the data but are important. One technique is to conduct a mind experiment. For example, perhaps a criminologist tries to imagine how things might be different if the general public tended to regard corporate crime as being more serious than other types of crime. Comparisons come in handy, as well. A researcher might try to imagine how ethnic minorities view the relative seriousness of corporate crime compared to how the majority ethnic group views it.

Lewis and Lewis (1980) provided seven kinds of *negative evidence* to consider.

Events That Do Not Occur. Some events are expected to occur on the basis of past experience, but do not. Perhaps an obvious example is this: Why has fear of crime in the United States not decreased in intensity in the face of declining crime rates?

Likewise, events may not occur if they happen to be in conflict with powerful segments of society. For instance, perhaps corporate crime in the United States is downplayed because the public implicitly realizes the enormous power base corporations have. This might help one understand the relative absence of an anticorporate crime movement in the United States.

Events of Which the Population Is Unaware. Some activities or events are not noticed by people in a setting or by researchers writing secondary documents. For example, a century ago in the United States, it was nearly unthinkable to imagine it possible that an genteel, affluent woman of "proper breeding" could commit brutal homicide. This blind spot in consciousness, if you will, helps explain the acquittal in the Lizzie Borden case. Lizzie Borden was the daughter of a millionaire banker in Fall River, Massachusetts, in the 1890s. She was a woman of high society, and the main suspect, as it turned out, in the brutal hatchet-slayings

of her stepmother and father. Despite strong evidence that she had in fact committed the murders, the community of Fall River could not bring itself to imagine a "lady would do it." Lizzie was never convicted of the crimes. The fact that members or participants in a setting are unaware of an issue does not mean that a researcher should ignore it or fail to look for its influence.[18]

Events the Population Wants to Hide. People may misrepresent events to protect themselves or others. For example, elites often refuse to discuss unethical behavior and may have documents destroyed or held from public access for a long period. Likewise, for many years, cases of domestic abuse went unreported in part because they violated such a serious taboo that it was simply hushed up.

Overlooked Commonplace Events. Everyday, routine events set expectations and create a taken-for-granted attitude. For example, a researcher may be analyzing the cultural context of corporate crime. In particular, he or she may be interested in studying the process of whistle-blowing in which an employee of the corporation comes forward to notify authorities that the corporation is in violation of a law. In some corporations, such as those typically found in Japan, cultural influences are so powerful over employees that they come to accept and take for granted the unethical and illegal practices of the corporation (Kerbo and Inoue, 1996).

Effects of a Researcher's Preconceived Notions. Researchers must take care not to let their prior theoretical framework or preconceived notions blind them to contrary events in a social setting. Strong prior notions of where to look and what data are relevant may inhibit a researcher from noticing other relevant or disconfirming evidence. A non-Islamic criminologist, for instance, might have great difficulty accepting Saudi Arabian forms of criminal punishment. That is to say, the criminologist's values related to human rights will probably cause him or her to view

Saudi punishments, such as public beheadings and hand amputation, as being totally incomprehensible, if not barbarous (Evans, 1995).

Unconscious Nonreporting.   Some events appear to be insignificant and not worthy of being reported in the mind of a researcher. Yet, if detailed observations are recorded, a critical rereading of notes looking for negative cases may reveal overlooked events.

For example, a researcher studying corporate crime in Japan might not initially think much about the *ringi* system of management. This system serves to generate consensus within the corporation by giving workers a voice in management decisions. However, upon deeper reflection, the researcher might realize that *ringi* inhibits whistle-blowing because it makes workers feel that they themselves are partly responsible for corporate decisions that may be unethical or illegal. In short, *ringi* diffuses responsibility for illegal corporate behavior (Kerbo and Inoue, 1996).

Conscious Nonreporting.   Researchers may omit aspects of the setting or events to protect individuals or relations in the setting. For example, a researcher may fail to present data that do not support his or her interpretation of the research findings. Researchers are bound by ethical principle to present all evidence, supportive or not, so that readers can decide for themselves what interpretation to put on the research findings.

Limitation by Omission

Analyzing qualitative data requires a researcher to make a special effort to include a diversity of perspectives in his or her interpretations of the data. For instance, a White male criminologist studying fear of crime might not grasp the unique perspectives that arise from racial, ethnic, age, and social class differences. That is to say, the researcher may not fully appreciate how a traditional female perspective conditions that person's fear of crime. Indeed, Eichler (1988) warned, "Gender insensi-

tivity in data interpretation takes two basic forms: ignoring sex as a socially significant variable, and ignoring a relevant sex-differentiated social context." Thus, when researchers interpret qualitative data, they need to be aware of alternative perspectives and not let the limits of the specific social group to which they belong blind them to a broader view.

DIAGRAMS AND OTHER TOOLS

Quantitative researchers use computers to analyze data statistically. The data are often presented in the form of charts, diagrams, tables, and graphs. These researchers have been quick to adopt new information-processing technology and to employ a wide array of graphs or diagrams to present data analysis.

By contrast, qualitative data analysis does not lend itself quite so readily to tables, charts, and so on as does quantitative analysis. That being said, however, qualitative researchers have taken the lead in introducing filmmaking technology into their research.

Diagrams and Qualitative Data

Qualitative data analysis can take different forms. Besides the written research report, qualitative data is often presented in the form of diagrams, maps, and charts. These tools help researchers organize ideas and systematically present relationships in the data.

Some researchers (e.g., Miles and Huberman, 1994) have begun to argue the importance of visual presentations of qualitative data. They stress that the way the data are presented or displayed is an integral aspect of qualitative analysis. Thus, they call for the increased use of a wide variety of techniques, including flowcharts, taxonomies, maps, lists, causal diagrams, organizational charts, as well as film and video recordings.

Outcroppings

Many qualitative researchers operate on an assumption that the empirical evidence they

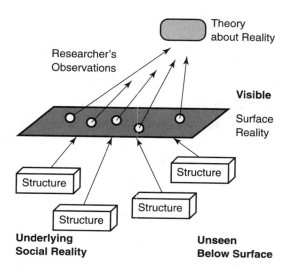

Researcher's
Observations

Theory
about Reality

Visible

Surface
Reality

Structure

Structure

Structure

Structure

**Underlying
Social Reality**

**Unseen
Below Surface**

FIGURE 16.3 Theory, Surface Reality, and Underlying Structures

gather is related to both their theoretical ideas and structures beneath observable reality. The relationship, modeled in Figure 16.3 suggests that a reseacher's data from the observable, surface reality are only samples of what happens on the visible, surface level. The researcher uses the data to generate and evaluate theories and generalizations. At the same time, he or she assumes that beneath the outer surface of reality lie deeper social structures or relationships.

The surface reality that we see only partially reflects what goes on unseen, beneath the surface. Events on the surface are *outcroppings,* to use a term from geology (see Fetterman, 1989:68). In geology, an outcropping is the part of bedrock that is exposed on the surface for people to see. It is the outward manifestation of central, solid features of the land. Geologists study outcroppings to get clues about what lies beneath the surface.

There are many things criminologists cannot directly observe yet are of research interest, nonetheless. For example, a researcher cannot actually observe the motivations behind a hate crime. Nor can a researcher observe firsthand the cultural norms and values that give rise to corporate crime.

Researchers use qualitative analysis for examining and organizing the observable data so that their concepts and theories reflect not only the empirical or surface level of reality but also shed light on the deeper structures and processes that may lie unseen beneath the surface of observable reality.

CONCLUSION

In this chapter, you have learned how researchers analyze qualitative data. In many respects, qualitative data are more difficult to deal with than data in the form of numbers. Numbers have mathematical properties that let a researcher use statistical procedures. Qualitative analysis requires more effort by an individual researcher to read and reread data notes, reflect on what is read, and make comparisons based on logic and judgment.

Most forms of qualitative data analysis involve coding and writing analytic memos. Both are labor-intensive efforts by the researcher to read over data carefully and think about them seriously. In addition, you learned about methods that researchers have used for the analysis of qualitative data. They are a sample of the many methods of qualitative data analysis. You also learned about the importance of thinking about negative evidence and events that are not present in the data.

Criminological research also involves preparing reports on a research project and dealing with ethical issues. These considerations are also part of the process of doing research and are discussed in Chapter 17 and in Appendix B.

KEY TERMS

analytic comparison	axial coding	illustrative method
analytic domain	empty boxes	method of agreement
analytic memo	ideal type	method of difference

negative evidence   outcropping   successive approximation
open coding   selective coding

REVIEW QUESTIONS

1. Identify four differences between quantitative and qualitative data analysis.
2. How does the process of conceptualization differ in qualitative and quantitative research?
3. How does data coding differ in quantitative and qualitative research, and what are the three kinds of coding used by a qualitative researcher?
4. What is the purpose of analytic memo writing in qualitative data analysis?
5. Describe *successive approximation*.
6. What are the *empty boxes* in the illustrative method and how are they used?
7. What is the difference between the method of agreement and the method of difference? Can a researcher use both together? Explain why or why not.
8. How would you analyze death squad activity?
9. How are ideal types used to contrast contexts?
10. Why is it important to look for *negative evidence,* or things that do not appear in the data, for a full analysis?

NOTES

1. See Miles and Huberman (1994) and Ragin (1987). These should not be confused with statistical techniques for "qualitative" data (see Haberman, 1978). These are sophisticated statistical techniques (e.g., logit and log linear) for quantitative variables where the data are at the nominal or ordinal level. They are better labeled as techniques for categorical data.
2. Sprague and Zimmerman (1989) discuss the importance of an explicit theory.
3. See Hammersley and Atkinson (1983:174–206) for a discussion of questions.
4. See also Horan (1987) and Strauss (1987:25) for multiple indicator measurement models with qualitative data.
5. For more on memoing, see Lester and Hadden (1980), Lofland and Lofland (1995:193–197), Miles and Huberman (1994:72–77), and Strauss (1987:107–129).
6. Also see Barzun and Graff (1970:255–274), Bogdan and Taylor (1975), Lofland and Lofland (1984: 131–140), Shafer (1980:171–200), Spradley (1979a, 1979b), and Schatzman and Strauss (1973: 104–120) on notes and codes.
7. For more on successive approximation and a debate over it, see Applebaum (1978a), McQuaire (1978,

1979), Paul Thompson (1978), Wardell (1979), and Young (1980).
8. For a discussion of empty boxes, see Bonnell (1980) and Smelser (1976).
9. For a discussion of the illustrative method, see Bonnell (1980) and Skocpol (1984). Bogdan and Taylor (1975:79) describe a similar method.
10. For a discussion of methods of difference and agreement, see Ragin (1987:36–42), Skocpol (1984), Skocpol and Somers (1980), and Stinchcombe (1978:25–29).
11. See Skocpol (1984) and Skocpol and Somers (1980).
12. For a discussion of analogies and models, see Barry (1975), Glucksmann (1974), Harré (1972), Hesse (1970), and Kaplan (1964).
13. For a discussion of the importance of analogies in social theory, see Lloyd (1986:127–132) and Stinchcombe (1978).
14. See Sanjek (1978) and Werner and Schoepfle (1987a).
15. See Gross (1984) and Miles and Huberman (1994:85, 119–126).
16. See Lofland and Lofland (1995:199–200) and Werner and Schoepfle (1987a:130–146).

17. See Canter and associates (1985) and Werner and Schoepfle (1987a:180–181).

18. See Blee and Billings (1986) for a discussion of analyzing "silences" and unnoticed features in ethnographic or historical text.

19. See Becker and Geer (1982) for a discussion of negative cases and preconceived notions.

RECOMMENDED READINGS

Miles, Matthew B., and A. Michael Huberman. (1994). *Qualitative data analysis,* 2nd ed. Thousand Oaks, CA: Sage. This unusual book is full of diagrams, lists, and charts. The authors present a collection of ways to analyze qualitative field research data. They move from field observation, to coding notes, to organizing codes into generalizations, and finally to presenting generalizations in the form of diagrams.

Ragin, Charles C. (1987). *The comparative method: Moving beyond qualitative and quantitative strategies.* Berkeley: University of California Press. Ragin presents an innovative method for the analysis of qualitative data, using Boolean algebra. His method is based on a systematic investigation of logical relationships. It gives researchers a way to analyze a small number of cases in which several conditions are measured as present or absent in each case. He applies the method to several major works in historical-comparative research to show its utility. The method helps researchers find instances where the combination of several conditions produces a specific outcome.

Stinchcombe, Arthur L. (1978). *Theoretical methods in social history.* New York: Academic Press. In this short book, Stinchcombe examines major works by Reinhard Bendix, Alexis de Tocqueville, Neil Smelser, and Leon Trotsky to discover how they used theory in the analysis of historical phenomena. He argues for a method of qualitative historical analysis that forms concepts from specific details then uses analogies to organize descriptions of historical events into causal explanations.

Strauss, Anselm. (1987). *Qualitative analysis for social scientists.* New York: Cambridge University Press. Strauss provides an approach for the analysis of qualitative data based on a grounded theory model from field research. Although parts of this book are somewhat sophisticated, it is a step-by-step guide for qualitative data analysis, from gaining access to writing up a report. Strauss gives extensive examples of field notes, which he then analyzes.

CHAPTER 17

ETHICAL AND POLITICAL ISSUES IN CRIMINOLOGICAL RESEARCH

Happy are those few nations that have not waited for the slow succession of coincidence and human vicissitude to force some little turn for the better after the limit of evil has been reached, but have facilitated the immediate progress by means of good laws. And humanity owes a debt of gratitude to that philosopher who, from the obscurity of his isolated study, had the courage to scatter among the multitude the first seeds, so long unfruitful, of useful truths.

—Cesare Beccaria, *On Crimes and Punishment,* p. 8.

INTRODUCTION

We have now come full circle. To raise a concern over research ethics forces us to confront the fundamentals of our science. It brings us to our starting questions: What is the nature of this science of justice? What purposes and "useful truths" should surface from the depths of criminological research? Has the researcher the courage to challenge the power elite, to question existing inequalities? Might anyone incur injury in the research process—emotional, political, social, cultural, or economic injury resulting from the study? Has the knowledge been gained ethically, and have these gains been spread evenly across lines of gender, age, race, ethnicity, and class? These are the classical questions. They have been at the center of criminology, criminal justice, or justice studies, for hundreds of years.

The philosophical context for discussing research ethics in contemporary criminology falls within the tradition of humanism that traces back to the Enlightenment movement of the eighteenth century. This sweeping celebration of human rights grew in counterposition to the brutal ethics of feudal systems of justice. Consider the following description of the death of Jean Calas, a French merchant wrongly executed for the murder of his son in 1762:

> In a chemise, with head and feet bare, [he] will be taken in a cart, from the palace prison to the Cathedral. There, kneeling in front of the main door, holding in his hands a torch of yellow wax weighing two pounds, he must take the "amende honorable," asking pardon of God, of the Kings, and of justice. Then the executioner should take him in the cart to the Place Saint Georges, where up on a scaffold his arms, legs, thighs, and loins will be broken and crushed. Finally, the prisoner should be placed upon a wheel, with his face turned to the sky, alive and in pain, and repent, for his said crimes and misdeeds, all the while imploring God for his life, thereby, to serve as an example and to instill terror in the wicked. (Beirne, 1993:11–12)

The Enlightenment philosophers were outraged by this brand of justice. They rejected these cruel methods of punishment and state-sponsored vengeance as violations of human rights. Synthesizing the thoughts of others, Beccaria (1764) articulated a reformist conception of justice which has laid the groundwork for contemporary criminal justice ethics. Criminology students around the world are well versed in these classical reforms: the disavowing of torture and the death penalty, the proportionate fit between crimes and punishments, the rule of law, and the certainty of punishment for rich and poor alike, to highlight just a few.

However necessary, such reforms are not sufficient in themselves, but rather mark the beginning of a long journey to institutionalize humane systems of justice everywhere and for everyone. To be sure, it is a journey fraught with debate and controversy: Have classical reforms gone far enough? Should not criminal justice ethics fit into a broader set of ethical concerns over social justice? And what responsibilities reside with the researcher in the face of these broader concerns over human rights and social justice? These are the sort of questions criminologists cannot avoid.

Beccaria's (1764) reference to the "philosopher . . . in isolated study" is understood in contemporary terms to mean the criminologist involved in ethical, scientific research. Clearly, there must be standards for ethical research within our scientific discipline. It is a social obligation that no criminologist has the authority to breach. In this last chapter, the authors lay out these standards or agreed-upon principles of ethical research. You will see how often there is a balancing act between the pursuit of criminological knowledge, on the one hand, and the dignity, privacy, and human rights of research participants, on the other.[1]

ETHICAL CONCERNS AND THE INDIVIDUAL RESEARCHER

The Individual Researcher

Ethics begin and end with you, the researcher. A researcher's personal moral code is the strongest defense against unethical behavior. Before, during, and after conducting a study, a researcher has opportunities to, and *should,* reflect on research actions and consult his or her conscience. Ethical research depends on the integrity of the individual researcher and his or her values.

Ethics come into play from the outset. The researcher's decision over what to study and what research questions to ask (and which to ignore) should itself be guided by ethical principles. No amount of concern over the ethics of the research process can transform an unethical research question into an ethical one. Criminologists need to keep this in mind as they establish their research agendas.

Why Be Ethical?

Given that most criminologists are genuinely concerned about human rights, why would a researcher act in an ethically irresponsible manner? Outside of the rare disturbed individual, most unethical behavior results from pressures on researchers to take ethical shortcuts. Criminologists are under considerable pressure to build a career, publish, and conform to the vested interests of the criminal justice system, which are factors that often drive ethical issues into the background. Ethical research may require criminologists to raise critical questions about the existing institutions of criminal justice. Raising the critical question often is tantamount to removing oneself from research funding opportunities that issue from these government institutions.

Moreover, written ethical standards typically are only vaguely worded philosophical principles. For example, the authors wanted to include in this book the codes of ethics for the two main criminology/criminal justice associations in the United States. However, neither professional organization has, at this writing, formally adopted a code of ethics.

There are few rewards available for ethical research. The unethical researcher, if caught, faces public humiliation, a ruined career, and possible legal action, but the ethical researcher wins no praise. Ethical behavior arises from a sensitivity to ethical concerns that researchers internalize during their professional training, from a professional role, and from personal contact with other researchers. Moreover, the norms of the scientific community reinforce ethical behavior with an emphasis on honesty and openness. Researchers who are oriented toward their professional role, who are committed to the scientific ethos, and who interact regularly with other researchers are likely to act ethically.

Scientific Misconduct.   The research community and government agencies that fund research oppose unethical behavior called scientific misconduct, which includes research fraud and plagiarism. *Scientific misconduct* occurs when a researcher falsifies or distorts the data or the methods of data collection, or plagiarizes the work of others. It also includes significant departures from the generally accepted practices of the scientific community for doing or reporting on research. Research institutes and universities have policies and procedures to detect misconduct, report it to the scientific community and funding agencies, and penalize researchers who engage in it (e.g., through a pay cut or loss of job).[2]

Research fraud occurs when a researcher fakes or invents data that were not really collected, or falsely reports how research was conducted. Though rare, it is treated very seriously. The most famous case of fraud was the scandal of Sir Cyril Burt, the father of British educational psychology. Burt died in 1971 as an esteemed researcher who was famous for his studies with twins that showed a genetic basis of intelligence. In 1976, it was discovered that he had falsified data and the names of coauthors. Unfortunately, the scientific community had been misled for nearly 30 years.[3]

Plagiarism is fraud that occurs when a researcher steals the ideas or writings of another or uses them without citing the source. A special type of plagiarism is stealing the work of another researcher, an assistant, or a student, and misrepresenting it as one's own. These are serious breaches of ethical standards, but they do sometimes occur.[4]

Unethical but Legal. Perhaps more common is the situation in which the researcher acts unethically—that is, against accepted professional standards—yet no law has been broken. Tewksbury and Gagne (1997) identified just such an aspect of criminological research. The issue has to do with covert field research. The ethical concern, as they put it, is this:

> *When researchers know, or strongly suspect, that research subjects have attributed identities to them that are in fact different from their actual social identities, the question of whether to self-disclose information that would "correct" these assumptions is raised. (p. 141)*

The issue of research deception will be discussed in much greater detail a bit later, but it is important to recognize at this point that unethical research behavior is not necessarily illegal behavior. (See Figure 17.1 for relations between legal and moral actions.)

Power

The relationship between the researcher and subjects or employee-assistants involves power and trust. The experimenter, survey director, or research investigator has power relative to subjects or assistants. The power is legitimated by credentials, expertise, training, and the role of science in modern society. Some ethical issues involve an abuse of power and trust.

The researcher's authority to conduct research, granted by professional communities and the larger society, is accompanied by a responsibility to guide, protect, and oversee the interests of the people being studied. For example, a physician was discovered to have conducted experimental gynecological surgery on 33 women without their permission. The women had trusted the doctor, but he had abused the trust that the women, the professional community, and society placed in him.[5]

The issue of power is particularly prominent in research projects involving individuals who are under criminal justice supervision or custody. One can imagine how a person on probation, for example, might feel pressure to participate in a

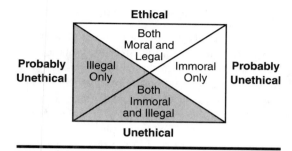

FIGURE 17.1   Typology of Legal and Moral Actions in Research

project even though he or she may not really want to. In real terms, such individuals may think they are in no position to refuse to be involved in the research.

ETHICAL ISSUES INVOLVING RESEARCH SUBJECTS

Have you ever been a subject in a research study? If so, how were you treated? More attention is focused on the possible negative effects of research on those being studied than any other ethical issue, beginning with concerns about biomedical research. Ethical research requires balancing the value of advancing knowledge against the value of noninterference in the lives of others. Giving research subjects absolute rights of noninterference could make empirical research impossible, but giving researchers absolute rights of inquiry could nullify subjects' basic human rights. The moral question becomes: When, if ever, are researchers justified in risking physical harm or injury to those being studied, causing them great embarrassment, or frightening them?

The law and codes of ethics recognize some clear prohibitions: Never cause unnecessary or irreversible harm to subjects; secure prior voluntary consent when possible; and never unnecessarily humiliate, degrade, or release harmful information about specific individuals that was collected for research purposes. These are minimal standards and are subject to interpretation (e.g., What does *unnecessary* mean in a specific situation?).

Origins of Human Subject Protection

Concern over the treatment of research subjects arose after the revelation of gross violations of basic human rights in the name of science. The most notorious violations were "medical experiments" conducted on Jews and others in Nazi Germany. In these experiments, terrible tortures were committed. For example, people were placed in freezing water to see how long it took them to die, people were purposely starved to death, and limbs were severed from children and transplanted onto others.[6]

Such human rights violations do not occur only in Germany, nor did they happen only long ago. A symbol of unethical research is the Tuskegee Syphilis Study, also known as *Bad Blood*. Until the 1970s, when a newspaper report caused a scandal to erupt, the U.S. Public Health Service sponsored a study in which poor, uneducated African American men in Alabama suffered and died of untreated syphilis, while researchers studied the severe physical disabilities that appear in advanced stages of the disease. The study began in 1929, before penicillin was available to treat the disease, but it continued long after treatment was available. Despite their unethical treatment of the subjects, the researchers were able to publish their results for 40 years.[7]

Unfortunately, the Bad Blood scandal was not unique. During the 1960s, live cancer cells were injected into ill patients without consent. The U.S. military gave LSD (a hallucinogenic drug) to unsuspecting individuals, a few of whom became mentally ill from the experience, and exposed soldiers to nuclear radiation, later resulting in high cancer rates. These examples are clear violations of ethical standards: The subjects suffered permanent physical harm and they did not give prior voluntary consent to participate in the study.[8]

Physical Harm, Psychological Abuse, Stress, or Legal Jeopardy

Social research can harm a research subject in several ways: physical harm, psychological harm, legal harm, and harm to a person's career or income. Physical harm is rare, even in biomedical

research, where the intervention is much greater; 3 to 5 percent of studies involved any subject who suffered any harm. Different types of harm are more likely in different types of research (e.g., in experiments versus field research). Researchers need to be aware of all types of harm and minimize them at all times.[9]

Physical Harm. A straightforward ethical principle is that researchers should not cause physical harm. An ethical researcher anticipates risks before beginning research, including basic safety concerns (safe buildings, furniture, and equipment). He or she screens out high-risk subjects (those with heart conditions, mental breakdown, or seizures) if stress is involved and anticipates the danger of injury or physical attacks on research subjects or assistants. The researcher accepts moral and legal responsibility for injury due to participation in research and terminates a project immediately if he or she can no longer guarantee the physical safety of the people involved (see the Zimbardo study in Box 17.1).

Psychological Abuse, Stress, or Loss of Self-Esteem. The risk of physical harm is rare in research, but social researchers may place people in stressful, embarrassing, anxiety-producing, or unpleasant situations. Researchers learn about how people respond in real-life, highly anxiety-producing situations by placing subjects in realistic situations of psychological discomfort or stress. Is it unethical to cause discomfort? The ethics of the famous Milgram obedience study are still debated (see Box 17.1). Some say that the precautions taken and the knowledge gained outweighed the stress and potential psychological harm that subjects experienced. Others believe that the extreme stress and the risk of permanent harm were too great.

Criminological research has the potential to create high levels of discomfort or anxiety in research subjects. Consider, for example, Gagne's (1996) research with battered women. The researcher conducted in-depth interviews with these women, asking them about their experiences as victims of domestic assault. Dekeseredy and col-

Box 17.1_____

Three Cases of Ethical Controversy

Stanley Milgram's *obedience study* (Milgram, 1963, 1965, 1974) attempted to discover how the horrors of the Holocaust under the Nazis could have occurred by examining the strength of social pressure to obey authority. After signing "informed consent forms," subjects were assigned, in rigged random selection, to be a "teacher" while a confederate was the "pupil." The teacher was to test the pupil's memory of word lists and increase the electric shock level if the pupil made mistakes. The pupil was located in a nearby room, so the teacher could hear but not see the pupil. The shock apparatus was clearly labeled with increasing voltage. As the pupil made mistakes and the teacher turned switches, she or he also made noises as if in severe pain. The researcher was present and made comments such as "You must go on" to the teacher. Milgram reported, "Subjects were observed to sweat, tremble, stutter, bite their lips, groan and dig their fingernails into their flesh. These were characteristic rather than exceptional responses to the experiment" (Milgram, 1963:375). The percentage of subjects who would shock to dangerous levels was dramatically higher than expected. Ethical concerns arose over the use of deception and the extreme emotional stress experienced by subjects.

In Laud Humphreys's (Humphreys, 1975) *tearoom trade study* (a study of male homosexual encounters in public restrooms), about 100 men were observed engaging in sexual acts as Humphreys pretended to be a "watchqueen" (a voyeur and lookout). Subjects were followed to their cars, and their license numbers were secretly recorded. Names and addresses were obtained from police registers when Humphreys posed as a market researcher. One year later, in disguise,

Humphreys used a deceptive story about a health survey to interview the subjects in their homes. Humphreys was careful to keep names in safety deposit boxes, and identifiers with subject names were burned. He significantly advanced knowledge of homosexuals who frequent "tearooms" and overturned previous false beliefs about them. There has been controversy over the study: The subjects never consented; deception was used; and the names could have been used to blackmail subjects, to end marriages, or to initiate criminal prosecution.

In the *Zimbardo prison experiment* (Zimbardo, 1972, 1973; Zimbardo et al., 1973, 1974), male students were divided into two role-playing groups: guards and prisoners. Before the experiment, volunteer students were given personality tests, and only those in the "normal" range were chosen. Volunteers signed up for two weeks, and prisoners were told that they would be under surveillance and would have some civil rights suspended, but that no physical abuse was allowed. In a simulated prison in the basement of a Stanford University building, prisoners were deindividualized (dressed in standard uniforms and called only by their numbers) and guards were militarized (with uniforms, nightsticks, and reflective sunglasses). Guards were told to maintain a reasonable degree of order and served 8-hour shifts, while prisoners were locked up 24 hours per day. Unexpectedly, the volunteers became too caught up in their roles. Prisoners became passive and disorganized, while guards became aggressive, arbitrary, and dehumanizing. By the sixth day, Zimbardo called off the experiment for ethical reasons. The risk of permanent psychological harm, and even physical harm, was too great.

---

leagues (1997) faced similar ethical concerns in their study of women's use of physical force in dating relationships.[10] The women were asked to recount personal situations of dating violence and what their reactions to it were. In both examples, the researchers were sensitive to the possible harm to their subjects' self-esteem.[11]

Only experienced researchers who take precautions before inducing anxiety or discomfort

should consider conducting experiments that induce significant stress or anxiety. They should consult with others who have conducted similar studies and mental health professionals when planning the study, screen out high-risk populations (e.g., those with emotional problems or a weak heart), and arrange for emergency interventions or termination of the research if dangerous situations arise. Researchers should always get informed consent (to be discussed) before the research and debrief subjects immediately afterward.

Researchers should never create *unnecessary* stress, beyond the minimal amount needed to create the desired effect, or stress that has no direct, legitimate research purpose. Knowing the minimal amount comes with experience. It is better to begin with too little stress, risking finding no effect, than to create too much. If the level of stress could have long-term effects, the researcher should follow up and offer free psychological counseling.

Research that creates stress and anxiety also carries the danger that experimenters will develop a callous or manipulative attitude toward others. Researchers report guilt and regrets after conducting experiments that caused psychological harm to subjects. Experiments that place subjects in anxiety-producing situations may produce discomfort for the ethical researcher.

Legal Harm.   A researcher is responsible for protecting subjects from increased risk of arrest. If participation in research increases the risk of arrest, subjects will distrust researchers and be unwilling to participate in future research. Researchers may be able to secure clearance from law enforcement authorities before conducting certain types of research. For example, the U.S. Department of Justice provides written waivers for researchers studying criminal behavior.

Potential legal harm is one criticism of the 1975 study by Humphreys (see Box 17.1). Polsky (1997:220) addressed the issue with respect to field research:

> The problem, although it exists in studying a criminal enmeshed with the law, is usually magnified in dealing with an uncaught criminal in his natural surroundings. . . . There is more of a possibility that he [the "uncaught criminal"] might be hurt by you, that is, he has more to lose than someone already in jail (emphasis added)

A related ethical issue arises when a researcher learns of illegal activity when collecting data. A researcher must weigh the value of protecting the researcher/subject relationship and the benefits to future researchers against potential harm to innocent people. A researcher bears the cost of his or her judgment. For example, in his field research on police, Van Maanen (1982:114–115) reported seeing police beat people and witnessing illegal acts and irregular procedures, but said, "On and following these troublesome incidents . . . I followed police custom: I kept my mouth shut." Polsky (1997:224) related the issue to one of establishing trust in field research, and offered this advice:[12]

> There is another kind of compromise that must be made, this by way of keeping faith with informants. . . . In reporting one's research it is sometimes necessary to write of certain things more vaguely and skimpily than one would prefer. But this is more of a literary than a scientific compromise; there need be no distortion of the sociological points involved.

Observing illegal behavior may be central to a research project. A researcher who covertly observes and records illegal behavior, then supplies information to law enforcement authorities, violates ethical standards regarding research subjects and undermines future research. Yet, a researcher who fails to report illegal behavior indirectly permits criminal behavior and could be charged as an accessory to a crime. Is the researcher a professional seeking knowledge or a free-lance undercover informant?

Other Harm to Subjects.   Research subjects may face other types of harm. For example, a survey interview may create anxiety and discomfort among subjects who are asked to recall unpleasant events. The ethical researcher is sensitive to any harm to subjects, considers possible precautions, and weighs potential harm against potential benefits. Another risk of harm to subjects is that of a negative effect on their careers or incomes.

Suppose, for example, a researcher conducts an experiment to determine the negative effects of being a known felon has on one's employment prospects. In this experiment, the researcher has two groups: a test group and a control group. For the test group, the researcher makes it known to the prospective employer that the subject is a convicted felon, whereas that same information is not made known about the control group. Whatever benefits might be garnered from the research, the experiment does diminish the employability of the test group, and, to that extent, raises serious ethical concerns.

The ethical researcher considers the consequences of research for the lives of those being studied. But there is no fixed answer to such questions. A researcher must evaluate each case, weigh potential harm against potential benefits, and bear the responsibility for the decision.

Deception

Has anyone ever told you a half-truth or lie to get you to do something? How did you feel about it? Researchers follow the ethical *principle of voluntary consent:* Never force anyone to participate in research, and do not lie unless it is required for legitimate research reasons. The people who participate in social research should, under most conditions, explicitly agree to participate. The right of a person not to participate becomes a critical issue whenever the researcher uses deception, disguises the research, or uses covert research methods.[13]

Criminologists sometimes deceive or lie to subjects in field and experimental research. A researcher might misrepresent his or her actions or true intentions for legitimate methodological reasons: If subjects knew the true purpose, they would modify their behavior, making it impossible to learn of their real behavior, or access to a research site might be impossible if he or she told the truth. Deception is never preferable if the researcher could accomplish the same thing without deception. Experimental researchers often deceive subjects to prevent them from learning the true hypothesis and to reduce reactive effects. Deception is acceptable only if there is a specific methodological purpose for it, and even then, it should be used only to the minimal degree necessary. A researcher who uses deception should obtain informed consent, never misrepresent risks, and always debrief subjects afterwards. He or she can describe the basic proce-

dures involved and conceal only specific information about hypotheses being tested.

Covert observation may be required in some field research settings to gain entry and access. If a covert stance is not essential, a researcher should never use it. If he or she does not know whether covert access is necessary, then a strategy of gradual disclosure may be best. It is better to err in the direction of disclosing one's true identity and purpose.

Tewksbury and Gagne (1997) have considered three alternatives to overcome the problem of deception inherent in covert field research commonly found in criminology. The three alternatives are:

> In the realm of criminal justice (especially corrections) research, there is a growing movement to incorporate a team research approach in which a community insider and an outsider cooperatively pursue research. Or, one can present oneself as a potential community member. Or, one can have a respected individual who holds a position of authority introduce one. (p. 134)

Covert research remains controversial, and some researchers feel that all covert research is unethical.[14] The code of ethics of the American Anthropological Association condemns it as "impractical and undesirable." Even those who accept covert research as ethical in some situations argue that it should be used only when overt observation is impossible. In addition, if possible, the researcher should inform subjects of the observation afterwards and give them an opportunity to express concerns.

Deception and covert research may increase mistrust and cynicism, and diminish public respect for criminologists. Misrepresentation in field research is analogous to being an undercover agent or informer in nondemocratic societies. Deception can increase distrust by people who are frequently studied. In one case, the frequent use of deception reduced helping behavior. When a student was shot at the University of Washington in Seattle in 1973, students crossing the campus made no attempt to assist. Later, it was discovered that many of the bystanders did not help because they thought that the shooting was staged as part of an experiment.[15]

Barbash and Taylor (1997:54–55) summarized some of the ethical complexities involving deception as they pertain to ethnographic filmmaking as well as criminological field research:

> *Can deception ever be justified? Most ethical codes say no. But what if you are deceiving someone whom most people call unethical anyway? If you don't reveal bias to your subjects are you deceiving them? Suppose you wanted to make a film about neo-Nazis in Europe or about the militia in Montana in the United States; do you try to "keep an open mind"? You could film them in plain observational style, with no obvious editorializing of your own, knowing full well that they would "undo" themselves before an "outside" audience. If you intend from the outset to be critical of them, or at least anticipate that your viewers will be, do you tell them this? Do you feel morally obliged to be as honest with them as you would be with anyone else? Are you certain that you're faithful to a higher ethical imperative than they are? On the other hand, if no one ever filmed acts that they considered immoral, imagine what an impoverished record one would have of human existence. There are surely situations in which the most ethical response to an immoral act is to bring it to the attention of the public. Clearly, all these questions have to be considered very carefully on a case-by-case basis.*

Informed Consent

A fundamental ethical principle of criminological research is: Never coerce anyone into participating; participation *must* be voluntary. It is not enough to get permission from subjects; they need to know what they are being asked to participate in so that they can make an informed decision. Subjects can become aware of their rights and what they are getting involved in when they read and sign a statement giving *informed consent,* a written agreement to participate given by subjects after they learn something about the research procedure.

Barbash and Taylor's (1997:52) discussion of the subtle forms of coercion in ethnographic filmmaking also generally apply to criminological research:

> *Numerous documentaries, for instance, have been made over the years about the police in the United States. Often the filmmakers establish initial contact with the police and then enjoy access thereby to all the people the police come in contact with. Many such films have been shot "over the shoulders" of law enforcement officers. Few people entangled with the police have the time or presence of mind to turn to a camera operator and ask them to stop shooting. And if a film crew, buttressed by the police, asks them to sign a release, they probably won't call a lawyer to look over the form. Can we really say that they were not coerced?*

Informed consent statements provide specific information (see Box 17.2).[16] A general statement about the kinds of procedures or questions involved and the uses of the data are sufficient for informed consent. In a study by Singer (1978), one random group of survey respondents received a detailed informed consent statement and another did not. No significant differences were discovered. If anything, people who refused to sign such a statement were more likely to guess or answer "no response" to questions.

Box 17.2 _____

Informed Consent

Informed consent statements contain the following:

1. A brief description of the purpose and procedure of the research, including the expected duration of the study
2. A statement of any risks or discomfort associated with participation
3. A guarantee of anonymity and the confidentiality of records
4. The identification of the researcher and of where to receive information about subjects' rights or questions about the study
5. A statement that participation is completely voluntary and can be terminated at any time without penalty
6. A statement of alternative procedures that may be used
7. A statement of any benefits or compensation provided to subjects and the number of subjects involved
8. An offer to provide a summary of findings

In their meta-analysis of the literature on giving assurances of confidentiality (see Chapter 5 on meta-analysis), Singer and colleagues (1995) found that assuring confidentiality modestly improved responses when researchers asked about highly sensitive topics. In other situations, extensive assurances of confidentiality failed to affect how or whether subjects responded.

Signed informed consent statements are optional for most survey, field, and secondary data research, but are often mandated for experimental research. They are impossible to obtain in documentary research and in most telephone interview studies. The general rule is: The greater the risk of potential harm to subjects, the greater the need for a written consent statement.

Issues of informed consent become particularly complex when researching people in positions of power.[17] The following five principles, for instance, guided the making of a documentary film about British corporations. They are instructive of the sort of understanding field researchers studying corporate crime might reach with corporate executives in order to gain access:

1. *The filmmakers would shoot only what had been agreed on by both sides.*
2. *No scoops to newspapers. This was essential when a great deal of confidential information was disclosed.*
3. *The films would be released only when both sides agreed to it. In other words, the filmmakers weren't setting out to embarrass the subjects.*
4. *In return for the above, the filmmakers asked for total access to one or two subjects they had agreed to film—that is, the right to film them at any time and walk in on any conversation.*
5. *The filming would be without lights and elaborate staging that might introduce an extremely unnatural setting, which could bias the process of making a documentary film. (*Barbash and Taylor, 1997)

Special Populations and New Inequalities

Special Populations and Coercion. Some populations or groups of subjects are not capable of giving true voluntary informed consent. They may lack the necessary competency or may be in-

directly coerced. Students, prison inmates, employees, military personnel, the homeless, welfare recipients, children, or the mentally retarded may agree to participate in research. Yet, they may not be fully capable of making a decision, or may agree to participate only because some desired good—such as higher grades, early parole, promotions, or additional services—requires an agreement to participate.

It is unethical to involve "incompetent" people (e.g., children, the mentally retarded, etc.) in research unless two conditions are met: A legal guardian grants written permission, and the researcher follows all ethical principles against harm to subjects. For example, a researcher wants to conduct a survey of smoking and drug/alcohol use among high school students. If it is conducted on school property, school officials must give permission, and written parental permission is needed for any subject who is a legal minor. It is best to ask permission from each student, as well.

It is unethical to coerce people to participate, including offering them special benefits that they cannot otherwise attain. Whether coercion to participate is involved can be a complex issue, and a researcher must evaluate the issue in each case. For example, a convicted criminal is given the alternative of imprisonment or participation in an experimental rehabilitation program. The convicted criminal may not believe in the benefits of the program, but the researcher may believe that it will help the criminal. This is a case of coercion, but the researcher must judge whether the benefits to the subject and to society outweigh the ethical prohibition on coercion.

Creating New Inequalities. Another type of harm occurs when one group of subjects is denied some service or benefit as a result of participation in a research project. This may be unavoidable for good research design. For example, a researcher wanting to do a field experiment on the effectiveness of policing might decide to compare test and control groups, as was similarly done in the famous Kansas City police study. Suppose the control group (i.e., one area of the city) received no police presence for a period of time, whereas another part of the city received intensive police presence. To ensure that neither area of the city is adversely affected by the field experiment, the researcher could employ a *crossover design*. This design involves having the control group become the test group and vice versa (i.e., crossover) at different points in the experiment.

Privacy, Anonymity, and Confidentiality

How would you feel if private details about your personal life were shared with the public without your knowledge? Because criminological researchers transgress the privacy of subjects in order to study social behavior, they must take precautions to protect subjects' privacy.

Privacy. Survey researchers invade a person's privacy when they probe into beliefs, backgrounds, and behaviors in a way that reveals intimate private details. Experimental researchers sometimes use two-way mirrors or hidden microphones to "spy" on subjects. Even if subjects are told they are being studied, they are unaware of what the experimenter is looking for. Field researchers may observe very private aspects of another's behavior or eavesdrop on conversations. In field experimentation and ethnographic field research, privacy may be violated without advance warning.

All of these situations call into play considerations of ethics. The ethical researcher violates privacy only to the minimum degree necessary and only for defensible research purposes. Moreover, the researcher must take great care in protecting the personal information on research subjects from public disclosure.[18]

In a few situations, privacy is protected by law. One case of the invasion of privacy led to the passage of a federal law. In the *Wichita Jury Study* of 1954, University of Chicago Law School researchers recorded jury discussions to examine group processes in jury deliberations. Although the findings were significant and great precautions were taken, a congressional investigation followed and a law was passed in 1956 to prohibit the "bugging" of any grand or petit jury for any purpose, even with the jurors' consent.[19]

Anonymity. Researchers protect privacy by not disclosing a subject's identity after information is gathered. This takes two forms, both of which require separating an individual's identity from his or her responses: anonymity and confidentiality.

Anonymity means that subjects remain anonymous or nameless. For example, the field researcher often uses a phony name to disguise, and thereby protect, the true identity of research subjects. Researchers commonly use this technique to protect the site location of their research, as was the case in Skolnick's (1994) famous study of policing in "Westville."

Essentially, all we know about Westville is this:

> Data for this book were drawn from a study of criminal law officials conducted by the author mainly in Westville, a city of approximately four hundred thousand with a nonwhite population of about 30 percent. . . .
>
> First, Westville is a "real" city. . . . Along with being a real city, Westville is reputed to have an exemplary machinery for administering criminal justice. . . . The salutary reputation of Westville's criminal justice machinery extends through the United States and even abroad. . . . Consequently, because Westville is generally regarded as a model of efficiency and modernity, its administration of criminal law cannot be claimed to be representative of the United States as a whole. On the contrary, it would be more accurate to consider it as an example of the top stratum of American criminal justice administration. (pp. 23–25)

Confidentiality. Even if anonymity is not possible, researchers should protect confidentiality. Anonymity protects the identity of specific individuals from being known. *Confidentiality* means that information may have names attached to it, but the researcher holds it in confidence or keeps it secret from the public. The information is not released in a way that permits linking specific individuals to specific responses and is publicly presented only in an aggregate form (e.g., percentages, means, etc.).

A researcher may provide anonymity without confidentiality, or vice versa, although they usually go together. Anonymity without confidentiality means that all the details about a specific individual are made public, but the individual's name is withheld. Confidentiality without anonymity means that information is not made public, but a researcher privately links individual names to specific responses.

Attempts to protect the identity of subjects from public disclosure has resulted in elaborate procedures: eliciting anonymous responses, using a third-party list custodian who holds the key to coded lists, or using the random-response technique. Past abuses suggest that such measures may be necessary. For example, Diener and Crandall (1978:70) reported that during the 1950s, the U.S. State Department and the FBI requested research records on individuals who had been involved in the famous Kinsey sex study. The Kinsey Sex Institute refused to comply with the government. The institute threatened to destroy all records rather than release any. Eventually, the government agencies backed down. The moral duty and ethical code of the researchers obligated them to destroy the records rather than give them to government officials. As Nelkin (1982b:705) remarked, "The right of researchers to protect their subjects is especially vulnerable when it conflicts with political or policy goals."

Confidentiality may protect subjects from physical harm. For example, one of the authors met a researcher who studied the inner workings of the secret police in a nondemocratic society. Had he released the names of informants, they would have faced certain death or imprisonment. To protect the subjects, he wrote all notes in code and kept all records secretly locked away. Although he resided in the United States, he was physically threatened by the foreign government and discovered attempts to burglarize his office.

In other situations, other principles may take precedence over protecting confidentiality. For example, if a criminologist discovers in the course of his or her field research that an assassination is being planned by the group under study, the researcher must weigh the benefit of confidentiality against the potential cost of the murder taking place. The ethical thing to do would be to contact

authorities with the specific information needed to prevent the assassination. It is worth noting that court precedents have refused to acknowledge the confidentiality of research data.[20]

In 1989, the U.S. government established a way to protect confidentiality. A researcher can apply for a *certificate of confidentiality,* issued by the U.S. National Institute of Health, by submitting a research proposal. The certificate guarantees the confidentiality of data on subjects from federal, state, or local government criminal or civil legal action. The research data are protected whether or not federal government funds were used to support the project. Unfortunately, the certificate protects the data on subjects, but it does not protect the researcher from legal action.

A special concern with anonymity and confidentiality arises when a researcher studies "captive" populations (e.g., students, prisoners, employees, patients, and soldiers). Gatekeepers, or those in positions of authority, may restrict access unless they receive information on subjects.[21] For example, a researcher studies drug use and sexual activity among high school students. School authorities agree to cooperate under two conditions: (1) students need parental permission to participate and (2) school officials get the names of all drug users and sexually active students in order to assist the students with counseling and inform the students' parents. An ethical researcher will refuse to continue rather than meet the second condition.

ETHICS AND THE SCIENTIFIC COMMUNITY

Police officers, criminal law attorneys, corrections personnel, and most other criminal justice practitioners have adopted a *code of ethics,* along with peer review boards and licensing requirements, which serve to allow a measure of governmental oversight and regulatory discipline.[22] Researchers in criminology, unfortunately, have not yet codified their ethical stance. This is unfortunate, for a code of ethics sets the benchmark for standards of professionalism and common decency. It represents, to borrow Max Weber's notion, the ideal type against which criminological research is to be evaluated.

Most international and national social science organizations have a code of ethics. The American Anthropological Association, the American Sociological Association, the American Political Science Association, and many more have codes of ethics. The codes state in principled terms the differences between proper and improper behavior on the part of the researcher.

Not all researchers may agree on every detail and interpretation, but researchers are expected to uphold the ethical standards embraced by their community of scientists. One can speculate as to why prominent criminological associations still linger in adopting a code of ethics. But, more to the point, being without a codified statement of ethical practices places research subjects at risk of victimization. Of course, the worst punishment an unethical researcher suffers at the hands of the scientific community is banishment. But even this carries dire consequences for reputation and professional livelihood.

Codes of research ethics can be traced to the *Nuremberg code,* which was adopted during the Nuremberg Military Tribunal on Nazi war crimes held by the Allied Powers immediately after World War II. The code, developed as a response to the cruelty of concentration camp experiments, outlines ethical principles and rights of human subjects. These include:

- The principle of voluntary consent
- Avoidance of unnecessary physical and mental suffering
- Avoidance of any experiment where death or disabling injury is likely
- Termination of research if its continuation is likely to cause injury, disability, or death
- The principle that experiments should be conducted by highly qualified people using the highest levels of skill and care
- The principle that the results should be for the good of society and unattainable by any other method

The principles in the Nuremberg code dealt with the treatment of human subjects and focused on medical experimentation, but they became the basis for the ethical codes in social research.

Similar codes of human rights, such as the 1948 Universal Declaration of Human Rights by the United Nations and the 1964 Declaration of Helsinki, also have implications for criminological researchers.[23] Figure 17.2 lists some of the basic principles of ethical criminology.

Codes of research ethics are more than advisory. They compel ethical criminologists to disseminate research findings irrespective of prevailing political climate. Ideally, universities and other nonprofit research organizations can continue to perform this vital function in society. As a case in point, there is the *Law Enforcement News,* a publication of John Jay College of Criminal Justice/City University of New York,

FIGURE 17.2   Basic Principles of Ethical Criminology

- Ethical responsibility rests with the individual researcher.
- Do not exploit subjects or students for personal gain.
- Some form of informed consent is highly recommended or required.
- Honor all guarantees of privacy, confidentiality, and anonymity.
- Do not coerce or humiliate subjects.
- Use deception only if needed, and always accompany it with debriefing.
- Use the research method that is appropriate to a topic.
- Detect and remove undesirable consequences to research subjects.
- Anticipate repercussions of the research or publication of results.
- Identify the sponsor who funded the research.
- Cooperate with host nations when doing comparative research.
- Release the details of the study design with the results.
- Make interpretations of results consistent with the data.
- Use high methodological standards and strive for accuracy.
- Do not conduct secret research.

which regularly publishes, in popular style, the latest news about criminological research. News about a recent "Congressionally mandated study [in the United States]" appeared in the May 15, 1997, issue. The study "classified as ineffective some of the nation's most popular anti-crime programs" and "questioned the wisdom of the nation's decade-old, multimillion-dollar prison construction binge, contending that much of the research on the deterrent effects of incarceration was inadequate or flawed" (p. 1).

Another example comes from research on the Milwaukee, Wisconsin, Public Defenders Office. After interviewing 24 staff members and conducting observations, a researcher in 1994 documented that the staff at the Milwaukee Public Defenders Office were seriously overworked and could not effectively provide legal defense for poor people. Learning of the findings, top officials at the office contacted the university and demanded to know who on their staff had talked to the researcher, with implications that there might be reprisals against the staff members. The university administration defended the researcher and refused to release the information, citing widely accepted codes that protect human research subjects.[24]

ETHICS AND THE SPONSORS OF RESEARCH

Special Considerations

The researcher/sponsor relationship must be given particularly close scrutiny for ethical improprieties. That is to say, special ethical problems are introduced whenever criminological research is conducted for profit or politics. Researchers need to set ethical boundaries beyond which they will refuse sponsor demands. When confronted with an illegitimate demand from a sponsor, a researcher has three basic choices: loyalty to an organization or larger group, exiting from the situation, or voicing opposition.[25] These present themselves as caving in to the sponsor, quitting, or becoming a whistleblower. The researcher must choose his or her own course of action, but it is best to consider ethical issues early in a relationship with a sponsor and to express concerns up front.

Whistle-blowing can be strenuous and risky. Three parties are involved: the researcher who

sees ethical wrongdoing, an external agency or the media, and supervisors in an employing organization. The researcher must be convinced that the breach of ethics is serious and approved of in the organization. After exhausting internal avenues to resolve the issue, he or she turns to outsiders. The outsiders may or may not be interested in the problem or able to help. Outsiders often have their own priorities (making an organization look bad, sensationalizing the problem, etc.)—ones that differ from the researcher's main concern (ending unethical behavior). Supervisors or managers may try to discredit or punish anyone who exposes problems and acts disloyal. As Frechette-Schrader (1994:78) noted, "An act of whistle blowing is a special kind of organizational disobedience or, rather, obedience to a higher principle than loyalty to an employer." Under the best of conditions, the issue may take a long time to resolve and create great emotional strain. By acting moral, a whistle-blower needs to be prepared to make many sacrifices—losing a job or promotions, lowered pay or undesirable transfer, being abandoned by friends at work, or incurring legal costs. There is no guarantee that doing the right thing will change the unethical behavior or protect the researcher from retaliation.

Applied social researchers in sponsored research settings need to think seriously about their professional roles. They may want to maintain some independence from an employer and affirm their membership in a community of dedicated professionals. Many find a defense against sponsor pressures by participating in professional organizations (e.g., the Evaluation Research Society), maintaining regular contacts with researchers outside the sponsoring organization, and staying current with the best research practices. The researcher least likely to uphold ethical standards in a sponsored setting is someone who is isolated and professionally insecure. Whatever the situation, unethical behavior is never justified by the argument that "If I didn't do it, someone else would have."

Arriving at Particular Findings

What should you do if a sponsor tells you, directly or indirectly, what results you should come up with? An ethical researcher refuses to participate if he or she must arrive at specific results as a precondition for doing research. All research should be conducted without restrictions on the findings that the research yields.[26]

Limits on How to Conduct Studies

Can a sponsor limit research by defining what can be studied or by limiting the techniques used, either directly or indirectly (by limiting funding)? Sponsors can legitimately set conditions on research techniques used (e.g., survey versus experiment) and limit costs for research. However, the researcher must follow generally accepted research methods. Researchers should give a realistic appraisal of what can be accomplished for a given level of funding.

The issue of limits is common in *contract research,* when a firm or government agency asks for work on a particular research project. In Washington, DC, private-sector research companies feed off of federal contracts. (In the local jargon, these companies are called the "beltway bandits.") The Department of Justice, for example, issues a request for proposal (RFP) on a certain topic, and various companies, as well as university and nonprofit organizations, will compete for the bid. The proposals are evaluated on technical merit as well as on how effectively they address the department's broader research agenda. Contracts are then signed and the research begun.

A trade-off may develop between quality and cost in contract research. Abt (1979), the president of a major private social research firm, Abt Associates, argued that it is difficult to get a contract by bidding what the research actually costs. Once the research begins, a researcher may need to redesign the project, or costs may be higher. The contract procedure makes midstream changes difficult. A researcher may find that he or she is forced by the contract to use research procedures or methods that are less than ideal. The researcher then confronts a dilemma: Complete the contract and do low-quality research, or fail to fulfill the contract and lose money and future jobs.

A researcher should refuse to continue if he or she cannot uphold generally accepted standards of research. If a sponsor wants biased samples or leading questions, the ethical researcher refuses to cooperate. If legitimate research shows the sponsor's pet idea or project to be a bad course of action, a researcher may anticipate the end of employment or pressure to violate professional research standards. In the long run, the sponsor, the researcher, the scientific community, and the larger society are harmed by the violation of sound research practice. The researcher has to decide whether he or she is a "hired hand" who gives the sponsors whatever they want, even if it is ethically wrong, or a professional who is obligated to teach, guide, or even oppose sponsors in the service of higher moral principles.[27]

A researcher should ask: Why would sponsors want the criminological research conducted if they are not interested in using the findings or in the truth? The answer is that such sponsors see research only as a cover they can use to legitimate a decision or practice that they could not otherwise carry out. They abuse the researcher's status as a professional to advance their own narrow goals. They are being deceitful and trying to "cash in" on the reputation of research for honesty and integrity. When it occurs, an ethical researcher has a moral responsibility to expose and stop the abuse.

Suppressing Findings

What happens if you conduct research and the findings make the sponsor look bad or the sponsor does not want to release the results? This is not an uncommon situation for applied researchers. For a sensational illustration of this, one need look no further than the tobacco industry in the United States. At present, the Attorneys General in a growing number of states are examining the unethical, if not outright illegal, behavior of the tobacco industry vis-à-vis contract research it had sponsored.

Since the 1950s, tobacco companies have sponsored its own research to counteract the mountain of independent scientific evidence testifying to the health hazards and addictiveness of nicotine. Consider the following:

> *A researcher in Cambridge, Massachusetts, finding precancerous lesions in Syrian hamsters after a 100-week inhalation study, was told by a research supervisor that he would not receive a penny more in grants if he tried to disseminate his findings. When the researcher went ahead and scheduled a press conference at a scientific gathering in Atlantic City, an industry publicist— spreading rumors about the shoddiness of his work—succeeded in having the event canceled. (Massing, 1996:33)*

It is not uncommon for government agencies to suppress scientifically based information that contradicts official policy or embarrasses high officials. Retaliation against social researchers employed by government agencies who make the information public also occurs. For example, a social researcher employed by the U.S. Census Bureau who studied death caused by the 1991 Gulf War against Iraq reported that government officials suppressed findings for political reasons. The researcher, whom the agency attempted to fire, reported that findings of high death rates were delayed and underestimated by the U.S. government's main agency for social statistics. Before information could be released, it had to go through an office headed by a political appointee. She charged that the political appointee was more interested in protecting the administration's foreign policy than in releasing relevant scientific findings to the public. In another example, the U.S. Defense Department ordered studies destroyed that showed 10 percent of the U.S. military to be gay or lesbian and that showed no support for the banning of gays from the military.[28]

In sponsored research, a researcher can negotiate conditions for releasing findings *prior to beginning* the study and sign a contract to that effect. It may be unwise to conduct the study without such a guarantee, although competing researchers who have fewer ethical scruples may do so. Alternatively, a researcher can accept the sponsor's criticism and hostility and release the findings over the sponsor's objections. Most researchers prefer the first choice, since the second one may scare away future sponsors.

Similar examples of institutional pressure brought to bear on researchers to manipulate, suppress, or delay findings is systemic in many countries. To be sure, the individual researcher shoulders the final responsibility to conduct the research ethically. However, by bringing unethical practices stemming from sponsor pressure to the attention of the public, the scientific community can help promote a more ethical world. (See Figure 17.3 for a diagram of the ethical pressures researchers face.)

Concealing the True Sponsor

Is it ethical to keep the identity of a sponsor secret? Suppose, for example, the federal revenue agency is sponsoring researchers to survey tax accountants to assess the role they play in tax noncompliance. Would it be ethical for the researchers to conceal this information from the survey respondents? There is not clear agreement on this. Presser and associates (1992) found that the answers respondents give may depend on their knowledge of the survey's sponsor. Thus, the tax accountants may be less forthcoming in their responses if they knew that the survey data were going, say, to the Internal Revenue Service. Of course, this becomes less of an issue for criminological research sponsored by neutral academic researchers.

EFFECTS OF THE LARGER SOCIETY OR GOVERNMENT

The preceding sections focused on harm to subjects, codes of ethics, and dealing with sponsors. A related issue is how powerful groups in society or the government shape research. In an extreme case, 40 percent of German scientists were dismissed from their jobs for political reasons when the Nazis "purified" universities and research centers in 1937.

Another example is the purge of hundreds of professors and researchers in the United States who did not publicly swear to anticommunism

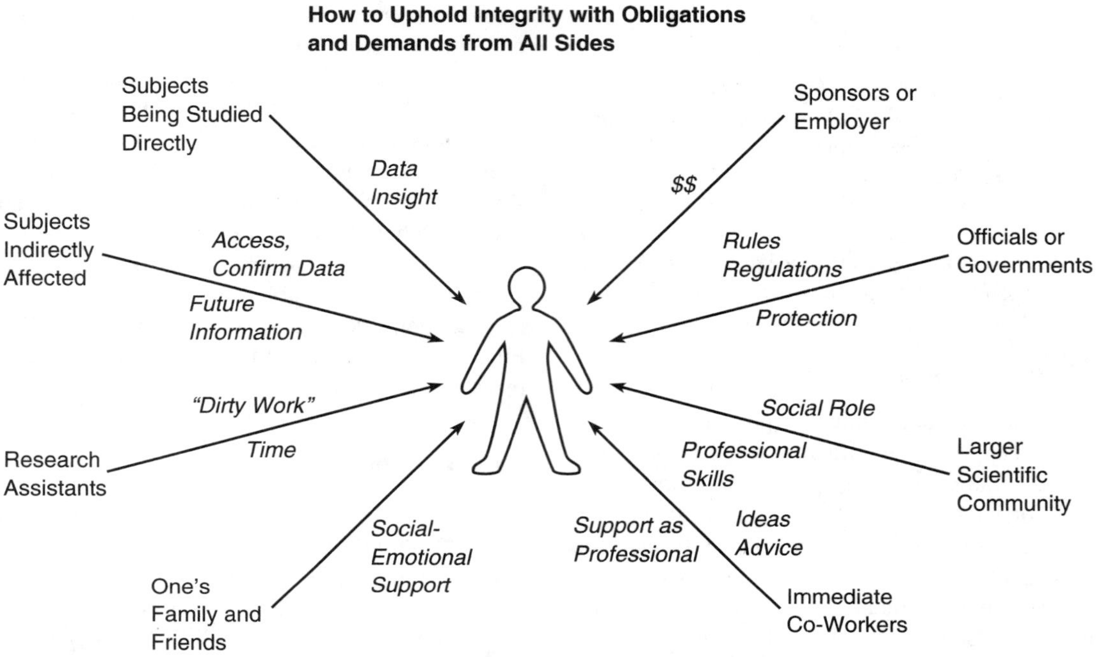

**How to Uphold Integrity with Obligations
and Demands from All Sides**

Subjects
Being Studied
Directly

*Data
Insight*

$$

Sponsors or
Employer

Subjects
Indirectly
Affected

*Access,
Confirm Data*

*Future
Information*

*Rules
Regulations*

Officials or
Governments

Protection

"Dirty Work"

Social Role

Research
Assistants

Time

*Professional
Skills*

Larger
Scientific
Community

*Social-
Emotional
Support*

*Support as
Professional*

*Ideas
Advice*

One's
Family and
Friends

Immediate
Co-Workers

FIGURE 17.3 Ethical Pressures the Social Researcher Faces. The researcher is provided with resources, but each entails responsibilities.

and collaborate with the McCarthy investigations of the 1950s. At that time, people who objected to mandatory loyalty oaths, supported racial integration, or advocated the teaching of sex education were suspected of subversion and threatened with dismissal. For example, at the University of California alone, 25 professors were fired for refusing to sign loyalty oaths.[29] Similar situations arose in universities in former communist countries, as well. For example, according to a criminologist friend in the former German Democratic Republic (GDR), nearly entire faculties in some university departments were forced to resign their posts after the reunification with West Germany.

The point is, governments exert tremendous political pressure on researchers. The pressure is largely tied to the allocation of research funds to those criminologists working within the preferred political persuasions. Consequently, critical crimi-

nologists find themselves in a distinct disadvantage when it comes to getting their research funded by governments. This raises important concerns regarding the proper role of government in influencing the direction of criminological research.

Governments can limit, constrain, or direct social research, both through legislation and by the allocation of research funds. The question is: What is the proper relationship between government or other powerful institutions and social research? What is the balance between the value of a government's overseeing science for society versus the value of free and autonomous research without political interference?

Mandated Protections of Subjects

The U.S. federal government has regulations and laws to protect research subjects and their rights. The legal restraint is found in rules and regulations issued by the U.S. Department of Health and Human Services Office for the Protection from Research Risks. Although this is only one federal agency, most researchers and other government agencies look to it for guidance. Current U.S. government regulations have evolved from Public Health Service policies adopted in 1966 and expanded in 1971. The National Research Act (1974) established the National Commission for the Protection of Human Subjects in Biomedical and Behavioral Research, which significantly expanded regulations, and required informed consent in most social research. The responsibility for safeguarding ethical standards was assigned to research institutes and universities. The Department of Health and Human Services issued regulations in 1981, which are still in force. Regulations on scientific misconduct and protection of data confidentiality were expanded in 1989.

Federal regulations follow a biomedical model and protect subjects from physical harm. Other rules require *institutional review boards (IRBs)* at all research institutes, colleges, and universities to review all use of human subjects. The IRB is staffed by researchers and community members. Similar committees oversee the use of animals in research. The IRB oversees, monitors, and reviews the impact of all research procedures on human subjects and applies ethical guidelines. The board also reviews research procedures at the preliminary stage when first proposed.

Seltzer (1996a) voiced a commonly heard complaint among criminologists and other social scientists. His particular problem arose after requesting permission and, hearing no word back from the IRB, conducting his survey. In Seltzer's words:

> In January, 1985, we decided to survey residents of the District of Columbia on their attitude toward AIDS. Immediately after choosing the topic, I wrote to the IRB explaining the nature of the course and how we would conduct the survey. I didn't hear from the IRB, so I assumed we had approval and the survey was conducted in March of that year. . . . The day after the Washington Post *article [which I wrote based on the survey*

> *findings], I received a request from the IRB to appear before it that week.*
>
> *After an initially contentious meeting, we came to a mutual understanding. Surveys that occurred in an academic course setting could receive more advance approval than other surveys. Furthermore, social science research had to be evaluated differently from research arising in the medical sciences. . . . Although social science research involves human subjects, they are rarely at any risk. For research that might put subjects at some risk, careful consideration by IRBs is called for. Otherwise, a more informal approach may be useful. (pp. 127–128)*[30]

Limits on What Can Be Studied

Governments or powerful groups in society may try to restrict free scientific inquiry. In nondemocratic societies, control over or the censorship of justice research is the rule, not the exception. This is particularly the case with politically sensitive topics, including public opinion surveys. Thus, in China, eastern Europe, South Africa, Taiwan, and other places, social researchers have been suspect, limited to "safe" topics, or forced to support official government policy.[31] In a number of countries (e.g., Greece and Chile), the study of sociology itself was banned as subversive after a military coup.

There are few restrictions on research in the United States. Most officials recognize that an open and autonomous social scientific community is the best path to unbiased, valid knowledge. The peer review process promotes autonomous research because proposals for funds to conduct research submitted to a government agency are reviewed by researcher peers who evaluate the proposal on its scientific merit. Although the federal government funds most basic research, research itself is decentralized and conducted at many colleges, universities, and research centers across the nation.

Two Limitations: Gatekeepers and Defining Indicators. Two limitations on research involve gatekeepers who control access to data or subjects and the types of data collected in official statistics.

As mentioned before, gatekeepers may limit what is studied.

Take the example of the United States School of the Americas. Lopez (1996) underscored the many Latin American military officers who have graduated from the school. In Colombia alone, some 10,000 soldiers have attended it since 1946. Suppose a criminologist wanted to do research on the socialization of military officers at the School of the Americas. Powerful gatekeepers in the military establishment would no doubt try to protect the school from criticism, political embarrassment, and a loss of funding. They would make research difficult, perhaps even blocking the research. In addition to outright denial of access, the gatekeepers may limit access to certain subjects, times, or areas. Access to the schools records, internal communication, and statistics can also be off limits to the criminologist.[32]

Limits Due to the Influence of Politicians. Unfortunately, political ideology can be put up as a roadblock to researchers wanting to investigate "forbidden topics" in criminology. These topics are sometimes difficult to identify beforehand, as they are usually conspicuously absent from the research literature.[33] One can imagine the resistance a researcher can expect from politicians and law enforcement administrators for wanting to study police brutality in a country. Indeed, criminological research tends to tip-toe around that topic, even though human rights organizations, such as *HumanRights Watch*, document serious violations on the part of police.

In the past, research on AIDS has been subject to heavy political pressure,[34] as have studies delving into juvenile sexual behavior, delinquency, and related issues.[35] More specific to comparative criminology, research on political corruption, organized crime, and corporate crime is often vehemently attacked and even blocked by government officials. Such attacks are a direct assault on ethical researchers, and must be countered by the scientific community.

In May 1992, members of the U.S. Congress identified 31 specific research projects to be funded by the National Science Foundation (NSF) as a waste of taxpayer money. The projects singled out to be cut included "Monogamy and Aggression," "A Systematic Study of Senate Elections," and "American Perceptions of Justice." Although the proposals had undergone a rigorous review on scientific merit, several politicians decided to overrule the judgment of the scientific community. The politicians had not studied the research proposals and lacked a background in the social or natural sciences. The politicians also criticized the NSF for supporting basic social research. After extensive lobbying by the research community, specific research projects were no longer targeted, but still Congress cut the research budget of the NSF by the amount allocated for these research projects.[36]

Adverse publicity that could destroy a researcher's career may keep researchers from investigating sensitive topics. Yet, scientific knowledge is especially important precisely because the topics are sensitive ones. Without scientifically based knowledge, fear, prejudice, and ideology dominate public policy and popular opinion.

National Security and Limits on Social Research. Military secrecy and national security became major issues during World War I and World War II. Most of the concern was with technology to create weapons, but social researchers have been limited in their study of foreign nations, issues of military interest, and research into government itself. U.S. security agencies such as the National Security Administration and the Central Intelligence Agency (CIA) have influenced social and natural science research into the Cold War period of the 1950s.

One government research project in the 1960s created a great controversy. The U.S. Army funded *Project Camelot,* which involved respected social researchers who went to Chile to study political insurgency and mobilization. Several aspects of the project created controversy. First, the project's goal was to find out how to prevent peasants and disadvantaged groups in Third World countries from taking independent political action to oppose a dictator. Such counterinsurgency research is usually conducted by the CIA. The researchers were accused of using their skills and knowledge to advance military interests against disadvantaged Third World people. Second, some researchers were unaware of the source of funds. Third, the people and the government of Chile were not informed about the project. Once they discovered it, they asked that it end and that all researchers leave.[37]

By the late 1960s and 1970s, freedom to conduct research expanded, restrictions on researchers were relaxed, and the government classified fewer documents. The U.S. Congress passed the *Freedom of Information Act (FOIA)* in 1966 and strengthened it in 1974. The law opened many government documents to scholars and members of the public if they file requests with government agencies. The trend toward greater openness of information and freedom of research was reversed in the 1980s. The U.S. government limited the publication of information, expanded the range of classified documents, and made less information publicly available in the name of national security and budget cutting. This has restrained academic inquiry, scientific progress, and democratic decision making.[38]

In the 1980s, the definition of national security was broadened, the system for classifying government documents was expanded, and new limits were imposed on research into "sensitive areas," even if no government agency or funds are involved. It became easier to classify information and classify documents that were already in the public domain. In addition, under the Export Control Act (1979 and 1985), military and security officials could restrict researchers from outside the U.S. from attending scholarly meetings or visiting U.S. classrooms, libraries, and research centers.[39]

In the past, CIA undercover agents have posed as social researchers to get information in foreign nations. Until 1986, the CIA had a blanket rule barring researchers from disclosing CIA sponsorship of their research. At that time, the rule was loosened to cover only cases where the CIA believed such disclosure "would prove damaging to the United States." For example, a Harvard professor had a contract with the CIA not to reveal that the agency paid for the research for a scholarly book on U.S. foreign policy.[40]

Cross-national research involves unique ethical issues. The research community condemns the use of undercover agents in the guise of researchers and the practice of hiding the source of funding for research. Researchers want to make funding sources known and provide results to subjects, to host nations in cross-national research, and to other scientists. Researchers have developed ethical guidelines for conduct in other nations, which specify cooperation with host officials, the protection of subjects, and leaving information in the host nation. Nevertheless, a researcher may find interference from his or her own government, or the researcher's respect for the basic human rights of the people being studied in a nondemocratic society may lead him or her to hide information from the host government involved.[41]

Funding as an Influence on the Direction of Research

Large-scale research projects in criminology are expensive, and the bulk of funded criminological research is sponsored by government. These two facts create a situation in which criminologists may feel a strong pressure to conform to the research agenda laid out by government.[42] In the United States, criminological research is funded by federal agencies such as the Department of Justice, the National Science Foundation, the Internal Revenue Service, the Department of Defense, and the Department of Health and Human Services. These powerful funding agencies exert great influence over the kinds of research questions criminologists ask.

For the most part, federal agencies prefer to fund applied research over basic research. What this produces is a close institutional connection between criminological research and the criminal justice system. In this way, the institutional interests of the system are communicated, via requests for research proposals, to individual researchers.

The decision at the National Institute of Justice in Washington, DC, for instance, to fund research projects in the area of community policing as opposed to, say, police corruption, is determined largely on the basis of pragmatic and political concerns of the criminal justice system, and not those of independent scientists. This is not to imply that such research is inherently nonscientific, but it does underscore the role of politics in setting the course of criminological research. Useem (1976a:159) noted:

> *Since federal research policies are oriented around producing policy-relevant quantitative research, the result of responsiveness to these policies is that academic research is more oriented toward topics and techniques useful to government agencies than would be the case in the absence of federal funding.*

Quite a number of critical criminologists express suspicion regarding this too-cozy connection between criminologists and the criminal justice status quo. In their minds, mainstream criminological research is ideologically tainted. Such sentiment is expressed in the following quote:

> *The forces behind this massive accumulation of data and information are generally motivated toward greater state control. That is, the aim is to develop more efficient mechanisms whereby state agencies can effectively maintain and protect inequalities in existing economic and political structures. The goal is rarely that of examining how our state crime control apparatus is oppressing the underclass and restricting people's abilities to gain control over their lives. The purpose of criminal justice programs and criminal justice studies is less to understand the oppressed than it is to render the control of the oppressor more efficient. (Quinney and Wildeman, 1991:82)*

Thus, for example, considerable funds may be made available by the federal government to study the issues surrounding the use of crack-cocaine in inner cities, which is consistent with the government's antidrug policies, yet at the very time research funds to study illegal business practices in the pharmaceutical industry are virtually nonexistent.[43]

Funds for basic research can also be allocated so as to promote specific theoretical or value perspectives. For example, research funds may be available to criminologists interested in studying the individual-level correlates of drug use (e.g., age, gender, etc.), while much less funding is provided for investigating structural factors within the community (e.g., deindustrialization) that correlate with illegal drug use. By supporting research questions that legitimate existing criminal justice structures and processes, and not supporting those that do not, political forces are able to control, in the main, large-scale criminological research. Not only does this have direct impact on the production of scientific knowledge but it also serves to delegitimize criminological perspectives that are critical of the criminal justice system.

In response to this politicalization of social science research, the professional associations of a number of scientific disciplines formed a lobbying organization called the *Consortium of Social Science Associations (COSSA)*. COSSA has had some successes and continues to work on behalf of researchers in the United States.[44] However, more has to be done on an international front to protect the integrity of criminological research in other countries, as well.

Some criminologists, especially historical researchers or those who rely on existing statistics, depend on the government less for funding than to supply information or documents. The U.S. Paperwork Reduction Act of 1980 created an Office of Information and Regulatory Affairs to determine whether it was necessary to collect information and maintain records. The act resulted in fewer publications of findings from government-sponsored research. In addition, the implementation of the law had been "used on occasion to restrict information not supportive of executive branch policy goals" (Shattuck and Spence, 1988:47). Thus, criminologists must remain vigilant that this legislation is not informally used to "justify" rejecting publication of research findings that are critical of either the government or powerful economic interests.

In the name of cost cutting, federal agencies stopped collecting information, removed information from public circulation, and shifted information collection to profit-making private businesses. This is exactly what happened, for example, to the IRS's Taxpayer Compliance Measurement Program (TCMP). What had been since the 1960s a regular government research project to estimate the tax gap for the United States is no longer conducted due to a variety of political pressures (Wiegand, 1987). Bureaucratic decisions not to conduct research can, of course, have serious scientific and policy implications. Criminologists interested in studying tax crimes in the United States were clearly hurt by the political decision to discontinue TCMP research. Therefore, national estimates and correlates of tax crime in the United States are based on theoretical models rather than on tax audit data as they had been when TCMP was in effect.

There is one other concern having to do with funding influences on criminological research. This concern centers on the privatization of data collected for or by the government. As it is, government is selling data at low bulk rates to the private sector. Private businesses thus become the only source of these data and often charge high prices to researchers wishing to analyze the data. Starr and Corson (1987:447) commented on this growing trend:

> The privatizing of statistical information poses some specific problems for the future of the social sciences and intellectual life. Without the capacity to make use of the new information resources in private hands, the universities and other nonprofit research centers may be left as intellectual backwaters.

In sum, there is still substantial free inquiry and independent criminological research. Nevertheless, there have been politically motivated attempts to limit what criminologists can study, as well.

THE DISSEMINATION AND USE OF RESEARCH FINDINGS

What do you do with your research findings? Positivist researchers recognize two areas where values legitimately come into play. First, researchers can select a topic area or research question. Although there are "frontier" areas of inquiry in topic areas, researchers can choose a research question on the basis of personal preference.[45] Second, once research is completed, the researchers' values shape where they disseminate their findings. They are expected to report findings to the scientific community, and funding agencies require a report, but beyond these requirements, it is up to the researcher.

Why researchers conduct research and what they do with findings is linked to how they see the entire research enterprise and their role in society as intellectuals.[46] The issue has been debated among leading social thinkers for over 50 years in such works as Howard Becker's (1967) "Whose Side Are We On?" Robert Lynd's (1939) *Knowledge for What?* Alfred McClung Lee's (1978) *Sociology for Whom?* and C. Wright Mills's (1959) *The Sociological Imagination.*

Models of Relevance

When the research completed involves an ethical-political concern, which Rule (1978a, 1978b) has called *models of relevance*, what happens? Rule reviewed the positions that social researchers took toward their research and its use and argued that the positions can be collapsed into five basic types (see Figure 17.4).

The models of relevance are ideal types of the positions social scientists take. Is the researcher a technician, who produces valid, reliable information about how society works, to be used by others? Or does the researcher belong to an independent community of professionals who have a say in what research questions are asked and how results are used? On a continuum, one extreme is the amoral researcher who lacks any concern or control over research or its use. He or she supplies the knowledge that others request and nothing more. This was the stance many scientists in Nazi Germany used to justify collaboration with Nazi practices later classified as "crimes against humanity." He or she "just follows orders" and "just does the job" but asks "no questions." At the other extreme are researchers who have total control over research and its use.

FIGURE 17.4   Models of Relevance

1. *No net effects.* Social science findings produce no greater social good. Several famous social scientists who argue this are William Graham Sumner, Vilfredo Pareto, Herbert Spencer, Edward Banfield, and James Q. Wilson. These conservative social scientists see the products of research as capable of being used for anyone's self-interest and believe that, in the long run, as much harm as good has come from the greater knowledge social science yields.

2. *Direct and positive effects.* Social science knowledge results in an improvement for all. Liberal social scientists, such as Robert Merton, who adopt this stance see knowledge about social relations leading to a more rational world. Research results on social problems help us understand the social world much better, enabling us to know how we can modify it toward some greater good. For example, Lindblom and Cohen (1979) urged a redirection of social science toward what they see as social problem solving.

3. *Special constituency, the proletariat.* Social science should be used to advance the interests and position of the working class. This is the Marxist model of the appropriate use of social research. According to it, all social science falls into three categories: the trivial, that which helps the bourgeoisie, and that which aids the proletariat. Consistent with a critical science approach, research findings should be used to advocate and defend the interests of the working class and assist workers by exposing and combatting exploitation, oppression, injustice, and repression.

4. *Special constituency, the uncoopted.* Social science should be used to aid any disadvantaged or underprivileged group in society. This model, associated with Karl Mannheim and C. Wright Mills, is more general than the Marxian position. It sees many social groups as lacking power in society (women, consumers, racial minorities, gays, the poor, etc.) and argues that these groups are oppressed by the powerful in society who have access to education, wealth, and knowledge. The social researcher should defend those who lack a voice in society and who are manipulated by those in power. The powerful can use or purchase social science research for their own ends. Because they have a unique role in society and are in a position to learn about all areas of society, social researchers have an obligation to help the weak and share knowledge with them.

5. *Special constituency, the government.* Social science's proper role is to aid the decision makers of society, especially public officials. This model is similar to the second model (direct and positive benefits), but adds the assumption that government is in the best position to make use of social research findings and is fully committed to eradicating social problems. It is also similar to the first (no net effects) model but implies "selling" or providing findings to the highest bidder within the limits of national loyalty. It assumes that the government operates in the best interests of everyone, and that researchers have a patriotic duty to give what they learn to those with political power.

The approaches to social science discussed in Chapter 4 are associated with different models of relevance, as are different political views.[47] Positivists tend to follow the "direct and positive effects" or "special constituency, the government" model. The interpretive researcher follows the "no net effects" or the "uncoopted" model. Critical social scientists follow the "special constituency, the proletariat" or "special constituency, the uncoopted" models.

Since Rule developed models of relevance, a new politicized model has appeared with the growth of nongovernment, private "think tanks" in the United States. This sixth model is *special constituency, wealthy individuals, and corporations.* It says social research can reflect a researcher's personal political values and advance the political goals of wealthy groups who seek to maintain or expand their power. The think tanks are research and publicity organizations funded by wealthy individuals, corporations, and political groups. For example, the Manhattan Institute, Cato Institute, Heritage Foundation, and American Enterprise Institute grew dramatically from the early 1980s to the 1990s. They seek to advance a political viewpoint and use social research or quasi-research among other means. Think tanks pay researchers and others, they sponsor research reports, and they draw public attention to results that support their political viewpoint. One such think tank is the National Center for Policy Analysis. It recently published a report on crime rates and "expected punishment"—that is, "the number of days in prison a criminal can expect to serve for committing a crime" (Reynolds, 1997:3–7). This report, however, adds little to serious debate regarding the deterrent doctrine in criminology.

Think tank studies vary greatly in quality, lack peer review, and are short on solid evidence but long on suggestions. The audience for this research is not the scientific community, and the goal is not to generally advance knowledge. Rather, think tank researchers conduct policy-oriented studies with an ideological viewpoint in an attempt to shape public thinking and influence political debate. Many receive significant media publicity, fame, and fortune, although their research may be inferior and lacks scientific peer review. At the same time, more traditional social scientists who operate with meager funds, but who lack connections to the mass media, find that their more rigorous, careful studies of the same public issues get overlooked. The public and policy officials are often overwhelmed by the greater publicity of think tank research results.

After Findings Are Published

The norm of the scientific community is to make findings public. Once findings are part of the public domain, the researcher loses control over them. This means that others can use the findings for their own purposes. Although the researcher may have chosen a topic based on his or her values, once the findings are published, others can use them to advance opposing values.

A few researchers try to retain control over research findings by keeping their findings secret. At best, this is a short-term solution and has several drawbacks. First, other researchers can conduct similar studies and discover the same results. Second, others cannot benefit from the knowledge. Third, the findings are not evaluated, replicated, and legitimized by the scientific community. A better solution is to make the findings public, but also make special efforts to supply specific others with the findings.

Subject Information as Private Property

If you freely give information about yourself for research purposes, do you lose all rights to it? Can it be used against you? People who participate in research have knowledge about them taken away and analyzed by others. The information can then be used for a number of purposes, including actions against the subject's interests. Is it ethical to use or exploit results from research for profit or for use by others against the subjects' interests?

An information industry exists in which information about people is collected, bought, sold, analyzed, and exchanged by large organizations on a regular basis. Information about buying habits, personal tastes, spending patterns, credit ratings, voting patterns, and the like is used by many private and public organizations. Information is a form of private property. Like other "intellectual" property (copyrights, software, patents, etc.) and unlike most physical property, information continues to have value or relevance for its original owner after it is exchanged.

Most people do not consider information about themselves to be their property; they freely give it away, like a gift. They give a researcher their time and information for little or no compensation. Yet, concerns about privacy and the collection of more information makes it reasonable to see personal information as private property. If it is private property, a subject's right to keep, sell, or give it away becomes clear. The ethical issue is strongest where the information is used against subjects or used in ways they would disapprove of if they were fully informed.

The issue of who controls data on research subjects is relevant to the approaches to criminology outlined in Chapter 4. In positivism and natural science, the description and understanding of the physical world have become the province of specialized experts. The experts control information removed from the average person, and use it outside democratic control to create miracle drugs, convenience items, fortunes for individuals or firms, or nightmarish weapons. Positivism implies the collection and use of information by experts separate from research subjects and the ordinary citizen. The two alternatives to positivism, each in its own way, argue for the involvement and participation of those who are studied in the research process and in the use of research data and findings.[48]

Findings That Influence Future Behavior

Did you ever do something differently than before because of research findings you read? If so, you are not alone. Sometimes the dissemination of findings affect social behavior. For instance, researchers may uncover changing patterns in the auditing of taxpayers. Perhaps they find that the tax agency is auditing taxpayers less often than previously. Such information itself could serve to encourage certain taxpayers to become noncompliant in their future behavior. Starr (1987:54) remarked, "Official statistics count even if the methods are faulty and the data incorrect. . . . If official statistics affect social perception and cognition, so they also powerfully affect social norms."[49]

Researchers have several responses to research findings that affect social behavior:

1. They ruin predictability and regularity of human social behavior, undermining replication.
2. Only trivial behaviors are changed, so this is an issue only to researchers working in very narrow applied areas.
3. Human behavior can change because there are few unalterable laws of human behavior, and people will use knowledge in the public domain to change their lives.

In any case, social research has not uncovered the full complexity of human relations and behavior. Even if it did, and such knowledge were fully and accurately disseminated to the entire population, social researchers would still have to study which human behaviors change and how.

Academic Freedom

Most students have heard about academic freedom, but few understand it. *Academic freedom* is the existence of an open and largely unrestricted atmosphere for the free exchange of ideas and information. In open democratic societies, many people value intellectual freedom and believe in providing scholars with freedom from interference. This idea is based on the belief that fundamental democratic institutions, the advance of unbiased knowledge, and freedom of expression require a free flow of ideas and information.

Academic freedom is related to the autonomy of research, and it is necessary for high-quality social research. New ideas for research topics, the interpretation of findings, the development of theories or hypotheses, and the open discussion of ideas require academic freedom.

Academic freedom in colleges, universities, and research institutes provides a context for the free discussion and open exchange of ideas that scientific research requires. For knowledge to advance, researchers, professors, and students need a setting where they feel free to advance or debate diverse, and sometimes unpopular, opinions or positions—a setting where people are not afraid to explore a full range of ideas in open discussion, in classrooms, in public talks, or in publications.

The importance of academic freedom is rather obvious when one witnesses countries in which these ethical norms do not apply. In Indonesia, for example, a criminologist wanting to investigate corruption between government and powerful corporations likely jeopardizes his or her personal safety or freedom.

Academic freedom was a significant issue in the late nineteenth and early twentieth centuries, when the social sciences were institutionalized in universities. In the early years, professors frequently lost their jobs because political officials or economic elites disliked the views expressed in their classrooms or publications. Famous scholars in the early period of American social science, like Thorsten Veblen, were forced out of several colleges because of what they said in the classroom or ideas they wrote about. The development of tenure, the idea that faculty could not be fired after a long probationary period without a very good reason, advanced academic freedom but did not guarantee complete academic freedom. Many professors and researchers have been fired for advocating unpopular ideas.[50]

Academic freedom is also threatened when a researcher fears not only losing his or her job but also when he or she is intimidated by a possible lawsuit for presenting findings. Cases of this sort of intimidation have already surfaced in recent years regarding research conducted for tobacco companies. Similarly, a study of corporate crime was delayed and the results changed after the threat of a lawsuit by managers who had been interviewed in the study.[51]

The fundamental point of ethics is this: Attacks on the independence of criminological research cannot be tolerated, be they political or economic in nature. Academic freedom is imperative to good research. Scientific research necessarily involves more technical knowledge (e.g., how to draw a random sample); it also requires a spirit of free inquiry, open discussion, criticism on the basis of scientific merit irrespective of political ideology, and the researcher's right to explore all aspects of social life. These values are the cornerstone to ethical criminological research.

OBJECTIVITY AND VALUE FREEDOM

Confusion sometimes arises in using the terms *objective, value free,* and *unbiased.* All three are important and are often used in debates over the nature of science. The easiest way to clear up the confusion is to recognize that each term has at least two alternative definitions. Sometimes, two different terms share the same definition (see Box 17.3).

Box 17.3 _____

Objective, Value Free, and Unbiased

1. *Objective:*
   a. Opposite of subjective; external, observable, factual, precise, quantitative
   b. Logical; created by an explicit rational procedure; absence of personal or arbitrary decisions; follows specific preestablished rules
2. *Value Free:*
   a. Absence of any metaphysical values or assumptions; devoid of a priori philosophical elements; amoral
   b. Lack of influence from personal prejudice or cultural values; devoid of personal opinion; no room for unsupported views; neutral
3. *Unbiased:*
   a. Nonrandom error eliminated; absence of systematic error; technically correct
   b. Lack of influence from personal prejudice or cultural values; devoid of personal opinion; no room for unsupported views; neutral

---

The positivist approach holds that science is value free, unbiased, and objective. It collapses the definitions together. Value neutrality is guaranteed by logical-deductive, formal theory and a complete separation of facts from value-based concepts. The scientific community is free of prejudice and governed by free and open discussion. With complete value freedom and objectivity, science reveals the one and only, unified, unambiguous truth.

Max Weber, Alvin Gouldner, and Karl Mannheim are three major nonpositivist social thinkers who discussed the role of the social scientist in society. Weber (1949) argued that the fact/value separation is not clear in the social sciences. He suggested that value-laden theories define social facts or socially meaningful action. Therefore, social theories necessarily contain value-based concepts, because all concepts about the social world are created by members of specific cultures. The cultural content of social concepts cannot be purged, and socially meaningful action makes sense only in a cultural context.

Weber (1949) also argued that social scientists cannot avoid taking stands on social issues they study. Researchers *must* be unbiased (i.e., neutral and devoid of personal opinion and unsupported views) when applying accepted research techniques and focus on the means or mechanisms of how the social world works, not on ends, values, or normative goals. A researcher's values must be separate from the findings, and he or she should advocate positions on specific issues only when speaking as a private citizen.

Gouldner (1976) attacked the notion of value-free, objective social science. He argued that the notion of value freedom was used in the past to disguise specific value positions. In fact, value freedom is itself a value—a value in favor of "value free." Gouldner said that complete value freedom was impossible and that scientists and other professionals use the term to hide their own values. He recommended making values explicit. A researcher can be motivated to do research by a desire to do more than dispassionately study the world. He or she can be motivated by a strong moral desire to effect change, which need not invalidate good research practice.

Mannheim (1936) also questioned the ideas of *value neutrality* and *objectivity*. He saw the intellectuals of a society, especially those involved in social research, as occupying a unique social role. A person's social location in society shapes his or her ideas and viewpoints. Yet, social researchers are separate from others and are less shaped by their social position because they try to learn the viewpoints of other people and empathize with all parts of society. Social researchers and intellectuals are not beholden to powerful elites, and they are also less subject to shifts in popular opinion, fads, and crazes. They can and should adopt a *relational position*—a position apart from any other specific social group, yet in touch with all groups. They should be detached or marginal in society, yet have connections with all parts of society, even parts that are often overlooked or hidden.

CONCLUSION

Whether you personally ever conduct criminological research or not, there is no escaping the effect research will have on your life and well-being. That being the case, the authors urge you to approach criminology from a higher plane, to be aware of this great responsibility criminologists have to society. The techniques and perspectives of criminological research are powerful tools for improving the social condition. You must accept the challenge and learn about these tools so as to pursue truth in as ethical a manner as possible. In the final analysis, the ultimate uses (and misuses) of criminological research depends, on you, the ethical criminologist.

KEY TERMS

academic freedom	informed consent	principle of voluntary consent
anonymity	institutional review board	Project Camelot
certificate of confidentiality	(IRB)	relational position
code of ethics	Milgram's obedience study	research fraud
confidentiality	models of relevance	scientific misconduct
Consortium of Social Science	National Science Foundation	tearoom trade study
Associations (COSSA)	(NSF)	value neutrality
contract research	Nuremberg code	Wichita Jury Study
crossover design	plagiarism	Zimbardo prison experiment

REVIEW QUESTIONS

1. What is the primary defense against unethical conduct in research?
2. How do deception and coercion to participate in research conflict with the principle of voluntary consent?
3. Explain the ethical issues in the Milgram, Humphreys, and Zimbardo examples.
4. What is *informed consent,* and how does it protect research subjects?
5. What is the difference between *anonymity* and *confidentiality?*
6. What are the origins of codes of ethics in social research?
7. In what ways might a sponsor attempt to influence a researcher illegitimately, and what can the researcher do about it?
8. In what ways can political groups or politicians affect social research?
9. What would happen if research subjects treated information about themselves as their private property?
10. What is the relationship between academic freedom and research ethics?

NOTES

1. See Reynolds (1979:56–57) and Sieber (1993).
2. Research fraud is discussed by Broad and Wade (1982), Diener and Crandall (1978:154–158), and Weinstein (1979). Also see Hearnshaw (1979) and Wade (1976) on Cyril Burt. Kusserow (1989) and the September 1, 1989, issue of the National Institutes of Health weekly *Guide* summarize some recent scientific misconduct issues.
3. See "Noted Harvard Psychiatrist" (December 7, 1988.)
4. See Blum (1989) and D'Antonio (1989) for another example of plagiarism.
5. See "Doctor Is Accused" (December 9, 1988). For a more general discussion of power and trust, see Reynolds (1979:32).
6. Lifton (1986) provided an account of Nazi medical experimentation.
7. See Jones (1981) on the Bad Blood case.
8. See Diener and Crandall (1978:128) for more discussion on these examples.
9. See Warwick (1982) on types of harm to research subjects. See Reynolds (1979:62–68) on rates of harm in biomedical research. Kelman (1982) discusses different types of harms from different types of research.
10. College counselors report that anxiety and low self-esteem over dating are major problems among college women (Diener and Crandall, 1978:21–22). Also see Kidder and Judd (1986:481–484).
11. See Dooley (1984:330) and Kidder and Judd (1986:477–484).
12. See Hallowell (1985) and "Threat to Confidentiality" (October, 1984).

13. For more on the general issue of the right not to be researched, see Barnes (1979), Boruch (1982), Moore (1973), and Sagarin (1973).
14. The debate over covert research is discussed in Denzin and Erikson (1982), Homan (1980), and Sieber (1982). Also see the section on ethics in Chapter 14.
15. See Diener and Crandall (1978:87) and Warwick (1982:112).
16. Informed consent requirements and regulations are discussed in detail in Maloney (1984). Also see Capron (1982) and Diener and Crandall (1978:64–66).
17. See Diener and Crandall (1978:173–177) and Kidder and Judd (1986:469).
18. See Boruch (1982), Caplan (1982), Katz (1972), and Vaughan (1967) on privacy.
19. For more on the Wichita Jury Study, see Dooley (1984:338–339), Gray (1982), Robertson (1982), Tropp (1982:391), and Vaughan (1967).
20. See Monaghan (1993a, 1993b, 1993c).
21. For more on gatekeepers, see Broadhead and Rist (1976).
22. See Freidson (1986).
23. See Beecher (1970:227–228) and Reynolds (1979:28–31, 428–441).
24. See "UW Protects Dissertation Sources" (December 19, 1994).
25. See Hirschman (1970) on loyalty, exit, or voice. Also see Rubin (1983:24–40) on ethical issues in applied research.
26. Additional discussion can be found in Schmeling and Miller (1988).

27. See Staggenborg (1988) on "hired hand" research.

28. See Nelson (April 14, 1992) and "Ex-Official Says Pentagon Dumped Findings" (April 1, 1993).

29. For more on the decade of the 1950s and its effect on social researchers, see Caute (1978:403–430), Goldstein (1978:360–369), and Schrecker (1986).

30. IRBs are discussed in Maloney (1984) and Chadwick and associates (1984:20).

31. For a review of changes in the former Soviet social science research, see Keller (1988, 1989) and Swafford (1987). Also see "Soviet Sociologist" (April 1987).

32. In addition to the discussion in Chapter 9, see Block and Burns (1986) and Starr (1987).

33. See Bermant (1982:138). Nelkin (1982a) provided a general discussion of "forbidden" topics in social science research.

34. See "Sex Survey" (July 26, 1989).

35. See Burd (October 2, 1991).

36. See "NIH FY 1991" (May 27, 1992).

37. Project Camelot is described in Horowitz (1965).

38. See Dickson (1984), Nelkin (1982b), and Shattuck and Spence (1988:2).

39. See Shattuck and Spence (1988) and Josephson (1988). Also see "Librarians Charge Plan" (February 21, 1989).

40. For more on the CIA and social researchers, see Shattuck and Spence (1988:39–40) and Stephenson (1978).

41. For sensitive situations involving cross-national research, see Fuller (1988) and Van den Berge (1967).

42. For a related discussion, see Bannister (1987), Blumer (1991b), D'Antonio (1992), Hyman (1991), Ross (1991), and Seybold (1987).

43. For more on the effects of politics and funding cuts on social research in the 1980s, see Cummings (1984), Himmelstein and Zald (1984), and Zuiches (1984). For more general discussion of the effect of funding on research, see Dickson (1984) and Galliher and McCartney (1973).

44. See Dynes (1984) on COSSA.

45. For more discussion on how researchers select research questions or problems, see Gieryn (1978) and Zuckerman (1978).

46. See Brym (1980) on role of intellectuals in society.

47. See Rule (1978a:67–139).

48. See Gustavsen (1986).

49. Marsh (1984), Noelle-Neumann (1974, 1984), and Price (1989) discussed the effects of research results on subsequent public behavior and opinion.

50. Bartiz (1960), Schrecker (1986), Schwendinger and Schwendinger (1974), and Silva and Slaughter have looked (1980) at this matter in historical detail.

51. See Punch (1986:18–19, 49–69).

RECOMMENDED READINGS

Alonso, William, and Paul Starr (Eds.). (1987). *The politics of numbers.* New York: Russell Sage. This book contains essays on how quantitative data collected by governments are influenced by political and cultural factors. Many different types of official or existing statistics are discussed, and the primary theme of the essays is that politics often has an effect on statistics that are used by researchers and policy makers.

Kimmel, Allen J. (1988). *Ethics and values in applied social research.* Newbury Park, CA: Sage. Kimmel provides a good introduction to ethical issues in research. He is very strong at showing how applied research often raises complex issues with sponsors and others. He also covers basic principles of ethical social research and describes how ethical concerns may conflict with methodological demands.

Rule, James. (1978). *Insight and social betterment.* New York: Oxford University Press. Rule raises important issues about the use of social research and the dissemination of findings. He describes alternative ways in which social researchers have defined their social role and discusses the implications of such definitions.

Sieber, Joan E. (1992). *Planning ethically responsible research: A guide for students and internal review boards.* Thousand Oaks, CA: Sage. This is an excellent introduction to the ethical issues of social research and the operation of IRBs. It can also serve as a "how-to" manual for new researchers or members of an IRB.

A TABLE OF RANDOMLY SELECTED FIVE-DIGIT NUMBERS

10819	85717	64540	95692	44985	88504	50298	20830	67124	20557
28459	13687	50699	62110	49307	84465	66518	08290	96957	45050
19105	52686	51336	53101	81842	20323	71091	78598	60969	74898
35376	72734	13951	27528	36140	42195	25942	70835	45825	49277
93818	84972	66048	83361	56465	65449	87748	95405	98712	97183
35859	82675	87301	71211	78007	99316	25591	63995	40577	78894
66241	89679	04843	96407	01970	06913	19259	72929	82868	50457
44222	37633	85262	65308	03252	36770	51640	18333	33971	49352
54966	75662	80544	48943	87983	62759	55698	41068	35558	60870
43351	15285	38157	45261	50114	35934	05950	11735	51769	07389
11208	80818	78325	14807	19325	41500	01263	09211	56005	44250
71379	53517	15553	04774	63452	50294	06332	69926	20592	06305
63162	41154	78345	23645	74235	72054	84152	27889	76881	58652
17457	68490	19878	04981	83667	00053	12003	84614	14842	29462
28042	42748	55801	94527	21926	07901	89855	21070	80320	91153
32240	24201	24202	45025	07664	11503	97375	83178	26731	45568
87288	22996	67529	38344	29757	74161	16834	40238	48789	99995
39052	23696	42858	85695	50783	51790	80882	97015	81331	76819
71528	74553	32294	86652	15224	07119	45327	69072	64572	07658
76921	04502	78240	89519	02621	40829	88841	66178	01266	10906
45889	22839	77794	94068	85709	96902	19646	40614	03169	45434
10486	79308	75231	33615	42194	49397	91324	79553	66976	83861
42051	14719	80056	74811	58453	04526	90724	36151	09168	04291
47919	11314	80282	09297	02824	59530	31237	26311	62168	46591
19634	40589	28985	40577	33213	52852	17556	85342	66881	18944
10265	45549	38771	38740	48104	63990	73234	19398	33740	97345
74975	33526	36190	25201	19239	06254	02198	99109	01005	20983
37677	76778	15736	57675	81153	59651	69262	89250	75156	59164
18774	15979	26466	80236	65400	24272	02088	09307	33426	11230
93728	14965	85141	27821	53791	38728	66369	29415	55330	99228
34212	15590	41336	23614	26153	19466	44176	80885	00015	40077
81984	54478	45226	97338	14064	45768	13538	49093	05691	69720
72755	15743	00552	89374	85400	37392	26598	71917	64275	16125
13162	57044	75982	15819	23385	40860	51585	44542	39656	91139
64686	62224	34124	79171	73909	26196	54057	63264	72089	06658
00157	64594	03178	75774	32315	34443	37224	85593	55251	42666
84194	83591	82152	24311	22414	43244	81542	31491	42075	17275
05776	60399	65218	89299	20273	30071	53077	18853	56652	63896
33365	18314	81074	49433	10884	75467	56085	14731	98085	60895
67928	38976	38480	59980	23156	72335	33489	59420	67819	51874
64394	45154	81851	54228	73095	97217	16908	90242	92869	17311

73000	20948	57065	70195	87563	41590	85047	71743	94916	50534
63555	03388	96638	16591	13641	73342	59131	63144	63587	62084
84005	02035	08182	16395	44928	08897	44750	71378	67522	20180
42593	35102	14577	38102	60403	04540	53992	27069	69574	76682
49519	49517	88147	83375	87045	57466	91259	06680	45586	36257
42149	01579	83056	19423	28165	25620	68035	17919	09120	59078
66192	98427	10152	96970	89990	34604	49632	46533	63362	43151
16124	88620	87074	37851	77131	73855	03740	10306	63858	04349
35492	47334	57189	26465	70078	14477	00881	00929	86907	73764
54503	40155	94734	20689	32475	62851	13216	21419	95502	36783
88063	53451	15642	67345	06935	70644	68570	79176	31975	83082
83689	14426	40357	34906	56282	96104	83796	57663	88627	17521
40393	72810	00681	15351	28858	72086	99090	39741	17914	27385
76648	61322	06817	64674	50317	52373	78223	84222	14021	43432
42091	27088	37686	88033	68007	71009	24018	49568	64351	94130
78925	41509	14319	92389	85492	40880	01487	85509	48316	62618
61915	98081	87996	53798	51485	38912	85858	43392	64678	44458
29504	66960	42645	54547	20615	77035	79942	33972	46112	78290
90170	97643	46284	34591	42692	72933	66166	98389	37460	14545
96439	06806	76714	80084	57685	37447	44901	64699	89142	64657
98365	28725	84376	50634	79289	31106	71351	10533	57545	27399
74794	91013	89791	54236	02369	35317	31103	82481	52256	94510
37499	85907	16293	17673	13373	06599	50138	19860	46716	36928
77530	25960	33671	54383	25144	82627	99266	75134	96539	47242
67990	35106	05214	82928	39824	11128	31390	76293	52809	54881
07355	29187	09357	94498	69697	92515	89812	90794	44738	46806
40716	05787	68975	38937	44033	50064	25582	09428	10220	42455
97748	64395	13937	60406	99182	92720	80805	26242	81943	40341
83682	18775	60095	78600	03994	30313	21418	58563	47258	75582
73506	30672	18213	37887	26698	87700	75784	86878	74004	88636
36274	02333	43132	93725	87912	90341	74601	77001	30717	60002
73508	00852	94044	98474	12621	91655	55258	85551	76122	68052
06488	12362	60020	66902	90734	73689	22382	40896	09028	72925
20201	31560	98885	32275	46818	76114	07959	65639	33267	98595
49947	13114	06773	06454	95070	26564	08974	11640	76202	86105
79928	50600	06586	72129	37233	02564	83265	32579	21234	83535
76360	86412	36240	20210	17692	80482	67007	15474	23198	74250
54601	84643	66759	57661	16434	61708	93185	75957	61056	90678
23441	63863	95238	59665	55789	26180	12566	58645	15125	76707
47093	90509	48767	09874	23363	84954	09789	30178	28804	93294
93603	11580	94163	85561	71328	88735	69859	84563	25579	52858
68812	15299	99296	45906	37303	49507	70680	74412	96425	38134
69023	84343	36736	52659	90751	20115	89920	44995	17109	96613
76913	03158	83461	27842	03903	34683	89761	80564	45806	88009
99426	99643	00749	79376	44910	27490	59668	93907	73112	46365
59429	08121	06954	28120	17606	22482	91924	00401	16459	15570
38121	05358	01205	00662	73934	97834	56917	64058	05148	87599
97781	32170	99914	75565	79802	38905	17167	08196	46043	72094
79068	21760	78832	93795	67798	54968	87328	46494	74338	89805
46601	04015	00484	39366	56233	22622	90706	02327	60807	39009
64821	72859	83471	60448	49159	38242	84473	05512	20200	91109

(continued)

49216	15978	76313	82040	79322	53190	99705	86694	39000	59173
85909	77399	56836	38084	24480	16180	58023	20122	78348	36906
72284	62418	84313	85377	00039	90894	72976	19553	22917	58585
20210	90083	06608	43380	76224	87362	81200	91427	34115	36488
63659	42186	61396	94269	58196	42997	96272	02004	63365	75665
60022	62412	97267	13525	36794	68402	10902	87223	95682	18000
32399	18357	80684	50976	28717	95782	31227	99800	62642	33563
88488	73641	06447	51771	17572	68734	75964	54434	21852	80662
87642	39726	67296	75473	82899	06689	09402	18953	07418	89659
89586	59644	02486	95252	57771	97979	44761	10361	99589	57982
72544	38997	64243	04873	97006	55074	63062	06692	69940	94364
50807	84525	33191	49539	51414	87457	36296	68915	78902	60245
59490	00996	40795	05159	14215	72282	99887	93436	73440	57270
38626	50552	71131	69450	00534	26851	63155	61856	31104	52773
51982	59414	61762	30549	38914	30613	48661	47104	84319	71299
37747	69944	81040	53066	72265	63828	33559	21167	44864	91959
35752	01162	55189	98224	83276	35108	65759	47387	78381	53662
39473	21252	53693	49359	00691	82273	87378	90967	06356	77705
55572	52235	46693	87891	13626	50676	16806	23052	49743	44683
86396	26942	31794	03215	14813	07506	40853	79461	69114	32357
33555	56824	39948	35309	27279	78587	02790	98720	57920	30931
23433	11441	30625	68538	85671	78168	60754	37067	99579	76294
08339	60862	33225	85288	47812	89681	04184	87755	59664	46025
12952	73728	73346	54435	12067	18137	24559	99949	29504	82736
31065	41220	40348	71545	27046	95290	38752	13456	16147	20025
38062	29620	11459	24800	99422	31514	42673	62254	50236	52802
22365	00954	49547	16844	04006	09907	87626	60601	21891	14980
86779	89664	29030	91894	73718	73392	65469	79340	90014	00229
43233	48154	74284	65921	63641	00481	08578	22188	38029	68894
74503	33076	28357	23271	05919	12247	65814	51837	17689	67065
80697	09861	44996	94438	79742	44904	43997	30676	47959	91749
66890	59837	08731	62577	45661	40331	20461	40292	58324	50957
65029	71853	28424	48445	86207	05328	12631	18104	56863	84071
03322	46034	72527	42011	69919	00090	04986	06121	81888	04985
37951	98690	60776	79282	17148	79300	67391	53561	46702	99623
36747	35157	67719	81282	86592	21054	10617	10464	79204	16241
49340	44927	10914	17275	58227	91974	75268	28733	43893	17837
92271	64437	96956	18631	88405	96753	81024	21948	63478	73161
92299	36704	68944	92681	77662	54685	48356	21081	76717	47337
48344	93928	34136	47466	72646	18566	96759	31149	74706	37745
61726	51613	52816	33027	24383	07647	95883	28605	62283	18197
54433	70788	83880	31335	21145	16946	98191	37417	11780	41066
58541	72719	59340	60681	11593	06237	94809	58680	87392	55946
61516	65817	41065	83854	15993	83786	78324	06439	17050	62552
29215	08513	25460	52439	15219	69991	59623	35029	02632	33829
50164	57477	50446	22847	43803	56626	88506	88224	84080	29224
46923	73217	29155	22288	27172	09824	49339	80134	53208	89901
39385	54156	74135	82779	58336	79663	26502	78853	95172	24059
75334	79987	15894	18571	81773	50842	49946	04147	92224	41201
41285	32053	40984	90635	22067	11948	11443	99064	14675	16826
27423	31830	04828	05954	38820	94218	32586	04261	80975	47008

35906	67533	20585	21162	75252	73296	37607	92368	10867	69657
08554	70414	77644	99739	27390	80574	80240	19485	45190	36046
70966	52860	29353	41888	80187	97313	32440	08527	47081	17205
34154	79907	00949	54009	49291	48157	17375	13343	44727	36956
86436	46594	80734	80081	02314	42041	67591	78793	15440	21127
06339	10486	48944	44373	78872	90269	36662	40163	95780	06374
17715	18488	29772	86669	12401	86000	78660	00923	77884	44633
39611	02846	95861	49731	95395	26893	13314	07928	77911	53123
87271	46990	77790	79885	68909	54505	83646	78409	72846	28686
11996	29733	05629	93964	14193	83846	99389	50959	31927	79226
46940	09460	89582	17701	60658	71768	45426	93490	35636	70854
03412	41860	78660	76735	61981	37962	16512	87707	27622	17311
25077	14423	76933	16748	00741	62390	43843	80842	10219	54622
36495	82476	90894	71327	38924	07373	84495	31424	21285	08333
58500	55613	12395	00199	57097	24914	01779	02403	93251	44807
75248	35900	97246	15383	43870	60826	54130	63156	50504	52135
92175	62718	99616	61643	26886	14107	90719	47074	91737	97462
32463	69375	39095	36324	78594	57722	23596	36217	96947	44887
03693	77597	35029	70206	04705	91187	18602	86022	87337	23965
06721	33386	12162	55884	10420	30100	28445	77620	05067	10724
98591	40854	94023	57651	02409	76108	19790	48544	26777	42597
82535	71772	85767	76266	29140	47778	73492	53870	45014	08608
20105	25926	56710	14862	44589	57022	17734	38841	92896	40737
01749	78458	35863	82790	02427	87027	40106	94542	70051	68439
66826	49905	97602	26543	32418	22873	58878	34287	98272	00311
19242	91018	31082	73167	82661	20369	22976	86145	11196	51282
07788	16036	93946	83038	33324	79508	15514	84539	76833	02366
10238	51425	12133	60556	66023	78920	45286	79512	93581	56294
70278	45813	02647	70584	58543	31479	69235	12031	72235	67157
68633	59965	98891	65043	20653	78122	38989	65198	18659	79978
45164	32766	09525	49788	28780	54551	09208	91609	28711	97751
44701	18094	65320	24871	03285	61221	76401	81827	52742	90754
51254	38946	10820	30486	43737	91703	54377	04192	24354	21605
84819	68816	08575	93437	41898	71419	69327	00712	64283	82111
18122	52721	39067	33039	57890	71647	29730	09964	42192	59661
74518	17688	24087	59431	94219	31903	31093	95252	78310	29618
29507	76366	37600	35446	66362	17595	37560	14716	94629	39897
17615	22514	51864	04371	67231	61647	94074	24199	35525	69556
10735	07934	13585	35967	14790	78730	59122	01989	95596	05732
27515	94008	99354	12854	19839	02870	09161	52671	74303	58650
87240	67750	02552	56223	09496	21435	43859	17700	55974	93075
30474	21865	41837	44887	38330	51929	92959	72672	65078	33986
81033	89276	51464	63498	12766	55494	86208	16462	55022	56727
03550	49560	71142	85413	90974	88062	52135	84299	37041	88678
91516	90902	16387	47167	06377	86048	97771	53715	57709	61076
60915	35579	76264	72403	02744	52525	70804	28840	15504	80628
20281	63058	68322	36364	88444	68667	48877	28781	98458	05481

APPENDIX B

THE RESEARCH REPORT
AND PROPOSALS

> *But that's our business: to arrange ideas in so rational an order that another person can make sense of them. We have to deal with that problem on two levels. We have to arrange the ideas in a theory or narrative, to describe causes and conditions that lead to the effects that we want to explain, and do it in an order that is logically and empirically correct. . . . Finally, we want our prose to make the order we have constructed clear. We don't want imperfection in our prose to interfere with our readers' understanding. These two jobs converge and cannot be separated.*
>
> —Howard Becker, *Writing for Social Scientists*, p. 133

INTRODUCTION

Why Write the Report?

After a researcher completes a project or a significant phase of a large project, it is time to communicate the findings to others through a research report. You can learn a lot about writing a research report by reading many reports and taking a course in scientific and technical writing. This appendix summarizes the principles of writ-ing a report, describes various types of reports, and discusses preparing a proposal for research.

A *research report* is a written document (or oral presentation based on a written document) that communicates the methods and findings of a research project to others. The research report is more than a summary of findings; it is a record of the research process. A researcher cannot wait until the research is done to think about the report;

he or she must think ahead to the report and keep careful records while conducting research. In addition to findings, the report includes the reasons for initiating the project, a description of the project's steps, a presentation of data, and a discussion of how the data relate to the research question or topic.

There are almost as many reasons for writing a report as there are for doing research. The basic reason for writing a report is to tell others what you, the researcher, did, and what you discovered. In other words, the research report is a way of disseminating knowledge. As you saw in Chapter 1, the research report plays a significant role in binding together the scientific community. Other reasons for writing a report are to fulfill a class or job assignment, to meet an obligation to an organization that paid for the research, to persuade a professional group about aspects of a problem, or to tell the public about findings. Communicating with the general public is rarely the primary method for communication of scientific results; it is usually a second stage of dissemination.

Your Audience

Professional writers say: Always know for whom you are writing. This is because communication is more effective when it is tailored to a specific audience. You should write a research report differently depending on whether the primary audience is an instructor, other students, professional social scientists, practitioners, or the general public. It goes without saying that the writing should be clear, accurate, and well organized.

Instructors assign a report for different reasons and may place requirements on how it is written. In general, instructors want to see writing and an organization that reflect clear, logical thinking. Student reports should demonstrate a solid grasp of substantive and methodological concepts. A good way to do this is to use technical terms explicitly *when appropriate;* they should not be used excessively or incorrectly.

When writing for other students, it is best to define technical terms and label each part of the report. The discussion should proceed in a logical, step-by-step manner with many specific examples.

Use straightforward language to explain how and why you conducted the various steps of the research project. One strategy is to begin with the research question, then structure the report as an answer.

Scholars do not need definitions of technical terms or explanations of why standard procedures (e.g., random sampling) were used. They are interested in how the research is linked to abstract theory or previous findings in the literature. They want a condensed, detailed description of research design. They pay close attention to how variables are measured and the methods of data collection. Scholars like a compact, tightly written, but extensive section on data analysis, with a meticulous discussion of results.

Practitioners prefer a short summary of how the study was conducted and results presented in a few simple charts and graphs. They like to see an outline of alternative paths of action implied by results with a discussion of the practical outcomes of pursuing each path. Practitioners must be cautioned not to overgeneralize from the results of one study. It is best to place the details of research design and a complete discussion of results in an appendix.

If you write for the general public, use simple language, provide concrete examples, and focus on the practical implications of findings for social problems. Do not include details of research design or of results when writing for the general public, and be careful not to make unsupported claims when writing for the public. Informing the public, however, is an important service, which can help nonspecialists make better judgments about public issues.

Style and Tone

Research reports are written in a narrow range of styles and have a distinct tone. Their purpose is to communicate clearly the research method and findings.

Style refers to the types of words chosen by the writer and the length and form of sentences or paragraphs used. *Tone* is the writer's attitude or relation toward the subject matter. For example, an informal, conversational style (e.g., colloquial words, idioms, clichés, and incomplete sentences) with a personal tone (e.g., these are my feelings) is appropriate for writing a letter to a close friend, but not for research reports. Research reports have a formal and succinct (saying a lot in few words) style. The tone expresses distance from the subject matter; it is professional and serious. Field researchers sometimes use an informal style and a personal tone, but this is the exception. Avoid moralizing and flowery language. The goal is to inform, not to advocate a position or to entertain.

A research report should be objective, accurate, and clear. Check and recheck details (e.g., page references in citations) and fully disclose how you conducted the research project. If readers detect carelessness or omissions in writing, they may question the research itself. The details of a research project can be complex, and such complexity means that confusion is always a danger. It makes clear writing essential. Clear writing can be achieved by thinking and rethinking the research problem and design, explicitly defining terms and labeling tables, writing with short declarative sentences, and limiting conclusions to what is supported by the evidence.

THE WRITING PROCESS

Organizing Thoughts

Writing is not something that happens magically or simply flows out of a person when he or she puts pen to paper (or fingers to keyboard) although many people have such an illusion. Rather, it is hard work, involving a sequence of steps and separate activities that result in a final product. Writing a research report is not radically different from other types of writing. Although some steps differ and the level of complexity may be greater, most of what a good writer does when writing a long letter, a poem, a set of instructions, or a short story applies to writing a research report.

First, a writer needs something about which to write. The "something" in the research report includes the topic, research question, design and measures, data collection techniques, results, and implications. With so many parts to write about, organization is essential. The most basic tool for organizing writing is the outline. Outlines help a writer ensure that all ideas are included and that the relationship between them is clear. Outlines are made up of topics (words or phrases) or sentences (see Figure B.1).

Outlines can help the writer, but they can also become a barrier if they are used improperly. An outline is simply a tool or mechanism to help the writer organize ideas. It helps the writer do three things: (1) put ideas in a sequence (e.g., what will be said first, second, and third); (2) group related ideas together (e.g., these are similar to each other, but differ from those); and (3) separate the more general, or higher-level, ideas from more specific ideas, and the specific ideas from very specific details.

Some students feel that they need a complete outline before writing, and that once an outline is

FIGURE B.1 Form of Outline

I. First major topic	One of the most important
A. Subtopic of topic I	Second level of importance
1. Subtopic of A	Third level of importance
a. Subtopic of 1	Fourth level of importance
b. Subtopic of 1	"
(1) Subtopic of b	Fifth level of importance
(2) Subtopic of b	"
(a) Subtopic of (2)	Sixth level of importance
(b) Subtopic of (2)	"
i. Subtopic of (b)	Seventh level of importance
ii. Subtopic of (b)	"
2. Subtopic of A	Third level of importance
B. Subtopic of topic I	Second level of importance
II. Second major topic	One of the most important

prepared, deviations from it are impossible. Few writers begin with a complete outline. The initial outline is necessarily sketchy because until you write everything down, it is impossible to put all ideas in a sequence, group them together, or separate the general from the specific. For most writers, new ideas develop or become clearer in the process of writing itself.

A beginning outline may differ from the final outline by more than degree of completeness. The process of writing may not only reveal or clarify ideas for the writer, but also stimulate the creation of new categories of ideas, new connections between ideas, a different sequence, or new relations between the general and the specific. In addition, the process of writing may involve reanalysis or a reexamination of the literature or findings. This does not mean beginning all over again. Rather, it means keeping an open mind to new insights and being candid, not defensive, about the research project.

Back to the Library

Few researchers finish their review and reading of the relevant literature before completing a research project. You, the researcher, should be familiar with the literature before beginning a project, but you will usually need to return to the literature after completing data collection and analysis, for several reasons. First, time has passed between the beginning and the end of a research project, and new studies may have been published. Second, after completing a research project, you will know better what is or is not central to the study. You may have new questions in mind when rereading the most critical studies in the literature. Finally, when writing the report, you may find that your notes are not complete enough or that you missed a detail in the citation of a reference source. The visit to the library after data collection is less extensive and more selective or focused than that conducted at the beginning of research.

When writing a research report, researchers frequently discard some of the notes and sources that were gathered prior to completing the research project. This does not mean that the initial library

work and literature review were a waste of time and effort. You should expect that some of the notes (e.g., 25 percent) taken before completing the project will become irrelevant as the project gains focus. Do not include notes or references in a report that are no longer relevant, because they distract from the flow of ideas and reduce clarity.

Returning to the library to verify and expand references will allow you to focus and elaborate ideas. It also helps you avoid plagiarism. *Plagiarism* is taking and passing off the ideas or writings of another as one's own. It is stealing another writer's words or ideas and treating them as if they were your own. Plagiarism is a serious form of cheating, and many universities expel students caught engaging in it. If a professional ever plagiarizes in a scholarly journal, it is treated as a very serious offense.[1] Take careful notes and identify the exact source of phrases or ideas to avoid unintentional plagiarism. Cite the sources of both directly quoted words and paraphrased ideas. For direct quotes, include the location of the quote with page numbers in the citation.

Using another's written words and failing to give credit is definitely wrong, but paraphrasing is less clear. *Paraphrasing* is not using another's exact words; it is restating another's ideas in your own words, usually condensing at the same time. Researchers regularly paraphrase, and good paraphrasing requires a solid understanding of what is being paraphrased. It means more than replacing another's words with synonyms; paraphrasing is borrowing an idea, boiling it down to its essence, and giving credit to the source.[2]

The Writing Process

Writing is a process. The way to learn to write is by writing.[3] It takes time and effort, and it improves with practice. There is no single correct way to write, but some methods are associated with good writing. The writing process has three steps:

1. *Prewriting.* Prepare to write by arranging notes on the literature, making lists of ideas, outlining, completing bibliographic citations, and organizing comments on data analysis.

2. *Composing.* Get your ideas onto paper as a first draft by freewriting, drawing up the bibliography and footnotes, preparing data for presentation, and forming an introduction and conclusion.

3. *Rewriting.* Evaluate and polish the report by improving coherence, proofreading for mechanical errors, checking citations, and reviewing voice and usage.

Many people find that getting started is difficult. Beginning writers often jump to the second step and end there, which results in poor-quality writing. *Prewriting* means that a writer begins with a file folder full of notes, outlines, and lists. You must think about the form of the report and audience. Thinking time is important. It often occurs in spurts over a period of time before the bulk of composing begins.

Some people become afflicted with a strange ailment when they sit down to compose writing: *writer's block*—a temporary inability to write. It comes when the mind goes blank and panic sets in. Writers from beginners through experts occasionally experience it. If you experience it, calm down and work on overcoming it (see Figure B.2).

Numerous writers begin to compose by *freewriting,* a process of sitting down and writing down everything you can as quickly as it enters into your mind. Freewriting establishes a link between a rapid flow of ideas in the mind and writing. When you freewrite, you do not stop to reread what you wrote, you do not ponder the best word, you do not worry about correct grammar, spelling, or punctuation. You just put ideas on paper as quickly as possible to get and keep the creative juices or ideas flowing. You can later clean up what you wrote.

Writing and thinking are so intertwined that it is impossible to know where one ends and the other begins. This means that if you plan to sit and stare at the wall, the computer output, the sky, or whatever until all thoughts become totally clear before beginning, you will rarely get anything written. All that you need to begin is the spark of an idea. The thinking process can be ignited during the writing itself.

Rewriting

Perhaps one in a million writers is a creative genius who can produce a first draft that communicates

---

FIGURE B.2 Suggestions for Ending Writer's Block

1. *Begin early.* Do not procrastinate or wait until the last minute. This not only gives you time to come back to the task but it also reduces the tension because you have time to write a poor-quality first draft that can be improved upon. Shafer (1980:205) chided, "Writing is hard work, and the excuses authors find for postponing it are legendary." Set yourself a deadline for a first draft that is at least a week before the final deadline, and keep it!

2. *Take a break, then return.* Some writers find that if they take a walk, get a snack, read a newspaper, and come back to the task a half hour later, the block is gone. Small diversions, if they remain small and short term, can help on occasion.

3. *Begin in the middle.* You do not have to begin at the beginning. Begin in the middle and just start

writing, even if does not seem to be directly relevant. It may be easier to get to your topic once the writing/thinking process is moving.

4. *Engage in personal magic rituals.* Some people have unusual habits or rituals that they engage in before writing (e.g., washing dishes, clearing a desk, or sharpening pencils). These can serve as mental triggers to help you get started. Do what gets you started writing.

5. *Break it into small parts.* Do not feel that you have to sit down and complete the writing task as a whole. Begin with pieces that come easily to you and stitch together the pieces later.

6. *Do not expect perfection.* Write a draft, which means that you can throw away, revise, and change what you wrote. It is always easier to revise a rough draft than to create perfect writing the first time.

with astounding accuracy and clarity. For the rest of us mortals, writing means that rewriting—and rewriting again—is necessary. For example, Ernest Hemingway is reported to have rewritten the end of *Farewell to Arms* 39 times.[4] It is not unusual for a professional researcher to rewrite a report a dozen times. Do not become discouraged. If anything, the idea of rewriting reduces the pressure; it means you can start writing soon and get out a rough draft that you can polish later. You should plan to rewrite a draft at least three or four times. A draft is a complete report, from beginning to end, not a few rough notes or an outline.

Rewriting helps a writer express himself or herself with a greater clarity, smoothness, precision and economy of words. When rewriting, the focus is on clear communication, not pompous or complicated language. As Leggett and colleagues (1965:330) stated, "Never be ashamed to express a simple idea in simple language. Remember that the use of complicated language is not in itself a sign of intelligence."

Rewriting means slowly reading what you have written and, if necessary, out loud to see whether it sounds right. It is a good idea to share your writing with others. Professional writers always have others read and criticize their writing. New writers soon learn that friendly, constructive criticism is very valuable. Sharing your writing with others may be difficult at first. It means exposing your written thoughts and encouraging criticism. Yet, the purpose of the criticism is to clarify writing, and the critic is doing you a favor.

Rewriting involves two related processes: revising and editing. *Revising* is the process of inserting new ideas, adding supporting evidence, deleting or changing ideas, moving sentences around to clarify meaning, or strengthening transitions and links between ideas. *Editing* is the process of cleaning up and tightening the more mechanical aspects of writing, such as spelling, grammar, usage, verb tense, sentence length, and paragraph organization. When you rewrite, go over a draft and revise it brutally to improve it. This is easier if some time passes between a draft and rewriting. Phrases that seemed satisfactory in a draft may look fuzzy or poorly connected after a week or two (see Figure B.3).

Even if you have not acquired typing skills or access to a word processor, it is a good idea to type, or print out if you use a word processor, at least one draft before the final draft. This is because it is easier to see errors and organization problems in a clean, typed draft. Feel free to cut and paste, cross out words, or move phrases on the typed copy.

Good typing skills and an ability to use a word processor are extremely valuable when writing reports and other documents. Serious researchers and other professionals find that the time they invest into building typing skills and learning to use a word processor pays huge dividends later. Word processors make editing much easier, and most have a feature for checking spelling and offering synonyms. In addition, there are programs that check grammar. You cannot rely on the computer program to do all the work, but it makes writing easier. The speed and ease that a word processor offers is so dramatic that few people who become skilled at using one ever go back to writing by hand or typing.

One last suggestion: Rewrite the introduction and title after completing a draft so that they accurately reflect what is said.[5] Titles should be short and descriptive. They should communicate the topic and the major variables to readers. They can describe the type of research (e.g., "An experiment on . . ." but should not have unnecessary words or phrases (e.g., "An investigation into the . . .").

THE QUANTITATIVE RESEARCH REPORT

The principles of good writing apply to all reports, but the parts of a report differ depending on whether the research is quantitative or qualitative. Before writing any report, read reports on the same kind of research for models.

We begin with the quantitative research report. The sections of the report roughly follow the sequence of steps of a research project.[6]

Abstract or Executive Summary

Quantitative research reports usually begin with a short summary called an *abstract*. The size of an abstract varies; it can be as few as 50 words (this

FIGURE B.3 Suggestions for Rewriting

1. *Mechanics.* Check grammar, spelling, punctuation, verb agreement, verb tense, and verb/subject separation with each rewrite. Remember that each time new text is added, new errors can creep in. Mistakes are not only distracting but they also weaken the confidence readers place in the ideas you express.

2. *Usage.* Reexamine terms, especially key terms, when rewriting to see whether you are using the exact word that expresses your intended meaning. Do not use technical terms or long words unnecessarily. Use the plain word that best expresses meaning. Get a thesaurus and use it. A *thesaurus* is an essential reference tool, like a dictionary, that contains words of similar meaning and can help you locate the exact word for a meaning you want to express. Precise thinking and expression requires precise language. Do not say *average* if you use the *mean*. Do not say *mankind* or *policeman* when you intend *people* or *police officer*. Do not use *principal* for *principle*.

3. *Voice.* Writers of research reports often make the mistake of using the passive instead of the active voice. It may appear more authoritative, but passive voice obscures the actor or subject of action. For example, the passive, *The relationship between grade in school and more definite career plans was confirmed by the data* is better stated as the active, *The data confirm the relationship between grade in school and more definite career plans.* The passive, *Respondent attitude toward abortion was recorded by an interviewer* reads easier in the active voice: *An interviewer recorded respondent attitude towards abortion.* Also avoid unnecessary qualifying language, such as *seems to* or *appears to.*

4. *Coherence.* Sequence, steps, and transitions should be logically tight. Try reading the entire report one paragraph at a time. Does the paragraph contain a unified idea? A topic sentence? Is there a transition between paragraphs within the report?

5. *Repetition.* Remove repeated ideas, wordiness, and unnecessary phrases. Ideas are best stated once, forcefully, instead of repeatedly in an unclear way. When revising, eliminate deadwood (words that add nothing) and circumlocution (the use of several words when one more precise word will do). Directness is preferable to wordiness. The wordy phrase, *To summarize the above, it is our conclusion in light of the data that X has a positive effect of considerable magnitude on the occurrence of Y, notwithstanding the fact that Y occurs only on rare occasions,* is better stated, *In sum, we conclude that X has a large positive effect on Y, but Y occurs infrequently.* As Selvin and Wilson (1984) warned, verbose and excessive words or qualifiers make it difficult to understand what is written.

6. *Structure.* Research reports should have a transparent organization. Move sections around as necessary to fit the organization better, and use headings and subheadings. A reader should be able to follow the logical structure of a report.

7. *Abstraction.* A good research report mixes abstract ideas and concrete examples. A long string of abstractions without the specifics is difficult to read. Likewise, a mass of specific concrete details without periodic generalization also loses readers.

8. *Metaphors.* Many writers use metaphors to express ideas. Phases like the *cutting edge, the bottom line,* and *penetrating to the heart* are used to express ideas by borrowing images from other contexts. Metaphors can be an effective method of communication, but they need to be used sparingly and with care. A few well-chosen, consistently used, fresh metaphors can communicate ideas quickly and effectively; however, the excessive use of metaphors, especially overused metaphors (e.g., *bottom line*), is a sloppy, unimaginative method of expression.

---

paragraph has 90 words) or as long as a full page. Most scholarly journal articles have abstracts that are printed on the first page of the article, or all abstracts for articles in an issue appear together on a separate page. The abstract has information on the topic, the research problem, the basic find-

ings, and any unusual research design or data collection features.

Reports of applied research that are written for practitioners have a longer summary called the *executive summary*. It contains more detail than an article abstract and includes the implications of research and major recommendations made in the report. Although it is longer than an abstract, an executive summary rarely exceeds four or five pages.

Abstracts and executive summaries serve several functions: For the less interested reader, they tell what is in a report; for readers looking for specific information, they help the reader determine whether the full report contains important information. Readers use the abstract or summary to screen information and decide whether the entire report should be read. It prepares serious readers who intend to read the full report by giving them a quick mental picture of the report which makes reading the report easier and faster.

Presenting the Problem

The first section of the report defines the research problem. It can be placed in one or more sections with titles such as "Introduction," "Problem Definition," "Literature Review," "Hypotheses," or "Background Assumptions." Although the subheadings vary, the contents include a statement of the research problem and a rationale for what is being examined. Here, you explain the significance of and provide a background to the research question.

You can explain the significance of the research by showing how different solutions to the problem lead to different applications or theoretical conclusions. Introductory sections frequently include a context literature review and link the problem to theory. Introductory sections also define key concepts and present conceptual hypotheses that are tested in the study.

Describing Methods

The next section of the report describes how you designed the study and collected the data. It goes by several names (e.g., "Methods," "Research Design" or "Data") and may be subdivided into other parts (e.g., "Measures," "Sampling," or "Manipulations"). It is the most important section for evaluating the methodology of the project because it gives the reader details on how you conducted the study. The section answers several questions for the reader:

1. What type of study (e.g., experiment, survey) was conducted?
2. Exactly how were data collected (e.g., study design, type of survey, time and location of data collection, experimental design used)?
3. How were variables measured? Are the measures reliable and valid?
4. What is the sample? How many subjects or respondents are involved in the study? How were they selected?
5. How were ethical issues and specific concerns of the design dealt with?

Results and Tables

After describing how data were collected, methods of sampling, and measurement, you then present the data. This section presents—it does not discuss, analyze, or interpret the data. Researchers sometimes combine the "Results" section with the next section, called "Discussion" or "Findings."

You have choices in how to present the data.[7] When analyzing the data, look at dozens of univariate, bivariate, and multivariate tables and statistics to get a feel for the data. This does not mean that you place every statistic or table in a final report. Rather, you select the minimum number of charts or tables that fully inform the reader and rarely present the raw data itself. You provide data analysis techniques that summarize the data and permit tests of hypotheses (e.g., frequency distributions, tables with means and standard deviations, correlations, and other statistics).

As a researcher, you want to give a complete picture of the data without overwhelming the reader. You do not provide data in excessive detail, nor do you present irrelevant data. Disclose the data so that readers can make their own interpretations, even if they contradict yours. You may place detailed summary statistics in appendixes or remind readers that they can write for the raw data.

Discussion

In the discussion section, talk about what you see in the data and give the reader a concise, unambiguous interpretation of its meaning. The discussion is not a selective emphasis or partisan interpretation; rather, it is a candid discussion of what is in the results section. The discussion section is separated from the results so that a reader can examine the data and arrive at different interpretations. Grosof and Sardy (1985:386) warned, "The arrangement of your presentation should reflect a strict separation between data (the record of your observations) and their summary and analysis on one hand, and your interpretations, conclusion, and comment on the other."

Beginning researchers often find it difficult to organize a discussion section. One approach is to organize the discussion according to hypotheses because you need to discuss how the data relate to each hypothesis. In addition, discuss unanticipated findings, possible alternative explanations of results, and weaknesses or limitations.

Drawing Conclusions

Researchers restate the research question and summarize findings in the conclusion. Its purpose is to summarize the report, and it is sometimes titled "Summary." Here, you should point to directions for future research so others can build on the findings.

The only sections after the conclusion are the references and appendixes. The references section contains only sources that were referred to in the text or notes of the report. Appendixes, if used, usually contain additional information on methods of data collection (e.g., questionnaire wording) or results (e.g., descriptive statistics). The footnotes or endnotes in quantitative research reports expand or elaborate on information in the text. Researchers use them sparingly to provide secondary information that clarifies the text but might distract from the flow of the reading. Publications require various formats for citations to sources, but they are usually in the form of authors' names in parentheses instead of in notes.

THE QUALITATIVE RESEARCH REPORT

Compared to quantitative research, it is more difficult to write a report on qualitative social research. It has fewer rules and less structure. Nevertheless, the purpose is the same: to clearly communicate the research process and the data collected through the process. As Bogdan and Taylor (1975:142) remarked, "A report, article, or monograph based on qualitative research is not, or should not be, an individual's off-the cuff view of a situation. Rather, it should be a descriptive and analytic presentation of data that have been laboriously and systematically collected and interpreted."

Quantitative research reports present hypotheses and evidence in a logically tight and condensed style. By contrast, qualitative research reports tend to be longer, and book-length reports are common. Qualitative research requires greater length for five reasons:

1. The data in a qualitative report are more difficult to condense. Data are in the form of words, pictures, or sentences and include many quotes and examples. If there are charts, diagrams, and tables, they are to supplement, not to replace, the qualitative data.

2. Qualitative researchers may want to create a subjective sense of empathy and understanding among readers in addition to presenting factual evidence and analytic interpretations. Detailed descriptions of specific settings and situations help readers better understand or get a feel for settings. Researchers attempt to transport the reader into the subjective world view and meaning system of a social setting.

3. Qualitative researchers use less standardized techniques of gathering data, creating analytic categories, and organizing evidence. The techniques applied may be particular to individual researchers or unique settings. Thus, researchers explain what they did and why, because it has not been done before.

4. Exploring new settings or constructing new theory is a common goal in qualitative research. The development of new concepts and examination of relationships among them adds to the length of reports. In addition, theory flows out of evidence, and detailed descriptions demonstrate

how the researcher created interpretations from evidence.

5. Qualitative researchers may use more varied and literary writing styles, which increases length. They have greater freedom to employ literary devices to tell a story or recount a tale when translating a meaning system for the reader.

Field Research

Field research reports rarely follow a fixed format with standard sections, and theoretical generalizations and data are not separated into distinct sections.[8] Generalizations are intertwined with the evidence, which takes the form of detailed description with frequent quotes.

Researchers balance the presentation of data and analysis. They want to avoid an excessive separation of data from analysis, called the *error of segregation*. This occurs when researchers separate data from analysis so much that readers cannot see the connection.[9]

The tone of field research reports also differs from those on quantitative research. It is less objective and formal, and more personal. Field research reports may be written in the first person (i.e., using the pronoun *I*) because you were directly involved in the setting, interacted with the people studied, and were the measurement "instrument." The decisions or indecisions, feelings, reactions, and personal experiences of the researcher are parts of the field research process.

Field research reports often face more skepticism than quantitative reports do. This makes it essential for you to assess an audience's demands for evidence and to establish credibility. The key is to provide readers with enough evidence so that they believe the recounted events and accept your interpretations as plausible. A degree of selective observation is accepted in field research, so the critical issue is whether other observers could reach the same conclusion if they examined the same data.[10] Schatzman and Strauss (1973:133) stressed the issue of establishing credibility:

An essential prerequisite to establishing credibility with any audience is the researcher's conviction that what he is saying or writing is so. And this conviction rests upon necessary and credible procedures performed, as well as upon the sense of certainty that the observer did in fact see what he says he saw.

As a field researcher, you face a data reduction dilemma when presenting evidence. Most evidence or data are in the form of an enormous volume of field notes, but you cannot directly share observations or recorded conversations with the readers. For example, in their study of medical students, *Boys in White,* Becker and Geer had about 5,000 pages of single-spaced field notes. Field researchers can only include 5 to 10 percent of their field notes in a report as quotes. The remaining 90 to 95 percent is not wasted; there is just no room for it. Thus, writers select quotes and indirectly convey the rest of the data to readers. In quantitative research, you condense numerical data with statistics, tables, and charts.

There is no fixed organization for a field research report, although a literature review often appears near the beginning. There are many acceptable organizational forms. Lofland (1976) suggests the following:

1. Introduction
   a. Most general aspects of situation
   b. Main contours of the general situation
   c. How materials were collected
   d. Details about the setting
   e. How the report is organized
2. The situation
   a. Analytic categories
   b. Contrast between situation and other situations
   c. Development of situation over time
3. Strategies
4. Summary and implications

Devices for organizing evidence and analysis also vary a great deal.[11] For example, writers can organize the report in terms of a *natural history,* an unfolding of events as you discovered them, or as a *chronology,* following the developmental cycle or career of an aspect of the setting or people in it. Another possibility is to organize the report as a *zoom lens,* beginning broadly and then focusing increasingly narrowly on a specific topic. Statements can move from universal statements about all cultures, to general statements about a specific culture, to statements about specific cultural scene, to specific statements about an aspect of culture, to specific statements about specific incidents.[12]

Field researchers also organize reports by themes. A writer chooses between using abstract analytic themes and using themes from the categories used by the people who were studied. The latter is sometimes preferred because it is crucial to give readers a vivid description of the setting and to display knowledge of the language, concepts, categories, and beliefs of those being written about.[13]

Field researchers discuss the methods used in the report, but its location and form vary. One technique, especially common when a natural history organization is used, is to interweave a description of the setting, the means of gaining access, your role as the researcher, and the subject/researcher relationship into the discussion of evidence and analysis. This is intensified if the writer adopts what Van Maanen (1988:73) called a "confessional" style of writing. When you use a chronological, zoom lens, or theme-based organization, the data collection method may be discussed near the beginning or the end. In book-length reports, methodological issues are usually discussed in a separate appendix.

Field research reports can contain transcriptions of tape recordings, maps, photographs, or charts illustrating analytic categories. They supplement the discussion and are placed near the discussion they complement. Qualitative field research is sometimes reported in creative formats that differ from the usual written text with examples from field notes. Harper's (1982) book contains many photographs with text. The photographs give a visual inventory of the settings described in the text and present the meanings of settings in the terms of those being studied. For example, field research articles have appeared in the form of all photographs (Jackson, 1978) or as a script for a play (Becker et al., 1989). A documentary film on a setting is another form of data presentation.[14]

Another issue in field research reports is that of *negative cases.* A negative case is evidence from field notes and observations that contradicts your interpretation. It can take two forms: members of a setting who have not yet been fully socialized into the meaning system being studied, or individuals who operate on the margins and use an alternative meaning system.[15] Although they do not contradict your primary investigation, negative cases reveal the complexity of the setting and your integrity as a researcher.

Your direct, personal involvement in the intimate details of a social setting heightens ethical concerns. Ethical concerns are discussed with methodological issues or as a separate topic. Researchers write their reports in a manner that protects the privacy of those being studied and helps prevent the publication of a report from harming those who were studied.[16] Field researchers usually change the names of members and exact locations in field reports. When writing a field research report, you must decide how much to disclose about the field setting and about yourself. Personal involvement in field research sometimes leads researchers to include a short autobiography as part of a report. For example, in the appendix to *Street Corner Society,* the author, William Foote Whyte, gave a detailed account of the occupations of his father and grandfather, his hobbies and interests, the jobs he held, how he ended up going to graduate school, and how his research was affected by his getting married.

Historical-Comparative Research

There is no single way to write a report on historical-comparative research. Most frequently, researchers "tell a story" or describe details in general analytic categories. The writing usually goes beyond description and includes limited generalizations and abstract concepts.

Historical-comparative (H-C) researchers rarely describe their methods in great detail. Explicit sections of the report or an appendix that describes the methods used are unusual. Occasionally, a book-length report contains a bibliographic essay that discusses major sources used. More often, numerous detailed footnotes or endnotes describe the sources and evidence. For example, a 20-page report on quantitative or field research typically has 5 to 10 notes, whereas an H-C research report of equal length may have 40 notes. Likewise, it is not unusual to find that notes (printed in small type) constitute one-fifth of the pages in a book-length H-C report.

Historical-comparative reports can contain photographs, maps, diagrams, charts, or tables of statistics. These are placed throughout the report and appear in the section that discusses evidence that relates to them. The charts, tables, and so forth in H-C research reports supplement a discussion or give the reader a better feel for the places and people being described. They are used in conjunction with frequent quotes as one among several types of evidence. Historical-comparative reports rarely summarize data to test specific hypotheses as quantitative research does. Instead, the writer builds a web of meaning or descriptive detail and organizes the evidence itself to convey interpretations and generalizations.

There are two basic modes of organizing historical-comparative research reports: by topic and chronologically. Most writers mix the two types. For example, information is organized chronologically within topics, or organized by topic within chronological periods. Occasionally other forms of organization are used—by place, by individual person, or by major events. If the report is truly comparative, the writer has additional options, such as making comparisons within topics. Figure B.4 provides a sample of some techniques used by historical-comparative researchers to organize evidence and analysis.[17]

Some H-C researchers mimic the quantitative research report and use quantitative research techniques. They extend quantitative research rather than adopt the logic of a distinct historical-comparative research method. Their reports follow the model of a quantitative research report. By contrast, many H-C researchers apply the model of narrative history, which is more consistent with the logic of qualitative social research. Stone (1987:74) described narrative history:

> Narrative is taken to mean the organization of material in a chronologically sequential order, and the focusing of the content into a single coherent story, albeit with subplots. Two essential ways in which narrative history differs from structural history is that its arrangement is descriptive rather than analytical and that its central focus is on man not circumstances. It therefore deals with the particular and specific rather than the collective and statistical.

THE RESEARCH PROPOSAL

What Is the Proposal?

A research *proposal* is a document that presents a plan for a project to reviewers for evaluation. It can be a supervised project submitted to instructors as part of an educational degree (e.g., a master's thesis or a Ph.D. dissertation) or it can be a research project proposed to a funding agency. Its purpose is to convince reviewers that you, the researcher, are capable of successfully conducting the proposed research project. Reviewers have more confidence that a planned project will be successfully completed if the proposal is well written and organized, and if you demonstrate careful planning.

The proposal is similar to a research report, but it is written before the research project begins. A proposal describes the research problem and its importance, and gives a detailed account of the methods that will be used and why they are appropriate.

The proposal for quantitative research has most of the parts of a research report: a title, an abstract, a problem statement, a literature review, a methods or design section, and a bibliography. It lacks results, discussion, and conclusion sections. The proposal has a plan for data collection and analysis (e.g., types of statistics). It frequently includes a schedule of the steps to be

FIGURE B.4 Ten Features to Consider When Writing a Report on Historical-Comparative Research

1. *Sequence.* Historical-comparative researchers are sensitive to the temporal order of events and place a series of events in order to describe a process. For example, a researcher studying the passage of a law or the evolution of a social norm may break the process into a set of sequential steps.

2. *Comparison.* Comparing similarities and differences lies at the heart of comparative-historical research. Make comparisons explicit and identify both similarities and differences. For example, a researcher comparing the family in two historical periods or countries begins by listing shared and nonshared traits of the family in each setting.

3. *Contingency.* Researchers often discover that one event, action, or situation depends on or is conditioned by others. Outlining the linkages of how one event was contingent on others is critical. For example, a researcher examining the rise of local newspapers notes that it depended on the spread of literacy.

4. *Origins and consequences.* Historical-comparative researchers trace the origins of an event, action, organization, or social relationship back in time, or follow its consequences into subsequent time periods. For example, a researcher explaining the end of slavery traces its origins to many movements, speeches, laws, and actions in the preceding fifty years.

5. *Sensitivity to incompatible meaning.* Meanings change over time and vary across cultures. Historical-comparative researchers ask themselves whether a word or social category had the same meaning in the past as in the present or whether a word in one culture has a direct translation in another culture. For example, a college degree had a different meaning in a historical era when it was extremely expensive and less than 1 percent of the 18- to 22-year-old population received a degree compared to the late twentieth century, when college became relatively accessible.

6. *Limited generalization.* Overgeneralization is always a potential problem in historical-comparative research. Few researchers seek rigid, fixed laws in historical, comparative explanation. They qualify statements or avoid strict determination. For example, instead of a blanket statement that the destruction of the native cultures in areas settled by European Whites was the inevitable consequence of advanced technological culture, a researcher may list the specific factors that combined to explain the destruction in particular social-historical settings.

7. *Association.* The concept of association is used in all forms of social research. As in other areas, historical-comparative researchers identify factors that appear together in time and place. For example, a researcher examining a city's nineteenth-century crime rate asks whether years of greater migration into the city are associated with higher crime rates and whether those arrested tended to be recent immigrants.

8. *Part and whole.* It is important to place events in their context. Writers of historical-comparative research sketch linkages between parts of a process, organization, or event and the larger context in which it is found. For example, a researcher studying a particular political ritual in an eighteenth-century setting describes how the ritual fit within the eighteenth-century political system.

9. *Analogy.* Analogies can be useful. The overuse of analogy or the use of an inappropriate analogy is dangerous. For example, a researcher examines feelings about divorce in country X and describes them as "like feelings about death" in country Y. This analogy requires a description of "feelings about death" in country Y.

10. *Synthesis.* Historical-comparative researchers often synthesize many specific events and details into a comprehensive whole. Synthesis results from weaving together many smaller generalizations and interpretations into coherent main themes. For example, a researcher studying the French Revolution synthesizes specific generalizations about changes in social structure, international pressures, agricultural dislocation, shifting popular beliefs and problems with government finances into a compact, coherent explanation. Researchers using the narrative form summarize the argument in an introduction or conclusion. It is a motif or theme embedded within the description. Thus, theoretical generalizations are intertwined with the evidence and appear to flow inductively out of the detailed evidence.

undertaken and an estimate of the time required for each step.

Proposals for qualitative research are more difficult to write because the research process itself is less structured and preplanned. You prepare a problem statement, literature review, and bibliography. You may demonstrate an ability to complete a proposed qualitative project in two ways. First, the proposal is well written, with an extensive discussion of the literature, significance of the problem, and sources. This shows reviewers that you are familiar with qualitative research and the appropriateness of the method for studying the problem. Second, the proposal describes a qualitative pilot study you have conducted. This demonstrates your motivation, familiarity with research techniques, and ability to complete a report about unstructured research.

Proposals to Fund Research

The purpose of a research grant is to provide the resources needed to help you complete a worthy project. You should evaluate why funds are needed before writing a proposal for funding. Researchers whose primary goal is to use funding for personal benefit or prestige or to escape from other activities are less successful. The strategies of proposal writing and getting grants has become an industry called *grantsmanship*.

There are many sources of funding for research proposals. Colleges, private foundations, and government agencies have programs to award grants to researchers. Funds may be used to purchase equipment, to pay your salary or that of others, for research supplies, for travel to collect data, or for help with the publication of results. The degree of competition for a grant varies a great deal, depending on the source. Some sources fund more than 3 out of 4 proposals they receive, others fund fewer than 1 in 20.

There are many sources of funding for social research, but there may be no source willing to fund a specific project. You will need to investigate funding sources and ask questions: What types of projects are funded—applied versus basic research, specific topics, or specific

research techniques? What are the deadlines? What kind (e.g., length, degree of detail, etc.) of proposal is necessary? How large are most grants? What aspects (e.g., equipment, personnel, travel, etc.) of a project are or are not funded? There are many sources of information on funding sources. Librarians or officials who are responsible for research grants at a college are good resource people. For example, private foundations are listed in an annual publication, *The Foundation Directory. The Guide to Federal Funding for Social Scientists* lists sources in the U.S. government. In the United States, there are many newsletters on funding sources and two national computerized data bases (SPIN and IRIS), which subscribers can search for funding sources. Some agencies periodically issue *requests for proposals (RFPs)* that ask for proposals to conduct research on a specific issue. You will need to learn about funding sources, because it is essential to send your proposal to an appropriate source in order to be successful.[18]

You will need to show a track record of past success in the proposal, especially if you are going to be in charge of the project. The researcher in charge of a research project is the *principal investigator (PI)* or project director. Proposals usually include a curriculum vitae or academic resumé, letters of support from other researchers, and a record of past research. Reviewers feel safer investing funds in a project headed by someone who already has research experience than in a novice. You can build a track record with small research projects or by assisting an experienced researcher before seeking funding as a principal investigator.

The reviewers who evaluate a proposal judge whether the proposal project is appropriate to the funding source's goals. Most funding sources have guidelines stating the kinds of projects they fund. For example, programs that fund basic research have the advancement of knowledge as a goal. Programs to fund applied research often have improvements in the delivery of services as a goal. Instructions will ask you to state project objectives and procedures. In addition, they will specify page length, number of copies, deadlines, and the like. Follow all instructions exactly. Why would reviewers give thousands of dollars to a researcher to carry out a complicated research project if he or she cannot even follow instructions on the page length of a proposal?

Proposals should be neat and professional looking. The instructions usually ask for a detailed plan for the use of time, services, and personnel. These should be clearly stated and realistic for the project. Excessively high or low estimates, unnecessary add-ons, or omitted essentials will lower how reviewers evaluate a proposal. Creating a budget for a proposed project is complicated and usually requires technical assistance. For example, pay rates, fringe benefit rates, and so on that must be charged may not be easy to obtain. It is best to consult a grants officer at a college or an experienced proposal writer. In addition, endorsements or clearances of regulations are often necessary (e.g., IRB approval; see Chapter 17 on ethics). Proposals should also include specific plans for disseminating results (e.g., publications, presentations before professional groups, etc.) and a plan for evaluating whether the project met its objectives.

The proposal is a kind of contract between you and the funding source to complete the project. Funding agencies often require a final report, including details on how funds were spent, the findings, and an evaluation of whether the project met its objectives. If you fail to spend funds properly, do not complete the project described in the proposal, or do not file a final report, you may find yourself barred from receiving future funding or may even face legal action. A serious misuse of funds may result in the banning of others at your institution from receiving future funding.

The process of reviewing proposals after they are submitted to a funding source takes anywhere from a few weeks to almost a year, depending on the funding source. In most cases, reviewers rank a large group of proposals, and only highly ranked proposals receive funding. A proposal often undergoes a blind peer review in which the reviewers are other researchers who know the proposer from the vitae in the proposal, but the proposer does not know the reviewers. Sometimes a proposal is reviewed by a group of nonspecialists or nonresearchers. Instructions on preparing a proposal will tell you whether to write for specialists in a field or for an educated general audience. A proposal may be evaluated by more than one group of reviewers. In general, proposals that ask for larger amounts of money receive closer review.

If a proposal is funded, you can celebrate, but only for a short time. Soon, you must begin the work of the project. If the proposal is rejected, which is more likely, do not despair. Most proposals are rejected the first or second time they are submitted. Many funding sources will provide you with written reviewer evaluations of the proposal. Always request them if they are provided. Sometimes, a courteous talk on the telephone with a person at the funding source will reveal the reasons for rejection. Often, you can strengthen and resubmit a proposal on the basis of the reviewer's comments. Most funding sources accept repeated resubmissions of revised proposals, and proposals that have been revised may be stronger in subsequent competitions.

In sum, a proposal for funds to support a research project is a plan for research and a type of contract. It competes with other proposals and is evaluated and ranked by reviewers. If a proposal has been submitted to an appropriate funding source and all instructions are followed, reviewers are more likely to rate it high when:

1. It addresses an important research question. It builds on prior knowledge and represents a substantial advance of knowledge for basic research. It documents a major social problem and holds promise for solutions for applied research.
2. It follows all instructions, is well written, and is easy to follow, with clearly stated objectives.
3. It completely describes research procedures that include high standards of research methodology, and it applies research techniques that are appropriate to the research question.

4. It includes specific plans for disseminating the results and evaluating whether the project has met its objectives.
5. The project is well designed and shows serious planning. It has realistic budgets and schedules.
6. You have the necessary experience or background to complete the project successfully.

CONCLUSION

In this appendix, you learned about writing the research report, different forms of the report, and proposals. Most people find that writing a research report is a difficult task. Yet, as with many difficult tasks that are well done, a genuine feeling of pride and sense of accomplishment develop when the task is completed. Writing is a learned skill that develops with practice.

You saw how the research report is an essential part of the research process. A research project is not finished until it is written as a research report. Writing the report requires time and skill. It also requires planning for it and thinking about it during earlier stages of research. Writing a proposal is similar to writing a research report and involves careful planning and investigation before doing research.

Writing the research report at the end of the research project can be exciting. It is exciting not only because it signals the end of the project and lets you tell others what you did and discovered but also because the process of writing the report generates new ideas and insights. Often, ideas are unclear and relationships in the data are fuzzy until they are written, and rewritten, into a report. Thus, the report gives you an opportunity to clarify and strengthen your thinking.

KEY TERMS

abstract	paraphrasing	research report
composing	plagiarism	revising
editing	prewriting	rewriting
error of segregation	principal investigator (PI)	style
executive summary	proofreading	thesaurus
freewriting	proposal	tone
negative cases	request for proposal (RFP)	writer's block

REVIEW QUESTIONS

1. Why should you write differently for different audiences?
2. What are some of the advantages and disadvantages of using outlines?
3. What can you do if you experience writer's block?
4. What is plagiarism and how can you avoid it?
5. What is the difference between editing and revising writing?
6. At least a partial statement of the findings of a study can appear in more than one section of a quantitative research report. In which section can findings appear?
7. Why are many qualitative research reports longer than those reporting quantitative research?
8. Why is it that field researchers cannot show all their data to readers in reports?
9. What organizational features are used in historical-comparative research reports?
10. Where are the methods used described for quantitative research reports, field research reports, and historical-comparative reports?

NOTES

1. See "Plagiarism Case Documented" (February 1989) and "Noted Harvard Psychiatrist" (December 7, 1989).
2. From Sociology Writing Group (1991).
3. For suggestions on writing, see Donald and colleagues (1983) and Leggett and colleagues (1965).
4. From Sociology Writing Group (1991:40).
5. See Fine (1988) for suggestions on writing.
6. See Mullins (1977:11–30) for a discussion of outlines and organizing quantitative research reports. Also see Williams and Wolfe (1979:85–116) for good hints on how to organize ideas in a paper.
7. Grosof and Sardy (1985:386–389) have provided suggestions on how to explain quantitative findings.
8. Lofland (1974) inductively discovered what he identifies as five major writing styles for reporting field research (generic, novel, elaborated, eventful, and interpenetrated) and discusses how they are evaluated.
9. The error of segregation is discussed in Lofland and Lofland (1984:146).
10. See Becker and Geer (1982:244) and Schatzman and Strauss (1973:130) for a discussion of this and related issues.
11. See Hammersley and Atkinson (1983) and Van Maanen (1988).
12. Discussed in Spradley (1970:162–167).
13. See Van Maanen (1988:13).
14. See Dabbs (1982) for a discussion of graphic and other visual forms of analyzing and presenting qualitative data.
15. See Becker and Geer (1982).
16. For a discussion of ethical concerns in writing field research reports, see Becker (1969), Punch (1986), and Wax (1971).
17. See Barzun and Graff (1970) and Shafer (1980) for excellent suggestions on writing about historical research.
18. For more on writing proposals to fund research projects, see Bauer (1988), Locke and associates (1987), and Quarles (1986). A dated but useful short introduction to proposal writing is Krathwohl (1965).

RECOMMENDED READINGS

Becker, Howard S. (1986). *Writing for social scientists: How to start and finish your thesis, book or article.* Chicago: University of Chicago Press. By recounting his own trials and errors with writing sociology for 35 years, Becker gives advice on all aspects of the very human activity of writing. Writers will benefit from his examples and discussions of such issues as how to get started and how to overcome writer's block. He shows that writing is central to the process of doing social research.

Locke, Lawrence F., Spirduso, Warren Wyrick, and Stephen J. Silverman (1987). *Proposals that work: A guide for planning dissertations and grant proposals,* 2nd ed. Beverly Hills, CA: Sage. This book includes suggestions on how to plan a proposal, what to include in it, and examples of proposals. In addition to suggestions for writing a proposal, there are descriptions of how proposals are evaluated and the process of grant getting.

Mullins, Carolyn J. (1977). *A guide to writing and publishing in the social and behavioral sciences.* New York: Wiley. Here is a handbook on all aspects of writing and publishing in the social sciences. It includes details on writing outlines for different types of research, how scholarly journals and other publication outlets operate, and the mechanics of preparing a manuscript for publication.

Sociology Writing Group, UCLA. (1991). *A guide to writing sociology papers,* 2nd ed. New York: St. Martin's Press. If you need an introductory book on writing an undergraduate sociology paper for a course, this is it. It includes suggestions for organizing time, writing notes, and using the library. It also has examples of student papers with comments noting strengths and weaknesses. The book discusses writing qualitative and quantitative research reports as well as literature review and theoretical analysis papers.

Van Maanen, John. (1988). *Tales of the field: On writing ethnography.* Chicago: University of Chicago Press. Van Maanen offers informal essays on how to write about ethnographic or field research. He also looks at the tension between an ethnographic approach to research and the rhetorical and literary devices available to the researcher to convey the meanings discovered in research.

COMPUTERS IN CRIMINOLOGICAL RESEARCH

> *The implementation of technical innovations implies not only changes in the social structure but in the culture of society. Social conduct is technically patterned. It takes place within the context of a configuration of technologies.*
> —Nico Stehr, *Knowledge Societies,* p. 71

INTRODUCTION

Computers have revolutionized the conduct of research and have become an essential tool in many areas of social research. Today, most researchers use computers as regularly as others operate telephones, televisions, or automobiles, and they do so for the same reason—to perform specific tasks more productively. Computers enable researchers to perform specialized tasks (e.g., organize data, calculate statistics, write reports, etc.) more quickly and efficiently.

Reading this appendix cannot teach you how to use computers. That requires hands-on assistance and instruction tailored to the specific computer system you will be using. Instead, this appendix will give you a general background on computers, present some basic terminology, and explain how computers are used in social research. It outlines the broad contours and guides you to the relevant questions. The uses and types of computers are changing so quickly that more

specific information would be out of date within a year or two.

A Short History

The ancestors of today's computer were mechanical devices developed in the 1800s to sort cards that had holes punched into them. Researchers punched holes in specific locations, and each hole represented information on a variable. The card-sorting machines organized information more quickly, reliably, and efficiently than previous paper-and-pencil methods. For example, in the 1890s, card-sorting machines reduced the time for the U.S. Census Bureau to count and process information from nine years to six weeks.[1]

During World War II and the Cold War years of the 1950s, huge amounts of money and human resources went into military research for the purpose of detecting and directing missiles and other weapons. Also, new and related technologies such as television and space exploration accelerated the advancement of electronics. By the 1960s, engineers redirected these new inventions and technology to build general application machines that could manipulate numerical information. Although they were crude and clumsy by modern standards, the early computers radically enlarged the capacity to manipulate data and changed thinking about information.

As late as the mid-1960s, the only use of computers in social research was for statistical data analysis. Researchers used newer card-sorting machines that were faster and more accurate than those of the 1800s. With the machines, the researchers analyzed survey and existing data using cross-tabulation techniques. The machines could sort and count many thin cardboard cards, called *IBM cards* after the largest maker of cards. The IBM card had 80 columns and 12 rows, or 960 spaces for information. Researchers punched holes exactly into one of the 960 spaces with a large, noisy *keypunch machine*. Thus, data were stored as holes in specific locations on cards. After punching the holes, a researcher used a card-sorting machine to sort large stacks of cards into piles based on the locations of holes.

(*Author's note:* When I (Professor Neuman) first began to analyze research data statistically, I used such cards. My data from a study of 100 cases was a stack of cards about 10 inches (20.5 centimeters) tall. I made three sets of the cards and bound them with rubber bands. With age and wear from the sorting machine, the cards tore and warped, causing problems and constant frustration. It would take me 20 to 30 minutes to create a few raw-count cross-tabulation tables. I took the frequencies and raw-count tables and spent another hour using a calculator to compute percentages or measures of association. The calculators were as large and expensive as today's laptop computers. They could perform only the statistics that one can do with modern handheld calculators that cost less than a decent restaurant meal. With today's computers, I can do the same thing in seconds.)

By 1990s standards, the early computers were very large, outrageously expensive, and exceedingly slow. They cost over $1 million, were the size of a dozen large refrigerators, consumed huge quantities of electricity, had to be kept in special rooms under controlled temperature conditions, and were constantly watched by a team of highly trained technicians. Nevertheless, these large computers, called *mainframe computers,* were more accurate, handled more information, and could precisely perform complex calculations much faster than the card-sorting and calculating machines combined. Most significantly, they could "read" and follow complex instructions called *computer programs.* The programs or instructions told the machine to carry out a huge number of precise logical steps on large amounts of information.

Highly trained computer programmers wrote programs to carry out specific types of tasks (e.g., data sorting, statistics, etc.). Programs depend on an overall *operating system.* It is special software that comes with computers. The operating system allows the software programs to communicate with the hardware, and it controls the traffic of information to and from programs.

By the 1970s, mainframe computers were cheaper and much more powerful. Most colleges, libraries, government agencies, and large companies acquired them for statistical, accounting, and information storage purposes. Today, many still use mainframe computers for analyzing large amounts of data. Modern mainframe computers are much more powerful and can be used by many people at the same time through *time sharing.* This means that the computer is so fast that it can do thousands of different tasks simultaneously. Researchers who use very complex statistics with dozens of variables and very large data sets (e.g., a million cases) still use mainframes, but many can now use smaller, microcomputers.

Advances in technology have turned the punched cards of the 1960s and 1970s into museum artifacts. Today, researchers type data and instructions directly into the computer where they are electronically stored. They use computer terminals or microcomputers. A computer terminal is a simple typewriterlike device connected to a mainframe computer. It has a keyboard (keys like those on a typewriter) and a televisionlike screen. Computer terminals can do very little by themselves. They exist to communicate with mainframe computers that do the work for them.

The electronic apparatus (boxes, switches, machines, wires, etc.) of the computer is called *hardware.* This is to distinguish it from *software,* the electronic messages that computers read, including computer programs or instructions that computers follow. A researcher needs both hardware and software, and without the correct software, the hardware can do nothing.

The Microcomputer Revolution

In the late 1970s, a new type of computer was invented: the micro- or personal computer. Modern microcomputers are as powerful as mainframe computers of the 1960s, cost about 1/1,000 as much, are about 1/1,000 the size, and can be used in many locations by people with just a little training. Microcomputer technology is still rapidly changing. Each year, microcomputers are faster and capable of performing more complex tasks. Microcomputers have replaced mainframes for many chores, have made computer technology accessible to more people, and have stimulated new uses for computers. Often, many microcomputers are linked together in a *local area network (LAN)* or network of computers. In this situation, several microcomputers are linked by electronic cables to a powerful microcomputer or mainframe that allows them to share software or information within the network.

Microcomputers look like terminals, but they are self-contained units that do not need a mainframe computer to perform most tasks. They have three basic parts:

1. *Monitor,* also known as a *CRT (cathode ray tube)* or *VDT (video display terminal).* A televisionlike screen that displays information (words or pictures) communicated to or from a computer.

2. *Keyboard.* A typewriterlike keyboard with additional special keys, used to type information into the computer. Most computers in the 1990s

also come with a *mouse.* It is a hand-sized device that rolls on a desk and controls a pointer within the computer. People who use computers (called *users*) can select options from a program using it.

3. *CPU (central processing unit).* The main box that holds the core computer parts. These include a box to manage electric power and parts that temporarily store electronic information (the memory), follow electronic instructions (the microprocessor), and a part to read and write electronic information on floppy diskettes (discussed later) called *disk drives.* The temporary memory or *RAM (random access memory)* can be thought of as "active thinking space." Its size can greatly affect the speed and performance of software.

Some microcomputers fuse the three parts together. Laptop or notebook computers are lightweight (4 to 7 pounds) and about the size of a medium-sized book. Most use battery power but need to be plugged into an electric outlet for extended use. Other types of microcomputers connect the main parts with heavy wires or cables. Additional equipment may include a *hard disk* (expanded internal storage memory that persists when the computer is turned off), a *CD-ROM* (compact disk–read only memory), a reader (to read words, music, numbers, or pictures from a CD), a printer, a scanner, and a modem.

Printers can vary widely in speed and quality or sharpness of printing. Some use a dot-matrix technology of pins hitting an inked ribbon, others use an ink-jet technology where tiny drops of ink are sprayed onto paper, and some use laser-jet technology where tiny specks of a fine powder called *toner* are melted onto the paper. Newer printers produce color as well as black and white images. A *scanner* is a machine that electronically "reads" a photograph or text page, similar to a photocopy machine, and converts the image into an electronic signal that computer software recognizes. A *modem* sends and receives electronic messages over telephone wires and is connected to a telephone jack or outlet. It may be a separate small box connected to the CPU unit by wires or contained in the CPU. Modems help different computers communicate with one other.

Most microcomputers are built to one of two basic standards: IBM-compatible and Apple, named after the major microcomputer manufacturers. Two standards use different types of microprocessors and operating systems, sometimes called *platforms*. In addition, within each standard, there are multiple computer types with different capabilities that arose as technology changed. IBM-compatible types of computers vary by the version of the Intel-brand or similar microprocessor used. You may have heard of a 486 or a Pentium chip. These are names of Intel-brand microprocessors. Apple or MacIntosh types of machines are based on a different type of chip called Motorola, which also goes by numbers, such as 6300. Processors operate at different speeds. Today, 300 megahertz is a reasonable speed, but fast, high-end models operate at over 400 megahertz. Roughly 15 years ago, a good microcomputer could operate at 12 megahertz!

The operating system in a MacIntosh computer has small pictures and offers choices that a user can select with the mouse. There are currently two main types of IBM-compatible operating systems: DOS and Windows. Windows operates a lot like the MacIntosh operating system. Most programs can work only on a specific a type of computer (MacIntosh or IBM-compatible) and operating system (e.g., Windows, DOS), and version of operating system (e.g., Windows 95, Windows 98). Equipment or programs designed for one type of computer or operating system will rarely work properly on another.

Information enters a microcomputer in six ways:

1. It is built into the computer memory itself.
2. A user types in on the keyboard or selects it using a mouse.
3. It comes across a telephone or communication line and through a modem or hardware device called a network card used in a LAN.
4. It is stored on floppy disks or diskettes, which computers can read.
5. It is stored on CD-ROM disks or other disks for computers.
6. It is read into the computer from a scanner.

Computers organize the information into files. A file can contain text (words) for word processing, computer programs, graphics or pictures, music or sound, video segments, or numerical data. The sizes of files vary greatly. For example, a text file, or one with words, can range in size from one letter to thousands of pages long. Files that contain good-quality graphics, photographic materials, or video information are many times larger than text or numerical files.

Most users store information on a *floppy disk* or diskette, a medium on which electronic information is stored and read by a microcomputer. The diskettes are specially treated paper-thin plastic material enclosed in a protective cover with an opening. The most common floppy disk size is about one-eighth inch (0.5 centimeter) thick by three and one-half inches square (about 1.5 centimeters). Older diskettes were larger and flexible (hence the name *floppy*) but stored much less information. A user places the disk into the slot of a disk drive, so the computer can read and write onto the disk.

Floppy disks can store different amounts of information. They can often hold the equivalent of several hundred typed pages of information. Yet, a disk costs less than many ballpoint pens, and information on it is easy to copy, revise, or update. Although they are inexpensive and easy to use, diskettes wear out. Also, information on them is easily destroyed by invisible magnetic fields. Microcomputer users should always make backup copies of the files on a diskette onto other diskettes.

Most modern microcomputers have a hard drive or hard disk. They are similar to floppy disks, but they are built in to the computer. Hard drives vary in size, but most store 50 to 1,000 times more information than a diskette. Hard drives are essential for storing large software programs and large documents or data sets. Although they can wear out or fail and need to be backed up, they are safer than floppy disks. Hard drive capacity has grown dramatically.

Memory size is measured in megabytes (millions of bytes) or gigabytes (billions of bytes). A byte is a very tiny piece of electronic information. The computer converts tens of thousands of bytes into something humans might recognize (e.g., a word or picture). The size of most diskettes is 1.44 MB or megabytes, and the minimum size of RAM for a lot of software is 32 MB.

HOW COMPUTERS HELP
THE SOCIAL RESEARCHER

Most social researchers trained before the 1980s learned research tools based on paper, charts, or card files. Looking back, it is as if the researchers trained 20 years ago had learned how to use horses and wagons or the telegraph rather than automobiles or telephones. Other technological advances (e.g., photocopiers, FAX machines, and videorecorders) have affected criminological research, but microcomputers have had an enormous impact.

Today, social researchers use computers for five purposes: locating published literature, analyzing quantitative data, analyzing qualitative data, communicating with others and retrieving distant information, and writing research reports and organizing information. Each task requires a specific type of software.

Locating Literature

Researchers use computers to locate literature or previous studies in three ways. They use computers to see what is in a library. By the 1990s, many university and major public libraries had converted their catalogs of holdings from cardboard cards in file drawers to electronic records. Libraries have many different systems, and often only more recent works are in the "on-line" catalog. In addition to a local library, researchers use the Internet (see Box C.1) to search the on-line catalogs of distant libraries.

Second, researchers search scholarly journal indexes or abstracts using computers. A researcher first converts his or her topic into a set of keywords, then uses a computer to search a database of journal article information on a local CD-ROM or at another location through the Internet. Many indexes or abstracts for scholarly journal articles

are available by computer. (Chapter 5 discussed the indexes that are available by computers.) Some major ones include *Social Science Index, CARL* (Colorado Area Research Library), *Socio-File* (includes *Sociological Abstracts*), *Sociological Abstracts, Social Science Citation Index,* and *PsychLit.*

A third use is discussed in more detail later in the section on communication. Researchers access the Internet and locate people or places that list specific bibliographies. A few scholarly journals are published electronically on the Internet and can be read only using a computer. These are still in the early stages of development.

Quantitative Data Analysis

Computers are a necessity for modern quantitative social research. Without a computer and software, a researcher cannot analyze the data from a large-scale research project or calculate complicated statistics in a reasonable amount of time. Although a researcher must invest time and effort into learning how to use computers, the investment can save enormous amounts of time and effort later. A trained researcher with the proper equipment can accomplish in a few hours what once took a *year* to do by hand.

Data formatting for modern computers can be traced to the earlier card technology. The IBM card had a location system of rows and columns. Each row represented a number (e.g., 0–9) and cards had 80 columns. The codebook matched the locations to code categories for variables. Usually, each respondent or case in a study (the unit of analysis) was given one IBM card or was a separate record.[2] Researchers divided the 80 columns into data fields for each variable. For example, a researcher might assign columns 15–21 as the data field for the variable "family income." The field had 7 columns to permit seven digits (i.e., incomes from $0 to $9,999,999), with the number of digits needed for the highest value determining the size of a field. Each column of the field was assigned a digit 0 to 9. Modern computers still use data fields, but there is no longer a limit of 80 columns.

Box C.1 _____

The Internet

The Internet is not a single thing in one place. Rather, the Internet is a system or interconnected web of computers around the world. It is changing very rapidly. One cannot describe everything on the Internet; many large books attempt to do that. Plus even if one tried, it would be out of date in six months. The Internet is changing, in a powerful way, how many people communicate and share information. At the time of this writing, _every day_ 67,000 more people join the Internet.

The Internet provides low-cost (often free), worldwide, fast communication among people with computers or between people with computers and information in the computers of organizations (e.g., universities, government agencies, businesses, etc.). There are special hardware and software requirements, but the Internet potentially can trans-

mit electronic versions of text material, up to entire books, as well as photos, music, video, and other information.

To get onto the Internet, a person needs an account in a computer that is connected to the Internet. Most college mainframe computers are connected, many business or government computers are connected, and individuals with modems can purchase a connection in some areas from private companies that provide access over telephone lines. In addition to a microcomputer, the person needs only a little knowledge about using computers. As more people learn to use computers, as computers become more powerful, and as the Internet expands to more people, it has the potential to accelerate significantly the exchange of various types of information around the globe.

Social researchers use one of the dozens of statistical software packages (e.g., SPSS, SAS, Minitab, or Microcase) to organize quantitative data into charts, tables, and graphs and to perform statistical calculations. The so-called packages collect many statistical procedures into a large, coordinated software program. Today, all quantitative social researchers have learned how to use at least one statistical software package. _SPSS (Statistical Package for the Social Sciences)_ is one of the more popular ones. The packages are easier to learn than computer languages and are specifically designed for analyzing quantitative data. Before learning how to use such software, a researcher must know the fundamentals of organizing quantitative data and have some background in statistics.

Choosing a software package for statistics can get complicated, and there is a wide range of prices. Companies that sell statistical software packages for mainframes and microcomputers periodically develop new, updated versions. What a user does to accomplish a task may vary by version, and a user may not be able to transfer information back and forth from old and new versions.

Also, many companies sell both large, full-featured and smaller, limited-feature forms of the same software.

All statistical packages can compute very basic statistics. They vary in ease of use, clarity of instructions, and format of output. They also vary a great deal in the features for modifying the data, presenting data as graphs, and the more advanced statistics that are calculated in the various software packages. Software packages differ in the maximum number of cases and variables they can process.

Some software packages use interactive processing, others use batch processing. Almost all used _batch_ processing in the past. In a batch form, the user writes a set of instructions and links them to the data. Next, the user submits them to the computer for processing and waits to receive the output after all data and instructions have been processed. Software has become increasingly _interactive_. This means that a user provides the data and a few core instructions at the start. The user then submits short, one-step instructions, one by one, and immediately gets back the output for that step. The speed of calculation depends on the efficiency of the software, the number of cases and type of statistical calculation, and the capacity of the computer hardware (microprocessor speed, RAM memory, and math coprocessor computer chip).

Qualitative Data Analysis

Researchers adopting a qualitative approach are also increasingly using computers for the analysis of nonnumerical data.[3] A researcher who enters notes into a word-processing document can search quickly for particular words and phrases or copy and duplicate sections of the notes using a computer. He or she can also enter codes on field notes in a word-processing document and later locate occurrences of the codes. With word processing, a researcher finds it easier to write analytic memos, add to them, divide them into parts, revise them, and move sections from one place to another. A researcher can also use software to keep track of files or documents, create categories within files, or show linkages among many different files.

During the last 10 years, the growth of specialized programs available for data analysis from a qualitative approach to research has been phenomenal. Weitzman and Miles (1995:4) noted, "Things have happened so fast that many qualitative researchers feel bewildered and uncertain." Next, we discuss the major categories of qualitative analysis of data outlined in Weitzman and Miles (1995). Focus will be on the types of programs and the kinds of analysis they can perform, rather than the details of specific programs. New programs are created each year and new features are being added to existing programs all the time.

Text Retrieval. Some programs perform searches of text documents. What they do is similar to the searching function available in most word-processing software. The specialized text retrieval programs are faster and have the capability of finding close matches, slight misspellings, similar sounding words, or synonyms. For example, when a researcher looks for the keyword *boat*, the program might also tell whether any of the following appeared: *ship, battleship, frigate, row-boat, schooner, vessel, yacht, steamer, ocean liner, tug, canoe, skiff, cutter, aircraft carrier, dinghy, scow, galley, ark, cruiser, destroyer, flagship,* and *submarine.* In addition, some programs permit the combination of words or phrases using logical terms *(and, or, not)* in what are called *Boolean searches.* For example, a researcher may search long documents for when the keywords *college student* and *drinking* and *smoking* occur within four sentences of one another, but only when the word *fraternity* is not present in the block of text. This Boolean search uses *and* to seek the intersection of *college student* with either of two behaviors that are connected by the logical term *or,* whereas the logical search word *not* excludes situations in which the term *fraternity* appears.

Most programs show the keyword or phrase and the surrounding text. The programs may also permit a researcher to write separate memos or add short notes to the text. Some programs count the keywords found and give their location. Most programs create a very specific index for the text, based only on the terms of interest to the researcher. Examples of such programs include Metamorph and ZyIndex.

Textbase Managers.   Textbase managers are similar to text retrieval programs. The key difference is their ability to organize or sort information about search results. Many programs create subsets of text data that help a researcher make comparisons and contrasts. They allow researchers to sort notes by a key idea or to add factual information. For example, where the data are detailed notes on interviews, a researcher can add information on the date and length of the interview, gender of interviewee, location of interview, and so on. The researcher can then sort and organize each interview or part of the interview notes using a combination of key words and added information.

In addition, some programs have *Hypertext* capability. Hypertext is a way of linking terms to other information. It works such that clicking the mouse on one term causes a new screen (one that has related information) to appear. The researcher can identify keywords or topics and link them together in the text. For example, a field researcher wants to examine the person Susan and the topic of hair (including haircuts, hairstyles, hair coloring, and hats or hair covering). The researcher can use Hypertext to connect all places Susan's name appears to discussions of hair. By clicking on Susan's name, one block of text quickly jumps to another in the notes to see all places where Susan and the hair topic appear together.

Some textbase manager software creates cross-tabulation or scatterplot cross-classifications from information in text documents. For example, students keep journals on a course. They write their feelings about each day using one of four categories (boring, stimulating, challenging, or creative). The students also describe the major activities of each day (e.g., group work, discussion, watch videotape, lecture, or demonstration). A researcher can cross-classify student feelings by activity. By adding other information (e.g., male or female), the researcher can see how students with different characteristics felt about various activities and examine whether the feelings changed with the topic being presented or time during the academic year. Two example programs are askSam and Folio VIEWS.

Code-and-Retrieve Programs.

Researchers often assign codes or abstract terms to qualitative data (text field notes, interview records, and video or audiotape transcripts). Code-and-retrieve programs allow a researcher to attach codes to lines, sentences, paragraphs, or blocks of text. The programs may permit multiple codes for the same data. In addition to attaching codes, most programs allow the user to organize the codes. For example, a program can help a researcher make outlines or "trees" of connections (e.g., trunks, branches, twigs) among the codes and the data to which the codes refer. The qualitative data are rearranged in the program based on the researcher's codes and the relations among codes that a researcher specifies. Two example programs are Kwalitan and Ethnograph.

Code-Based Theory Builders.

Qualitative researchers are often interested in the evaluation and generation of theory. Code-based theory builders require that a researcher first assign codes to the data. The programs provide ways for manipulating or drawing contrasts and comparisons among the codes. The relationships among the codes then become the basis for a researcher to test or generate theory.

The types of relations created among the codes may vary by program. A program may permit *if-then* type of logical relations or analytic comparison techniques (discussed in Chapter 16). For example, Corsaro and Heise (1990) described how they coded field research data on young children into separate events. They then examined the logical sequence and relations among the events to search for principles or a "grammar" of implicit rules. They looked for rules that guided the sequencing, combination, or disconnection among events. The program they used, ETHNO, asks for logical connections among the events (e.g., time order, necessary precondition, cooccurrence, etc.), then the program shows the pattern among events.

In contrast to other qualitative programs, code-based theory builders have a powerful ability to manipulate codes to reveal patterns or show relations in data that are not immediately evident. It becomes easier for researchers to compare and classify categories of data. The program QCA (Qualitative Comparative Analysis) uses Boolean logic or algebra to help a researcher analyze the characteristics of several cases and apply the method of difference and method of agreement (see Chapter 16). It performs algebraic computations to identify common and unique characteristics among a set of cases. The algebra is not difficult but it can be time consuming and subject to human error without the program. NUD*IST is another program of this type.

Conceptual Network Builders.

This category of programs helps a researcher build and test theory by presenting graphic displays or networks. The displays do more than diagram data, they help organize a researcher's concepts or thinking about the data. The programs use nodes, or key concepts, that the researcher identifies in data. They then show links or relationships among the nodes. Most programs give graphic presentations with boxes or circles and connected by lines with arrows. The output looks similar to a flowchart diagram, with a web or network of connections among concepts. For example, the data might be a family tree in which the relationships among several generations of family members are presented. Relations among family members (X is a sibling of Y, Z is married to Y, G is an offspring of X) can be used to discuss and analyze features of the network. Example programs include MetaDesign and SemNet.

Communication and Data

E-Mail.   Electronic communication across distances is one of the fastest growing uses of computers. This takes many forms, the most common being electronic mail, or e-mail. E-mail spread in the 1990s with computer networks on college campuses and in large companies, and with the creation of the Internet. E-mail can operate within a single organization (e.g., a university, government agency, or corporation) or between organizations. E-mail lets people send messages (e.g., memos, letters, data files, and sometimes pictures) to one another almost instantly. The messages must be in an electronic format that computers can read, and both the sender and receiver must have e-mail addresses in a large computer.

An Internet e-mail address has several parts. The beginning is a personal name or identification number. This can be one word or a set of words or numbers separated by a period. It is followed by the @ symbol. Next comes a computer system name and an organization name separated by periods. The last part or parts may be the type of organization (e.g., EDU for educational, GOV for government, AC for academic, and COM for commercial) or the organization type and country (e.g., JP for Japan, NZ for New Zealand, etc.). For

example, our e-mail addresses at the University of Wisconsin–Whitewater are as follows:

> Neumanl@uwwvax.uww.edu
> Wiegandb@uwwvax.uww.edu

Social researchers and those in government and private companies increasingly have e-mail addresses. For example, www.abacon.com will get you information from Allyn and Bacon publishing company.

If the receiving person is not using e-mail at the time the message arrives, the e-mail system stores the message and lets the user know that a message is waiting. Similar to voice messages held in a telephone answering machine, computer e-mail holds written messages. Larger computers that are connected to the Internet operate all the time and have backup systems, so they can receive messages 24 hours a day, every day.

Most publishers and other organizations can be reached by Internet. For example, let us say you want to locate a book that you saw advertised several months ago. You cannot recall the author's name or its exact title, but you remember it was published by the University of Chicago Press. You may use the Internet to locate the University of Chicago Press computer and select their catalog. From the catalog you can find the book, along with its title, author, and other information on it. There is even a way you can get information on ordering a copy of the book. You can do all this in five minutes from your home, your flight to your Spring Break destination, or your dorm room in New Zealand.

The Internet can also connect you to others who are interested in a topic and sometimes to bibliographies or data sets that they have created. One way to locate information on the Internet is to use Gopher (discussed later); the other way is to join one of the thousands of Internet "discussion groups."

LISTSERV.   A popular feature of the Internet is LISTSERV. It works when a user subscribes (at no cost) to a mailing list by sending an e-mail message. The list or discussion group is a topic of interest. For example, there is a list for teachers of research methods, one for people who like Italian cooking, one for science-fiction readers, one for people with an interest in qualitative social research methods, or one for users of a statistical software package (e.g., Minitab, SPSS). Subscribers receive announcements and e-mail messages from other subscribers and can ask questions or provide information. Because anyone with Internet access can join and submit messages, a LISTSERV can become a free for all. New Internet users are advised to read one of the many sets of rules about proper etiquette on the Internet that are "posted" on the Internet.

Searching GopherSpace with Veronica.   The Gopher is a very popular tool for using the Internet. It is an electronic menu system first developed by the University of Minnesota. It does not provide fancy graphics or photos, but it is widely available, is easy to use, and requires only a low-level computer. The Gopher presents a list of choices, and a user indicates a choice.

There are several ways to get to Gopher. Often, it requires only typing the word *Gopher* on a Internet computer system. A common choice will be Gophers Around the World. Selecting this option (by moving an arrow symbol next to the option and hitting the return key) opens up a list of nations or world regions. Selecting a nation from the list in the same way opens up a list of places in the country. The places may be states in the United States or organizations. For example, when looking for the book by the University of Chicago Press, one chooses North America, then United States, then Illinois, then University of Chicago Press. Once at the University of Chicago Press's Gopher, one selects Sociology titles and looks for the book. Note that you have to know a little geography and that each Gopher list of options takes you to a more specific level. Returning to the previous menu is easy. You just type the letter *U* (for up) or the left arrow ← key. To leave Gopher, just type the letter *Q* (for quit) and answer *Y* (for yes) when asked whether you really want to quit.

Veronica (or Very Easy Rodent Oriented Network Index of Computerized Archives) is a way to search all the Gopher menus on the Internet or GopherSpace. Gopher can take the user to a huge array of resources, but it can be very time consuming to find specific information. Veronica is an index and retrieval system that locates items throughout the Internet. A user reaches Veronica through a Gopher menu and can search for keywords in directories, or Gopher menus, or in all titles. Searching all titles can be slow.

The Web.   The "web" (or World Wide Web) is a Hypertext-based Internet information retrieval system. Like Gopher, it allows a user to find information on the Internet, including Gophers. It uses Hypertext. This means that words or phrases in a document or text shown on the screen are connected to other screens of information. For example, in the middle of a sentence you read the word **Hypertext** and notice that it is in boldface. Clicking a mouse on the word will quickly connect to a new screen on Hypertext.

A more showy way to browse the web is with a system that has pictures or graphics. Some graphic "browers" are Mosaic, Cello, MacWeb, and Netscape. They permit a user, who has the right software and a very powerful computer, to search the Internet with a friendlier, easier "interface" or set of screens and instructions. As more powerful computers spread, these will probably replace Gophers.

Telnet and FTP.   Telnet is a program that allows an Internet user to log on to, or connect to, large computers in remote locations. For example, a researcher might have accounts on mainframe computers in two different countries. Using Telnet, he or she could do most tasks on the remote computer in Japan that he or she could do on a computer in Wisconsin. The advantage is that a researcher in Japan can access information from the other side of the world.

Telnet requires the user to have permission to use an account in the remote computer, unless the remote computer is an *anonymous FTP server*. This means it permits public access or anonymous FTP. Such access is usually limited to viewing a directory of file names and copying files from a remote to a local computer.

FTP stands for *file transfer protocol.* It is software available on most computers that are connected to the Internet. It lets an Internet user transfer files to or from a remote computer to a local computer. The file may contain data, text, or graphic information. Its main advantage is a fast speed of transferring information across the Internet. Some Gopher menus offer it as a choice. Unless a researcher has a private account on such computers with a password and other information, he or she is limited to public or "anonymous FTP" accounts that can be entered temporarily as a guest.

Writing and Organizing

Writing, storing, and organizing information are an essential part of the research process. Most social researchers today use a word processor for their writing. The word processor is a type of software for computers (and a few low-end computers specially designed for writing purposes only). Word-processing software spread very rapidly during the 1980s as microcomputer hardware became more powerful.

In the past, researchers typed their reports using a typewriter or had a typist type it from a handwritten copy. The typewriter was invented in the late 1800s and spread to office settings in the early 1900s. Electric versions appeared in the 1930s and spread in the 1950s. By the 1960s, electronic versions that could store small amounts of text were developed. Today, word-processing software for microcomputers has replaced many typewriters.

To write reports, papers, and the like, a researcher needs word-processing software (e.g., Word Perfect, Wordstar, Microsoft Word). Most word-processing software allows a user to delete, edit, and revise much easier. The user can move text to different locations, copy text for multiple uses, and format the text in many ways. Most software also provides spell-checking. Storage is also a major advantage of word processing. Once a user enters text, it can be stored indefinitely for later additions, revision, copying, or printing. The storage usually takes much less space than a paper version of the same text.

Despite the many advantages, there are a few drawbacks to word processing. First, one needs access to a microcomputer, software, and printer. Second, the user needs minimal typing skills and has to invest some time into learning the software. Some of the learning may not be transferable, because how one does the same task in different software might vary. Last, it is not always possible to convert material written with one word-processoring software into another without some complications.

CONCLUSION

This appendix has offered a brief introduction to computer terms and ways that social researchers use computers. The number and scope of computer uses has expanded greatly during the past decade. Thirty years ago, computers were only used by quantitative researchers to perform what now appear to be simple calculations. Today, all types of social researchers use computers, including the Internet, for many steps in the research process. Researchers use computers when doing literature reviews, when performing quantitative and qualitative data analysis, when communicating with others, and when writing a research report.

KEY TERMS

batch processing	floppy disk	IBM cards
Boolean searching	FTP (file transfer protocol)	interactive processing
CD-ROM	Gopher	Internet
computer program	hard drive	LAN (local area network)
CPU (central processing unit)	hardware	LISTSERV
e-mail	Hypertext	mainframe computer

modem

mouse

operating system

scanner

software

SPSS (Statistical Package for
the Social Sciences)

Telnet

time sharing

user

Veronica

World Wide Web

REVIEW QUESTIONS

1. Name three advances in the history of computers that had a direct impact on criminological science research and describe the impact of each.

2. Describe e-mail and give two major ways that criminological researchers use it.

3. What three ways could you use computer technology to help you conduct a literature review more quickly or comprehensively than you could without computers?

4. Describe Gopher and give two examples of how one might use it when conducting a social research project.

5. How would you respond to someone who said, "I do not need to learn about computers because I only collect and examine qualitative data." Give at least two specific examples in your answer.

NOTES

1. For a discussion of computer use in social research, see Cozby (1984), Grosof and Sardy (1985:191–206), Heise (1981), Karweit and Meyers (1983), and Norusis (1986).

2. When the data for a case took more than one 80-column card, the researcher created multiple-card records. This required adding an identification number of the case and the card number as separate fields on each card to keep track of information for each case.

3. See Weitzman and Miles (1995) for a comprehensive review of 24 software programs for qualitative data analysis. Also see Fielding and Lee (1991) and Richards and Richards (1994).

RECOMMENDED READINGS

Butler, Mark. (1994). *How to use the Internet.* Emeryville, CA: Ziff-Davis. This is one of many books on using the Internet. It is one that I have used, but there is so much to choose from, it is largely a matter of personal preference.

Fielding, Nigel G., and Raymond M. Lee (eds.). (1991). *Using computers in qualitative research.* Newbury Park, CA: Sage. This early collection of essays describes the basic issues involved when social researchers use computers to examine broadly defined qualitative date.

Grafton, Carl, and Anne Permaloff. (1993). Statistical Analysis and Data Graphics. *Advances in Criminological Science and Computers,* 3:267–284. This essay is a short introduction for beginnners on ways to use computers to display quantitative data in creative ways.

National Journal. (1995). *The federal Internet source*, 3rd ed. Washington, DC: National Journal. This is one of a subset of books on Internet resources. Many government agencies in the United States now make information available on the Internet.

Weitzman, Eben A., and Matthew B. Miles. (1995). *A software sourcebook: Computer programs for qualitative data analysis*. Thousand Oaks, CA: Sage. This is more of a catalog, handbook, or reference manual than text. It provides a detailed analysis of software that provides many new ways of organizing, thinking about, and looking at qualitative forms of data.

Wiggins, Richard W. (1995). *The Internet guide for everyone*. New York: McGraw Hill. See earlier comments on the book by Mark Butler.

BIBLIOGRAPHY

Abelson, Robert P., Elizabeth F. Loftus, and Anthony G. Greenwald. (1992). Attempts to improve the accuracy of self-reports of voting. In *Questions about questions: Inquiries into the cognitive bases of surveys,* edited by Judith M. Turner, pp. 138–153. New York: Russell Sage Foundation.

Abrams, Philip. (1982). *Historical sociology.* Ithaca, NY: Cornell University Press.

Abt, Charles. (1979). Government constraints on evaluation quality. In *Improving evaluation,* edited by L. Datta and R. Perloff. Beverly Hills, CA: Sage.

Achen, Christopher H. (1982). *Interpreting and using regression.* Beverly Hills, CA: Sage.

Adams, Gerald R., and Jay D. Schvaneveldt. (1985). *Understanding research methods.* New York: Longman.

Adler, Patricia A. (1985). *Wheeling and dealing.* New York: Columbia University Press.

Adler, Patricia A., and Peter Adler. (1983). Shifts and oscillations in deviant careers: The case of upper-level drug dealers and smugglers. *Social Problems,* 31:195–207.

Adler, Patricia A., and Peter Adler. (1987). *Membership roles in field research.* Beverly Hills, CA: Sage.

Adler, Patricia A., and Peter Adler. (1993). Ethical issues in self-censorship: Ethnographic research on sensitive topics. In *Research on Sensitive Topics,* edited by Claire Renzetti and Raymond Lee, pp. 249–266. Thousand Oaks, CA: Sage.

Adler, Patricia A., and Peter Adler. (1994). Observational techniques. In *Handbook of qualitative research,* edited by Norman Denzin and Yvonna Lincoln, pp. 377–392. Thousand Oaks, CA: Sage.

Adorno, Theodor W. (1976a). Sociology and empirical research. In *The positivist dispute in German sociology,* edited by Theodor Adorno et al., trans. Glyn Adey and David Frisby, pp. 68–86. New York: Harper and Row.

Adorno, Theodor W. (1976b). The logic of the social sciences. In *The positivist dispute in German sociology,* edited by Theodor Adorno et al., trans. Glyn Adey and David Frisby, pp. 87–104. New York: Harper and Row.

Agar, Michael. (1980). Getting better quality stuff: Methodological competition in an interdisciplinary niche. *Urban Life,* 9:34–50.

Agar, Michael. (1986). *Speaking of ethnography.* Beverly Hills, CA: Sage.

Agger, Ben. (1991). Critical theory, poststructuralism, postmodernism: Their sociological relevance. *Annual Review of Sociology,* 17:105–131.

Agnew, Neil McK., and Sandra W. Pyke. (1991). *The science game: An introduction to research in the social sciences,* 5th ed. Englewood Cliffs, NJ: Prentice-Hall.

Aguilar, Filomeno V. (1989). Curbside capitalism: The social relations of street trading in metropolitan Manila. *Philippine Sociological Review,* 37(3–4):6–25.

Albrecht, Gary L. (1985). Videotape safaris: Entering the field with a camera. *Qualitative Sociology,* 8: 325–344.

Albrecht, Hans-Jorg. (1997). Ethnic minorities, crime, and criminal justice in Germany. In *Ethnicity, crime, and immigration,* edited by Michael Tonry, pp. 31–99. Chicago: University of Chicago Press.

Aldenderfer, Mark S., and Roger K. Blashfield. (1984). *Cluster analysis.* Beverly Hills, CA: Sage.

Allen, Michael Patrick. (1974). Construction of composite measures by the canonical-factor-regression method. In *Sociological methodology, 1973–74,* edited by H. L. Costner, pp. 51–78. San Francisco: Jossey-Bass.

Alm, James. (1996). Explaining tax compliance. *Exploring the underground economy,* edited by Susan Pozo, pp. 103–127. Kalamazoo, MI: W. E. Upjohn Institute for Employment Research.

Almond, Gabriel A., and Sidney Verba. (1963). *The civic culture.* Princeton, NJ: Princeton University Press.

Alpern, Anita. (Oct. 1978). The Taxpayer Compliance Measurement Program: The backbone of an audit selection system. *Tax Adviser,* pp. 605–607.

Altheide, David L. (1976). *Creating reality.* Beverly Hills, CA: Sage.

Altheide, David L. (1980). Leaving the newsroom. In *Fieldwork experience,* edited by W. B. Shaffir, R. Stebbins, and A. Turowetz, pp. 301–310. New York: St. Martin's Press.

Alwin, Duane F. (1977). Making errors in surveys. *Sociological Methods and Research,* 6:131–150.

Alwin, Duane F. (1988). The general social survey: A national data resource for the social sciences. *PS: Political Science and Politics,* 21:90–94.

Alwin, Duane F., and David J. Jackson. (1980). Measurement models for response errors in surveys: Issues and applications. In *Sociological methodology, 1980,* edited by Samuel Leinhardt. San Francisco: Jossey-Bass.

Alwin, Duane F., and Jon A. Krosnick. (1985). The measurement of values in surveys: A comparison of ratings and rankings. *Public Opinion Quarterly,* 49:535–552.

Aminzade, Ronald. (1984). Capitalist industrialization and patterns of industrial protest: A comparative urban study of nineteenth century France. *American Sociological Review,* 49:437–453.

Anderson, Andy B., Alexander Basilevsky, and Derek P. J. Hum. (1983). Measurement: Theory and techniques. In *Handbook of survey research,* edited by Peter Rossi, James D. Wright, and Andy B. Anderson, pp. 231–287. New York: Academic Press.

Anderson, Barbara A., Brian D. Silver, and Paul R. Abramson. (1988). The effects of the race of interviewer on race-related attitudes of black respondents in SRC/CPS national election studies. *Public Opinion Quarterly,* 52:289–324.

Anderson, Elijah. (1989). Jelly's place. In *In the field,* edited by Carolyn Smith and William Kornblum, pp. 9–20. New York: Praeger.

Anderson, N. (1923). *The hobo.* Chicago: University of Chicago Press.

Anderson, Perry. (1974a). *Linkages of the absolutist state.* London: New Left Books.

Anderson, Perry. (1974b). *Passages from antiquity to feudalism.* London: New Left Books.

Anderson, R. Bruce W. (1973). On the comparability of meaningful stimuli in cross-cultural research. In *Comparative research methods,* edited by D. Warwick and S. Osherson, pp. 149–186. Englewood Cliffs, NJ: Prentice-Hall.

Anderson, Sarah, and John Cavanagh. (1997). The top ten list. *The Nation*, pp. 8, 9.

Anderson, Victor. (1991). *Alternative economic indicators*. New York: Routledge.

Andren, Gunnar. (1981). Reliability and content analysis. In *Advances in content analysis*, edited by Karl Erik Rosengren, pp. 43–67. Beverly Hills, CA: Sage.

Andrews, Frank M., Laura Klem, Terrence Davidson, Patrick O'Malley, and Willard Rodgers. (1981). *A guide for selecting statistical techniques for analyzing social science data*. Ann Arbor: Institute for Social Research, University of Michigan.

Anglin, M. Douglas, and George Speckart. (1988). Narcotics use and crime: A multisample, multimethod approach. *Criminology*, 26:197–233.

Annandale, Ellen C. (1988). How midwives accomplish natural birth: Managing risk and balancing expectations. *Social Problems*, 35:95–110.

Applebaum, Richard. (1978a). Marxist method: Structural constraints and social praxis. *American Sociologist*, 13:73–81.

Applebaum, Richard. (1978b). Marx's theory of the falling rate of profit. *American Sociological Review*, 43:67–80.

Aquilino, William S. (1993). Effects of spouse presence during the interview on survey response concerning marriage. *Public Opinion Quarterly*, 57:358–376.

Aquilino, William S., and Leonard Losciuto. (1990). Effects of interview mode on self-reported drug use. *Public Opinion Quarterly*, 54:362–395.

Ardener, Shirley. (1984). Gender orientations in fieldwork. In *Ethnographic research: A guide to general conduct*, edited by R. F. Ellen, pp. 118–129. Orlando: Academic Press.

Aries, E. (1977). Male-female interpersonal styles in all male, all female, and mixed groups. In *Beyond sex roles*, edited by Alice G. Sargent, pp. 292–299. Boulder, CO: West.

Armer, Michael. (1973). Methodological problems and possibilities in comparative research. In *Comparative social research*, edited by M. Armer and A. D. Grimshaw, pp. 49–79. New York: Wiley.

Aronson, Elliot, and J. Merrill Carlsmith. (1968). Experimentation in social psychology. In *The handbook of social psychology, Vol. 2: Research methods*, edited by Gardner Lindzey and Elliott Aronson, pp. 1–78. Reading, MA: Addison-Wesley.

Ashdown, Peter. (1980). Bootlegging in Belize, 1920–1933. *Belizean Studies*, 8:14–19.

Athens, Lonnie. (1992). *The creation of dangerous violent criminals*. Urbana: University of Illinois Press.

Auriat, Nadia. (1993). My wife knows best: A comparison of event dating accuracy between the wife, the husband, the couple, and the Belgium population register. *Public Opinion Quarterly*, 57:165–190.

Auster, Carol J. (1985). Manual for socialization: Examples from Girl Scout handbooks, 1913–1984. *Qualitative Sociology*, 8:359–367.

Ayella, Marybeth. (1993). "They must be crazy:" Some of the difficulties in researching cults. In *Research on Sensitive Topics*, edited by Claire Renzetti and Raymond Lee, pp. 108–124. Thousand Oaks, CA: Sage.

Babbie, Earl. (1989). *The practice of social research*, 5th ed. Belmont, CA: Wadsworth.

Babbie, Earl. (1990). *Survey research methods*, 2nd ed. Belmont, CA: Wadsworth.

Babbie, Earl. (1995). *The practice of social research*, 7th ed. Belmont, CA: Wadsworth.

Backstrom, Charles H., and Gerald Hursh-Cesar. (1981). *Survey research*, 2nd ed. New York: Wiley.

Bailar, Barbara A., and C. Michael Lanphier. (1978). *Development of survey methods to access survey practices*. Washington, DC: American Statistical Association.

Bailey, Kenneth D. (1975). Cluster analysis. In *Sociological methodology, 1975*, edited by David R. Heise, pp. 59–128. San Francisco: Jossey-Bass.

Bailey, Kenneth D. (1983). Sociological classification and cluster analysis. *Quality and Quantity*, 17:251–268.

Bailey, Kenneth D. (1984). A three-level measurement model. *Quality and Quantity*, 18:225–245.

Bailey, Kenneth D. (1986). Philosophical foundations of sociological measurement: Notes on the three-level model. *Quality and Quantity*, 20:327–337.

Bailey, Kenneth D. (1987). *Methods of social research*, 3rd ed. New York: Free Press.

Bailey, Kenneth D. (1988). Ethical dilemmas in social problems research: A theoretical framework. *American Sociologist*, 19:121–137.

Bailey, Kenneth D. (1992). Typologies. *Encyclopedia of Sociology*, Vol. 4, edited by Edgar and Marie Borgatta, pp. 2188–2194. New York: Macmillan.

Bakanic, Von, Clark McPhail, and Rita Simon. (1987). The manuscript

review and decision-making process. *American Sociological Review*, 52:631–642.

Bakanic, Von, Clark McPhail, and Rita Simon. (1989). Mixed messages: Referees' comments on the manuscripts they review. *Sociological Quarterly*, 30:639–654.

Ball, Donald. (1967). An abortion clinic ethnography. *Social Problems*, 14:293–301.

Ball, Michael, and Gregory W. H. Smith. (1992). *Analyzing visual data*. Thousand Oaks, CA: Sage.

Ball, Richard A., and G. David Curry. (1995). The logic of definition in criminology: Purposes and methods for defining "gangs." *Criminology*, 33:225–245.

Banaka, William H. (1971). *Training in depth interviewing*. New York: Harper & Row.

Bankston, William B., and Carol Y. Thompson. (1989). Carrying firearms for protection. *Sociological Inquiry*, 59:75–87.

Bannister, Robert C. (1987). *Sociology and scientism: The American quest for objectivity, 1880–1940*. Chapel Hill: University of North Carolina Press.

Barbash, Ilisa, and Lucien Taylor. (1997). *Cross–cultural filmmaking*. Berkeley: University of California Press.

Bardack, Nadia R., and Francis T. McAndrew. (1985). The influence of physical attractiveness and manner of dress on success in a simulated personnel decision. *Journal of Social Psychology*, 125:777–778.

Barkey, Karen. (1991). Rebellious alliances: The state and peasant unrest in early seventeenth-century France and the Ottoman Empire. *American Sociological Review*, 56:699–715.

Barlow, Melissa Hickman, David E. Barlow, and Theodore G. Chiricos. (1995). Economic conditions and ideologies of crime in the media: A content analysis of crime news. *Crime and Delinquency*, 41:3–19.

Barnes, Barry. (1974). *Scientific knowledge and sociological theory*. Boston: Routledge and Kegan Paul.

Barnes, J. A. (1970). Some ethical problems in modern fieldwork. In *Qualitative methodology*, edited by W. J. Filstead, pp. 235–251. Chicago: Markham.

Barnes, J. A. (1979). *Who should know what? Social science, privacy and ethnics*. New York: Cambridge University Press.

Barry, Brian. (1975). On analogy. *Political Studies*, 23:208–224.

Bart, Pauline. (1987). Seizing the means of reproduction: An illegal feminist abortion collective—How and why it worked. *Qualitative Sociology*, 10:339–357.

Bart, Pauline, and Linda Frankel. (1986). *The student sociologist's handbook*, 4th ed. New York: Random House.

Bartiz, Loren. (1960). *Servants of power: A history of the use of social science in American industry*. Middletown, CT: Wesleyan University Press.

Barzun, Jacques, and Henry F. Graff. (1970). *The modern researcher*, rev. ed. New York: Harcourt, Brace and World.

Basirico, Laurence A. (1986). The art and craft fair: An institution in an old art world. *Qualitative Sociology*, 9:339–353.

Bateson, Nicholas. (1984). *Data construction in social surveys*. Boston: George Allen and Unwin.

Bauer, David G. (1988). *The "how to" grants manual*, 2nd ed. New York: Macmillan.

Bauer, Raymond, ed. (1966). *Social indicators*. Cambridge: MIT Press.

Bausell, R. Barker. (1994). *Conducting meaningful experiments: Forty steps to becoming a scientist*. Thousand Oaks, CA: Sage.

Bayless, David L. (1981). Twenty-two years of survey research at the Research Triangle: 1959–1980. In *Current topics in survey sampling*, edited by D. Krewski, R. Platek, and J. N. K. Rao, pp. 87–103. New York: Academic Press.

Beasley, David. (1988). *How to use a research library*. New York: Oxford University Press.

Beccaria, Cesare. (1764). *On crimes and punishment*, trans. Henry Paolucci [1963]. Indianapolis: Bobbs-Merrill.

Beck, Bernard. (1970). Cooking welfare stew. In *Pathways to data*, edited by R. W. Habenstein, pp. 7–29. Chicago: Aldine.

Beck, E. M., and Stewart E. Tolnay. (1990). The killing fields of the Deep South: The market for cotton and the lynching of blacks, 1882–1930. *American Sociological Review*, 55: 526–539.

Becker, Howard. (1967). Whose side are we on? *Social Problems*, 14: 239–247.

Becker, Howard S. (1969). Problems in the publication of field studies. In *Issues in participant observation*, edited by G. McCall and J. L. Simmons, pp. 260–275. Reading, MA: Addison-Wesley.

Becker, Howard S. (1970a). Practitioners of vice and crime. In *Pathways to data*, edited by R. W. Habenstein, pp. 30–49. Chicago: Aldine.

Becker, Howard S. (1970b). Problems of inference and proof in participant observation. In *Qualitative methodology: Firsthand involvement with the social world*, edited by William J. Filstead, pp. 189–201. Chicago: Markham.

Becker, Howard S. (1970c). Whose side are we on? In *Qualitative methodology*, edited by W. J. Filstead, pp. 15–26. Chicago: Markham.

Becker, Howard S. (1986). *Writing for social scientists: How to start and finish your thesis, book or article*. Chicago: University of Chicago Press.

Becker, Howard S. (1993). How I learned what a crock was. *Journal of Contemporary Ethnography*, 22:28–35.

Becker, Howard S., and Blanche Geer. (1970). Participant observation and interviewing: A comparison. In *Qualitative methodology*, edited by W. J. Filstead, pp. 133–142. Chicago: Markham.

Becker, Howard S., and Blanche Geer. (1982). Participant observation: The analysis of qualitative field data. In *Field research: A sourcebook and field manual*, edited by Robert G. Burgess, pp. 239–250. Boston: George Allen and Unwin.

Becker, Howard S., Blanche Geer, Everett C. Hughes, and Anselm Strauss. (1961). *Boys in white: Student culture in medical school*. Chicago: University of Chicago Press.

Becker, Howard S., Michal M. McCall, and Lori V. Morris. (1989). Theatres and communities: Three scenes. *Social Problems*, 36:93–116.

Beecher, H. K. (1970). *Research and the individual: Human studies*. Boston: Little, Brown.

Beirne, Piers. (1993). *Inventing criminology*. Albany: State University of New York Press.

Beisel, Nicola. (1990). Class, culture, and campaigns against vice in three American cities, 1872–1892. *American Sociological Review*, 55: 44–62.

Bellah, Robert N. (1957). *Tokugawa religion*. Glencoe, IL: Free Press.

Ben-David, Joseph. (1971). *The scientist's role in society*. Englewood Cliffs, NJ: Prentice-Hall.

Ben-Yehuda, Nachman. (1983). History, selection and randomness—Towards an analysis of social historical explanations. *Quality and Quantity*, 17:347–367.

Bendix, Reinhard. (1956). *Work and authority in industry*. New York: Wiley.

Bendix, Reinhard. (1963). Concepts and generalizations in comparative sociological studies. *American Sociological Review*, 28:91–116.

Bendix, Reinhard. (1978). *Kings or people: Power and the mandate to rule*. Berkeley: University of California Press.

Benson, Michael L. (1985). Denying the guilty mind: Accounting for involvement in a white–collar crime. *Criminology*, 23:589–599.

Benton, Ted. (1977). *Philosophical foundations of the three sociologies*. Boston: Routledge and Kegan Paul.

Berelson, B. (1952). *Content analysis in communication research*. Glencoe, IL: Free Press.

Berg, Bruce L. (1989). *Qualitative research methods*. Boston: Allyn and Bacon.

Berger, Peter, and Thomas Luckman. (1967). *The social construction of reality: A treatise in the sociology of knowledge*. Garden City, NY: Anchor.

Berk, Richard A. (1983). An introduction to sample selection bias in sociological data. *American Sociological Review*, 48:386–397.

Bermant, Gordon. (1982). Justifying social science research in terms of social benefit. In *Ethical issues in social science research*, edited by Tom L. Beauchamp, R. Faden, R. J. Wallace, and L. Walters, pp. 125–142. Baltimore: Johns Hopkins University Press.

Bernard, H. Russell. (1988). *Research methods in cultural anthropology*. Newbury Park, CA: Sage.

Bernard, H. Russell, Peter Killworth, David Kronenfeld, and Lee Sailer. (1984). The problem of information accuracy: The validity of retrospective data. *Annual Review of Anthropology*, 13:495–517.

Bhaskar, Roy. (1975). *A realist theory of science*. Atlantic Highlands, NJ: Humanities.

Biersack, Aletta. (1989). Local knowledge, local history: Geertz and beyond. In *The new cultural history*, edited by L. Hunt, pp. 72–96. Berkeley: University of California Press.

Bigus, Odis. (1972). The milkman and his customer: A cultivated relationship. *Urban Life and Culture*, 1:131–165.

Billiet, Jacques, and Geert Loosveldt. (1988). Improvement of the quality of responses to faculty survey questions by interviewer training. *Public Opinion Quarterly*, 52:190–211.

Bishop, George F. (1987). Experiments with the middle response alternative in survey questions. *Public Opinion Quarterly*, 51:220–232.

Bishop, George F., Robert W. Oldendick, and Alfred J. Tuchfarber. (1983). Effects of filter questions in public opinion surveys. *Public Opinion Quarterly*, 47:528–546.

Bishop, George F., Robert W. Oldendick, and Alfred J. Tuchfarber. (1984). What must my interest in politics be if I just told you "I don't know?" *Public Opinion Quarterly*, 48:510–519.

Bishop, George F., Robert W. Oldendick, and Alfred J. Tuchfarber. (1985). The importance of replicating a failure to replicate: Order effects on abortion items. *Public Opinion Quarterly*, 49:105–114.

Bishop, George F., Alfred J. Tuchfarber, and Robert W. Oldendick. (1986). Opinions on fictitious issues: The pressure to answer survey questions. *Public Opinion Quarterly*, 50:240–251.

Blaikie, Norman. (1993). *Approaches to social enquiry*. Cambridge, MA: Polity.

Blalock, Hubert M., Jr. (1968). The measurement problem: A gap between the language of theory and research. In *Methodology in social research*, edited by Hubert Blalock and Ann Blalock, pp. 5–27. New York: McGraw-Hill.

Blalock, Hubert M., Jr. (1969). *Theory construction: From verbal to mathematical formulations*. Englewood Cliffs, NJ: Prentice-Hall.

Blalock, Hubert M., Jr. (1979a). Measurement and conceptualization problems: The major obstacle to integrating theory and research. *American Sociological Review*, 44:881–894.

Blalock, Hubert M., Jr. (1979b). *Social statistics*, 2nd ed. New York: McGraw-Hill.

Blalock, Hubert M., Jr. (1982). *Conceptualization and measurement in the social sciences*. Beverly Hills, CA: Sage.

Blalock, Hubert M., Jr., and Ann B. Blalock, eds. (1968). *Methodology in social research*. New York: McGraw-Hill.

Blankenship, Albert B. (1977). *Professional telephone surveys*. New York: McGraw-Hill.

Blau, Judith R. (1978). Sociometric structure of a scientific discipline. *Research in Sociology of Knowledge, Sciences and Art*, 1:191–206.

Blee, Kathleen M. (1991). *Women of the Klan: Racism and gender in the 1920s*. Berkeley: University of California Press.

Blee, Kathleen M., and Dwight B. Billings. (1986). Reconstructing daily life in the past: An hermeneutical approach to ethnographic data. *Sociological Quarterly*, 27:443–462.

Bleicher, Josef. (1980). *Contemporary hermeneutics*. Boston: Routledge and Kegan Paul.

Bloch, Marc. (1953). *The historian's craft*, trans. Peter Putnam. New York: Vintage.

Block, Alan. (1985). *East side–west side: Organizing crime in New York, 1930–1950*. New Brunswick, NJ: Transaction.

Block, Alan A., and William J. Chambliss. (1981). *Organizing crime*. New York: Elsevier.

Block, Fred. (1977). Beyond corporate liberalism. *Social Problems*, 24:353–361.

Block, Fred, and Gene A. Burns. (1986). Productivity as a social problem: The uses and misuses of social indicators. *American Sociological Review*, 51:767–780.

Bloor, Michael J. (1983). Notes on member validation. In *Contemporary field research*, edited by R. M. Emerson, pp. 156–171. Boston: Little, Brown.

Blum, Debra E. (1989). A dean is charged with plagiarizing a dissertation for his book on Muzak. *Chronicle of Higher Education*, 35: A17.

Blume, Stuart S. (1974). *Toward a political sociology of science*. New York: Free Press.

Blumer, M. (1984). *The Chicago school of sociology*. Chicago: University of Chicago.

Blumer, Martin. (1991a). W. E. B. DuBois as a social investigator: The Philadelphia Negro 1889. In *The social survey in historical perspective, 1880–1940*, edited by M. Blumer, K. Bales, and K. Sklar, pp. 170–188. New York: Cambridge University Press.

Blumer, Martin. (1991b). The decline of the social survey movement and the rise of American empirical sociology. In *The social survey in historical perspective, 1880–1940*, edited by M. Blumer, K. Bales, and K. Sklar, pp. 271–315. New York: Cambridge University Press.

Blumer, Martin. (1992). The growth of applied sociology after 1945: The prewar establishment of the postwar infrastructure. *Sociology and its publics: The forms and fates of disciplinary organization*, edited by Terence C. Halliday and Morris Janowitz, pp. 317–346. Chicago: University of Chicago.

Blumer, Martin, K. Bales, and K. Sklar. (1991). The social survey in historical perspective. In *The social survey in historical perspective, 1880–1940*, edited by M. Blumer, K. Bales, and K. Sklar, pp. 1–48. New York: Cambridge University Press.

Blumstein, Alfred. (1974). Seriousness weights in an index of crime. *American Sociological Review*, 39: 854–864.

Bogardus, Emory S. (1959). *Social distance*. Yellow Springs, OH: Antioch.

Bogdan, Robert, and Steven J. Taylor. (1975). *Introduction to qualitative research methods: A phenomenological approach to the social sciences*. New York: Wiley.

Bohrnstedt, George. (1992a). Reliability. *Encyclopedia of Sociology*, Vol. 3, edited by Edgar and Marie Borgatta, pp. 1626–1632. New York: Macmillan.

Bohrnstedt, George. (1992b). Validity. *Encyclopedia of Sociology*, Vol. 4, edited by Edgar and Marie Borgatta, pp. 2217–2222. New York: Macmillan.

Bohrnstedt, George W., and Edgar F. Borgatta, eds. (1981). *Social measurement: Current issues*. Beverly Hills, CA: Sage.

Bohrnstedt, George, and David Knoke. (1994). *Statistics for social data analysis*, 3rd ed. Itasca, IL: Peacock.

Bollen, Kenneth A., Barbara Entwisle, and Arthur S. Alderson. (1993). Macrocomparative research methods. *Annual Review of Sociology*, 19:321–351.

Bonnell, Victoria E. (1980). The uses of theory, concepts and comparison in historical sociology. *Comparative Studies in Society and History*, 22:156–173.

Borgatta, Edgar F., and George W. Bohrnstedt. (1980). Level of measurement: Once over again. *Sociological Methods and Research*, 9:147–160.

Boruch, Robert F. (1982). Methods for revolving privacy problems in social research. In *Ethical issues in social science research*, edited by Tom L. Beauchamp, R. Faden, R. J. Wallace, and L. Walters, pp. 292–313. Baltimore: Johns Hopkins University Press.

Boruch, Robert F. (1989). Experimental and quasi–experimental designs in taxpayer compliance research. In *Taxpayer compliance*, edited by Jeffrey A. Roth, John T. Scholz, and Anne D. Witte, pp. 339–379. Philadelphia: University of Pennsylvania Press.

Bottomore, Thomas. (1984). *The Frankfurt School*. New York: Travistock.

Bouchard, Thomas J., Jr. (1976). Unobtrusive measures: An inventory of uses. *Sociological Methods and Research*, 4:267–300.

Bradburn, Norman M. (1983). Response effects. In *Handbook of survey research*, edited by Peter Rossi, James Wright, and Andy Anderson, pp. 289–328. Orlando, FL: Academic.

Bradburn, Norman M., and Carrie Miles. (1979). Vague qualifiers. *Public Opinion Quarterly*, 43: 92–101.

Bradburn, Norman M., and Seymour Sudman. (1980). *Improving interview method and questionnaire design.* San Francisco: Jossey-Bass.

Bradburn, Norman M., and Seymour Sudman. (1988). *Polls and surveys: Understanding what they tell us.* San Francisco: Jossey-Bass.

Brannigan, Augustine. (1992). Postmodernism. *Encyclopedia of Sociology,* Vol. 3, edited by Edgar and Marie Borgatta, pp. 1522–1525. New York: Macmillan.

Braudel, Fernand. (1980). *On history,* trans. Sarah Matthews. Chicago: University of Chicago Press.

Bredo, Eric, and Walter Feinberg, eds. (1982). *Knowledge and values in social and educational research.* Philadelphia: Temple University Press.

Brenner, Michael. (1985). Survey interviewing. In *The research interview: Uses and approaches,* edited by Michael Brenner, Jennifer Brown, and David Canter, pp. 9–36. New York: Academic Press.

Brenner, Michael, Jennifer Brown, and David Canter, eds. (1985). *The research interview: Uses and approaches.* Orlando, FL: Academic Press.

Briggs, Charles L. (1986). *Learning how to ask: A sociolinguist appraisal of the role of the interview in social science research.* New York: Cambridge University Press.

Brinberg, David, and Joseph E. McGrath. (1982). A network of validity concepts. In *Forms of validity in research,* edited by David Brinberg and Louise H. Kidder, pp. 5–21. San Francisco: Jossey-Bass.

Broad, W. J., and N. Wade. (1982). *Betrayers of the truth.* New York: Simon and Schuster.

Broadhead, Robert, and Ray Rist. (1976). Gatekeepers and the social control of social research. *Social Problems,* 23:325–336.

Broadhurst, Roderic. (1997). Aborigines and crime in Australia. In *Ethnicity, crime, and immigration,* edited by Michael Tonry, pp. 407–468. Chicago: University of Chicago Press.

Brodsky, Stanley L., and H. O'Neal Smitherman. (1983). *Handbook of scales for research in crime and delinquency.* New York: Plenum.

Brody, Charles J. (1986). Things are rarely black or white: Admitting gray into the converse model of attitude stability. *American Journal of Sociology,* 92:657–677.

Bromley, David G., and Anson D. Shupe, Jr. (1979). *Moonies in America: Culture, church and crusade.* Beverly Hills, CA: Sage.

Brown, Jennifer, and David Canter. (1985). The uses of explanation in the research interview. In *The research interview: Uses and approaches,* edited by Michael Brenner, Jennifer Brown, and David Canter, pp. 217–245. New York: Academic Press.

Brown, M. Craig, and Barbara Warner. (1992). Immigrants, urban politics, and policing in 1900. *American Sociological Review,* 57:293–305.

Brown, Richard Harvey. (1978). Symbolic realism and sociological thought. In *Structure, consciousness and history,* edited by R. H. Brown and S. M. Lyman, pp. 14–37. New York: Cambridge University Press.

Brown, Richard Harvey. (1989). *Social science as civic discourse: Essays on the invention, legitimation and uses of social theory.* Chicago: University of Chicago Press.

Brown, Steven R. (1980). *Political subjectivity: Applications of Q methodology in political science.* New Haven, CT: Yale University Press.

Brown, Steven R. (1986). Q technique and method: Principles and procedures. In *New tools for social scientists: Advances and applications in research methods,* edited by William D. Berry and Michael S. Lewis-Beck, pp. 57–76. Beverly Hills, CA: Sage.

Brym, Robert J. (1980). *Intellectuals and politics.* Boston: George Allen and Unwin.

Burawoy, Michael. (1977). Social structure, homogenization, and the process of status attainment in the United States and Great Britain. *American Journal of Sociology,* 82:1031–1042.

Burawoy, Michael. (1979). *Manufacturing consent.* Chicago: University of Chicago Press.

Burawoy, Michael. (1985). Karl Marx and the satanic mills: Factory politics under early capitalism in England, the United States, and Russia. *American Journal of Sociology,* 90:247–282.

Burawoy, Michael. (1989). Two methods in search of science: Skocpol versus Troksky. *Theory and Society,* 18:759–806.

Burawoy, Michael. (1990). Marxism as science: Historical challenges and theoretical growth. *American Sociological Review,* 55:775–793.

Burawoy, Michael. (1991). The extended case method. In *Ethnography unbound: Power and resistance in the modern metropolis,* edited by Michael Burawoy et al., pp. 271–287. Berkeley: University of California Press.

Burawoy, Michael, and Janos Lukács. (1985). Mythologies of work: A comparison of firms in state social-ism and advanced capitalism. *American Sociological Review,* 50:723–737.

Burd, Stephen. (October 2, 1991). Scientists fear rise of intrusion in work supported by NIH. In *Chronicle of Higher Education,* p. A1ff.

Burgess, Robert G. (1982a). Approaches to field research. In *Field research,* edited by R. G. Burgess, pp. 1–11. Boston: George Allen and Unwin.

Burgess, Robert G. (1982b). Keeping field notes. In *Field research,* edited by R. G. Burgess, pp. 191–194. Boston: George Allen and Unwin.

Burgess, Robert G. (1982c). The unstructured interview as a conversation. In *Field research,* edited by R. G. Burgess, pp. 107–110. Boston: George Allen and Unwin.

Burke, Peter. (1980). *Sociology and history.* Boston: George Allen and Unwin.

Burke, Peter. (1992). *History and social theory.* Ithaca, NY: Cornell University Press.

Burnstein, Leigh, Howard E. Freeman, and Peter H. Rossi, eds. (1985). *Collecting evaluation data: Problems and solutions.* Beverly Hills, CA: Sage.

Burrage, Michael C., and David Corry. (1981). At sixes and sevens: Occupational status in the city of London from the 14th to the 17th century. *American Sociological Review,* 46:375–392.

Burton, Michael L., and Douglas R. White. (1987). Cross-cultural surveys today. *Annual Review of Anthropology,* 16:143–160.

Butterfield, Fox. (Oct. 27, 1997). Drop in homicide rate linked to crack's decline. *New York Times,* p. A10.

Byrne, Noel. (1978). Sociotemporal considerations of everyday life suggested by an empirical study of the bar milieu. *Urban Life,* 6:417–438.

Camic, Charles. (1980). The institutionalization of the role of scientist: England in the seventeenth century and ancient Greece. *Comparative Social Research,* 3: 271–285.

Camic, Charles, and Yu Xie. (1994). The statistical turn in American social science: Columbia University, 1890–1915. *American Sociological Review,* 59: 773–805.

Campbell, Donald T., and D. W. Fiske. (1959). Convergent and discriminant validation by the multitrait-multimethod matrix. *Psychological Bulletin,* 56:81–105.

Campbell, Donald T., and Julian C. Stanley. (1963). *Experimental and quasi-experimental designs for research.* Chicago: Rand McNally.

Campbell, John P., Richard L. Daft, and Charles L. Hulin. (1982). *What to study: Generating and developing research questions.* Beverly Hills, CA: Sage.

Cancian, Francesca M., and Cathleen Armstead. (1992). Participatory research. *Encyclopedia of Sociology*, Vol. 3, edited by Edgar and Marie Borgatta, pp. 1427–1432. New York: Macmillan.

Cannell, Charles F., and Robert L. Kahn. (1968). Interviewing. In *Handbook of social psychology*, 2nd ed., edited by Gardner Lindzey and Elliot Aronson, pp. 526–595. Reading, MA: Addison-Wesley.

Cannell, Charles F., Peter V. Miller, and Lois Oksenberg. (1981). Research on interviewing techniques. In *Sociological methodology, 1981*, edited by Samuel Leinhardt, pp. 389–436. San Francisco: Jossey-Bass.

Canter, David, Jennifer Brown, and Linda Goat. (1985). Multiple sorting procedure for studying conceptual systems. In *The Research Interview: Uses and Approaches*, edited by Michael Brenner, Jennifer Brown, and David Canter, pp. 79–114. New York: Academic Press.

Cantor, Norman F., and Richard I. Schneider. (1967). *How to study history.* New York: Thomas Y. Crowell.

Caplan, Arthur L. (1982). On privacy and confidentiality in social science research. In *Ethical issues in social science research*, edited by Tom L. Beauchamp, R. Faden, R. J. Wallace, and L. Walters, pp. 315–327. Baltimore: Johns Hopkins University Press.

Cappell, Charles L., and Thomas M. Guterbock. (1992). Visible colleges: The social and conceptual structure of sociology specialties. *American Sociological Review*, 57:266–273.

Capron, Alexander Morgan. (1982). Is consent always necessary in social science research? In *Ethical issues in social science research*, edited by Tom L. Beauchamp, R. Faden, R. J. Wallace, and L. Walters, pp. 215–231. Baltimore: Johns Hopkins University Press.

Carl, Jim. (1994). Parental choice as national policy in England and the United States. *Comparative Education Review*, 38:294–322.

Carley, Michael. (1981). *Social measurement and social indicators: Issues of policy and theory.* London: George Allen and Unwin.

Carlson, Susan M., and Raymond J. Michalowski. (1997). Crime, unemployment, and social structures of accumulation: An inquiry into historical contingency. *Justice Quarterly*, 14:209–242.

Carmines, E., and R. Zeller. (1979). *Reliability and validity assessment.* Beverly Hills, CA: Sage.

Carney, Thomas F. (1972). *Content analysis: A technique for systematic inference from communications.* Winnipeg: University of Manitoba Press.

Carr, Edward Hallett. (1961). *What is history?* New York: Vintage.

Carr-Hill, Roy A. (1984a). The political choice of social indicators. *Quality and Quantity*, 18:173–191.

Carr-Hill, Roy A. (1984b). Radicalising survey methodology. *Quantity and Quality*, 18:275–292.

Caute, David. (1978). *The great fear.* New York: Touchstone.

Cavan, Sherri. (1974). Seeing social structure in a rural setting. *Urban Life*, 3:329–361.

Cerulo, Karen A. (1989). Sociopolitical control and the structure of national symbols: An empirical analysis of anthems. *Social Forces*, 68:76–99.

Chadwick, Bruce A., Howard M. Bahr, and Stan L. Albrecht. (1984). *Social science research methods.* Englewood Cliffs, NJ: Prentice-Hall.

Chafetz, Janet Saltzman. (1978). *A primer on the construction and testing of theories in sociology.* Itasca, IL: Peacock.

Chambers, Marcia. (1986). Jesuit priest standing by the survey that Vatican attempted to suppress. *New York Times*, October 22, 1986.

Channels, Noreen L. (1993). Anticipating media coverage: Methodological decisions regarding criminal justice research. In *Research on Sensitive Topics*, edited by Claire Renzetti and Raymond Lee, pp. 267–280. Thousand Oaks, CA: Sage.

Chase-Dunn, Christopher. (1989). *Global formation: Structures of the world economy.* Cambridge, MA: Blackwell.

Chermak, Steven. (1994). Body count news: How crime is presented in the news media. *Justice Quarterly*, 11:561–582.

Chermak, Steven. (1997). The presentation of drugs in the news media: News sources involved in the construction of social problems. *Justice Quarterly*, 14:687–718.

Chesney-Lind, Meda. (1998). *The female offender.* Newbury Park, CA: Sage.

Chicago manual of style for authors, editors and copywriters, 13th ed., revised and expanded. (1982). Chicago: University of Chicago Press.

Church, Allan H. (1993). Estimating the effect of incentives on mail survey response rates: A meta analysis. *Public Opinion Quarterly*, 57:62–80.

Churchill, Gilbert A., Jr. (1983). *Marketing research: Methodological foundations*, 3rd ed. New York: Dryden.

Cicourel, Aaron. (1964). *Method and measurement in sociology.* Glencoe, IL: Free Press.

Cicourel, Aaron. (1973). *Cognitive sociology.* London: Macmillan.

Cicourel, Aaron. (1982). Interviews, surveys, and the problem of ecological validity. *American Sociologist*, 17:11–20.

Clammer, John. (1984). Approaches to ethnographic research. In *Ethnographic research: A guide to general conduct*, edited by R. F. Ellen, pp. 63–85. Orlando: Academic Press.

Clark, Herbert H., and Michael F. Schober. (1992). Asking questions and influencing answers. In *Questions about questions: Inquiries into the cognitive bases of surveys*, edited by Judith M. Turner, pp. 15–48. New York: Russell Sage Foundation.

Clark, John, James Austin, and D. Alan Henry. (1997). *Three strikes and you're out.* Washington, DC: National Institute of Justice.

Clarke, Michael. (1975). Survival in the field: Implications of personal experience in field work. *Theory and Society*, 2:95–123.

Clinard, Marshall B., and Daniel J. Abbott. (1973). *Crime in developing countries: A comparative perspective.* New York: John Wiley & Sons.

Clinard, Marshall B., and Peter C. Yeager. (1980). *Corporate crime.* New York: Free Press.

Clogg, Clifford C., and D. O. Sawyer. (1981). A comparison of alternative models for analyzing the scalability of response patterns. In *Sociological methodology 1981*, edited by S. Leinhardt, pp. 240–280. San Francisco: Jossey-Bass.

Clubb, Jerome M., E. Austin, C. Geda, and M. Traugott. (1985). Sharing research data in the social sciences. In *Sharing research data*, edited by Stephen E. Fineberg, M. Martin, and M. Straf, pp. 39–88. Washington, DC: National Academy Press.

Cogan, Johan, Judith Torney-Purta, and Douglas Anderson. (1988). Knowledge and attitudes toward global issues: Students in Japan and the United States. *Comparative Education Review*, 32:283–297.

Cohen, Lawrence E., and Marcus Felson. (1979). Social change and crime: A routine activity approach. *American Sociological Review*, 44:588–608.

Cohen, Patricia Cline. (1982). *A calculating people: The spread of numeracy in early America.* Chicago: University of Chicago Press.

Cohen, Stephen R. (1991). The Pittsburg survey and the social survey movement: A sociological road not taken. In *The social survey in historical perspective, 1880–1940*, edited by M. Blumer, K. Bales, and K. Sklar, pp. 245–268, New York: Cambridge University Press.

Cole, Jonathan R., and Stephen Cole. (1973). *Social stratification in science*. Chicago: University of Chicago Press.

Cole, Stephen. (1978). Scientific reward systems: A comparative analysis. *Research in the Sociology of Knowledge, Science and Art*, 1:167–190.

Cole, Stephen. (1983). The hierarchy of the sciences? *American Journal of Sociology*, 89:111–139.

Cole, Stephen. (1994). Why sociology doesn't make progress like the natural sciences. *Sociological Forum*, 9:133–154.

Cole, Stephen, Jonathan Cole, and Gary A. Simon. (1981). Chance and consensus in peer review. *Science*, 214:881–885.

Coleman, James William. (1998). *The criminal elite*. New York: St. Martin's Press.

Collins, H. M. (1983). The sociology of scientific knowledge: Studies of contemporary science. *American Review of Sociology*, 9:265–285.

Collins, Randall. (1984). Statistics versus words. *Sociological Theory*, 2:329–362.

Collins, Randall. (1986). Is 1980s sociology in the doldrums? *American Journal of Sociology*, 91:1336–1355.

Collins, Randall. (1988). *Theoretical sociology*. New York: Harcourt Brace Jovanovich.

Collins, Randall. (1989). Sociology: Proscience or anti-science? *American Sociological Review*, 54:124–139.

Collins, Randall. (1994). Why the social sciences won't become high-consensus, rapid-discovery science. *Sociological Forum*, 9:155–177.

Collins, Randall, and Sal Restivo. (1983). Development, diversity and conflict in the sociology of science. *Sociological Quarterly*, 24:185–200.

Comaroff, John, and Jean Comeroff. (1992). *Ethnography and the historical imagination*. Boulder, CO: Westview.

Committees on the Status of Women in Sociology. (1986). *The treatment of gender in research*. Washington, DC: American Sociological Association.

Contrad, Peter, and Shulamit Reinharz. (1984). Computers and qualitative data: Editors' introductory essay. *Qualitative Sociology*, 7:3–15.

Converse, Jean M. (1984). Strong arguments and weak evidence: The open/closed questioning controversy of the 1940s. *Public Opinion Quarterly*, 48:267–282.

Converse, Jean M. (1987). *Survey research in the United States: Roots and emergence, 1890–1960*. Berkeley: University of California Press.

Converse, Jean M., and Stanley Presser. (1986). *Survey questions: Handcrafting the standardized questionnaire*. Beverly Hills, CA: Sage.

Converse, Jean M., and Howard Schuman. (1974). *Conversations at random: Survey research as interviewers see it*. New York: Wiley.

Cook, Judith A., and Mary Margaret Fonow. (1990). Knowledge and women's interests: Issues of epistemology and methodology in feminist sociological research. In *Feminist research methods*, edited by Joyce McCarl Nielsen, pp. 69–93. Boulder, CO: Westview.

Cook, Thomas D., and Donald T. Campbell. (1979). *Quasi-experimentation: Design and analysis issues for field settings*. Chicago: Rand McNally.

Coombs, R. H., and L. J. Goldman. (1973). Maintenance and discontinuity of coping mechanisms in an intensive care unit. *Social Problems*, 20:342–355.

Cooper, Harris M. (1984). *The integrative research review: A systematic approach*. Beverly Hills, CA: Sage.

Cordes, Colleen. (Dec. 14, 1988). Legacy of "Golden Fleece" awards to survive Proxmire's retirement. *Chronicle of Higher Education*.

Corsaro, William A. (1988). Routines in the peer culture of American and Italian nursery school children. *Sociology of Education*, 61:1–14.

Corsaro, William A. (1992). Cross-cultural analysis. In *Encyclopedia of Sociology*, Vol. 1, edited by Edgar and Marie Borgatta, pp. 390–395. New York: Macmillan.

Corsaro, William A., and David Heise. (1990). Event structure models from ethnographic data. *Sociological Methodology*, 20:1–57.

Corsino, Louis. (1987). Fieldworkers blues: Emotional stress and research underinvolvement in fieldwork settings. *Social Science Journal*, 24:275–285.

Coser, Lewis A., and Rosenberg, Bernard. (1976). *Sociological theory: A book of readings*. New York: Macmillian.

Costner, Herbert L. (1969). Theory, deduction and rules of correspondence. *American Journal of Sociology*, 75:245–263.

Costner, Herbert L. (1985). Theory, deduction and rules of correspondence. In *Causal models in the social sciences*, 2nd ed., edited by H. M. Blalock, Jr., pp. 229–250. New York: Aldine.

Cotter, Patrick R., Jeffrey Cohen, and Philip B. Coulter. (1982). Race of interview effects in telephone interviews. *Public Opinion Quarterly*, 46:278–286.

Couch, Carl J. (1987). Objectivity: A crutch and club for bureaucrats/subjectivity: A haven for lost souls. *Sociological Quarterly*, 28:105–118.

Cox, Stephen, and William Davidson. (1995). A meta-analysis of alternative education programs. *Crime and Delinquency*, 41:219–230.

Cozby, Paul C. (1984). *Using computers in the behavioral sciences*. Palo Alto, CA: Mayfield.

Crane, Diana. (1967). The gatekeepers of science: Some factors affecting the selection of articles for scientific journals. *American Sociologist*, 2:195–201.

Crane, Diana. (1972). *Invisible colleges*. Chicago: University of Chicago Press.

Creswell, John W. (1994). *Research design: Qualitative and quantitative approaches*. Thousand Oaks, CA: Sage.

Crime and Justice International. (June 11–12, 1998a). UNICRI reports on activities.

Crime and Justice International. (May 22–23, 1998b). U.S. to increase Drug War.

Cromwell, Paul. (1996). *In their own words: Criminals on crime*. Los Angeles: Roxbury.

Cromwell, Paul F., James N. Olson, and D'Aunn W. Avary. (1993). Who buys stolen property? A new look at criminal receiving. *Journal of Crime and Justice*, 56: 75–95.

Croyle, Robert T., and Elizabeth Loftus. (1992). Improving episodic memory performance of survey respondents. In *Questions about questions: Inquiries into the cognitive bases of surveys*, edited by Judith M. Turner, pp. 95–101. New York: Russell Sage Foundation.

Cullen, Francis T., Bruce Link, and Craig Polanzi. (1982). The seriousness of crime revisited: Have attitudes toward white collar crime changed? *Criminology*, 20:83–102.

Cummings, Scott. (1984). The political economy of funding for social science research. *Sociological Inquiry*, 54:154–170.

Curran, Daniel J., and Sandra Cook. (1993). Doing research in post-Tiananmen China. In *Research on Sensitive Topics*, edited by Claire Renzetti and Raymond Lee, pp. 71–81. Thousand Oaks, CA: Sage.

Curry, G. David, Richard A. Ball, and Scott H. Decker. (1996). *Estimating the national scope of gang crime from law enforcement data.* Washington, DC: U.S. Department of Justice.

Czaja, Ronald, Johnny Blair, and Jutta P. Sebestik. (1982). Respondent selection in a telephone survey: A comparison of three techniques. *Journal of Marketing Research,* 19:381–385.

Dale, Angela, S. Arber, and Michael Procter. (1988). *Doing secondary analysis.* Boston: Unwin Hyman.

Daly, Kathleen, and Meda Chesney-Lind. (1988). Feminism and criminology. *Justice Quarterly,* 5:497–538.

D'Antonio, William V. (Aug. 1989). Executive office report: Sociology on the move. *ASA Footnotes,* 17, p. 2.

D'Antonio, William V. (1992). Recruiting sociologists in a time of changing opportunities. In *Sociology and its publics: The forms and fates of disciplinary organization,* edited by Terence Halliday and Morris Janowitz, pp. 99–136. Chicago: University of Chicago Press.

Dabbs, James M., Jr. (1982). Making things visible. In *Varieties of qualitative research,* edited by John Van Maanen, James M. Dabbs, Jr., and Robert R. Faulkner, pp. 31–64. Beverly Hills, CA: Sage.

Dannefer, Dale. (1981). Neither socialization nor recruitment: The avocational careers of old car enthusiasts. *Social Forces,* 60:395–413.

Danziger, Kurt. (1988). The question of identity: Who participated in psychological experiments? In *The rise of experimentation in American psychology,* edited by Jill G. Morawski, pp. 35–52. New Haven, CT: Yale University Press.

Darnton, Robert. (1978). The history of *mentalities.* In *Structure, consciousness and history,* edited by R. H. Brown and S. M. Lyman, pp. 106–136. New York: Cambridge University Press.

Davis, Fred. (1959). The cabdriver and his fare: Facets of a fleeting relationship. *American Journal of Sociology,* 65:158–165.

Davis, Fred. (1973). The Martian and the convert: Ontological polarities in social research. *Urban Life,* 2: 333–343.

Davis, James A. (1985). *The logic of causal order.* Beverly Hills, CA: Sage.

Davis, James A., and Tom W. Smith. (1986). *General social surveys 1972–1986 cumulative codebook.* Chicago: National Opinion Research Center, University of Chicago.

Davis, James A., and Tom W. Smith. (1992). *The NORC General Social Survey: A user's guide.* Newbury Park, CA: Sage.

Dawes, R. M., and T. W. Smith. (1985). Attitude and opinion measurement. In *Handbook of social psychology,* 3rd ed., Vol. 1, edited by G. Lindzey and E. Aronson, pp. 509–566. New York: Random House.

de Tocqueville, Alex. (1981/1835). *Democracy in America.* New York: Modern Library.

Dean, John P., Robert L. Eichhorn, and Lois R. Dean. (1969). Fruitful informants for intensive interviewing. In *Issues in participant observation,* edited by G. McCall and J. L. Simmons, pp. 142–144. Reading, MA: Addison-Wesley.

Dean, John P., and William Foote Whyte. (1969). How do you know if the informant is telling the truth? In *Issues in participant observation,* edited by G. McCall and J. L. Simmons, pp. 105–115. Reading, MA: Addison-Wesley.

Deegan, Mary Jo. (1988). *Jane Adams and the men of the Chicago School, 1892–1918.* New Brunswick: Transaction.

Dekeseredy, Walter S., Daniel G. Saunders, Martin D. Schwartz, and Shid Alvi. (1997). The meaning and motives for women's use of violence in Canadian college dating relationships: Results from a national study. *Sociological Spectrum,* 17:199–222.

DeLamater, John, and Pat MacCorquodale. (1975). The effects of interview schedule variations on reported sexual behavior. *Sociological Methods and Research,* 4:215–236.

DeMaio, Theresa J. (1980). Refusals: Who, where and why? *Public Opinion Quarterly,* 44:223–233.

DeMaio, Theresa J. (1984). Social desirability and survey measurement: A review. In *Surveying Subjective Phenomena,* Vol. 2, edited by Charles Turner and Elizabeth Martin, pp. 257–282. New York: Russell Sage Foundation.

Denzin, Norman K. (1970). Symbolic interactionism and ethnomethodology. In *Understanding everyday life,* edited by Jack D. Douglas, pp. 261–286. Chicago: Aldine.

Denzin, Norman K. (1989). *The research act: A theoretical introduction to sociological methods,* 3rd ed. Englewood Cliffs, NJ: Prentice-Hall.

Denzin, Norman K., and Kai Erikson. (1982). On the ethics of disguised observation: An exchange. In *Social research ethics,* edited by M. Blume. New York: Macmillan.

Denzin, Norman K. and Yvonna S. Lincoln, eds. (1994). Introduction: Entering the field of qualitative research. In *Handbook of qualitative research,* pp. 1–18. Thousand Oaks, CA: Sage.

Derksen, Linda, and John Gartrell. (1992). Scientific explanation. In *Encyclopedia of Sociology,* Vol. 4, edited by Edgar and Marie Borgatta, pp. 1711–1720. New York: Macmillan.

Desan, Susanne. (1989). Crowds, community and ritual in the work of E. P. Thompson and Natalie Davis. In *The new cultural history,* edited by L. Hunt, pp. 24–46. Berkeley: University of California Press.

Devault, Marjorie L. (1990). Talking and listening from women's standpoint: Feminist strategies for interviewing and analysis. *Social Problems,* 37:96–116.

deVaus, D. A. (1986). *Surveys in social research.* Boston: George Allen and Unwin.

Dexter, Lewis A. (1970). *Elite and specialized interviewing.* Evanston, IL: Northwestern University Press.

Diamond, Sigmund. (1988). Informed consent and survey research: The FBI and the University of Michigan Survey Research Center. In *Surveying social life: Papers in honor of Herbert H. Hyman,* edited by Hubert J. O'Gorman, pp. 72–99. Middletown, CT: Wesleyan University Press.

Dibble, Vernon K. (1963). Four types of inference from documents to events. *History and Theory,* 3:203–221.

Dickson, David. (1984). *The new politics of science.* Chicago: University of Chicago Press.

DiCristina, Bruce. (1995). *Method in criminology: A philosophical primer.* New York: Harrow and Heston.

DiCristina, Bruce. (1997). The quantitative emphasis in criminal justice education. *Journal of Criminal Justice Education,* 8:181–200.

Diener, Edward, and Rick Crandall. (1978). *Ethics in social and behavioral research.* Chicago: University of Chicago Press.

Dijkstra, Wil, and Johannes van der Zouwen, eds. (1982). *Response behavior in the survey interview.* New York: Academic Press.

Dillman, Don A. (1978). *Mail and telephone surveys: The total design method.* New York: Wiley.

Dillman, Don A. (1983). Mail and other self-administered questionnaires. In *Handbook of survey research,* edited by Peter H. Rossi, James D. Wright, and Andy B. Anderson, pp. 359–377. Orlando, FL: Academic Press.

Dillman, Donald A. (1991). The design and administration of mail surveys. *Annual Review of Sociology*, 17:225–249.

Ditton, Jason. (1977a). *Part-time crime: An ethnography of fiddling and pilferage*. New York: Macmillan.

Ditton, Jason. (1977b). Perks, pilferage, and theft: The historical structure of invisible wages. *Theory and Society*, 4:39–71.

Doctor is accused of "immoral" tests. (Dec. 9, 1988). *New York Times*.

Domhoff, G. William. (1974). *The Bohemian Grove and other retreats*. New York: Harper and Row.

Donald, Robert B. et al., (1983). *Writing clear paragraphs*, 2nd ed. Englewood Cliffs, NJ: Prentice-Hall.

Donziger, Steven R., ed. (1996). *The real war on crime: The report of the National Criminal Justice Commission*. New York: HarperCollins.

Dooley, David. (1984). *Social research methods*. Englewood Cliffs, NJ: Prentice-Hall.

Douglas, Jack D. (1976). *Investigative social research*. Beverly Hills, CA: Sage.

Douglas, Jack D. (1985). *Creative interviewing*. Beverly Hills, CA: Sage.

Douglas, Jack D., and Paul K. Rasmussen. (1977). *The nude beach*. Beverly Hills, CA: Sage.

Downey, Gary L. (1986). Ideology and the Clamshell identity: Organizational dilemmas in the antinuclear power movement. *Social Problems*, 33:357–373.

Drass, Kriss. (1980). The analysis of qualitative data: A computer program. *Urban Life*, 9:332–353.

DuBois, W. E. Burghardt. (1899). *The Philadelphia Negro*. New York: Benjamin Bloom.

Dunaway, David K., and Willa K. Baum, eds. (1984). *Oral history*. Nashville, TN: Association for State and Local History.

Duncan, Otis Dudley. (1975). *Introduction to structural equation models*. New York: Academic Press.

Duncan, Otis Dudley. (1984). *Notes on social measurement: Historical and critical*. New York: Russell Sage Foundation.

Duncan, Otis Dudley, and Magnus Stenbeck. (1988). No opinion or not sure? *Public Opinion Quarterly*, 52:513–525.

Durkheim, Emile. (1938). *Rules of the sociological method*, trans. Sarah Solovay and John Mueller, edited by George E. G. Catlin. Chicago: University of Chicago Press.

Dynes, Russell R. (1984). The institutionalization of COSSA. *Sociological Inquiry*, 54:211–229.

Easterday, Lois, Diana Papademas, Laura Schorr, and Catherine Valentine. (1982). The making of a female researcher. Role problems in fieldwork. In *Field research*, edited by R. G. Burgess, pp. 62–67. Boston: George Allen and Unwin.

Eastrope, Gary. (1974). *History of social research methods*. London: Longman.

Eckberg, Douglas Lee, and Lester Hill, Jr. (1979). The paradigm concept and sociology. *American Sociological Review*, 44:937–947.

The Economist. (Oct. 15, 1994). Measuring crime: A shadow on society, pp. 21–23.

Eder, Donna. (1981). Ability grouping as a self-fulfilling prophecy: A microanalysis of teacher-student interaction. *Sociology of Education*, 54:151–162.

Eder, Donna. (1985). The cycle of popularity: Interpersonal relations among female adolescents. *Sociology of Education*, 58:154–165.

Edward, G. Franklin. (1974). E. Franklin Frazier. In *Black sociologists: Historical and contemporary perspectives*, edited by James E. Blackwell and Morris Janowitz, pp. 85–117. Chicago: University of Chicago Press.

Edwards, Allen L. (1957). *Techniques of attitude scale construction*. New York: Appleton-Century-Crofts.

Edwards, Rosalind. (1993). An education in interviewing: Placing the researcher and research. In *Research on sensitive topics*, edited by Claire Renzetti and Raymond Lee, pp. 181–196. Thousand Oaks, CA: Sage.

Eichler, Margrit. (1988). *Nonsexist research methods: A practical guide*. Boston: George Allen and Unwin.

Elder, Glen H., Jr., Eliza Pavalko, and Elizabeth Clipp. (1993). *Working with archival data: Studying lives*. Thousand Oaks, CA: Sage.

Elder, Joseph W. (1973). Problems of crosscultural methodology: Instrumentation and interviewing in India. In *Comparative social research*, edited by M. Armer and A. D. Grimshaw, pp. 119–144. New York: Wiley.

Ellen, R. F., ed. (1984a). *Ethnographic research: A guide to general conduct*. Orlando: Academic Press.

Ellen, R. F. (1984b). Some other interactionist methods. In *Ethnographic research: A guide to general conduct*, edited by R. F. Ellen, pp. 273–293. Orlando: Academic Press.

Emerson, Robert M. (1981). Observational field work. *Annual Review of Sociology*, 7:351–378.

Emerson, Robert M. (1983). Introduction. In *Contemporary field research*, edited by R. M. Emerson, pp. 1–16. Boston: Little, Brown.

Ennis, James G. (1992). The social organization of sociological knowledge: Modeling the intersection of specialties. *American Sociological Review*, 57:259–265.

Erikson, Kai T. (1970). A comment on disguised observation in sociology. In *Qualitative methodology*, edited by W. J. Filstead, pp. 252–260. Chicago: Markham.

Erikson, Kai T. (1978). *Everything in its path*. New York: Touchstone.

Evans, Kathy. (Apr. 27, 1995). I feel numb. I have seen Islamic justice firsthand. *Guardian*, p. 26

Evans, Peter, and John D. Stephens. (1989). Studying development since the sixties: The emergence of a new comparative political economy. *Theory and Society*, 17:713–746.

Evans, Peter B., Dietrich Rueshemeyer, and Theda Skocopol. (1985). *Bringing the state back in*. New York: Cambridge University Press.

Evans-Pritchard, E. E. (1940). *The Nuer: A description of the modes of livelihood and political institutions of a Nilotic people*. Oxford: Clarendon Press.

Ex-official says Pentagon dumped findings on gays. (Apr. 1, 1993). *Captial Times*.

Faris, R. E. L. (1967). *Chicago sociology, 1920–1932*. San Francisco: Chandler.

Farnsworth, Clyde H. (Aug. 10, 1997). This penal colony learned a lesson. *New York Times*, p. 6.

Faupel, Charles E., and Carl B. Klockars. (1987). Drugs-crime connections: Elaborations from the life history of hard-core heroin addicts. *Social Problems*, 34:54–68.

Fay, Brian. (1975). *Social theory and political practice*. London: George Allen and Unwin.

Featherman, David L., and Richard C. Rockwell. (1992). Social science research council. *Encyclopedia of Sociology*, Vol. 4, edited by Edgar and Marie Borgatta, pp. 1942–1945. New York: Macmillan.

Feige, Edgar. (1996). Overseas holding of U.S. currency and the underground economy. In *Exploring the underground economy*, edited by Susan Pozo, pp. 5–62. Kalamazoo, MI: W. E. Upjohn Institute for Employment Research.

Ferrell, Jeff. (1997). Criminological *Verstehen*: Inside the immediacy of crime. *Justice Quarterly*, 14:3–23.

Ferriss, Abbott L. (1988). The uses of social indicators. *Social Forces*, 66:601–617.

Fetterman, David M. (1989). *Ethnography: Step by step*. Newbury Park, CA: Sage.

Fichter, Joseph H., and William L. Kolb. (1970). Ethical limitations on sociological reporting. In *Qualitative methodology*, edited by W. J. Filstead, pp. 261–270. Chicago: Markham.

Fielding, Nigel G., and Raymond M. Lee, eds. (1991). *Using computers in qualitative research*. Newbury Park, CA: Sage.

Fine, Gary Alan. (1979). Small groups and culture creation: The idioculture of Little League baseball teams. *American Sociological Review*, 44: 733–745.

Fine, Gary Alan. (1987). *With the boys: Little League baseball and preadolescent culture*. Chicago: University of Chicago Press.

Fine, Gary Alan. (1988). The ten commandments of writing. *The American Sociologist*, 19:152–157.

Fine, Gary Alan. (1990). Organizational time: The temporal experience of restaurant kitchens. *Social Forces*, 69:95–114.

Fine, Gary Alan. (1992). The culture of production: Aesthetic choices and constraints in culinary work. *American Journal of Sociology*, 97:1268–1294.

Fine, Gary Alan, and Barry Glassner. (1979). Participant observation with children: Promise and problems. *Urban Life*, 8:153–174.

Finkel, Steven E., Thomas M. Guterbock, and Marian J. Borg. (1991). Race-of-interviewer effects in a preelection poll: Viriginia 1989. *Public Opinion Quarterly*, 55: 313–330.

Finley, M. I. (Summer 1977). Progress in historiography. *Daedalus*, pp. 125–142.

Finsterbusch, Kurt, and Annabelle Bender Motz. (1980). *Social research for policy decisions*. Belmont, CA: Wadsworth.

Finsterbusch, Kurt, and C. P. Wolf. (1981). *Methodology of social impact assessment*. Stroudsburg, PA: Hutchinson Ross.

Firebaugh, Glenn. (1980). Cross-national versus historical regression models. *Comparative Social Research*, 3:333–344.

Firebaugh, Glenn, and Kevin Chen. (1995). Vote turnout of nineteenth amendment women: The enduring effect of disenfranchisement. *American Journal of Sociology,* 100:972–996.

Fischer, Claude S. (1992). *America calling: A social history of the telephone to 1940*. Berkeley: University of California Press.

Fischer, David H. (1970). *Historians' fallacies: Towards a logic of historical thought*. New York: Harper & Row.

Fischer, Frank. (1985). Critical evaluation of public policy: A methodological case study. In *Critical theory and public life*, edited by John Forester, pp. 231–257. Cambridge, MA: MIT Press.

Fiske, Donald W. (1982). Convergent-discriminant validation in measurements and research strategies. In *Forms of validation in research*, edited by David Brinberg and Louise H. Kidder, pp. 72–92. San Francisco: Jossey-Bass.

Fiske, Edward B. (July 12, 1989). The misleading concept of "average" on reading tests changes, and more students fall below it. *New York Times*.

Fitchen, Janet M. (1991). *Endangered spaces, enduring places: Change, identity and survival in rural America*. Boulder, CO: Westview.

Fletcher, Colin. (1974). *Beneath the surface: An account of three styles of sociological research*. Boston: Routledge and Kegan Paul.

Flora, Cornelia Butler. (1979). Changes in women's status in women's magazine fiction: Differences by social class. *Social Problems*, 26:558–569.

Foddy, William. (1993). *Constructing questions for interviews and questionnaires: Theory and practice in social research*. New York: Cambridge University Press.

Fontana, Andrea, and James H. Frey. (1994). Interviewing: The art of science. In *Handbook of qualitative research*, edited by Denzin and Lincoln, pp. 361–376. Thousand Oaks, CA: Sage.

Form, Willam H. (1973). Field problems in comparative research. In *Comparative social research*, edited by M. Armer and A. D. Grimshaw, pp. 83–117. New York: Wiley.

Fowler, Edward. (1998). *San'ya blues: Laboring life in contemporary Toyko*. Ithaca, NY: Cornell University Press.

Fowler, Floyd J., Jr. (1984). *Survey research methods*. Beverly Hills, CA: Sage.

Fowler, Floyd J., Jr. (1992). How unclear terms can affect survey data. *Public Opinion Quarterly*, 56: 218–231.

Fox, James Alan, and Paul E. Tracy. (1986). *Randomized response: A method for sensitive surveys*. Beverly Hills, CA: Sage.

Fox, John. (1992). Statistical graphics. In *Encyclopedia of Sociology*, Vol. 4, edited by Edgar and Marie Borgatta, pp. 2054–2073. New York: Macmillan.

Fox, Richard, Melvin R. Crask, and Jonghoon Kim. (1988). Mail survey response rate: A meta-analysis of selected techniques for inducing

response. *Public Opinion Quarterly*, 52:467–491.

Franke, Charles O. (1983). Ethnography. In *Contemporary field research*, edited by R. M. Emerson, pp. 60–67. Boston: Little, Brown.

Franke, Richard H., and James D. Kaul. (1978). The Hawthorne experiments: First statistical interpretation. *American Sociological Review*, 43:623–643.

Frankel, Martin. (1983). Sampling theory. In *Handbook of survey research*, edited by Peter H. Rossi, James D. Wright, and Andy B. Anderson, pp. 21–67. Orlando, FL: Academic Press.

Frazier, E. Franklin. (1957). *The black bourgeoisie*. Glencoe, IL: Free Press.

Frechette-Schrader, Kristin. (1994). *Ethics of scientific research*. Lanham, MD: Rowland and Littlefield.

Fredrickson, George. (1981). *White supremacy*. New York: Oxford University Press.

Freeman, Howard. (1983). *Applied sociology*. San Francisco: Jossey-Bass.

Freeman, Howard. (1992). Evaluation research. In *Encyclopedia of Sociology*, Vol. 2, edited by Edgar and Marie Borgatta, pp. 594–598. New York: Macmillan.

Freeman, Howard, and Peter H. Rossi. (1984). Furthering the applied side of sociology. *American Sociological Review*, 49:571–580.

Freeman, Howard, and Merrill J. Shanks, eds. (1983). The emergence of computer assisted survey research. *Sociological Methods and Research*, 23:115–230.

Freidson, Eliot. (1986). *Professional powers: A study of the institutionalization of formal knowledge*. Chicago: University of Chicago Press.

Freire, Paulo. (1970). *Pedagogy of the oppressed*, trans. Myra Bergman Ramos. New York: Seabury.

Freitag, Peter. (1983). The myth of corporate capture: Regulatory commissions in the United States. *Social Problems*, 30:480–491.

Frey, Frederick W. (1970). Cross-cultural survey research in political science. In *The methodology of comparative research*, edited by R. Holt and J. Turner, pp. 173–294. New York: Free Press.

Frey, James H. (1983). *Survey research by telephone*. Beverly Hills, CA: Sage.

Friedrichs, David O. (1995). *White collar crime in contemporary society*. Belmont, CA: Wadsworth.

Friedrichs, Robert W. (1970). *A sociology of sociology*. New York: Free Press.

Frost, Peter, and Ralph Stablein, eds. (1992). *Doing exemplary research*. Newbury Park, CA: Sage.

Fuchs, Stephan, and Jonathan H. Turner. (1986). What makes a science "mature"? Patterns of organizational control in scientific production. *Sociological Theory*, 4:143–150.

Fuller, John R. (1998). *Criminal justice: A peacemaking perspective*. Boston: Allyn and Bacon.

Fuller, Linda. (1988). Fieldwork in forbidden terrain: The U.S. state and the case of Cuba. *American Sociologist*, 19:99–120.

Gadamer, Hans-Georg. (1979). The problem of historical consciousness. In *Interpretative social science: A reader*, edited by Paul Rabinow and William Sullivan, pp. 103–160. Berkeley: University of California Press.

Gagne, Patricia. (1996). Identity, strategy, and feminist politics: Clemency for battered women who kill. *Social Problems*, 43:77–93.

Galaskiewicz, Joseph. (1985). Professional networks and the institutionalization of a single mind set. *American Sociological Review*, 50:639–658.

Galaskiewicz, Joseph. (1987). The study of a business elite and corporate philanthropy in a United States metropolitan area. In *Research methods for elite studies*, edited by George Moyser and Margaret Wagstaffe, pp. 147–165. Boston: George Allen and Unwin.

Galaskiewicz, Joseph, and Stanley Wasserman. (1993). Social network analysis: Concepts, methodology and directions for the 1990s. *Sociological Methods and Research*, 22:3–22.

Gallie, W. B. (1963). The historical understanding. *History and Theory*, 3:149–202.

Galliher, John F., and James L. McCartney. (1973). The influence of funding agencies on juvenile delinquency research. *Social Problems*, 21:77–90.

Gamson, William A. (1992). *Talking politics*. Cambridge: Cambridge University Press.

Gans, Herbert J. (1982). The participant observer as a human being: Observations on the personal aspects of fieldwork. In *Field research*, edited by R. G. Burgess, pp. 53–61. Boston: George Allen and Unwin.

Garfinkel, Harold. (1967). *Studies in ethnomethodology*. Englewood Cliffs, NJ: Prentice-Hall.

Garfinkel, Harold. (1974a). The origins of the term "ethnomethodology." In *Ethnomethodology*, edited by Roy Turner, pp. 15–18. Middlesex: Penguin.

Garfinkel, Harold. (1974b). The rational properties of scientific and common sense activities. In *Positivism and sociology*, edited by Anthony Giddens, pp. 53–74. London: Heinemann.

Gartman, David. (1998). Postmodernism; Or, the cultural logic of post–Fordism? *The Sociological Quarterly*, 39:119–137.

Gaston, Jerry. (1978). *The reward system in British and American science*. New York: Wiley.

Geer, John G. (1988). What do open-ended questions measure? *Public Opinion Quarterly*, 52:365–371.

Geertz, Clifford. (1973). *The interpretation of cultures*. New York: Basic Books.

Geertz, Clifford. (1979). From the native's point of view: On the nature of anthropological understanding. In *Interpretative social science: A reader*, edited by Paul Rabinow and William Sullivan, pp. 225–242. Berkeley: University of California Press.

Geiger, Roger L. (1986). *To advance knowledge: The growth of American research universities, 1900–1940*. New York: Oxford University Press.

Georges, Robert A., and Michael O. Jones. (1980). *People studying people*. Berkeley: University of California Press.

Gephart, Robert P., Jr. (1988). *Ethnostatistics: Qualitative foundations for quantitative research*. Newbury Park, CA: Sage.

Gibbs, Jack. (1989). Conceptualization of terrorism. *American Sociological Review*, 54:329–340.

Giddens, Anthony. (1976). *New rules of sociological method: Positivist critique of interpretative sociologies*. New York: Basic Books.

Giddens, Anthony. (1978). Positivism and its critics. In *A history of sociological analysis*, edited by Tom Bottomore and Robert Nisbet. New York: Basic Books.

Gieryn, Thomas F. (1978). Problem retention and problem change in science. In *The sociology of science*, edited by Jerry Gaston. San Francisco: Jossey-Bass.

Gilbert, Margaret. (1992). *On social facts*. Princeton, NJ: Princeton University Press.

Gillespie, Richard. (1988). The Hawthorne experiments and the politics of experimentation. In *The rise of experimentation in American psychology*, edited by Jill G. Morawski, pp. 114–137. New Haven, CT: Yale University Press.

Gillespie, Richard. (1991). *Manufacturing knowledge: A history of the Hawthorne experiments*. New York: Cambridge University Press.

Gillis, A. R. (1996). Urbanization, sociohistorical context, and crime. In *Criminological controversies*, edited by John Hagan, A. R. Gillis, and David Brownfield, pp. 47–74. Boulder, CO: Westview.

Gilljam, Mikael, and David Granberg. (1993). Should we take Don't Know for an answer? *Public Opinion Quarterly*, 57:348–357.

Glaser, Barney, and Anselm Strauss. (1967). *The discovery of grounded theory*. Chicago: Aldine.

Glaser, Barney, and Anselm Strauss. (1968). *A time for dying*. Chicago: Aldine.

Glasser, Gerald J., and Gale O. Metzger. (1972). Random digit dialing as a method of telephone sampling. *Journal of Marketing Research*, 9:59–64.

Glock, Charles Y. (1987). Reflections on doing survey research. In *Surveying social life: Papers in honor of Herbert H. Hyman*, edited by Hubert J. O'Gorman, pp. 31–59. Middletown, CT: Wesleyan University Press.

Glucksmann, Miriam. (1974). *Structuralist analysis in contemporary social thought: A comparison of the theories of Claude Levi-Strauss and Louis Althusser*. Boston: Routledge and Kegan Paul.

Gold, Raymond L. (1969). Roles in sociological field observation. In *Issues in participant observation*, edited by G. J. McCall and J. L. Simmons, pp. 30–38. Reading, MA: Addison-Wesley.

Goldstein, Paul J., Henry H. Brownstein, Patrick J. Ryan, and Patricia A. Bellucci. (1997). Crack and homicide in New York City: A case study in the epidemiology of violence. In *Crack in America: Demon drugs and social justice*, edited by Craig Reinarman and Harry G. Levine, pp. 11–130. Berkeley, CA: University of California Press.

Goldstein, Robert Justin. (1978). *Political repression in modern America*. New York: Schenckman.

Goldthorpe, John. (1977). The relevance of history to sociology. In *Sociological research methods*, edited by M. Bulmer, pp. 178–191. London: Macmillan.

Gonor, George. (1977). "Situation" versus "frame": The "interactionist" and the "structuralist" analysis of everyday life. *American Sociological Review*, 42:854–867.

Goodsell, Charles B. (1983). Welfare waiting rooms. *Urban Life*, 12:464–477.

Gorden, Raymond. (1980). *Interviewing: Strategy, techniques and tactics*, 3rd ed. Homewood, IL: Dorsey Press.

Gorden, Raymond. (1992). *Basic interviewing skills*. Itasca, IL: Peacock.

Gordon, David F. (1987). Getting close by staying distant: Fieldwork with proselytizing groups. *Qualitative Sociology*, 10:267–287.

Gordon, Randall A., T. A. Bindrim, M. L. McNicholas, and T. L. Walden. (1988). Perceptions of blue-collar and white-collar crime: The effect of defendant race on simulated juror decisions. *Journal of Social Psychology*, 128:191–197.

Gorelick, Sherry. (1989). "Join our war": The construction of ideology in a newspaper crimefighting campaign. *Crime and Delinquency*, 35:421–436.

Gorelick, Sherry. (1991). Contradictions of feminist methodology. *Gender and Society*, 5:459–477.

Gould, Roger V. (1991). Multiple networks and mobilization in the Paris Commune, 1871. *American Sociological Review*, 56:716–729.

Gouldner, Alvin. (1970). *The coming crisis of Western sociology*. New York: Basic Books.

Gouldner, Alvin W. (1976). The dark side of the dialectic: Toward a new objectivity. *Sociological Inquiry*, 46:3–16.

Goward, Nicola. (1984a). Publications on fieldwork experiences. In *Ethnographic research: A guide to general conduct*, edited by R. F. Ellen, pp. 88–100. Orlando: Academic Press.

Goward, Nicola. (1984b). Personal interaction and adjustment. In *Ethnographic research: A guide to general conduct*, edited by R. F. Ellen, pp. 100–118. Orlando: Academic Press.

Goyder, John C. (1982). Factors affecting response rates to mailed questionnaires. *American Sociological Review*, 47:550–554.

Graham, Sandra. (1992). Most of the subjects were white and middle class: Trends in published research on African Americans in selected APA journals, 1970–1989. *American Psychologist*, 47:629–639.

Granovetter, Mark. (1976). Network sampling: Some first steps. *American Journal of Sociology*, 81:1287–1303.

Grant, Linda, Kathryn B. Ward, and Xue Lan Rong. (1987). Is there an association between gender and methods of sociological research? *American Sociological Review*, 52:856–862.

Gray, Bradford H. (1982). The regulatory context of social and behavioral research. In *Ethical issues in social science research*, edited by Tom L. Beauchamp, R. Faden, R. J. Wallace, and L. Walters, pp. 329–354. Baltimore: Johns Hopkins University Press.

Gray, Paul S. (1980). Exchange and access in field work. *Urban Life*, 9:309–331.

Greenwald, Howard P. (1992). Ethics in social research. In *Encyclopedia of sociology*, Vol. 2., edited by Edgar and Marie Borgatta, pp. 584–588. New York: Macmillan.

Griffin, Larry J. (1992). Comparative-historical analysis. In *Encyclopedia of sociology*, Vol. 1, edited by Edgar and Marie Borgatta, pp. 263–271. New York: Macmillan.

Griffin, Larry J. (1993). Narrative, event structure analysis and causal interpretation in historical sociology. *American Journal of Sociology*, 98:1094–1133.

Griffin, Larry J., Michael E. Wallace, and Beth A. Rubin. (1986). Capitalist resistance to the organization of labor before the New Deal: Why? How? Success? *American Sociological Review*, 51:147–167.

Grimshaw, Allen D. (1973). Comparative sociology. In *Comparative social research*, edited by M. Armer and A. Grimshaw, pp. 3–48. New York: Wiley.

Grinnell, Frederick. (1987). *The scientific attitude*. Boulder, CO: Westview.

Griswold, Wendy. (1983). The devil's techniques: Cultural legitimation and social change. *American Sociological Review*, 48:668–680.

Griswold, Wendy. (1987). A methodological framework for the sociology of culture. In *Sociological methodology*, edited by Clifford C. Clogg, pp. 1–35. San Francisco: Jossey-Bass.

Griswold, Wendy. (1994). *Cultures and societies in a changing world*. Thousand Oaks, CA: Pine Forge Press.

Grosof, Miriam Schapiro, and Hyman Sardy. (1985). *A research primer for the social and behavioral sciences*. Orlando, FL: Academic Press.

Gross, Daniel R. (1984). Time allocation: A tool for the study of cultural behavior. *Annual Review of Anthropology*, 13:519–558.

Gross, Edward. (1986). Waiting at Mayo. *Urban Life*, 15:139–164.

Groves, Robert M., Nancy H. Fultz, and Elizabeth Martin. (1992). Direct questioning about comprehension in a survey setting. In *Questions about questions: Inquiries into the cognitive bases of surveys*, edited by Judith M. Turner, pp. 49–61. New York: Russell Sage Foundation.

Groves, Robert M., and Robert L. Kahn. (1979). *Surveys by telephone: A national comparison with personal interviews*. New York: Academic Press.

Groves, Robert M., and Nancy Mathiowetz. (1984). Computer assisted telephone interviewing: Effects on interviewers and respondents. *Public Opinion Quarterly*, 48:356–369.

Guba, Egon G., and Yvonna S. Lincoln. (1994). Competing paradigms in qualitative research. In *Handbook of qualitative research*, edited by Norman K. Denzin and Yvonna S. Lincoln, pp. 105–117. Thousand Oaks, CA: Sage.

Gubrium, Jaber F., and James A. Holstein. (1992). Qualitative methods. In *Encyclopedia of sociology*, Vol. 3, edited by Edgar and Marie Borgatta, pp. 1577–1582. New York: Macmillan.

Gudkov, Lev D. (1997). Ethnic phobias in the structure of national identity. *Sociological Research*, 36:60–73.

Gurevitch, Z. D. (1988). The other side of the dialogue: On making the other strange and the experience of otherness. *American Journal of Sociology*, 93:1179–1199.

Gurney, Joan Neff. (1985). Not one of the guys: The female researcher in a male-dominated setting. *Qualitative Sociology*, 8:42–62.

Gurr, Ted. (1976). *Rogues, rebels, and reformers*. Beverly Hills, CA: Sage.

Gusfield, Joseph. (1976). The literary rhetoric of science: Comedy and pathos in drinking driver research. *American Sociological Review*, 41:16–34.

Gustavsen, Bjørn. (1986). Social research as participatory dialogue. In *The use and abuse of social science*, edited by Frank Heller, pp. 143–156. Beverly Hills, CA: Sage.

Gustin, Bernard H. (1973). Charisma, recognition and the motivation of scientists. *American Journal of Sociology*, 86:1119–1134.

Guttman, Louis. (1950). The basis for scalogram analysis. In *Measurement and prediction*, edited by S. A. Stouffer, L. Buttman, E. A. Suchman, P. F. Lazarfeld, S. A. Star, and J. A. Clausen, pp. 60–90. Princeton, NJ: Princeton University Press.

Guttman, Louis. (1970). A basis for scaling qualitative data. In *Attitude measurement*, edited by Gene Summers, pp. 174–186. Chicago: Rand McNally.

Haberman, Shelby J. (1978). *Analysis of qualitative data*. New York: Academic Press.

Habermas, Jurgen. (1971). *Knowledge and human interests*. Boston: Beacon.

Habermas, Jurgen. (1973). *Theory and practice*. Boston: Beacon.

Habermas, Jurgen. (1976). *Legitimation crisis*. Boston: Beacon.

Habermas, Jurgen. (1979). *Communication and the evolution of society*. Boston: Beacon.

Habermas, Jurgen. (1988). *On the logic of the social sciences*. Oxford: Polity.

Hagan, Frank. (1997). *Political crime*. Boston: Allyn and Bacon.

Hagan, John. (1990). The gender stratification of income inequality among lawyers. *Social Forces*, 63:835–855.

Hagan, John. (1994). *Crime and disrepute*. Thousand Oaks, CA: Pine Forge.

Hagan, John. (1996). Testing propositions about gender and crime. In *Criminological controversies*, edited by John Hagan, A. R. Gillis, and David Brownfield, pp.17–46. Boulder, CO: Westview.

Hagan, John, A. R. Gillis, and David Brownfield. (1996). *Criminological controversies*. Boulder, CO: Westview.

Hage, Jerald. (1972). *Techniques and problems of theory construction in sociology*. New York: Wiley.

Hagedorn, John M. (1988). *People and folks: Gangs, crime, and the underclass in a rustbelt city*. Chicago: Lakeview.

Hagstrom, Warren. (1965). *The scientific community*. New York: Basic Books.

Hakim, Catherine. (1987). *Research design: Strategies and choices in the design of social research*. Boston: Allen and Unwin.

Halfpenny, Peter. (1979). The analysis of qualitative data. *Sociological Review*, 27:799–823.

Halfpenny, Peter. (1982). *Positivism and sociology: Explaining social life*. London: George Allen and Unwin.

Hallin, Daniel C. (1985). The American news media: A critical theory perspective. In *Critical theory and public life*, edited by John Forester, pp. 121–146. Cambridge, MA: MIT Press.

Hallowell, Lyle. (1985). *Ethical and legal problems of research: Professional workshop*. Presentation at the American Sociological Association annual meeting, Washington, DC, August 26.

Hammersley, Martyn. (1992). *What's wrong with ethnography? Methodological explorations*. New York: Routledge.

Hammersley, Martyn, and Paul Atkinson. (1983). *Ethnography: Principles in practice*. London: Tavistock.

Hammond, Holly A., and C. Thomas Caskey. (1997). *Automated DNA typing: Method of the future?* Washington, DC: U.S. Department of Justice.

Hannan, Michael T. (1985). Problems of aggregation. In *Causal models in the social sciences*, 2nd ed., edited by Hubert M. Blalock, Jr., pp. 403–439. Chicago: Aldine.

Harari, Herbert, Oren Harari, and Robert V. White. (1985). The reaction to rape by American bystanders. *Journal of Social Psychology*, 125:653–658.

Harding, Sandra. (1986). *The science question in feminism*. Ithaca, NY: Cornell University Press.

Harkens, Shirley, and Carol Warren. (1993). The social relations of intensive interviewing: Constellations of strangeness and science. *Sociological Methods and Research*, 21: 317–339.

Harper, Douglas. (1982). *Good company*. Chicago: University of Chicago Press.

Harper, Douglas. (1994). On the authority of the image: Visual methods at the crossroads. In *Handbook of qualitative research*, edited by Norman Denzin and Yvonna Lincoln, pp. 403–412. Thousand Oaks, CA: Sage.

Harré, Rom. (1972). *The philosophies of science*. London: Oxford University Press.

Harré, R., and P. F. Secord. (1979). *The explanation of social behavior*. Totowa, NJ: Littlefield, Adams.

Harrington, Michael. (1984). *The new American poverty*. New York: Holt, Rinehart and Winston.

Harris, Benjamin. (1988). Key words: A history of debriefing in social psychology. In *The rise of experimentation in American psychology*, edited by Jill G. Morawski, pp. 188–212. New Haven, CT: Yale University Press.

Harvey, Lee. (1990). *Critical social research*. London: Urwin Hyman.

Hauck, Matthew, and Michael Cox. (1974). Locating a sample by random digit dialing: Some hypotheses and a random sample. *Public Opinion Quarterly*, 38:253–260.

Hayano, David M. (1982). *Poker faces: The life and work of professional card players*. Berkeley: University of California Press.

Hazelrigg, Lawrence E. (1973). Aspects of the measurement of class consciousness. In *Comparative social research*, edited by M. Armer and A. D. Grimshaw, pp. 219–246. New York: Wiley.

Hearnshaw, L. S. (1979). *Cyril Burt: Psychologist*. London: Holder and Stoughten.

Heberlein, Thomas A., and Robert Baumgartner. (1978). Factors affecting response rates to mailed questionnaires: A quantitative analysis of the published literature. *American Sociological Review*, 43:447–462.

Heberlein, Thomas A., and Robert Baumgartner. (1981). Is a questionnaire necessary in a second mailing? *Public Opinion Quarterly*, 45:102–107.

Hector, Michael. (1975). *Internal colonialism*. Berkeley: University of California Press.

Hegtvedt, Karen A. (1992). Replication. In *Encyclopedia of sociology*, Vol. 3, edited by Edgar and Marie Borgatta, pp. 1661–1663. New York: Macmillan.

Heise, David. (1965). Semantic differential profiles for 1,000 most frequent English words. *Psychological Monographs*, 70, No. 8.

Heise, David. (1970). The semantic differential and attitude research. In *Attitude measurement*, edited by Gene F. Summers, pp. 235–253. Chicago: Rand McNally.

Heise, David. (1974). Some issues in sociological measurement. In *Sociological methodology, 1973–74*, edited by H. L. Costner, pp. 1–16. San Francisco: Jossey-Bass.

Heise, David, ed. (1981). *Microcomputers in social research*. Beverly Hills, CA: Sage.

Held, David. (1980). *Introduction to critical theory: Horkheimer to Habermas*. Berkeley: University of California Press.

Heller, Nelson B., and J. Thomas McEwen. (1973). Applications of crime seriousness information in police departments. *Journal of Criminal Justice*, 1:241–253.

Henry, Gary T. (1990). *Practical sampling*. Newbury Park, CA: Sage.

Henry, Gary T. (1995). *Graphing data: Techniques for display and analysis*. Thousand Oaks, CA: Sage.

Henry, Stuart. (1978). *The hidden economy*. New York: Martin Robertson.

Herting, Jerald R. (1985). Multiple indicator models using LISREL. In *Causal models in the social sciences*, 2nd ed., edited by Hubert M. Blalock, Jr., pp. 263–320. New York: Aldine.

Herting, Jerald R., and Herbert L. Costner. (1985). Re-specification in multiple indicator models. In *Causal models in the social sciences*, 2nd ed., edited by Hubert M. Blalock, Jr., pp. 321–394. Chicago: Aldine.

Hertz, Rosanna, and Jonathan B. Imber. (1993). Fieldwork in elite settings. *Journal of Contemporary Ethnography*, 22:3–6.

Herzberger, Sharon D. (1993). The cyclical pattern of child abuse: A study of research methodology. In *Research on sensitive topics*, edited by Claire Renzetti and Raymond Lee, pp. 33–51. Thousand Oaks, CA: Sage.

Herzog, A. Regula, and Jerald G. Bachman. (1981). Effects of questionnaire length on response quality. *Public Opinion Quarterly*, 45:549–559.

Hesse, Mary B. (1970). *Models and analogies in science*. Notre Dame, IN: Notre Dame Press.

Hicks, David. (1984). Getting into the field and establishing routines. In *Ethnographic research: A guide to general conduct*, edited by R. F. Ellen, pp. 192–199. Orlando: Academic Press.

Hill, Michael R. (1993). *Archival strategies and techniques*. Thousand Oaks, CA: Sage.

Hiller, Harry H. (1979). Universality of science and the question of national sociologies. *American Sociologist*, 14:124–135.

Hilts, Philip J. (1996). *Smokescreen: The truth behind the tobacco industry cover-up*. New York: Addison-Wesley.

Himmelstein, Jerome L., and Mayer Zald. (1984). American conservatism and government funding of the social sciences and arts. *Sociological Inquiry*, 54:171–187.

Hindess, Barry. (1973). *The use of official statistics in sociology: A critique of positivism and ethnomethodology*. New York: Macmillan.

Hippler, Hans, J., and Norbert Schwartz. (1986). Not forbidding isn't allowing: The cognitive basis of the forbid-allow asymmetry. *Public Opinion Quarterly*, 50:87–96.

Hirschman, Albert O. (1970). *Exit, voice, and loyalty: Response to decline in firms, organizations and states*. Cambridge, MA: Harvard University Press.

Hochschild, Arlie. (1983). *The managed heart*. Berkeley: University of California Press.

Hochschild, Jennifer L. (1981). *What's fair? American beliefs about distributive justice*. Cambridge, MA: Harvard University Press.

Hoffmann, Joan Eakin. (1980). Problems of access in the study of social elites and boards of directors. In *Fieldwork experience*, edited by W. B. Shaffir, R. A. Stebbins, and A. Turowetz, pp. 45–56. New York: St. Martin's Press.

Hoffman-Lange, Ursula. (1987). Surveying national elites in the Federal Republic of Germany. In *Research methods for elite studies*, edited by George Moyser and Margaret Wagstaffe, pp. 27–47. Boston: Allen and Unwin.

Hollander, Myles, and Frank Proschan. (1984). *The statistical exorcist: Dispelling statistics anxiety*. New York: Marcel Decker.

Hollis, Martin. (1977). *Models of man: Philosophical thoughts on social action*. New York: Cambridge University Press.

Holstein, James A., and Jaber F. Gubrium. (1994). Phenomenology, ethnomethodology and interpretative practice. In *Handbook of qualitative research*, edited by Norman Denzin and Yvonna Lincoln, pp. 262–272. Thousand Oaks, CA: Sage.

Holsti, Ole R. (1968). Content analysis. In *Handbook of social psychology*, 2nd ed., Vol. 2, edited by Gardner Lindzey and Elliot Aronson, pp. 596–692. Reading, MA: Addison-Wesley.

Holsti, Ole R. (1969). *Content analysis for the social sciences and humanities*. Reading, MA: Addison-Wesley.

Holt, Robert T., and John E. Turner. (1970). The methodology of comparative research. In *The methodology of comparative research*, edited by R. Holt and J. Turner, pp. 1–20. New York: Free Press.

Holub, Robert C. (1991). *Jürgen Habermas: Critic in the public sphere*. New York: Routledge.

Holy, Ladislav. (1984). Theory, methodology and the research process. In *Ethnographic research: A guide to general conduct*, edited by R. F. Ellen, pp. 13–34. Orlando: Academic Press.

Homan, Roger. (1980). The ethics of covert methods. *British Journal of Sociology*, 31:46–57.

Honigmann, John J. (1982). Sampling in ethnographic fieldwork. In *Field research*, edited by R. G. Burgess, pp. 79–90. Boston: Allen and Unwin.

Horan, Patrick. (1987). Theoretical models in social history research. *Social Science History*, 11:379–400.

Horn, Robert V. (1993). *Statistical indicators for the economic and social sciences*. Cambridge: Cambridge University Press.

Hornstein, Gail A. (1988). Quantifying psychological phenomena: Debates, dilemmas and implications. In *The rise of experimentation in American psychology*, edited by Jill G. Morawski, pp. 1–34. New Haven, CT: Yale University Press.

Horowitz, Irving Louis. (1965). The life and death of Project Camelot. *Transaction*, 3:3–7, 44–47.

House, Ernest R. (1980). *Evaluating with validity*. Beverly Hills, CA: Sage.

Hoy, David Couzens. (1994). *Critical theory*. Cambridge, MA: Blackwell.

Hubbard, Raymond, and Eldon Little. (1988). Promised contributions to charity and mail survey responses: Replication with extension. *Public Opinion Quarterly*, 52:223–230.

Huck, Schuyler W., and Howard M. Sandler. (1979). *Rival hypotheses: Alternative interpretations of data based conclusions*. New York: Harper & Row.

Humphreys, Laud. (1970). *Tearoom trade*. Chicago: Aldine.

Humphreys, Laud. (1975). *Tearoom trade: Impersonal sex in public places*, enlarged ed. Chicago: Aldine.

Hunt, Jennifer. (1984). The development of rapport through the negotiation of gender in field work among police. *Human Organization*, 45:283–296.

Hunt, Lynn. (1989). Introduction. In *The new cultural history*, edited by Lynn Hunt, pp. 1–22. Berkeley: University of California Press.

Hunter, Albert. (1993). Local knowledge and local power: Notes on the ethnography of local community elites. *Journal of Contemporary Ethnography*, 22:36–58.

Hunter, James Davidson. (1991). *Culture wars: The struggle to define America*. New York: Basic Books.

Hunter, John E., Frank L. Schmidt, and Gregg B. Jackson. (1982). *Meta-analysis: Cumulating research findings across studies*. Beverly Hills, CA: Sage.

Hutchinson, Sharon. (1996). *Nuer dilemmas: Coping with money, war, and the state*. Berkeley: University of California Press.

Hyman, Herbert H. (1975). *Interviewing in social research*. Chicago: University of Chicago Press.

Hyman, Herbert H. (1991). *Taking society's measure: A personal history of survey research*. New York: Russell Sage.

Hymes, Dell. (1970). Linguistic aspects of comparative political research. In *The methodology of comparative research*, edited by Robert T. Holt and John E. Turner, pp. 295–341. New York: Free Press.

Hymes, Dell. (1983). *Essays in the history of linguistic anthropology*. Philadelphia: John Benjamins Publishers.

Inciardi, James A., Anne E. Pottieger, and Hilary L. Surratt. (1996). African Americans and the crack-crime connection. In *The American pipe dream: Crack cocaine in the inner city*, edited by Dale Chitwood, James E. Rivers and James A. Inciardi, pp. 56–70. Fort Worth, TX: Harcourt Brace.

Internal Revenue Service. (1988). *Income tax compliance research: Gross tax gap estimates for 1973–1992*. Washington, DC: IRS Research Division.

Inverarity, James M. (1976). Populism and lynching in Louisiana, 1889–1896: A test of Erikson's theory of the relationship between boundary crisis and repressive justice. *American Sociological Review*, 41:262–280.

Isaac, Larry W., and Larry J. Griffin. (1989). A historicism in time series analysis of historical process: Critique, redirection, and illustrations from U.S. labor history. *American Sociological Review*, 54:873–890.

Jackson, Bruce. (1978). Killing time: Life in the Arkansas penitentiary. *Qualitative Sociology*, 1:21–32.

Jackson, Bruce. (1987). *Fieldwork*. Urbana: University of Illinois Press.

Jackson, David J., and Edgar F. Borgatta, eds. (1981). *Factor analysis and measurement in sociological research*. Beverly Hills, CA: Sage.

Jacob, Herbert. (1984). *Using published data: Errors and remedies*. Beverly Hills, CA: Sage.

Jacobs, Jerry. (1974). *Fun City: An ethnographic study of a retirement community*. New York: Holt, Rinehart and Winston.

Jaeger, Richard M. (1983). *Statistics as a spectator sport*. Beverly Hills, CA: Sage.

Jesilow, Paul, Henry M. Pontell, and Gilbert Geis. (1993). *Prescription for profit: How doctors defraud Medicaid*. Berkeley: University of California Press.

Johnson, Bruce. (1982). Missionaries, tourists and traders. *Studies in Symbolic Interaction*, 4:115–150.

Johnson, David Richard, and James C. Creech. (1983). Ordinal measures in multiple indicator models: A simulation study of categorization error. *American Sociological Review*, 48: 398–407.

Johnson, David W., and Roger T. Johnson. (1985). Relationships between black and white students in intergroup cooperation and competition. *Journal of Social Psychology*, 125:421–428.

Johnson, Jean. (Sept. 1997). Americans' view on crime and law enforcement. *National Institute of Justice Journal*, pp. 9–12.

Johnson, John M. (1975). *Doing field research*. New York: Free Press.

Johnson, P. Timonty, James G. Hougland, Jr., and Richard R. Clayton. (1989). Obtaining reports of sensitive behavior: A comparison of substance-use reports from telephone and face-to-face interviews. *Social Science Quarterly*, 70:173–183.

Johnson, Stephen D. (1985). Religion as a defense in a mock-jury trial. *Journal of Social Psychology*, 125: 213–220.

Jones, Gareth Stedman. (1976). From historical sociology to theoretical history. *British Journal of Sociology*, 27:295–305.

Jones, Gareth Stedman. (1983). *Languages of class*. New York: Cambridge University Press.

Jones, J. H. (1981). *Bad blood: The Tuskegee syphilis experiment*. New York: Free Press.

Jones, Wesley H. (1979). Generalizing mail survey inducement methods: Populations' interactions with anonymity and sponsorship. *Public Opinion Quarterly*, 43:102–111.

Jordan, Lawrence A., Alfred C. Marcus, and Leo G. Reeder. (1980). Response styles in telephone and household interviewing: A field experiment. *Public Opinion Quarterly*, 44:210–222.

Jorgensen, Danny L., and Lin Jorgensen. (1982). Social meanings of the occult. *Sociological Quarterly*, 23:373–389.

Josephson, Paul R. (Nov. 1, 1988). The FBI menaces academic freedom. *New York Times*.

Junger-Tas, Josine. (1997). Ethnic minorities and criminal justice in the Netherlands. In *Ethnicity, crime, and immigration*, edited by Michael Tonry, pp. 257–310. Chicago: University of Chicago Press.

Junguito, Roberto, and Carlos Caballero. (1982). Illegal trade transactions and the underground economy of Colombia. In *The underground economy in the U.S. and abroad*, edited by Vito Tanzi, pp. 285–313. Lexington, MA: D. C. Heath.

Junker, Buford H. (1960). *Field work*. Chicago: University of Chicago Press.

Juster, F. Thomas, and Kenneth C. Land, eds. (1981). *Social accounting systems: Essays on the state of the art*. New York: Academic Press.

Kalberg, Stephen. (1994). *Max Weber's comparative-historical sociology*. Chicago: University of Chicago Press.

Kalton, Graham. (1983). *Introduction to survey sampling*. Beverly Hills, CA: Sage.

Kandel, Denise B. (1980). Drug and drinking behavior among youth. *Annual Review of Sociology*, 6: 235–265.

Kane, Emily W., and Laura J. MacAulay. (1993). Interview gender and gender attitudes. *Public Opinion Quarterly*, 57:1–28.

Kaplan, Abraham. (1964). *The conduct of inquiry: Methodology for behavioral science*. New York: Harper & Row.

Karp, David A. (1973). Hiding in pornographic bookstores: A reconsideration of the nature of urban anonymity. *Urban Life*, 1:427–452.

Karp, David A. (1980). Observing behavior in public places: Problems and strategies. In *Fieldwork experience*, edited by W. B. Shaffir, R. A. Stebbins, and A. Turowetz, pp.

82–97. New York: St. Martin's Press.

Karweit, Nancy, and Edmund D. Meyers, Jr. (1983). Computers in survey research. In *Handbook of survey research*, edited by Peter H. Rossi, James D. Wright, and Andy B. Anderson, pp. 379–414. Orlando, FL: Academic Press.

Katovich, Michael A., and Ron L. Diamond. (1986). Selling time: Situated transactions in a noninstitutional setting. *Sociological Quarterly*, 27:253–271.

Katz, Jay. (1972). *Experimentation with human beings*. New York: Russell Sage Foundation.

Katzer, Jeffrey, Kenneth H. Cook, and Wayne W. Crouch. (1982). *Evaluating information: A guide for users of social science research*, 2nd ed. Reading, MA: Addison-Wesley.

Katzer, Jeffrey, Kenneth H. Cook, and Wayne W. Crouch. (1991). *Evaluating information: A guide for users of social science research*, 3rd ed. New York: McGraw Hill.

Keat, Russell. (1981). *The politics of social theory: Habermas, Freud and the critique of positivism*. Chicago: University of Chicago Press.

Keat, Russell, and John Urry. (1975). *Social theory as science*. London: Routledge and Kegan Paul.

Keeter, Scott. (1995). Estimating telephone noncoverage bias with a telephone survey. *Public Opinion Quarterly*, 59:196–217.

Keller, Bill. (May 27, 1988). Ups and downs of conducting the poll. *New York Times*.

Keller, Bill. (Jan. 19, 1989). Prying where it counts: Into census. *New York Times*.

Keller, Evelyn Fox. (1983). *A feeling for the organism: The life and work of Barbara McClintock*. New York: W. H. Freeman.

Keller, Evelyn Fox. (1985). *Reflections on gender and science*. New Haven, CT: Yale University Press.

Keller, Evelyn Fox. (1990). Gender and science. In *Feminist research methods*, edited by Joyce McCarl Nielsen, pp. 41–57. Boulder, CO: Westview.

Kelman, Herbert. (1982). Ethical issues in different social science methods. In *Ethical issues in social science research*, edited by Tom Beauchamp, R. Faden, R. J. Wallace, and L. Walters, pp. 40–99. Baltimore: Johns Hopkins University Press.

Kemp, Jeremy, and R. F. Ellen. (1984). Informants. In *Ethnographic research: A guide to general conduct*, edited by R. F. Ellen, pp. 224–236. Orlando: Academic Press.

Kenen, Regina. (1982). Soapsuds, space and sociability: A participant observation of a laundromat. *Urban Life*, 11:163–184.

Kent, Stephen A. (1992). Historical sociology. In *Encyclopedia of sociology*, Vol. 2, edited by Edgar and Marie Borgatta, pp. 837–843. New York: Macmillan.

Kerbo, Harold, and Mariko Inoue. (1996). Japanese social structure and white collar crime: Recruit cosmos and beyond. In *Criminology: A cross-cultural perspective*, edited by Robert Heiner, pp. 66–78. New York: West.

Kercher, Kyle. (1992). Quasi-experimental research designs. In *Encyclopedia of sociology*, Vol. 3, edited by Edgar and Marie Borgatta, pp. 1595–1613. New York: Macmillan.

Kerlinger, Fred N. (1979). *Behavioral research: A conceptual approach*. New York: Holt, Rinehart and Winston.

Kidder, Louise H. (1982). Face validity from multiple perspectives. In *Forms of validity in research*, edited by David Brinberg and Louise H. Kidder, pp. 41–57. San Francisco: Jossey-Bass.

Kidder, Louise H., and Charles M. Judd. (1986). *Research methods in social relations*, 5th ed. New York: Holt, Rinehart and Winston.

Kiecolt, K. Jill, and Laura E. Nathan. (1985). *Secondary analysis of survey data*. Beverly Hills, CA: Sage.

Kim, Jae-On, and Charles W. Mueller. (1978). *Introduction to factor analysis: What it is and how to do it*. Beverly Hills, CA: Sage.

Kimmel, Allan J. (1988). *Ethics and values in applied social research*. Newbury Park, CA: Sage.

Kincheloe, Joe L., and Peter L. McLaren. (1994). Rethinking critical theory and qualitative research. In *Handbook of qualitative research*, edited by Norman Denzin and Yvonna Lincoln, pp. 138–157. Thousand Oaks, CA: Sage.

Kindermann, Charles, James Lynch, and David Cantor. (1997). *Effects of the redesign on victimization estimates*. Washington, DC: U.S. Bureau of Justice Statistics.

King, Gary, Robert O. Keohane, and Sidney Verba. (1994). *Designing social inquiry: Scientific inference in qualitative research*. Princeton, NJ: Princeton University Press.

Kinsey, R., J. Lea, and Jock Young. (1986). *Losing the fight against crime*. Oxford: Blackwell.

Kirk, Jerome, and Marc L. Miller. (1986). *Reliability and validity in qualitative research*. Beverly Hills, CA: Sage.

Kish, L. (1965). *Survey sampling*. New York: Wiley.

Klein, Dorie. (1973). The etiology of female crime: A review of the literature. *Criminology*, 8:3–30.

Kleinman, Sherry. (1980). Learning the ropes as fieldwork analysis. In *Fieldwork experience*, edited by W. B. Shaffir, R. A. Stebbins, and A. Turowetz, pp. 171–183. New York: St. Martin's Press.

Kleinman, Sherry, and Martha A. Copp. (1993). *Emotions and field work*. Thousand Oaks, CA: Sage.

Klockars, Carl B. (1974). *The professional fence*. New York: Free Press.

Knapp, Peter. (1990). The revival of macrosociology: Methodological issues of discontinuity in comparative-historical theory. *Sociological Forum*, 5:545–567.

Knoke, David. (1993). Networks of elite structure and decision-making. *Sociological Methods and Research*, 22:23–45.

Koetting, Mark G., and Vincent Schiraldi. (1997). Singapore West: The incarceration of 200,000 Californians. *Social Justice*, 24:40–53.

Kohn, Melvin L. (1987). Cross-national research as an analytic strategy. *American Sociological Review*, 52:713–731.

Kohn, Melvin L., ed. (1989). *Cross-national research in sociology*. Newbury Park, CA: Sage.

Koretz, Daniel. (Summer 1988). Arriving in Lake Wobegon: Are standardized tests exaggerating achievement and distorting instruction? *American Educator*, 12:8–15.

Kornblum, William. (1974). *Blue collar community*. Chicago: University of Chicago Press.

Kraemer, Helena Chmura, and Sue Thiemann. (1987). *How many subjects? Statistical power analysis in research*. Newbury Park, CA: Sage.

Kraska, Peter B., and Louis J. Cubellis. (1997). Militarizing Mayberry and beyond: Making sense of American paramilitary policing. *Justice Quarterly*, 14:607–629.

Kraska, Peter B., and Victor E. Kappeler. (1997). Militarizing American police: The rise and normalization of paramilitary units. *Social Problems*, 44:1–18.

Krathwohl, D. R. (1965). *How to prepare a research proposal*. Syracuse, NY: Syracuse University Bookstore.

Krippendorff, Klaus. (1980). *Content analysis: An introduction to its methodology*. Beverly Hills, CA: Sage.

Krosnick, Jon A., and Robert P. Abelson. (1992). The case for measuring attitude strength in surveys. In *Questions about questions: Inquiries into the cognitive bases of surveys*, edited by Judith M. Turner, pp. 177–203. New York: Russell Sage Foundation.

Krosnick, Jon A., and Duane F. Alwin. (1988). A test of the form-resistant correlation hypothesis: Ratings, rankings and the measurement of values. *Public Opinion Quarterly*, 52:526–538.

Krueger, Richard A. (1988). *Focus groups: A practical guide for applied research*. Beverly Hills, CA: Sage.

Kuhn, Thomas S. (1970). *The structure of scientific revolutions*, 2nd ed. Chicago: University of Chicago Press.

Kuhn, Thomas S. (1979). The relations between history and the history of science. In *Interpretive social science: A reader*, edited by Paul Rabinow and William Sullivan. Berkeley: University of California Press.

Kurz, Demie. (1987). Emergency department responses to battered women: Resistance to medicalization. *Social Problems*, 34:69–81.

Kusserow, Richard P. (March 1989). *Misconduct in scientific research*. Report of the Inspector General of the U.S. Department of Health and Human Services. Washington, DC: Department of Health and Human Services.

Kviz, Frederick J. (1984). Bias in a directory sample for mail survey of rural households. *Public Opinion Quarterly*, 48:801–806.

Labaw, Patricia J. (1980). *Advanced questionnaire design*. Cambridge, MA: Abt Books.

Lachmann, Richard. (1988). Graffiti as career and ideology. *American Journal of Sociology*, 94:251–272.

Lachmann, Richard. (1989). Elite conflict and state formation in 16th and 17th century England and France. *American Sociological Review*, 54:141–162.

Lagemann, Ellen Condliffe. (1989). *The politics of knowledge: The Carnegie Corporation, philanthropy and public policy*. Chicago: University of Chicago.

Land, Kenneth. (1992). Social indicators. *Encyclopedia of sociology*, Vol. 4, edited by Edgar and Marie Borgatta, pp. 1844–1850. New York: Macmillan.

Lane, Michael. (1970). *Structuralism*. London: Jonathan Cape.

Lang, Eric. (1992). Hawthorne effect. *Encyclopedia of sociology*, Vol. 2, edited by Edgar and Marie Borgatta, pp. 793–794. New York: Macmillan.

Laslett, Barbara. (1980). Beyond methodology. *American Sociological Review*, 45:214–228.

Laslett, Barbara. (1992). Gender in/and social history. *Social Science History,* 16:177–196.

Law Enforcement News. (1996). Criminal justice with Chinese characteristics. In *Criminology: A cross-cultural perspective,* edited by Robert Heiner, pp. 172–181. New York: West.

Law Enforcement News. (May 15, 1997). Do you get what you pay for? With criminal justice efforts, not necessarily, pp. 1, 18.

Lawyers Committee for Human Rights. (1989). *The Jesuit murders: A report on the testimony of a witness.* New York: Lawyers Committee for Human Rights.

Layder, Derek. (1993). *New strategies in social research.* Cambridge, MA: Polity.

Lazarsfeld, Paul F., and Jeffrey G. Reitz. (1975). *An introduction to applied sociology.* Amsterdam: Elsevier.

Lazere, Donald, ed. (1987). *American media and mass culture: Left perspectives.* Berkeley: University of California Press.

Lee, Alfred McClung. (1978). *Sociology for whom?* New York: Oxford University Press.

Lee, Harper. (1960). *To kill a mockingbird.* New York: Warner Books.

Leggett, Glenn, C. David Mean, and William Charvat. (1965). *Prentice-Hall handbook for writers,* 4th ed. Englewood Cliffs, NJ: Prentice-Hall.

Leiter, Kenneth. (1980). *A primer on ethnomethodology.* New York: Oxford University Press.

LeMasters, E. E. (1975). *Blue collar aristocrats.* Madison: University of Wisconsin Press.

Lemert, Charles. (1979). Science, religion and secularization. *Sociological Quarterly,* 20:445–461.

Lemert, Charles, ed. (1981). *French sociology: Rupture and renewal since 1968.* New York: Columbia University Press.

Lenski, Gerhard E. (1966). *Power and privilege.* New York: McGraw-Hill.

Lenzer, Gertrud, ed. (1975). *Auguste Comte and positivism: Essential writings.* New York: Harper & Row.

Lesiuer, Henry R., and Joseph F. Sheley. (1987). Illegal appended enterprises: Selling the lines. *Social Problems,* 34:249–260.

Lessler, Judith T. (1984). Measurement error in surveys. In *Surveying subjective phenomena,* Vol. 2, edited by Charles Turner and Elizabeth Martin, pp. 405–440. New York: Russell Sage Foundation.

Lester, Marilyn, and Stuart C. Hadden. (1980). Ethnomethodology and grounded theory methodology: An integration of perspective and method. *Urban Life,* 9:3–33.

Lever, Janet. (1978). Sex differences in the complexity of children's play and games. *American Sociological Review,* 43:471–483.

Lever, Janet. (1981). Multiple methods of data collection: A note on divergence. *Urban Life,* 10:199–213.

Levine, Joel H. (1993). *Exceptions are the rule: An inquiry into methods in the social sciences.* Boulder, CO: Westview.

Lewis, George H., and Jonathan F. Lewis. (1980). The dog in the nighttime: Negative evidence in social research. *British Journal of Sociology,* 31:544–558.

Librarians charge plan would cut flow of data. (Feb. 21, 1989). *New York Times.*

Lieberson, Stanley. (1985). *Making it count: The improvement of social research and theory.* Berkeley: University of California Press.

Lieberson, Stanley. (1991). Small N's and big conclusions: An examination of the reasoning of comparative studies based on a small number of cases. *Social Forces,* 70:307–320.

Liebetrau, Albert M. (1983). *Measures of association.* Beverly Hills, CA: Sage.

Liebman, Robert, John R. Sutton, and Robert Wuthnow. (1988). Exploring social sources of denominationalism: Schisms in American Protestant denominations, 1890–1980. *American Sociological Review,* 53:343–352.

Liebow, Elliot. (1967). *Talley's corner.* Boston: Little, Brown.

Lifton, Robert J. (1986). *Nazi doctors.* New York: Basic Books.

Light, Ivan. (1977). The ethnic vice industry, 1880–1944. *American Sociological Review,* 42:464–479.

Light, Ivan, and Edna Bonacich. (1988). *Immigrant entrepreneurs: Koreans in Los Angeles, 1965–1982.* Berkeley: University of California Press.

Light, Richard J., and David B. Pillemer. (1984). *Summing up: The science of reviewing research.* Cambridge, MA: Harvard University Press.

Likert, Rensis. (1970). A technique for the measurement of attitudes. In *Attitude measurement,* edited by Gene Summers, pp. 149–158. Chicago: Rand McNally.

Lindblom, Charles E., and David K. Cohen. (1979). *Usable knowledge: Social science and social problem solving.* New Haven, CT: Yale University Press.

Lindzey, Gardner, and Donn Byrne. (1968). Measurement of social choice and interpersonal attractiveness. In *The handbook of social psychology,* Vol. 2: Research methods, edited by Gardner Lindzey and Elliott Aronson, pp. 452–525. Reading, MA: Addison-Wesley.

Lipset, Seymour Martin. (1968). History and sociology: Some methodological considerations. In *Sociology and history: Methods,* edited by S. M. Lipset and R. Hofstadter, pp. 20–58. New York: Basic Books.

Little, Daniel. (1991). *Varieties of social explanation: An introduction to the philosophy of science.* Boulder, CO: Westview.

Livingston, Steven, and Todd Eachus. (1996). Indexing news after the Cold War: Reporting U.S. ties to Latin American paramilitary organizations. *Political Communication,* 13:423–436.

Lloyd, Christopher. (1986). *Explanation in social history.* New York: Basil Blackwell.

Locke, Lawrence F., Warren Wyrick Spirduso, and Stephen J. Silverman. (1987). *Proposals that work: A guide for planning dissertations and grant proposals,* 2nd ed. Beverly Hills, CA: Sage.

Loewenstein, Gaither. (1985). The new underclass: A contemporary sociological dilemma. *Sociological Quarterly,* 26:35–48.

Lofland, John. (1966). *Doomsday cult.* Englewood Cliffs, NJ: Prentice-Hall.

Lofland, John. (1974). Styles of reporting qualitative field research. *American Sociologist,* 9:101–111.

Lofland, John. (1976). *Doing social life: The qualitative study of human interaction in natural settings.* New York: Wiley.

Lofland, John, and Lyn H. Lofland. (1984). *Analyzing social settings,* 2nd ed. Belmont, CA: Wadsworth.

Lofland, John, and Lyn H. Lofland. (1995). *Analyzing social settings,* 3rd ed. Belmont, CA: Wadsworth.

Lofland, Lyn H. (1972). Self management in public settings: Parts I and II. *Urban Life,* 1:93–108, 217–231.

Lofquist, William S. (1997). Constructing "crime": Media coverage of individual and organizational wrongdoing. *Justice Quarterly,* 14:243–263.

Loftus, Elizabeth, Mark Klinger, Kyle Smith, and Judith Fiedler. (1990). A tale of two questions: Benefit of asking more than one question. *Public Opinion Quarterly,* 54:330–345.

Loftus, Elizabeth, Kyle D. Smith, Mark R. Klinger, and Judith Fiedler. (1992). Memory and mismemory of health events. In *Questions about questions: Inquiries into the cognitive bases of surveys,* edited by

Judith M. Turner, pp. 102–137. New York: Russell Sage Foundation.

Long, J. Scott. (1976). Estimation and hypothesis testing in linear models containing measurement error: A review of Joreskog's model for the analysis of covariance structures. *Sociological Methods and Research*, 5:157–206.

Long, J. Scott. (1978). Productivity and academic positions in a scientific career. *American Sociological Review*, 43:889–908.

Longino, Helen E. (1990). *Science as social knowledge: Values and objectivity in scientific inquiry*. Princeton, NJ: Princeton University Press.

Lopez, Michael C. (Winter 1996). The U.S. School of the Americas: Teaching terror. *Colombia Bulletin*, pp. 35–44.

Lorr, Maurice. (1983). *Cluster analysis for social scientists: Techniques for analyzing and simplifying complex blocks of data*. San Francisco: Jossey-Bass.

Lovin-Smith, Lynn, and Charles Brody. (1989). Interruptions in group discussions: The effects of gender and group composition. *American Sociological Review*, 54:424–435.

Lowenthal, David. (1985). *The past is a foreign country*. New York: Cambridge University Press.

Luebke, Barbara F. (1989). Out of focus: Images of men and women in newspaper photographs. *Sex Roles*, 20:121–133.

Luger, Michael I. (1996). Quality-of-life differences and urban and regional outcomes: A review. *Housing Policy Debate*, 7:749–771.

Lynd, Robert S. (1964). *Knowledge for what? The place of social science in American culture*. New York: Grove. (Originally published in 1939 by Princeton University Press.)

MacFarlane, Alan. (1977). *Reconstructing historical communities*. New York: Cambridge University Press.

MacIver, A. M. (1968). Levels of explanation in history. In *Readings in the philosophy of the social sciences*, edited by M. Brodbeck, pp. 304–316. New York: Macmillan.

MacKeun, Michael B. (1984). Reality, the Press and Citizens Political Agendas. In *Surveying subjective phenomena*, Vol. 2, edited by Charles Turner and Elizabeth Martin, pp. 443–473. New York: Russell Sage Foundation.

Maguire, Kathleen, and Ann L. Pastore, eds. (1997). *Sourcebook of criminal justice statistics 1996*. U.S. Department of Justice, Bureau of Justice Statistics. Washington, DC: U.S. Government Printing Office.

Maier, Mark H. (1991). *The data game: Controversies in social science statistics*. Armonk, NY: M. E. Sharpe.

Maines, David R., William Shaffir, and Allan Turowetz. (1980). Leaving the field in ethnographic research. In *The fieldwork experience: Qualitative approaches to social research*, edited by William B. Shaffir, R. Stebbins, and A. Turowetz, pp. 261–280. New York: St. Martin's.

Makkai, Toni, and John Braithwaite. (1993). Praise, price and corporate compliance. *International Journal of the Sociology of Law*, 21:73–91.

Maloney, Dennis M. (1984). *Protection of human research subjects: A practical guide to federal laws and regulations*. New York: Plenum.

Mann, Floyd C. (1970). Human relations skills in social research. In *Qualitative methodology*, edited by W. J. Filstead. Chicago: Markham.

Mannheim, Karl. (1936). *Ideology and utopia*. New York: Harcourt, Brace and World.

Manson, Donald A., and Darrell K. Gilliard. (1997). *Presale handgun checks, 1996*. Washington, DC: U.S. Department of Justice.

Mariampolski, Hyman, and Dana C. Hughes. (1978). The use of personal documents in historical sociology. *The American Sociologist*, 13:104–113.

Markoff, John, Gilbert Shapiro, and Sasha R. Weitman. (1974). Toward the integration of content analysis and general methodology. In *Sociological methodology, 1974*, edited by David Heise, pp. 1–58. San Francisco: Jossey-Bass.

Marradi, Alberto. (1981). Factor analysis as an aid in the formation and refinement of empirically useful concepts. In *Factor analysis and measurement in social research: A multi-dimensional perspective*, edited by David Jackson and Edgar Borgatta, pp. 11–50. Beverly Hills, CA: Sage.

Marsh, Catherine. (1982). *The survey method: The contribution of surveys to sociological explanation*. Boston: George Allen and Unwin.

Marsh, Catherine. (1984). Do polls affect what people think? In *Surveying subjective phenomena*, Vol. 2, edited by Charles Turner and Elizabeth Martin, pp. 565–592. New York: Russell Sage Foundation.

Marshall, Catherine. (1985). Appropriate criteria of trustworthiness and goodness for qualitative research on educational organizations. *Quality and Quantity*, 19:353–373.

Marshall, Catherine, and Gretchen B. Rossman. (1989). *Designing qualitative research*. Beverly Hills, CA: Sage.

Martens, Peter L. (1997). Immigrants, crime, and criminal justice in Sweden. In *Ethnicity, crime and immigration*, edited by Michael Tonry, pp. 183–256. Chicago: University of Chicago Press.

Martin, Elizabeth. (1985). Surveys as social indicators: Problems of monitoring trends. In *Handbook of survey research*, edited by Peter Rossi, James Wright, and Andy Anderson, pp. 677–743. Orlando, FL: Academic.

Martin, Jay. (1973). *The dialectical imagination*. Boston: Little, Brown.

Martin, John L., and Laura Dean. (1993). Developing a community sample of gay men for an epidemiological study of AIDS. In *Research on sensitive topics*, edited by Claire Renzetti and Raymond Lee, pp. 82–100. Thousand Oaks, CA: Sage.

Marvell, Thomas R., and Carlisle E. Moody. (1995). The impact of enhanced prison terms for felonies committed with guns. *Criminology*, 33: 247–281.

Marx, Karl, and Friedrich Engels. (1947). *The German ideology, Parts I & III*, edited with introduction by R. Pascal. New York: International Publishers.

Massing, Michael. (July 11, 1996). How to win the tobacco war. *New York Review of Books*, pp. 32–36.

Masterman, Margaret. (1970). The nature of a paradigm. In *Criticism and the growth of knowledge*, edited by Imre Lakatos and Alan Musgrove, pp. 59–90. Cambridge: Cambridge University Press.

Mauro, Paolo. (1996). *The effects of corruption on growth, investment, and government expenditure*. Washington, DC: International Monetary Fund.

Mayer, Charles S., and Cindy Piper. (1982). A note on the importance of layout in self-administered questionnaires. *Journal of Marketing Research*, 19:390–391.

Mayhew, Bruce H. (1980). Structuralism versus individualism, Part I: Shadowboxing in the dark. *Social Forces*, 59:335–375.

Mayhew, Bruce H. (1981). Structuralism versus individualism, Part II: Ideological and other obfuscations. *Social Forces*, 59:627–648.

Maynard, Douglas W. (1985). On the functions of conflict among children. *American Sociological Review*, 50:207–223.

McCabe, Donald L. (1992). The influence of situational ethics on cheating among college students. *Sociological Inquiry*, 62:365–374.

McCall, George. (1969). Quality control in participant observation. In

Issues in participant observation, edited by George McCall and J. L. Simmons, pp. 128–141. Reading, MA: Addison-Wesley.

McCall, George. (1984). Systematic field observation. *Annual Review of Sociology*, 10:263–282.

McCall, Michal. (1980). Who and where are the artists? In *The fieldwork experience: Qualitative approaches to social research*, edited by William B. Shaffir, R. Stebbins, and A. Turowetz, pp. 145–158. New York: St. Martin's.

McCarthy, Thomas. (1978). *The critical theory of Jurgen Habermas*. Cambridge, MA: MIT Press.

McCartney, James L. (1984). Setting priorities for research: New politics for the social sciences. *Sociological Quarterly*, 25:437–455.

McConaghy, Maureen. (1975). Maximum possible error in Guttman scales. *Public Opinion Quarterly*, 39:343–357.

McCracken, Grant. (1988). *The long interview*. Thousand Oaks, CA: Sage.

McDaniel, Timothy. (1978). Meaning and comparative concepts. *Theory and Society*, 6:93–118.

McDiarmid, Garnet. (1971). *Teaching prejudice: A content analysis of social studies textbooks authorized for use in Ontario*. Ontario: Ontario Institute for Studies in Education.

McFarland, Sam G. (1981). Effects of question order on survey responses. *Public Opinion Quarterly*, 45: 208–215.

McGrath, Joseph, Joanne Martin, and Richard A. Kulka. (1982). *Judgment calls in research*. Beverly Hills, CA: Sage.

McIllwain, Jeffrey Scott. (1997). From tong war to organized crime: The historical perception of violence in Chinatown. *Justice Quarterly*, 14: 25–51.

McIver, John P., and Edward G. Carmines. (1981). *Unidimensional scaling*. Beverly Hills, CA: Sage.

McKee, J. McClendon, and David J. O'Brien. (1988). Question order effects on the determinants of subjective well being. *Public Opinion Quarterly*, 52:351–364.

McKelvie, Stuart J., and Linda A. Schamer. (1988). Effects of night, passengers and sex on driver behavior at stop signs. *Journal of Social Psychology*, 128:658–690.

McKeown, Bruce. (1988). *Q methodology*. Thousand Oaks, CA: Sage.

McLennan, Gregor. (1981). *Marxism and the methodologies of history*. London: Verso.

McMurtry, John. (1978). *The structure of Marx's world view*. Princeton, NJ: Princeton University Press.

McNall, Scott G. (1988). *The road to rebellion*. Chicago: University of Chicago Press.

McNamara, Sean Cush. (1986). Learning how to bribe a policeman. *Anthropology Today*, 2.

McQuaire, Donald. (1978). Marx and the method of successive approximations. *Sociological Quarterly*, 20:431–435.

McQuaire, Donald. (1979). Reply to Wardell. *Sociological Quarterly*, 20:431–435.

Mead, George Herbert. (1918). The psychology of punitive justice. In *Sociological theory: A book of readings*, edited by Lewis A. Coser and Bernard Rosenberg, pp. 578–584. New York: Macmillan.

Meadows, A. J. (1974). *Communication in science*. Toronto: Butterworths.

Mehan, Hugh. (1973). Assessing children's language using abilities (with discussion). In *Comparative social research*, edited by M. Armer and A. Grimshaw, pp. 309–345. New York: Wiley.

Mehan, Hugh, and Houston Wood. (1975). *The reality of ethnomethodology*. New York: Wiley.

Meier, Barry. (Dec. 5, 1997). Hundreds of secret tobacco industry papers on marketing cigarettes to minors are released. *New York Times*, p. 1.

Melbin, Murray. (1978). Night as frontier. *American Sociological Review*, 43:3–22.

Mendenhall, William, Lyman Ott, and Richard L. Scheaffer. (1971). *Elementary survey sampling*. Belmont, CA: Duxbury Press.

Merton, Robert K. (1957). *Social theory and social structure*. New York: Free Press.

Merton, Robert K. (1967). *On theoretical sociology: Five essays, old and new*. New York: Free Press.

Merton, Robert K. (1970). *Science, technology and society in seventeenth century England*. New York: Harper & Row.

Merton, Robert K. (1973). *The sociology of science*. Chicago: University of Chicago Press.

Miles, Matthew B., and A. Michael Huberman. (1984). *Qualitative data analysis*. Beverly Hills, CA: Sage.

Miles, Matthew B., and A. Michael Huberman. (1994). *Qualitative data analysis*, 2nd ed. Thousand Oaks, CA: Sage.

Milgram, Stanley. (1963). Behavioral study of obedience. *Journal of Abnormal and Social Psychology*, 6:371–378.

Milgram, Stanley. (1965). Some conditions of obedience and disobedience to authority. *Human Relations*, 18:57–76.

Milgram, Stanley. (1974). *Obedience to authority*. New York: Harper & Row.

Miller, Delbert C. (1991). *Handbook of research design and social measurement*, 5th ed. Newbury Park, CA: Sage.

Miller, Gale. (1983). Holding clients accountable: The micro-politics of trouble in a work incentive program. *Social Problems*, 31:139–151.

Miller, Gale. (1992). Case studies. In *Encyclopedia of sociology*, Vol. 1, edited by Edgar and Marie Borgatta, pp. 167–172. New York: Macmillan.

Miller, Richard. (1987). *Fact and method: Explanation, confirmation and reality in the natural and social sciences*. Princeton, NJ: Princeton University Press.

Miller, Susan L. (1998). *Crime control and women*. Newbury Park, CA: Sage.

Miller, William L. (1983). *The survey method in the social and political sciences: Achievements, failures and prospects*. London: Frances Pinter.

Milligan, John D. (1979). The treatment of historical source. *History and Theory*, 18:177–196.

Mills, C. Wright. (1959). *The sociological imagination*. New York: Oxford University Press.

Mishler, Elliot G. (1986). *Research interviewing: Context and narrative*. Cambridge, MA: Harvard University Press.

Mitchell, J. Clyde. (1984). Case studies. In *Ethnographic research: A guide to general conduct*, edited by R. F. Ellen, pp. 237–241. Orlando, FL: Academic Press.

Mitchell, Mark, and Janina Jolley. (1988). *Research design explained*. New York: Holt, Rinehart and Winston.

Mitchell, Richard G., Jr. (1993). *Secrecy and fieldwork*. Thousand Oaks, CA: Sage.

Mitchell, Richard H. (1996). *Political bribery in Japan*. Honolulu: University of Hawaii Press.

Mitroff, Ian. (1974). Norms and counter-norms in a select group of the Apollo moon scientists: A case study of ambivalence of scientists. *American Sociology Review*, 39:579–595.

Monaghan, Peter. (Apr. 7, 1993a). Facing jail, a sociologist raises question about a scholar's right to protect sources. *Chronicle of Higher Education*, p. A10.

Monaghan, Peter. (May 26, 1993b). Sociologist is jailed for refusing to testify about research subject. *Chronicle of Higher Education*, p. A10.

Monaghan, Peter. (Sept. 1, 1993c). Sociologist jailed because he "wouldn't snitch" ponders the way research ought to be done. *Chronicle of Higher Education*, pp. A8–A9.

Mooney, Linda, and Robert B. Gramling. (1991). Asking threatening questions and situational framing: The effects of decomposing survey items. *Sociological Quarterly*, 32:277–288.

Moore, Barrington, Jr. (1966). *The social origins of dictatorship and democracy*. Boston: Beacon Press.

Moore, Joan. (1973). Social constraints on sociological knowledge: Academic and research concerning minorities. *Social Problems*, 21:65–77.

Moore, Joan, Diego Vigil, and Robert Garcia. (1983). Residence and territoriality in Chicago gangs. *Social Problems*, 31:182–194.

Morrow, Raymond Allan. (1994). *Critical theory and methodology*. Thousand Oaks, CA: Sage.

Morse, Janice M. (1994). Designing funded qualitative research. In *Handbook of qualitative research*, edited by Norman K. Denzin and Yvonna S. Lincoln, pp. 220–235. Thousand Oaks, CA: Sage.

Moser, C. A., and G. Kalton. (1972). *Survey methods in social investigation*. New York: Basic Books.

Mostyn, Barbara. (1985). The content analysis of qualitative research data: A dynamic approach. In *The research interview: Uses and approaches*, edited by Michael Brenner, Jennifer Brown, and David Canter, pp. 115–145. New York: Academic Press.

Mugford, Stephen. (1997). Crack in comparative perspective: The absence of a crack problem in Australia. In *Crack in America: Demon drugs and social justice*, edited by H. Levine and C. Reinarman, pp. 140–165. Berkeley: University of California Press.

Mulkay, Michael. (1979). *Science and the sociology of knowledge*. London: George Allen and Unwin.

Mullins, Carolyn J. (1977). *A guide to writing and publishing in the social and behavioral sciences*. New York: Wiley.

Mullins, Nicholas C. (1971). *The art of theory: Construction and use*. New York: Harper & Row.

Mullins, Nicholas C. (1973). *Theory and theory groups in American sociology*. New York: Harper & Row.

Murdock, George P. (1967). Ethnographic atlas. *Ethnology*, 6:109–236.

Murdock, George P. (1971). *Outline of cultural materials*, 4th ed. New Haven, CT: Human Relations Area Files.

Murphey, Murray G. (1973). *Our knowledge of the historical past*. Indianapolis: Bobbs-Merrill.

Murray, Shoon. (1992). Turning an elite cross-sectional survey into a panel study while protecting anonymity. *Journal of Conflict Resolution*, 36:586–595.

Myerhoff, Barbara. (1989). So what do you want from us here? In *In the field*, edited by Carolyn Smith and William Kornblum, pp. 83–90. New York: Praeger.

Myers, Gloria, and A. V. Margavio. (1983). The black bourgeoisie and reference group change: A content analysis of Ebony. *Qualitative sociology*, 6:291–307.

Myrdal, Gunnar. (1973). The beam in our eyes. In *Comparative research methods*, edited by D. Warwick and S. Osherson, pp. 89–99. Englewood Cliffs, NJ: Prentice-Hall.

Nadeau, Richard, Richard Miemi, and Jeffrey Levine. (1993). Innumeracy about minority population. *Public Opinion Quarterly*, 57:332–347.

Naffine, Ngaire. (1987). *Female crime: The construction of women in criminology*. Boston: Allen and Unwin.

Nafziger, E. Wayne. (1988). *Inequality in Africa: Political elites, proletariat, peasants and the poor*. New York: Cambridge University Press.

Nagin, Daniel S., David P. Farrington, and Terrie E. Moffitt. (1995). Life course trajectories of different types of offenders. *Criminology*, 33:111–139.

Namenwirth, J. Z. (1970). Prestige newspapers and assessment of elite opinions. *Journalism Quarterly*, 47:318–323.

Naroll, Raoul. (1968). Some thoughts on comparative method in cultural anthropology. In *Methodology in social research*, edited by H. Blalock and A. Blalock, pp. 236–277. New York: McGraw-Hill.

Nash, Jeffrey E., and David W. McCurdy. (1989). Cultural knowledge and systems of knowing. *Sociological Inquiry*, 59:117–126.

Neapolitan, Jerry. (1988). The effects of different types of praise and criticism on performance. *Sociological Focus*, 21:223–232.

Nederhof, Anton J. (1986). Effects of research experiences of respondents. *Quality and Quantity*, 20:277–284.

Nelkin, Dorothy. (1982a). Forbidden research: Limits on inquiry in the social sciences. In *Ethical issues in social science research*, edited by Tom L. Beauchamp, R. Faden, R. J. Wallace, and L. Walters, pp. 163–174. Baltimore: Johns Hopkins University Press.

Nelkin, Dorothy. (May 1982b). Intellectual property: The control of scientific information. *Science*, 216: 704–708.

Nelson, Dale W. (Associated Press). (Apr. 14, 1992). Analyst: War death counts falsified. *Wisconsin State Journal*, p. 3A.

Neuberg, Leland Gerson. (1988). Distorted transmission: A case study in the diffusion of "social scientific" research. *Theory and Society*, 17: 487–526.

Neuman, W. Lawrence. (1992). Gender, race and age differences in student definitions of sexual harassment. *Wisconsin Sociologist*, 29: 63–75.

Neuman, W. Russell, Marion R. Just, and Ann N. Crigler. (1992). *Common knowledge: News and the construction of political meaning*. Chicago: University of Chicago Press.

NIH FY 1991 budget rescinded by $3.1 million, Congress objects to 31 research projects funded by NSF. (May 27, 1992). *The Blue Sheet* (F-D-C Reports, Inc.), p. 3.

Noelle-Neumann, Elisabeth. (1974). Spiral of silence: A theory of public opinion. *Journal of Communication*, 24:43–51.

Noelle-Neumann, Elisabeth. (1984). *The spiral of silence: Public opinion our social skin*. Chicago: University of Chicago Press.

Norris, M. (1981). Problems in the analysis of soft data and some suggested solutions. *Sociology*, 15:337–351.

Norusis, Marija J. (1986). *The SPSS-X guide to data analysis*. Chicago: SPSS, Inc.

Noted Harvard psychiatrist resigns post after faculty group finds he plagiarized. (Dec. 7, 1988). *Chronicle of Higher Education*.

Novick, Peter. (1988). *That noble dream: The "objectivity question" and the American historical profession*. New York: Cambridge University Press.

Nowak, Stefan. (1989). Comparative studies and social theory. In *Cross-national research in sociology*, edited by Melvin Kohn, pp. 34–56. Newbury Park, CA: Sage.

Nowotny, Helga, and Hilary Rose, eds. (1979). *Counter-movements in the sciences*. Boston: D. Reidel.

Nunnally, Jum C. (1978). *Psychometric theory*. New York: McGraw-Hill.

Oakley, Ann. (1981). Interviewing women: A contradiction in terms. In *Doing feminist research*, edited by Helen Roberts, pp. 30–61. London: Routledge.

O'Brien, Robert M. (1992). Levels of analysis. *Encyclopedia of sociology*, Vol. 3, edited by Edgar and Marie Borgatta, pp. 1107–1112. New York: Macmillan.

O'Donnell, John M. (1985). *The origins of behaviorism: American psy-*

chology, 1870–1920. New York: New York University Press.

Offe, Claus. (1981). The social sciences: Contract research or social movements? *Current Perspectives on Social Theory*, 2:31–37.

Office of National Drug Control Policy. (1997). *National drug control strategy, 1997.* Washington, DC: U.S. Government Printing Office.

Oksenberg, Lois, Lerita Coleman, and Charles F. Cannell. (1986). Interviewers' voices and refusal rates in telephone surveys. *Public Opinion Quarterly*, 50:97–111.

Olsen, Marvin E., and Michael Micklin, eds. (1981). *Handbook of applied sociology.* New York: Praeger.

Olsen, Virginia. (1994). Feminism and models of qualitative research. In *Handbook of qualitative research*, edited by Norman Denzin and Yvonna Lincoln, pp. 158–174. Thousand Oaks, CA: Sage.

Orloff, Ann Shola. (1993). *The politics of pensions: A comparative analysis of Britain, Canada and the United States, 1880–1940.* Madison: University of Wisconsin Press.

Osgood, C. E., G. Suci, and H. Tannenbaum. (1957). *The measurement of meaning.* Urbana: University of Illinois Press.

Ostrander, Susan. (1993). "Surely you're not in this just to be helpful": Access, rapport and interview in three studies of elites. *Journal of Contemporary Ethnography*, 22: 7–27.

O'Sullivan, Katherine. (1986). *First world nationalisms.* Chicago: University of Chicago Press.

O'Toole, Kevin, Neville Millen, and Ranjut Murugason. (1994). *Fraud against organizations in Victoria.* Geelong: Deakin University Press.

Øyen, Else. (1990). The imperfection of comparisons. In *Comparative methodology: Theory and practice in international social research*, edited by Else Øyen, pp. 1–18. Newbury Park, CA: Sage.

Paige, Jeffrey M. (1975). *Agrarian revolution.* New York: Free Press.

Palmer, C. Eddie. (1978). Dog catchers: A descriptive study. *Qualitative Sociology*, 1:19–104.

Parcel, Toby L. (1992). Secondary data analysis and data archives. *Encyclopedia of sociology*, Vol. 4, edited by Edgar and Marie Borgatta, pp. 1720–1728. New York: Macmillan.

Peacock, Walter Gillis, Greg A. Hoover, and Charles D. Killian. (1988). Divergence and convergence in international development. *American Sociological Review*, 53:838–852.

Pearsall, Marion. (1970). Participant observation as role and method in behavioral research. In *Qualitative methodology*, edited by W. J. Filstead, pp. 340–352. Chicago: Markham.

Pearson, Geoffrey. (1993). Goths and vandals: Crime in history. In *Crime and capitalism*, edited by David Greenberg, pp. 122–141. Philadelphia: Temple University Press.

Pearson, Michael Ross, and Robyn M. Dawes. (1992). Personal recall and the limits of retrospective questions in surveys. In *Questions about questions: Inquiries into the cognitive bases of surveys*, edited by Judith M. Turner, pp. 65–94. New York: Russell Sage Foundation.

Pepinsky, Harold E. (1980). A sociologist on police control. In *Fieldwork experience*, edited by W. B. Shaffir, R. Stebbins, and A. Turowetz, pp. 223–234. New York. St. Martin's Press.

Pepinsky, Harold. E., and Richard Quinney, eds. (1991). *Criminology as peacemaking.* Bloomington: Indiana University Press.

Perry, Donna L. (1997). Rural ideologies and urban imaginings: Wolof immigrants in New York City. *Africa Today*, 44:229–259.

Peterson, Robert A. (1984). Asking the age question: A research note. *Public Opinion Quarterly*, 48:379–383.

Pfohl, Stephen. (1990). Welcome to the parasite cafe: Postmodernity as a social problem. *Social Problems*, 37:421–442.

Phillips, Bernard. (1985). *Sociological research methods: An introduction.* Homewood, IL: Dorsey.

Phillips, D. C. (1987). *Philosophy, science and social inquiry: Contemporary methodological controversies in social science and related applied fields of research.* New York: Pergamon.

Phillips, Derek. (1971). *Knowledge from what?* Chicago: Rand McNally.

Phillips, Derek L. (1986). *Toward a just society.* Princeton, NJ: Princeton University Press.

Piliavin, Irving M., J. Rodin, and Jane A. Piliavin. (1969). Good samaritanism: An underground phenomenon? *Journal of Personality and Social Psychology*, 13: 289–299.

Plagiarism case documented. (Feb. 1989). *ASA Footnotes, 17* (2), p. 2.

Plath, David W. (1990). Field notes, filed notes and the conferring of note. In *Field notes: The makings of anthropology*, edited by Roger Sanjek, pp. 371–384. Ithaca, NY: Cornell University Press.

Platt, Jennifer. (1981). Evidence and proof in documentary research. *Sociological Review*, 29:31–66.

Poe, Gail S., et al. (1988). "Don't know" boxes in factual questions in a mail questionnaire: Effects on level and quality of response. *Public Opinion Quarterly*, 52:212–222.

Polsky, Ned. (1967). *Hustlers, beats and others.* Chicago: Aldine.

Polsky, Ned. (1997). Research method, morality, and criminology. In *The subcultures reader*, edited by Ken Gelder and Sarah Thornton, pp. 217–230. London: Routledge.

Pottick, Kathleen, and Paul Lerman. (1991). Maximizing survey response rates for hard-to-reach inner-city populations. *Social Science Quarterly*, 72:172–180.

Pozo, Susan. (1996). *Exploring the underground economy.* Kalamazoo, MI: W. E. Upjohn Institute for Employment Research.

Prechel, Harland. (1990). Steel and the state: industry politics and business policy formation, 1940–1989. *American Sociological Review*, 55:648–668.

Presser, Stanley. (1984). Is inaccuracy on factual survey items item-specific or respondent-specific? *Public Opinion Quarterly*, 48:344–355.

Presser, Stanley. (1990). Measurement issues in the study of social change. *Social Forces*, 68:856–868.

Presser, Stanley, Johnny Blair, and Timothy Triplett. (1992). Survey sponsorship, response rates and response effects. *Social Science Quarterly*, 73: 699–702.

Prewitt, Kenneth. (1983). Management of survey organizations. In *Handbook of social research*, edited by P. Rossi, J. Wright, and A. Anderson, pp. 123–143. Orlando, FL: Academic Press.

Price, Vincent. (1989). Social identification and public opinion: Effects of communicating group conflict. *Public Opinion Quarterly*, 53: 197–224.

Prucha, Francis Paul. (1987). *Handbook for research in American history: A guide to bibliographies and other reference works.* Lincoln: University of Nebraska Press.

Prus, Robert C., and Steve Vassilakopoulos. (1979). Desk clerks and hookers. *Urban Life*, 8:52–71.

Przeworski, Adam, and Henry Teune. (1970). *The logic of comparative inquiry.* New York: Wiley.

Przeworski, Adam, and Henry Teune. (1973). Equivalence in cross-national research. In *Comparative research methods*, edited by D. Warwick and S. Osherson, pp. 119–137. Englewood Cliffs, NJ: Prentice-Hall.

Punch, Maurice. (1986). *The politics and ethics of fieldwork.* Beverly Hills, CA: Sage.

Puri, Harish K., Paramjit S. Judge, and Jagroop S. Sekhon. (1997). Terrorism in Punjab: Understanding reality at the grass-roots level. *Guru Nanak Journal of Sociology,* 18:37–59.

Pusey, Michael. (1987). *Jügen Habermas.* New York: Tavistock.

Pyke, Sandra W., and Neil McK. Agnew. (1991). *The science game,* 5th ed. Englewood Cliffs, NJ: Prentice-Hall.

Qouta, Samir, Raija-Leena Punamaki, and Eyad El Sarraj. (1997). Prison experiences and coping styles among Palestinian men. *Peace and Conflict: Journal of Peace Psychology,* 3:19–36.

Quadagno, Jill S. (1984). Welfare capitalism and the Social Security Act of 1935. *American Sociological Review,* 49:632–648.

Quadagno, Jill S. (1988). *The transformation of old age security.* Chicago: University of Chicago Press.

Quarles, Susan D., ed. (1986). *Guide to federal funding for social scientists.* New York: Russell Sage Foundation.

Quinney, Richard. (1993). A life of crime: Criminology and public policy as peacemaking. *Journal of Crime and Justice,* 16:3–9.

Quinney, Richard, and John Wildeman. (1991). *The problem of crime: A peace and social justice approach.* Mountain View, CA: Mayfield.

Rabinow, Paul, and William M. Sullivan. (1979). The interpretative turn: Emergence of an approach. In *Interpretative social science: A reader,* edited by Paul Rabinow and William Sullivan, pp. 1–24. Berkeley: University of California Press.

Ragin, Charles C. (1987). *The comparative method.* Berkeley: University of California Press.

Ragin, Charles. (1989). New directions in comparative research. In *Cross-national research in sociology,* edited by Melvin Kohn, pp. 57–76. Newbury Park, CA: Sage.

Ragin, Charles C. (1992a). Introduction: Cases of "what is a case?" In *What is a case: Exploring the foundations of social inquiry,* edited by Charles Ragin and Howard Becker, pp. 1–18. New York: Cambridge University Press.

Ragin, Charles C. (1992b). Casing and the process of social inquiry. In *What is a case: Exploring the foundations of social inquiry,* edited by Charles Ragin and Howard Becker, pp. 217–226. New York: Cambridge University Press.

Ragin, Charles C. (1994). *Constructing social research.* Thousand Oaks, CA: Pine Forge Press.

Ragin, Charles C., and David Zaret. (1983). Theory and method in comparative research. *Social Forces,* 61:731–754.

Rathje, W. L., and W. W. Hughes. (1976). The garbage project as nonreactive approach: Garbage in–garbage out. In *Perspective on attitude assessment: Surveys and their alternatives,* edited by H. W. Sinaiko and L. A. Broeding. Champaign, IL: Pendleton Publications.

Rathje, William, and Cullen Murphy. (1992). *Rubbish: The archaeology of garbage.* New York: Vintage.

Raudzens, George. (1997). In search of better quantification for war history: Superiority and casualty rates in early modern Europe. *War and Society,* 15:1–30.

Rawls, John. (1971). *A theory of justice.* Cambridge, MA: Harvard University Press.

Reason, Peter. (1994). Three approaches to participative inquiry. In *Handbook of qualitative research,* edited by Norman K. Denzin and Yvonna S. Lincoln, pp. 324–339. Thousand Oaks, CA: Sage.

Reese, Stephen, W. Danielson, P. Shoemaker, T. Chang, and H. Hsu. (1986). Ethnicity of interview effects among Mexican Americans and Anglos. *Public Opinion Quarterly,* 50:563–572.

Reiman, Jeffery. (1998). *The rich get richer, the poor get prison.* Boston: Allyn and Bacon.

Reinharz, Shulamit. (1979). *On becoming a social scientist.* San Francisco: Josey-Bass.

Reinharz, Shulamit. (1992). *Feminist methods in social research.* New York: Oxford University Press.

Reisman, W. Michael, and Chris T. Antoniou. (1994). *The laws of war.* New York: Vantage Books.

Reiss, Albert J., Jr. (1992). Training incapacities of sociologists. In *Sociology and its publics: The forms and fates of disciplinary organization,* edited by Terence C. Halliday and Morris Janowitz, pp. 297–315. Chicago: University of Chicago Press.

Reskin, Barbara. (1977). Scientific productivity and the reward structure of science. *American Sociological Review,* 42:491–504.

Reuter, Peter. (1996). The mismeasurement of illegal drug markets. In *Exploring the underground economy,* edited by Susan Pozo, pp. 63–80. Kalamazoo, MI: W. E. Upjohn Institute for Employment Research.

Reynolds, Morgan O. (1997). *Crime and punishment in America: 1997 update.* Dallas: National Center for Policy Analysis.

Reynolds, Paul Davidson. (1971). *A primer in theory construction.* Indianapolis: Bobbs-Merrill.

Reynolds, Paul Davidson. (1979). *Ethical dilemmas and social science research.* San Francisco: Jossey-Bass.

Reynolds, Paul Davidson. (1982). *Ethics and social science research.* Englewood Cliffs, NJ: Prentice-Hall.

Rhodes, William, and Michael Gross. (1997). *Case management reduces drug use and criminality among drug-involved arrestees: An experimental study of an HIV prevention intervention.* Washington, DC: National Institute of Justice.

Richards, Thomas J., and Lyn Richards. (1994). Using computers in qualitative research. In *Handbook of qualitative research,* edited by Norman K. Denzin and Yvonna S. Lincoln, pp. 445–462. Thousand Oaks, CA: Sage.

Ricoeur, Paul. (1970). The model of the text: Meaningful action considered as a text. In *Interpretative social science: A reader,* edited by Paul Rabinow and William Sullivan, pp. 73–102. Berkeley: University of California Press.

Rifkin, Jeremy. (1995). *The end of work.* New York: Putnam's Sons.

Ringel, Cheryl. (1997). *Criminal victimization 1996.* Washington, DC: U.S. Bureau of Justice Statistics.

Ritzer, George. (1975). *Sociology: A multi-paradigm science.* Boston: Allyn and Bacon.

Roadburg, Alan. (1980). Breaking relationships with field subjects: Some problems and suggestions. In *Fieldwork experience,* edited by W. B. Shaffir, R. Stebbins, and A. Turowetz, pp. 281–291. New York: St. Martin's.

Roberts, Carl W. (1989). Other than counting words: A linguistic approach to content analysis. *Social Forces,* 68:147–177.

Robertson, John A. (1982). The social scientist's right to research and the IRB system. In *Ethical issues in social science research,* edited by Tom L. Beauchamp, R. Faden, R. J. Wallace, and L. Walters, pp. 356–372. Baltimore: Johns Hopkins University Press.

Robinson, John P., Jerrold G. Rusk, and Kendra B. Head. (1972). *Measures of political attitudes.* Ann Arbor: Center for Political Studies, Institute for Social Research, University of Michigan.

Robinson, John P., and Philip R. Shaver. (1969). *Measures of social psychological attitudes.* Ann Arbor: Survey Research Center, Institute for Social Research, University of Michigan.

Roderick, Rick. (1986). *Habermas and the foundations of critical theory.* New York: St. Martin's.

Roethlisberger, F. J., and Dickenson, W. J. (1939). *Management and the worker.* Cambridge, MA: Harvard University Press.

Rosen, Lawrence. (1995). The creation of the Uniform Crime Report: The role of social science. *Social Science History,* 19:215–238.

Rosenau, Pauline Marie. (1992). *Postmodernism and the social sciences.* Princeton, NJ: Princeton University Press.

Rosenberg, Morris. (1968). *The logic of survey analysis.* New York: Basic Books.

Rosenthal, Robert. (1984). *Meta-analytic procedures for social research.* Beverly Hills, CA: Sage.

Rosnow, Ralph L. (1981). *Paradigms in transition: The methodology of social inquiry.* New York: Oxford University Press.

Ross, Dorothy. (1991). *The origins of American social science.* New York: Cambridge University Press.

Rossi, Peter H., ed. (1982). *Standards for evaluation practice.* San Francisco: Jossey-Bass.

Rossi, Peter H., and Howard E. Freeman. (1985). *Evaluation: A systematic approach,* 3rd ed. Beverly Hills, CA: Sage.

Rossi, Peter H., James D. Wright, and Andy Anderson. (1983). Sample surveys: History, current practice and future prospects. In *Handbook of social research,* edited by P. Rossi, J. Wright, and A. Anderson, pp. 1–20. Orlando, FL: Academic Press.

Rossi, Peter H., James D. Wright, and Eleanor Weber-Burdin. (1982). *Natural hazards and public choice.* New York: Academic.

Rossi, Robert J., and Kevin J. Gilmartin. (1980). *The handbook of social indicators: Sources, characteristics and analysis.* New York: Garland STPM Press.

Roth, Guenther, and Wolfgang Schluchter. (1979). *Max Weber's vision of history: Ethics and methods.* Berkeley: University of California Press.

Roth, Jeffrey A., John T. Scholz, and Anne D. Witte. (1989). *Taxpayer compliance.* Philadelphia: University of Pennsylvania Press.

Roy, Donald. (1970). The study of southern labor union organizing campaigns. In *Pathways to data,* edited by R. W. Habenstein, pp. 216–244. Chicago: Aldine.

Roy, William G. (1983). The unfolding of the interlocking directorate structure of the United States. *American Sociological Review,* 48:248–257.

Roy, William G. (1984). Class conflict and social change in historical perspective. *Annual Review of Sociology,* 10:483–506.

Rubin, Herbert J. (1983). *Applied social research.* Columbus, OH: Charles E. Merrill.

Rule, James. (1978a). *Insight and social betterment: A preface to applied social science.* New York: Oxford University Press.

Rule, James. (1978b). Models of relevance: The social effects of sociology. *American Journal of Sociology,* 84:78–98.

Runciman, W. G. (1980). Comparative sociology or narrative history. *European Journal of Sociology,* 21:162–178.

Runyon, Richard P., and Audry Haber. (1980). *Fundamentals of behavioral statistics.* Reading, MA: Addison-Wesley.

Ryan, Mary. (1989). The American parade. In *The new cultural history,* edited by L. Hunt, pp. 131–153. Berkeley: University of California Press.

Ryder, Norman B. (1992). Cohort analysis. In *Encyclopedia of sociology,* Vol. 1, edited by Edgar and Marie Borgatta, pp. 227–231. New York: Macmillan.

Sabia, Daniel R., Jr., and Jerald T. Wallulis. (1983). *Changing social science: Changing theory and other critical perspectives.* Albany: State University of New York at Albany.

Sagarin, Edward. (1973). The research setting and the right not to be researched. *Social Problems,* 21: 52–64.

Sanchez, Maria Elena. (1992). Effects of questionnaire design on the quality of survey data. *Public Opinion Quarterly,* 56:206–217.

Sanday, Peggy Reeves. (1983). The ethnographic paradigm(s). In *Qualitative methodology,* edited by John Van Maanen, pp. 19–36. Beverly Hills, CA: Sage.

Sanjek, Roger. (1978). A network method and its uses in urban anthropology. *Human Organization,* 37: 257–268.

Sanjek, Roger. (1990). On ethnographic validity. In *Field notes: The makings of anthropology,* edited by Roger Sanjek, pp. 385–418. Ithaca, NY: Cornell University Press.

Sarre, Rick. (1997). Justice as restoration. *Peace Review,* 9:541–547.

Saxe, Leonard, and Michelle Fine. (1981). *Social experiments: Methods for design and evaluation.* Beverly Hills, CA: Sage.

Sayer, Andrew. (1992). *Method in social science: A realist approach,* 2nd ed. New York: Routledge.

Scaramella, Gene L. (1997). Cooperative efforts between criminal organizations. *Crime & Justice International,* 13:7–8.

Schaffer, Nora Cate. (1980). Evaluating race-of-interviewer effects in a national survey. *Sociological Methods and Research,* 8:400–419.

Rule, James. (1978a). *Insight and social betterment: A preface to applied social science.* New York: Oxford University Press.

Schatzman, Leonard, and Anselm L. Strauss. (1973). *Field research: Strategies for a natural sociology.* Englewood Cliffs, NJ: Prentice-Hall.

Scheibe, Karl E. (1988). Metamorphosis in the psychologist's advantage. In *The rise of experimentation in American psychology,* edited by Jill G. Morawski, pp. 53–71. New Haven, CT: Yale University Press.

Scheuch, Erwin K. (1990). The development of comparative research: Towards causal explanations. In *Comparative methodology,* edited by Else Øyen, pp. 19–37. Newbury Park, CA: Sage.

Schissel, Bernard. (1997). Youth crime, moral panics and the news: The conspiracy against the marginalized in Canada. *Social Justice,* 24:165–183.

Schmeling, Sharon L., and Mike Miller. (Aug. 11, 1988). Whistleblower wins suit against UW. *Capital Times* (Madison, Wisconsin).

Schneider, Mark A. (1987). Culture-as-text in the work of Clifford Geertz. *Theory and Society,* 16:809–883.

Schrager, Laura, and James Short. (1980). How serious a crime? Perceptions of organizational and common crimes. In *White collar crime,* edited by G. Geis and E. Stotland, pp. 14–31. Beverly Hills, CA: Sage.

Schrecker, Ellen. (1986). *No ivory tower: McCarthyism and the university.* New York: Oxford University Press.

Schuessler, Karl. (1982). *Measuring social life feelings.* San Francisco: Jossey-Bass.

Schuman, Howard, and Lawrence Bobo. (1988). Survey-based experiments on white racial attitudes towards racial integration. *American Journal of Sociology,* 94:273–299.

Schuman, Howard, and Jean M. Converse. (1971). Effects of black and white interviewers on black response in 1968. *Public Opinion Quarterly,* 65:44–68.

Schuman, Howard, and Otis Dudley Duncan. (1974). Questions about attitude survey questions. In *Sociological methodology, 1973–1974,* edited by Herbert L. Costner, pp. 232–251. San Francisco: Jossey-Bass.

Schuman, Howard, and Jacob Ludwig. (1983). The norm of even-handedness in surveys as in life. *American Sociological Review,* 48:112–120.

Schuman, Howard, and Stanley Presser. (1977). Question wording as an independent variable in survey analysis. *Sociological Methods and Research,* 6:151–170.

Schuman, Howard, and Stanley Presser. (1979). The open and closed question. *American Sociological Review*, 44:692–712.

Schuman, Howard, and Stanley Presser. (1981). *Questions and answers in attitude surveys: Experiments on question form, wording and content.* New York: Academic Press.

Schwandt, Thomas A. (1994). Constructivist, interpretivist approaches to human inquiry. In *Handbook of qualitative research*, edited by Norman Denzin and Yvonna Lincoln, pp. 118–137. Thousand Oaks, CA: Sage.

Schwartz, Dona. (1986). Camera clubs and fine art photography: The social construction of an elite code. *Urban Life*, 15:165–196.

Schwartz, Howard, and Jerry Jacobs. (1979). *Qualitative sociology: A method to the madness.* New York: Free Press.

Schwartz, Martin D., and David O. Friedrichs. (1994). Postmodern thought and criminological discourse: New metaphors for understanding violence. *Criminology*, 32:221–246.

Schwartz, Morris, and Charolotte Green Schwartz. (1969). Problems in field observation. In *Issues in participant observation*, edited by George J. McCall and J. L. Simmons, pp. 89–105. Reading, MA: Addison-Wesley.

Schwartz, Richard, and S. Orleans. (1967). On legal sanctions. *University of Chicago Law Review*, 34:274–300.

Schwarz, Norbert, and Hans-J. Hippler. (1995). Subsequent questions may influence answers to preceding questions in mail surveys. *Public Opinion Quarterly*, 59:93–97.

Schwarz, Norbert, Bäurbel Knäuper, Hans-J. Hippler, Elizabeth Noelle-Neumann, and Leslie Clark. (1991). Rating scales: Numeric values may change the meaning of scale labels. *Public Opinion Quarterly*, 55: 570–582.

Schwendinger, H., and J. Schwendinger. (1974). *Sociologists of the chair.* New York: Basic Books.

Scott, Peter Dale, and Jonathan Marshall. (1991). *Cocaine politics.* Berkeley: University of California Press.

Scott, William A. (1968). Attitude measurement. In *The handbook of social psychology, Vol. 2: Research methods*, edited by Gardner Lindzey and Elliott Aronson, pp. 204–273. Reading, MA: Addison-Wesley.

Seeman, Melvin, and Carolyn S. Anderson. (1983). Alienation and alcohol: The role of work, mastery and community in drinking behavior. *American Sociological Review*, 48:60–77.

Seider, Maynard S. (1974). American big business ideology: A content analysis of executive speeches. *American Sociological Review*, 39:802–815.

Sellin, Thorsten. (1938). *Culture conflict and crime.* New York: Social Science Research Council.

Sellin, Thorsten, and Marvin E. Wolfgang. (1964). *The measurement of delinquency.* New York: Wiley.

Seltzer, Richard A. (1996a). Institutional review boards. In *Mistakes social scientists make*, edited by R. Seltzer, pp. 127–128. New York: St. Martin's Press.

Seltzer, Richard A. (1996b). *Mistakes social scientists make.* New York: St. Martin's Press.

Selvin, Hanan C., and Everett K. Wilson. (1984). On sharpening sociologists' prose. *Sociological Quarterly*, 25:205–223.

Sepstrup, P. (1981). Methodological developments in content analysis. In *Advances in content analysis*, edited by Karl E. Rosengren, pp. 133–158. Beverly Hills, CA: Sage.

Sewell, William H., Jr. (1980). *Work and revolution in France.* New York: Cambridge University Press.

Sewell, William H., Jr. (1987). Theory of action, dialectic, and history: Comment on Coleman. *American Journal of Sociology*, 93:166–171.

Sex survery is dealt a setback. (July 26, 1989). *New York Times*, p. 7.

Seybold, Peter. (1987). The Ford Foundation and the transformation of political science. In *The structure of power in America*, edited by Michael Schwartz, pp. 185–198. New York: Holmes and Meier.

Shafer, Robert Jones. (1980). *A guide to historical method*, 3rd ed. Homewood, IL: Dorsey.

Shaffir, William B., Robert A. Stebbins, and Allan Turowetz. (1980). Introduction. In *Fieldwork experience*, edited by W. B. Shaffir, R. Stebbins, and A. Turowetz, pp. 3–22. New York: St. Martin's Press.

Sharon, Batia. (1979). Artist-run galleries: A contemporary institutional change in the visual arts. *Qualitative Sociology*, 2:3–28.

Sharp, Kathleen. (1995). *In good faith.* New York: St. Martin's Press.

Shattuck, John, and Muriel Morisey Spence. (1988). *Government information controls: Implications for scholarship, science and technology.* Washington, DC: Association of American Universities.

Shavit, Yossi. (1990). Segregation, tracking, and the educational attainment of minorities: Arabs and oriental Jews in Israel. *American Sociological Review*, 55:115–126.

Shaw, C. (1930). *The jack roller.* Chicago: University of Chicago Press.

Sheatsley, Paul B. (1983). Questionnaire construction and item writing. In *Handbook of social research*, edited by P. Rossi, J. Wright, and A. Anderson, pp. 195–230. Orlando, FL: Academic Press.

Shoemaker, Donald J. (1992). Delinquency in the Philippines: A description. *Philippine Sociological Review*, 40:83–103.

Shupe, Anston D., Jr., and David G. Bromley. (1980). Walking a tightrope: Dilemmas of participation observation of groups in conflict. *Qualitative Sociology*, 2:3–21.

Sieber, Joan, ed. (1982). *The ethics of social research: Fieldwork, regulation, and publication.* New York: Springer-Verlag.

Sieber, Joan E. (1992). *Planning ethically responsible research: A guide for students and internal review boards.* Thousand Oaks, CA: Sage.

Sieber, Joan E. (1993). The ethics and politics of sensitive research. In *Research on sensitive topics*, edited by Claire Renzetti and Raymond Lee, pp. 14–26. Thousand Oaks, CA: Sage.

Sieber, Sam D. (1973). The integration of fieldwork and survey methods. *American Journal of Sociology*, 78:1335–1359.

Sigelman, Lee. (1982). The uncooperative interviewee. *Quality and Quantity*, 16:345–353.

Silva, Edward T., and Sheila Slaughter. (1980). Prometheus bound: Limits of social science professionalization. *Theory and Society*, 9:781–819.

Silverman, David. (1972). Some neglected questions about social reality. In *New directions in sociological theory*, edited by Paul Filmer et al. Cambridge, MA: MIT Press.

Silverman, David. (1993). *Interpreting qualitative data.* Thousand Oaks, CA: Sage.

Simpson, Sally S. (1989). Feminist theory, crime, and justice. *Criminology*, 27:605–631.

Singer, Benjamin D. (1989). The criterial crisis of the academic world. *Sociological Inquiry*, 59:127–143.

Singer, Eleanor. (1978). Informed consent: Consequences for response rate and response quality in social survey. *American Sociological Review*, 43: 144–162.

Singer, Eleanor. (1988). Surveys in the mass media. In *Surveying social life: Papers in honor of Herbert H. Hyman*, edited by Hubert J. O'Gorman, pp. 413–436. Middletown, CT: Wesleyan University Press.

Singer, Eleanor, and Martin R. Frankel. (1982). Informed consent procedures in telephone interviews. *American Sociological Review*, 47:416–426.

Singer, Eleanor, and Luane Kohnke-Aguirre. (1979). Interviewer expectation effects: A replication and extension. *Public Opinion Quarterly*, 43:245–260.

Singer, Eleanor, Dawn R. Von Thurn, and Ester R. Miller. (1995). Confidentiality assurances and response: A quantitative review of the experimental literature. *Public Opinion Quarterly*, 59:66–77.

Singleton, Royce, Jr., B. Straits, Margaret Straits, and Ronald McAllister. (1988). *Approaches to social research*. New York: Oxford University Press.

Sinha, Anita. (1979). Control in craft work: The case of production potters. *Qualitative Sociology*, 2:3–25.

Sitton, Thad, G. Mehaffy, and O. L. Davis, Jr. (1983). *Oral history*. Austin: University of Texas Press.

Siu, Paul C. P. (1987). *The Chinese laundryman: A study of social isolation*, edited by John Kuo Wei Tchen. New York: New York University Press.

Skidmore, William. (1979). *Theoretical thinking in sociology*, 2nd ed. New York: Cambridge University Press.

Sklar, Kathryn Kish. (1991). Hull House maps and papers: Social science as women's work in the 1890s. In *The social survey in historical perspective, 1880–1940*, edited by M. Blumer, K. Bales, and K. Sklar, pp. 111–147. New York: Cambridge University Press.

Skocpol, Theda. (1979). *States and social revolutions*. New York: Cambridge University Press.

Skocpol, Theda. (1984). Emerging agendas and recurrent strategies in historical sociology. In *Vision and method in historical sociology*, edited by T. Skocpol, pp. 356–392. Cambridge: Cambridge University Press.

Skocpol, Theda. (1988). The "uppity generation" and the revitalization of macroscopic sociology: Reflections at mid-career of a woman from the sixties. *Theory and Society*, 17:627–644.

Skocpol, Theda, and Margaret Somers. (1980). The uses of comparative history in macrosocial inquiry. *Comparative Studies in Society and History*, 22:174–197.

Skolnick, Jerome H. (1994). *Justice without trial*. New York: Macmillan.

Slater, Phil. (1977). *Origin and significance of the Frankfurt School*. Boston: Routledge and Kegan Paul.

Smart, Barry. (1976). *Sociology, phenomenology, and Marxian analysis: A critical discussion of the theory and practice of a science of society*. Boston: Routledge and Kegan Paul.

Smelser, Neil J. (1959). *Social change in the industrial revolution*. Chicago: University of Chicago Press.

Smelser, Neil J. (1976). *Comparative methods in the social sciences*. Englewood Cliffs, NJ: Prentice-Hall.

Smith, Dennis. (1991). *The rise of historical sociology*. Philadelphia: Temple University Press.

Smith, Douglas. (1986). The neighborhood context of police behavior. In *Communities and cities*, edited by Albert J. Reiss and Michael Tonry. Chicago: University of Chicago Press.

Smith, Louis M. (1994). Biographical method. In *Handbook of qualitative research*, edited by Norman Denzin and Yvonna Lincoln, pp. 286–305. Thousand Oaks, CA: Sage.

Smith, Mary Lee, and Gene V. Glass. (1987). *Research and evaluation in education and the social sciences*. Englewood Cliffs, NJ: Prentice-Hall.

Smith, Robert B. (1987). Linking quality and quantity. Part I: Understanding and explanation. *Quantity and Quality*, 21:291–311.

Smith, Robert B. (1988). Linking quality and quantity, Part II: Surveys as formalizations. *Quantity and Quality*, 22:3–30.

Smith, S. J. (1984). Crime in the news. *British Journal of Criminology*, 24:289–295.

Smith, Tom W. (1984). The subjectivity of ethnicity. In *Surveying subjective phenoemona*, Vol. 2, edited by Charles Turner and Elizabeth Martin, pp. 117–128. New York: Russell Sage Foundation.

Smith, Tom W. (1987). That which we call welfare by any other name would smell sweeter: An analysis of the impact of question wording on response patterns. *Public Opinion Quarterly*, 51:75–83.

Snow, David A., E. Burke Bochford, Jr., Steven K. Worden, and Robert D. Benford. (1986a). Frame alignment process, micromobilization and movement participation. *American Sociological Review*, 51:464–481.

Snow, David A., Susan G. Baker, Leon Anderson, and Michael Martin. (1986b). The myth of pervasive mental illness among the homeless. *Social Problems*, 33:407–423.

Sobal, Jeffery. (1984). The content of survey introductions and the provision of informed consent. *Public Opinion Quarterly*, 48:788–793.

Sociology Writing Group, UCLA. (1991). *A guide to writing sociology papers*, 2nd ed. New York: St. Martin's Press.

Sohn-Rethel, Alfred. (1978). *Intellectual and manual labor: A critique of epistemology*. New York: Macmillan.

Sonquist, J. A., and C. Dunkelberg. (1977). *Survey and opinion research: Procedures for processing and analysis*. Englewood Cliffs, NJ: Prentice-Hall.

South, Scott, and Kim Lloyd. (1995). Spousal alternatives and marital dissolution. *American Sociological Review*, 60:126–140.

Soviet sociologist calls attention for her science. (Apr. 1987). *ASA Footnotes*, p. 2.

Spector, Paul E. (1981). *Research designs*. Beverly Hills, CA: Sage.

Spector, Paul E. (1992). *Summated rating scale construction*. Newbury Park, CA: Sage.

Spencer, Gary. (1982). Methodological issues in the study of bureaucratic elites: A case study of West Point. In *Field research*, edited by R. G. Burgess, pp. 23–30. Boston: Allen and Unwin.

Spradley, James P. (1970). *You owe yourself a drunk*. Boston: Little, Brown.

Spradley, James P. (1979a). *The ethnographic interview*. New York: Holt, Rinehart and Winston.

Spradley, James P. (1979b). *Participant observation*. New York: Holt, Rinehart and Winston.

Spradley, James P., and B. J. Mann. (1975). *The cocktail waitress*. New York: Wiley.

Sprague, Joey, and Mary K. Zimmerman. (1989). Quality and quantity: Reconstructing feminist methodology. *American Sociologist*, 20:71–86.

Stack, Carol. (1989). Doing research in the flats. In *In the field*, edited by Carolyn Smith and William Kornblum, pp. 21–26. New York: Praeger.

Stack, Steven. (1987). Celebrities and suicide: A taxonomy and analysis, 1948–1983. *American Sociological Review*, 52:401–412.

Staggenborg, Susan. (1988). "Hired hand research" revised. *American Sociologist*, 19:260–269.

Stake, Robert E. (1994). Case studies. In *Handbook of qualitative research*, edited by Norman Denzin and Yvonna Lincoln, pp. 236–247. Thousand Oaks, CA: Sage.

Staples, William G. (1987). Technology, control, and the social organization of work at a British hardware firm, 1791–1891. *American Journal of Sociology*, 93:62–88.

Starr, Paul. (1982). *The social transformation of American medicine*. New York: Basic Books.

Starr, Paul. (1987). The sociology of official statistics. In *The politics of numbers*, edited by William Alonso and Paul Starr, pp. 7–58. New York: Russell Sage Foundation.

Starr, Paul, and Ross Corson. (1987). Who will have the numbers? The rise of the statistical services industry and the politics of public data. In *The politics of numbers*, edited by William Alonso and Paul Starr, pp. 415–447. New York: Russell Sage Foundation.

Stech, Charlotte G. (1981). Trends in nonresponse rates, 1952–1979. *Public Opinion Quarterly*, 45:40–57.

Stehr, Nico. 1994. *Knowledge societies.* Thousand Oaks, CA: Sage.

Stempel, G., III. (1971). Visibility of blacks in news and news-picture magazines. *Journalism Quarterly*, 48:337–339.

Stephens, John. (1989). Democratic transition and breakdown in western Europe, 1870–1939: A test of the Moore thesis. *American Journal of Sociology*, 94:1019–1077.

Stephens, Mary Ann Parris, N. S. Cooper, and J. M. Kinney. (1985). The effects of effort on helping the physically disabled. *Journal of Social Psychology*, 125:495–503.

Stephenson, Richard M. (1978). The CIA and the professor: A personal account. *American Sociologist*, 13: 128–133.

Stern, Paul C. (1979). *Evaluating social science research.* New York: Oxford University Press.

Stewart, David W. (1984). *Secondary research: Information sources and methods.* Beverly Hills, CA: Sage.

Stewart, Donald E. (1983). *The television family.* Melborne: Institute of Family Studies.

Stimson, Gerry B. (1986). Place and space in sociological fieldwork. *The Sociological Review*, 34:641–656.

Stinchcombe, Arthur L. (1968). *Constructing social theories.* New York: Harcourt, Brace and World.

Stinchcombe, Arthur L. (1973). Theoretical domains and measurement, Part 1. *Acta Sociologica*, 16:3–12.

Stinchcombe, Arthur L. (1978). *Theoretical methods in social history.* New York: Academic Press.

Stoianovich, Traian. (1976). *French historical method.* Ithaca, NY: Cornell University Press.

Stone, John. (1985). *Racial conflict in contemporary society.* Cambridge, MA: Harvard University Press.

Stone, Lawrence. (1987). *The past and present revisited.* Boston: Routledge and Kegan Paul.

Stone, Philip, et al. (1966). *The general inquirer: A computer approach to content analysis in the behavioral sciences.* Cambridge, MA: MIT Press.

Stone, Philip J., and Robert P. Weber. (1992). Content analysis. In *Encyclopedia of sociology*, Vol. 1, edited by Edgar and Marie Borgatta, pp. 290–295. New York: Macmillan.

Stoner, Norman W. (1966). *The social system of science.* New York: Holt, Rinehart and Winston.

Strauss, Anselm. (1987). *Qualitative analysis for social scientists.* New York: Cambridge University Press.

Strauss, Anselm, and Juliet Corbin. (1990). *Basics of qualitative research: Grounded theory procedures and techniques.* Newbury Park, CA: Sage.

Strauss, Anselm, and Juliet Corbin. (1994). Grounding theory methodology: An overview. In *Handbook of qualitative research*, edited by Norman Denzin and Yvonna Lincoln, pp. 273–285. Thousand Oaks, CA: Sage.

Suchman, Luch, and Brigitte Jordan. (1992). Validity and the collaborative construction of meaning in face-to-face surveys. In *Questions about questions: Inquiries into the cognitive bases of surveys*, edited by Judith M. Turner, pp. 241–267. New York: Russell Sage Foundation.

Sudholm, Charles A. (1973). The pornographic arcade: Ethnographic notes on moral men in immoral places. *Urban Life*, 2:85–104.

Sudman, Seymour. (1976a). *Applied sampling.* New York: Academic Press.

Sudman, Seymour. (1976b). Sample surveys. *Annual Review of Sociology*, 2:107–120.

Sudman, Seymour. (1983). Applied sampling. In *Handbook of survey research*, edited by Peter H. Rossi, James D. Wright, and Andy B. Anderson, pp. 145–194. Orlando, FL: Academic Press.

Sudman, Seymour, and Norman M. Bradburn. (1983). *Asking questions: A practical guide to questionnaire design.* San Francisco: Jossey-Bass.

Sudman, Seymour, and Norman M. Bradburn. (1987). The organizational growth of public opinion research in the United States. *Public Opinion Quarterly*, 51:S67–S78.

Sudnow, David. (1978). *Ways of the hand: The organization of improvised conduct.* Cambridge, MA: Harvard University Press.

Sullivan, John L., and Stanley Feldman. (1979). *Multiple indicators: An introduction.* Beverly Hills, CA: Sage.

Sullivan, John P. (1997). Third generation street gangs: Turf, cartels, and netwarriors. *Crime & Justice International*, 13:9–10, 31–33.

Sullivan, Mercer. (1989). *Getting paid: Youth crime and work in the inner city.* Ithaca, NY: Cornell University Press.

Suls, Jerry M., and Ralph L. Rosnow. (1988). Concerns about artifacts in psychological experiments. In *The rise of experimentation in American psychology*, edited by Jill G. Morawski, pp. 153–187. New Haven, CT: Yale University Press.

Sumner, Colin. (1979). *Reading ideologies.* New York: Academic.

Suppe, Frederick, ed. (1977). *The structure of scientific theories*, 2nd ed. Urbana: University of Illinois Press.

Survey Research Center, Institute for Social Research. (1976). *Interviewer's manual*, rev. ed. University of Michigan.

Sutherland, Edwin. (1937). *The professional thief.* Chicago: University of Chicago Press.

Sutherland, Edwin. (1940). White collar criminality. *American Sociological Review*, 5:2–10.

Sutherland, Edwin. (1949). *White collar crime.* New York: Holt.

Swafford, Michael. (Nov. 1987). Soviet, U.S. sociologists work together. American Sociological Association *Footnotes*, 15:9.

Swanson, Guy E. (1971). Frameworks for comparative research. In *Comparative methods in sociology*, edited by I. Vallier, pp. 141–203. Berkeley: University of California Press.

Swidler, Ann. (1986). Culture in action: Symbols and strategies. *American Sociological Review*, 51: 273–286.

Szymkowiak, Kenneth F. (1996). *Necessary evil: Extortion, organized crime and Japanese corporations.* Doctoral dissertation, University of Hawaii.

Tagg, Stephen K. (1985). Life story interviews and their interpretation. In *The research interview: Uses and approaches*, edited by Michael Brenner, Jennifer Brown, and David Canter, pp. 163–199. New York: Academic Press.

Tanur, Judith H., ed. (1992). *Questions about questions: Inquiries into the cognitive bases of surveys.* New York: Russell Sage Foundation.

Tanur, Judith M. (1983). Methods for large scale surveys and experiments. In *Sociological Methodology, 1983–1984*, edited by Samuel Leinhardt, pp. 1–71. San Francisco: Jossey-Bass.

Taylor, Charles. (1979). Interpretation and the sciences of man. In *Interpretative social science: A reader*, edited by Paul Rabinow and William Sullivan, pp. 25–72. Berkeley: University of California Press.

Taylor, Charles Lewis, ed. (1980). *Indicator systems for political, economic and social analysis.*

Cambridge, MA: Oelgeschlager, Gunn and Hain.

Taylor, Charles L., and David Jodice. (1983). *World handbook of political and social indicators*, 3rd ed. New Haven, CT: Yale University Press.

Taylor, Marylee C. (1995). White backlash to workplace affirmative action: Peril or myth? *Social Forces*, 73: 1385–1414.

Taylor, Steven. (1987). Observing abuse: Professional ethics and personal morality in field research. *Qualitative Sociology*, 10:288–302.

Terkel, Studs. (1970). *Hard times*. New York: Pantheon.

Tewksbury, Richard, and Patricia Gagne. (1997). Assumed and presumed identities: Problems of self-presentation in field research. *Sociological Spectrum*, 17:127–155.

Thomas, Robert J. (1993). Interviewing important people in big companies. *Journal of Contemporary Ethnography*, 22:80–96.

Thompson, E. P. (1963). *The making of the English working class*. New York: Vintage.

Thompson, E. P. (1967). Time, work-discipline, and industrial capitalism. *Past and Present*, 38:56–97.

Thompson, E. P. (1978). *The poverty of theory and other essays*. New York: Monthly Review Press.

Thompson, Paul. (1978). *The voice of the past: Oral history*. New York: Oxford University Press.

Thorne, Barrie, and Zella Luria. (1986). Sexuality and gender in children's daily world. *Social Problems*, 33: 176–190.

Thrasher, F. M. (1927). *The gang*. Chicago: University of Chicago Press.

Threat to confidentiality of fieldnotes. (Oct. 1984). *ASA Footnotes, 12*, p. 6.

Thurstone, L. L. (1970). Attitudes can be measured. In *Attitude measurement*, edited by Gene Summers, pp. 127–141. Chicago: Rand McNally.

Tilly, Charles. (1964). *The vendee*. Cambridge, MA: Harvard University Press.

Tilly, Charles. (1981). *As sociology meets history*. New York: Academic Press.

Tilly, Charles, Louise Tilly, and Richard Tilly. (1975). *The rebellious century, 1830–1930*. Cambridge, MA: Harvard University Press.

Tolnay, Stewart E., and E. M. Beck. (1992). Racial violence and black migration in the American South, 1910–1930. *American Sociological Review*, 57:103–117.

Topolski, Jerzy. (1976). *Methodology of history*, trans. Olgierd Wojtasiewicz. Boston: D. Reidel.

Toulmin, Stephen. (1953). *The philosophy of science: An introduction*. New York: Harper & Row.

Traugott, Michael W. (1987). The importance of persistence in respondent selection for preelection surveys. *Public Opinion Quarterly*, 51:48–57.

Treiman, Michael. (1977). Towards methods for a quantitative comparative sociology: A reply to Burawoy. *American Journal of Sociology*, 82:1042–1056.

Trice, H. M. (1970). The "outsider's" role in field study. In *Qualitative methodology*, edited by W. J. Filstead, pp. 77–82. Chicago: Markham.

Tropp, Richard A. (1982). A regulatory perspective on social science research. In *Ethical issues in social science research*, edited by Tom L. Beauchamp, R. Faden, R. J. Wallace, and L. Walters, pp. 391–415. Baltimore: Johns Hopkins University Press.

Tuchman, Gaye. (1994). Historical social science: Methodologies, methods and meanings. In *Handbook of qualitative research*, edited by Norman Denzin and Yvonna Lincoln, pp. 306–323. Thousand Oaks, CA: Sage.

Tucker, Clyde. (1983). Interviewer effects in telephone interviewing. *Public Opinion Quarterly*, 47:84–95.

Tufte, Edward. (1983). *The visual display of quantitative information*. Cheshire, CT: Graphics Press.

Tufte, Edward. (1991). *Envisioning information*, rev. ed. Cheshire, CT: Graphics Press.

Tuma, Nancy B., and Andrew Grimes. (1981). A comparison of models of role orientations of professionals in a research oriented university. *Administrative Science Quarterly*, 21:187–206.

Turner, Charles. (1984). Why do surveys disagree? Some preliminary hypotheses and some disagreeable examples. In *Surveying subjective phenomena*, Vol. 2, edited by Charles Turner and Elizabeth Martin, pp. 157–214. New York: Russell Sage Foundation.

Turner, Charles, and Elizabeth Martin, eds. (1984). *Surveying subjective phenomena*, Vol. 1. New York: Russell Sage Foundation.

Turner, Jonathan H. (1985). In defense of positivism. *Sociological Theory*, 3:24–30.

Turner, Jonathan H. (1992). Positivism. In *Encyclopedia of sociology*, Vol. 3, edited by Edgar and Marie Borgatta, pp. 1509–1512. New York: Macmillan.

Turner, Roy. (1974). *Ethnomethodology*. Middlesex: Penguin.

Turner, Stephen P. (1980). *Sociological explanation as translation*. New York: Cambridge University Press.

Turner, Stephen P. (1991). The world of academic quantifiers: The Columbia University family and its connections. In *The social survey in historical perspective, 1880–1940*, edited by M. Blumer, K. Bales, and K. Sklar, pp. 269–290. New York: Cambridge University Press.

Turner, Stephen Park, and Jonathan H. Turner. (1991). *The impossible science: An institutional analysis of American sociology*. Newbury Park, CA: Sage.

United States Department of Justice. (1988). *Report to the nation on crime and justice*. Washington, DC: Bureau of Justice Statistics.

United States Departments of Justice, Health and Human Services, Education, Labor, Housing and Urban Development, and Agriculture. (1994). *Partnerships against violence: Promising programs*. Washington, DC: Government Printing Office.

United States Internal Revenue Service. (1979). *Estimates of income unreported on individual income tax returns*. Washington, DC: IRS.

United States Internal Revenue Service. (1987). *Survey of tax practitioners and advisers*. Washington, DC: IRS Research Division.

United States Internal Revenue Service. (1988). *Survery of tax practitioners and advisers*. Washington, DC: IRS Research Division.

United States National Institute of Justice. (1998a). *NIJ request for proposals for comparative, cross-national crime research challenge grants*. Washington, DC: Department of Justice.

United States National Institute of Justice. (1998b). *Solicitation for research and evaluation on violence against women*. Washington, DC: Department of Justice.

Useem, Michael. (1976a). Government influence on the social science paradigm. *Sociological Quarterly*, 17:146–161.

Useem, Michael. (1976b). State production of social knowledge: Patterns of government financing of academic social research. *American Sociological Review*, 41:613–629.

Useem, Michael. (1984). *The inner circle: Large corporations and the rise of business political activity in the U.S. and the U.K.* New York: Oxford University Press.

UW protects dissertation sources. (Dec. 19, 1994). *Capital Times*, p. 4.

Valentine-French, Suzanne, and H. Lorraine Radtke. (1989). Attributions of responsibility for an incident of sexual harassment in a university setting. *Sex Roles*, 21: 545–555.

Vallier, Ivan, ed. (1971a). *Comparative methods in sociology: Essays on trends and applications*. Berkeley: University of California Press.

Vallier, Ivan. (1971b). Empirical comparisons of social structure. In *Comparative methods in sociology*, edited by I. Vallier, pp. 203–263. Berkeley: University of California Press.

Van den Berg, Harry, and Cees Van der Veer. (1985). Measuring ideological frames of references. *Quality and Quantity*, 19:105–118.

Van den Berge, Pierre L. (1967). Research in South Africa: The story of my experiences with tyranny. In *Ethics, politics and social research*, edited by Gideon Sjøberg. New York: Schenckman.

Van Maanen, John. (1973). Observations on the making of policemen. *Human Organization*, 32:407–418.

Van Maanen, John. (1982). Fieldwork on the beat. In *Varieties of qualitative research*, edited by John Van Maanen, James M. Dabbs, Jr., and Robert R. Faulkner, pp. 103–151. Beverly Hills, CA: Sage.

Van Maanen, John. (1983a). Epilogue: Qualitative methods reclaimed. In *Qualitative methodology*, edited by John Van Maanen, pp. 247–268. Beverly Hills, CA: Sage.

Van Maanen, John. (1983b). The moral fix: On the ethics of fieldwork. In *Contemporary field research*, edited by R. M. Emerson, pp. 269–287. Boston: Little, Brown.

Van Maanen, John. (1988). *Tales of the field: On writing ethnography*. Chicago: University of Chicago Press.

Vaughan, Diane. (1992). Theory elaboration: The heuristics of case analysis. In *What is a case? Exploring the foundations of social inquiry*, edited by Charles Ragin and Howard S. Becker, pp. 173–202. Cambridge: Cambridge University Press.

Vaughan, Ted R. (1967). Government intervention in social research: Political and ethical dimensions of the Wichita jury recordings. In *Ethics, politics and social research*, edited by Gideon Sjøberg. New York: Schenckman.

Veltmeyer, Henry. (1978). Marx's two methods of sociological analysis. *Sociological Inquiry*, 48:101–112.

Verba, Sidney. (1971). Cross-national survey research. In *Comparative methods in sociology*, edited by I. Vallier, pp. 309–356. Berkeley: University of California Press.

Verba, Sidney, and Gary R. Orren. (1985). *Equality in America: The view from the top*. Cambridge, MA: Harvard University Press.

Vidich, Arthur Joseph, and Joseph Bensman. (1968). *Small town in mass society*, rev. ed. Princeton, NJ: Princeton University Press.

Vold, George B., Thomas J. Bernard, and Jeffrey B. Snipes. (1998). *Theoretical criminology*. New York: Oxford University Press.

Wade, Nicholas. (1976). IQ and heredity: Suspicion of fraud beclouds classic experiment. *Science*, 194: 916–919.

Waegel, William B. (1984). How police justify the use of deadly force. *Social Problems*, 32:133–143.

Waksberg, J. (1978). Sampling methods for random digit dialing. *Journal of the American Statistical Association*, 73:40–46.

Wallace, Walter. (1971). *The logic of science in sociology*. Chicago: Aldine.

Wallerstein, Immanuel. (1974). *The modern world system*. New York: Academic Press.

Walsh, David. (1972). Varieties of positivism. In *New directions in sociological theory*, edited by Paul Filmer et al. Cambridge, MA: MIT Press.

Walster, Elaine. (1965). The effect of self-esteem on romantic liking. *Journal of Experimental Social Psychology,* 1:194–197.

Walters, Ronald G. (1980). Signs of the times. *Social Research,* 47:537–556.

Walton, John. (1973). Standardized case comparison. In *Comparative social research,* edited by M. Armer and A. Grimshaw, pp. 173–191. New York: Wiley.

Walton, John. (1992). Making the theoretical case. In *What is a case? Exploring the foundations of social inquiry*, edited by Charles Ragin and Howard S. Becker, pp. 121–138. Cambridge: Cambridge University Press.

Ward, Benjamin. (1972). *What's wrong with economics*. New York: Basic Books.

Ward, Kathryn B., and Linda Grant. (1985). The feminist critique and a decade of published research in sociology journals. *Sociological Quarterly*, 26:139–158.

Wardell, Mark L. (1979). Marx and his method: A commentary. *Sociological Quarterly*, 20:425–436.

Warner, R. Stephen. (1971). The methodology of Marx's comparative analysis of modes of production. In *Comparative methods in sociology*, edited by Ivan Vallier, pp. 49–74. Berkeley: University of California Press.

Warren, Carol A. B., and Paul K. Rasmussen. (1977). Sex and gender in field research. *Urban Life*, 6:349–369.

Warwick, Donald P. (1982). Types of harm in social science research. In *Ethical issues in social science research*, edited by Tom L. Beauchamp, R. Faden, R. J. Wallace, and L. Walters, pp. 101–123. Baltimore: Johns Hopkins University Press.

Warwick, Donald P., and Charles A. Lininger. (1975). *The sample survey: Theory and practice*. New York: McGraw-Hill.

Warwick, Donald P., and Samuel Osherson. (1973). Comparative analysis in the social sciences. In *Comparative research methods*, edited by D. Warwick and S. Osherson, pp. 3–11. Englewood Cliffs, NJ: Prentice-Hall.

Wax, Rosalie H. (1971). *Doing fieldwork: Warnings and advice*. Chicago: University of Chicago Press.

Wax, Rosalie H. (1979). Gender and age in fieldwork and fieldwork education: No good thing is done by any man alone. *Social Problems*, 26:509–522.

Weatherford, Jack McIver. (1986). Cocaine and the economic deterioration of Bolivia. In *Conformity and conflict: Readings in cultural anthropology*, edited by James Spradley and David W. McCurdy, pp. 185–195. New York: Harper Collins.

Webb, Eugene J., Donald T. Campbell, Richard D. Schwartz, Lee Sechrest, and Janet Belew Grove. (1981). *Nonreactive measures in the social sciences*, 2nd ed. Boston: Houghton Mifflin.

Weber, Max. (1949). *The methodology of the social sciences*, trans. and edited by Edward A. Shils and Henry A. Finch. New York: Free Press.

Weber, Max. (1974). Subjectivity and determinism. In *Positivism and sociology*, edited by Anthony Giddens, pp. 23–32. London: Heinemann.

Weber, Max. (1978). *Economy and society*, Vol. 1, edited by Guenther Roth and Claus Wittich. Berkeley: University of California Press.

Weber, Max. (1981). Some categories of interpretative sociology. *Sociological Quarterly*, 22: 151–180.

Weber, Robert P. (1983). Measurement models for content analysis. *Quality and Quantity*, 17:127–149.

Weber, Robert P. (1984). Computer assisted content analysis: A short primer. *Qualitative Sociology*, 7: 126–149.

Weber, Robert P. (1985). *Basic content analysis*. Beverly Hills, CA: Sage.

Weeks, M. F., and R. P. Moore. (1981). Ethnicity of interviewer effects on ethnic respondents. *Public Opinion Quarterly*, 45:245–249.

Weil, Frederick D. (1985). The variable effects of education on liberal attitudes. *American Sociological Review*, 50:458–474.

Weinstein, Deena. (1979). Fraud in science. *Social Science Quarterly*, 59:639–652.

Weiss, Carol H. (1972). *Evaluation research: Methods of assessing program effectiveness.* Englewood Cliffs, NJ: Prentice-Hall.

Weiss, Janet A., and Judith E. Gruber. (1987). The managed irrelevance of educational statistics. In *The politics of numbers*, edited by William Alonso and Paul Starr, pp. 363–391. New York: Russell Sage Foundation.

Weiss, Robert S. (1994). *Learning from strangers: The arts and method of qualitative interview studies.* New York: Free Press.

Weitz, Rose, and Deborah A. Sullivan. (1986). The politics of childbirth: The re-emergence of midwifery in Arizona. *Social Problems*, 33:163–175.

Weitzman, Eben, and Matthew Miles. (1995). *Computer programs for qualitative data analysis.* Thousand Oaks, CA: Sage.

Weitzman, Lenore, D. Eifler, E. Hokada, and C. Ross. (1972). Sex role socialization in picture books for preschool children. *American Journal of Sociology*, 77:1125–1150.

Wellford, Charles F. (1997). Controlling crime and achieving justice: The American Society of Criminology 1996 presidential address. *Criminology*, 35:1–11.

Wenger, G. Clare, ed. (1987). *The research relationship: Practice and politics in social policy research.* Boston: Allen and Unwin.

Wentworth, Ellen J. (1993). *Survey responses: An evaluation of their validity.* New York: Academic Press.

Werner, Oswald, and G. Mark Schoepfle. (1987a). *Systematic fieldwork, Vol. 1: Foundations of ethnography and interviewing.* Beverly Hills: Sage.

Werner, Oswald, and G. Mark Schoepfle. (1987b). *Systematic fieldwork, Vol. 2: Ethnographic analysis and data management.* Beverly Hills: Sage.

West, W. Gordon. (1980). Access to adolescent deviants and deviance. In *Fieldwork experience*, edited by W. B. Shaffir, R. A. Stebbins, and A. Turowetz, pp. 31–44. New York: St. Martin's Press.

Whalley, Peter. (1984). Deskilling engineers? The labor process, labor markets, and labor segmentation. *Social Problems*, 32:117–132.

Wharton, Carol S. (1987). Establishing shelters for battered women. *Qualitative Sociology*, 10:146–163.

Whiting, John W. M. (1968). Methods and problems in cross-cultural research. In *The handbook of social psychology*, 2nd ed., edited by G. Lindzey and E. Aronson, pp. 693–728. Reading, MA: Addison-Wesley.

Whyte, William Foote. (1955). *Street corner society: The social structure of an Italian slum*, 2nd ed. Chicago: University of Chicago Press.

Whyte, William Foote. (1982). Interviewing in field research. In *Field research*, edited by R. G. Burgess, pp. 111–122. Boston: George Allen and Unwin.

Whyte, William Foote. (1986). On the uses of social science research. *American Sociological Review*, 51: 555–563.

Whyte, William F. (1989). Advancing scientific knowledge through participatory action research. *Sociological Forum*, 4:367–385.

Wieder, D. Lawrence. (1977). Ethnomethodology and ethnosociology. *Mid-American Review of Sociology*, 2:1–18.

Wiegand, Bruce. (1987). Political considerations of studying tax compliance. *American Sociologist,* 18:375–384.

Wiegand, Bruce. (1993). Petty smuggling as social justice: Research findings from the Belize-Mexico border. *Social and Economic Studies,* 42:171–193.

Wiegand, Bruce. (1994). Black money in Belize: The ethnicity and social structure of black-market crime. *Social Forces,* 73:135–154.

Wiegand, Bruce, and Richard Bennett. (1993). The will to win: Determinants of public support for the drug war in Belize. *Crime, Law and Social Change*, 19:203–220.

Wigginton, Eliot, ed. (1972). *Foxfire book.* New York: Doubleday.

Wilcox, Clyde, Lee Sigelman, and Elizabeth Cook. (1989). Some like it hot: Individual differences in responses to group feeling thermometers. *Public Opinion Quarterly*, 53:246–257.

Williams, Bill. (1978). *A sampler on sampling.* New York: Wiley.

Williams, Carol I., and Gary K. Wolfe. (1979). *Elements of research: A guide for writers.* Palo Alto, CA: Mayfield.

Williams, Christopher. (1996). An environmental victimology. *Social Justice*, 23:16–40.

Williamson, John B., David Karp, John Dalphin, and Paul Gray. (1982). *The research craft: An introduction to social research methods.* Boston: Little, Brown.

Willimack, Diane K., Howard Schuman, Beth-Ellen Pennell, and James M. Lepkowski. (1995). Effects of prepaid non-monetary incentives on response rates and response quality in face-to-face survey. *Public Opinion Quarterly*, 59:78–92.

Willis, Paul. (1977). *Learning to labor: How working class kids get working class jobs.* New York: Columbia University Press.

Wilson, John. (1982). Realist philosophy as a foundation for Marx's social theory. *Current Perspectives in Social Theory*, 3:243–263.

Wilson, Julius W. (1978). *The declining significance of race.* Chicago: University of Chicago Press.

Wilson, Thomas P. (1970). Normative and interpretative paradigms in sociology. In *Understanding everyday life: Toward the reconstruction of sociological knowledge*, edited by Jack D. Douglas, pp. 57–79. New York: Aldine.

Wimberly, Dale W. (1990). Investment dependence and alternative explanations of third world mortality: A cross-national study. *American Sociological Review*, 55:75–91.

Winkler, Karen J. (Jan. 11, 1989). Dispute over validity of historical approaches pits traditionalists against advocates of new methods. *Chronicle of Higher Education*, pp. A4ff.

Winston, Chester. (1974). *Theory and measurement in sociology.* New York: Wiley.

Witte, Anne. (1996). Beating the system? In *Exploring the underground economy*, edited by Susan Pozo, pp. 129–144. Kalamazoo, MI: W. E. Upjohn.

Wolcott, Harry F. (1994). *Transforming qualitative data: Description, analysis and interpretation.* Thousand Oaks, CA: Sage.

Wolf, Eric R. (1982). *Europe and the people without history.* Berkeley: University of California Press.

Wolfgang, Marvin. (1995). *Delinquency in China: Study of a birth cohort.* Washington, DC: National Institute of Justice.

Woodrum, Eric. (1984). "Mainstreaming" content analysis in social science: Methodological advantages, obstacles, and solutions. *Social Science Research*, 13:1–19.

Wray, Henry R. (1993). *Money laundering: The use of Bank Secrecy Act reports by law enforcement could be increased.* Washington, DC: U.S. General Accounting Office.

Wright, Erik O., and Donmoon Cho. (1992). The relative permeability of class boundaries to cross-class friendships: A comparative study of the United States, Canada, Sweden and Norway. *American Sociological Review*, 57:85–102.

Wright, James D., and Peter H. Rossi, eds. (1981). *Social science and natural hazards*. Cambridge, MA: Abt Books.

Wright, J. P., F. T. Cullen, and M. B. Blankenship. (1995). The social construction of corporate violence: Media coverage of the Imperial Foods Products fire. *Crime and Delinquency,* 41:20–36.

Wright, Richard T., and Scott H. Decker. (1997). *Armed robbers in action*. Boston: Northeastern University Press.

Wright, Richard T., Scott H. Decker, Allison K. Redfern, and Dietrich L. Smith. (1996). A snowball's chance in hell: Fieldwork with active residential burglars. In *In their own words*, edited by Paul Cromwell, pp. 1–7. Los Angeles: Roxbury.

Wuthnow, Robert. (1979). The emergence of modern science and world system theory. *Theory and Society*, 8:215–243.

Wuthnow, Robert. (1987). *Meaning and moral order: Explorations in cultural analysis*. Berkeley: University of California Press.

Yammarino, Francis, Steven Skiner, and Terry Childers. (1991). Understanding mail survey response behavior: A meta-analysis. *Public Opinion Quarterly*, 55:613–640.

Yancey, William L., and Lee Rainwater. (1970). Problems in the ethnography of the urban underclasses. In *Pathways to data*, edited by R. W. Habenstein, pp. 245–269. Chicago: Aldine.

Yeo, Eileen James. (1991). The social survey in social perspective, 1830–1930. In *The social survey in historical perspective, 1880–1940*, edited by M. Blumer, K. Bales, and K. Sklar, pp. 49–65. New York: Cambridge University Press.

Yin, Robert K. (1988). *Case study research*, rev. ed. Newbury Park, CA: Sage.

Young, T. R. (1980). Comment on the McQuaire-Wardell debate. *Sociological Quarterly*, 21:459–462.

Yow, Valerie Raleigh. (1994). *Recording oral history: A practical guide for social scientists*. Thousand Oaks, CA: Sage.

Yu, J., and H. Cooper. (1983). A quantitative review of research design effects on response rates to questionnaires. *Journal of Marketing Research*, 20:36–44.

Zaller, John, and Stanley Feldman. (1992). A simple theory of survey responses: Answering questions versus revealing preferences. *American Journal of Political Science*, 36:579–616.

Zane, Anne, and Euthemia Matsoukas. (1979). Different settings, different results? A comparison of school and home responses. *Public Opinion Quarterly*, 43:550–557.

Zaret, David. (1978). Sociological theory and historical scholarship. *The American Sociologist*, 13:114–121.

Zeisel, Hans. (1985). *Say it with figures*, 6th ed. New York: Harper & Row.

Zelizer, Viviana A. (1985). *Pricing the priceless child*. New York: Basic Books.

Zeller, Richard, and Edward G. Carmines. (1980). *Measurement in the social sciences: The link between theory and data*. New York: Cambridge University Press.

Ziman, John. (1968). *Public knowledge: An essay concerning the social dimension of science*. New York: Cambridge University Press.

Ziman, John. (1976). *The force of knowledge: The scientific dimension of society*. New York: Cambridge University Press.

Zimbardo, Philip G. (1972). Pathology of imprisonment. *Society*, 9:4–6.

Zimbardo, Philip G. (1973). On the ethics of intervention in human psychological research. *Cognition*, 2:243–256.

Zimbardo, Philip G., et al. (Apr. 8, 1973). The mind is a formidable jailer: A pirandellian prison. *New York Times Magazine*, 122:38–60.

Zimbardo, Philip G., et al. (1974). The psychology of imprisonment: Privation, power and pathology. In *Doing unto others*, edited by Zick Rubin. Englewood Cliffs, NJ: Prentice-Hall.

Zuckerman, Harriet. (1972). Interviewing an ultra-elite. *Public Opinion Quarterly*, 36:159–175.

Zuckerman, Harriet. (1978). Theory choice and problem choice in science. In *Sociology of science*, edited by Jerry Gaston, pp. 65–95. San Francisco: Jossey-Bass.

Zuiches, James J. (1984). The organization and funding of social science in the NSF. *Sociological Inquiry*, 54:188–210.

Zurcher, Louis A. (1979). The airline passenger: Protection of self in an encapsulated group. *Qualitative Sociology*, 1:77–99.

NAME INDEX

SUBJECT INDEX